SHARING OUR KNOWLEDGE

Sharing Our Knowledge
The Tlingit and Their Coastal Neighbors

EDITED BY SERGEI KAN

With Steve Henrikson

University of Nebraska Press | Lincoln

© 2015 by the Board of Regents of the University of Nebraska. All rights reserved. The University of Nebraska Press is part of a land-grant institution with campuses and programs on the past, present, and future homelands of the Pawnee, Ponca, Otoe-Missouria, Omaha, Dakota, Lakota, Kaw, Cheyenne, and Arapaho Peoples, as well as those of the relocated Ho-Chunk, Sac and Fox, and Iowa Peoples. ∞

First Nebraska paperback printing: 2023

Library of Congress Cataloging-in-Publication Data

Sharing our knowledge: the Tlingit and their coastal neighbors / edited by Sergei Kan with Steven Henrikson.

pages   cm

Includes bibliographical references and index.

ISBN 978-0-8032-4056-8 (cloth: alkaline paper)
ISBN 978-1-4962-3688-3 (paperback)
ISBN 978-0-8032-6674-2 (pdf)
1. Tlingit Indians—Social life and customs. 2. Tlingit Indians—History. 3. Tlingit Indians—Languages. 4. Tlingit art. 5. Indians of North America—Alaska—Pacific Coast—Social life and customs. 6. Indians of North America—British Columbia—Pacific Coast—Social life and customs. 7. Indians of North America—Alaska—Pacific Coast—Languages. 8. Indians of North America—British Columbia—Pacific Coast—Languages. 9. Pacific Coast (North America)—Social life and customs. 10. Pacific Coast (North America)—Ethnic relations. I. Kan, Sergei. II. Henrikson, Steve.

E99.T6S53 2015
979.8004'9727—dc23
2014036321

Set in Charis by Renni Johnson.

We dedicate this book to
Mark Jacobs Jr.
(Saa.aat', Keet Wú, Gusht'eihéen,
Wóochx Kaduhaa)
(1923–2005)
Andrew Hope III
(Xaastanch)
(1949–2008)
and Richard Danenhauer
(Xwaayeenák)
(1942–2014)

May Their Memory Be Eternal!

CONTENTS

List of Illustrations   x

Introduction   1
SERGEI KAN

Part 1. Our Elders and Teachers

1. Shotridge in Philadelphia: Representing Native Alaskan Peoples to East Coast Audiences   41
ROBERT W. PREUCEL

2. Louis Shotridge: Preserver of Tlingit History and Culture   63
LUCY FOWLER WILLIAMS

3. This Is Kux̱aankutaan's (Dr. Frederica de Laguna's) Song   79
CHEW SHAA (ELAINE ABRAHAM) AND DAXOOTSU (JUDITH RAMOS)

4. Mark Jacobs Jr./Gusht'ei'héen (1923–2005)   88
HAROLD JACOBS

5. X'eigaa K̲aa (Tlingit Warrior)   95
HAROLD JACOBS

6. Mark Jacobs Jr./Gusht'eihéen: My Teacher, Friend, and Older Brother   97
SERGEI KAN

7. World War II Scuttlebutt: Naval Section Bases, Southeast Alaska   118
MARK JACOBS JR.

8. Poems by Andrew Hope III 137
   INTRODUCED BY ISHMAEL HOPE

9. As Long as the Work Gets Done 149
   PETER METCALFE

10. Revival and Survival: Two Lifetimes in Tlingit 153
    NORA MARKS DAUENHAUER AND
    RICHARD DAUENHAUER

Part 2. Native History

11. Tlingit Interaction with Other Native Alaskan
    and Northwest Coast Ethnic Groups before
    and during the Russian Era 171
    ELENA PITERSKAYA

12. Relating Deep Genealogies, Traditional History, and
    Early Documentary Records in Southeast Alaska:
    Questions, Problems, and Progress 187
    JUDITH BERMAN

13. Whose Justice? Traditional Tlingit Law
    and the Deady Code 247
    DIANE PURVIS

14. Bringing to Light a Counternarrative of Our History: B. A.
    Haldane, Nineteenth-Century Tsimshian Photographer 265
    MIQUE'L ICESIS DANGELI

Part 3. Subsistence, Natural Resources, and Ethnogeography

15. Haida and Tlingit Use of Seabirds from the
    Forrester Islands, Southeast Alaska 297
    MADONNA L. MOSS

16. Deiki Noow: Tlingit Cultural Heritage
    in the Hazy Islands 320
    STEVE J. LANGDON

17. Place as Education's Source   364
   THOMAS F. THORNTON

Part 4. Material Culture, Art, and Tourism

18. Skidegate Haida House Models   381
   ROBIN K. WRIGHT

19. The Evolution of Tlingit Daggers   394
   ASHLEY VERPLANK MCCLELLAND

20. Tourists and Collectors: The New Market for Tlingit and Haida Jewelry at the Turn of the Century   417
   KATHRYN BUNN-MARCUSE

21. Opening the Drawer: Unpacking Tlingit Beadwork in Museum Collections and Beyond   441
   MEGAN A. SMETZER

22. Balancing Protocol and Law for Intellectual Property: Examples and Ethical Dilemmas from the Northwest Coast Art Market   461
   ALEXIS C. BUNTEN

Part 5. Repatriation

23. A Killer Whale Comes Home: Neil Kúxdei woogoot, Kéet S'aaxw, Mark Jacobs Jr., and the Repatriation of a Clan Crest Hat from the Smithsonian Institution   483
   R. ERIC HOLLINGER AND HAROLD JACOBS

24. Building New Relationships with Tlingit Clans: Potlatch Loans, NAGPRA, and the Penn Museum   496
   STACEY O. ESPENLAUB

   Appendix   509

   Contributors   517

   Index   521

ILLUSTRATIONS

Figures

0.1 Andrew Hope III speaking at the 1993 clan conference   xviii
0.2 Tlingit elders at the 1993 Klukwan/Haines clan conference   xviii
0.3 Clan Conference attendees in Klukwan/Haines, 1993   2
0.4 Traditional Native dancing at the 2003 clan conference in Haines/Klukwan   2
0.5 Herman Davis at the 2007 clan conference in Sitka   3
0.6 Daniel Johnson Jr. wearing a ceremonial Double-headed Raven hat   4
0.7 Edwell John Jr. wearing a ceremonial headdress and button blanket   5
0.8 Frederica de Laguna at the University of Pennsylvania Museum, 1931   9
0.9 Mark Jacobs Jr. and Harvey Jacobs, 1942   12
0.10 Mark Jacobs Jr. and Sergei Kan at the 1997 clan conference   14
0.11 Richard Dauenhauer speaking at the 2007 clan conference   15
0.12 Clan conference in Sitka, 2007   16
0.13 Andrew Hope III in 1984   17
0.14 Andrew Hope III at the 2007 clan conference   18
0.15 Gerry Hope speaking at the 2007 clan conference   26
0.16 Harold Jacobs speaking at the 2007 clan conference   29

1.1 Louis Shotridge in Kaagwaantaan clan regalia, ca. 1912   43
1.2 Native American exhibit in the Furness Library, ca. 1890   47
1.3 Model of Kluckwan, Alaska   48
1.4 Grizzly Bear House in the Klukwan model   49
1.5 Model of Haina, Haida Gwaii, BC   51
1.6 American Section exhibits, ca. 1922   52

1.7   Reinstallation of the Northwest Coast Gallery, ca. 1931   53
1.8   Louis and Florence Shotridge with schoolchildren, ca. 1912   55
2.1   Louis Shotridge at expedition camp, Chilkoot village, ca. 1915   64
2.2   The Ganook hat purchased by Louis Shotridge in 1924   72
2.3   Kaagwaantaan Shark helmet collected by Louis Shotridge in 1929   73
3.1   Elaine Abraham   80
3.2   JOM Mount Saint Elias Dancers   81
3.3   Susie Abraham and Freddy de Laguna at Sharon Goodwin's memorial potlatch   83
3.4   The musical score from de Laguna's *Under Mount Saint Elias*   84
4.1   Mark Jacobs Jr. holding the Killer Whale dagger   93
4.2   Mark Jacobs Jr. shortly before his death   94
6.1   Mark Jacobs Jr. and Alla Kan in spring 1987   104
6.2   Mark Jacobs Jr. at the grave of his brother, Ernest Jacobs   110
6.3   The 1997 Dakl'aweidí memorial *koo.éex'* in Angoon   111
6.4   Mark Jacobs Jr. announcing his financial contribution   112
7.1   Photograph of Mark Jacobs Jr. and the Navy ship he served on   121
8.1   Ishmael Hope speaking at the 2007 clan conference   138
10.1 Nora Marks Dauenhauer speaking at the 2007 clan conference   155
12.1 A page of the George McKay genealogy   192
12.2 Louis Shotridge genealogy card   193
12.3 First page of Shotridge chart of Raven House matriline   194
12.4 McKay's descent from S'eiltín I and Taaxsha   196
12.5 Lineages of the Klukwan Kaagwaantaan and Gaanaxteidí   198
12.6 Lineages of the Taant'a Kwáan Gaanax.ádi, Teikweidí, and Dakl'aweidí, ca. 1730–1870   200
12.7 Relationships of the Stikine Naanyaa.aayí and the Klukwan Gaanaxteidí and Kaagwaantaan clans, ca. 1750–1900   206
12.8 Affinal relationships of leaders of the Naanyaa.aayí and Kaagwaantaan and of the Naanyaa.aayí, Gaanaxteidí, and Kaagwaantaanca. 1770–1850   207

Illustrations   xi

12.9 Lineages of the Taant'a Ḵwáan G̲aanax̲.ádi and Teiḵweidí clans, ca. 1770–1900   208
12.10 Andáa and Teiḵweidí men at Kadukguká on Tongass Island, 1868   229
14.1 David Kininnook of Saxman, Alaska, taken by B. A. Haldane, 1907   269
14.2 George Hamilton, Haidah (Haida) from Howkan, Alaska   270
14.3 Nisga'a family, Laxgalt'sap (Greenville BC), 1903   271
14.4 Chief James Skean and his family, Gitlaxt'aamiks (Aiyansh BC), 1914   272
14.5 Group in native dress on occasion of Edward Marsden's wedding day   273
14.6 B. A.'s self-portrait in his Metlakatla studio   275
14.7 Young girls with model totem pole   276
14.8 Boy wearing button robe and holding a paddle   277
14.9 Sidney Campbell with his totem pole in Metlakatla, Alaska, ca. 1905   278
14.10 Totems carved by Chief Neesh-Loot and his tribesmen   279
14.11 Sidney Campbell and Josephine Hewson Hayward, ca. 1930   280
14.12 Sidney Campbell   281
14.13 John Hayward at Metlakatla, Alaska, ca. 1920   283
14.14 Portrait of mother and child taken in B. A.'s studio, ca. 1910   284
14.15 A detail of "Looking to Our Past to Inspire Our Future"   285
14.16 B. A.'s granddaughter and great-granddaughters with his self-portrait   286
16.1 *Deiki Noow* from *Kuxk'*   321
16.2 *Deiki Noow* from the air   322
16.3 *At.óow*–Kagwaantaan Ganuk hat   334
16.4 *At.óow* -Naasteidí pole originally located at Tajig' aan   337
16.5 Deiki Noow and Yaandayein up close   342
16.6 Seagull egg in grass nest on Kuxk'   353
17.1 Place-based model of education and health   374
18.1 Haida canoe at the World's Columbian Exposition, Chicago, 1893   380
18.2 Map sketch of the World's Columbian Exposition grounds   382

18.3 Skidegate Haida model houses at the World's Columbian Exposition   382
18.4 Skidegate Haida model houses   383
18.5 End of Skidegate Haida model house   384
18.6 View from the back of the display at the World's Columbian Exposition   385
18.7 Deans's sketch   386
18.8 Hlgagilda 'Llnagaay (Skidegate village) in 1878, Haida Gwaii, BC   387
18.9 Hlgagilda 'Llnagaay (Skidegate) in 2006   387
18.10 Skidegate site rendering   388
18.11 Captain Gold's House, First Beach, Haida Gwaii   389
18.12 Model of Captain Gold's House   390
19.1 Dagger vocabulary   395
19.2 Double-bladed dagger   397
19.3 Hafted-pommel dagger   398
19.4 Made-for-sale dagger   399
19.5 Malaspina daggers, collected in 1791   401
19.6 Single-raised-median blade   403
19.7 Double-raised-line blade   404
19.8 Fluted blade   405
19.9 Elaborate double-bladed dagger   408
19.10 Hafted-pommel dagger   409
19.11 Gusht'eiheen and Keet Gwalaa   411
19.12 Made-for-sale dagger   413
20.1 Silver bracelet by Rudolph Walton   423
20.2 Tlingit woman selling baskets and bracelets, Sitka, 1886–1890   424
20.3 Tlingit silversmith Johnny Kasank   426
20.4 Silver spoon with fish handle by Jim Williams   427
20.5 Commercially produced fiddle-back spoon with engraved handle   427
20.6 Tlingit silver bracelets   431
20.7 Silver bracelet designed by Bill Wilson   431
20.8 Floral bracelet designed by Jim Jacobs   432
20.9 Silver bracelet by Jim Jacobs   432
20.10 Silver bracelets illustrated in Scidmore (1885)   434

20.11 Tlingit silver bracelets collected at Fort Wrangell in 1879   435
20.12 Tlingit silver bracelet collected by Emmons in 1942   435
20.13 "Love Birds" bracelet designed by Bill Wilson   437
21.1 Moccasins purchased at Sitka, Alaska, in 1888   446
21.2 Sealskin moccasins made by Annie White, ca. 1960s   448
21.3 Late nineteenth- or early twentieth-century dance collar with pouches   449
21.4 Angoon dancers from the Teikweidí clan   449
21.5 Sam Davis seated with octopus bags and other regalia   450
21.6 Octopus bag, early twentieth century, Angoon   451
21.7 Sitka hosts and Yakutat guests at the 1904 Sitka potlatch   454
21.8 Dance collar, late nineteenth or early twentieth century   455
21.9 Two native Sitka women   456
21.10 Mid twentieth-century dolls, probably made by Mary Baker of Juneau   457
23.1 Mark Jacobs Jr. wearing the Killer Whale hat   484
23.2 The Killer Whale hat as illustrated in Swanton   485
23.3a and 23.3b
    Mark Jacobs Jr. with the Killer Whale hat   486
23.4 Kéet Hít (Killer Whale House) lineage   489
23.5 Tlingit clan leader lying in state with Killer Whale clan property   491
23.6 Clan leaders placing the Killer Whale hat on Mark Jacobs Jr.   493
24.1 Interior view of box containing the Petrel hat, 2004   498
24.2 Boxes containing the Tlingit clan hats en route to Sitka, 2004   499
24.3 The Wolf hat on display at the Sitka National Historic Park   500
24.4 Andrew Gamble, Lucy F. Williams, and Robert W. Preucel, 2004   501
24.5 Ray Wilson and Herman Davis, 2004   503
24.6 Joe Bennett Jr. holding the Shark helmet   503
24.7 Joe Howard Sr. dancing the Petrel hat, 2004   504
24.8 Andrew Gamble Jr., Herman Davis, and Tom Young Jr., 2008   505

Maps

12.1 Taant'a Ḵwáan town sites, ca. 1700–1900   209
15.1 Forrester Islands   299
16.1 Deiki Noow (Hazy Islands)   323
16.2 Naasteidí and L'eeneidí clan territories   327
16.3 Tlingit place-names in the Hazy Islands   340

Tables

15.1 Radiocarbon ages from five sites having seabird remains, Forrester Islands   302
15.2 Bird remains from five archaeological sites, Forrester Islands   304
16.1 Tlingit place-names associated with the Hazy Islands   341
16.2 Tlingit cultural heritage in practice: Deiki Noow, 2007   359

SHARING OUR KNOWLEDGE

Fig. 0.1 (*top*) Andrew Hope III speaking at the 1993 clan conference in Klukwan/Haines. Photograph by Sergei Kan.

Fig. 0.2 (*bottom*) Tlingit elders at the 1993 Klukwan/Haines clan conference. *From left to right*: Austin Hammond, Joe Hotch, and Paul Jackson. Behind them is a group of Native dancers. Photograph by Peter Metcalfe.

Introduction

SERGEI KAN

Most of the papers appearing in this volume were first presented at the 2007 Conference of Tsimshian, Haida, and Tlingit Tribes and Clans, which took place in Sitka, Alaska, March 21–25, 2007. That conference was a continuation of a project initiated in the late 1980s by Andrew Hope III (Xaastanch). As Andy wrote two decades ago (*Juneau Empire*, September 23, 1992: 2), "The original premise for the conference was to reaffirm the customs and traditions of the Alaska Tlingit and the Kaigani Haida clans." Eventually Alaska and British Columbia Tsimshians, Inland Tlingits, as well as the Tagish, Tutchone, and Tahltan Athabascan peoples from British Columbia and the Yukon Territory were invited as well to what became the first of a series of "clan conferences." Held in Haines and Klukwan in 1993, the first clan conference was a tremendous success and was followed by several others: in Sitka in 1995 and again in 1997 as well as a smaller one in Ketchikan in 1995 dedicated solely to language preservation. None of these subsequent gatherings, however, matched the initial one in terms of the number of participants. According to the organizers, close to five hundred people signed the attendance book at the 1993 conference. The format for the meeting developed by Andy and his colleagues and adopted by the Haines-Klukwan conference continued to be followed at all of the subsequent clan conferences including that of 2007: a combination of plenary and smaller sessions and workshops in the morning and the afternoon, followed by Native dances, poetry readings, and other cultural performances in the evening. Most important, the 1993 clan conference differed from a regular academic one by virtue of the fact that, as Andy Hope wrote in 2000, "Probably for the first time ever, *practitioners came together with scholars as equals to discuss their mutual knowledge of and experience with* the cultures indigenous to this part of the world" (10, italics mine).

Fig. 0.3 (*top*) Clan conference, 1993, in Klukwan/Haines. *From left to right*: Forrest DeWitt Jr., Betsy McFarlane, Joe Murray, Andy Hope III, Richard Jackson, and Esther Shea. Photograph by Peter Metcalfe.

Fig. 0.4 (*bottom*) Traditional Native dancing at the 1993 clan conference in Haines/Klukwan. The two men dancing in the front of the group are Paul Marks (*left*) and Paul Jackson. Photograph by Peter Metcalfe.

Fig. 0.5 Herman Davis, the head of the L'uknax̱.ádi clan of Sitka, speaking at the 2007 clan conference in Sitka. To his right is a photograph of Mark Jacobs Jr. Photograph by Peter Metcalfe.

A few of the papers appearing here have been previously published. The decision to include them has been prompted by several factors, such as my wish to showcase the current work by a major scholar in the field whose paper from the 2007 conference had already been committed to another publication (Madonna Moss), to present recent work in a new area of research by a young Alaska Native scholar (Alexis Bunten), and to honor several Native and non-Native elders and scholars who died in the past few years and to whom this book is dedicated (Frederica de Laguna, Mark Jacobs Jr., and Andy Hope).

For various reasons the periodic clan conferences stopped after 1997, but in 2006 the idea of organizing another one came simultaneously from me and from Steve Henrikson, both of us having decided to pay tribute to our recently deceased Tlingit teacher, friend, and clan relative through adoption, Mark Jacobs Jr. (Gusht'eihéen, 1923–2005). A prominent Tlingit and Alaska Native politician as well as the head of the Angoon branch of the Dak̲l'aweidí clan, Mr. Jacobs was a man well versed in traditional cultural knowledge, which he had shared generously with both of us (see Kan 2001, this volume; Mark Jacobs, this volume; Harold Jacobs, this volume; Hollinger and Harold Jacobs, this

Introduction 3

Fig. 0.6 Daniel Johnson Jr., the spokesman for the Kak'weidí (Basket Bay) clan of Angoon, wearing a ceremonial Double-headed Raven hat, which belongs to his grandfathers from the Raven House of Angoon. Photograph by Peter Metcalfe.

Fig. 0.7 Edwell John Jr., the head of the Killer Whale Chasing Seal House of the Dakl'aweidí clan of Angoon, wearing a ceremonial headdress and button blanket of his clan, at the 2007 clan conference in Sitka. Photograph by Peter Metcalfe.

volume). Having invited Andy Hope to serve as the third co-organizer of this conference, we began the preparations. Generous funding from the Arctic Social Science Program of the National Science Foundation as well as additional support from the Sitka tribe of Alaska and other sources enabled us to put together an impressive gathering of academic scholars, Native elders, and traditional culture experts as well as younger culture and language activists and artists to share their knowledge and current work. Andy Hope, joined by his colleague Peter Metcalfe, succeeded in raising the money that funded video coverage of the conference, which was produced by Metcalfe. Complete sets and individual DVDs that cover more than sixty hours of workshops and events can be accessed through a website sponsored by the University of Alaska Fairbanks (http://ankn.uaf.edu; search "sharing our knowledge"). All in all over one hundred participants took part in the conference, with several hundred attending all or at least some of its sessions and events.

The timing of the Sitka conference and of this publication has been quite favorable for assessing the field of Tlingit (and to some extent, greater northern Northwest Coast, i.e., Haida and Coast Tsimshian) anthropology and related fields in the first decade of the twenty-first century. Such an assessment has not been undertaken for quite some time, even though the field has changed a good deal in the last couple of decades. One major overview of the state of Northwest Coast ethnology and the related fields is, of course, the relevant volume of the *Handbook of North American Indians* (Suttles 1990).[1] Despite being a goldmine of information, it stops its coverage with the mid- to late 1980s and thus barely reflects the work of several generations of scholars who have entered the field since then and who began publishing in the late 1980s or early 1990s. Moreover, the *Handbook* has very little to say about the work done by nonacademic indigenous scholars and cultural activists.

As far as academic conferences have been concerned, the closest to our 2007 venue was the above-mentioned 1993 clan conference and the book based on it, published seven years later (Hope and Thornton 2000). Useful as that publication was, it contained only eight of the papers presented in Haines and Klukwan. More recently an international conference of Northwest Coast ethnologists from the United States, Canada, France, and other European countries, which had taken place in Paris in 2000, resulted in the publication of a volume entitled *Coming to Shore: Northwest Coast Ethnology, Traditions, and Visions* (Mauzé, Harkin, and Kan 2004). Several of the papers appearing in it address the Tlingit, Haida, and Tsimshian cultures, while the editors' introduction discusses a number of the new developments in the field of Northwest Coast ethnology, which the present book also addresses. However, only two of the contributors to *Coming to Shore* are Native, so that, in the end, the volume still fits the mold of a traditional academic publication.

The goal of *Sharing Our Knowledge* is different. In the last twenty years and especially the last decade, cultural anthropologists, museum specialists, archaeologists, and linguists working in southeast Alaska and the adjacent areas have engaged in a good deal of collaborative research with Native scholars, elders, and community activists. One might refer to this kind of work as "anthropology of mutual engagement" (cf. Lassiter 2000; Strong 2005; see also Field 2004). This collaborative work has focused on a number of time-honored topics, such as language and folklore, archaeology, ethnohistory, life history, and art history. At the same time, in recent years, several new areas or research and activism have developed, in which collaboration between academic and tribal scholars is not only desirable but also necessary and profitable for both sides. They include subsistence-related research, ethnogeography, archaeology, repatriation of human remains, clan regalia and other forms of cultural property, indigenous tourism, language preservation, and biography and family history.

The biggest change that has taken place in anthropology and related disciplines involved in studying the history and culture of the indigenous people of southeastern Alaska is the obligation most professional researchers feel to make sure that their research benefits the so-called source communities. This new ethics or philosophy of doing research, known as collaborative, community-based, or participatory action research, has emerged out of the changing ideological climate in the United States as well as the needs and demands of the native communities that researchers conduct their work in such a way as to benefit them and allow community input into the research design and the research process. In the words of Alison Brown and Laura Peers, "These new ways of working begin with the acknowledgment that dominant-society heritage professionals are not the only ones who know about, own, and control heritage resources: that local communities have rights in their culture and heritage and in its representation and dissemination" (2006, 101). This new approach to research has often been referred to as "the repatriation of knowledge." This term is particularly appropriate when it comes to enabling indigenous communities to gain access to archival documents, photographs, recordings of songs and stories and other forms of valuable cultural/historical data, which must find their way back to them, and engaging in (re)interpreting these data in collaboration with experts from these communities (cf. Ryan and Robinson 1990; Anderson and Nyce 1999; Krupnik and Jolly 2002; Schneider 2002).

Our volume begins by paying tribute to the lives and contributions of Tlingit intellectuals, tribal scholars, and elders as well as non-Native scholars who have all inspired the conference organizers and participants by their deep knowledge of and appreciation for Tlingit history and culture (Tlingit *Lingit kusteeyí*). One of them is Frederica de Laguna (1906–2004),[2] who bridged the Boasian era in northern Northwest Coast studies and the work of the current generation of scholars featured in this volume (Boas 1902, 1916; Swanton 1905a, 1905b, 1908, 1909; Garfield 1939, 1947; Olson 1967).[3] From her initial survey of the northern Tlingit territory in 1949 (which included Yakutat, Haines-Klukwan, Hoonah, Angoon, and Sitka), to summers of archaeological and ethnological research in Angoon in 1949 and 1950, to a series of longer periods of in-depth ethnographic study in Yakutat in 1949, 1952, and 1954, combined with library research, Freddy (as she was known to her colleagues, students, and friends) put together the most detailed record of Tlingit culture and history than any of her predecessors in the field. Moreover, in the tradition of the "Americanist anthropology," she did her best to comprehend this culture from the Tlingit point of view (de Laguna 1972).[4]

It was in Yakutat that Freddy developed her closest ties with a number of Tlingit elders and, as a result, produced her monumental opus, *Under Mount St. Elias: The History and Culture of the Yakutat Tlingit* (1972), which continues to serve as a major source of information for academic and community researchers. De Laguna's adoption by Katy Dixon Isaac into the Gineix̱ Ḵwáan clan of the Raven moiety confirmed the fact of her acceptance by the Yakutat elders she worked with, while her ability to compose a Tlingit love song is a clear indication of her deep understanding not only of the key principles of the Tlingit culture but of the subtleties of its worldview, ritual etiquette, and performative culture.[5] The history of "Freddy's song" and her relationship with the Yakutat community is described in the article by noted Yakutat cultural historians Elaine Abraham (Chew Shaa) and her daughter, Judy Ramos

Fig. 0.8 Frederica de Laguna at the University of Pennsylvania Museum, 1931. She is wearing the Marmot and Bat (or "Marmot and Its Prey") frontlet headdress (NA8498) and is holding the Raven of the Roof hat (NA10511). The Raven of the Roof hat will be repatriated to the L'ukna<u>x</u>.ádi clan of Sitka in the near future. Photographer unknown. Photo courtesy of the Penn Museum Archives.

(Daxootsu). We have reprinted it from an earlier publication dedicated to de Laguna (see Kaplan 2006).[6]

One major difference between the state of ethnological research in southeastern Alaska prior to the 1980s and in the past three decades is a significant increase in the number of Native scholars involved in it as well as the number of collaborative projects between them and the non-Native representatives of the academy. Prior to World War II, the field of Tlingit studies had only one indigenous scholar, Louis Shotridge (Stoowukáa, 1882–1937), who became an employee of and a collector for a major American anthropology museum and wrote a series of informative and thoughtful articles about the material and spiritual culture of his people. Even though his collecting activity met with some resistance from Tlingit traditionalists and remains a subjects of debate in the modern-day Native community, Stoowukáa's deep appreciation for and understanding of the nuances of his own heritage and his impressive ability to convey them in the English language continue to impress scholars and general readers alike, whether Native or non-Native. While much has already been written about this remarkable man,[7] our volume introduces two new essays on the subject: one by Robert W. Preucel on Shotridge's work at the University of Pennsylvania Museum of Anthropology and Archaeology and another by Lucy Fowler Williams on collecting activities and the same museum's current work on digitizing his very substantial archive of photographs and ethnographic notes. A special strength of these two essays, compared with some of the previous publications about Shotridge, has to do with the fact that Preucel and Williams, affiliated with the same museum, have for several years worked in close cooperation with members of the Tlingit community, verifying the accuracy of the information about Stoowukáa that they had found in their museum's archive and researching the history of the ceremonial objects that he had collected in southeastern Alaska.

This kind of close cooperation between Native elders and tribal scholars, on the one hand, and anthropologists, ethnohistorians, linguists, and other scholars working on southeastern Alaska culture and history, on the other, was relatively rare until the tone of the Native-Euroamerican relations in Alaska changed rather dramatically in the 1970s and 1980s. Among other things, there had been a significant increase in the number of knowledgeable Native elders/tradition bearers who had grown up speaking Tlingit as their first language but had also gone through the American educational system—at least through high school and in some cases through college and graduate school. Among them one ought to mention such men as William Paul, Andrew P. Johnson, Cyrus Peck Sr., Walter Soboleff, and Mark Jacobs Jr. (see Dauenhauer and Dauenhauer 1994). Some of them recorded their own versions of well-known Tlingit myths and stories or wrote down their own accounts of Tlingit culture and history, while others, like Mark Jacobs, chose to publish a few works of their own and also collaborate with linguists and anthropologists (Jacobs and Jacobs 1982; Jacobs 1987; Kan 1985, 1999, 2001b, this volume). Others, who lacked extensive formal schooling, relied on the latter to record their impressive knowledge of Tlingit oratory, stories, and myths, cultural information about traditional subsistence, place-names, ethnobotany, crafts, and other subjects. Notable among them were Robert Zuboff, Charlie Joseph Sr., Jesse Dalton, Jimmie George, Lydia George, Austin Hammond, Sally Hopkins, Alex Andrews, Amy Marvin, Jenny Thlunaut, Willie and Emma Marks, Herman Kitka, Mary Willis, Charlotte and Thomas Young Sr., Mary Marks, and Esther Littlefield (Dauenhauer and Dauenhauer 1987, 1990, 1994; Dauenhauer, Dauenhauer, and Black 2008; Kan 1985, 1989, 1999; Thornton 2000a, 2004, 2008).

As the number of these elderly traditionalists gradually decreased, the few remaining ones took it upon themselves to carry on the work of recording the *Lingít Kusteeyí*, translating it into English, and explaining it to their non-Tlingit colleagues in the academic community. For several of the contributors to this book and myself, Mark Jacobs Jr. was such an elder. As Jacobs's biographical sketch, written by his son Harold, as well as my own contribution explain, he was born and raised in a high-ranking family where everyone spoke Tlingit as their first language and where the older generations possessed deep knowledge of Tlingit history and ceremonial protocol. True to this upbringing and his family's legacy, Mark grew up to be a very proud Tlingit aristocrat (*aanyádi*), on the one hand, and an American patriot and a devout Christian, on the other. As I have argued in an earlier article as well as in the one appearing here, these various strands of his identity rarely seemed to clash within his mind (Kan 2001a and this volume).

A fine example of Mark's ability to blend traditional Tlingit and modern American cultures was his deep patriotism that grew out of his younger years when he and his brother volunteered to serve in the Navy during World War II. Having served with distinction in the Pacific, Mark saw a great deal of bloodshed and tragedy but also heroism, and

Fig. 0.9 Mark Jacobs Jr. (*right*) and his brother Harvey in 1942. Photograph courtesy of Harold Jacobs.

he maintained close ties with his wartime Navy comrades. To honor this important part of his life and identity, I have included his reminiscences about the war as well as a song in Tlingit composed by his son Harold, in which Harold draws on the traditional images of Tlingit warfare and warrior's pride and honor.

By the time I met Gusht'eihéen, he had already begun writing down the information on Tlingit history and culture that he had been obtaining from knowledgeable Tlingit elders, and he had been preparing an essay on traditional Tlingit foods, which he had started writing while his father was still alive. This piece was published in a 1982 collection edited by Andy Hope (Jacobs and Jacobs 1982) and was followed five years later by a publication based on a presentation Mark gave at the Second International Conference on Russian America on the Tlingit version of the circumstances of the 1804 battle between the Tlingit and the Russians in Sitka (Jacobs 1987, reprinted in Dauenhauer, Dauenhauer, and Black 2008). By this time, he was already busy keeping a journal consisting of his own reminiscences, stories told to him by various elders, and bits of ethnographic data. Steve Henrikson and I are convinced that he was a natural-born anthropologist/historian with a particular legal bend. After all, he did begin studying law in college and always regretted not being able to complete his education in that area. It is also clear, as I demonstrate in my contribution to this book, that the work I began with Mark in 1979–80 stimulated him to become interested in an even deeper probe into the Tlingit social and ideational culture. The relationship that the two of us established differed greatly from that of an "anthropologist–informant (consultant)," which was more common in American anthropology before the 1970s. As I argue, ours was a dialogue in which Gusht'eihéen acted as a mentor. This student-teacher relationship, which continued for much longer than anthropologist-informant relationships often lasted in the past,[8] was further affirmed when Mark adopted me into his clan and gave him his younger brother's name. At the same time, as the information I was acquiring from Mark, combined with that which I was collecting from other sources, began to generate articles and books, my mentor and older brother was gaining greater and greater respect for anthropology ("when it was done right," as he would put it).

I had not been the only anthropologist with whom Mark Jacobs shared his deep knowledge of Tlingit history and culture. Various researchers, ranging from those working for the National Park Service to those representing the State of Alaska Department of Fish and Game, benefitted greatly not only from his phenomenal memory but also from his openness, friendliness, and the great care he took to "tell it like it is" without embellishment or being self-serving. In the last decade of his life, he also spent a good deal of time interacting with curators and other museum professionals involved in researching, taking care of, and repatriating the precious material representations of the crests

Fig. 0.10 Mark Jacobs Jr. and Sergei Kan at the 1997 clan conference in Sitka. Photograph courtesy of Sergei Kan.

of Tlingit clans and houses. This work involved him in visits to a large number of American museums and introduced him to museum professions (see Hollinger and Jacobs, this volume).

If Mark Jacobs was one of the giants of the last generation of the traditional Tlingit elders/fluent speakers of the Tlingit language who generously shared their knowledge with the younger Native and non-Native scholars, Nora and Richard Dauenhauer have served as a bridge between those elders and several generations of the younger researchers and Tlingit language and culture activists. Born in 1927 into a family that combined a subsistence way of life with commercial fishing and cannery work and used Tlingit as the primary language of communication, Nora Marks Dauenhauer (Ḵeixwnéi) began to speak English only when she went to public school.[9] Steeped in the Tlingit oral tradition and oratory, she was able to transfer that knowledge to an academic setting when in the early 1970s, encouraged by her recently deceased husband, linguist and folklorist Richard Dauenhauer, she earned an undergraduate degree in anthropology and began transcribing and translating the potlatch ora-

Fig. 0.11 Richard Dauenhauer speaking at the 2007 clan conference in Sitka. Photograph by Peter Metcalfe.

tory she herself had recorded a few years earlier (see Nora Marks Dauenhauer 2000, 31–53, and Dauenhauer and Dauenhauer, this volume).

This type of work had never been done before. To begin with, very few ethnographers had an opportunity to be present at the potlatch (*koo.éex'*). And even those who were able to witness one did not record the ceremonial oratory verbatim. Moreover, they did not have the necessary command of the Tlingit language or a sufficiently deep understanding of the intricacies of the local social structure and interpersonal relations to be able to place those speeches in their proper sociocultural context.[10] Nora's work, which first appeared in small mono- and bilingual brochures produced by the Tlingit Readers,[11] demonstrated a major advantage that a Native scholar who combined a perfect command of the native language with academic training would have over his or her non-Native counterpart. In Keixwnéi's case, the success of her work was further increased by close cooperation with Richard, whose own expertise complemented hers very well. Their joint work on translating and interpreting the meaning of Tlingit oratory (both the speeches delivered in the potlatch and those given outside of it) resulted in the 1990 publication of a major work, *Haa Tuwunáagu Yís, for Healing Our Spirit: Tlingit Oratory*.

Fig. 0.12 Clan conference in Sitka, 2007. *From left to right*: Dolores Churchill, Nora Dauenhauer, and Dawn Glinsmann. Photograph by Peter Metcalfe.

Along with the study of Tlingit oratory, the Dauenhauers have made a major contribution to the work on the development and promotion of Tlingit literacy (Dauenhauer and Dauenhauer 1976) and the collection, transcription, and translation of Tlingit oral literature, with the latter ranging from the classic myths to the stories about the first encounters between the Tlingit and the Europeans (Dauenhauer and Dauenhauer 1987). While some of the stories appearing in Nora and Richard's books have been recorded and published before by such scholars as Swanton (1909) and Emmons (1911), only the Dauenhauers' publications are fully bilingual and present as accurate a rendition of the storytellers' words as possible. In addition each story is accompanied by a detailed linguistic and cultural commentary, making these publications a treasure trove for scholars and lay readers alike (and especially for the Native ones wishing to learn their own language and folklore). Given the inspiration that the Dauenhauer team has become for the younger generation of Tlingit storytellers, writers (in Tlingit and English), linguists, song composers, and language learners, it was only fitting for the conference organizers to request that the two of them deliver the keynote address, which I am delighted to reprint in this volume.[12]

For years, Andrew Hope III (1949–2008), our partner in organizing the 2007 conference, has been a close colleague of the Dauenhauers in

Fig. 0.13 Andrew Hope III in 1984. Photograph by Peter Metcalfe.

their efforts to promote the recording and publication of Tlingit texts and in various other language and culture preservation projects. Along with the Dauenhauers, Katherine Mills, and Henry Davis, Andy was a charter member of the Tlingit Readers, Inc., and a prime mover in its incorporation in 1972. He remained the organization's vice president until his death.

As I have already mentioned, the clan conference was Andy's brainchild, and it is not surprising that he took part in many of the panels

Fig. 0.14 Andrew Hope III at the 2007 Clan Conference in Sitka. Photograph by Peter Metcalfe.

and other events of the 2007 Sitka conference. He was looking forward to a similar gathering in 2009 in Juneau and during much of 2007 was already laying some of the groundwork for it. Tragically, his life was cut short by cancer, and he left us in August 2008. Consequently our 2009 conference, entitled *Sharing Our Knowledge / Telling Our Stories*, was officially dedicated to Andy's memory, and a decision was made to include a brief tribute by one of his closest friends and longtime colleagues, Peter Metcalfe, into the present volume. Given Andy's love of poetry and especially the fact that his own poems so eloquently reflect his identity as a Tlingit and Alaska Native intellectual, educator, and political/cultural activist, I have also decided to include several of them here. Andy's son, Ishmael Hope, himself a poet, actor, storyteller, and cultural activist, has selected these poems and written a brief introduction to them. While Peter's tribute sums up the highlights of Andy's life and contributions aptly, I would like to point out that to me Andy's sense of his own identity as well as his multifaceted activities and commitments represent a perfect bridge between the older generation of his grandparents that included both monolingual Tlingit traditionalists and bilingual political activists (like his paternal grandfather, Andrew Percy Hope, who served in the Alaska state legislature), the generation of his parents who devoted their lives to Native politics and education, and the younger generation of Tlingit students, teachers, and community activists. The latter, like his own son Ishmael, have been committed to the preservation of the indigenous culture of southeastern Alaska but are also open to cultural innovation, drawing on the best or the most useful aspects of non-Native "high" culture (e.g., theater), media, and technology.

One representative of this younger generation of Alaska Native scholars and cultural activists featured here is Mique'l Icesis Dangeli. A doctoral student in art history at the University of British Columbia, she has been researching the work of a Metlakatla Tsimshian photographer, Benjamin Alfred Haldane (1874–1941). A Tsimshian woman from the same Native community as Haldane, Dangeli has been able to interview a number of his descendants and other Metlakatla Tsimshian people who knew or heard of him. Using her community connections and an insider's understanding of the local culture and history, she has also been able to identify many of the individuals portrayed by Haldane, thus putting his photographs in a proper sociocultural and historical context. As a result, Dangeli's interpretation of Melakatla's history in the late nineteenth century and the first third of the twentieth turns out to be quite different from most of the previous one: instead of a story of assimilation and irreversible cultural loss of traditional culture, she constructs a story of resistance and cultural persistence.

Her essay offers an example of one relatively new approach to northern Northwest Coast ethnohistory, that which combines the use of documentary evidence (in this case, photographs and the photographer's correspondence) with the data obtained from interviews.[13] This approach is "relatively new" because, echoing a point made by Berman (this volume), I would argue that until quite recently, the majority of the anthropological and historical (or ethnohistorical) works that have dealt with the interaction between Northwest Coast Natives and newcomers have focused on broad trends rather than the history of indigenous clans or communities (Wike 1951; Fisher 1977; Gibson 1992).

When it comes to the ethnohistorical work dealing specifically with the Tlingit-White relations, two trends can be identified. On the one hand, there is a large body of work by an American historian, the late Ted Hinckley, whose primary focus has been "the Americanization of Alaska," including the impact of the American colonization on the Tlingit. While the difference between his earlier works and his last book on the subject shows an attempt to comprehend the Tlingit side of the Native encounter with the Americans, on the whole, the Tlingit cultural motivations for action remained rather unclear to him (Hinckley 1972, 1996; see also Kan 1986). On the other hand, James Gibson's studies of the role played by the Tlingit in the socioeconomic history of Russian America, while providing a good deal of valuable information (much of it from archival sources), tells us a lot more about the Russian than the Native side of this frontier encounter (1987).

Unlike these historians who, by and large, did not conduct interviews with the modern-day Tlingit, an anthropologist seriously interested in Native history did have the advantage of having plenty of opportunities to do so. However, the only scholar of the pre-1980s era who had an interest in combining ethnographic and historical research was de Laguna. She first articulated and tried it in her Angoon project (1960), but carried it out on a much larger scale during her work in Yakutat (1972). Nonetheless, most of the historical sources she used were the published ones.

It must be said, then, that the first major project of combining a large body of archival materials with ethnographic data was my own

1979–80 doctoral dissertation research on Russian Orthodox Christianity among the northern Tlingit (with a particular focus on Sitka, Angoon, and Juneau). Being a native Russian speaker, I could read the documents from the Alaska Russian Orthodox Church Collection, which covered the 1800s through the 1930s and remained in the United States after the sale of Alaska and the 1917 Bolshevik coup. During my stay in southeastern Alaska, I was able to complement the rich historical data gleaned from that collection with information obtained from a variety of published sources (e.g., Russian Orthodox and American periodicals), photographs, interviews with the elderly Tlingit members of several Orthodox parishes, and my own observations. After an initial one-year stay in southeast Alaska, I continued to come back for additional research, while seeking new published and archival sources on the subject of Tlingit-Russian relations and Tlingit Orthodoxy. This large-scale research project resulted in a series of articles and a book that shed light on a previously largely unknown and misunderstood but very important dimension of Tlingit history and culture (Kan 1985, 1987, 1996, 1999).[14]

Unlike the ecclesiastical documents pertaining to the era of the post-contact Tlingit history, only a portion of the records dealing with the various "secular" events and activities that took place in Russian America and involved the Tlingit has been available to Western researchers. For that reason, it was a Russian scholar, Andrei V. Grinev, who finally produced the first detailed monograph on the Russian-Tlingit relation, which drew quite heavily on these records and particularly the archive of the Russian Foreign Ministry and the Navy (1991).[15] It is as much the introduction of these valuable new sources of information as the author's interpretations and hypotheses that makes this an important contribution to the new body of works on Tlingit history. Following in Grinev's footsteps and drawing on a variety of published and unpublished Russian sources, our young Russian contributor, Elena Piterskaya, explores the Tlingit interaction with their Native neighbors during the Russian era.[16] Of course, what these Russian works lack is the use of the Tlingit oral narratives that could be played against the data from the written documents. An example of the work of the latter kind is a 2008 book by the Dauenhauers and their co-author, the late Lydia T. Black, a noted specialist on the history and ethnology of Russian Alaska. Thanks to Black's participation in this project as well as Richard's command of the Russian language, the Dauenhauers were able to reconstruct the events of the famous battles of 1802 and 1804 between the Tlingit and the Russians using Russian documents (both published and the newly available archival ones) and the Tlingit oral narratives by knowledgeable elders recorded some fifty years ago. The result is a monumental one-of-a-kind ethnohistorical work that offers a comprehensive reconstruction and culturally sensitive interpretation of the meaning of some of the key events in Tlingit colonial history and the history of Russian America.

Aside from the Russian materials, the numerous archival documents pertaining to the era of the American rule over southeastern Alaska are another major source of information on southeastern Alaska Native history. Some of the most interesting are those related to the court cases involving the Natives because they often reveal a clash between two completely different and mutually unintelligible legal systems. Particularly revealing are the cases pertaining to the pre-1884 era when Alaska did not have its own courts, judges, or juries, when the Oregon Code had to be applied to it, and when the issue of whether or not it constituted "Indian country" had to be decided by each judge on a case-by-case basis. It is this era that Diane Purvis addresses in an essay appearing in this book.

The (ethno)historical section of this volume concludes with a contribution by Judith Berman that sets new standards for the study of Tlingit history and, in my opinion, Northwest Coast Native history in general. Her essay combines the information gleaned from the manuscript records compiled by fur traders and other visitors to the Tlingit shores with that which can be derived from the indigenous historical tradition. Berman is an anthropologist by training, and this contribution, just as much of her previous work on both Kwakwaka'wakw and Tlingit history and oral literature, benefits greatly from her adopting the perspective of the ethnography of communication (Berman 1991, 2004). As an anthropologist Berman is also able to make good sense of the field notes of her predecessors, Ronald Olson and Louis Shotridge, who recorded detailed information on the genealogies and family history of the people of Taant'a Ḵwáan (Tongass area), which has been one of the most poorly represented in the published anthropological literature.[17] By carefully comparing this data with all the information on the Taant'a Ḵwáan that she could find in the non-Native written records, Berman is not only able to significantly enrich our knowledge of the history of this particular *Ḵwáan* but demonstrate that the unpublished work of some of the anthropologists of the earlier times could still be utilized as a *major* source of important historical/cultural information and that this method of combining traditional Native forms of history with primary non-Native documentary sources is valid and could yield important and interesting results.

The papers by Steve Langdon and Tom Thornton share a focus on the centrality of place in Tlingit culture. They also represent a relatively new field of systematic subsistence studies with practical ("applied") implications, which did not really exist in southeastern Alaska anthropology prior to the late 1970s. The one exception to this generalization is an important pioneering work of the recently deceased anthropologist Walter R. Goldschmidt and his lawyer colleague Theodore Haas, who in 1946 were sent by the Commission of Indian Affairs to interview a significant number of Native people of southeastern Alaska about their possessory land rights. The impetus for this project was a major increase in non-Native migration to the region that galvanized Native political leaders and brought issues of land and resources to courts of law, where neither precedence nor evidence was sufficient to settle claims. Unfortunately, the two researchers' detailed observations and invaluable interview data became available exclusively to a small group of specialists and only in mimeographed form, and the book was published only in 1998, thanks to the efforts of its editor, Tom Thornton (Goldschmidt and Haas 1998).[18]

Thornton's own work, which began in the early 1990s, has combined extensive "applied" research with the Division of Subsistence, Alaska Department of Fish and Game, with a consistent scholarly focus on Tlingit "ethnogeography" as it pertains to social organization, language and cognition, economy, and ceremonies. Studying Tlingit and Haida subsistence is something that Steve Langdon, Tom's senior colleague, has actually been doing since the late 1970s. For decades he has been publishing academic articles on southeast Alaska Native fishing technologies (past and present), while also "assisting Alaska and Canadian Native organizations by providing research information, and by developing ideas and strategies for enhancing Alaska Native participating in commercial fisheries" (Feldman, Langdon, and Natcher 2005, 141).[19]

The notion that anthropological research, whether referred to as "applied," "practical," or "engaged," should be of interest to and benefit the indigenous people whose culture is being studied may sound like common sense today, but like the study of southeastern Alaska subsistence, the field of "applied" anthropology is relatively young. For obvious reasons, in Alaska it has been linked to the Alaska Native Claims Settlement Act of 1971 and has to a significant extent focused on subsistence. As Wheeler and Thornton (2005,85) have convincingly argued, ethnographic research, a careful study of people's cultural ways through interviewing and participant observation, "continues to be the way to evaluate the ongoing adaptation and evolution of subsistence economies and the changing patterns of subsistence in relation to regional and global developments." At the same time the ways of carrying out this research have clearly been changing. In the words of the same two scholars, "The model of the lone researcher in a remote village is gradually giving way to collaborative team-oriented approaches in which local people are empowered partners in all facets of the research. . . . Already, collaborative approaches are proving effective at the community level" (85).

In Langdon's project among the southern Tlingit, represented by the paper published here, these Tlingit collaborators are not only the elders he interviewed about *Deiki Noow* (Hazy Islands) in 2004–2005 but also a group of younger Tlingit whom he accompanied in June 2007 on a trip to these islands. Steve's description of that trip is an important part of the paper, as it demonstrates how "that experience was informed by the past and looked to the future and linked activities conducted at that time to the core components of Tlingit culture." Of course, as in much of his previous work, Steve effectively supplements his ethnographic study with careful archival research as well as the data gleaned from Tlingit myths pertaining to *Deiki Noow*. As a result, he is able to explore the multiple reasons for the significance of this particular place to the southern Tlingit people, as far as their economy, society and worldview have been concerned.

Another major source of scholarly inspiration for the Langdon paper is Tom Thornton's work on "being and place" among the Tlingit. In a series of articles and a recently published book, Thornton eloquently demonstrates that the Tlingit notion of space actually consists of three dimensions—space, time, and experience—each of which is both ecological and culturally constituted (Thornton 1997, 2000a, 2004, 2008). By analyzing each of these dimensions, he demonstrates how individual and collective notions of place, being, and identity are formed and maintained over time. He also argues that, despite some major sociocultural, political, and environmental changes that have taken place in Tlingit country since 1867, many Tlingit continue to connect to places on the land in ways that are different from those of their non-Tlingit neighbors (Kan 2008/09).

Here, Thornton continues his exploration of Tlingit notions of space, but this time he treats them as an educational resource. He builds on his own field project aimed at creating a cultural atlas prototype based on Tlingit-named places around the village of Angoon (Thornton 2000b). Initiated in the early 1990s, this project involved such well-respected and highly knowledgeable Angoon elders as the late Lydia George and had the enthusiastic support of Andy Hope, who at the time was developing his own vision for incorporating place-based Native Alaskan theories of knowledge into the curriculum. As Tom explains in this essay, the idea of the Angoon Cultural Atlas (which is now stored on the Alaska Native Knowledge Network web site, one of Andy's major and favorite projects) is that "a person could start within a Tlingit cultural geography, either a named place, a named house, or even a crest, and move to the corresponding cultural property associated with that entity." Obviously such an exercise would be particularly valuable for a Native person trying to learn the fundamentals of his or her native culture and to locate himself or herself within the Tlingit geographic, social, and spiritual (ancestral) universe of crests and names.

The third paper in our collection to deal with the southeastern Alaska Natives' use of natural resources is by Madonna Moss, one of the region's most prominent and prolific senior archaeologists. In fact, as an archeologist, Dr. Moss addresses the issues of Native use of a food resource—seabirds in this particular case—in a detailed and systematic fashion. Drawing on several recent archaeological excavations on Forrester Islands, an area historically utilized by both the Haida and the Southern Tlingit, she analyzes the zooarchaeological data, supplemented by ethnographic and biological data, to demonstrate a widespread hunting of migratory seabirds by the indigenous people of the region for the past 1,600 years. Moss's final argument nicely illustrates the point that in southeastern Alaska (as elsewhere in the state) even archaeological research could play a positive role in helping the Native people support their continuous use of a particular natural resource or reclaim a traditional use no longer permitted by American laws. In Moss's words, her results "provide longitudinal support for the rights of southeast Alaska Natives to harvest seabirds" (see also Moss 2010, 2011).[20]

Conferences dealing with indigenous Northwest Coast cultures almost always include presentations on Native art, and ours was no exception.

Fig. 0.15 Gerry Hope (Andrew Hope's younger brother) speaking at the 2007 Clan Conference in Sitka. Photograph by Peter Metcalfe.

In fact, there were several panels dealing with the more practical issues of art and craft making as well as studying and collecting them. This volume features the works of the latter kind. One is by a senior scholar, Robin Wright, professor of Art History at the University of Washington and curator of Native American Art at the Burke Museum in Seattle, two by her former students, Kathryn Bunn-Marcuse and Ashley Verplank McClelland,[21] and the fourth one by Megan Smetzer, a young scholar with a 2007 PhD from the University of British Columbia's Department of Art History, Visual Art, and Theory. Wright's paper builds on her monumental work, *Northern Haida Master Carvers* (2001), to explore a series of Haida house models created in 1892 by a group of Haida carvers for the World's Columbian Exposition. Representing the best in the present-day research on the history of Northwest Coast art, this project is a collaboration between Wright's own museum, Chicago's Field Museum, and the Haida Gwaii Museum at Kaay 'Llnagaay, a Skidegate Haida community.

Drawing on a large body of museum pieces, published literature, and interviews with Native tradition bearers, Verplank McClelland offers a detailed examination of Tlingit daggers from a chronological as well as a contextual framework in order to define their physical and functional evolution. Bunn-Marcuse and Smetzer deal with the types of Tlingit and Haida arts that for a long time were considered a "tourist trade" and something inferior to the work of the precontact and early contact artists. In Bunn-Marcuse's case it is gold and silver jewelry, and in Smetzer's it is beadwork. Contrary to this prevailing older view, Bunn-Marcuse makes a strong argument that jewelry making of many Tlingit and Haida artists in Alaska and northern British Columbia was not experiencing a decline in the beginning of the twentieth century; instead, new techniques and aesthetics as well as a search for new markets was taking place. Megan Smetzer's approach to a previously neglected topic of Tlingit beadwork is to reject the Euro-American view of it as a sign of indigenous assimilation and cultural decline and carefully examine the ways in which it "has circulated and gained meaning from the late nineteenth century to the present." Like Wright and Verplank McClelland, Bunn-Marcuse and Smetzer rely not only on museum collections but also on interviews with Native artists.

Alexis Bunten's paper, which is based entirely on interviews she conducted with Native artists living in southeast Alaska, continues the theme of "tourist art." Her focus, however, is quite different from the other essays in this section. It is not the specific objects themselves that she discusses but the Native artists' strategies to abide by at least some of the key rules of the indigenous protocol involved in making crest-bearing artifacts, while trying to make a living in a commercial market where they are competing with non-Native artists and craftsmen as well as companies mass-producing cheap imitations of Native art. While presenting interesting ethnographic data, Bunten also raises an important practical question of whether the traditional protocol could be in any way reconciled with the U.S. copyright law.[22]

The two essays in the last section of the book examine a major issue confronting museum professionals today: the repatriation of certain types of Native American artifacts back to the indigenous communities, tribes, clans, and families. As Stacey Espenlaub's chapter argues, the Native American Graves Protection and Repatriation Act (NAGPRA) legislature has dramatically altered the relationship between Native American communities, on the one hand, and museum professionals and anthropologists, on the other. This is particularly true for southeastern Alaska where many of the most precious Tlingit and Haida artifacts represent what the Tlingit call *at.óow*, sacred property owned collectively by a matrilineal group (house, clan) rather than an individual, and hence are often the most obvious candidates for repatriation. In fact, some of the earliest successful cases of repatriation in the United States have involved Tlingit objects. For this reason, I am especially pleased to be able to include an essay by Eric Hollinger and Harold Jacobs. Harold (b. 1964) is a prominent Tlingit cultural activist with deep knowledge of Tlingit ceremonial protocol and traditional culture as well as command of the Tlingit language, rare among the people of his generation. For the past two decades Harold has worked as a cultural specialist for the Central Council of the Tlingit and Haida Tribes of Alaska, handling all of the repatriation cases for this major native organization. Eric Hollinger is a staff member of the repatriation office of the Smithsonian's National Museum of Natural History and has had a good deal of experience working with Native American repatriation cases, including Native Alaskan ones. The repatriation case their essay describes is a textbook one, since the identity and the history of the object in question, a beautiful wooden headdress in the shape of a killer whale, was well documented, and the identity of its rightful owner, the Dakl'aweidí clan of the Angoon Tlingit, was accurately established by combining the data from John Swanton's ethnographic notes and the testimony from several knowledgeable Tlingit cultural experts, including Harold himself. Particularly noteworthy is the fact that the headdress in question had been collected by one of the pioneers of Tlingit ethnology while the head of the Dakl'aweidí clan at the time of the repatriation was none other than Harold's father himself. Mark, who carried the same name as the man from whom Swanton had bought the artifact, served as one of the main sources of information about the headdress. The story of the headdress's return and especially the Smithsonian's willingness to speed up the bureaucratic portion of the repatriation process, so as to get the *at.óow* to Mr. Jacobs before his health had completely deteriorated, is a moving example of collaboration between the representatives of a Native American community and knowledgeable and conscientious museum professionals.

While the Hollinger/Jacobs paper deals with a single case of repatriation, the contribution by Espenlaub discusses the more general practical and ethical issues involved in those cases when museums loan ceremonial objects from their collections to legitimate Native Alaskan kinship groups and organizations for their use in memorial potlatches and other rituals. As these essays on repatriation demonstrate, despite the initial fears that many museum professionals had about repatriation

Fig. 0.16 Harold Jacobs speaking at the 2007 clan conference in Sitka. Next to him is his mother, the late Adelaide Jacobs. Photograph by Peter Metcalfe.

resulting in the loss of a large portion of their collections, in many cases the return of the *at.óow* to their rightful owners and/or the loaning of them to Tlingit clans for ceremonial purposes have only increased the museologists' and the anthropologists' knowledge of Tlingit culture and have contributed significantly to the development of much more cooperative, collaborative, and collegiate relationships between the Native and the museum/anthropological communities. These relationships are a major theme running through this entire volume.

NOTES

1. For an earlier review of the state of the field, see Adams (1981) and Suttles and Jonaitis (1990).
2. On de Laguna's life and career, see her own writing (2000, 2004) as well as McClellan (1989), Guedon (2004), and Darnell (2005). See also a special issue of *Arctic Anthropology* dedicated to de Laguna and edited by Kaplan (2006).
3. It has long been noted that up to the 1950s and 1960s, much of the ethnological research on the Northwest Coast had been dominated by Boas, his students, and his students' students (Suttles and Jonaitis

1990; see also Adams 1981). Major exceptions, however, did exist, particularly in Tlingit anthropology. It began with the pioneering work of a Russian missionary ethnographer and linguist priest (later bishop), Ivan Veniaminov, in the 1830s (Veniaminov 1984), and continued with an impressive and quite comprehensive ethnological work by George Emmons (1991) in the late nineteenth and early twentieth century. It also included a study of the native economy and social organization by Kalervo Oberg (1973), trained at the University of Chicago in the 1930s.

4. On the Americanist tradition in American and Canadian anthropology, see Valentine and Darnell (1999).
5. Freddy's close ties with the people of Yakutat and her emotional return there in the mid-1990s are depicted in a documentary film, *Reunion under Mount St. Elias*, produced by Laura Bliss Spaan in 1997 (see Spaan 2006).
6. Of the scholars whose work is featured in this volume, Freddy had had a particular close relationship with Richard and Nora Dauenhauer. I began corresponding with her about my research in the early 1980s and consider her pioneering essay on the Tlingit ideas about the individual to be among her most profound contributions to Tlingit ethnology and particularly ethnopsychology; it inspired and informed my own work in that area (de Laguna 1954; cf. Kan 1989, 66–102).
7. See, for example, Carpenter (1975), Milburn (1986), and Dauenhauer and Dauenhauer (1994, 548–64; 2003).
8. Unlike many of my predecessors in this research, including Laura Klein (1976, 1980), Kristin Barsness (1997), and Kirk Dombrowski (2001), but like the other participants in this volume (Langdon, Moss, Thornton) and Kenneth Tollefson, who has continued to interact regularly with the Tlingit residents and visitors in his hometown of Seattle, I have repeatedly returned to the Tlingit country to continue my ethnographic work and maintain close ties with numerous Tlingit relatives, friends, and colleagues (Kan 2001a, this volume). Of course, my experience is not unique. See, for example, Thomas Buckley's 2002 account of his long-term involvement with Yurok elders and several essays in my edited volume on the adoption and naming of anthropologists by Native Americans (Kan 2001b).
9. For the biographies of Nora Marks's parents, see Dauenhauer and Dauenhauer 1994, 378–406, 452–62).
10. In the course of my own ethnographic research, I did record quite a few potlatch speeches, but I could only translate them with the help of knowledgeable elders. Moreover, my own work on the potlatch did not begin until 1980, more than a decade after Nora Dauenhauer initiated hers (see Kan 1983, 1989).
11. Other activists of the Tlingit Readers included Richard Dauenhauer, Andy Hope III, Katherine Mills, Henry and Clarabell Davis, Jeff Leer, Rosita Worl, Elaine Abraham, Vesta Dominics, and JoAnn George.

12. Of course, the Dauenhauers rarely worked alone but with a group of Native and non-Native colleagues mentioned earlier. Some of the work on Tlingit language preservation and education, which they had initiated while working for the Sealaska Heritage Foundation (established in 1980), is now being continued by this organization's successor, the Sealaska Heritage Institute.
13. The "photographic ethnohistory" of the northern Northwest Coast nations was pioneered by Margaret Blackman (1981), who worked on the Haida, and continued more recently by Sharon B. Gmelch (2008), who focused on the Tlingit. However, in comparison with Blackman, Gmelch's archival research was limited largely to the study of the photographs themselves and not the archival materials on the photographers and the subjects they portrayed. I wrote a book dealing with Vincent Soboleff's photographs of the Tlingit of Angoon and Killisnoo, taken in the late nineteenth and the early twentieth century (Kan 2013; see also Fair 2000).
14. I also undertook the task of translating the works of Russian Orthodox missionaries into English, beginning with the excerpts from Bishop Ivan Veniaminov's (St. Innocent's) 1840s description of the Tlingit, which Andy Hope published in *Neek*, the newsletter of the Sitka Community Association that he produced in the 1980s, and in *Raven's Bones*, a 1982 volume of Tlingit-related essays and other materials that he edited, and culminating with the translation of Anatolii Kamenskii's 1906 *The Tlingit Indians* (1985).
15. In 2005 an English translation of Grinev's book was published in the United States.
16. Elena Piterskaya also published a detailed Russian-language report on the 2007 Sitka conference, published in the online portion of the leading Russian anthropology journal *Etnograficheskoe Obozrenie*.
17. It should be pointed out that while Berman's project has been historical and did not involve interviews with the present-day Tongass people, she did receive assistance from several prominent Tongass elders in deciphering Olson's field notes and checking his and Shotridge's genealogical data. She had also been given strong encouragement for this project from the leading members of the Tongass tribe.
18. The 1998 publication of the work of Goldschmidt and Haas received a great deal of support from Dennis Demmert, a Native Alaskan educator, who in the late 1990s was president of the Sealaska Heritage Foundation.
19. Thus in the early 1980s Langdon's research helped prepare a court case to reopen Inian Islands purse seining, which had been halted by the state of Alaska in 1973 (Feldman, Langdon, and Natcher 2005, 141).
20. It should be added that a number of Madonna Moss's publications deal with such subjects that address Tlingit subsistence, past and present,

and are otherwise of interest to those members of the Tlingit community who might be inclined to read professional articles and reports on archaeological subjects (see, for example, Newton and Moss 2005).
21. Bunn-Marcuse and Verplank McClelland received their PhDs from the University of Washington's Art History Department.
22. For Bunten's work on a related subject of tribal (Tlingit) tourism and ethnic self-representation, see Bunten (2006, 2008).

REFERENCES

Adams, John W. 1981. "Recent Ethnology of the Northwest Coast." *Annual Review of Anthropology* 10: 361–92.
Anderson, Margaret Seguin, and Marjorie Halpin, eds. 2000. *Potlatch at Gitsegukla: William Beynon's 1945 Field Notebooks*. Vancouver: University of British Columbia Press.
Anderson, Margaret Seguin, and Deanna Nyce. 1999. "Nisga Studies and the Americanist Tradition: Bringing First Nations Research and Teaching in the Academy." In *Theorizing the Americanist Tradition,* ed. Lisa Philips Valentine and Regna Darnell. Toronto: University of Toronto Press.
Barsness, Kristin. 1997. "A Tlingit Community, a Century of Change." PhD diss., Bryn Mawr College.
Berman, Judith. 1991. "The Seals' Sleeping Cave: The Interpretation of Boas's Kwakw'ala Texts." PhD diss., University of Pennsylvania.
———. 2004. "'Some Mysterious Means of Fortune': A Look at North Pacific Oral History." In *Coming to Shore: Northwest Coast Ethnology, Traditions, and Visions,* ed. Marie Mauzé, Michael E. Harkin, and Sergei Kan, 129–62. Lincoln: University of Nebraska Press.
Blackman, Margaret. 1981. *Window on the Past: The Photographic Ethnohistory of the Northern and Kaigani Haida*. National Museum of Man. Mercury Series. Ethnology Service Papers 74. Ottawa.
Boas, Franz. 1902. *Tsimshian Texts*. BAE Bulletin, 27. Washington DC: Government Printing Office.
———. 1916. *Tsimshian Mythology*. Washington DC: Government Printing Office.
Brown, Alison K. and Laura Peers, eds. 2006. *"Pictures Bring Us Messages": Photographs and Histories from the Kainai Nation*. Toronto: University of Toronto Press.
Buckley, Thomas C. T. 2002. *Standing Ground: Yurok Indian Spirituality, 1850–1990*. Berkeley: University of California Press.
Bunten, Alexis. 2006. "'So, How Long Have You Been Native?' Self-Commodification in the Native-Owned Cultural Tourism Industry." PhD diss., University of California, Los Angeles.
———. 2008. "Sharing Culture or Selling Out? Developing the Commodified Persona in the Heritage Industry." *American Ethnologist* 35 (3): 380–95.

Campbell, Robert. 2007. *In Darkest Alaska: Travel and Empire along the Inside Passage*. Philadelphia: University of Pennsylvania Press.

Carpenter, Edmund. 1975. Introduction to *Form and Freedom: A Dialogue on Northwest Coast Art*, 9–27. Houston: Institute for the Arts, Rice University.

Darnell, Regna, 2005. "Frederica de Laguna (1906–2004)." *American Anthropologist* 107 (3): 554–62.

Dauenhauer, Nora Marks. 2000. *Life Woven with Song*. Tucson: University of Arizona Press.

Dauenhauer, Nora Marks, and Richard Dauenhauer. 1976. *Beginning Tlingit*. Sitka AK: Tlingit Readers.

———. 1987. *Haa Shuká, Our Ancestors: Oral Narratives*. Seattle: University of Washington Press.

———. 1990. *Haa Tuwunáagu Yís, for Healing Our Spirit: Tlingit Oratory*. Seattle: University of Washington Press.

———. 1994. *Haa Kusteeyí, Our Culture: Tlingit Life Stories*. Seattle: University of Washington Press.

———. 2003. "Louis Shotridge and Indigenous Tlingit Ethnography." In *Constructing Cultures Then and Now: Celebrating Franz Boas and the Jesup North Pacific Expedition*, ed. Laurel Kendall and Igor Krupnik, 165–84. Contributions to Circumpolar Anthropology 4. Washington DC: Smithsonian Institution.

Dauenhauer, Nora Marks, Richard Dauenhauer, and Lydia T. Black. 2008. *Anóoshi Lingít Aaní Ká, Russians in Tlingit America: The Battles of Sitka, 1802 and 1804*. Seattle: University of Washington Press.

de Laguna, Frederica. 1954. "Tlingit Ideas about the Individual." *Southwestern Journal of Anthropology* 19 (2): 172–91.

———. 1960. *The Story of a Tlingit Community*. BAE Bulletin, 172. Washington DC: Government Printing Office.

———. 1972. *Under Mount St. Elias: The History and Culture of the Yakutat Tlingit*. 3 vols. Smithsonian Contributions to Anthropology. Washington DC: Smithsonian Institution Press.

———. 1990. The Tlingit. In *Handbook of North American Indians*, vol. 7, *Northwest Coast*, ed. Wayne Suttles, 203–28. Washington DC: Smithsonian Institution Press.

———. 2000. "Fieldwork among Tlingit Friends." In *Celebration 2000: Restoring Balance Culture*, ed. Susan Fair and Rosita Worl, 21–40. Juneau AK: Sealaska Heritage Foundation.

———. 2004. "Becoming an Anthropologist: My Debt to European and Other Scholars Who Influenced Me." In *Coming to Shore: Northwest Coast Ethnology, Traditions, and Visions*, ed. Marie Mauzé, Michael Harkin, and Sergei Kan, 23–52. Lincoln: University of Nebraska Press.

Dombrowski, Kirk. 2001. *Against Culture: Development, Politics, and Religion in Indian Alaska*. Lincoln: University of Nebraska Press.

Emmons, George T. 1911. "Native Account of the Meeting between La Perouse and the Tlingit." *American Anthropologist* 13 (2): 294–98.

———. 1991. *The Tlingit Indians*. Ed. Frederica de Laguna. Seattle: University of Washington Press.

Fair, Susan W. 2000. "Vincent Soboleff: An Intimate Look at Turn-of-the-Century Southeast Alaska." In *Celebration 2000: Restoring Balance through Culture*, ed. Susan W. Fair and Rosita Worl, 73–76. Juneau: Sealaska Heritage Foundation.

Feldman, Kerry D., Steven J. Langdon, and David Natcher. 2005. "Northern Engagement: Alaska Society and Applied Cultural Anthropology, 1973–2003." *Alaska Journal of Anthropology* 3 (1): 121–55.

Field, Les W. 2004. "Beyond 'Applied' Anthropology." In *A Companion to the Anthropology of American Indians*, ed. Thomas Biolsi, 472–89. Malden MA: Blackwell.

Fisher, Robin. 1977. *Contact and Conflict: Indian-European Relations in British Columbia, 1774–1890*. Vancouver: University of British Columbia Press.

Garfield, Viola. 1939. *Tsimshian Clan and Society*. University of Washington Publications in Anthropology 7 (3).

———. 1947. "Historical Aspects of Tlingit Clans in Angoon, Alaska." *American Anthropologist* 49 (3): 438–52.

Gibson, James R. 1987. "Russian Dependence upon the Natives of Alaska." In *Russia's American Colony*, ed. S. Frederick Starr, 77–104. Durham NC: Duke University Press.

———. 1992. *Otter Skins, Boston Ships, and China Goods: The Maritime Fur Trade of the Northwest Coast, 1785–1841*. Seattle: University of Washington Press.

Gmelch, Sharon Bohn. 2008. *The Tlingit Encounter with Photography*. Philadelphia: University of Pennsylvania Museum of Archaeology and Anthropology.

Goldschmidt, Walter, and Theodore H. Haas. 1998. *Haa aaní = Our Land: Tlingit and Haida Land Rights and Use*, ed. Thomas F. Thornton. Seattle: University of Washington Press.

Grinev, Andrei. 1991. *Indeitsy tlinkity v period Russkoi Ameriki (1741–1867 gg.)*. Novosibirsk: Nauka.

———. 2005. *The Tlingit Indians in Russian America, 1741–1867*. Lincoln: University of Nebraska Press.

Guedon, Marie-Françoise. 2004. "Crossing Boundaries: Homage to Frederica de Laguna." In *Coming to Shore: Northwest Coast Ethnology, Traditions, and Visions*, ed. Marie Mauzé, Michael Harkin, and Sergei Kan, 53–61. Lincoln: University of Nebraska Press.

Hinckley, Ted C. 1972. *The Americanization of Alaska, 1867–1897*. Palo Alto CA: Pacific Books.

———. 1996. *The Canoe Rocks: Alaska's Tlingit and Euramerican Frontier*. Lanham MD: University Press of America.

Hope, Andrew, III, ed. 1982. *Raven's Bones*. Sitka: Sitka Community Association.

———. 2000. Introduction to *Will the Time Ever Come? A Tlingit Source Book*, ed. Andrew Hope III and Thomas F. Thornton, 6–10. Fairbanks: Alaska Native Knowledge Network, University of Alaska.

Hope, Andrew, III, and Thomas F. Thornton, eds. 2000. *Will the Time Ever Come? A Tlingit Source Book*. Fairbanks: Alaska Native Knowledge Network, University of Alaska.

Jacobs, Mark, Jr. 1987. "Early Encounters between the Tlingit and the Russians." In *Russia in North America: Proceedings of the 2nd International Conference on Russian America*, ed. Richard A. Pierce, 1–6. Kingston, Ontario: Limestone Press.

Jacobs, Mark, and Mark Jacobs Sr. 1982. "Southeast Alaska Native Foods." In *Raven's Bones*, ed. Andrew Hope III, 112–20. Sitka: Sitka Community Association.

Kamenskii, Anatolii. 1985. *The Tlingit Indians*. Rasmusson Library Historical Translation Series, vol. 2. Fairbanks: University of Alaska Press.

Kan, Sergei. 1983. "Words That Heal the Soul: Analysis of the Tlingit Potlatch Oratory." *Arctic Anthropology* 20 (2): 47–59.

———. 1985. "Russian Orthodox Brotherhoods among the Tlingit: Missionary Goals and Native Response." *Ethnohistory* 32 (3): 196–223.

———. 1986. Review of *Ted C. Hinckley, Alaskan John G. Brady: Missionary, Businessman, Judge, and Governor, 1878–1918*. *Alaska Native Magazine (Raven's Bones Journal)* 4 (5): 14–15.

———. 1987. "Memory Eternal: Russian Orthodoxy and the Tlingit Mortuary Complex." *Arctic Anthropology* 24 (1): 32–55.

———. 1989. *Symbolic Immortality: Tlingit Potlatch of the Nineteenth Century*. Washington DC: Smithsonian Institution Press.

———. 1996. "Clan Mothers and Godmothers: Tlingit Women and Russian Orthodox Christianity." Ed. Michael Harkin and Sergei Kan. *Ethnohistory* 43 (4): 613–41.

———. 1999. *Memory Eternal: Tlingit Culture and the Russian Orthodox Church through Two Centuries*. Seattle: University of Washington Press.

———. 2001a. "Friendship, Family, and Fieldwork: One Anthropologist's Adoption by Two Tlingit Families." In *Strangers to Relatives: The Adoption and Naming of Anthropologists in Native North America*, ed. Sergei Kan, 185–217. Lincoln: University of Nebraska Press.

———. 2001b. *Strangers to Relatives: The Adoption and Naming of Anthropologists in Native North America*, ed. Sergei Kan. Lincoln: University of Nebraska Press.

———. 2004. "'It's Only Half a Mile from Savagery to Civilization': American Tourists and the Southeastern Alaska Natives in the Late Nineteenth Century." In *Coming to Shore: Northwest Coast Ethnology, Traditions, and*

Visions, eds. Marie Mauzé, Michael Harkin, and Sergei Kan, 201–20. Lincoln: University of Nebraska Press.

———. 2008/2009. Review of Thomas F. Thornton, *Being and Place among the Tlingit*. BC *Studies* 160: 131–33.

———. 2009a. Review of Page Raibmon, *Authentic Indians: Episodes of Encounter from the Late Nineteenth-Century Northwest Coast*. *Ethnohistory* 56(1): 207–9.

———. 2013. *A Russian American Photographer in Tlingit Country: Vincent Soboleff in Alaska*. Norman: Oklahoma University Press.

Kaplan, Susan. 2006. Introduction. *Arctic Anthropology* 43 (2): 6. (Special issue dedicated to Frederica de Laguna.)

Klein, Laura. 1976. "She Is One of Us, You Know: The Public Life of Tlingit Women." PhD diss., New York University.

———. 1980. "Contending with Colonization: Tlingit Men and Women in Change." In *Women and Colonization: Anthropological Perspectives*, ed. Mona Etienne and Eleanor Leacock, 88–108. New York: Praeger.

Krupnik, Igor, and Dyanna Jolly. 2002. *The Earth Is Faster Now: Indigenous Observations on Arctic Environmental Change*. Fairbanks: Arctic Research Consortium of the United States.

Langdon, Steve. 1979a. "The Development of Salmon Fishing Technologies in the Prince of Wales Archipelago." In *The Sea in Alaska's Past*, ed. M. Kennedy. History and Archaeology Series, no. 25. Anchorage: Office of History and Archaeology.

———. 1979b. "Comparative Tlingit and Haida Adaptation to the West Coast of the Prince of Wales Archipelago." *Ethnology* 19 (2): 101–19.

———. 1987. "Traditional Tlingit Fishing Structures in the Prince of Wales Archipelago." In *Fisheries in Alaska's Past: A Symposium*. Alaska Historical Commission Studies in History, no. 227. Anchorage: Office of History and Archaeology.

———. 2006. "Tidal Pulse Fishing: Selective Traditional Tlingit Salmon Fishing Techniques on the West Coast of the Prince of Wales Archipelago." In *Traditional Ecological Knowledge and Natural Resource Management*, ed. C. Menzies, 21–46. Lincoln: University of Nebraska Press.

Lassiter, Luke E. 2000. "Authoritative Texts, Collaborative Ethnography, and Native American Studies." *American Indian Quarterly* 24(4): 601–14.

McClellan, Catherine. 1989. "Frederica de Laguna and the Pleasures of Anthropology." *American Ethnologist* 16: 766–85.

Mauzé, Marie, Michael E. Harkin, and Sergei Kan, eds. 2004. *Coming to Shore: Northwest Coast Ethnology, Traditions, and Visions*. Lincoln: University of Nebraska Press.

Milburn, Maureen. 1986. "Louis Shotridge and the Objects of Everlasting Esteem." In *Raven's Journey*, ed. Susan Kaplan and Kristin J. Barsness, 54–90. Philadelphia: University of Pennsylvania Press.

Moss, Madonna. 2010. "Re-Thinking Subsistence in Southeast Alaska: The Potential of Zooarchaeology." *Alaska Journal of Anthropology* 8 (1): 121–35.
———. 2011. *Northwest Coast: Archaeology as Deep History.* Washington DC: Society for American Archaeology Press.
Newton, Richard G., and Madonna L. Moss. 2005. *Haa Atxaayi Haa Kusteeyix Sitee: Our Food Is Our Tlingit Way of Life: Excerpts of Oral Interviews.* Juneau: USDA Forest Service, Alaska Region, R10-MR-30.
Oberg, Kalervo. 1973. *The Social Economy of the Tlingit Indians.* Seattle: University of Washington Press.
Olson, Ronald L. 1967. *Social Structure and Social Life of the Tlingit in Alaska.* Anthropological Records 26. Berkeley: University of California.
Peers, Laura, and A. K. Brown, eds. 2003. *Museums and Source Communities: Routledge Reader.* London: Routledge.
Piterskaya, Elena. 2007. "Traditional Knowledge: The Conference of Tlingit, Haida, and Tsimshian Clans (March 21–25, 2007, Sitka, Alaska)." *Etnograficheskoe Obozrenie* (http://journal.iea.ras.ru./online). Unpublished English translation by Sergei Kan.
Raibmon, Page. 2005. *Authentic Indians: Episodes of Encounter from the Late Nineteenth-Century Northwest Coast.* Durham NC: Duke University Press.
Ryan, J., and M. Robinson. 1990. "Implementing Participatory Action Research in the Canadian North: A Case Study of the Gwich'in Language and Culture Project." *Culture* 10 (2): 57–71.
Schneider, William. 2002. *. . . So They Understand: Cultural Issues in Oral History.* Logan: Utah University Press.
Seguin, Margaret, ed. 1984. *The Tsimshian: Images of the Past: Views for the Present.* Vancouver: University of British Columbia Press.
Seguin, Margaret. 1985. *Interpretive Contexts for Traditional and Current Coast Tsimshian Feasts.* Mercury Series. Ethnology Service Papers 98. Ottawa: National Museum of Man.
Spaan, Laura Bliss. 2006. "The Two Lives of Frederica de Laguna." *Arctic Anthropology* 43 (2): 54–56.
Strong, Pauline Turner. 2005. "Recent Ethnographic Research on North American Indigenous Peoples." *Annual Reviews in Anthropology* 34: 254–68.
Suttles, Wayne, ed. 1990. *Handbook of North American Indians*, vol. 7: *Northwest Coast.* Washington DC: Smithsonian Institution.
Suttles, Wayne, and Aldona C. Jonaitis. 1990. "History of Research in Ethnology." In *Handbook of North American Indians*, vol. 7: *Northwest Coast*, 73–87. Washington DC: Smithsonian Institution.
Swanton, John R. 1905a. "Contributions to the Ethnology of the Haida." *Jesup North Pacific Expedition* 5(1).
———. 1905b. *Haida Texts and Myths: Skidegate Dialect.* BAE Bulletin 29. Washington DC: Government Printing Office.

———. 1908. "Social Conditions, Beliefs, and Linguistic Relationships of the Tlingit Indians." In *26th Annual Report of the BAE for the Years 1904–1905*. Washington DC.

———. 1909. *Tlingit Myths and Texts*. BAE *Bulletin* 145. Washington DC: Government Printing Office.

Thornton, Thomas F. 1997. "Know Your Place: The Organization of Tlingit Geographic Knowledge." *Ethnology* 36 (4): 295–307.

———. 2000a. "Person and Place: Lessons from Tlingit Teachers." In *Celebration 2000: Restoring Balance through Culture*, ed. Susan W. Fair and Rosita Worl, 79–86. Juneau: Sealaska Heritage Foundation.

———. 2000b. "Building a Tlingit Resource Atlas." In *Will the Time Ever Come? A Tlingit Source Book*, ed. Andrew Hope III and Thomas F. Thornton, 98–116. Fairbanks: Alaska Native Knowledge Network; Fairbanks: University of Alaska.

———. 2004. "The Geography of Tlingit Character." In *Coming to Shore: Northwest Coast Ethnology, Traditions, and Visions*, ed. Marie Mauzé, Michael Harkin, and Sergei Kan, 363–84. Lincoln: University of Nebraska Press.

———. 2008. *Being and Place among the Tlingit*. Seattle: University of Washington Press.

———. 2012. *Haa Léelk'w Has Aaní Saax'u: Our Grandparents' Names on the Land*. Juneau: Sealaska Heritage Institute; Seattle: University of Washington Press.

Tollefson, Kenneth. 1976. "The Cultural Foundation of Political Revitalization among the Tlingit." PhD diss., University of Washington.

Valentine, Lisa Philips, and Regna Darnell, eds. 1999. *Theorizing the Americanist Tradition*. Toronto: University of Toronto Press.

Veniaminov, Ivan. 1984. *Notes on the Islands of the Unalaska District*. Trans. Lydia Black and R. M. Geoghegan. Ed. Richard A. Pierce. Kingston ON: Limestone Press. (First published in Russian in 1840.)

Wheeler, Polly, and Tom Thornton. 2005. "Subsistence Research in Alaska: A Thirty-Year Retrospective." *Alaska Journal of Anthropology* 3 (1): 69–103.

Wike, Joyce. 1951. "The Effect of the Maritime Fur Trade on Northwest Coast Indian Society." PhD diss., Anthropology Department. Columbia University.

Wright, Robin K. 2001. *Northern Haida Master Carvers*. Seattle: University of Washington Press.

Part 1 | *Our Elders and Teachers*

1

Shotridge in Philadelphia
Representing Native Alaskan Peoples to East Coast Audiences

ROBERT W. PREUCEL

Louis Shotridge is a remarkable figure in the history of American ethnology. He was the first Northwest Coast Indian to receive professional anthropological training and the first to gain employment by a museum (Milburn 1997, 124). While working for the University Museum of the University of Pennsylvania in Philadelphia, he led four expeditions to Alaska and British Columbia and collected over 475 ethnographic objects (see Williams, this volume). In addition, he took more than five hundred photographs and published eleven articles on aspects of Northwest Coast culture.[1] Shotridge has been prominently featured in books (Carpenter 1975; Cole 1985; Kaplan and Barsness 1986; Price 1989; Williams 2003; Winegrad 1993), scholarly essays (Berman 2004; Brown 2005; Dauenhauer and Dauenhauer 2003; Dean 1990; Lenz 2004; Mason 1960; Milburn 1986, 1994; Napier 1997; Seaton 2001) and newspaper and magazine articles (Anonymous 1912a, 1912b, 1916, 1917; Enge 1993; Smith 1912).[2] A dissertation was written about his collecting activities (Milburn 1997), and a play has been performed about his life (Dunham 1995; Hanley 1995).

Much of the interest in Shotridge is due to the many contradictions and controversies surrounding his life as a Tlingit Indian man working for a major East Coast museum during a traumatic period of rapid modernization for Northwest Coast Indian communities. Louis, himself, was intimately aware of these contradictions. For example, in his *Museum Journal* article on the Kaagwaantaan shark helmet, he confessed, "It is true that the modernized part of me rejoiced over my success in obtaining this important ethnological specimen for the museum, but as one who had been trained to be a true Kaguanton, in my heart I cannot help but have the feeling of a traitor who has betrayed confidence" (1929,

343). Some Tlingit people today remain ambivalent about his collecting activities since he removed objects from their proper cultural context but his actions ensured they would be preserved and available for potential repatriation under the Native American Graves Protection and Repatriation Act.

In this chapter, I discuss Louis Shotridge's educational activities at the University Museum with a special emphasis on his exhibits and public lectures. These activities have been largely neglected by previous scholars, but are nonetheless important in understanding his motives and goals. I suggest that through his exhibits and lectures, Louis actively shaped the representation of Northwest Coast peoples for East Coast audiences. He sought to challenge popular stereotypes of Indians, to provide accurate information about Northwest Coast peoples, and to "raise up" Northwest Coast cultures alongside the great civilizations of the world, especially those of Greece, Italy, Egypt, and China. To accomplish these goals, he crafted a series of personae that mediated popular prejudices and misunderstandings. This thesis is consistent with Elizabeth Seaton's 2001 argument that Louis embodies a postcolonial subjectivity in which he developed multiple roles, each appropriate to the expectations of particular audiences.

Louis Shotridge

Louis V. Shotridge (Stoowukáa) was born in 1882 to an influential Tlingit family in Klukwan, Alaska.[3] He had two sisters and two brothers, one of whom died in infancy. It is said that he was named after Louis Paul, the first Presbyterian missionary in Haines (Mason 1960, 11). His father was George Shotridge (Yeilgooxú), the housemaster of the famous Whale House (Yaay hít), the leading house of the powerful Gaanax.teidí clan. His paternal grandfather was Shartrich (Laatxítshx), the housemaster of Killer Whale Fin House (Keet Gooshi hít), the leading house of the Kaagwaantaan clan. According to George Emmons, Shartrich was the most important chief not only of Klukwan but of all the Tlingit (Milburn 1994, 551). Louis's mother was Kudeit.sáakw of the Killer Whale Fin house. Her mother, Shaxéexi, was Shartrich's sister, so he was both a member of Kaagwaantaan clan and a grandchild of the clan. Louis subsequently inherited the title of housemaster of the Kaagwaantaan Killer Whale Fin House (Milburn 1986, 60).

Louis attended high school at the Presbyterian Mission School in Haines, a newly established Christian town at Portage Cove on Lynn

Fig. 1.1 Louis Shotridge posing in Kaagwaantaan clan regalia at the Penn Museum, ca. 1912. Photograph no. 140236, courtesy of the Penn Museum Archives.

Canal. The school was a place where Indians "could speedily learn the white man's ways and Christian habits and where their children could be educated as Boston men and women" (Young 1927, 210). There Louis met Florence "Suzie" Scundoo (Kaatxwaantséx), the daughter of a high-ranking shaman from Mountain House (Shaa hít) of the Lukaax̱.ádi clan in Chilkoot. After spending four years at school, she became quite an accomplished pianist and singer (Smith 1912). In accordance with their families' wishes, they had been betrothed as children and were married on Christmas Day in 1902 (Dauenhauer and Dauenhauer 2003, 166).

In 1905, Governor John G. Brady selected the Shotridges to be part of the Alaskan exhibit at the Lewis and Clark Centennial Exposition in Portland, Oregon. He asked Florence to demonstrate Chilkat weaving and Louis to describe Tlingit dyes and exhibit masks. At the Centennial, George Heye introduced the young couple to George Byron Gordon, curator of ethnology at the University Museum (Cole 1985, 255). Gordon was just embarking on a four-month collecting expedition among the Yup'ik of the Kuskokwim River area of Alaska. He purchased forty-nine objects from the Shotridges and discussed hiring them as his collecting agents and bringing them to Philadelphia "to tell the history and meanings of the different things" (LSC: Gordon to Shotridge, January 9, 1906). However, nothing was immediately forthcoming, so the Shotridges took a series of temporary positions. They participated in Antonio Apache's Indian Crafts Exhibition in 1906, toured the country with an Indian grand opera company in 1911, and participated in the World in Cincinnati Exposition in 1912.

In 1912, Gordon offered Louis temporary employment as a curatorial and interpretive assistant. The Shotridges moved to Philadelphia and spent the summer with Frank Speck, professor of anthropology at Penn, until they found lodgings in West Philadelphia.[4] Louis's task was nothing less than to inspect "every article in the American section" and "prepare a detailed account of its significance, purposes, origins, and uses" (Anonymous 1912b). Florence volunteered as an educational guide taking schoolchildren through the galleries. In the fall, Louis enrolled in the Wharton Business School, where he studied for two years. He wrote that he "trained himself for only one thing," namely, to help his people negotiate the complex forces of Western capitalism as they impacted the Indian communities of southeast Alaska. Milburn (1997, 103) has suggested that his pursuit of an entrepreneurial career was consistent with the activities of his father and grandfather, and this may be seen as an attempt to maintain his prestige within a rapidly changing Tlingit society.

In 1914, Gordon introduced the Shotridges to Franz Boas in New York City. Louis subsequently attended Boas's ethnology lectures at Columbia University and worked with him on a phonetic key and the recording of songs. He also assisted Boas in compiling the first reliable Tlingit grammar (Boas 1917). A year later, Gordon promoted Louis to assistant curator. This was a full-time position, and his duties involved preparing objects from the George Heye Collection for exhibit and evaluating private collections for possible donation. In the fall of 1915, he made two trips to Klukwan when he attended potlatches and made wax cylinder recordings of Tlingit songs. Following the death of his father, he also began exploring the possibility of acquiring the Whale House artifacts for the museum.

In 1916, he and Florence co-directed the Wanamaker expedition to southeast Alaska. This was funded by John Wanamaker, the Philadelphia department store magnate and a member of the museum's board of trustees. The Shotridge expedition was apparently the first anthropological expedition to be led by Native Americans (Anonymous 1916; Milburn 1994, 558). Louis and Florence collected ethnographic objects and gathered detailed information on myths and religious beliefs. Unfortunately, Florence contracted tuberculosis and died in Alaska in 1917 (Anonymous 1917).

In 1918, at Gordon's request, Louis traveled among the Tsimshian communities along the Nass and Skeena Rivers (Dean 1990). He collected forty-five specimens and took more than one hundred photos that document the leading families of each town. He spent the winter in Sitka and became enamored of Elizabeth Cook, a married woman of the X'at'ka.aayi clan. After her divorce, which he financed, they married in February 1919. They had three children, Louis Jr., born in 1921 or 1922, Richard, born in 1923, and Lillian, born in 1925. In 1922, Louis made a second collecting expedition funded by Wanamaker. He purchased a thirty-foot boat, which he christened the *Penn*, and made the rounds from Hoonah, Kake, Killisnoo, Angoon, and Klukwan, taking photographs and purchasing objects for the museum.

In November, he made another attempt to acquire the Whale House artifacts. He called together the leading men of the Gaanax̱.tedí clan and gave a speech urging the sale of the objects. He offered the impressive sum of $3,500, which he said could be used to rebuild the clan house that had been destroyed in a mudslide. The artifacts would go to Philadelphia where they "will stand as evidence of the Tlingit claim of a place in primitive culture," he later wrote to Gordon (LSC: Shotridge to Gordon, January 27, 1927). The clan leaders were not impressed and turned him down. He then tried to enlist his uncle Edward's help in going around the clan leaders to acquire the artifacts on the basis of Western rather than Tlingit law, but his uncle refused to help.

Beginning in 1927, a series of tragic events occurred. First, Louis's mentor, George Bryon Gordon, died after falling down the staircase of the Philadelphia Racquet Club. A year later, Elizabeth died of tuberculosis in an Albuquerque sanitarium. Then, in 1929, the Great Depression hit and the U.S. economy slowed dramatically. During this period, Louis became increasing involved in Native Alaskan political activities. He helped organize the Grand Camp of the Alaska Native Brotherhood in Sitka in 1929 and was elected Grand president in 1930. Sometime in 1931 or 1932, Louis married Mary Kasakan, a Kiks.ádi woman from Sitka, and they had two children.

The museum was severely impacted by the Great Depression and forced to make wholesale financial cutbacks. Horace Jayne, the acting director, reluctantly let Louis go in January 1932. Desperate for work, Louis made a living by fishing, doing odd jobs, and selling an occasional curio. He sent beadwork trinkets and moccasins to the museum staff to raise additional funds for his family. In 1935, he took a job as a government fisheries inspector. Jayne served as his reference. While on the job, Louis fell from a scaffold and broke his neck. He died at the Alaska Pioneers' Home Hospital on August 6, 1937.[5]

Shotridge as Exhibitor

In order to put Louis's exhibition philosophy in context, it is first necessary to review the history of the American section exhibitions at the University Museum. Unfortunately, this history is not well documented, and what follows must be regarded as preliminary. The first Native American exhibit dates to shortly after the founding of the museum in 1889. Charles C. Abbott was its curator (Abbott 1890). The exhibit, located in a single room in College Hall, depicted the prehistory of the Delaware Valley of southeastern Pennsylvania. It likely included his collection of artifacts from Abbott's farm in New Jersey as well as Daniel Garrison Brinton's collection from Bucks County.

In 1890, Abbott curated an expanded Native American exhibit in the University Library (now the Furness Art History Library). This exhibit featured prehistoric antiquities from different states and was organized according to their "characteristic forms and materials" (Culin 1891). Ethnographic objects were also displayed to help the viewer interpret the uses of the prehistoric ones. Frank Hamilton Cushing of the Smith-

Fig. 1.2 Native American exhibit in the Furness Library, ca. 1890. Photograph no. 153359, courtesy of the Penn Museum Archives.

sonian Institution guest curated two subsequent exhibits, one devoted to the Cliff Dwellers of the Southwestern United States that showcased the newly acquired Hearst-Hazzard collection (Anonymous 1895) and the second featuring the "lost civilization" of Key Marco, Florida, that displayed the results of his recent excavations (Anonymous 1896). When the new museum building opened in 1899, these exhibits were reinstalled in the new galleries to great fanfare.

In 1903, George Byron Gordon was hired as curator of general ethnology. Gordon came to the museum from Harvard University, where he had trained in classics and Native American ethnology. He was a strong advocate of salvage ethnography and felt that ethnographic museums needed to make every effort "to save all that is possible before it becomes too late," since "it is a question of a very few years when the last opportunity for collecting will have disappeared" (King and Little 1986, 28). For this reason, he sought to acquire representative collections from Native American communities across the Americas.

In 1907, Gordon announced an agreement with George G. Heye, a New York businessman, to supplement the museum's Native American

Fig. 1.3 Model of Kluckwan, Alaska, made by Louis Shotridge. Photograph by Robert Preucel.

holdings (Williams 2003, 10). Heye had acquired a vast but little known collection of artifacts, and he agreed to loan a portion of his collection to the museum and to donate duplicate specimens. In return for this largess, he was appointed vice president of the board of managers and given gallery space to exhibit his collection (Jacknis 2006; Pezzati 2002). The acquisition of this collection was a great coup since, in one fell swoop, Gordon was able to gain objects representing Native American cultures from most of the Americas. Because he assumed that this loan would eventually become permanent, Gordon focused his collecting activities on the Arctic, an area not well represented by the Heye Collection (Williams 2003, 10).

The museum exhibited the Heye Collection in two rooms located in the west wing. The curator is not recorded; however, Gordon, along with Mark Harrington and George Pepper, both assistants to Heye, likely played major roles. From extant photographs, it is possible to see that one of these rooms was devoted to Plains Indian cultures, since it shows exhibit cases containing clothing, shields, and headdresses, all organized by tribe. The other room seems to have been a catchall for

Fig. 1.4 Crest designs on screens and houseposts of Grizzly Bear House in the Klukwan model. Photograph no. 12590, courtesy of the Penn Museum Archives.

the rest of North America. It displayed everything from a Northeast birch bark canoe to California curio baskets.

Louis was hired in May 1912 during the Heye period. One of his first duties was to build a model of his own village of Klukwan (Mason 1960).

Although he had no formal training, Louis created a superb model exquisitely detailed down to the very methods of joining cedar planks. The model depicts three clan houses in the central section of the village and includes grave houses, houses for drying fish, canoes, and people performing daily activities. He identifies the house on the right as the Kaagwaantaan Grizzly Bear House (Xoots hít) (Shotridge and Shotridge 1913). Its interior is left open to reveal the Grizzly Bear screen at the back, a smaller Killer Whale screen on the left side, and the four houseposts.

According to Louis, the four houseposts tell the story of Lgayak, the two-headed bear, wolf and pups, and bear and cubs, respectively (Shotridge and Shotridge 1913). The house on the left is likely the Frog

Shotridge in Philadelphia 49

House (Xixch'i hít) of the Gaanax.tedí clan, since the grave house behind the clan house displays the Frog crest. Marsha Hotch (personal communication) has suggested that the house in the center is Whale House (Yaay hít), Louis's father's house. The available Klukwan house lists (e.g., Olson 1967) indicate several houses between Frog House and Bear House, so this is likely an ideal representation of his village.

Louis also created a detailed model of a Haida village of Haina (Xa'ina) or Sunshine Town, also known as New Gold Harbor. It shows two of the thirteen clan houses. This, too, is an ideal representation of the village. It depicts a hunter just returning in a canoe with a deer and the shredding of cedar bark for food mats, rain cloaks, and diapers. According to Louis, the double finned killer whale was one of a pair of carvings that originally accompanied a chief's tomb. The memorial pole between the two houses was raised in honor of a nobleman named "One Man" who had died away from the village and whose remains could not be recovered.[6] Louis identifies the house on the right as the home of the head chief of Haina. According to MacDonald, the town chief was "Chief Ganai of the Pebble Town Eagles," and he had two houses. The house should be "House Always Looking for Visitors," which was adjacent to "House Passers-by Always Look Up At." However, Louis seems to have represented Ganai's second house, "Lightning" (Ts'amiti).[7] Louis doesn't identify the house on the left, but it is likely "House Passers-by Always Look Up At" and its owner, "He Whose Word Is Obeyed" of Those Born on the Stasoas Coast (MacDonald 1983, 62).[8]

When George Heye's mother died in 1915, he received a substantial inheritance (Force 1999, 8). Because of disputes with members of the museum's board of trustees, he withdrew his collection and used it to found the Museum of the American Indian, Heye Foundation at Audubon Terrace, on land donated by Archer M. Huntington.[9] The loss of the Heye Collection was a severe blow to Gordon and required a major reinstallation of the American section exhibits. This was in process in 1918 when Gordon informed Louis that the Northwest Coast collection was being installed in one of the exhibition rooms previously used for the Heye Collection and that it was to include the new objects he was acquiring for the museum (LSC: Gordon to Shotridge, February 4, 1918). The installation was completed before 1920 (Anonymous 1920).

Extant drawings show that the American section exhibits then occupied four rooms in the western half of the building. The first room to the right of the main entrance contained South American collections,

Fig. 1.5 Model of Haina, Haida Gwaii, BC, made by Louis Shotridge. Photograph by Robert Preucel.

the second contained the Western, Southwestern, Prairie, and Eastern collections, the third room contained the Eskimo collections chiefly from Alaska, and the fourth room contained the Northwest Coast collection together with the Copper Eskimo and some of the other Eskimo groups. Louis prepared plans and detailed inventories of the Eskimo and Northwest Coast exhibits. It is clear from his documentation that Gordon organized the exhibits by object type. For example, Case 25 in the Northwest Coast exhibit contained nine ceremonial hats. These included the Killer Whale hat, the Undersea Grizzly Bear helmet, the Murrelet hat, the Ganook hat, the Loon Spirit Brass hat, the Barbecuing Raven helmet, and the Raven on the Roof hat.

In 1928, Gordon invited Louis to curate the reinstallation of the Northwest Coast gallery (Shotridge 1928). This may be the first time that a Northwest Coast Native exhibited his own culture in a museum setting, and Louis took full advantage. He designed his Tlingit Hall exhibit to illustrate two fundamental principles of Tlingit society. The first of these was the moiety system, the fact that Tlingit culture is organized according to two major divisions—Raven and Eagle/Wolf—that serve to regulate marriage practices. The second is what he called the "aesthetic emotions" underlying Tlingit narrative art. This refers to the high value and esteem Tlingit people place upon certain kinds of material culture, particularly clan hats, helmets, house posts, and canoes.[10]

Shotridge in Philadelphia 51

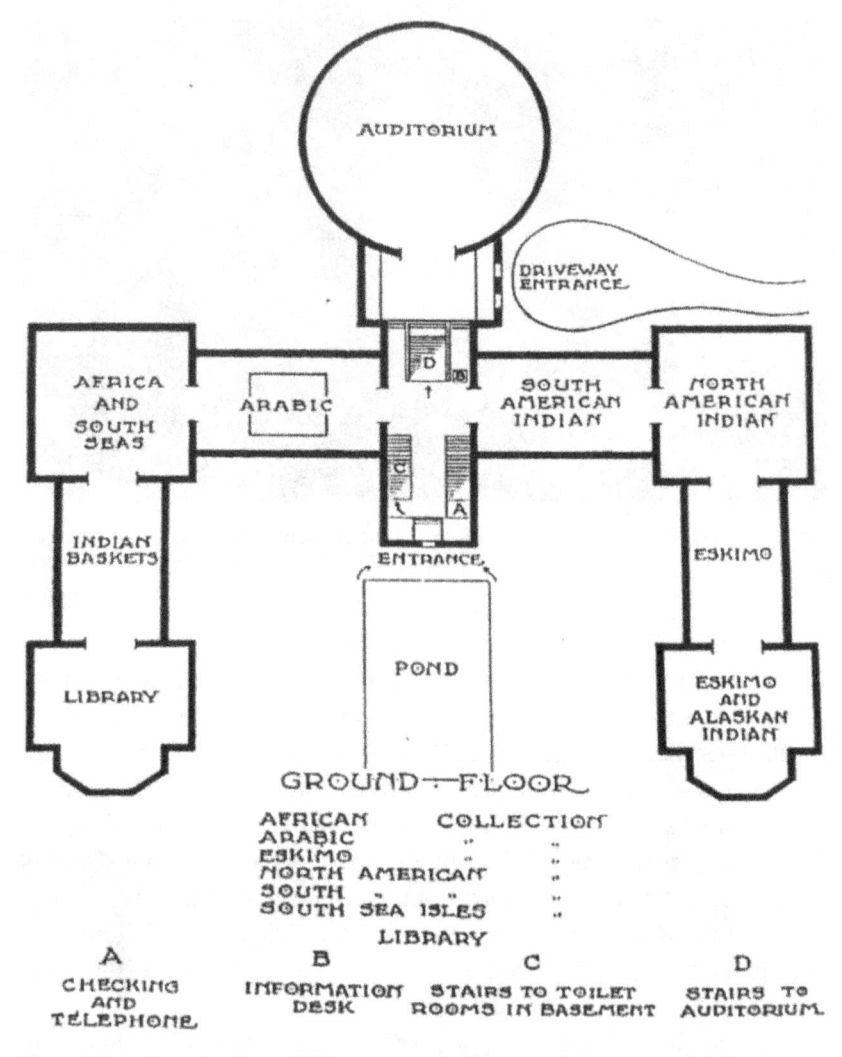

Fig. 1.6 American section exhibits, ca. 1922. Photograph courtesy of the Penn Museum Archives.

Although there are no recorded photographs, Louis described his exhibit method in some detail (Shotridge 1928, 352–53). He placed Raven moiety objects, according to rank, in cases on the right side of the main aisle. These included the Luknax̱.ádi Raven hat representing "culture," the Luknax̱.ádi Whale hat indicating "greatness," the Luknax̱.ádi Sea Lion hat representing "endurance," and the Kiks.ádi Frog hat emphasizing "persistence." In a case on the left side of the aisle, he placed

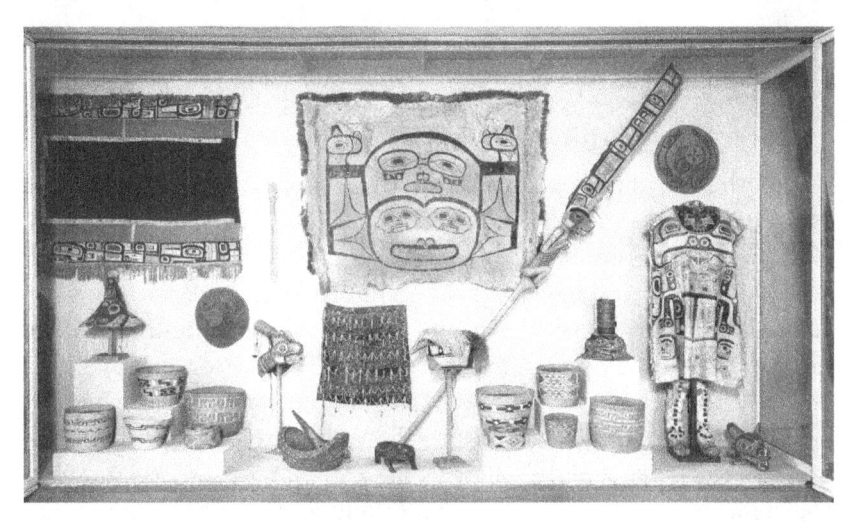

Fig. 1.7 Reinstallation of the Northwest Coast Gallery, ca. 1931. Photograph no. 12702, courtesy of the Penn Museum Archives.

Eagle moiety objects. These included the Kaagwaantaan Eagle hat representing "determination," the Teikweidí Grizzly Bear hat representing "power," and the Kaagwaantaan Wolf hat signifying "courage." In this way, he emphasized balance between opposite moieties as well as the enduring cultural values embodied by particular objects. In addition, he also exhibited the headdress known as the Lord of Hawks and the Ganook hat, which represents the most ancient being in Tlingit mythology. He exhibited in a small case the hat of Shaxéex, the first woman diplomat, and, in another, the hairpieces of Tseitlin, the famous bride of Tongass. Further cases were devoted to wood carving, wearing apparel, the arts of weaving and quill embroidery, feast dishes, war implements and trophies, shaman paraphernalia, and ceremonial headdresses.

Louis's exhibit remained in place for three years. In 1930, Horace Jayne wrote to notify him of the possible renovation of the Northwest Coast gallery (LSC: Jayne to Shotridge, November 18, 1930). A little over a year later, Jayne wrote again to report that the Tlingit exhibits had been reinstalled in the "old Plains Indian hall" (LSC: Jayne to Shotridge, September 22, 1931, December 22, 1931). The cases appear to have been installed to emphasize ceremonial regalia, since one features a Haida basketry hat, the Gaanax.tedí Whale house leather tunic, the Wolf hat, the Kaagwaantaan Wolf baton, and various baskets and feast dishes.

Shotridge in Philadelphia

Unfortunately, Louis's organizing principle was not preserved, and Eagle and Raven moiety objects were indiscriminately mixed together.

Shotridge as Teacher

In 1911, Gordon undertook a series of experiments to extend the educational mission of the museum beyond the university to engage the city public schools (Gordon 1913, 35; Madeira 1964, 40). This project was accomplished with the support of the Philadelphia superintendent of education and proved very successful. Between January and June 1913, 1,331 schoolchildren were brought to the museum (Gordon 1913, 36). They ranged from third graders to high school seniors. The museum provided a choice of eleven lectures, each lasting forty minutes and illustrated with lantern slides.[11] Following the lecture, thirty or forty museum objects were used to discuss cultural origins and methods of manufacture and then passed around among the children for them to examine.

The most popular of these lectures for the younger children were those on the American Indian. According to Gordon (1913, 37–38), this was because "all children are interested in the Indians and have their imagination stimulated by the mere mention of an Indian." But even more exciting was the fact that the students were able to learn about their subject firsthand from two Native American instructors, Louis and Florence Shotridge. Gordon (1913, 38) wrote that this feature was "immensely popular with the children, who become greatly attached to the Indians and establish at once the most friendly relations." The Shotridges often dressed in Plains Indian style costumes when they gave lectures and led tours through the Native American galleries.

Here we have an interesting example of postcolonial subjectivity: Indians "playing Indian" in order to appeal to the desires and expectations of a popular audience and, at the same time, to control the discourse on representation.[12] The local press reported accurate information but also stereotyped them. For example, Florence was called an "Indian Princess" and "Minnehaha" (Anonymous 1917).

Four of Louis's public school lectures are preserved in his unpublished papers (LSC). These are titled "Alaska: The Country and Its People," "The American Territory of Alaska: Its Peoples and Its History," "The First White Man," and "Moldy Head: Adventures of 'Alive-in-the-Pond' in the Salmon World." It is instructive to stylistically compare his public school lectures with his *Museum Journal* articles. The Dauenhauers have analyzed the latter and shown that he intentionally adopted archaic

Fig. 1.8 Louis and Florence Shotridge with Philadelphia schoolchildren, ca. 1912. Photograph no. 10992, courtesy of the Penn Museum Archives.

English and "poetic diction" in an attempt to represent the integrity of the original Tlingit language (Dauenhauer and Dauenhauer 2003, 165). In his public school lectures, however, Louis adopts a more accessible conversational tone and, in places, engages directly with his student audience. In these cases, he is usually emphasizing a moral lesson.

For example, in his presentation on "Alaska: The Country and Its People," he begins with a personal anecdote. He relates that when he was nine years old, his father took him on a fur-trading trip among the Tanana people. His father told him to go off and play with the local boys while he engaged in negotiations. Louis quickly found a group and stood back watching them. One boy came forward and started pulling on the red handkerchief around his neck. Louis couldn't understand what he was saying and thought that he was being threatened. So he struck him, and they began fighting until a man fluent in both the Tanana and Tlingit languages broke it up. The man then demanded that the boys explain what had happened. After listening to their stories, he turned to Louis and said that the boy only wanted to buy the handkerchief and had offered him a beaver skin as payment. Louis was deeply embarrassed because of the misunderstanding and immediately took off the handkerchief to give to the boy. He then related that he and this boy became good friends and that he even saw him during his last collecting trip for the museum. He used this story didactically both as evidence for the linguistic diversity in Alaska and to stress the importance of respecting other peoples' cultures.

Shotridge in Philadelphia 55

In his account of the First White Man, Louis uses the first encounter to highlight the virtue of bravery. He relates that one day a man named Skotte' and his three brothers from Spruce Fort (Klawock) were hunting for sea otter when they looked up and saw a monster. "Its great body was drifting over the surface of the calm ocean like that of a monster duck, but it could not be a living [monster] duck, because the great wings were like that of a dragon fly which were stretched out as if to dry." They then observed a "beetle-like thing" land on the shore and "people-like beings" disembark. So the Tlingit men saw the ship as a living monster, and its sails were great wings, the masts were its horns, the rattling sound of the chain when the anchor was lowered was the grinding of its teeth, and the rowboat was a beetle.

Skotte' then asked his men if they should leave or if they should investigate the situation. One of them, Tánah, volunteered to go and find out. He went over to them and then called out to his comrades to join him. They did so and were all taken to the deck of the ship where they were brought some "blackwater" in a mica container, some "old cork" in a second container, and maggots or white worms in a third container. They were then instructed to take the old cork and dip it into the blackwater and eat it with the maggots! Tánah then stepped forward and ate the food. The blackwater was molasses, the old cork was pilot bread, and the maggots in the mica container were boiled rice in a tin dish. Shotridge's lesson here is that the brave man challenges the unknown and does not run away. As Berman (2004, 159) points out, Louis is seeking to re-portray Native people since "he, a Native man is holding up the naive but courageous Native character to white children as an example of a 'real man.'"

Louis tells the story of Moldy Head to emphasize honor and responsibility.[13] Moldy Head is the account of a spoiled child, named Alive-in-the-Pond, who insults his mother, drowns, and is then transformed into a salmon. After a series of adventures in the salmon world, he returns to his people as a great prophet. Louis prefaces the story by telling his audience that oral teachings from the elders were the main method of education in his culture and that stories like this were a way of holding the attention of restless children.

Louis concludes the story with an admonition told to him as a child by his father's servant Ooshaw: "Be careful in what you say; do not let your talk go wild—loose tongue or foolish talking will always cause you shame; make no remarks about what you have to eat; abuse no living creatures, lest their spirits shall demand retaliation; never be careless with anything entrusted to your care." Louis uses the story not only to teach about Tlingit morals and values but also to encourage the schoolchildren to consider the moral lessons they themselves have received in their own lives.

Conclusions

Louis Shotridge is often celebrated for making one of the most important and best-documented ethnographic collection of Tlingit material culture in the world. George Emmons, for example, wrote that he collected "the most valuable and interesting helmets and ceremonial hats and headpieces that is or ever will be in any museum (Emmons to J. Alden Mason, May 10, 1942). However, Louis was more than a collector. He actively shaped the representation of Northwest Coast peoples and cultures for a Philadelphia audience. He challenged popular stereotypes about Indians, provided detailed information about the lives of the Native peoples of Alaska, and sought to "raise up" Northwest Coast cultures alongside the great civilizations of the world. He and his wife, Florence, accomplished these goals by crafting a series of personae that mediated popular prejudices and misunderstandings. He successfully embraced his role as a "Museum Indian," a living ethnographic exhibit, while acquiring the cultural capital of elite Anglo American scholar (Seaton 2001, 35).

An analysis of Louis's exhibits and public lectures reveals aspects of his educational philosophy. His 1928 exhibit was structured according to the fundamental principle of Tlingit culture, the moiety system. It also emphasized the relationship between objects and culture by highlighting the psychological component of clan objects in social practice. His public school lectures demonstrate his sincere interest in instructing Philadelphia schoolchildren about the diverse peoples and cultures of Alaska. They highlighted the cross-cultural significance of moral education in child development. Together, his exhibits and public lectures reveal his desire to record and communicate what he called a "faithful history of the Tlingit people" (Shotridge 1917:105) during a time when that same history was being devalued by state and federal administrators and some reform-minded leaders within his own community.

NOTES

I am grateful to Sergei Kan, Steve Henrickson, and the late Andy Hope for inviting my participation in the Sitka clan conference. I would also like to especially thank Judith Berman, Steve Brown, Richard and Nora Dauenhauer,

Sergei Kan, Stacey Espenlaub, Andy Hope, Marsha Hotch, Harold Jacobs, Alex Pezzati, Lucy Williams, and Robin Wright for their assistance with various aspects of this research.

1. These articles address art, architecture, landscape, ritual, and mythology (Shotridge 1917, 1919a, 1919b, 1920, 1921, 1922, 1928, 1929a, 1929b, 1930).
2. There are new publications coming out as well. Judith Berman is currently editing a book of Shotridge's *Museum Journal* articles, and Maureen Milburn is working on a book on Shotridge for the University of Pennsylvania Museum.
3. There is very little biographical information available for Shotridge. The information here is derived largely from the dissertation and publications of Maureen Milburn (1986, 1994, 1997).
4. Their West Philadelphia address was 1608 S. 56th Street, apt. B.
5. There are several sensational accounts of his death (cf. Carpenter 1975; Cole 1985). Milburn (1997, 321) argues convincingly that the historical record contradicts them.
6. MacDonald (1983, 62) describes this same pole as having a beaver at the base and tall potlatch rings on its head. At the top is a carving of a bird. Nailed above the beaver is a copper for "One man" of the Striped Town people. This copper is not represented in the Shotridge model.
7. The crests on the front pole included a raven at the top, a story figure wearing a dance hat, a raven with a downturned beak, a story figure, and a thunderbird (MacDonald 1983, 62). This pole is at the Field Museum of Natural History in Chicago (MacDonald 1983, 65).
8. The figures on the pole are two watchmen with a humanoid killer whale at the top, a heron, a supernatural snag, three human figures, and one holding the dorsal fin of the whale at the bottom. The whale has an owl at its chest (MacDonald 1983, 62).
9. This collection now forms the central part of the holdings of the National Museum of the American Indian in Washington DC.
10. These objects are of the kind that today would be called *at.óow*. Curiously, Shotridge does not use this term in any of his writings.
11. These lectures consisted of the American Indians, the people of Borneo, the peoples of Oceania, the peoples of Africa, the peoples of China and Japan, the peoples of Europe, the peoples of Asia, ancient Greece and Rome, ancient Egypt and Babylonia, the world's peoples and the habits of primitive man (Gordon 1913, 38).
12. "Playing Indian" is the topic of a recent book by Philip Deloria (1998), but this focuses on how non-Indians adopted Indian culture in order to create a distinctive national identity.
13. The story of Moldy Head is well known among the Tlingit people. It was recorded by Swanton (1909) and has recently been published as a book

by Sealaska Heritage Institute (Marks et al. 2004). It is generally agreed to be a *Kiks.ádi* story. Shotridge's version is very similar to the Swanton version. It possesses the same ten structural elements identified by Dauenhauer and Dauenhauer (2001).

REFERENCES

Abbott, C. C. 1890. *Annual Report of the Curator of the Museum of American Archaeology in Connection with the University of Pennsylvania*. Philadelphia: University of Pennsylvania Press.

Anonymous. 1895. "Cliff Dweller and His Relics: A Marvelous Exhibit Opened Today in the Library Building of the University, the Hazzard Collection." *Philadelphia Evening Telegraph*, November 8, 1895.

———. 1896. "Another Lost Race Discovered: Explorer Cushing's Find in the Ten Thousand Islands." *Philadelphia Times*, July 5, 1896.

———. 1910. "The Heye Collection." *Museum Journal* 1 (1): 11–12.

———. 1912a. "Alaska Chief Here on Visit." *Sun*, February 10, 1912.

———. 1912b. "Indians at Museum to Interpret Lore." *Evening Bulletin*, February 28, 1912.

———. 1916. "Indian Leads Exploring Team into Alaska." *Christian Science Monitor*, August, 14, 1916.

———. 1917. "'Minnehaha' Shotridge Dies at Home in Alaska." *Telegraph*, June 14, 1917.

———. 1920. Handbook American Section, University Museum, Philadelphia.

Berman, Judith. 2004. "'Some Mysterious Means of Fortune': A Look at North Pacific Coast Oral History." In *Coming to Shore: Northwest Coast Ethnology, Traditions, and Visions*, ed. Marie Mauzé, Michael E. Harkin, and Sergei Kan, 129–62. Lincoln: University of Nebraska Press.

Boas, Franz. 1917. *Grammatical Notes on the Language of the Tlingit Indians*. Philadelphia: University of Pennsylvania Museum.

Brown, Steven C. 2005. "A Tale of Two Carvers: The Rain Wall Screen of the Whale House, Klukwan, Alaska." *American Indian Art Magazine* 30 (4): 48–59.

Carpenter, Edmund. 1975. "Collecting Northwest Coast Art." In *Indian Art of the Northwest Coast: A Dialogue on Craftsmanship and Aesthetics*, ed. Bill Holm and Bill Reid, 9–27. Houston: Rice University Institute for the Arts.

Cole, Douglas. 1985. *Captured Heritage: The Scramble for Northwest Coast Artifacts*. Vancouver: University of British Columbia Press.

Culin, Stewart. 1891. "University Archaeological Association." *Philadelphia Sunday Mercury*, May 2, 1891.

Dauenhauer, Nora Marks, and Richard Dauenhauer. 2003. "Louis Shotridge and Indigenous Tlingit Ethnography: Then and Now." In *Construct-*

ing Cultures Then and Now: Celebrating Franz Boas and the Jesup North Pacific Expedition, ed. Laurel Kendall and Igor Krupnik, 165–83. Circumpolar Anthropology 4. National Museum of Natural History, Smithsonian Institution, Washington DC.

Dauenhauer, Richard, and Nora Marks Dauenhauer. 2001. *The Salmon Story and Alaska Standards: Activities and Suggestions*. Juneau School District.

Dean, Jonathan. 1990. "Louis Shotridge, Museum Man: A 1918 Visit to the Nass and Skeena Rivers." *Pacific Northwest Quarterly* 89 (4): 202–10.

Deloria, Philip. 1998. *Playing Indian*. New Haven: Yale University Press.

Dunham, Mike. 1995. "Shotridge: UAA Play Walks Line between Tragic Hero and Tlingit Traitor." *Anchorage Daily News*, April 14, 1995.

Enge, Marilee. 1993. "Collecting the Past." *Anchorage Daily News*, April 6, 1993.

Force, Roland W. 1999. *Politics and the Museum of the American Indian: The Heye and the Mighty*. Honolulu: Mechas Press.

Gordon, George Byron. 1913. "The Museum and the Public Schools." *Museum Journal* 4 (3): 35–39.

Hanley, Anne. 1995. *Shotridge*. Dir. Michael Hood. Produced by the University of Alaska, Anchorage.

Jacknis, Ira. 2006. "A New Thing? The NMAI in Historical and Institutional Perspective." *American Indian Quarterly* 30 (3–4): 511–42.

Kaplan, Susan, and Kristin Barsness, eds. 1986. *Raven's Journey: The World of Alaska's Native People*. Philadelphia: University Museum.

King, Eleanor M., and Bryce P. Little. 1986. George Byron Gordon and the Early Development of the University Museum. In *Raven's Journey*, ed. Susan Kaplan and Kristin Barsness, 16–53. Philadelphia: University of Pennsylvania Museum.

Lenz, Mary Jane. 2004. "No Tourist Material: George Heye and His Golden Rule." *American Indian Art Magazine* 29 (4): 86–95, 105.

Louis Shotridge Collection, University Museum Archives, University of Pennsylvania (LSC).

MacDonald, George F. 1983. *Haida Monumental Art: Villages of the Queen Charlotte Islands*. Vancouver: University of British Columbia Press.

Madeira, Percy, Jr. 1964. *Men in Search of Man: The First Seventy-Five Years of the University Museum of the University of Pennsylvania*. Philadelphia: University of Pennsylvania Press.

Marks, Johnny, Hans Chester, David Katzeek, Nora Dauenhauer, and Richard Dauenhauer. 2004. *Shanyaak'utlaax (Moldy End)*. Juneau: Sealaska Heritage Institute.

Mason, J. Alden. 1960. "Louis Shotridge." *Expedition* 2 (2):11–16.

Milburn, Maureen E. 1986. "Louis Shotridge and the Objects of Everlasting Esteem." In *Raven's Journey: The World of Alaska's Native People*, ed. Susan Kaplan and Kristin Barsness, 54–90. Philadelphia: University Museum.

———. 1994. "Weaving the 'Tina' Blanket: The Journey of Florence and Louis Shotridge." In *Haa Kusteeyí, Our Culture: Tlingit Life Stories*, ed. Nora Marks Dauenhauer and Richard Dauenhauer, 548–64. Seattle: University of Washington Press.

———. 1997. "The Politics of Possession: Louis Shotridge and the Tlingit Collections of the University of Pennsylvania Museum." PhD diss., Department of Fine Arts, University of British Columbia, Vancouver.

Napier, A. David. 1997. "Losing One's Marbles: Cultural Property and Indigenous Thought." In *Contesting Art: Art, Politics, and Identity in the Modern World*, ed. Jeremy MacClancy, 165–82. Oxford: Berg.

Olson, Ronald L. 1967. *Social Structure and Social Life of the Tlingit in Alaska*. Anthropological Records 26. Berkeley: University of California Press.

Pezzati, Alex. 2002. "The Big One That Got Away: Heye-Day Ends with Loss of Prized American Indian Collection." *Expedition* 44 (2): 5.

Price, Sally. 1989. *Primitive Art in Civilized Places*. Chicago: University of Chicago Press.

Seaton, Elizabeth P. 2001. "The Native Collector: Louis Shotridge and the Contests of Possession." *Ethnography* 2 (1): 35–61.

Shotridge, Louis. 1917. "My Northland Revisited." *Museum Journal* 8 (2): 105–15.

———. 1919a. "War Helmets and Clan Hats of the Tlingit Indians." *Museum Journal* 10 (1–2): 43–48.

———. 1919b. "A Visit to the Tsimshian Indians." *Museum Journal* 10 (1–2): 49–67, 117–48.

———. 1920. "Ghost of Courageous Adventurer." *Museum Journal* 11 (1): 11–26.

———. 1921. "Tlingit Woman's Root Basket." *Museum Journal* 12 (3): 162–78.

———. 1922. "Land Otter-Man." *Museum Journal* 13 (1): 55–59.

———. 1928. "The Emblems of Tlingit Culture." *Museum Journal* 19 (4): 350–77.

———. 1929a. "The Bride of Tongass: A Study of the Tlingit Marriage Ceremony." *Museum Journal* 20 (2): 131–56.

———. 1929b. "The Kaguanton Shark Helmet." *Museum Journal* 20 (3–4): 339–43.

———. 1930. "How Ats-ha Followed the Hide of His Comrade to Yek Land." *Museum Journal* 21 (3–4): 215–26.

Shotridge, Louis, and Florence Shotridge. 1913. "Indians of the Northwest." *Museum Journal* 4 (3): 71–100.

Smith, F. Maude. 1912. "A Little Chat with Katkwachsnea." *North American*, January 2, 1912.

Swanton, John R. 1909. *Tlingit Myths and Texts*. Smithsonian Institution, Bureau of American Ethnology, Bulletin 39. Washington DC: Government Printing Office.

Williams, Lucy Fowler. 2003. "Of Spirits and Science: Meaning and Material Culture Crossing Boundaries." In *Guide to the North American Ethnographic Collections at the University of Pennsylvania Museum of Archaeology and Anthropology*, 1–18. Philadelphia: University Museum Press.

Winegrad, Dilys. 1993. *Through Time, across Continents: A Hundred Years of Archaeology and Anthropology at the University Museum*. Philadelphia: University Museum, University of Pennsylvania.

Young, Reverend S. Hall. 1927. *Hall Young of Alaska: The Autobiography of S. Hall Young*. New York: Fleming H. Revell.

2

Louis Shotridge

Preserver of Tlingit History and Culture

LUCY FOWLER WILLIAMS

> It is clear now that unless someone go[es] to work, [to] record our history in the English language and place these old things as evidence, the noble idea of our forefathers shall be entirely lost.
>
> LOUIS SHOTRIDGE, 1923

> From the time the white man was attracted by the unique workmanship in things among the Northwest pacific coast peoples, artifact of various types ha[ve] been generously taken out from the seeming inexhaustible supply in the store-house of the Tlingit people. Yet, strange to say, the collectors and curio buyers have never approached that which is most important, and that is objects which represent the honorable history of the people.
>
> LOUIS SHOTRIDGE, 1924

As these quotes indicate, Louis Shotridge, a Tlingit Indian man working for the University Museum of the University of Pennsylvania, was deeply concerned about the preservation of his culture's history (Fig. 2.1). More than George Emmons, Charles Newcomb, or any other collector, he appreciated the fact that Tlingit history could best be preserved by acquiring those special clan objects and their related stories that embody a clan's claim to fame. Not all scholars have appreciated Shotridge's motives. Douglas Cole, for example, criticizes him within the frame of nineteenth- and early twentieth-century museum collecting along the Northwest Coast. His evaluation of Shotridge's collecting strategy to acquire "impressive prestige items" underestimates his purpose and presents a distorted picture of Shotridge as a selfish, overly ambitious man (Cole 1985, 258).[1]

Fig 2.1 Louis Shotridge at his expedition camp, Chilkoot village, ca. 1915. Courtesy of the Penn Museum Archives, neg. S4-14747.

This chapter is an outgrowth of Penn Museum's initiative to create the new Louis Shotridge Digital Archive to make his work accessible to Tlingit people and the public over the Internet. My purpose is to publish a thorough description of Louis Shotridge's work in Alaska for the Penn Museum. I introduce his training and fieldwork and describe his collections of objects, photographs, papers, and writings. By doing so, I want to reveal Shotridge's overarching vision to record a Tlingit ethnography representing all Tlingit geographical divisions and argue that a comprehensive view of his work is essential to appreciate his unique contribution to the study of Tlingit history and culture. This discussion counters what I believe is a distorted representation of Shotridge's collecting efforts by some authors and strives instead to illuminate the breadth of his collecting vision and his goals to preserve Tlingit clan objects and culture.

Background

Louis Shotridge was born in 1882 to an elite Tlingit family in the remote northern community of Kluckwan, Alaska. His father, Yeilgooxú, belonged to the Gaanaxteidí clan of the Raven moiety and was the hereditary chief of the Klukwan Whale House. His mother, Kudeit.sáakw, belonged to the opposite Eagle moiety and was a member of the Killer Whale Fin House of the Kaagwaantaan clan.[2] In Tlingit society, descent is followed through the mother's line, making Louis a member of the Killer Whale Fin House.

Shotridge was born at a time of dramatic change in Tlingit communities when imposed Western economic, political, religious, and educational agendas were catalysts for the gradual abandonment of traditional subsistence lifestyle, social organization, and religion. Louis was educated at the Presbyterian Missionary School in neighboring Haines, where he was immersed in nontraditional ideas and standards that set his future path in two worlds: his ancestral one and that of the American newcomers. As a young adult he proved himself as a talented and articulate individual in both spheres. At the age of twenty-two he inherited the position of the head of his house.[3] At twenty-three the governor of the District of Alaska invited Louis's Tlingit wife, Florence, to demonstrate weaving at the 1905 Lewis and Clark Centennial Exposition in Portland, Oregon. It was there that the Shotridges first met George Byron Gordon, archaeologist and curator of Penn's Free Museum of Science and Art. Gordon asked them to make a small collection, and thus began Louis's thirty-year relationship with Penn.[4]

Although his letters and collections remain unpublished, several authors have studied and written about Louis Shotridge. Some do little justice to the complexity of the contexts in which he was engaged. Anthropological studies have more successfully recognized the complexity of Shotridge's position. Milburn's detailed, systematic research outlines Shotridge's collecting efforts for Penn, yet is limited in describing his collections (Milburn 1986, 1994, 1997). Katz (1986) presents an in-depth analysis of the Deisheetaan Raven Cape, a remarkable object in Shotridge's collection. Seaton (2001) explores Shotridge as a colonized postmodern subject performing fragmented and conflicting identities. Dauenhauer and Dauenhauer (2003) evaluates Shotridge's collaboration with Franz Boas on Tlingit grammar as a cornerstone of Tlingit research and publication. Preucel, in this volume, explores Shotridge's exhibits and teaching at the Penn Museum. To date, no article explores his ethnographic vision and the cumulative resource of his collections at Penn, and to this we now turn.

Training

Louis Shotridge corresponded with George Gordon after their 1905 meeting at the Portland fair and visited the Museum in Philadelphia in 1911. Now the director of Penn's Free Museum of Science and Art, Gordon eagerly hired Louis as a part-time assistant in 1912. For three years he was trained in museum and anthropological methods and was promoted to full-time assistant curator in the American section in 1915.

At Penn, Louis catalogued specimens, recording provenience and source information, explained the uses of native objects, and wrote exhibit labels. He learned about museum display and photography, made dioramas of Tlingit and Haida communities, and installed board member George Heye's vast Indian collections in the Museum galleries. Louis and Florence gave tours to Philadelphia schoolchildren and offered four lectures about Alaska. They examined Northwest Coast collections for possible purchase and collaborated on an article for the *Museum Journal*. In the fall of 1914, Gordon arranged for Louis to study in New York City with anthropologist Franz Boas. Boas helped Louis finalize his Tlingit phonetic system, which would enable him to write and record the spoken word with accuracy. Shotridge offered Boas living Tlingit texts, songs, and myths and illuminated Tlingit verb structure. Their collaboration resulted in the first accurate written Tlingit phonology, which was published by the University Museum in 1917.[5]

Throughout this period, Shotridge was immersed in ideas about the collection and display of world cultures, and he developed his tools of the ethnographic collecting trade. Noted ethnologists at Penn who were also collectors, such as Frank Speck, Mark R. Harrington, and Frederica de Laguna, supported him. After three years of training, Gordon asked Shotridge to turn his attention to his home environment to conduct a study of the Tlingit and to make collections of their arts and industries for the Free Museum.

Field Work

Over the next seventeen years Shotridge undertook four extended collecting and research trips in Alaska for Penn. He returned to Philadelphia on only three occasions. As a Tlingit speaker of high rank, he was well positioned to study and collect among his own people, and he gained their confidence with greater ease than would an outsider. Shotridge's goals to collect and preserve Tlingit history further distinguished him from other collectors working for commercial purposes. In his own words, Shotridge always had the "upper hand" on access to collections.

Shotridge had full financial backing in the field, and this set up a unique situation among native collectors of the time. He received a monthly salary and, with all expenses paid, established his ethnographic collecting methods and practices with relative ease. The first trip ran for nearly four years, from June 1915 to the spring of 1919. Based in Haines, close to his home community, Shotridge's early research focused on the Tlingit communities of his northern home region. He purchased a small skiff and camping equipment and spent long periods, often three to four weeks at a time, living and camping among the northern communities. In the winter he traveled by ice skate and dog sled through the northern region and reached further distances by commercial boat when necessary. He worked with informants, made a small number of sound recordings, and collected objects and research notes with precision.

After three years of museum work back at Penn, Louis returned to Alaska for five years from June 1922 to October 1927. Headquartered this time to the south in Sitka, where he lived with his second wife and a growing family, his second research period focused on the Tlingit region more broadly. At this time Shotridge articulated three specific and ambitious goals: to collect the art and history of the leading Tlingit clans across the region, to record the origins and migrations of the Tlingit people, and to document the origins of the clan names, which are based in geography. His mobility improved dramatically on this trip with the purchase of the *Penn*, a thirty-foot inboard, which he outfitted for sleeping and cooking. He traveled widely to document and map abandoned and living Tlingit villages.

Shotridge's third and fourth field seasons were shortened due to a series of personal difficulties and financial complications. He lost his mentor, George Gordon, in a tragic fall in Philadelphia in the winter of 1927, and his second wife died of tuberculosis in the spring of 1928. With continued support from the Museum's new director, Horace Jayne, Shotridge continued his fieldwork and wrote rather productively during this difficult time. The third field season ran for only eight months, from August 1928 to May 1929. After installing the American wing at the Museum, his fourth field season began in the summer of 1930 and continued for two years.

In December 1930, Shotridge was elected president of the Alaska Native Brotherhood camp in Sitka. This was a leading position among his people, as the ANB fought for native rights and helped individuals meet the requirements of citizenship. In a letter to Jayne, he wrote that the appointment favored his collecting efforts, since once suspicious headmen now offered him objects he could not have on previous visits.[6] At Penn there was talk of financial crisis as early as November 1930. The city eliminated its yearly appropriation to the Museum in 1931, and Museum salaries were cut. Shotridge's annual salary was reduced by 15 percent in December 1931 to $2,400.[7] Along with all but the chief curators, Louis's position was terminated in May 1932. Jayne offered compassionate support in his writings to Shotridge in these years, and though he was never able to do so, he expressed hope of soon reinstating his position.[8]

Field Practices

Throughout his career, Shotridge meticulously recorded data and notes in his own hand and using a typewriter outfitted with Tlingit characters.[9] He wrote letters to Gordon every two weeks, often three or four detailed pages at a time. His letters, postcards, and telegrams provide details of his collecting and research activities and strategies. Shotridge also documented his living and collecting expenses with exactitude and regularly sent Gordon packing lists, specimen lists, invoices, bills of sale, receipts, inventories, and monthly lists of cash expenditures. At Gordon's urging, he wrote several manuscripts for the *Museum Journal,* yet noted that this was hard work for him and that he much preferred being in the field visiting with his people. When his articles were published, he mailed copies to his Alaskan informants.[10]

Shotridge established and maintained two research files, one held in his Museum office in Philadelphia, and a second at his home in Alaska. The Philadelphia file included fifty broad categories for an eventual book on Tlingit culture (see below). The data in his Alaskan field file was more specific. Within its four hundred pages, Shotridge recorded family histories on 110 genealogical cards recorded at Chilkoot, Klawak, Klukwan, Sitka, and Wrangell, clan and house histories on over 60 cards, personal names on approximately 30 cards, object histories on 94 specimen cards, and more than one hundred geographical place-names at Admiralty Island, Annette Island, Baranof Island, Chichagof Island, Cleveland Peninsula, Dasa-xaku, Duke Island, Gravina Island, Kuiu Island, Kupreanof Island, the mainland, and Prince of Wales Island.

Another important field tool was the camera, and Shotridge took three hundred black-and-white photographs with at least two instruments on this trip. When the weather was warm, he developed and printed the negatives in the field and mailed these back to Gordon. In his later years in Sitka, he filmed Tlingit basket weaving and planned with his ANB members to film traditional potlatch dances.

To gain access to Tlingit objects and information, Shotridge knew to seek out the leading men in Tlingit communities. He was offered numerous collections for a variety of reasons.[11] Most frequently, leading men were elderly or sick and lacked confidence in their clan members to take care of clan objects.[12] Others had died, having left objects to "those individuals who did not appreciate them."[13] Some objects were left as collateral on loans that were not repaid, others were sold by female inheritors, and some were sold because their owners had converted to Christianity.[14] In the 1930s, the Great Depression compelled families to sell old collections.[15] Many individuals felt they had no one to pass objects to for safekeeping, and they found a solution in their tribal member's plan to bring objects to the Penn Museum. Shotridge sent lists and photographs of available specimens to Dr. Gordon, and through their correspondence he made collecting decisions over a period of several weeks.[16] If prices were too high, he declined, then made purchases once prices had fallen.[17]

On some occasions individuals chose not to sell their collections to Shotridge. He tried to acquire objects from his late father's house in Klukwan, the celebrated Whale House of the G̲aanax̲teidí clan. He made eloquent speeches to the remaining men of the house, and when they did not yield, his persistent efforts caused serious conflict that required a peace ceremony. Shotridge felt considerable strain over this event.

Finally, in 1931, the Sheldon Jackson Museum of Sitka contacted Penn Museum's director to ask if he wished to purchase a specific set of Tlingit human remains, a common museum practice at the time. Director Jayne wrote to Shotridge and asked him to inspect the remains. After doing so, Shotridge recommended against the purchase. Soon thereafter, he collected the remains of a Kaagwaantaan shaman and quietly shipped these to Philadelphia.

Ethnographic Collections

In his many years of association with Penn, Louis Shotridge purchased approximately 570 objects for its Museum. Approximately 88 percent are of Tlingit origin, 10 percent are Tsimshian, and 2 percent are Athabascan. He acquired Tlingit objects in nine communities: Angoon, Chilkoot, Killisnoo, Klukwan, Haines, Hoonah, Juneau, Sitka, and Taku. Approximately two-thirds of his Tlingit collection is utilitarian in nature, including tools, hunting and fishing equipment, baskets, boxes, spoons, knives, art supplies and raw materials. One-third consists of Tlingit regalia and clan objects, including hats and headdresses, blankets, masks, rattles, dance batons and ornaments.

A unique attribute of Shotridge's Tlingit collection is its several house collections. These are objects owned by clan families at the time and held together in clan houses. Nine such collections were sold to Shotridge between 1917 and 1931 from the following houses: Klukwan Kaagwaantaan Drum House, 1917; the Sitka L'uknax̱.ádi Sea Lion House, 1918; the Sitka Kaagwaantaan Eagle's Nest House, 1918; the Angoon Deisheetaan Tuquka House, 1923; the Hoonah T'akdeintaan Snail House, 1924; the Sitka L'uknax̱.ádi Whale House, 1925; the Killisnoo Teiḵweidí Raven House, 1925; the Sitka Kaagwaantaan Wolf House, 1926; and the Sitka Kagwaantaan Burned House, 1931. Shotridge valued the house collections as historic documents of the leading families.

Photographs

Shotridge's photographs include five hundred black-and-white images of named individuals, townscapes, landscapes, objects, and events. Surprisingly, he did not photograph traditional Tlingit ceremonies or objects in use in ceremonial contexts. Shotridge captured real life in Tlingit communities through images of parades, funerals, the catching and processing of fish, harbor scenes, and portraits of individuals. He gave the majority of his images descriptive titles. His early work focused on the northern communities of Klukwan and Haines, where he took more than one hundred portraits of individuals identified by name. His portraits include A-gux-daet, An-g, An-qin-q, An-g-xd, Ca-i-ti, Cqin-a, John Dana-Wag, Dewu Enix, Gac-tu-kix-x, Ga-qux-k, Ga-ucti, Gidion Meneshgu, Gago-Gem-Dzwust, Gin-du-at, Gingu-at, Gin-Tu-W, Giyi-s n-an, Gutc-uxu, Gu tin, Gun-gu, Gu-tin, Jos. King, Ke-t-xut-Tc Keyqu, Ku xs, Mene-eck, Thomas Na g-k, Nic-yetxc, Nic-yo-go, Peter Nisshiyok, Nukt yi-la, Nxc-k-num-caka-ayi, Qas-gu, Sa-lan-x, Sdayatla, Miss Peter Simpson, Sxan-du-n-la, Sxe-la, Tagum-Tege, Tawu-k-dutnuk, Tc t-yi, Tiy-ca, Tqex-k, Tsutsx-xu, Ttxih-du-n, Tu-nat, Tus-try, Tu X ani-Gin, Tu-xua-nigin, T w-tu, Txut-ki, Xa-kan-dusox, Y d k-can, Yak-xudede-sak, Yand gin-yet, Yedi-w-du-keit, Yet-guw-d-u, and Wiget. Shotridge's numerous landscape images from his later fieldwork supported his goals to document Tlingit history and migration by mapping Tlingit communities and recording place-names.

Curatorial Records, Manuscripts and Publications

Shotridge's Museum curatorial research files were a work in progress. At his desk at Penn, he organized his research notes into fifty categories marked by tabbed index cards. Arranged in the following order, they reveal a sense of the book he planned to write on Tlingit culture. Headings included Tlingit character, condition, grammar, phonetics, terminology, vocabulary, animals, plants, history, warfare, emblems, education, ceremonies, names, religion, beliefs, charms, conceptions, customs, cosmology, mythology, trade, commodities, barter, industry, resources, habits, artifacts, implements, utensils, subsistence[s], foods, wearing apparel, methods, medicines, constructions, amusements, games, sports, arts, sculpture, origins of totem poles, textiles, painting, music, cooking, paraphernalia, and organization. Shotridge's research notes include a notebook from his work with Franz Boas and a section on northern genealogies developed on his first trip. Five categories hold the greatest number of research notes, including beliefs, emblems, warfare, history, and Tlingit terminology.

Louis Shotridge wrote thirteen manuscripts, eleven of which were published in the University of Pennsylvania's *Museum Journal*.[18] Eight of the manuscripts relate to Tlingit objects in his collection. His first research trip resulted in the publication of seven manuscripts. "My Northland Revisited" (1917), written and mailed from Alaska, documents the revival of potlatch ceremonies. "War Helmets and Clan Hats of the Tlingit" (1919) describes the Kaagwaantaan and L'uknax̱.ádi hats he purchased in Klukwan and Sitka. "A Visit to the Tsimshian Indians" (1919) summarizes Shotridge's six weeks of research among the neighboring Tsimshian. Three essays from this early period reveal the significance of Tlingit objects as allegories of proper behavior. "Ghost of Courageous Adventurer" (1920) tells the harrowing tale of a Kluckwan exploring party and the Tlingit dagger[19] made to honor their sacrifice. "Land Otter-Man" (1922) tells the tale of a great L'uknax̱.ádi warrior whose courage and prowess in battle were memorialized in the carving of the land otter canoe prow.[20] "Tlingit Woman's Root Baskets" (1920) explores the form, design, construction, and uses of basketry and its meaningful ties to the northern Tlingit landscape.

Shotridge's published manuscripts from his later field seasons reveal his maturing interest in recording clan histories. "The Emblems of Tlingit Culture" (1928) outlines the mythological origins of the Tlingit clans through

Fig. 2.2 The Ganook hat, Kaagwaantaan, purchased by Louis Shotridge in 1924. Photograph NA 6864.

their hats, some of which Shotridge had recently placed on exhibit in Philadelphia. "The Bride of Tongass" (1929) tells the Tlingit legend of an unlikely marriage that unites warring factions from north and south and presents Tlingit marriage as a model of proper behavior. Objects he collected play a central role in this story. The groom, Tàx.cà, wore the Petrel (Ganook) hat[21] (said today to be the oldest Tlingit hat in existence) as he entered the bride's territory by canoe to ask Saetl-tin's father for her hand in marriage (Fig. 2.2). Later, the bride honors her husband with a gift of her hair as a symbol of her enduring commitment. "The Kaguantan Shark Helmet" (1929)[22] describes an old object obtained from the last of the

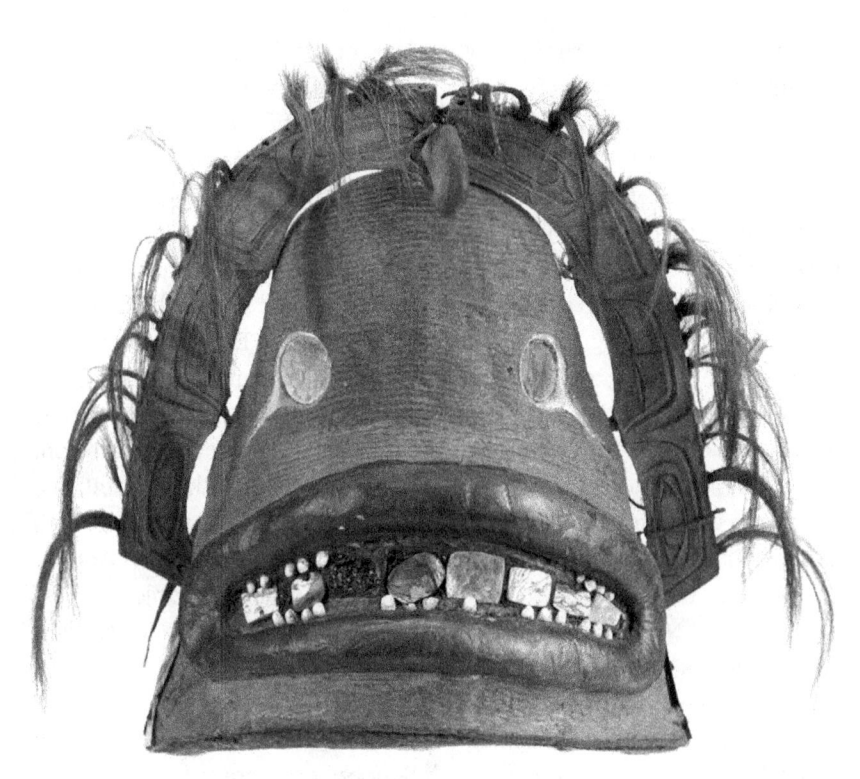

Fig. 2.3 Kaagwaantaan Shark helmet collected by Louis Shotridge in 1929. Photograph 29-1-1.

Kaagwaantaan house group known to be the founders of this great clan (Fig. 2.3). Shotridge acknowledges the considerable personal strain he felt over collecting this object. "How Ats-ha Followed the Hide of His Comrade to Yek Land" (1930) records an old Tlingit legend involving shamanism. Two manuscripts went unpublished: "The Vanishing Nobility of the Tlingit" (undated but written after 1929), and "Vengeance" (1933), which Shotridge described as the only love story in the Tlingit narrative.[23]

The New Shotridge Digital Archive

The Shotridge collection has always been of significance to Tlingit people because it represents their cultural heritage. Today almost a third of the object collection has been claimed for repatriation under the Native American Graves Protection and Repatriation Act (NAGPRA) of 1990 by several separate Tlingit entities. At present, some of these claims are incomplete or inactive, and the Museum is working to evaluate others. In 2009 eight objects in the T'aḵdeintaan Snail House Collection were found by the University of Pennsylvania to fit the definitions of Object of Cultural Patrimony or Sacred Object and will be repatriated to Hoonah in the coming months. In addition, the university proposed a partnership with the clan including a joint custodial agreement for an additional thirty-seven objects and to work together on projects that build on the legacy of NAGPRA and Louis Shotridge's vision to preserve Tlingit history. The claimants rejected this proposal. In October 2010, the university passed a "Resolution to Repatriate Clan Objects and Establish a Partnership between the Tlingit Kaagwaantaan Clan and the Tlingit L'ooknax.ádi Clan of Sitka, Alaska, and the University of Pennsylvania Museum." Eight of eleven objects in this instance were found to fit NAGPRA's definitions of "Objects of Cultural Patrimony" and/or "Sacred Objects." In addition, the university proposed a partnership with the clan including a joint custodial agreement for the remaining three objects. The claimants accepted this proposal. However, a second Tlingit entity, the Sitka tribe of Alaska, has made a competing claim for five of the Kaagwaantaan objects.

Because of NAGPRA and the significance of Shotridge's accomplishments, the Museum created a digital archive of Shotridge's collection in its entirety. The three-year project involved commitments from the Institute of Museum and Library Services (IMLS), the Museum's American section and archives, Penn Library's Schoenberg Center for Electronic Text and Image (SCETI), Penn's Center for Native American Studies, the Central Council of Tlingit and Haida Indian Tribes of Alaska (CCTHIA), and the Alaska State Library (ASL). The digital archive was launched on the Penn Museum's website in 2011.

Archives and museums are important repositories that create safe houses for records and valued resources. They are also places where meaningful research can be conducted. The digital archive of the Shotridge collection preserves all of Shotridge's objects, photographic images, and more than three thousand pages of his writings and makes them accessible online to the Tlingit people and the general public for research and educational purposes.

There are innumerable ways in which the Shotridge digital archive can be of assistance to the Tlingit people in their ongoing efforts to strengthen and revitalize their culture. Shotridge's records are an important source of Tlingit language and clan history that can renew relationships to clan ancestors and places, help revitalize and strengthen the clan system and cultural traditions, and provide new resources for language study and retention.

Conclusion

Louis Shotridge felt the onrushing tide of modernity in Alaska and he devoted his life to recording the history of his Tlingit people and to finding a safe place for Tlingit clan regalia where it would be seen on a world stage. Adopting anthropological methods, he worked as systematically as possible to record and collect Tlingit histories with emphasis on the clan system from the Tlingit point of view. With Gordon's support, he intended to write a book on the subject. Yet the extenuating circumstances of the Great Depression and Shotridge's death in 1937 prevented him from completing his work.

In this essay, I have suggested that it is valuable to take an all-inclusive view of Shotridge's fieldwork and practices, collections, and writings to best understand his commitment to Tlingit history and culture. Sifting through the details of his meticulous records, one begins to understand the importance of his actions. Shotridge's collections and writings at the Penn Museum are much more than the clan objects alone or the acts of their taking and display as metonyms of Tlingit culture. They embody rich and textured histories and identities and constitute an ever-important legacy of Tlingit cultural heritage. With the help of the digital archive, as we at Penn are already beginning to see, Shotridge's records can be used and newly appreciated by future generations of Tlingit scholars and the larger Tlingit community. As Shotridge himself would have wished, the objects he collected and the historical records he compiled can once again play a major role in the life of the Tlingit community.

ACKNOWLEDGMENTS

I thank the Institute for Museum and Library Services for their generous support of this project, as well as Sergei Kan and Steve Henrickson for inviting me to participate in the 2007 and 2009 clan conferences in Alaska. I am grateful to my many colleagues on the Shotridge digital archive team for their support including Robert Preucel, Kathryn Venzor, Cassandra Turcotte, Alex Pezzati; David Mcknight, Dennis Mullen, Chris Lippa, and Mishajlo Matijkiw of the Penn Library's Schoenberg Center for Electronic Text and Image; Ariela Houseman, Sharon Kornelly, Emma McClafferty, and Deven Parker; Tlingit consultants Harold Jacobs of Central Council of Tlingit and Haida Indian Tribes of Alaska, Nora and Richard Dauenhauer, Teri Rofkar, and Lilly Hudson;

and Jim Simard and Anastasia Tarmann of the Alaska State Library. I also thank additional colleagues at the Penn Museum who have supported the project in a variety of important ways including Bill Wierzbowski, Stacey Espenlaub, Ginny Ebert, Judith Berman, Francine Sarin, Jen Chiappardi, Shawn Hayla, Rajeev Thomas, Jen Bournstein, Jerry Sabloff, Richard Leventhal, and Richard Hodges.

NOTES

1. Some Tlingit people have also been critical of Shotridge's collecting activities.
2. Milburn 1994, 551.
3. Low 1991, xxviii.
4. That year, Gordon accessioned forty-five objects collected by Shotridge in Klukwan.
5. Letters LS to GBG, November 4, 1914, November 27, 1914, January 21, 1915, UPM Archives.
6. Letter LS to HJ, December 19, 1930, UPM Archives.
7. Letters HJ to LS, November 18, 1930, December 22, 1931, UPM Archives.
8. Letter HJ to LS, January 30, 1933, UPM Archives.
9. Letter, E. S. Hewett Company to LS, April 23, 1917, UPM Archives.
10. Letter LS to JM, August 2, 1929, UPM Archives.
11. Letters LS to GBG, July 7, 1922, October 14, 1922; January 7, 1924, UPM Archives.
12. Letters LS to GBG, February 17, 1922; November 27, 1926, UPM Archives.
13. Letter LS to GBG, October 8, 1923, UPM Archives.
14. Letters LS to GBG, April 2, 1917, July 19, 1926, January 5, 1918; Letter LS to HJ, March 29, 1929, UPM Archives.
15. Letters LS to HJ, July 21, 1931, January 25, 1932, UPM Archives.
16. Letter LS to GBG, October 14, 1922, UPM Archives.
17. Letters LS to GBG, October 14, 1922, July 9, 1925, UPM Archives.
18. Florence wrote one article, "*The Life of a Chilkat Indian Girl*" (1913).
19. UPM NA8488.
20. UPM NA8500.
21. UPM NA6864.
22. UPM 29–1–1.
23. Letter LS to HJ, August 2, 1933, UPM Archives.

REFERENCES

Carpenter, Edmund. 1975. "Collecting Northwest Coast Art." In *Indian Art of the Northwest Coast: A Dialogue on Craftsmanship and Aesthetics*, ed.

Bill Holm and Bill Reid, 9–27. Houston: Rice University Institute for the Arts.

Cole, Douglas. 1985. *Captured Heritage: The Scramble for Northwest Coast Cultural Heritage.* Seattle: University of Washington Press.

Dauenhauer, Nora M., and Richard Dauenhauer. 2003. "Louis Shotridge and Indigenous Tlingit Ethnography: Then and Now." In *Constructing Cultures Then and Now: Celebrating Franz Boas and the Jesup North Pacific Expedition,* ed. Laurel Kendall and Igor Krupnik, 165–83. Washington DC: Arctic Studies Center, National Museum of Natural History, Smithsonian Institution.

———. 1994. *Haa Kusteeyí, Our Culture.* Seattle: University of Washington Press; Juneau: Sealaska Heritage Foundation.

Dean, John. 1998. "Louis Shotridge, Museum Man: A 1918 Visit to the Nass and Skeena Rivers." *Pacific Northwest Quarterly* 89 (4): 202–9.

Emmons, George Thornton. 1991. *The Tlingit Indians.* Ed. Frederica de Laguna. Seattle: University of Washington Press.

Gmelch, Sharon Bohn. 2008. *The Tlingit Encounter with Photography.* Philadelphia: University of Pennsylvania Museum of Archaeology and Anthropology.

Goldschmidt, Walter R., and Theodore H. Haas. 1998. *Haa Aaní = Our Land: Tlingit and Haida Land Rights and Use.* Seattle: University of Washington Press; Juneau: Sealaska Heritage Foundation.

Kan, Sergei. 1999. *Memory Eternal: Tlingit Culture and Russian Orthodox Christianity through Two Centuries.* Seattle: University of Washington Press.

Kaplan, Susan, and Kristin Barsness, eds. 1986. *Raven's Journey: The World of Alaska's Native People.* Philadelphia: University of Pennsylvania Museum.

Katz, Adria H. 1986. "The Raven Cape: A Tihitian Breastplate Collected by Louis Shotridge." In *Raven's Journey,* ed. Susan Kaplan and Kristin Barsness, 78–90. Philadelphia: University of Pennsylvania Museum.

Low, Jean. 1991. "Lieutenant George Thornton Emmons, USN, 1852–1945." In *The Tlingit Indians,* by George T. Emmons, xxvii–xl. Seattle: University of Washington Press.

Mason, Alden. 1960. "Louis Shotridge." *Expedition* 2 (2): 11–15.

Milburn, Maureen E. 1986. "Louis Shotridge and the Objects of Everlasting Esteem." In *Raven's Journey,* ed. Susan Kaplan and Kristin Barsness, 54–77. Philadelphia: University of Pennsylvania Museum.

———. 1994. "Weaving the Tina Blanket: The Journey of Florence and Louis Shotridge." In *Haa Kusteeyí, Our Culture,* ed. Richard and Nora Dauenhauer, 548–61.

———. 1997. "The Politics of Possession: Louis Shotridge and the Tlingit Collections of the University of Pennsylvania Museum." PhD diss., University of British Columbia.

Seaton, Elizabeth. 2001. "The Native Collector: Louis Shotridge and the Contests of Possession." *Ethnography* 2 (1): 35–61.

Shotridge, Florence. 1913. "The Life of a Chilkat Indian Girl." *Museum Journal* 4(3): 101–3.

Shotridge, Louis V. 1917. "Chilkat Houses." *Museum Journal* 4 (3): 81–100.

———. 1917. "My Northland Revisited." *Museum Journal* 8 (2): 105–15.

———. 1919. "War Helmets and Clan Hats of the Tlingit." *Museum Journal* 10 (1–2): 43–48.

———. 1917. "A Visit to the Tsimshian Indians, Part 1." *Museum Journal* 10: 49–67.

———. 1919. "A Visit to the Tsimshian Indians, Part 2." *Museum Journal* 10: 117–48.

———. 1919. "Tlingit Woman's Root Baskets." *Museum Journal* 12 (3): 162–78.

———. 1920. "Ghost of Courageous Adventurer." *Museum Journal* 11 (1): 11–26.

———. 1922. "Land Otter-Man." *Museum Journal* 13 (1): 55–59.

———. 1928. "The Emblems of the Tlingit Culture." *Museum Journal* 19 (4): 350–77.

———. 1929. "The Bride of Tongass." *Museum Journal* 20 (2): 131–56.

———. 1929. "The Kaguantan Shark Helmet." *Museum Journal* 20 (3–4): 339–43.

———. 1930. "How Ats-ha Followed the Hide of His Comrade to Yek Land." *Museum Journal* 21 (3–4): 215.

3

This Is Ku_xaankutaan's (Dr. Frederica de Laguna's) Song

CHEW SHAA (ELAINE ABRAHAM) AND
DAXOOTSU (JUDITH RAMOS)

X̱an Kootaan (Freddy's Tlingit name, short for Ku_xaankutaan) composed a song in Tlingit for the people of Yakutat. The song was in honor of the children of the K'ineix̱ Ḵwáan, a clan of the Raven moiety[1] that owns and occupies the Yakutat area, and of L'ukna_x.ádi, a Raven clan from the Dry Bay area. She finished the song just before she left Yakutat during the summer of 1954, when the ethnological research that she started in 1949 was completed.

In 1986 my mother, Susie Bremner Abraham, invited Freddy to attend her granddaughter Sharon Goodwin's memorial potlatch. A potlatch is usually held a year after burial to "pay off" a clan's obligations to the opposite moiety. Freddy was pleased and arrived several days before the memorial potlatch. While the family prepared for the ceremony, my mother informed us that Freddy would open the "pay off" portion of the potlatch by singing the song she had composed. Freddy was excited and yet nervous about her clan role. She began humming her song, then whispered to me, "My dear educated granddaughter in the Western and Tlingit world, did you think I went native with the song?" I replied, "Of course, we all know you are Tlingit."

When a person is adopted and given a name, the adoption and naming are validated at a public ceremony so that guests can be witnesses. My mother wanted to validate Freddy's adoption by Katy Dixon Isaac into the K'ineix̱ Ḵwáan clan of Raven Moiety and the name Katy Dixon gave her was Katy's own name, Ku_xaankutaan. The K'ineix̱ Ḵwáan is also known in Yakutat as the Kwáashk'i Ḵwáan clan, from when the clan bought Humpy Creek in Yakutat Bay. Freddy was also to be adopted into the Moon House. Because Katy Dixon Isaac was an elderly matriarch of the clan, her adoption of Frederica was unquestioned but unvalidated.[2]

Fig 3.1 Elaine Abraham (*left*) and Judy Ramos (*center*). Photograph courtesy of Judy Ramos.

Freddy's Song

Freddy's favorite birdsong was the golden-crowned sparrow's song. The tune to the song she composed was inspired by this bird, Shakida Tinaa, the golden-crowned sparrow (*Zonotrichia aticapilla*). Although she identified more than a dozen Yakutat songbirds, she adored what she referred to as "the most beautiful sparrow," with a golden crown and with black stripes on the side of the crown. Most of all, she enjoyed its song.

The winter of 1954, Freddy's last spring in Yakutat, was a good year for songbirds. My parents said there were more birds than usual that spring. The birds arrived in March and congregated in the back of their house among the spruce, alders, and willow trees that were also near Freddy's rented house. Early in the morning, my father would go outside to chop wood or get water from the lake behind Freddy's house. She would be out on the side of the house replenishing the bird feeder. Sometimes when a bird would start singing, Freddy would come running out with her recorder. My mother said that it always brought a smile to my father, a man who was known in the community not to show any emotion. The birds she recorded that spring included the varied thrush, the song sparrow, the golden-crowned sparrow, the yellow warbler, and the robin.

At a celebration sponsored by Sealaska, the regional Native corporation for southeast Alaska, Freddy was honored for her work. She sat

Fig. 3.2 JOM Mount Saint Elias Dancers. Photograph courtesy of Yakutat Tlingit Tribe. *Left to right, front row*: Martha Mallot and Sylivia Schumacker; *second row*: Kalen Adams and Maka Monture (Judy Ramos's daughter); *third row*: Nathan Bremner, Kai Monture (Judy Ramos's son), Sharnel Vale, and Kirsten Slate; *fourth row*: J. P. Buller, Alin Vale, Shane Brown, and Tim Brown.

in one of the front row seats whenever her "grandchildren," the Mount Saint Elias Dancers, were going to dance. She cheered louder than anyone; however, she lamented to me that all her old Tlingit teachers from Yakutat had passed on to the spirit world. With tears in her eyes, she added, "Now all my grandchildren are orphans," nodding toward the dancing children. She added with pride, "But look at them now."

In her article "Field Work with My Tlingit Friends," she wrote:

> After Olaf's death, Susie invited me to visit her on my way home from Copper River, and I brought her a blanket I'd been given at a potlatch, which pleased her. But our last reunion was when I attended the potlatch she gave in 1986. At that time I got to know and appreciate her daughter, Elaine Abraham, who acted as Susie's "executive officer" in charge of the complicated logistics of the ceremony. Susie suffered from a bad heart, and Elaine was most solicitous. All of "our" clan, including myself, were taught a few songs and simple dances, but Elaine's pretty daughter, Judy Ramos, and her son, David Ramos, costumed alike, performed an impressive shaman's dance. (de Laguna 2000, 30)

This was the night Freddy sang her song for the first time in Yakutat, and the applause lasted a long time. Thus she opened the "pay off" time and the "happy time" at her clan's potlatch.

Ten years later, when David Ramos was doing an internship in research and care of collections at the National Museum of American Indians in New York, he went to Bryn Mawr College outside Philadelphia to see Gram X̲ankootan. It was a surprise visit, yet as soon as she saw him, she recognized him, greeting him with a hug and asking in Tlingit, "Ax̲ dachx̲ánk', goosú ee tláa?" (My grandchild, where is your mother?) She took David to lunch, introducing him as her grandson.

When Judy Ramos received her bachelor's and master's degrees, Freddy was also proud of her. When Judy did a traditional ecological knowledge study on salmon for the Yakutat Tlingit tribe, Judy wrote to her for advice. Freddy wrote back:

> Dear Judy, of course I know who you are. Your grandparents were among the great leaders of the Yakutat and some of the nicest people I know. You are undertaking too much, I think, in your studies. Please remember that you are to explain the Native ways of think-

Fig. 3.3 Susie Abraham (*left*) and Freddy de Laguna at Sharon Goodwin's memorial potlatch. Photograph courtesy of Eva Sensmeier.

ing about territorial rights, fishing, and all the other topics on your list. Give up the jargon of "resource management." That is the white man's way of thinking about such matters. If you could only consult *Under Mount Saint Elias,* you would see that the Tlingit and other Native peoples felt that they were in one world with the plants and animals and fish.

Fig. 3.4 The musical score from de Laguna's *Under Mount Saint Elias* (1972:1368-369). Courtesy of the Smithsonian Institution Press.

Grandma X̱ankootan composed and recorded a song in 1954 (Fig. 3.4) to honor her clan and the people of Yakutat. Her song, translated below from Tlingit into English, will always be part of the clan's oral tradition. Her memory will live on; at her clan's potlatches when "fire dishes" are brought out, her name will be called: "Kux̱aankutaan, Kux̱aankutaan."

To the People of Yakutat: Song for K'ineix Ḵwáan Children and L'uknax̱.ádi-Children[3]

Composed by Frederica de Laguna

Yá shí kax̱wlishiyi shí áyá. Ldakát Kwáashk'i Ḵwáan yátx'i ḵa L'uknax̱.ádi yátx'i ḵa Lukaax̱.ádi yátx'i daadáx̱ áyá kax̱wlishi áyá. Kux̱aanguwutaan x̱'ashiyí.

This song is for all Kwáashk'i Ḵwáan children and L'uknax̱.di children and Lukaax̱.ádi children. It is Kux̱aankutaan's song.

Whereas Yakutat birds are supposed to have learned their songs from those of human beings, I have based my melody upon the song of the golden-crowned sparrow. I wish to acknowledge my indebtedness to John Ellis for his assistance with the words.

Frederica de Laguna's Song for K'ineix Kwáan-Children and L'uknax.ádi-Children

♪=116
C#

    Refrain
A. Ha ya ha ya ya ya ha-ni ha-ya
B. ha ya ha ha ya ha ya
C. ye ya he, ha ya ha
D. he ya ha ya ha ya
E. ha ya ha ya ha ha ya ha,
F. ha ya ha he ha hay, ha ya
G. he a-ni a—ya, ye a-ni a—ye

    Stanza I (sung twice)
A. Ha ya ha ya ye, ye ha-ni a-ya
B. Kawayikdei kuḵwateeni

(When I go away) To the unknown (space) (meaning the whole universe)
C. I daadei tuwuneekw
D. K'inei̱x̱ Ḵwaani yatx'i
for you I am sad children of K'inei̱x̱ Ḵwáan (clan)
E. I daa toowooch x̱at gugajaaḵ
longing for you will kill me
F. Lax̱aayikde tsuk' kuḵwateen
Inside Tlax̱ayik (Yakutat) I will look for (come again),
G. he a-ni a-ya, ye a-ni a-ye,
this is your (land) dwelling, your dwelling

Stanza II (sung twice)
A. Ha ya he ya he, ye a-ni a–ya
B. Ax̱ Gooji naḵajooni
My wolf (clan) I dream of
C. Ax̱ toowoo alik'ei,
D. L'ukna̱x.adi yatx'i
My inner being you make well (happy),
child of L'ukna̱x.adi.
E. Uwayaa gagaan ḵagani
It is as if you are the sun beam (the sun is shining)
F. I Yeili toowu yisigoo
Your Raven you have made happy
G. he a-ni a-ya, ye a-ni a-ye,
this is your land (universe).
End
A. ha ya ha ya ye, he a-ni a-ya

ACKNOWLEDGMENTS

We would like to acknowledge Elaine's father and mother, the late Olaf Abraham and Susie Bremner Abraham, and Harry K. Bremner, Elaine's maternal uncle, for teaching Freddy and us the history, culture, and mythology of Yakutat's Tlingit.

Elaine Abraham (Chew Shaa) is a retired professor from University of Alaska. Judith Ramos (Daxootsu) is Elaine's daughter. She works for the Yakutat Tlingit tribe and has also collaborated on subsistence and traditional ecological knowledge projects with the USDA Forest Service and the National Park Service. Judith is an assistant professor in the Department of Alaska Native Studies and Rural Development Program at the University of Alaska Fairbanks. She is a graduate student in the Indigenous Studies PhD program and Resilience and Adaptations Program Fellow at the same university.

NOTES

This paper was first published in Arctic Anthropology 43(2) (2006):14–19. In 2011, upon the editor's request, Richard and Nora Marks Dauenhauer transliterated de Laguna's orthography to the modern-day one and in the process corrected her spelling of some of the clan names as well as some of her word divisions.

1. Children belong to the mother's clan and moiety, so the reference in such songs is to the father's clan.
2. Tlingits believe in reincarnation. Katy Dixon Isaac was reborn as Katie Lord, the daughter of Nellie Lord of the Moon House.
3. The explanation and song were composed by Frederica de Laguna and were first published in the third volume of *Under Mount Saint Elias* (de Laguna 1972:1362–363). Elaine Abraham has a recording of the song as sung by de Laguna. She transcribed it for the 2006 *Arctic Anthropology* article and added the translation. For the present publication, the editors have transliterated the original de Laguna orthography to the contemporary standard coastal Tlingit writing system. The translation is as published in 2006.

REFERENCES

de Laguna, Frederica. 1972. *Under Mount Saint Elias: The History and Culture of the Yakutat Tlingit*. Smithsonian Contributions to Anthropology 7. 3 vols. Washington DC: Smithsonian Institution Press.
———. 2000. "Field Work with My Tlingit Friends." In *Celebration 2000: Restoring Balance Culture*, ed. Susan W. Fair and Rosita Worl, 21–40. Juneau: Sealaska Heritage Foundation.

4

Mark Jacobs Jr./Gusht'ei'héen (1923-2005)

HAROLD JACOBS

Lineage and Traditional Training

Mark Jacobs Jr. was born on November 28, 1923, in Sitka, to Mark and Annie Paul Jacobs. He was born into the Dakl'aweidí (Killer Whale) clan; his father was Deisheetaan (Beaver clan).[1]

He had several Tlingit names. Saa.aat' (Cold) refers to the migration of the clan to the coast when they were camped by a glacier and had an encounter with the ice field. The name Keet Wú (White Killer Whale) derives from when he took movies of a white killer whale in the 1950s while out seining.[2] Oodéi Shkaduneek translates as "Everyone Wants to Claim It," referring to the killer whale. When he became leader of the Killer Whale House in Angoon, he was given the traditional housemaster's name of Gusht'eihéen, meaning "Spray behind the Dorsal Fin." Fourteen months before his death, at the most recent Killer Whale clan memorial, he succeeded Dan Brown Sr. to the name Wóochx Kaduhaa, a shaman's name that Brown had inherited from Jimmie George Sr.

At the time of his death, Mark Jacobs Jr. was the *Naa shaadei háni* ("one standing at the head," clan leader) of the Dakl'aweidí clan in Angoon. He was the hít s'aatí or housemaster of Kéet Hít (Killer Whale House), also known as Woochdakádin Kéet Hít, the Killer Whales Facing Away from Each Other House. The design on the house was painted by his great-grandfather Dick Yeilnaawú, and it is probably the last traditional clan house on the Northwest Coast with a painted front. Mark was a noted historian, fluent speaker of Tlingit, and the last male speaker of his lineage and house group. He enjoyed speaking Tlingit with others and telling stories. He was highly knowledgeable in Tlingit culture, political history, and traditional law. He actively participated in potlatches and understood how this tradition functions to keep clan property in correct clan ownership. He worked actively on repatriation efforts and witnessed the successful return of many items, including the return of a Killer Whale hat to his clan in the final week of his life.

Mark could trace his ancestry for five generations on his mother's side and eight generations on his father's side. Through his father's line he has Kiks.ádi connections. His father was Mark Jacobs Sr. (Kashkwei, Kootax̱'teek, Nahóowu, G̲oochtoowú) of the Deisheetaan (Beaver clan) and Took̲ká Hít (Needlefish House) also known as S'igeidí Hít (Beaver House) in Angoon. The father of Mark Sr. was a Teik̲weidí man from the Bear House in Angoon named Toonax (Frank Noble Johnson), making Mark Jr. a grandchild of the Teik̲weidí. Frank Johnson's parents were a woman named K̲aastaak and a Kiks.ádi man named Naats Éesh. This made Mark Jacobs Sr. a grandchild of Kiks.ádi. A noted fisherman and historian, he often wore the Kiks.ádi clan's Frog hat to honor his grandfather's people.

Mark often spoke of listening to Grandpa George Lewis calling for Al Perkins III, Mark's cousin and playmate, to sit and listen, telling Al that one day he would be the leader of the clan. Mark would listen in, and George would also tell him history on his own. George Lewis (Aanaatl'éek') was a Chookaneidí yádi, his father Naadageix̱' Éesh coming from G̲aayeis' Hít (Iron House) in Sitka whose wife, George's mother, was known as X̱éetl'i. George was a T'ak̲deintaan grandchild through a man named K̲aayiskéek whose wife was known as Jaanaaleik.

George's wife, Caroline Skinna, known as Carrie, was an aunt to Mark Jr.'s mother. Carrie, a woman of the Dak̲l'aweidí, had the Tlingit name Daalneix̱, the same name as the woman in history of the battle of 1804 who told of their bad fortune coming. Carrie, a well-educated woman and former schoolteacher, was a child of Kiks.ádi, and her father, Chanak Éesh, was a Kaagwaantaan yádi (child of Kaagwaantaan). Carrie's mother was known as K̲aachkaník.

From the time that K'alyáan's Raven helmet was placed in the Sheldon Jackson Museum in 1905 up until 1999, George Lewis was the only person to have worn the helmet, using it in 1948. He was a well-versed historian and clan leader. He and Carrie passed away within a month of each other in 1953, Carrie asking, "Why didn't you tell me he was gone?" and leaving soon after. Having listened to their stories in Tlingit from the time he was a child, as well as listening to his own father, who knew the history well, Mark Jacobs Jr. told and retold what he learned from these people.

Schooling

Mark first attended the segregated school for Natives in the Sitka village and then Sheldon Jackson High School. His schooling was interrupted by military service during World War II, after which he returned to Sheldon Jackson, graduating in 1947. He attended law school in Dubuque, Iowa, in hopes of becoming an attorney, but was unable to achieve this goal.

Military Service

Mark spent four years in the U.S. Navy, nearly all of it on sea duty and in war zones. He and his brother Harvey enlisted immediately after Pearl Harbor. They never attended basic training, but were immediately put to work on "picket boats" in the Icy Straits area. Using "code," Mark and his brother communicated only in the Tlingit language, never using English, and were part of a group of the lesser-known "code talkers."

After a stint in the Aleutians on the USS *New Mexico* (BB-40), Mark served on the USS *Newberry* (APA 158) with the rank of quartermaster 3. During the last two years of the war he served with the amphibious forces in the South Pacific. While on the USS *Newberry* they landed combat troops in Tacloban (Philippines, on Leyte Gulf), on Guam, and on Saipan after the beachheads were secure. They participated in initial landings with combat troops of the Fifth and Eighty-Fourth Marines on Iwo Jima Day, February 19, 1945. Mark witnessed the raising of the American flag on Mt. Suribachi, Iwo Jima, and entered this event into the ship's log. They landed the Second Marines on southern Okinawa, D-day Easter Sunday morning, April 1, 1945. Later they landed the first occupation forces at Aomori, Japan, the famed U.S. Army Black Cat Division.

My father told me how he remembered William A. Childers heading to the landing craft and yelling to my father that he had forgotten his helmet. My dad threw his to Childers and found Childers's helmet and wore it. He said he never forgot that they looked at each other, knowing that Childers would die on the first wave on the beach. He watched all those troops go ashore, knowing that most would not be coming back. Twenty-four landing craft were sent ashore; two came back. The ship carried 1,500 troops.

He saw the USS *Bismarck Sea* get hit, and eventually its magazines exploded; 318 crewmen were lost on that ship. The daily routine. Okinawa was the worst. Mark said that from April 1 to 18 it was "round-the-clock antiaircraft fire." He told one story of a kamikaze attack, the plane diving toward them, but veering off suddenly and hitting the ship next to them. This oral history was confirmed years later. I found the story on an internet search, told by a crewman on the ship that was hit. I showed it to my father. He retold the story . . . again.

He had to record sea burials in the ship's log. Some of the burials were made right over the Marianas Trench, the deepest spot in the ocean. They had so many casualties that they ran out of flags. They had to use the same flag over and over as the bodies sewn up in canvas bags and weighted with a five-inch round were buried at sea. As they say, "They're still on duty."

The worst time he had, though, was when his brother's ship was sunk, hit by five kamikazes off of Okinawa. He said he pleaded for information and could only go hide by himself and cry for his brother. Later he learned that his brother had been taken off at Midway and missed that sailing. He received a letter from his brother saying, "My ship was _____." The word *sunk* was cut out by the censors.

Mark was discharged from the navy on his twenty-second birthday, November 28, 1945. Along with his honorable discharge as a quartermaster, Mark was given credit for unused annual leave, paid off in war bonds.

Marriage and Family

Mark Jacobs Jr. married Adelaide Bartness (X̲aasteen) on June 14, 1949. The couple had five children, two of whom survive, as well as five grandchildren and five great-grandchildren. Surviving sons are Harold Jacobs of Sitka and Tony Jacobs of Seattle. Mark was preceded in death by his sons Richard and Philip Jacobs and his daughter, Karen Mann. The grandchildren are John Jacobs and Rene Eubanks of Sitka; Mark Mann of San Jacinto CA; Heather Jacobs of Sedro Woolley WA; and Michelle Moore of Seaside OR. Mark is also survived by his sister, Bertha Karras, of Sitka, and his brother, Wally Jacobs, of Seattle.

Organizations and Community Service

Mark was active in many Alaska Native organizations, bringing strong leadership ability to the meetings he attended. During the war, the Alaska Native Brotherhood and Sisterhood enrolled all local Natives serving in the military as members of Sitka ANB Camp #1 and ANS Camp #4. After discharge from the U.S. Navy, Mark became active in the local ANB, and he held various offices including president of Sitka ANB Camp #1.

He worked actively in the land claims effort, which began with the Alaska Native Brotherhood. The full history of Mark's involvement is too complex to cover in this brief biography. In short, the government ruled for a number of reasons that ANB could not be the sponsor of the land claims movement. Eventually the Central Council of Tlingit and Haida Indians of Alaska and the Alaska Federation of Natives were formed to pursue the struggle. Mark served on the Tlingit and Haida Planning Committee with Alfred Widmark, Andrew Hope, Ted Denny, Joseph Demmert Jr., and Victor Haldane.

Serving as an ANB delegate in many annual conventions and as a Tlingit and Haida delegate from Sitka, his strong voice needed no microphone, nor did he need notes to rattle off dates of one event or another. He was active in the Alaska Federation of Natives conventions as well as the National Congress of American Indians.

He completed more than thirty-four years of faithful service on the Executive Council of Tlingit and Haida, and the Council voted unanimously to appoint him as the first Executive Council Member Emeritus in recognition of his many years of service. He also served on the Tlingit and Haida Housing Authority.

He served on the Interim Board of Directors of Sealaska Corporation, followed by two three-year terms on the Board of Directors. He also served on the Interim Board of Directors of Sitka's Native urban corporation, Shee Atika, declining to serve on the full board due to his full load of other commitments.

In addition to his involvement with Native organizations, Mark was heavily involved in civic activities. He was a steadfast supporter and member of the Sitka Assembly of God Church. When the church burned in 1954, he, his wife, and three sons traveled through Washington, Oregon, and Idaho raising money to rebuild. He took an active role in rebuilding that church as well as the one at its present location.

He served on the Boats and Harbors Commission and the Historic Preservation Society. He was a member of the Veterans of Foreign Wars and a charter member of the Civil Air Patrol in Sitka. He served many years as a subsistence representative on the Sitka Fish and Game Advisory Board and presented position statements on many issues that resulted in federal legislation such as the Veterans Omnibus Bill and the Native American Graves Protection and Repatriation Act (NAGPRA). He was knowledgeable on many issues and courageous in speaking out and stating the facts.

Fig. 4.1 Mark Jacobs Jr., holding the Killer Whale dagger, 2003 General Assembly of the Central Council of Tlingit and Haida Indian Tribes of Alaska. Photograph courtesy of the CCTHITA Archives.

Earning a Living

Aside from many years as a commercial fisherman with his father on the F/V *Rondout*, Mark worked in construction for over thirty years. He was a union member and for twenty years was union steward, retiring in 1985. He was a professional driller and powder man and was involved in construction and blasting of many roads around Sitka, at the Blue Lake and Green Lake Dams, and at the Sitka airport. When asked once

Fig. 4.2 Mark Jacobs Jr. shortly before his death. Photograph by Harold Jacobs.

what qualified him to be on the board of a particular corporation, he replied, "I know the best how to handle explosive situations!"

Mark remained ceremonially active until the final months of his life. He passed away at Mt. Edgecumbe Hospital in Sitka on January 13, 2005, with his wife and son at his side. He continues to be praised by those who knew and worked with him. One internationally known anthropologist deeply moved by his death emphasized that Mark was "open, honest, and generous with his knowledge." Another commented that he was extremely knowledgeable in Tlingit traditions and protocol and "knew how to be assertive and deflect things from going in the wrong direction." Perhaps the shortest and simplest statement we have heard was that "his life generated song."

NOTES

1. This biographical sketch originally appeared in the book *Anóoshi Lingít Aaní Ká, Russians in Tlingit America: The Battles of Sitka, 1802 and 1804*, ed. Nora Marks Dauenhauer, Richard Dauenhauer, and Lydia T. Black (Seattle: University of Washington Press; Juneau: Sealaska Heritage Institute, 2008), 444–46.
2. There are two Tlingit names that translate into English as White Killer Whale. Harold Jacobs explained, "My dad used the name Kéet Wú, not Dleit Kéet."

5

X'eigaa Ḵaa (Tlingit Warrior)

HAROLD JACOBS

In Tlingit, the name for warrior is *xeigaa ḵaa*. Many "Lower 48" tribes have songs for the warrior, but we seemed not to have any specifically for them.[1]

Since my dad was a World War II combat veteran, I always viewed him as a Tlingit warrior. I grew up while the Vietnam War was going on and watched it on the evening news. So much second-guessing and critiquing of the war occurred while our troops were in combat. It was an impossible war to win, and we lost more than 53,000 men.

A Tlingit clan had a war in which many were lost. About a year and a half later they were discussing the war, saying, "They should have done this and that and maybe if they had done this the war would have gone this way." A baby in a swing started speaking to them: "Do you know what happened during the war? Were you there when the battle took place?" To them, the baby was a reincarnated warrior who saw the battle and was chastising them for their conversation. This story is used to illustrate that we can't second-guess battles and that at times we should listen to the younger people.

My dad helped me with some of the harder words and phrases to this song.

The first verse says, "From my swing, I saw the bloodiest parts of the battle; this war was not meant for you, but you still died in our place. Children of all nations, now you know it well."

The second verse says, "Warriors! Stand up! Your hair is always tied in a knot, ready for battle. Because of this, you can all still see the flag. Children of all nations say, 'Thank you!'" (A warrior would tie his hair up in a knot to keep it out of the way for battle and as a sign of preparedness.)

> Hei yaaw hei yaaw hei hee yaaw hei yaaw hei yaaw
> Hei hee yaaw hei yaaw hei yaaw hei hee yaaw hei yaaw hei yaaw

Hei hee yaaw hei yaaw hei yaaw hei hee yaaw aaya
Hei yaaw hei yaaw hei hee yaaw aya hei ee yaaw aaya hei hee yaaw aya

Kejaa daxh kunaxh koolijeeyee ye adaawootl tgat kaawahaa
Tlel has du daadi xaa aaya haa eeti ganeki wunaa
Ldakat naa yax'i; yaayeedat gidein yiysikoo
Hei hee yaaw aaya hei ee yaaw aaya (2x)

Refrain

Xeigaa kaax'u gaayeedaanaak aya, tiakw shawdichin yeewhaan has
Ach awe aankweiyi tlein ch'u yei yiysiteen
Ldakat naa yatx'i; gunalcheesh yoo daa yatooka
Hei hee yaaw aaya hei ee yaaw aaya (2x)

Hei yaaw hei yaaw hei hee yaaw hei yaaw hei yaaw
X'eigaa kaa wusitee ax eesh.

Thank you, Pop, for these words, through which we'll hear your voice for many, many more years.

NOTES

1. Harold Jacobs insisted that we reproduce his own spelling of Tlingit words and sounds, even though it is somewhat different from the standard ones used throughout this book.

6

Mark Jacobs Jr./Gusht'eihéen (1923–2005)

My Teacher, Friend, and Older Brother

SERGEI KAN

Meeting Gusht'eihéen

I first met Mark Jacobs Jr. (Gusht'eihéen) at an Alaska Native Brotherhood (ANB) meeting in early December 1979.[1] I had been in Sitka for four months already, and my fieldwork was going fairly well. I had already established good rapport with the Youngs-Littlefields, one of the leading Tlingit families involved in the Russian Orthodox Church, and had conducted lengthy interviews with Tlingit elders on subjects related to my research interests that focused on the pre-Christian Native religion and Tlingit Christianity (see Kan 2001).

I had been told by a respected non-Native Sitka old-timer and an ANB member that when it came to Tlingit history and culture, Mark was very knowledgeable and that I definitely had to meet him. And so, having gathered up my courage, I did. Mark was gracious and friendly, and after the meeting was over, we sat in his Jeep outside the ANB building for at least two hours talking about subjects ranging from the old Tlingit beliefs in witches and scary land-otter people to the history of the Sitka Tlingit. To be more precise, Mark did most of the talking while I was listening and trying to remember all the fascinating information he was sharing with me. No one in this community had been so open with me, especially when it came to some controversial issues involving interclan and intercommunity conflicts.

Two things struck me about my new Tlingit acquaintance and future teacher. He was obviously proud of his heritage. As he told me, "Whenever I travel throughout southeastern Alaska, I brush up on my knowledge." On the other hand, he was clearly a devout Christian who used the Bible as his moral compass and was critical of some of the "old

97

superstitions and customs" of his people, while struggling to explain the others by trying to rationalize them or comparing them to those of the Old Testament.

Here was a Tlingit man in his mid-fifties who had already become a Native scholar in his own right and who seemed to enjoy sharing his knowledge with a young non-Native anthropologist whom he had just met. Why was he so open with me? It would have been flattering to think that we had really hit it off on that very first night, and maybe we did. However, it is also possible that at the time when Gusht'eihéen had already accumulated a great deal of knowledge about the *Lingit kusteeyí* (Tlingit culture) but had not yet gained a status of the "elder," he enjoyed having a (literally) "captive" audience. Moreover, the fact that he had spent his entire life in Sitka but that both his mother's and father's clans originated from Angoon must have prevented him from speaking at length in public on the subject of Sitka history, which he actually knew very well and was happy to share with an educated outsider, like myself, who seemed eager to learn and serious about learning. Finally, what might have also helped me that evening was telling Mark about my plan to travel to Angoon in late December for the first time in order to interview some elders there about the history of the local Orthodox parish. Eager to assert his father's clan's very prominent place in Angoon's social structure and history as well as his strong personal ties with prominent elders from that village, Gusht'eihéen gave me detailed instructions on who to interview and how to conduct myself in what he described as a very conservative community but also a "treasure-trove of information about the old ways." He was particularly insistent that I spend time with a house leader from his clan, the Dakl'aweidí, Jimmie George Sr. (Wóochx Kaduhaa, 1889–1990) (Dauenhauer and Dauenhauer 1994, 193–206). At the same time, Mark was clearly curious about any new information about Angoon history or the "old customs" that I might learn in his parents' community. As he coached me about the best ways of approaching Angoon elders, I was getting a feeling of the two of us being a research team, with him acting as the senior scholar. This was truly exciting. It was, in part, thanks to Mark's recommendations and instructions that my trip to Angoon was, indeed, a success and generated goodwill as well as a lot of valuable new information. Since then I have visited it many times, even though Sitka has remained my primary home and research site in Tlingit country.

Our Cooperation Begins

Back in Sitka Mark continued sharing ethnographic and historical information with me, including details of traditional Tlingit customs pertaining to funerals and memorial rites. I dutifully recorded everything he told me, even though I had no idea that in a few months I would receive an invitation to attend my very first memorial *koo.éex'* (potlatch). Since he was clearly enjoying our weekly discussions of *Lingít kusteeyí*, I decided to try a more formal method of working with him and suggested that we review Swanton's 1908 ethnography of the Tlingit together. Recorded in Wrangell and Sitka, it contained a variety of data, much of it on the subjects that Mark had already touched upon in our previous conversations. Mark happily agreed to my proposition, and in the next few weeks we went over the Swanton work line by line. Although he did identify a number of errors in that seventy-year-old ethnography, he also agreed with much of it and even found new information. As he later put it, "There have been many attempts by reputable writers and anthropologists in recording the Tlingit customs, religion, superstitions, beliefs, and also the language. Much of what I have read is misinformation, inaccurate or simply stated as unknown. Yet I [still] believe that the early collections are valuable in spite of inaccuracies and incompleteness. No doubt this information came from the Tlingit Indians themselves" (Jacobs to Kan, January 1, 1984). Most important, this exercise gave us our first opportunity to discuss the pros and cons of anthropological research, a topic Mark would come back to a number of times over the course of our twenty-five-year friendship.

What struck me about Mark's view of anthropology was his thoughtfulness and open-mindedness. Unlike a few other elders I had met who had voiced familiar complaints about the "fly-by-night anthropologists" who "got it all wrong" and "published lies" about the Tlingit, he made a careful distinction between those among them who made only a brief visit to southeastern Alaska versus those who stayed for a long time, learned the Tlingit language, and spoke to the "right people" in the native community. Thus Mark had a high opinion of George Emmons's 1991 book but found numerous errors in the work of Aurel Krause. He was not opposed to anthropology in general but only to "bad" (superficial, biased) anthropology.

Mark obviously realized that a native speaker of the Tlingit language, like himself, who had grown up among the traditional elders and had made an effort to learn about the old ways from as many of them as possible, would have a great advantage over any anthropologist. But he was also well aware of the fact that at the time he and I met, the number of such elders was declining, and there were few men and women of his generation who possessed the kind of knowledge that he had and were both capable and willing to share it with the younger generation of Natives and the non-Native public and researchers. He was also adamant about those individuals in the Tlingit community who "twisted the history for their own benefit" or "did not know enough but claimed they did." To him they were just as guilty as the "bad anthropologists."

This explains why in his own oral presentations to various audiences (including my own Dartmouth College students in the early 1990s) and in his manuscript, where he recorded his encyclopedic knowledge from time to time, Mark detailed the exact sources of his own knowledge. In that activity he was indeed a traditional Tlingit. Here are some examples:

> In order to convey that my writing is not a secondhand account or that I am not a novice in the [Tlingit] language and customs, I will give an account of my family tree. My mother and father married in conformity with the Tlingit marriage customs. My dad is of the Deisheetaan clan under the Raven tribe. Although he was born in Sitka, his tribal house is originally located in Angoon. His linage goes into the Chilkat country and other areas. My mother's clan is the Killer Whale of the Eagle tribe. It is also of Angoon. Her Killer Whale House is still located in Angoon. My mother was born in Angoon, but lived in Sitka all of her married life of over sixty years. It was a lasting marriage in which she had five natural sons and two daughters, with everyone versed in Tlingit ways and language. Our [Killer Whale] lineage also runs into the Chilkat country.
>
> My older brother Harvey (Tleyaakéet), born on November 24, 1921, was exactly two years older than me. We spoke Tlingit exclusively when we were youngsters. Our paternal grandmother, S'eiltín, did not speak any English at all. She was already quite old but was still very agile. She owned one of the very last original dugout canoes which she called *ts'axweil yaakw* or "crow boat." It was fitted with modern oars and oarlocks. Harvey and I were her constant companions, and she taught us the Indian ways, including many expressions, beliefs, subsistence practices, and Indian lore.

My dad, Mark Jacobs Sr., was born in Sitka on April 15, 1896; he was eighty-one when he died. His knowledge of Tlingit history, customs, beliefs, and language was phenomenal. I would dare to say his knowledge was the equivalent of today's academic doctorate degree. My mother, born in Angoon in 1903, spent her childhood there and was equal to my dad in the intricacies of the customs, beliefs, and language.

One of the caretakers of our Killer Whale House was Archie Bell (Daanawú). After he died, my grand-uncle, Pete Kanosh (Tleyaakéet), moved into that house. Being the eldest, he was in effect the chief of the Killer Whale clan. He was a walking encyclopedia of information in Indian customs, laws; he had a great sense of humor and had real Indian style of jesting, telling funny stories and jokes. I spent many hours listening to him tell stories. His ability to interject humor made his style all the more interesting; it also served as a catalyst of memory to the stories.

Another outstanding grand-uncle of mine from the Chookaneidí clan was Phillip Jones. He was seventy-one years when he died in 1932. He was married to my grand-auntie, a true sister to my real grandmother S'eiltín. He was eight years old at the time of the transfer of Russian America to the United States. . . . Even in his old age Phillip Jones was a very active person. He owned a double tender rowboat; these double tenders were used for hand trolling, a livelihood common to every [Tlingit] family. This type of cash income led to the establishment of handtrollers' camps. Transportation was slow and no such thing as radio communication existed. The evenings at the camps were devoted to visiting and storytelling. It is interesting to note the protocol that was used when a storyteller was off base or omitting important parts of the story or history. He was never interrupted or told he was wrong. He was simply allowed to finish his version. When he was done, someone would announce that this was a very interesting story and that he would like to hear it again, so "let's have so-and-so retell it." So when the person selected got to the portion that wasn't told correctly, he would carefully restate the segment of the story and someone would invariably say, "That's the way I know it, too" or "That's the way I heard it." Then another one would verify the story, and it would then go to its conclusion. Phillip Jones was one of the outstanding storytellers.

Down the hill from us lived closely related grandparents of ours, George Lewis Sr. (a Kiks.ádi whose name was Aanaatl'ek') and Carrie Lewis (a Dakl'aweidí by the name of Daalneix̱). They were almost as second parents to us. They both spoke good English. Grandma Carrie Lewis was one of or probably the first Tlingit Indian to become a schoolteacher. Yet the old ways were strong for her. She was an expert in basketry. Grandpa Lewis was an expert metal smith. He was of the Kiks.ádi clan and was well versed in his own clan's history and especially the Kiks.ádi battle with the Russians.

Everyone I have mentioned so far is an old-timer and is either closely related [to me] or is an important tribal relative of our family on my mother's or father's side. Everyone was eighty plus or older. The importance of maintaining one's social standing by knowing one's tribal identity was very strong because of the caste system and the tribal obligations required to be satisfied for the clan heads and other high-ranking persons. It was very important to know what to do, what to say, how to say it, and to whom the address and protocol was due.[2]

There was another major reason Mark valued *accurate* information on Tlingit culture and history. This special appreciation came from his years of active participation in the work on the Native land claims and other political struggles undertaken by the ANB, the Tlingit and Haida tribes of Alaska, and other Native Alaskan organizations. The notion that this information would someday be of utmost importance for the Native people in their pursuit of their land claims, subsistence, and other rights taken away or limited by the state and federal governments was something he acquired from his father, a prominent Native Alaskan politician and Native rights advocate. This is how Mark explained it to me:

During the land claims movement [of the 1940s and 1950s] there was still a segment of Tlingit, even among our [ANB] leadership, who were trying to do away with the old customs and language. I vividly remember my dad on many occasions giving an oration on the need to continue the old customs. He would tell the people in the meeting, "Your old Indian customs is *law*. You will have to fall back on it when our [court] case calls for evidence." He was right when the time did come to gather the information. He was a member of this most important committee [which dealt with the land claims–

S.K.]. They made a thirty-three-day trip throughout the claims area. This was an experience they cherished. He and I spent many, many hours discussing the findings. It was educational to him, even though he already knew Indian customs as law. The findings they gathered dovetailed with his knowledge. This is a source of information I am sure that hasn't been available to writers and anthropologists. (Kan, field notes, 1984)

Mark further strengthened his view of "old customs" as "Indian law" after he had studied in a prelaw program at the University of Dubuque. Unfortunately, he never completed the program and thus could not go on to law school. I believe that he would have made a great lawyer. Nonetheless, his education made a big impression on him and helped him develop a legal way of thinking about the issues involving Native Alaskans and the various governmental institutions they have had to deal with since 1867 and even before. I am convinced that this view of the traditional Tlingit culture as "law" helped Mark reconcile many of its practices that he sometimes characterized as being "harsh by modern standards" (e.g., blood revenge) with his deeply held Christian beliefs and many of the modern American values that he also adhered to. Here is a powerful statement from a letter he wrote to me in 1988: "A [native people's] way of life is the strongest evidence of a sovereign people exercising its inherent political system." And here is how he explained the social and legal significance of the traditional memorial potlatch to me in a letter dated December 22, 1995: "A potlatch was a form of probate. In other words, it was a law that transferred clan property to the next succeeding clan nephew or younger brother of the deceased chief."

Despite this emphasis on legal and political functions of the *koo.éex'*, Mark was also among the first of my Tlingit teachers/consultants to emphasize its fundamental emotional and spiritual dimensions. The latter had often escaped the previous scholars who preferred to write about "fighting with property." I was truly fortunate to have been invited to two memorials held in Sitka in the spring of 1980 while I was still conducting my initial field research and to have Mark as my interpreter and guide. It was in one of these potlatches, given by Charlotte (Littlefield) Young and her family in memory of her three brothers and a maternal uncle, that I was adopted into the Box House (Ḵook Hit) of the Kaagwaantaan clan of the Eagle moiety. As I have already mentioned,

Fig. 6.1 Mark Jacobs Jr. and Alla Kan in front of the Kans' home in Ann Arbor, Michigan, spring 1987. The bear headdress they are holding had been carved for the author by Harold Jacobs. Photograph by Sergei Kan.

by this time I had developed a very close relationship with the Young family. Still this formal adoption came as a total surprise.

Doing Ethnographic Research by Correspondence

What is important for the present discussion is Mark's appreciation of the fact that a family whom he respected chose to incorporate me into its social network. Moreover, he could see that my wife and I took this adoption very seriously, and for the rest of our stay in Sitka we did our best to act according to the kinship and clanship roles that had been assigned to us. This close familiar relationship with the Young-Littlefield family continued after we departed from Alaska and persists to this day, long after Charlotte and Thomas Sr. have left this world. For Mark, my conduct was an indication of the seriousness with which I viewed my adoption and hence the traditional Tlingit ceremonial system and the obligation one's participation in it entailed. On many occasions he would remind me (and sometimes others) that my adoption was "carried out properly" and that "I had demonstrated sensitivity toward the Tlingit ceremonial protocol" (Sergei Kan, field notes, 1984–1987). At the same time, from the start of our correspondence, Gusht'eihéen made sure that I acted like a properly socialized Tlingit man when it came to offering condolence to the people I knew in Sitka and several other northern Tlingit communities. Thus, in one of his very first letters, which informed me of the death of a prominent member of the Sitka Kiks.ádi clan, he recommended that I send a letter of condolence to his family. As he put it, "As you have learned, words and expressions of concern are highly respected by the Tlingit people" (Jacobs to Kan, December 5, 1980).

I believe that my adoption and my subsequent efforts to fulfill my kinship obligations to the best of my ability as well as a strong feeling of friendship and mutual respect we had developed toward each other in 1979–1980 were the main reasons that after I left Alaska, Mark became my closest Tlingit friend and teacher for twenty-five years.

Since the focus of much of my ethnographic and ethnohistorical research has been the Tlingit memorial rituals (including the *koo.éex'*) and since attending a *koo.éex'* has been both my obligation and an opportunity to visit my Tlingit family and friends, I have often returned to Sitka and Angoon to attend these rituals. Such participant observation helped me better understand this complex phenomenon, especially its emotional and spiritual dimensions. As one Tlingit friend, who had read my book on the potlatch, once told me, "Your work is the first one that talks about our feelings." Of course, it was hard for me not to focus on the participants' emotions, especially when I took part in the rites memorializing my own adopted sister, Charlotte Young (Littlefield) (1916–1982) or another elder I had become very fond of (Kan 2001). A careful observer of human behavior, Mark must have noticed that. Here is what he wrote to me in October 1984, soon after Charlotte's memorial *koo.éex'*:

> You are the very first researcher I know who is willing to be part of us, to know our feelings and participate in all of our ways. It is easy to sense that. I am sure that is the reason you have been fully adopted into one of our clans. My family and some other elderly relatives who have met you have commented on how well you understand our customs. This understanding is not possible by observation only; you must feel the strong emotions, the deep feelings and their expressions in order to understand them well.

Besides Mark's phenomenal knowledge of *Lingit kusteeyí,* he had another quality that made him an ideal consultant for an anthropologist, especially one, like me, who worked far away from Alaska and could return there only occasionally and for relatively brief periods. He loved writing letters and would send me written reports about his daily life and the native community at least twice a month. In addition he encouraged me to ask him questions on any subject pertaining to Tlingit history and culture. As he put it in a letter dated September 8, 1981:

> Please, don't apologize for the questions you ask. I really enjoy them; they refresh my mind. You are asking about the things that have kept our culture alive. Many times you have asked me questions that really got my mind working.... Your questions also help me think of things I would not normally be thinking of. If I can't answer them, I can seek others who can and in the process I'll learn too.... I never tire of talking to the old-timers.

It soon became clear to me that Mark truly enjoyed our intellectual exchanges and that our relationship had stimulated his own research and writing. In a way, our dialogue had further pushed him toward becoming an even more thorough tribal historian, encouraging him to spend more time with a dwindling group of traditionalist elders and compile detailed accounts of the traditional rituals (especially potlatches). In addition, our long-distance conversation encouraged him to put together a more systematic and detailed record of his own life, which he interspersed with ethnographic and historical data as well as numerous anecdotes.

Over the years Mark shared his knowledge with a few other researchers, including several who are featured in this book. Nonetheless, he always insisted on saving the most sensitive information for me. Thus when a visiting Russian anthropologist tried to elicit some data on Tlingit religion and social organization from him, he stated flatly that "he was already working with a Dartmouth anthropologist" and would not be able to discuss those matters with this newcomer (Kan, field notes, 1993).

Mark was obviously not the only knowledgeable Tlingit elder and tradition-bearer I have relied on in my thirty-five years of research on Tlingit history and culture. Which topics of research, then, did he offer me most help with? First and foremost it was the memorial potlatch. While Charlotte Young, Lydia George, and several other elders who took part in the two 1980 memorials (a Kookhittaan-Kaagwaantaan and a L'uknax̱.ádi) as well as the two Kookxittaan-Kaagwaantaan ones I attended in the 1980s, helped translate the speeches delivered there and explained the basic features of those ceremonies, Mark was able to unravel some of the more complicated aspects of their sociopolitical dimension. It is here that his willingness to discuss any issue, no matter how controversial, was particularly helpful. If a certain piece of information he shared with me was especially sensitive, he would tell me so and I would promise to keep it confidential. Here is, for example, a passage from a letter he wrote to me in 1984:

> You have gained a unique trust of many of our people, not to mention my own. As you know, in the past I have guarded what I know. But I believe you are a person that will honestly tell things as they are. I suggest you don't avoid touchy subjects. I think it can be done by leaving names of the people and the specific clans blank. I think a confidential supplement should be kept for record's sake.

When it came to the subject of the memorial potlatch, he felt it was important for me to know the truth about each major participant's true motivations and objectives, so that I would better understand the "Tlingit law" and the way in which some individuals did or did not live up to it.

After completing my doctoral dissertation and then a book on the potlatch, my next big project was a cultural history of Russian Orthodox Christianity among the Tlingit. Here again Mark's phenomenal memory turned out to be helpful. He remembered many of the Sitka old-timers who belonged to the Orthodox Church, and since his own family had been Orthodox, he could describe in vivid detail the ways in which Orthodox holidays had once been celebrated in the community. Only with Mark's help was I able to identify many of the people depicted in photographs of the Orthodox parishioners taken in Sitka by Elbridge W. Merrill in the 1920s.[3] This information was essential for developing my analysis of the split between the two Orthodox brotherhoods in Sitka (Kan 1985, 1999).

Mark responded to endless questions about some old ritual practice, belief, name, dispute, or controversy. If he could not come up with an answer himself, he tried very hard to locate an elder who would. Sometimes such a search lasted for months. I believe he enjoyed such "detective work" a great deal. He was clearly learning new things about his cultural heritage along with his ethnographer friend. In fact, when in the early 2000s I turned to a large project on the history of Russian anthropology and had fewer questions dealing with Tlingit history and culture for Mark, he would complain that I was not doing my homework anymore.

From Colleagues to Close Friends and Brothers

Over the years my collegiate relationship with Mark evolved into close friendship marked by a feeling of deep mutual respect. As he once told me, "Please feel free to write often; your letters are the first thing I ask about when I get home from my trips." He shared with me many of the most difficult trials and tribulations of his family life and my willingness to discuss my Jewish identity with him, a subject that until the last few years had almost never come up in conversations with my other Tlingit friends. Like a number of other Tlingit elders who are well versed in the Bible, Mark had a special interest in and identification with Old Testament Israelites, and he liked to compare their customs (e.g., levirate) with those of "old time Tlingits." His fundamentalist Christianity also contributes to a sympathetic attitude toward modern-day Jews and the state of Israel.[4] In addition, Mark was fond of comparing his own people and the Jews, pointing out that both have been victims of oppression and prejudice. The one important difference he saw between the two peoples is that the Jews have been able to establish their own state and the Tlingit have not. In one of his 1989 letters Mark told me about an encounter with a Jewish couple visiting Sitka.

He said he felt a sense of kinship with them even before they revealed their identity. In subsequent letters, Mark often stated his belief that "according to the biblical prophecy, the Lord would always punish those trying to destroy the Jews, his Chosen People." When I was denied tenure at the University of Michigan in late 1988, he interpreted this as a manifestation of anti-Semitism and compared it to his own encounters with anti-Indian prejudice. In 1994, Mark stayed at our house in New Hampshire, I was finally able to reciprocate his efforts to include me in Tlingit ceremonial life. I invited him to join our Friday night Jewish family ritual of lighting the Sabbath candles followed by a festive meal. Mark was visibly moved by the experience and often mentioned it in his subsequent letters.

Given our special relationship, it was not surprising that eventually Gusht'eihéen decided to adopt me into his own clan and house. What I did not expect was his decision to give me the name of his deceased younger brother, James Ernest Jacobs (1929–1975). The formal adoption took place at a large 1991 Dak̲l'aweidí *koo.éex'* in Angoon (given in memory of Jimmie George Sr.), but already for several years prior to that he had been signing his letters with the words "your tribal brother" or simply "your brother." This new form of address gave me a hint of an upcoming change in my status. Unfortunately, an illness prevented Mark from being present at that potlatch, and for that reason he decided to repeat the naming ritual at the next large gathering of Tlingit people (including elders) that he and I attended. This was the second clan conference, held in Sitka in the summer of 1995. During a banquet at the ANB hall Mark rubbed some cash on my forehead and announced my Dak̲l'aweidí name, G̲unáak'w, to the people present.[5]

Finally my adoption into the Killer Whale House of the Dakl'aweidí clan was officially confirmed and further made public in the course of a major memorial *koo.éex'* in Angoon given by Mark's house group in cooperation with other house groups of his clan in November 1997. From Mark's point of view, this was a particularly important ritual for two reasons. First, he and his sister Bertha Karras gave it in memory of their beloved mother, Annie Jacobs (Sxaalgen, Khaatukl.aa), a well-known Dakl'aweidí matriarch and tradition-bearer who passed away in 1989. Second, the ceremony memorialized two recently deceased Dakl'aweidí men of high rank, Robert Jamestown (Shaakhwaani, Yeildáadzee) and Dan Brown Jr. (Gús'kóoskaan, Yéetsaa). Third, the ceremony served as the occasion for Mark and his clan to officially install Edwell John

Fig. 6.2 Mark Jacobs Jr. beside the grave of his brother Ernest Jacobs (1929–1975) at the Old City Cemetery in Sitka. Late 1980s–early 1990s. Photograph by Sergei Kan.

Fig. 6.3 The 1997 Dakl'aweidí memorial *koo.éex'* in Angoon. *Left to right*: the author, Edwell John Jr., and Mark Jacobs Jr. Photograph courtesy of Sergei Kan.

Jr. (Woochx Káduxaa, Tleeyaa Kéet, Yéetsaa) as the head of the second house of the Killer Whale clan (known as Killer Whale Chasing the Seal House or the Killer Whale Dorsal Fin House) (H. Jacobs 2000, 44). Finally this *koo.éex'* gave Gusht'eihéen an opportunity to publicly display several precious regalia (*at.óow*) repatriated by his house group from the Denver Museum of Natural History.

For me this was a very important *koo.éex'* for several reasons. First, I witnessed a traditional-style installation of a new house head for the first time and, second, this was the last potlatch I took part in where Mark was in good health and very much in charge. The next time we found ourselves at the same *koo.éex'* was five years later. Once again, it was in Angoon, but this time we were both guests and the occasion was a memorial for Matthew Fred Sr. of the Deisheetaan clan. Mark's health had significantly deteriorated by then, and he was much more subdued. Moreover, we were unable to sit together or spend much time conversing after the potlatch was over. Our next reunion took place two years later in Sitka, and my friend was in a hospital bed.

This fall 2004 trip to Sitka was a very important one for me for several reasons. First, I came to attend a very important *koo.éex* hosted by the Wolf House of the Sitka Kaagwaantaan clan to commemorate the

Fig. 6.4 Mark Jacobs Jr. announcing his financial contribution at the 1997 Daḵl'aweidí memorial *koo.éex'* in Angoon. To the left of him is Ellen George. Photograph by Sergei Kan.

hundredth anniversary of the so-called Last Potlatch, which had been given by the same house (Preucel and Williams 2005; Kan 2008). The new head of the Wolf House, Andrew Gamble/Annahóotz, whose title and position were to be confirmed at this *koo.éex'*, is closely related to Mark, which meant that Mark would have played a major role in this ceremony.[6] I was looking forward to seeing him act as the headman of the Killer Whale clan and, as always, learn new things about Tlingit ceremonial life.

Second, this was the first time I managed to bring my daughter to Sitka. She had just turned sixteen, and this was my present to her: I wanted her to meet her Tlingit family and especially her father's older brother, Gusht'eihéen; the last time the two of them had met was during Mark's visit to Dartmouth, when Elianna was only five years old. The three of us did meet, but it was a short get-together: Elianna and

I had to be at the potlatch, and Mark could not leave the hospital to attend the ceremonies even for a brief period. Still I was happy that my older brother was able to meet my only child, who had heard so much about him. After all, our two families had become quite close over the years. Mark's letters always included questions about my wife and daughter, while I had grown very fond of his wife, Adelaide, and followed the ups and downs of his children and the accomplishments of his grandchildren.

Since the 1980s and 1990s, I had become especially close to his youngest son, Harold (Gooch shaayí, Goos'shú, b. 1964), whose own phenomenal knowledge of the traditional Tlingit culture and history has always amazed me. A dedicated student of *Lingít kusteeyí* from an early age, Gooch shaayí had absorbed so much of his father's and other elders' knowledge that, in the last decade of his life, Mark would often respond to my questions by saying, "We better ask Harold." Harold has become one of the most knowledgeable people of his generation when it comes to ritual protocol and Tlingit genealogies and names. For almost two decades now he has been involved on a full-time basis in the work of the repatriation of the Tlingit ceremonial regalia (*at.óow*) back to the matrilineal groups that are their rightful owners (see Hollinger and Jacobs, this volume).[7] This work has often taken him on trips to the various American museums as a member of a delegation representing the Tlingit houses and clans whose *at.óow* were being examined and considered for repatriation. On many occasions Harold's father was among the delegates. Thanks to Harold's efforts and dedication, Mark was able to be part of these trips, which he enjoyed immensely, long after he became seriously ill and lost much of his strength and energy. Thus almost to the end of his life was my older brother able to share his knowledge not only with his own people but also with museum professionals.

It was difficult for me to accept that my fall 2004 visit with Mark was most likely to be my last. I had known from his family that he had been quite sick, but I had never been told how bad the situation had become. My old friend's emaciated body said it all. After I returned home to New Hampshire, I received a couple of letters from Mark, but they were unusually short for a man who always loved long and detailed correspondence. On January 13, 2005, Harold called me with the sad news. Two days later I was on my way to Sitka to attend Mark's funeral, which was to take place January 19 after a series of memorial observances. What struck me most about the events of those difficult days was how each of the ceremonies I attended reflected a different aspect of this remarkable man. From the prayer service by the Assembly of God minister in the funeral home, to the lying in state ceremony in the Mother Coho House of the L'oooknax̱.ádi clan, to the ANB memorial service, to the traditional Tlingit memorial at the new community house (the Sheet'ka Kwaan Naa Kahidi), to the actual funeral service in the Centennial Hall (where I was one of the speakers), and the final military-style ceremony at the Sitka National Cemetery, each ritual and speech told a story about a different dimension of Mark's life and the values he held dear.

With Mark's death, a major chapter in my research in southeastern Alaska and my relationship with the Tlingit people ended. Of course, I do have other wonderful relatives, friends, colleagues, teachers, and consultants in the Tlingit community and will continue coming back to them and their beautiful country. I will undoubtedly be pursuing new research projects on *Lingit kusteeyí*, but without my older brother, Gusht'eihéen, as my teacher and guide, this work will never be the same.

Conclusion

I would like to discuss the reasons why Mark had been so open with me. Was it simply because we had been friends of many years? If that was the case, why had he been so open and generous with his knowledge from the very beginning?

My own guess is that from very early on he had decided that my commitment to Tlingit research was a long-term one and that I could be trusted. He must have also decided that there were at least some anthropologists who could be given the job of "setting the record straight" and "getting it right." In fact, these were the expressions he used when talking not only about some of my own predecessors in the profession but also about some of the Tlingit folks who, in his view at least, were not qualified to act as spokesmen for his people and lacked the proper knowledge to be called "tradition-bearers."

While always insisting that there were some areas of traditional knowledge that were much more accessible to a qualified Tlingit, Mark never said that only a Tlingit should be studying Tlingit history and culture. In that respect his position differed from that of modern-day radical Native American academics (and some of their non-Native allies) for whom "indigenizing the academy" means keeping the non-Native researchers out.[8] Instead he saw the field as having enough room for both Tlingit and non-Tlingit scholars.[9] Thus he would defer to my knowledge of Russian history and command of the Russian language and would often question me about my latest discoveries in the archives. He was happy to participate in the 1987 International Conference on Russian America as well as the clan conferences held in Sitka in 1995 and 1997 (Jacobs 1990). I have no doubt that he would have been a strong supporter of the 2007 clan conference, which we dedicated to his memory. Quoting from the Eastern Orthodox funeral service: "May his memory be eternal!"

NOTES

Some of the material presented here first appeared in my chapter "Friendship, Family, and Fieldwork: One Anthropologist's Adoption by Two Tlingit Families" (Kan 2001). I would like to thank Richard Dauenhauer, Steve Henrikson, Harold Jacobs, and Robert W. Preucel for reading and commenting on an earlier draft of this chapter.

1. In addition to "Gusht'eihéen," Mark Jacobs had four other prestigious Dak̲l'aweidí (Killer Whale clan) names.
2. Manuscript in the author's possession. For a more detailed genealogy of Mark, see H. Jacobs (this volume).
3. Individuals photographed during an earlier era were identified with the help of an older generation of Tlingit consultants and particularly Mary Marks.
4. Mark also mentioned to me on several occasions that one of his favorite law professors was Jewish.
5. Mark was fond of pointing out to me how proud I should be of this name, since it also belonged to Chester Worthington (1868–1935), one of the founders of the ANB. Worthington was a member of the Kayaashkéditaan clan of Wrangell, which is related to Mark's, and their matrilineages (houses) had the same name, Kéet Hít (Harold Jacobs, personal communication, June 2011).
6. Andrew Gamble was originally given the title "Annaxoots" at the memorial potlatch for his maternal uncle, Patrick Paul, which took place in Angoon in 1993. Mark's mother's father, John Paul (a Deisheetaan), married Patrick Paul's mother (a Kaagwaantaan) after his own wife (a Dak̲l'aweidí) had died. I had known Patrick Paul and conducted several interviews with him in 1980 and 1984.
7. See, for example, the following news items: "SE Native Relic Returned" (posted Thursday, September 16, 1999, http://www.sealaskaheritage

.org/news/articles/article%20beaver%20prow.htm); Át yánwoo-nei ḵáachx̱ana.aak'wx̱ (It Was Completed in Wrangell). http://74.125.47.132/search?q=cache:9lpofqSox0oJ : www.ccthita.org/pdf/Repatriation/wrangell.Final%2520report.webx.pdf+harold+jacobs+on+repatriation&cd=3&hl=en&ct=clnk&gl=us&client=firefox-a.

8. See Cook-Lynn (1997) and Smith (1999).
9. This view was shared by another Tlingit scholar and cultural activist, Andy Hope, to whom this book is also dedicated. See his 1998 review of my book *Symbolic Immortality*.

REFERENCES

Cook-Lynn, Elizabeth. 1997. "Who Stole Native American Studies?" *Wicazo Sa Review* 12 (1): 9–28.

Dauenhauer, Nora Marks, and Richard Dauenhauer. 1994. *Haa kusteeyi/Our Culture: Tlingit Life Stories*. Seattle: University of Washington Press.

Emmons, George. 1991. *The Tlingit Indians*. Ed. Frederica de Laguna. Seattle: University of Washington Press.

Hope, Andy. 1998. Review of *Symbolic Immortality* by Sergei Kan. *Sharing Our Pathways: A Newsletter of the Alaska Rural Systemic Initiative* 3 (3): 14–16.

Jacobs, Harold. 2000. "Inhabitants of Burning Wood Fort." In *Will the Time Ever Come? A Tlingit Source Book*, ed. Andrew Hope III and Thomas F. Thornton, 34–47 Fairbanks: University of Alaska Press.

Jacobs, Mark, Jr. 1990. "Early Encounters between the Tlingit and the Russians." In *Russia in North America: Proceedings of the 2nd International Conference on Russian America*, ed. Richard Pierce, 1–6. Kingston, ON: Limestone Press.

———. n.d. Manuscript. Copy in the author's possession.

Kan, Sergei. 1979–2007. Field notes from southeastern Alaska in author's possession.

———. 1982. "'Wrap Your Father's Brothers in Kind Words': An Analysis of the Nineteenth-Century Tlingit Mortuary and Memorial Rites." PhD diss., Anthropology, University of Chicago.

———. 1985. "Russian Orthodox Brotherhoods among the Tlingit: Missionary Goals and Native Response." *Ethnohistory* 32 (3): 196–223.

———. 1989. *Symbolic Immortality: The Tlingit Potlatch of the Nineteenth Century*. Washington DC: Smithsonian Institution Press.

———. 1999. *Memory Eternal: Tlingit Culture and Russian Orthodox Christianity through Two Centuries*. Seattle: University of Washington Press.

———. 2001. "Friendship, Family, and Fieldwork." In *From Strangers to Relatives: The Adoption and Naming of Anthropologists in Native North America*, 185–207. Lincoln: University of Nebraska Press.

———. 2008. "The 2004 Centennial Potlatch: History, Memory, and Politics among the Northern Tlingit." Paper presented at the Annual Meeting of the American Society for Ethnohistory, Eugene, OR.

Krause, Aurel. 1956. *The Tlingit Indians.* Translated by Erna Gunther. (First published in German in 1885). Seattle: University of Washington Press.

Preucel, Robert W., and Lucy F. Williams. 2005. "The Centennial Potlatch." *Expedition* 47 (2): 9–19.

Smith, Linda Tuhiwai. 1999. *Decolonizing Methodologies: Research and Indigenous Peoples.* London: Zed Books.

Swanton, John R. 1908. "Social Conditions, Beliefs, and Linguistic Relationship of the Tlingit Indians." In *Twenty-Sixth Annual Report of the Bureau of American Ethnology for the Years 1904–1905,* 391–512. Washington DC: Government Printing Office.

7

World War II Scuttlebutt

Naval Section Bases, Southeast Alaska

MARK JACOBS JR.

Naval section bases are small outpost stations formed during World War II for the purpose of coastal defense and as a home base for the scout planes. These small bases were part of the larger main naval bases along the extensive stretches of Alaska's coastline.

From the time we were very young boys, my older brother Harvey and I had keen interest in the U.S. Navy. We both agreed that we would join the Navy when we were old enough. When we were in the fifth and sixth grades in an all-Native school, our teacher, Mrs. Ernestine Wolff, used to express her concern to the boys that we would be the ones who would fight in the next war. I was skeptical because I didn't think they would take us as young as we were.

Things were getting hot in Europe. The names of Adolf Hitler, Tojo, and Mussolini were on everybody's lips. We used to receive a publication for classroom use called *My Weekly Reader,* which kept us up-to-date on current events in Europe. Before all the talk of war, Hitler had sent one of his light cruisers on a goodwill tour around the world. Sitka, being one of the older naval bases in the North Pacific, was one of their ports of call. The *Karlsruhe* was the second German man-of-war to visit Sitka; the *Emden* was here in 1925. Of great interest is that the *Karlsruhe* negotiated the islands, rocks, and reefs of Sitka Sound without the aid of a pilot who would have had local knowledge; in fact, they didn't even use the regular steamer channels that were well marked with navigational aids. They came into Sitka anchorage through the middle channel, which is used only by small local fishing boats.

We were allowed a strictly controlled visit on board the *Karlsruhe.* This was an exciting experience for boys like us. The German sailors were given liberty (shore leave); they were landed on a very old float about halfway out on the old McGrath wharf. We befriended some of the sailors, who all spoke English but were more interested in gaining girlfriends than in wasting their time on fascinated young boys.

Japonski Island used to be a coaling station before the U.S. Navy ships were switched to an oil-burning fleet. For the most part, the facilities were only maintained by a handful of personnel; a wireless radio station was operated there, also. The various types of naval vessels that used to frequent Sitka were heavy and light cruisers, destroyers, fleet tugs: USS *Teal*, USS *Oriole*, USS *Swallow*, and the gunboat *Charleston*. One of the more notable Navy ships to visit Sitka was the USS *Langley*, which was here in the early 1930s; it was the Navy's first aircraft carrier. It was acting as an aircraft tender for a large naval air squadron, biplane flying boats that were to pay a visit to Sitka. Long before they appeared around the Pyramid Mountains, their motors could be heard. It was said they made the non-stop flight from Seattle in less than eight hours, which was fantastic at the time. I think it was a historic occasion to have four dozen airplanes in our harbor at one time, when the airplane was still quite rare.

As the talk of war heated up in Europe, there was talk about Japan as a possible enemy. There were rumors of Japanese submarine sightings and fishing boats spying out our coastal waters; probably some innocent Japanese American fishermen were under strong suspicion. On one occasion an old Indian named Cider Johnson, a naval veteran, failed to return from one of his hunting-fishing trips. His boat and camp were located, but it was left undisturbed, probably for evaluation of what may have happened to him. As the next search party was on their way out, they met Johnson in his rowboat, rowing toward town; he was picked up by the gas boat. The story he told was believed by many but dubbed as far-fetched by others. His claim was that he was taken captive by a Japanese submarine whose shore party was dressed like movie Indians and that they interrogated him. They then released him on a promise not to talk about his detainment. Those that doubted his honesty said he often drank a lot, and therefore his account could not be reliable.

The Japanese fishermen were allegedly violating our territorial waters more frequently. Japonski Island was eventually made into a PBY base with six of these flying boats permanently based in Sitka. One day it was noted that all of the PBYs didn't return as usual. The rumor was that they were sent to Bristol Bay to warn the Japanese out or be blasted out. A lot of the war talk centered on the U.S. Navy's being able to flatten the islands of Japan in sixty days. This gave me a sense of security and was exciting; I didn't realize what the real horrors of war were.

When Hitler's Germany began conquering Europe, and Japan was making strategic moves in the Far East by invading Manchuria and China, it was finally decided that Alaska was of strategic importance. The U.S. Navy and the U.S. Army began to enlarge the defense facilities of Japonski Island; the smaller islands in the vicinity were joined to Japonski. Eventually the work expanded into an emergency preparation for war. Hundreds of construction workers were being shipped in, but the local Natives were unable to get hired, even though many were seeking employment. The local Alaska Native Brotherhood then pleaded to give at least two Native laborers a test performance. Soon there was a call for more Native workmen. Some were eventually put in charge as foremen.

The Army placed heavy artillery at Shoals Point to help guard the Sitka Sound area. During the initial landing, a heavy ocean surf was running, and almost every boatload attempting a landing capsized in the breakers. One of the officers in charge had so much confidence in the Natives' handling of the boats that he decided to wait for a boat manned by them, none of which capsized.

About one month before the bombing of Pearl Harbor, while we were having our noon dinner at Sheldon Jackson School, there was a very sharp jolt, not like an earthquake, followed by a very loud explosion and concussion. We rushed out of the dining room to see what had happened. What we saw was a mushroom cloud forming like the pictures of an atomic bomb explosion. An explosives magazine had exploded, taking with it an undetermined number of lives.

There was a dredging, drilling, and blasting operation going on in the Sitka Channel to accommodate larger vessels. Not long after the tragedy of the magazine explosion, the dredge in the channel caught on fire; it was reported to have forty tons of high explosives on board. The Indian village was hastily evacuated.

The dredging rig was successfully scuttled before detonation could occur. If this amount of unconfined explosives had detonated, it could have broken most windows in town besides whatever destruction it could have caused. There were quite a number of premature explosions during this construction period. Whether or not these accidents were caused by gross negligence of good safety practices was not determined, but one might speculate that some of this was enemy sabotage.

Fig. 7.1 Photograph of Mark Jacobs Jr. and the Navy ship he served on during World War II. Photograph courtesy of Harold Jacobs.

I was a sophomore at Sheldon Jackson School when Pearl Harbor was attacked. On Sunday morning, some of us had the privilege of having our breakfast downtown. Louis Paul Jr. and I were discussing the big news that morning. We both knew we would be in the military service before too long. Should we volunteer or wait to be inducted? I told him I would volunteer as soon as I could get my parents' consent to go into the Navy, assuming that it would be mostly sea warfare. Louie is one of the young men who made the supreme sacrifice; he was killed in Salerno Bay in Italy.

One week after the Pearl Harbor attack, Harvey and I dropped out of school to enlist. Quite a few local men were volunteering for the Navy. Since the Navy was taking over some fishing boats to use for patrol duty, they needed local volunteers to man these vessels, so they didn't bother to send local enlistees to boot camp; the sea was their way of life.

Harvey and I went together to enlist; he was accepted, but I was rejected because I had one tooth that wasn't considered permanent to round out the required number. I asked the Navy doctor why they couldn't overlook one tooth since there was a war on. He said to come back in one month, and he would request a waiver from the division of personnel. It was evident that the strict peacetime physical require-

World War II Scuttlebutt 121

ments hadn't been changed yet. Though I was very disappointed, I wasn't discouraged. As soon as a month had gone by, I went to check on the waiver. There was still no response, but the Navy doctor said they would give me the works again; he meant another complete physical examination. I was the happiest boy in Sitka when the doctor said to me, "You're accepted into the Navy."

The naval station's chief master-at-arms came to the clinic to escort me to the commanding officer, Captain Jackson R. Tate. (Tate eventually became a rear admiral and was assigned to some joint Allied war effort post in Soviet Russia, an assignment from which he was subsequently ousted because of his involvement with a Russian movie actress. His daughter by the actress came to visit him in Florida before his death.) Before swearing me into the Navy, the chief master-at-arms was very friendly. He addressed me as Mr. Jacobs. But as soon as I was sworn in, he became a military man. His friendliness was gone. I was marched down to the Navy small-stores to be issued a full sea-bag of naval uniforms. The chief barked orders to me to get rid of those civilian rags and to report to him immediately in full dress. I was so elated with my new status (though frightened) I didn't mind the verbal abuse. I quickly learned the harshness wasn't meant to abuse me but was for the purpose of instilling the military way of life.

Harvey was assigned to duty on the patrol boat known as the P6, the former seine boat *Daisy O*); on my first day in the Navy they were in port. When we met, he expressed his joy by giving me a brotherly hug and then instructing me in detail about what was expected of me. Prior to our enlistment we had to have the consent of our parents. The executive officer called for our dad to make a statement in our behalf; our dad's statement was, "Being unqualified because of my age to go myself, this is the very best I can offer for my country. They volunteered by their own decision, and I'm proud of my sons' willingness to sacrifice." This statement was published in the *Island News*, a short mimeographed newspaper. Needless to say, our mother was extremely concerned for our safety. My brother and I attracted a lot of attention from the upper naval brass. Although Harvey was exactly two years older than I, we looked and passed as twins.

A Japanese freighter heading for Japan was about one day out before reaching its destination. The scuttlebutt (rumors and shop talk) was that its crew consisted of Japanese officers, a Korean crew, and a Dutch radio operator. When the radioman picked up the news of the Pearl

Harbor attack, he didn't notify the officers in charge; instead, the crew organized and took control of the ship. They reversed the ship's course. Since none were skilled in navigation, they were lost in the North Pacific until they sighted some shore installations on Biorka Island, about twelve miles from Sitka. The freighter then sent up a distress flare. Being an unidentified vessel, general quarters alarm was sounded and word was passed that this was not a drill. The P6 was sent out to investigate. None on board spoke English. The skipper of the P6, John Bahrt, piloted the ship into the Sitka harbor. A lieutenant commander was taken to the ship in a Navy launch; they put a Jacobs-ladder over the side, and as he was about to climb aboard, he looked up at a fierce-looking Oriental. He appeared to chicken out and backed off, ordering the launch back to the station. Commander Robbins was later taken out to claim the war prize. As far as I know, this was the very first vessel taken intact in World War II.

At the onset of the war in the Pacific, the Navy took over quite a few fishing boats for coastal patrol duty and manned them mostly with local volunteers. These boats were numbered P1, P2, P3, etc. Sheldon Jackson School owned a seine boat named the SJS. When the Navy took the boat over, it was numbered the P5. The school also had a beautiful boat under construction by an expert boat builder, a Native Indian leader, Andrew Hope Sr. The Board of National Missions of the Presbyterian Church, which owned the boat, asked the Navy to spare the vessel from takeover. Boats owned by the school were absolutely necessary for its survival because of transportation for the students to the school and returning them after the school year. It was evident that the Navy had plans to grab the vessel as soon as it was waterborne, for when they did take it over it was numbered P1. All of the fine finish work was disregarded, and it was painted in battleship gray. A 20mm antiaircraft gun was mounted on its forward deck and a depth charge rack on its stern. It was a sad day for many.

I was serving in the yard craft when a couple of high-speed picket boats were shipped in by the Navy. They were armed with a machine gun nest and a depth charge rack. Harvey was assigned to Picket No. 1, and I was assigned to Picket No. 2. We were tested for our local knowledge of the inside passages by trial runs in pitch darkness without dependence on channel markers; all lighted buoys and beacons were blacked out anyway because of the war. Since Harvey and I spoke our Tlingit Indian language fluently, the Navy used us for communicating some verbal radio messages. I don't think any of our messages were of military value, but it was good for propaganda purposes.

When those in charge of our assignments determined we were capable of running these speedy craft, we were sent to Icy Straits with both boats and were told that this was a top-secret mission. We were to report to a vessel in Icy Straits located halfway between Hoonah and Porpoise Islands. We were cautioned to flash our recognition signal before approaching too close or we would be blown out of the water. We made sure we followed the instructions. When we were near the rendezvous site, we kept flashing the coded signal for that day but got no response. We speculated that we might have had to contact a submarine when we couldn't see any surface craft in the entire area. Our fuel tanks were near empty, so we decided to anchor behind Pleasant island. Toward evening a couple of loaded freighters dropped their anchors in the same area. We started communicating with one by blinker system. We couldn't reveal our mission, but we did ask if they had encountered any other vessels in the outer straits. They informed us that the Coast Guard lightship *Swiftsure* was anchored out in the middle. This gave us a clue, so we hauled anchor and reported to the naval routing officer stationed on board. The reason we didn't make immediate contact was that the *Swiftsure* had gone into the village of Hoonah to replenish their fresh water supply. We learned that our duties were to be organizing the convoys prior to their crossing the Gulf of Alaska, with anti-submarine escort vessels.

The USS *Swiftsure* in peacetime was used for aids to navigation and was usually anchored in a vital location near major harbor entrances. It was a short and beamy vessel designed to ride out rough seas while at anchor; its anchor gear was exceptionally large for this purpose. When under way on its own power, it was very slow. The crew consisted of thirty or forty men.

Our main duty was to pick up the master or captain of each vessel in a newly assembled convoy for their briefing with the naval routing officer and the escort commander, then return them to their ships. There was some attempt at communicating in our Tlingit Indian language between my brother and me. Very little of our communications were of any military value. I do remember that we had no single word for *radar*. It took almost a paragraph of description. We finally developed the phrase *Eyes in Darkness* for radar. We had to note every vessel that possessed a radar antenna. At that time only Navy ships had them and only a few were privileged to have one. A large percentage of the convoys consisted of lend-lease ships to Russia. We also noted that quite a few of them actually had female captains and masters.

The picket boats had twin gasoline engines with a total of nearly 400 hp. We estimated that our fuel consumption was 24 to 30 gallons per hour at normal cruising speed depending on weather conditions. Because of our limited fuel tank capacity, we had to run into Hoonah to refuel frequently; we also went in whenever the weather was rough.

Although Harvey and I chose the machinist branch for our regular rating, we were considered pilots with knowledge of southeastern Alaska waters. The senior petty officer on Picket No. 1 was a boatswain mate first class by the name of Bob Starr. On Picket No. 2 it was Palmer Knutson, a PM 2fc. Both men were seasoned seamen because of their civilian livelihood. If my brother and I had chosen the seaman branch, we most likely would have eventually been rated as boatswain mates. After I attained the rating of fireman first class, I switched to the navigation division and became a quartermaster. All our records and payroll were kept at Port Althorp, a naval section base. My pay was thirty-six dollars a month at that time.

During one of our frequent trips into Hoonah, we learned of an incident that took place after the war started. One of the first priorities was to round up all persons of Japanese descent whether they were U.S. citizens or not. Regardless of their fierce allegiance to the United States, they were treated as potential enemies. There was an elderly Japanese man running a small bakery business in Hoonah that was overlooked in this roundup. When it was discovered that he was still free, a patrol boat was sent in, and he was arrested at gunpoint with Thompson submachine guns. As old as he was, he was neither a burden nor a threat to anyone. He was sent to a concentration camp somewhere in the Midwest, probably to live out his few remaining days on this earth.

There was a military officer and his Japanese wife living down the street from us on Kelly Street in Sitka. When the news of the attack on Pearl Harbor was flashed on the radio, a neighbor ran over to their place to see if they had been listening. He was still denying such a probability when a military police car came to his doorway, arrested his wife, and ordered him to report for the emergency. The realities of war hit suddenly and hard; no doubt there were many innocent victims.

Our duties in Icy Straits were a part of the section base operations in Port Althorp. We received all our mail, paychecks, and some supplies from the base. Spending the winter out in Icy Straits is the toughest physical endurance we were ever subjected to. We didn't have access to government issue foul weather gear, although our Navy routing officer put in repeated requests to get us some, without success; he finally boarded one of the Navy ships passing through the area and got us some jungle-cloth cold weather gear. Before we were able to get this, I bought the warmest jacket I could find in Hoonah; I then cut up one of my dress blues and stitched it as lining in the coat for extra warmth. Lieutenant Kesselbaum also had a drip-type oil heater fabricated and installed on each boat. Prior to this we had to depend on an automobile-type heater that worked haphazardly and only when the main motors were running. With the oil heaters we were able to make coffee and do a limited amount of cooking. For the most part we were fed our meals on board the *Swiftsure*. Its showers and laundry facilities were available to us, but the picket boat was our home, and sometimes we were unable to get back to the *Swiftsure* due to extremely bad weather.

There were many times when we had to brave some severe weather at risk of our lives mostly due to one officer who didn't realize the perils of the sea in a small boat from his comfortable quarters on the larger vessel. During the coldest part of the winter, we constantly faced the hazards of icing down, a condition that can make a vessel top-heavy with ice and eventually will capsize the craft. There were many times when we had to kick at the hatch doors to get out because the ice would imprison us inside; even testing the doors every few minutes didn't help any. All of our anchor gear and mooring lines were kept inside, out of the weather, so they would be more convenient to handle. The officer who subjected us to this hazardous duty was not Lieutenant Kesselbaum but his replacement, who also referred to seagulls as ducks.

The P13, known in peacetime as the *Messenger*, was finally sent to relieve the smaller picket boats. The PI 3 was a 65-foot motor vessel with comfortable living quarters and facilities. Picket No. 1 was sent to Port Althorp, and Picket No. 2 was laid up at Hoonah, so the picket boat crew took turns serving with the crew on the P13, one at a time. We expected to resume our regular duties when milder weather returned.

I was aboard P13 for temporary duty when an emergency call was received from the U.S. Army in Excursion Inlet. An Army cook was severely burned and required transportation to the nearest hospital, which was in Juneau. The regular skipper of the P13, a veteran commercial fisherman, happened to be on leave when this emergency call came. The P13 was ordered to pick up the burned cook and transport him to Auke Bay, north of Juneau, where an ambulance would be waiting. The acting skipper was a green man lacking local knowledge and navigational skills. Because it was an emergency, he undertook the task, obeying orders in spite of the severe north wind that was blowing. We all knew this was a dangerous because we expected icing down. But as it turned out, instead of freezing spray, we encountered green water over the bow, which prevented the ice buildup on the upper portions of the boat. As we neared Auke Bay, we realized we either needed more daylight or lighted navigational aids to find the safe entrance. The total blackout of all navigational aids and residences was still strictly enforced. The acting skipper decided it was safer to head for downtown Juneau, which meant about two and a half hours of extra running time. Later when the ambulance picked up the patient in Juneau, the entire crew took the opportunity to hit the bars. I began to worry about our supposed quick turn-around. The Taku winds had died down, yet the one in charge deemed it too risky to start our trip back. I knew it was not fear of the inclement weather but an excuse to further enjoy their unauthorized shore leave. A word of inquiry finally got to the authorities in Juneau, and the crew was rounded up. By the time we headed back out, we had a very sick crew who slept most of the way back.

The inquiry required us, one at a time, to give our version of the episode. We realized a serious naval court-martial was in the making. It was determined that this was a hazardous trip for all of us and that the acting skipper exercised good judgment in proceeding to downtown Juneau because of the risk in trying to navigate beyond his abilities. In spite of the unauthorized extended shore leave, he was exonerated. I think he should have gotten a letter of commendation or a medal for this feat instead of facing a Navy court. I can't offer any excuses for the unauthorized extended shore leave, however.

When we got back to the *Swiftsure*, we learned that Picket No. 1 had blown up and was destroyed by fire and Picket No. 2 had been sent to Port Althorp to replace it. It was more than two weeks before I was able to rejoin my crew. My brother and I were transferred to the P5.

When I finally rejoined my crew on Picket No. 2 in Port Althorp, there was what to me appeared to be a naval inquiry in progress on the cause of Picket No. 1 being destroyed by fire. The inspecting officers were examining the remains of the burned-out hull resting in the shallow water on the beach. The built-in firefighting system was never activated. During their inspection, one of them tripped on the wire cable that releases the carbon dioxide when the emergency lever is pulled; a loud roar from the CO_2 bottles ensued, causing the men to scramble in all directions, some into waist-deep water. I heard of the heroic action by Bob Starr BMI/C. He first rescued the unconscious mechanic from the flaming engine compartment; then he singlehandedly removed the depth charges, fearing that they might be detonated by the heat. Nothing further was heard about the incident.

The incidents I mention are not necessarily in chronological sequence. As I write, my memory is being refreshed about some highlights of my experience.

During one of our rest periods we were moored at the float in Excursion Inlet cannery. I went for a hike to see if I could see a lake above there that I had heard about, and I hoped to see a porcupine in the wild. This was a relaxing hike after being confined to a small boat for days at a time. On my way down I could hear a lot of activity: machinery, ships' whistles, and even explosions. I rushed to see what was happening and was about halfway down when I met a bulldozer, painted in army colors, pushing a road inland rapidly. What I was witnessing was a big landing operation that appeared as an actual invasion. The U.S. Army was taking over the area to make a large supply depot. There was constant activity in the unloading of equipment and supplies. Not long after that, it was evident that tidal conditions had not been taken into account. One night thousands of 55-gallon fuel drums were set adrift. It was impossible to salvage all; hundreds of them drifted into the open waters of the Icy Straits. We saw many adrift, but we had no means of picking them up. Ours would have been a puny effort. In fact, they were even hard to spot because of their low buoyancy. Seine boats from Hoonah began salvaging them by the dozen. Storing these fuel drums among the houses created a potential firebomb. One of the houses eventually caught fire, and when the fuel drums began to burst, there was no way to effectively fight the fire. The village of Hoonah was destroyed. Along with the loss of their homes, they also lost priceless tribal regalia items and artifacts. This tragedy must have been at least two years after the Excursion inlet operation, because I was already in the South Pacific when I heard about the fire.

During the landing and unloading operation in Excursion inlet, one of the supply barges was stuck on top of a submerged piling with the tide rapidly receding. It was impossible to lighten the load fast enough to float it off. Navy patrol boat P7, skippered by fisherman volunteer

Don Mills, arrived in the bay, saw the predicament, and passed a towline to the men on the barge. He began tugging in a pivoting manner and was able to move and save the barge and materials. For this quick action, the P7 and its crew were awarded a letter of commendation from the U.S. Army.

In addition to U.S. Army personnel, civilian defense workers were arriving in large numbers. I also saw German prisoners of war. I noted that some were quite old while others appeared to be young. I couldn't help but feel some compassion for such young prisoners. The realities of war began to form in my mind; I asked myself if I would ever have the nerve to take a human life in the war if the situation ever made it necessary. In some of our frequent propaganda pep talks we were being indoctrinated into hating the enemy, an attitude considered indispensable in time of war.

The prisoners were told that some of the fierce Tlingit warriors had not yet been subdued and chances of escape were nil. In spite of this fake warning, a couple of prisoners did sneak off into the wilderness. After they had been gone for days, they decided they had had enough and surrendered back to the camp in pitiful condition; their faces were swollen from mosquito bites, they had encountered bears, and they had no idea how to subsist in the rainforest of southeastern Alaska.

One dark night we hit a hard object out in the middle of Icy Straits; we assumed it was one of the drifting fuel drums, and we limped into Hoonah with the stern-end vibrating heavily. The next day we put the boat on the gridiron (a series of cross timbers constructed on the beach for the purpose of supporting any boats beached for repairs). During the early evening low tide, we took off the damaged propeller and put on the spare. On the pier above us were three teenage Native boys who were speaking in the Tlingit language. I heard them talking about how vicious the miniature PT looked and wondered about its machinery and speed. When we were done, I climbed up to introduce myself to them in their own language. This surprised them so much that it appeared as if they wanted to run. I discovered that all three boys were expert in blinker and semaphore signaling; their interest was sparked by seeing the ship's communication system. It wasn't long before all three boys entered the military service. They were James Austin Jr., Archie Brown, and John Fawcett Jr.

Gustavus (or Strawberry Point, as some called it) was a ranch and a homestead. On at least two occasions it was necessary for the *Swiftsure* to purchase beef there. A work crew detailed there to select, slaughter, and transport the meat back to the *Swiftsure* were very impressed by the young "tomboy" who escorted their party to show them where the herd was located. She carried a rifle, which she proved she could use with exceptional marksmanship. Some of the fellows stated that they felt pretty inferior in her presence. She would have been more than a match to the enemy in guerrilla warfare.

One of our deckhands on Picket No. 2 was a big and husky farmer boy. His lingo was, in itself, some entertainment. After he had his liberty in Juneau, he was telling us of his encounter with a young lady. His story goes, "Ah was the onliest sailor sitting at the bar when a purty gal come in and fetched a stool bah me and asked me where ah was stationed. When ah tole her, she noted ah wasn't a Coast Guardsman. She asked me if ah ever heard or knew of the wild gal over at Gustavus. Ah says, 'Ah sure do.'" Then she led him into making some vivid descriptions of the tomboy. When she got up to leave, she announced that *she* was that girl. The farmer boy said, "Ah done blown mah chance for a new gal friend."

On some days, when ships arriving for the next convoy were not expected, we were sent on patrol to investigate any suspicious activities in the Icy Straits area. On one occasion we stopped at the Willoughby homestead, located on Lemesuir Island. The log cabin was of beautiful workmanship and the artifacts, big game trophies, and mineral collections I think qualified the home as a private museum. Mr. Willoughby also showed us a bullet that he claimed had killed the notorious crime boss Jefferson Randolph "Soapy" Smith in 1898.

In Dundas Bay we befriended the watchman at the old abandoned cannery, Joe Ibach; he and his wife were mentioned in the Glacier Bay history. They seemed content with their isolation. The hospitality extended to us resulted in other visits whenever we were in the vicinity.

Hoonah did not have any liquor stores, so it was not considered a liberty (shore leave) town. Whenever a stateside-bound convoy arrived, they no longer needed antisubmarine escorts through the inside passages. The escorts then headed for Juneau to refuel. A small liberty party from the *Swiftsure* and one or two from the picket boats were sent in for a much-needed shore leave. When the officers in charge at Port Althorp found out about the liberty parties, they also started sending in small groups at a time. The commanding officer on the *Swiftsure* was very much aware of servicemen of other service branches getting into brawls when on leave. He lectured each party, saying that if he heard of any fights, the privilege would be cancelled. Port Althorp sailors eventually lost this cherished privilege. The culprits couldn't be repentant enough.

Port Althorp had been the site of a high-capacity cannery that was destroyed by fire at the peak of the salmon season in 1938. The fresh water line and the dam were still intact and usable when the Navy occupied the site.

When we were finally established for duties with the picket boat in Port Althorp, it was a paradise after a miserable winter spent out in Icy Straits. The base had some recreational facilities for the morale and comfort of the men stationed there: a movie theater and some pool tables and Ping-Pong tables. Our duties consisted of running supplies, mail, and personnel to George Island and occasional small liberty parties to Elfin Cove and Pelican City. We also patrolled the Cross Sound area and the bays, coves and passages among the islands, including the Inian Islands. We used to make some imaginary battle runs at high speed through the narrow passages, especially one very narrow passage known locally as Mosquito Pass.

Elfin Cove is a small fishing community located in a harbor that is almost completely enclosed; it has a very narrow entrance. The place consisted of some year-round residences, two stores, liquor stores, fish buying facilities, and a fueling station. One night we took a small liberty to the Cove. While the group was shopping, the picket boat got orders to pursue a vessel for identification. It was dark before they were able to get back, and due to the darkness plus wartime blackout of all lights, they were unable to locate the entrance to the harbor. The owner of the grocery store was kind enough to allow us to wait in his place until daybreak, when the picket boat finally found its way; the fact that I missed this trip may have made the difference in their not finding the entrance.

George Island was part of the Port Althorp facility. It was one of the larger islands in the Cross Sound area, and it had an 8 inch gun emplacement and a Navy gun crew that guarded the entrance to the inside passages. Its existence was not publicly known. One day a curious fishing boat approached for a better look. The officer in charge phoned the CO at Port Althorp for instructions; he was told to fire warning shots with 20 mm tracers across their bow. The boat took off at high speed. After that, it was a standing order to warn other boats in the same manner.

After a few boats were "shooed away," the location of this shore battery was no longer a military secret.

I was eventually assigned to the P5 with my brother. Our assignments were the same as on the picket boats except that we were now on a much slower boat. One day the scuttlebutt was that a raft was to be built to resemble the silhouette of a submarine and that the P5 was to tow this as a live target so that the gun crew on George Island could get some practice. Our crew became deeply concerned about the length of the towline we would be using. When our skipper asked the division officer if this was just a rumor, he said that we had all been practicing with our antiaircraft guns on targets towed by our scout planes, and that now it was time for the big gun crew to get the same kind of practice. We had on board a seaman deckhand by the name of Joe Lesser. He had what I thought of as nerves of steel, a guy with a "don't-care-what-comes" attitude. Joe would say, "When we get out there, we're going to be a very small target; if one of them big shells should hit us, we'd never be missed."

There were a number of submarine sighting alerts in the Cross Sound area. We would be sent out with orders to attack on sighting the enemy, being assured that there were no friendly submarines in the area. We were armed with four depth charges, a 20 mm antiaircraft gun, and some small arms, no sonar or radar. We knew we had to be traveling at least 11 knots to safely get away from any depth charges we might drop with a 350 to 400 foot detonation setting. Our top speed was barely 7 knots. Joe Lesser was in charge of setting the detonation depth. He concluded we could never get away from the depth charge explosion at any depth setting, so he said, "We'll make it quick," and he set them to detonate at 200 feet. We all agreed to this. These were exciting moments. We later noted that just prior to a new convoy starting across the Gulf of Alaska we were sent on a wild goose chase to find and attack a phantom submarine.

As I try to describe some of my experiences, my memory is bringing back some incidents I had long forgotten. During one target practice with the shore battery on George Island, the gun barrel burst. Fortunately, the only injury was a bruised heel of one of the gun crew. The Navy, as usual, began an inquiry about this near-tragic mishap. One young seaman, during the inquiry, told the investigating officers, "Sir, I swear that the powder bag was much longer and heavier than the others." Laughter followed. Two days after this accident, the floating crane *Marianne* brought in a replacement gun barrel. We took hold of a cable from a caterpillar winch on the beach with the P5 and pulled it out to the crane. After it was attached to the gun barrel, it was simply dropped over the side and was pulled ashore with the winch. In a very short time the big gun was back in readiness.

Some of the bombs and gas fuel drums were cached in secluded coves with good beaches. There were no warning signs, and they remained hidden until someone happened to be at the exact location. We inspected these secret sites as frequently as our other duties allowed. In battle conditions it would not have been necessary for the scout planes to return to the base to rearm and refuel.

One of the most vital functions we were to perform was the search and rescue effort for overdue scout planes. Some that were missing were never found, while others would return after waiting out the weather in some sheltered bay or by getting on the lee side of any available protection. One of these planes was forced to land in Dundas Bay during a severe blizzard. The high winds capsized the plane before they were able to inflate their raft and they were forced into the frigid waters. The pilot succumbed before rescue came; the gunner/mechanic recovered from the exposure. If they had known they had landed in Dundas Bay, they could have sought refuge with the Ibachs, who said they heard the plane flying around the area but assumed it had flown on by.

Elfin Cove and Pelican City offered a bit of relaxation for small liberty parties; they were not considered a real liberty, except that liquor was available. As a result, we had to put up with some unruly inebriated sailors. Because of a few that were problem passengers, I wouldn't want the rest to be stereotyped. There were about a half-dozen sailors that I consider to be the toughest gang of misfit characters I've known in my entire naval career. Taking booze back to the base was strictly forbidden. Any sailor caught with such faced a Captain's Mast and was usually given extra duty. For more serious or second offenses, the men were put into the brig on ten days of bread and water. Everyone was frisked for contraband bottles, yet some considered it worth the risk. Some used various tricks to get their booze past the officers doing the frisking. Clorox bottles were emptied and filled with whiskey, and soapboxes were opened at the bottom, contents emptied, and replaced with a flask. These tricks may have worked for a while. Sometimes they hoped the officer would let them by with a wink.

On at least two occasions we took a liberty party into Juneau on the P5, an average of eighteen to twenty hours of steady running time. We had only eight bunks available. Twenty-seven sailors and one officer all seeking the comfort of those bunks was a big problem. We tried to rotate them, without success. Some of the men sought refuge in the hold (a fish cargo space); it was not heated. My brother took the fan that normally transferred heat from the galley and placed it in the pilot house, cutting a hole from the engine room into the fish hold; this fan was able to take some of the chill out. Why did these men go through this ordeal for just a few hours of pleasure on the beach? I think the answer is because of isolation in semi-camp conditions.

Feeding this crowd was quite a task. Joe Lesser, our seaman deckhand, volunteered to be the acting cook. His tough nature organized the eating shifts and also designated who would wash the dishes. Though he was only a seaman, I think his natural traits of authority would have made him a good officer. I mentioned earlier that Joe, in my opinion, had nerves of steel. At times he worried us because of the way he would answer the upper brass. When the officer in charge of the liberty party sat down for his breakfast, he began to instruct Joe on how he wanted his meal prepared. Joe was already pretty edgy. He quickly turned around and pointed his pancake turner at the officer, saying, "Listen Mister, I am not a cook. I am a crew member charged with your safety and welfare as a passenger. You will be treated as any other." Joe got away with this insolence. We were afraid of some sort of retaliation by the officer; it never happened. Our return trip was even more nerve-wracking because some crewmembers were still inebriated. With every liberty trip we made into Juneau, upon our return to the base, at least one or two sailors were left behind as over-leave.

While the term *scuttlebutt* may mean a rumor, to old salts it means secondhand truth. The following account will be hard to believe, but such is the nature of scuttlebutt. I would like to refer back to the half-dozen troublemakers I mentioned earlier. They were incorrigible. It seems no matter what they were assigned, they invariably caused problems for others, such as giving the Port Althorp and George Island personnel a bad reputation in Pelican City and Elfin Cove. This is the reason I am careful to avoid stereotyping the personnel. These incorrigibles ran the dice and card games on the base, and at least one of them amassed a small fortune. It got to the point where they were shunned, not trusted.

This is the gang that helped a young girl stow away on board the old freighter *Tongass* in Seattle. They concealed her in a cement mixer in the cargo space below decks. They padded the mixing vanes with Mae West type life jackets and several blankets. As troop passengers, they saved portions of their meals to feed her. They freely talked about how they almost got away with it. They laughed about the "honey-bucket" duty being forced on the subordinate of this gang. The girl was discovered before arriving in Petersburg, Alaska. Their destination was the naval air station at Sitka. It was after they served their time in the brig in Sitka that they were sent to Port Althorp. It is hard to believe that the Navy kept this gang together. Maybe they considered the section base duty an additional punishment. Whatever the case, they were the cause of trouble wherever they were, mostly in their pursuit of excitement, fun, and their version of entertainment.

The commanding officer of Port Althorp was a veteran bush pilot. He had two of his personal airplanes on a wartime loan to the Navy, and he flew them himself. One was a biplane passenger type; the other was a small Piper that had to be started by manually spinning the wooden propeller. He also had his speedboat cabin cruiser, which was capable of speeds of over 30 mph. The commanding officer was frequently required to be absent from the base, thus affording this group unauthorized joy riding in his speedboat. In a short time ordinary joy riding didn't seem to provide enough excitement. They began to maneuver the boat between the pilings under the dock and then gradually increased their speed until they were making repeated runs under the dock at full speed. It became a game of "chicken" as they took turns at the wheel. Although it was expected that they would eventually wind up in a pile of splinters, they didn't have any mishaps until they hit the reef off the point at high speed. The bottom of the hull was ripped off and the machinery dropped out the bottom. They now realized that they were in serious trouble. They manually pulled the damaged boat almost into the woods. It appeared as if they were trying to hide their crime.

The commanding officer was not due to return that night, and the other officers returning from their patrol duties didn't notice the damaged boat. During the night the gang broke into the mess hall galley for provisions for their planned escape, then loaded empty 55-gallon fuel drums into an open 50-foot Navy motor launch. Early the next morning they requisitioned unauthorized gasoline from the fuel station at Elfin Cove. They were dangerous because they took advantage of their access to firearms and ammunition. They were headed down Icy Straits when the much faster picket boat with armed officers and men gave chase. A scout plane had spotted them, but they could only notify the base of their position.

They were returned to Port Althorp under a heavy armed guard and locked up with an armed guard to watch them until they could be transported to Sitka. No one felt safe with these idiots still on the base. I heard later that during their court-martial they accused the upper brass at Port Althorp of letting an illegal fisherman fish in the restricted waters of Port Althorp. I was never aware of any such illegal activity; it was probably a defense tactic. I never heard how the court-martial turned out.

The big scuttlebutt now was that most of the personnel would be going out with a big draft of men. War production was getting into high gear, and every new ship needed a mixture of seasoned sailors and new seamen from the boot camps. The scuttlebutt was in fact a secondhand truth, and the excitement caused a lot of wishful talk on just what kind of ships each would prefer.

The day of our transfer came quicker than we expected, and we were on our way to the hotter areas of the war. We considered this a chance to get into the real war. Little did I realize how formidable and highly efficient the Japanese navy was. Things were still pretty bleak for the U.S. Navy in the South Pacific. The USS *Juneau*, a light cruiser, was sunk with the loss of over seven hundred; there were only ten survivors. All five of the Sullivan brothers were lost in this battle. Naval headquarters issued a communiqué that all members of the same family are to be assigned to different ships and stations. Harvey and I were to be separated for the duration of the war. Because of the strict censorship, we couldn't tell each other where we were or about the battles we were involved in until the restriction was lifted and then only in a limited way. We were constantly worried about each other's welfare.

When we were finally sent to stateside duty, we were entitled to at least one year of shore duty individually. Without consulting each other, Harvey and I opted for more sea duty. My last thirteen months were in the amphibious forces with landings in Saipan, Iwo Jima, Okinawa, and the occupation of northern Japan at the devastated city of Amori.

Many of us that survived the war have strong feelings that if the atomic bomb had not been dropped, we never would have made it home. The horrors of war that we had firsthand experience in would be mild compared with a nuclear holocaust. Let's hope it can be avoided.

Originally published in the *Newsletter of the Sitka Historical Society* 7 (3) (1994): 5–15; edited by Sergei Kan in 2011.

8

Poems by Andrew Hope III

INTRODUCED BY ISHMAEL HOPE

Andrew Hope III, X̱aastánch of the S'iknax̱.ádi, was a poet, educator and organizer all his adult life. He came from a family well known for its activity in Alaskan Native politics, and he engaged in that politics for much of his life. However, in his later years, he spent less and less time in the pursuit and exercise of social power and more with the sharing of knowledge. He was known for his outspoken honesty about any given issue, and no doubt this harmed him more than helped if he had any political ambitions to begin with.

More likely, I believe, his heart was in learning. Though he spoke English and was a writer rather than an oral poet, as his ancestors would have been, he absorbed the old stories. In those stories, the true spiritual power resides not in the rich man, or the political leader, but in the one who is overlooked, the one who appears lazy, who spends the day playing with gambling sticks, the one who is cast away or orphaned, the one who never reveals his true power until he is needed by his clan. For his last accomplishment, while the cancer was growing, unknown, inside him, he organized the Honoring Alaska's Indigenous Literature Awards with me and Richard and Nora Dauenhauer. We honored the great Koyukon storyteller Catherine Attla, the respected Yup'ik elder Annie Blue, the Dena'ina speaker Walter Johnson, Tlingit writer Ernestine Hayes, and Tlingit weaver Clarissa Hudson, along with linguists Michael Krauss and James Kari. The HAIL awards epitomized what Andy was all about. He put elders and speakers front and center, while honoring new writers and innovators, along with linguists who devoted their working lives to Native knowledge.

The HAIL Awards was a small and humble event with forty or so people in attendance. On the face of things, the event was a blip in the midsized town of Juneau. This is how Andy worked, driving on, with or without popular approval. Andy lived, however, and taught me how to

Fig. 8.1 Ishmael Hope speaking at the 2007 clan conference in Sitka. Photograph by Peter Metcalfe.

see, beyond the smoke and mirrors of colonial values. He told me that his father, John Hope, who died in 1997, said often that in the beginning of the Alaska Native Brotherhood, when Alaska Native leaders first fought for Native civil rights and land, you could often count on one hand how many people were doing the work and leading the way. As long as you had some people in the towns and villages who recognized and supported your work, you could do a lot with those few people. There is no doubt that Andy carried this weight and burden, and he seemed ashamed at his most challenging moments, such as when he found in his late fifties, with all his experience and a recently acquired master's degree in cross-cultural studies from the University of Fairbanks, that he was unable to get a regular job doing what he loved. But this is how Andy persisted. Against all the diminishment and devaluation of a colonial world, he remained focused on the beauty of his rich Native history and culture.

It took me a while to recognize that beauty. With a demeanor not unlike the reserve and reticence of the best storytellers, my father never outright said what I should do or what I should think. He just showed me that when the learning stops, you're stopping short. At an early *koo.éex'* memorial party for my grandfather John Hope (Ḵaalgéikw) and great-uncle Herb Hope (Stoonook) in Sitka, the late and gentle elder Jim Walton was eating breakfast with my father and me. Teenager that I was, I relished sharing my newfound wisdom with whoever was in earshot. I said something about speaking love to my people, and Jim was impressed. I said I didn't know where these thoughts came from. My dad said, "What, are you kidding? Your mom gave that to you since you were born." My mother, Sister Goodwin, was also a poet and a teacher. My dad gave it to me, too.

Hats and Masks

"Sure are a lot of son of a bitches out there."[1]
—WILLIAM CARLOS WILLIAMS

Ugly
Scary
Masks out there
Everywhere you look
Resentment
Chewing on your back
Masks sticking to the face
Faces turning to masks
Heads and hats
Lookers and admirers
Comparing postures
Making deals
Trading hats and masks
And dancing away with them
A posture becoming an art form
Masks making politics
What happens to the ones without masks or hats?
Where does one find sanctuary
From these hats and masks?
How does one
Keep skin on flesh and bone?

November 1985, rev. December 1991 and August 1995

Oral Tradition

"Fidelity to the given word.
The man standing by his word."[2]
—AFTER CONFUCIUS, THROUGH POUND

How do storytellers
And song people
Edit talk?
What to think?
What to say?

What to sing?
And old man walks to the microphone
At a Native convention
  "I don't speak good English,"
   He tells the crowd
   Before beginning his story
He talks about diplomacy
Words going out
Public statements
Words coming out
He knows word power
Sometimes words spear people, hurt people
Puncture skin
Tearing
Bleeding
War songs
Hate poems
Wild words
Sometimes you can't get around those words
Like Baraka's *Hard Facts*
Words coming down lickety-split on public scandal
Those lines rail like a saxophone
A geography of words
Literary maps
Describe the way you move
Along word landscapes
Telling about place
Place words carefully
Making peace with words
Healing words
Ceremonial words
Plan
Think how your words come out
Transform words
Thoughts
Gossip
Rumor
Talk Talk Talk
Oral tradition

Spoken word
Conversation
Remembering
Surrender?
(Watch their faces)
Stories
Acting
The translated word?
Think well
Speak well
Remember
Know your words

September 1977

Shagoon 1-4

   Shagoon 1
Thunderbirds flying
Like giant planes
Moving silently
Across the gray sky
Thunderbirds flying

   Shagoon 2
Brown bears dancing
Leaving footprints
In the mud and snow
Brown bears dancing
Into the woods
Brown bears dancing

   Shagoon 3
Killer whales flying
To the mountains
Becoming rock
Turning to stone
Permanent landscape
Eternal killer whales flying

Shagoon 4
Killer whales multiplying
Like grains of sand along the shore
Killer whales multiplying
Killer whales multiplying

January 1991

Holy Bread

Mother
Feeds the fire
With holy bread
Memory food
For the ancestors

October 1990

Children of Leaves and Blossoms

First things
Raven came upon
A strong, sturdy log
Which he used to make
What he thought would be
The eternal Tlingit
The Tlingit log started walking away
But he was too clumsy and fell flat on his face
Raven smashed the log and moved to a rock
Hard and heavy
Which he used to make
What he thought would be
Indestructible Tlingit
The Tlingit rock took a few steps
But soon he was limping along weakly
Raven destroyed the rock
What could he use to create the Tlingit?
He heard the leaves
Floating through the air
They were light
Quietly growing out of the branches of trees

Children of the forest
Tlingit man
Formed of leaves
Multiplying
Growing
Branching
With Tlingit woman
Delicate to the touch
Pleasant to the eye
Born to blossoms

Sweet Rain

Sweet rain
Came down upon us
Last night
Clean rain
Fell through us
Sweetened berry blossoms
Washed salt from seaweed
Soaked leaves
Crackle volcanic ash
Dust churned into air
Dried in the heat of the islands
Crackle burning wood
Salmon cooking in a pan
Stone breaking flat into pieces
Burnt by the sun
Crackle moist heat rising off the ocean
Low tide
Bending
Lifting
Distant islands over the horizon

These Masks

—FOR CY PECK SR.

We use the tools that are available
To provide options for those

That will follow
Masks
Symbol
Metaphor
Survival strategies
We share
Religious sanctuary
Holy places
Mountain valleys and streams
Presbyterian Church
Salvation Army Church
Russian Orthodox Church
And the other churches
Did someone say spirit masks?
Those high church surveyors
Those low church surveyors
Those love missions
Those fear missions
Those education missions
Those religious colonies
Founded by the U.S.A.
Organizers
Founders
Of the Alaska Native Brotherhood and
Sisterhood
Traded tribal masks
For political masks
Look at their faces
In those turn of the century photos
No long hair there
Is diplomacy not a mask?
Sometimes we lose
The face
Behind all those masks
Should we learn
the lessons
of the ANB and ANS ancestors
Children
Grandchildren

Coming generations
May benefit from our work

Brotherhood

In brotherly love let your feelings of deep affection for one another come to expression and regard others as more important than yourself.

—ROMANS 12:10, *The New Jerusalem Bible* (1985)

Come on boys
It's all right
We know very well
There's a lot of bad
Out there
Come on men
It's all right
Don't despair
Come on guys
It's a fight
Let's go to work
Come on men
Let's take care of the children
The nieces
The nephews
The sisters
The brothers
The families
The wives and mothers
The sons and fathers
Don't be afraid
To learn respect and pride
Know your ancestors
Keep the clan in mind
Come out boys
No need to hide
From that education
From that family
From your sisters
From your brothers

Keep the friendship
Keep the family
Keep the clan

The School of Custom and Tradition

Where do traditions come from?
Where do customs originate?
How are customs and traditions learned?
Carried forward?
What are the sources of inspiration
Look to the ones that know
Look to creative ones
Look to ones with ideas
Look to the artistic
Look to elders
Look to the young
Look to the energetic
I attended the school of custom and tradition
A school of vitality and richness
A school of ideas
A school where one will always learn something new
Where people meet
Where people teach
Where people learn from each other
And move on to become
The school of custom and tradition
Reflected
In their lives
In their minds
In their eyes

NOTES

1. The exact quote is "There's a lot of bastards out there!" As quoted in the introduction to the poem "Death News" by Allen Ginsberg: "Visit to W.C.W. circa 1957, poets Kerouac Corso Orlovsky on sofa in living room inquired wise words stricken Williams pointed thru window curtained on Main Street: 'There's a lot of bastards out there!'"
2. The Chinese character *xin* depicts a man beside the sign for "word." Ezra Pound defined this as "Fidelity to the given word. The man here stand-

ing by his word." According to Wendell Berry, "Such fidelity to the word, as evidenced by clarity of meaning and intent, would go far to reconnect language to life. Without a renewed sense of language we cannot hope to restore balance, harmony, and coherence to our lives, our land, and our communities, for these must be joined as marriage joins them—in words by which a man or woman can stand, words confirmable in acts." *Standing by Words: Essays* (San Francisco: North Point Press, 1986), 30.

9

As Long as the Work Gets Done

PETER METCALFE

Andrew John Hope III died at the age of fifty-eight on August 7, 2008, following a brief battle with cancer. At the time of his death, he was executive director of Sharing Our Knowledge: Conference of Tlingit Tribes and Clans. Hope previously served as regional coordinator of the Alaska Rural Systemic Initiative of the University of Alaska as a tribal enrollment officer for the Bureau of Indian Affairs and as administrator of the Sitka tribe of Alaska.

Andy Hope was born to be a leader. His grandfather, Andrew Hope, founded the Central Council of Tlingit and Haida Indian Tribes of Alaska, the organization his father, John Hope, later led as president/CEO. Hope's grandfather and father both served as Grand Camp presidents of the Alaska Native Brotherhood, a civil rights organization founded in 1912. Rather than feeling entitled by this legacy of leadership, Andy assumed the responsibility that came with it by doing the hard work of organizing, promoting, and advocating the interests of Alaska Natives.

The traditional ceremony held in Sitka two days after he passed away served to remind us of Andy's many, many contributions to the revival and current widespread recognition and acceptance of Tlingit cultural traditions. It is now commonplace for people of Tlingit heritage to know their Tlingit names and matrilineal clans and clan houses, as well as their fathers' clan associations. Through his years of research and advocacy, Andy played a leading role in popularizing Tlingit culture, but he rarely, if ever, sought to take credit for his accomplishments.

One of Andy's greatest contributions to those studying clan lineages lives on in the "Tlingit Country" map he published. The map is an essential guide, the Rosetta Stone, by which the social organization of Tlingit clans and clan houses are revealed. To look at this poster, one could be forgiven for not appreciating the decades it took Andy to complete the research, find consensus among Native tradition bearers, achieve agreement on a spelling system (orthography), and then raise the money to pay for four successive printings as increasingly minor typos and errors of omission were corrected.

I met Andy's father, John, well before Andy and I became acquainted. My father, Vern, shared a broadcast booth with John during the annual Gold Medal basketball tournaments in Juneau. As a young boy I would climb the ladder to the booth with its commanding view of the basketball court, join my father and John, and listen in awe to their masterful play-by-play and "color commentary" of Southeast Alaska's most beloved sporting event.

When Andy and I first became acquainted in 1977, it was through our mutual admiration of Jim Pepper (1941–1992), the late, great Native American jazz musician. Andy and I collaborated on sponsoring Pepper's concerts in Juneau and Sitka. Much later, in 1993, we produced an hourlong radio show in tribute to Jim.

Over the more than thirty years that Andy and I were close friends and associates, he enlisted me in many publishing projects, media productions, and cultural events. Recognizing the obvious intrinsic worth in each of these undertakings, it never occurred to me to say no to him. Later, during his memorial services in Sitka, I listened as one person after another recalled how Andy had similarly roped them into working with him. It all sounded very familiar, especially when someone referred to the simple question that began so many of Andy's phone calls: "Is it done yet?"

Andy's leadership was not dramatic. He led by example and persistence. But, as low key as he was, he never withheld his opinion about anything, including baseball, politics, jazz, poetry, Tlingit history and culture, and Alaska Native education, about which he was especially passionate. His trenchant observations, almost always laced with profanities, were wickedly amusing. Upon hearing yet another lacerating opinion about a Native leader who had fallen short of his expectations, I'd throw back at him one of his favorite expressions: "Don't sugar coat it, Andy; tell me how you really feel!" Time and again, however, Andy revealed his ability to change his mind and to generously acknowledge when someone he may have previously criticized had stepped up to do the right thing.

If Andy wasn't Alaska's first tribal leader of the post–Self-Determination era, he was the movement's guiding light. Under his leadership, the Sitka Community Association (now the Sitka Tribe of Alaska) became the model for other tribal organizations. There are now more than two hundred federally recognized tribes in Alaska, but back in the early 1980s, only about a dozen tribes were active in the state, and few if any were as advanced as SCA. Andy was quick to seize on the mandates of new federal laws that empowered tribes. He led the way for other tribes by presiding over the creation of social service, economic development, employment, energy assistance, and housing programs, as well as the development of a tribal court, the adoption of tribal ordinances, and the funding of preschool and cultural education.

One of the things Andy did best was to get people working toward a common goal. In 1972, he co-founded *Tlingit Readers*, a nonprofit publishing house that to this day continues to produce books and events about Tlingit culture, language, and oral history. Several years later, he organized the first Conference of Southeast Alaska Tradition Bearers. In 1983, he co-founded the United Tribes of Alaska and, in the early 1990s, the Southeast Alaska Native Educators Association. And all along, from the early 1970s forward, he organized seminars on Native culture, arts and language, tribal courts, and Alaska Native education.

One of Andy Hope's most important endeavors was the Sharing Our Knowledge conferences of Tlingit tribes and clans, the first of which was held in 1993 in Haines/Klukwan. From the start, these conferences staked out a unique position in the study of indigenous cultures. To my knowledge, no similar event exists that brings together academicians and tradition bearers, students and tradition learners, and the interested public to share and absorb knowledge of a minority culture on the basis of equal footing and mutual respect. Several Sharing Our Knowledge conferences were held in the 1990s, but ten years were to elapse before the "clan conference" of March 2007, a five-day event that attracted over five hundred people to Sitka's convention center. Academics from leading universities in Canada, Europe, and the United States shared research with culture bearers and others who study, promote, and live Southeast Alaska Native languages and traditions.

Andy, the conference executive director, asked me to supervise the video documentation. In the middle of the five-day event in Sitka, as I was racing between three camera crews covering concurrent workshops, he and I shared a few words as we were jostled by the crowd. "There's a hunger for this," he observed.

For over fifteen years, Andy had championed the concept of a tribal college. I had had my doubts, but with Andy I had learned to wait and see. At that moment, while talking with Andy at the Sharing Our Knowledge conference in Sitka, it finally made sense as I saw participants jam the lobby making their way to workshops, the topics of which included linguistics, archaeology, museum studies, cultural anthropology, education, ethnohistory, art and music, traditional ecological knowledge, indigenous protocols, and fisheries. Seemed like college to me.

For the last evening of the 2007 conference, Andy had organized several poets and writers to give readings. The tribal theater on Katlian Street, modeled on a Tlingit longhouse, was packed until the wee hours. I recall the shocked appreciation he expressed to me the day after for what had happened: the crowd rising to call for repeated ovations. "For poetry?" he said. "Amazing!"

Preparing his obituary, Andy's family quickly agreed that a comment they had heard from him more than a few times best summed up his attitude toward so much of what he had accomplished: "You don't need to take the credit; let others take the credit *as long as the work gets done.*"

We, his friends and family, continue his work. His legacy lives on with the Sharing Our Knowledge conferences and his many publishing efforts. The 2009 conference in Juneau was dedicated to his memory, and the 2012 conference in Sitka included workshops and the presentation of papers recognizing the contributions of the Alaska Native Brotherhood—one of Andy's first publications profiled the organization's founders—on its centennial.

In life, Andy did not seek credit for much, so in his memory, let us acknowledge his contributions. Whenever I hear a young person speaking Tlingit or reciting her or his clan lineage or talking about Northwest Coast culture, I think of Andy. He is not forgotten.

10

Revival and Survival

Two Lifetimes in Tlingit

NORA MARKS DAUENHAUER
AND RICHARD DAUENHAUER

Nora Dauenhauer

I want to say hurray for Tlingit literature—*Lingít shkalneegí*—that is, Tlingit literature in Tlingit.[1] I am very happy about this.

I was hired to teach Tlingit in Juneau-Douglas High School in 1969. I was a sixth grade dropout and was teaching high school students. I quickly discovered I needed more education, so I went to the only thing I knew that was accessible to me–the GED. It took me seven months to complete it, but I had a real good teacher. She was a wonderful teacher; she was a very good woman. And I had very good students who were my classmates, so we helped each other, trying to figure out what we were supposed to do with our lessons. After half a year in the Juneau-Douglas, I got a letter of discharge. It said that although I had done a good job, they really needed a certified teacher in order to keep their accreditation. Some thirty-five years later they still didn't have a certified teacher of Tlingit language, but they seemed to keep their accreditation. I'm happy to say that some of our students are now being certified and hired.

Being terminated was painful, but I pulled through it. I went up to Anchorage where the National Congress of American Indians was meeting. There I met Dick, and I entered college (Alaska Methodist University, which is now Alaska Pacific University) and started my higher education.

It was really hard after dropping out of school and going through the GED program, but I finally made it. After five years of college, I graduated. By that time Dick and I were working on a project I had started—Tlingit oratory that had been recorded at my father's potlatch for his older brother, my uncle Jim Marks. I had been transcribing and translating one of the speeches delivered at the potlatch. I showed it to Dick, and lo and behold he thought it was wonderful, but he is really a student of literature, and I was not. I didn't know or appreciate what I had wandered into. So anyway, I showed it to him and he was impressed with it.

So I kept working on the Tlingit oratory. I began with Jesse Dalton's speech for the removal of grief, using the old Naish-Story orthography. And it was difficult, very emotional for me, because I discovered—actually not right away—but I discovered it was sad the way the words were put together in the speech. And then I realized that this was something we were going to lose. So I kept on working on it, and then I transcribed speeches by Matthew Lawrence, David Kadashan, William Johnson, and Austin Hammond. We first published these, in the Tlingit language only, in our Tlingit Language Workshop Reader in 1972. Expanded with English translations, annotations, and an introduction, they became the heart of our *Haa Tuwunáagu Yís, For Healing Our Spirit: Tlingit Oratory* published eighteen years later in 1990.

And then sometime along the way Carlton Smith, at that time corporate secretary of Sealaska Corporation and incorporator of the Sealaska Heritage Foundation, called and asked if we could write down the oratory delivered during the Sitka Native Education Program evening as part of the conference called "Sealaska Elders Speak to the Future," held in Sitka in 1980. The students of SNEP had recorded this conference when the children came out to sing and dance. Charlie Joseph, who was the head teacher of the Sitka students, narrated during the presentation, and afterward several elders gave speeches in response, including George Davis, William Johnson, Charlie Jim, and George Jim. Carlton Smith wanted us to work on that set of speeches. And, my! We were still just beginners then! We didn't have computers yet, though Dick did have an IBM correcting Selectric typewriter with a special Tlingit element and a dead key disconnect for typing tones and underlines. By the time we finished the manuscript, it looked like a mummy, because it had correction tape all over it. It was thick. But we got it in print anyway as *Because We Cherish You: Sealaska Elders Speak to the Future* (1981).

So this was a streak of luck for us, because Carlton Smith was convinced we could do anything. One time he even tracked us down by telephone in Vienna, Austria, at a visiting writers' crash pad with an

Fig. 10.1 Nora Marks Dauenhauer speaking at the 2007 clan conference in Sitka. Photograph by Peter Metcalfe.

unlisted number and told us, "We want you to do this and that," launching us on another project. In that way we kept on going. And it was wonderful and at the same time sad for me. It was really great. I discovered *Lingit tundatáani* — the thoughts of my Tlingit people and how they are conveyed. The words are beautiful and show how the visual art is an image of our ancestors. I was a goner. I had to keep going.

So that is the short of it that I could tell you. I cannot think of anything else I could tell you now, except that we need more storytellers, and I am going to give you a little bit of advice: when you write, find the best proofreaders and editors you know to make sure your writing is in the best spelling order, both in Tlingit and English. I know there are a lot of you writing; I could see you when I look at you. Some of us who are writing today were trained by linguists. I began by studying the books by Connie Naish and Gillian Story, the Bible translators who were working in Angoon in the early 1960s. I think that SNEP hired Jeff Leer. And he is my son — he adopted me as his mother. I don't know if I am a good mother to him. Those of you who do not know how to speak Tlingit, try to learn it so you could understand what we are talking about up here. George Ramos said yesterday, "We have to remem-

Revival and Survival 155

ber our ownership of our lands." This is true. You can remember your ownership of your lands better in Tlingit than in English. And that is why we should learn Tlingit and learn about our land. And Ray Wilson said yesterday, "The White Man recognizes us by our votes. If we come together, we have more strength." I agree with him. We have more strength in numbers.

Our books are written in Tlingit. We worked at Sealaska Heritage Foundation (now Sealaska Heritage Institute) for about fifteen years. We moved to Juneau to do that in 1983. David Katzeek hired us to do materials. And instead of doing children's literature—"kiddie lit"—we started doing serious things of Tlingit culture and oral literature that we knew had to be saved. Our first book was *Haa Shuká* (1987), then *Haa Tuwunáagu Yís* (1990) and *Haa Kusteeeyí* (1994). Rather than copyright these in our own names, we left ownership of our books at Sealaska because we feel that this material belongs to all of the Tlingit people. SHI has the copyright. Also, all royalties from sales go to Sealaska Heritage Institute, not to us.

We need more writers. We now have Ruth Demmert in Tlingit and Bert Adams in English, Ernestine Hays in English, Andy Hope in English, Ishmael Hope in English, Hans Chester in Tlingit, and Harold Jacobs—he is a writer, too. We need more song composers as well. We now have Harold Jacobs and Hans Chester, and also Chuck Miller and Lyle James. This is wonderful. Maybe this will catch on with teenagers, too. We have Robert Davis, who is also a wonderful poet, and Vida Davis, a composer of children's songs. Lance Twitchell is an up-and-coming writer in English. They are all wonderful people, and they will be wonderful elders.

Gunalcheesh. Thank you all for listening.

Richard Dauenhauer

This is going to be a hard act to follow, but I'll do it as a confession. I guess this is going to be "his side" of the story; it's going to be a "she said, he said" type of thing—especially how we met. Basically, it's illegal these days: I put the hustle on my freshman student.

As Nora said, there is a lot of work involved here. I don't know how many times proofreading has brought us to the brink of divorce. But we've managed to tough it out for thirty-three going on thirty-four years and still counting. We appreciated all of Harold's jokes last night about old people, as we grow old.

Now I'd like to tell a little bit about how I came into this because my half of the working together is totally different. I grew up in upstate New York, and my ancestry is Irish and German, so I guess I am and Irish and German *yádi*. I have been interested in languages since I was a kid. I studied German and Russian in high school, and I had a chance to be an exchange student in high school, which shaped my life a lot by giving me an appreciation for doing things in more languages than one and living with a German family. I was also interested in writing since high school—even elementary school, in fact—so in college I studied lots of languages. My major was Russian, and my minor was German, and I also studied such things as Greek and was involved with classical Greek all the way through my PhD exams. One thing led to another, and I fell in love with translation, so to this day I do a lot of translation of poetry. In graduate school I ran out of money, and there was a job opening in Anchorage at Alaska Methodist University. I applied and got the job, and off I went and eventually met Nora, and that's the short version.

My big desire coming to the university was to apply Euro-American status to Alaska Native languages and literatures, or what Ishmael Hope mentioned earlier as "the professional treatment of Alaska Native oral literature with dignity and with respect." And this is often a hard sell. Even Albert Lord, who worked on oral literature at Harvard, had trouble convincing his colleagues that there is anything to oral tradition or that *Beowulf* and the Homeric epics were probably composed and published orally before they were written down at some great intersection of oral tradition and the innovative technology of literacy, and that the processes that the composer of *Beowulf* or Homer used to compose these works were basically the same processes that we see in the Tlingit community today.

So it aggravated me very much and still does today to see Alaska Native language and literature trivialized, to say, "It's children's literature" or to hear school administrators say, "Oh, we tried that in the fourth grade, and it didn't work." And I reply, "Do you also teach *Julius Caesar* or *Macbeth* in the fourth grade?" Obviously there are children's stories and there is a place for them, but to take adult literature from another culture and to treat it as if it's children's literature is basically racism. We used to see a lot of this, and we still do in some places. What bothered me very much is that we do not want Native literature marginalized or trivialized. We want it to be taken seriously.

Another thing that bothered me very much when I arrived in Alaska was the whole sociopolitical dimension, and we are still fighting that battle—the right to bilingual education, the right for children to learn concepts in their own language first and then learn English as a second language and be able to apply those concepts in the new language. It always amazed me that I had Japanese students who had learned everything in Japanese first and then learned English as a second language, and they were performing much better in college than the Yup'ik students who had everything taught to them in English and who were products of twelve years of American education. So what would happen if these Yup'ik kids had learned all these concepts first in their own language and then learned English? If I could do it in German, they could do it in English. When I was in a German school, I did very well in German and history because I like languages, but I did very poorly in math. My German math was as much of a disaster as my English math. I also wonder what Tlingit would be like today if American educators had fostered bilingual education rather than English-only, targeting Tlingit language for extermination.

The very first thing I was asked to do in Anchorage was to give a presentation to a meeting of speech therapists, who told me, "We can't tell the difference between a Yup'ik accent and a speech impediment." And I said, "Wow, these people are asking the right questions!" A lot of people were not asking the right question, and all the students with brown faces were ending up in speech therapy. But they don't put Bill Clinton or Henry Kissinger in speech therapy. Perish the thought that Zsa Zsa Gabor should ever be put in special education and speech therapy. The point is that there are legitimate reasons for speech therapy, but there are features of speech that are just regional accents. A lot of the schools had trouble sorting this out, and it was easier to stick all the Natives into special education, where a lot of the money was, in contrast to bilingual education, which has been a hot sociopolitical battle from the start. These were some of the issues that we began fighting, and we are still in the trenches fighting some of these battles.

So then I met Nora and we started working together and this is something that has shaped our work for the past thirty-five years. The first rule that we came up with—and it has helped me a lot, of course, to have Nora insisting on this—is that we present the Tlingit point of view. We let the elders speak for themselves; we are not putting words in their mouths; we are not paraphrasing them or retelling their stories.

What goes on the page are the words of the elders—in Tlingit. We are simply the transcribers. We are like a microphone—we are transmitting their words. For the most part, this had not been done before. In the past, elders had usually been paraphrased or only given in translation.

So we came up with three standards when we were working at Sealaska Heritage Foundation with David Katzeek, which Nora mentioned. The three main criteria that we wanted to follow in our work were (1) that it would be acceptable to the Tlingit community, so that we work in the community with the people who want to be worked with and what we do is open and above board and meets the standards of the community; (2) that it also meets professional, scholarly academic standards, because it can work both ways: you can have work that the university thinks is great but is not acceptable to the community and you can have community-based work that is not up to professional standards; (3) and finally, that the work is accessible to the average interested and intelligent reader, because sometimes writing can get so jargony that nobody can read it. As someone said about the thesis of one of our friends: "It's brilliant but impenetrable."

Another thing that we are doing—and some of you at this conference are involved with this—is teaching distance-delivered university classes to which all interested community members are invited. In these classes we work on developing teaching and learning materials. One activity is to establish texts. For Tlingit, this means taking a story recorded in performance from oral tradition, writing it down in Tlingit, translating it into English, and proofreading both the Tlingit and the English. If you're studying English or world literature and you read Shakespeare's *Macbeth*, that's been around for four hundred years. It's there to read. If you read Homer's *Iliad* or *Odyssey*, they've been around for over two thousand years. What we are doing with the Tlingit literature is the process that Nora talked about of recording it and of writing it down for the first time from recordings of oral performance. And we want to be sure that we are hearing correctly what they are saying on the tape, that we are spelling it right and translating it properly.

And that opens up a whole other can of worms. How do you translate all of this so that it makes sense? In our proofreading Nora and I argue about this back and forth. "It doesn't make sense." "Yes, it does." "No, it doesn't." "That's your problem." And so forth. And we eventually work these things out.

I'd like to talk a little bit about style now. Style and personality are two of my favorite topics in oral literature. My students know that I really get excited about this, even if sometimes I see them falling asleep when I talk about the subject. Typically in older and popular editions of oral tradition from Native people, the attributions are often like "Here is a native story." And you would ask, "Who is it from? Who told it?" Often the answer is something like, "We don't know. It's the folk. It's anonymous." But that's baloney. There are individual storytellers and individual people, and there always have been. It's just that in earlier periods, collectors often did not bother to record information about the tradition bearers, so we no longer know who they are. Moreover, the stories are usually "retold" and in translation, so we are very far from the actual words of actual storytellers.

But we think it is important to feature individual tradition bearers, to consider how they put their material together, how they think about it, and how it fits into the larger world. It is exciting to explore how and why storytellers say things and how they use language. We grow to appreciate and even savor such characteristics of oral style as repetition, a device frowned on in written composition.

When we have the actual words or actual storytellers, we realize how their styles can be radically different. You can see some of that when you look at our books. Compare Robert Zuboff and Andrew P. Johnson, who have quite different styles. We are discovering some things now while working with a text from Angoon from 1963 by Jimmy Johnson. I excitedly pointed out to the class, "Look, he loves dependent clauses!" and everyone says, "Give me a break! What's a dependent clause?" And I say "Look, here it is. It's a sequential form of the verb. We don't have that in some of the other stories we've been reading, but here are seven of them!" The point is that we can appreciate how different composers put their stories together, the same way that we can distinguish T. S. Eliot from Robert Frost.

We can also stand in awe of the wonderful range of language at the command of the masters of Tlingit oral tradition. A good example is Katherine Mills, who in her wonderful version of the story of "Raven and the Deer" uses the verb *hop* seven times and in five different verb forms within fourteen lines, some of these forms being without precise English equivalents, but approximately Raven hopping up and down in place, hopping out and back, hopping, skipping, and jumping along, etc., and this is great. Hopefully some of our students will get as excited about these things as I do. I am in awe at the stylistic range commanded by these master verbal artists, and I am humbled by the realization that as a learner I will never approach their level of linguistic genius and skill.

We believe that individual personality is as important in Tlingit oral literature as it is in the familiar classics of world literature. We are used to asking how Tolstoy and Dostoevsky wrote about theology. We should also pay attention to Robert Zuboff in his story about the origin of the mosquito when he reminds us that it was not God who created evil in the world, it was humans who messed things up. This is his theology. We would not have mosquitoes if it weren't for human greed, revenge, and one-upmanship. So if your life is going bad, don't blame it on God. It may be your own fault. The point is that the stories are not generic and the storytellers are not mindless, neutral pipelines through which the stories flow; rather, the stories are shaped by and are part of the personality, life experience, and worldview of each.

We also see the storytellers' personalities coming through in the two versions of the Glacier Bay history: one by Amy Marvin of Hoonah and one by Susie James of Sitka. The stories are "the same" but very different. Susie James's is very "mythic" and is about the eternal return and the fertility of the land and people, while Amy Marvin's is very socially oriented. Both are powerful.

In the book we are working on now, about the battles of Sitka of 1802 and 1804, we have two main versions recorded in Tlingit, one from Sally Hopkins, who was Kiks.ádi, and another by Alex Andrews, who was Kaagwaantaan, Kiks.ádi yádi ("child of the Kiks.ádi clan"). And as we mentioned in our session this afternoon, Alex Andrews's version is like Homer: it is a blow-by-blow description of the battle. But in Sally Hopkins, if you blink, you miss the battle. You say, "Wait a minute. Where is the battle of 1804? Where is K'alyaan?" On the other hand she has seventy-five or eighty personal names in the story, all the genealogies, and what the social impact of the events was on the people, the civilians (so to speak), the noncombatants. Of course, the other information is there, too. But this is what to me is very exciting. This is what we want to do with the oral literature. We want to say: This is the glory of the people in the oral tradition. These are the words of the elders.

We are also involved with writing grammatical and instructional materials. I will not mention too much about that. Our *Beginning Tlingit* grammar has been around for over thirty years and is a bit dated pedagogically, but still usable (4th ed., rev., 2000). We also have the

Tlingit Spelling Book (4th ed., 1999), the *Say It in Tlingit* phrase book (2002), and our *Sneaky Sounds* (2006), and we are working now to finish *Intermediate Tlingit*. Another very, very important part of our work is trying to empower Native people to do this also. This has been our political agenda. We are very proud of our students who presented here the other day. And we are trying to work at the college level with the next generation of Tlingit, Haida, and Tsimshian youth, not only to provide training in the languages and literature, but also to involve them professionally in education so that they can find a place in the educational system.

This is part of my current job. I am very happy to be President's Professor at the University of Alaska, Southeast. It is a three-year appointment, but it is also a three-year window to try to develop courses and a program. Last year, I am proud to say, for the first time we offered Tlingit, Haida, and Tsimshian–all three native languages of southeast Alaska. We hope to expand working with distance delivery. We do have a minor in Tlingit now, and our next effort is a certificate modeled on the one they have at the University of Alaska, Fairbanks for other Native languages or at the University of Northern British Columbia. So that is part of our political agenda. This is unfortunately more difficult now than twenty or thirty years ago. Back then, there were speakers of Tlingit, Haida, and Tsimshian who could be placed in classrooms. It is relatively easy to offer courses in literacy and teaching methods to fluent speakers of a language. Now we must build language acquisition into the program. Our next generation of speakers, scholars, and teachers will come from this age group learning the language now.

The future. I would like to spend a little bit of time talking about where we are going and to address the big question: where is the next generation of speakers, scholars, learners, teachers, and leaders coming from? That's the overwhelming concern as I see it. In thirty-five years, if I am (God willing) still living, I will be one hundred years old! This staggers my imagination. I do not know how many of us will be around in thirty-five years or where will the second generation, the people behind us, will be. So there is a frightening, rapidly closing window of opportunity, and we figure it is about ten years, in which the learners can work with the birth speakers of the language. By this we mean the people who grew up speaking the language. There will perhaps be people after that who have heard and understood the language all their lives and may possibly become more active speakers, but right now is our last opportunity to work with the people who were born and raised as speakers of the language and who are active, fluent speakers now. When we lose a language, it is gone forever. Unfortunately, languages are easy to lose and hard to get back.

I did a paper years ago, and it was published recently as "Seven Hundred Million to One" (R. Dauenhauer 2005). In it I compare the impact any one of us could ever have on Mandarin Chinese, which has seven hundred million speakers, in contrast to a language like Eyak, which has one.[2] In the latter category we would include Tsimshian, Haida, Tlingit, and all of the Alaska Native languages. What any of us does can have an impact on an Alaska Native language. If I were to do a German grammar, it would not have any impact whatsoever on the German language and its survival. The German language is doing quite well, as is Chinese. One of my friends who spent his life studying Chinese says it is comforting to know that he could mess up his work and it would not mess up the Chinese language. They are doing quite well without him—all seven hundred million. But we need to be very careful about what we do. If we are teaching poorly, it's going to take a generation to fix it. We hope we are not doing too many disastrous things as errors of commission. As for errors of omission, what we fail to document of Tlingit language and literature may be lost forever. The same, of course, applies to Haida and Tsimshian.

So let me get a little bit preachy here. My first message would be to use all the tools and education we have—literacy, computers, technology, etc. Sometimes people worry about innovation. Purists wonder, "Should we use English?" The Native American writer Simon Ortiz had a great comment about writing in English, "It's a weapon. Use it." And of course, the founders of the Alaska Native Brotherhood knew this. If you want to compete, you need to know these things. Literacy is a tool. It wasn't traditional for Tlingit. But nobody came out of the womb writing, whether it was English or Russian or any other language. There is a long tradition of literacy in English, but not in Tlingit. It is something new. It was, of course, something new for English, too, and missionaries also introduced it to the speakers of English, but that was over a thousand years ago for English. It is a tool.

Likewise all the electronic stuff we saw yesterday and today: it is a tool, and it is great. Get the skills to learn and to maintain and to teach. And this could be in the family, in the community, in the schools. There could be all kinds of venues. This does not have to be for university credit. Universities are in the credit and certification business, so I'm working in that arena as a tool. But the language is not going to survive through a certificate. It is going to survive through personal and community effort. So whatever you do, speak it, talk it, use it.

And that is, of course, where we get to the theme of the conference: sharing knowledge, working together. And that can be informal, or it can be formal as in our university classes, or a combination. We all benefitted so much by having the Sitka elders such as Ethel Makinen, Irene Paul, and others participate in our distance delivery classes with Roby Littlefield and others. The Tlingit-speaking elders add a dimension to the class that I certainly could not provide alone. We just need the wisdom and support of the elders with their priceless knowledge of the language and culture.

Here are some kinds of working together: elders and young ones, speakers and learners, the community and the university, family history and archival history. I'd like to repeat the last one, because these two complement each other. We have found in several cases that the family history may have one set of information and the archive or library may have the other, and that neither may be complete, but if you put them together, you get the whole picture. For example, the birth certificates, the genealogical information may be in the archives, but the family history makes it come alive and helps make the connections. So it's like putting a puzzle together and each group of people has a different piece of that. So, for example, in our session today on Russian America, Judy Ramos and Elaine Abraham went through some of the Yakutat oral history, and I could give them the names from the Russian documents of who the Russians were. The Russian documents, of course, do not have the information on who the Tlingits were, but if we put both together, we get the names of the people on both sides of the battle.

Likewise oral literature and written literature can work together, even though each is composed according to different rules. What makes good oral style is not necessarily what makes good written style, and it is important to appreciate (and enjoy) the differences. The classics of world literature can have meaning for the local community, and Tlingit, Haida, and Tsimshian literature can fit in the context of world literature.

And I would like to give you an example of one of the most important things we discovered while doing our book on the battles of Sitka: personal names. Get your clan and family names, record as many from the elders as you can. In the case of the book, not all of the names that are in the texts from fifty years ago are still in circulation, and we no longer can go to the people who knew those names and ask them because they are gone. And as I mentioned this afternoon, we are now, finally, in a position to ask important questions, but the people who could answer these questions are no longer alive.

So that's what is going to be important: to get the accurate pronunciation from a reliable speaker on a CD. Try to get an accurate spelling, because if you are using your own private system, while it may be good for you or for somebody who already knows the language and the name, nobody else is going to know what it is. It will be like writing in a secret code rather than to communicate. Also, get as much information about these people as you can—the departed who had the name, and the people who have it now. This is precious information for current and future generations of your family, and it is something only the people in the family can do. Get as much outside help as you can if you need to, but do it. In the case of some of the names in the Sally Hopkins history, we could find no one alive today who remembers them.

Likewise, old tape recordings are precious. Try to copy them to CD. Try to archive them. The traditional fears of people getting rich off them or stealing them are not as real now as the fear of losing priceless clan and family history forever. We are just now working with one recording from 1963 and another one from 1958. These are like a window in time and you're going back. I have been thinking a lot about this: if you have a person who is seventy years old and he or she recorded something fifty years ago, you are going back 120 years, as far as the language is concerned, assuming the speaker was fluent by the age of five. So, for example, the recordings of Sally Hopkins preserve a now-extinct dialect of Tlingit.

There is another important thing someone outside the community can't do regardless of how well he or she writes Tlingit. Let's say you have an old tape recording of a party from Angoon in 1960. Who are these voices? If you are from the community, you might know: that's Uncle Harry talking and Aunt so-and-so. So Nora was able to do this in working with the speeches from Hoonah from 1968 that she mentioned. She'd play the tape for me, and all I'd hear would be dishes rattling and ambient noise, but she'd say, "That's so-and-so making a speech." And at best I'd be just hearing some squeaky voice in the background speaking. But if you know those voices, you can give them life, whereas the best linguists in the world can't do that. We can transcribe the sounds, but we would have no idea who the speaker is. But somebody locally does. So local knowledge is very critical, and teamwork is often the most productive way to document these things. We benefitted very much by having the Sitka people helping us, and we thank them again.

In closing, I'd like to say just a few things about some of the barriers to success. Some of the barriers to doing this kind of work can be fear, insecurity, guilt, or shame over the language. Hopefully this is on the wane, but it's something we have to come to grips with, especially with persons who may be able to help younger learners but are reluctant to do so. Another factor is that language learning is not everyone's cup of tea. I don't expect that everyone would want to learn the ancestral language, and I would be hypocritical to say so. I don't have enough lifetimes to learn Irish, my heritage language on my mother's side. I drink my beer on St. Patrick's Day. As for Irish whiskey, I learned that the Catholics drink Jameson's and the Protestants drink Bushmills. I drink both of them, being eclectic and ecumenical. But on the German side I am fluent. I have studied the language since I was fourteen years old, I have visited and lived in Germany, and I have a BA minor and MA degree in German. I have not done this for the Irish side of my heritage. So not everyone is going to learn his or her heritage language. But somehow coming to grips with that fact, I think, is very important psychologically and emotionally. Another barrier—one of our biggest barriers, to be perfectly honest about this—is institutional politics. And somehow we've got to cut through that crap. We have a limited amount of time, energy, money, and human resources, and we can't be fighting over them. Likewise we can't have rivalry, jealousy, sabotage, and all these turf wars. We don't have time for that. It's a luxury we cannot afford.

Finally, since I'd much rather end on an optimistic note, I'll say that Nora and I have been so very impressed with the high energy level at this conference and the talent of the younger people, the wisdom of the elders, and the tremendous outpouring of goodwill. We are just amazed. One of our friends compared this to an acre of fruitcake. There is just too much going on to take it all in. We are getting a little bit of indigestion from all of the activity and the energy. But it's wonderful. And again my hat is off to the organizers. I know that Sergei, and Steve and Andy were wondering "what if," back a year, a year and a half ago. It was their leadership and effort that went into raising the money to do this and organizing it, despite people like me trying to lay low because

I had a full plate already. So thank you to the organizers. You have done a wonderful job. We are just so proud to be here. And we are also proud of you, the participants, who make it all possible.

Nora Dauenhauer

I just want to say a few words about what Dick said about politics. We are going to have to put all that aside. We have been shut down many times, but we kept on going anyway. And we hope that it will stop. And I think that Tlingit literature and our Tlingit identity that comes from the literature are too precious to play around with. So this is all I wanted to say. Thank you.

NOTES

1. This paper was delivered as the keynote address at the 2007 Conference of Tlingit Tribes and Clans. It was transcribed by the editor in August 2009 and edited by Nora and Richard Dauenhauer in 2009, 2011, and 2012.
2. See Dauenhauer (2005). Eyak is now extinct as a spoken language. The last speaker of Eyak, Marie Smith Jones, died in January 2008 in Anchorage at the age of eighty-nine.

PUBLISHED WORKS

Dauenhauer, Nora Marks. 2000. *Life Woven with Song.* Tucson: University of Arizona Press.

Dauenhauer, Nora Marks, and Richard Dauenhauer. 1981. *Because We Cherish You: Sealaska Elders Speak to the Future.* Juneau: Sealaska Heritage Foundation.

———. 1987. *Haa Shuká, Our Ancestors: Oral Narratives.* Seattle: University of Washington Press.

———. 1990. *Haa Tuwunáagu Yís, For Healing Our Spirit: Tlingit Oratory.* Seattle: University of Washington Press.

———. 1994. *Haa Kusteeyí, Our Culture: Tlingit Life Stories.* Seattle: University of Washington Press.

———. 1999. *Tlingit Spelling Book.* 4th ed. Juneau: Sealaska Heritage Foundation.

———. 2000. *Beginning Tlingit.* 4th ed., with CDs. Juneau: Sealaska Heritage Foundation.

———. 2002. *Lingít X'éináx Sá! Say It in Tlingit: A Tlingit Phrase Book.* Juneau: Sealaska Heritage Foundation.

———. 2006. *Sneaky Sounds: A Non-Threatening Introduction to Tlingit Sounds and Spelling*. Juneau: Sealaska Heritage Institute.

Dauenhauer, Nora Marks, Richard Dauenhauer, and Lydia T. Black. 2008. *Anóoshi Lingít Aaní Ká = Russians in Tlingit America: The Battles of Sitka, 1802 and 1804*. Seattle: University of Washington Press.

Dauenhauer, Richard. 2005. "Seven Hundred Million to One." *Etudes/Inuit/Studies* 29 (1/2): 267–84.

Part 2 | *Native History*

11

Tlingit Interaction with Other Native Alaskan and Northwest Coast Ethnic Groups before and during the Russian Era

ELENA PITERSKAYA

For more than two centuries, Alaska and the Northwest Coast of North America have been a region of special interest for Russian researchers.[1] Nonetheless, the majority of their published works have focused on the ethnography, history, politics, and economy of the former Russian colonies in North America. Only a few studies attempt to reconstruct the traditional social structure and culture of the different ethnic groups of Alaska. Despite a limited number of reliable sources on Native cultures before the arrival of the first Europeans, these works are highly successful and make a significant contribution to the study of Alaska and the Northwest Coast (Liapunova 1975, 1987; Grinev 1991; Dzeniskevich 1987). New primary sources published over the past several decades, including collections of archival documents and oral history records, provide better opportunities for a broader historical reconstruction and help researchers fill some gaps.

It seems to me that one of the most interesting phenomena requiring further detailed research is the interaction between Native Alaskan peoples on the eve of the European colonization. It is a difficult task because one has to rely on a limited number of primary sources. In any case, a study of trade, intermarriage, and warfare can provide a deeper understanding of the larger sociocultural processes (i.e., cross-cultural influence and acculturation) in this vast region.

This paper focuses on the Tlingit interaction with other Native Alaskan and Northwest Coast ethnic groups before and during the Russia era. My approach is to identify and analyze the available sources and to determine to what extent contemporary researchers can reconstruct a complex network of connections that existed on the Northwest Coast and Alaska mainland long before the first Europeans began visiting the region. Using the available Russian data, I also attempt to trace the degree to which the aboriginal cultures influenced each other through trade and other forms of interaction. Although a large number of works has been published on the Tlingits' interaction with the Russians and other Europeans (Gibson 1992; Grinev 1991, 2005; Istomin 1985; Kan 1999; Zorin 2002), their relations with other indigenous peoples of the region have not been sufficiently researched, with only a few works on this topic published in Russian (Grinev 1986) or any other language.

Alaska and the Northwest Coast as a Network of Trade Relations

In the seventeenth and eighteenth centuries, Alaska and the Northwest Coast were an arena of multiple contacts with various ethnic groups that inhabited this region, such as the Aleuts, the Alutiit (pl. of Alutiiq), the Athapascans, the Tlingits, the Haidas, and the Tsimshians. No one was isolated. They had contacts with their immediate neighbors and also traveled to more distant places. All the contacts of the Alaskan and Northwest Coast peoples could be divided into two major categories: peaceful interaction with other groups focused on trade, and armed conflicts aimed at a forceful acquisition of valuables. They had a similar economic rationale: an acquisition of necessary valuables (slaves, material goods). I will focus on trade as the most effective method of cultural exchange.

Russian Sources
WRITTEN NARRATIVES

I draw on various narrative sources, including memoirs of travelers and navy officers, private and business correspondence of the Russian-American Company personnel (hereafter RAC), and writings by Russian Orthodox missionaries. Some of the documents are published in separate volumes, such as those by Ivan Veniaminov, and some are included in the sets or collections of documents on the Russian exploration of the North Pacific and occupation of Alaska as well as activities of the RAC. I also use the official reports and records sent by the Russian colonial administrators such as Aleksandr Baranov, Kiril Khlebnikov, and Ferdinand von Wrangel to the board of the RAC, the Russian imperial authorities, and the RAC shareholders (Khlebnikov 1985; Wrangel 1839). I have paid special attention to the detailed descriptions by early Russian travelers and military men such as Gavriil Davydov (1810), Vasilii

Golovnin (1861), and Iurii Lisyanski (1977), as well as the writings by such Orthodox missionaries as Ivan Veniaminov (1840) and Ieromonakh Gedeon (1994). I also draw upon the writings by such historians as Petr Tikhmenev (1861–1863) and Semen Okun (1939), who used the documentary materials that no longer exist today. The largest part of the unpublished records is stored in the Archive of the Foreign Policy of the Russian Empire, the Russian State Historical Archive, the Russian Navy Archive, and others.

An ethnological study of the cultures of the Northwest Coast and Alaska has a long history in Russia (Averkieva 1941, 1960; Dzeniskevich 1987; Grinev 1991; Korsun 2002; Zorin 1994, 2002). Like other present-day Russian researchers, I rely on published documents as well as unpublished archival records. However, the data from these sources can be dubious, and the information drawn from them should be used very carefully, given their subjective nature and a negative attitude toward the Native population often exhibited by the Russian navigators and fur traders. In addition, the RAC personnel often exaggerated the heroic deeds of the Russian hunters and tried to hide the real social and political situation in the colonies, simply to make a better impression on the shareholders and state authorities. Some of the RAC employees misinterpreted the facts because of the lack of knowledge of the aboriginal languages and cultures. Moreover, the Russian sources paid little attention to the issue of trade and social interaction of Alaskan Natives before the European colonization. They simply presented a few facts that one has to retrieve from very scarce references. Although the selection of such information is time-consuming, the overall information collected in the course of writing this paper helped me reconstruct a complicated network of social ties between the various indigenous peoples of Alaska before the Russians established their rule over this region.

ORAL HISTORY

For many years Russian researchers had limited access to the oral history records. However, thanks to some new publications, they recently have been given an opportunity to use oral history materials as one of the primary sources of information on the culture and history of the Tlingit people (H. Hope 2000; Dauenhauer, Dauenhauer, and Black 2008). These records supplement the more traditional written records and archaeological data, which provided fewer opportunities for a full-scale reconstruction of the process of interethnic interaction in

Alaska. Often oral history records help uncover some episodes previously unknown to researchers or allow them to (re)interpret some established ideas from a new perspective. One of the best examples is the battle of 1804 between the Russians and the Tlingit of the Kiks.ádi clan at Sitka. For a long time the Tlingit withdrawal from their fort at Indian River was not understood by researchers and was interpreted in various ways including as an escape. But in recent years Herbert Hope, a Kiks.ádi historian and elder, who compared the oral history of the battle of 1804 he had learned as a boy with other oral and written accounts of the same event, presented the Tlingit retreat as a survival march.

It was only thanks to the oral history records that I first encountered a reference to a marriage between an Aleut man and a Tsimshian woman as well as the fact that under certain conditions the Aleuts were allowed to hunt in the Tsimshian hunting areas (Bradley 1992).

MUSEUM COLLECTIONS

Another important source of information on the Tlingit interaction with other Native peoples are museum collections. Objects relevant to our topic are found in the major museums both in Russia and the United States, including the Museum of Anthropology and Ethnography in St. Petersburg (hereafter MAE), the Russian Ethnographic Museum, the Anchorage Museum of Art, and the Sitka National Historical Park. Their description and attributive characteristics can help researchers establish the origin and travel routes of the various artifacts. For instance, in the collection of items brought to Russia in the late 1840s by Ilya Voznesensky from the Northwest Coast of North America, there are women's jewelry, robes, moose skin garments, rugs, smoking pipes, various dishes, shaman's masks, and sets of festive ritual attire that were clearly produced by the Tlingits. Yet in the same collection there are also items that were manufactured by the Haidas and Athapaskan people but that were definitely acquired by Voznesensky from the Tlingits. The MAE also owns some Athapaskan-made artifacts collected by Mikhail Lazarev and Tlingit ones acquired later by Igumen Georgii Chudnovskii.

STATISTICAL DATA

Although statistical data are important for historical reconstruction, there are not many relevant statistical records that could be used to study the Tlingit connections with other Native groups of the region during the early (precolonial) period of their history. Most of the statistical data, including the number of Tlingit, Athapaskan, and Aleut people living in the vicinity of Russian settlements, comes from the Russian period, particularly 1830–1867. For this matter, in regard to the precolonial era, the official records of the RAC and Alaska Russian Church Archives could hardly be used for the purposes of this paper.

Traditional or Precolonial Period
TRADE

Many historians and anthropologists recognize that the Tlingits had excellent entrepreneurial qualities. They maintained intensive trade relations with other Alaska Natives and Northwest Coast groups. They extended their trading routes in several directions, and the territory of their active trade included British Columbia, the upper Yukon, and the Mackenzie River valley. Each year in May and June, their special trading expeditions walked to the Alaskan interior and canoed far to the south.

As Andrei Grinev mentions, the Tlingits of Chilkat, Stikine, and Taku ḵwáan(s), who lived in the territories through which the most popular trails into the interior Athapaskan area ran, actively traded with the Tutchone, the Tagish, and the Tahltan Athapaskan groups. Trading routes also followed the Stikine, Taku, and Alsek Rivers. In addition, the Tlingits traded with the Ahtna, the Tanana, and the Han Athabascans (Grinev 1986: 113). The Hans acted as the intermediaries between the Chilkat ḵwáan Tlingits and the Upper Tutchones. The Hans acquired fish, fish oil, and dentalia shells from the Tlingits and sold them to the Tutchones, while obtaining processed reindeer skins and furs from the Tlingits (Mishler and Simeone 2004: 2). A peculiar feature of the Tlingit trade with Athapaskan groups was the ownership of certain trails leading into the interior by specific Tlingit clans. The Tlingits from other clans could use these paths but only as members of the trading expeditions headed by the chief of the clan that owned the path (Grinev 1986: 114).

Tlingit trading goods included basketry, wooden boxes, fish, fish oil, seaweed, and tobacco. There is documentary evidence that the Sitka Tlingits grew small-leafed plants about the height of tobacco, which they mixed with lime derived from shells and used for smoking and chewing. According to Tikhmenev, this mixture was not very strong but, when burnt, produced a pleasant odor. The Tlingits traded it with the Native groups living to the north of them (Tikhmenev 1861–1863: 84). Based on the experts' opinion, Frederica de Laguna suggests that it was not a true tobacco, *Nicotiana tabacum*, but some other species, possibly *Nicotiana multivalvis* or *Nicotiana quadrivalvis* (de Laguna in Emmons 1992: 153). The main goods the Tlingits acquired from the Athapaskans were various furs, beaver pelts, mountain goat wool, moose and caribou skins, and clothing and boots made of tanned hide with traditional Athapaskan decorations. For instance, objects collected by Voznesensky from the Yakutat Tlingits include Athapaskan-style moccasins made of reindeer chamois and decorated with beads (MAE, no. 2520-11/1-2). In the same collection one finds an Athapaskan-style blanket made of moose skin acquired by Voznesensky probably in the fall of 1844 (MAE, no. 593-27). Russian sailors, RAC officials, and missionaries collected similar clothing items. For instance, a shirt made of elk hide decorated with porcupine needles was collected by Mikhail P. Lazarev in 1823-1824 in the Alexander Archipelago (MAE, no. 633-31/1). In 1890 Chudnovskii acquired Athapaskan style reindeer hide trousers decorated with porcupine needles on Admiralty Island (MAE, no. 211-27). The most important trading item the Tlingits acquired from the Athapaskan groups of the Copper River region was copper, which their craftsmen used for manufacturing knives, arrows, jewelry, and highly valued plates. Part of the copper traded from the Athapaskans was sold by the Tlingits to the Haidas and the Tsimshians in exchange for slaves, red cedar canoes, and finely carved ceremonial paraphernalia, such as dancing headdresses decorated with feathers and abalone shell inlays. Copper River groups produced axes, knives, and breast pieces for themselves as well as for the trade with the Eyaks and the Tlingits (de Laguna 1972: 348; Wrangel 1839: 52).

The Tlingit people dominated the inland Alaskan and Yukon trade networks by controlling access to the coast and allowing only a few selected Athapaskan leaders to visit their own territory (Hirschman 1999: 76). When the first Russians appeared in the Yukon and Kuskokwim River valleys and tried to establish trading connections with the local groups, they had to take into consideration and compete with an effective traditional trading system that had existed in the region long before their arrival.

The main trading partners of the Aleut people were the Tanainas and Ahtnas and sometimes the Alutiiqs as well. There are very few references in the literature to the Aleut trade with the Tlingits. The reasons for this were the long distance between the two peoples and the fact that the area between their territories was occupied by the Alutiiqs, with whom the Aleuts were in a state of constant conflict. When occasional contacts between the Aleuts and the Tlingits did occur, the former offered the latter gut skin clothing and pelts of sea mammals in exchange for deer skins, clothing made of fur, and highly valued amber and mineral paints used to decorate Aleut hunting hats made of thin wood bent into the shape of a wide cone.

The inhabitants of the Island of Kodiak traded primarily with the Kenai and the Chugach ethnic groups and only occasionally with the Eyaks and the Tlingits. The Alutiiqs had a great demand for deerskins and fur, which they used for decorating their coats (Davydov 1810: 14). Ieromonakh Gedeon's notes confirm that the Kodiak Alutiiqs acquired dentalia shells from the Tlingits: "They received small plates of pearly shells from the Sitka people" (Gedeon 1994: 75–76).

Aside from the interior Alaskan peoples, the major trading partners of the Tlingits were the Northwest Coast tribes. For instance, the Tlingits of the Chilkat ḵwáan sold the Tsimshians and Haidas their Chilkat blankets, while the Tlingits from Yakutat, Sitka, and Hoonah ḵwáan traded basketry. The Tsimshians sold spoons made of mountain goat horn, woven goat hair blankets, and carved rattles to the Haidas (Marsden 1992). The Tlingits acquired dentalia shells from the Haidas, who obtained them mostly from Vancouver Island. The Tlingits used them in their trade with other ethnic groups. The Tlingits also obtained canoes made of red cedar, paying the Haidas with mountain goat wool and processed skins of caribou and moose that they acquired from the Athapaskans. This wool, used for blanket weaving, was highly valued all along the Northwest Coast and was sometimes even used as currency. It was measured by the double handful and traded for such items as canoes, paddles, and fish (Vanderhoop 2007).[2]

The copper acquired by the Tlingits from the Athapaskans was one of the most significant trade items, as were slaves, traded mainly from the Kwakwaka'wakw and Salish groups (Khlebnikov 1985: 85). References to a coastal trade in nephrite can be found in the work of George Emmons (1991). This mineral is not common in southeast Alaska and came from the Upper Fraser and Thompson River valleys. Nephrite chisels and knives were traded by the Interior Salish to the Lower Fraser River people and coastal tribes. Such tools were highly valuable and too expensive for common people. A piece of unfinished nephrite weighing about twenty pounds, found under the foundation of an old house in Sitka in 1885, was worth four slaves. Emmons also heard from the Tlingits of a pipe made of jade that had been buried with a Chilkat chief (Emmons 1991: 170). As soon as the iron tools had become part of the trade and eventually the everyday life of the Tlingits and other Native peoples of the region, the demand for nephrite declined.

The Tlingits' role as the middlemen in the regional trade contributed to the development of their strong entrepreneurial skills and helped quickly increase their wealth. For example, Veniaminov described a headman's son who started his trading career with several beaver pelts and within three or four years he bought eight slaves, a new canoe, a wife [i.e., gave large bridewealth to her family—SK], several guns, and many other things considered valuable among this people (Veniaminov 1840:117–18).

MARRIAGE

We know that the Tlingits occasionally married members of other Native Alaskan and Northwest Coast ethnic groups. Sergei Kan mentions that members of the Tlingits elite occasionally married aristocrats from the neighboring non-Tlingit nations if such marriage could bring significant political, economic, or social gains (Kan 1999: 7). Tlingit relations with the Eyaks extended far beyond trade. Similar dual social organizations of these two societies contributed to the development of various social contacts between them, including potlatching, raising of totem poles, and marriage. Marriages between members of appropriate moieties created a kind of mutual demographic dependence between these two societies (Olson 1967:20; Nikolai 1994:237).

Generally speaking, there are some examples of marriage unions between representatives of ethnic groups who could hardly have been ideal partners. For instance, there exist records of a marriage between a Tsimshian woman and an Aleut man. Being perfect sea otter hunters, the Aleuts were constantly looking for better hunting areas, and this eventually brought them to the Tsimshian territory rich in sea otter. One of these Aleuts married a local woman, thus acquiring the right to hunt in this area. However, the next year a greater number of Aleut canoes came, and the Tsimshians could not allow such large-scale hunting and chased them away (Bradley 1992: 12). Though it is the only example of marriage connections between the Aleuts and the Tsimshians I managed to find, it does support my argument of the existence of certain ties between the Northwest Coast and the Aleutian Islands.

WARFARE

Although military conflicts are not the focus of this paper, it is still important to mention them in order to paint a more comprehensive picture of the interethnic interactions in Alaska. Warfare, both local (against the other groups of the same tribal nation) and "foreign" (with other tribal nations), was an integral part of the social and political life of the Aleuts, the Tlingits, and the Alutiiqs. For centuries it served as a reliable source of slaves. Thanks to the armed conflicts, the winners gained access to mineral deposits and acquired valuable goods. As a rule during such conflicts, the old people were killed and the women and youth were taken as slaves.

The Tlingits and the Haidas were considered the best warriors of the Northwest Coast and Alaska along with the Eastern Aleuts (inhabitants of Unalaska and Unimak Islands). The enemies of the Tlingits included the Chugach and sometimes the Alutiiqs to the north and the Haidas and the Tsimshians to the south (Emmons 1991: 324–27). The Tlingits, especially those living along the Gulf of Alaska, disliked their Alutiiq neighbors with whom they did trade but whose incursions into their own sea otter hunting grounds and occasional raids they deeply resented (Kan 1999:45). Ronald Olson wrote an account, "A War with the Tsimshian," shared with him by a Tlingit elder from Wrangel sometime between the early 1930s and the early 1950s (Olson 1967: 80–81). A conflict began when a Tsimshian party from British Columbia stole a box containing the skull of a Tlingit chief from his grave post. In revenge the Tlingits raided a Tsimshian village and killed several people. The Tsimshians returned and went up the Stikine River, where they burned Tlingit houses and stole dried fish and berries. For several years the two groups raided each other, until a large group of Tsimshian warriors was taken captive, while messengers were sent to Kitkatla, Wakutl[?], Port Simpson, and the original village of Metlakatla with an invitation to come to an agreement and release all captives. Only after the Tsimshians accepted the conditions of the offer was a lasting peace achieved (Mobley 1999).

In the mid-eighteenth century, the Tsimshian started expanding north, which in turn resulted in a northbound migration of the Tlingits. Sometime in the 1730s, some of the Haidas also migrated from the Queen Charlotte Islands (Haida Gwaii) further north to the areas inhabited by the Tlingits, and they occupied the southern part of Prince of Wales Island. Grinev hypothesizes that it was due to the pressure from these Haidas that some Tlingit clans (and first of all, the Teiḵweidée) moved from that island to the mainland where they assimilated the Tsetsauts, a local indigenous Athapaskan people (Grinev 1991:20).

In the mid-eighteenth century, the Yakutat-area Eyaks as well as the Eyak groups living northwest of Controller Bay acted as intermediaries in the trade between the Ahtna and the Tlingits. However, in the second half of eighteenth century, the Tlingits migrating from the south arrived in Yakutat and partly assimilated and partly mixed with the largest local Eyak clan, the Kwaashk'i Ḵwáan. The pressure from the Tlingits resulted in other Eyak groups moving to the right bank of the Copper River and the Chugach withdrawal from Controller Bay by the end of the eighteenth century. According to Grinev, this active Tlingit expansion was forced not only by the influence of the Haidas and the Tsimshians in the southern areas but also by a strong Tlingit desire to establish control over the trading routes and become the sole traders of copper mined by Athna (Grinev 1993: 73).

CULTURAL CHANGES AS A RESULT OF
INTER-TRIBAL INTERACTION

As a result of living as neighbors and cooperating as trading partners, the ethnic groups in the vast territory of Alaska experienced significant mutual cultural influences. The Eyaks experienced the strongest Tlingit influence. Several Athapaskan groups acquired many Tlingit cultural traits, such as games, several rituals, and some art elements typical for the Northwest Coast. Such Athapaskan groups as the Tahltans, the Tagish, and the southern Tutchones acquired the matrilineal clan system of the Tlingits. Trade contacts between the Tlingits and the Athapaskan peoples boosted the development of slavery among the latter. As a result of the expansion of the Tlingit trade, some of the Athapaskan groups as well as the Eyaks acquired some loan words from the Tlingit language. But the Athapaskan influence on the Tlingits was limited to some types of clothing and footwear, which the Tlingits occasionally traded with Russians. The Tlingits considered the Haidas and the Tsimshians to be the people of highly developed cultures similar to themselves. They borrowed some of their songs, dances, and ceremonial objects.[3] Through trade the Tlingits also acquired the knowledge of the Eskimo bows, which were far better than Tlingit ones. Via their contacts with the Athapaskans, the Tlingits bought Athapaskan bows and Aleut spear throwing boards or atlatls. Some groups of the northern Tlingits came to use the leather baidarkas and baidaras probably obtained from the Alutiiqs.

COLONIAL PERIOD

The Tlingit-Russian relations during the period from the early contacts (1741) until 1804 could be described as an armed standoff. Hence we could hardly speak of significant economic ties between them during these years. Starting with 1804 and until the sale of Alaska, the Russians managed to establish and sustain more or less peaceful and regular contacts with the Tlingits, with trade becoming the integral part of this interaction.

The Russian ethnographic literature on the peoples of Russian America pays major attention to the contacts between the Russians and the indigenous population of Alaska as if such intercultural contacts were the only ones that took place. Yet according to various sources, even during the period of significant Russian presence in southeastern Alaska, the Tlingits maintained their exclusive trading rights in the region. Their interaction included both the other indigenous peoples and the newly arrived Russians. It is primarily because of the Tlingits that the intercultural exchange between the Native groups of this part of Alaska did not stop with the Russian arrival but dynamically developed further and acquired new features that had not existed during the earlier period of intertribal trade.

At the beginning of the nineteenth century, the Tlingits established a strong position as the middlemen between the Europeans (including the Russians), with whom they traded extensively, and the other peoples of the Northwest Coast and interior Alaska. The Tlingits' main European trading partners were Russian hunters and RAC employees, American and English captains, and starting in the 1830s, the Hudson's Bay Company agents. The Americans and the British provided the Tlingits with firearms and even cannons in exchange for sea otter skins. The development of trade with the Europeans boosted the dissemination of iron among the Tlingits, used to produce knives, hooks, and carving tools. Due to their geographic location, entrepreneurial qualities, and active trade with the Europeans, the Tlingits became the dominant power in the Alaskan trading network in the mid-nineteenth century.

Contacts with the Europeans led to changes in the nature of goods the Tlingits traditionally obtained from the Athapaskan tribes. From now on, furs became the most significant trading item, while European goods such as iron pots, manufactured blankets, knives, tobacco, flour, tea, and coffee rose enormously. Firearms and black powder remained the most valuable commodities that they sought.

Trade with the Europeans was important for the Tlingits, who acquired goods not only for their internal consumption but also to exchange with other Alaskan and Northwest Coast Natives. For the majority of the European commodities sold by the Russians, the Tlingits paid with food items, primarily potatoes, and sea otter pelts (Tikhmenev 1863: 314, 323, 326). However, the Tlingits did not sell all of their furs to the Russians, because of the low price paid by the RAC. Here is how Langsdorf described the barter between Tlingit traders and Alexander Baranov: "They brought along sea otter pelts, gave them to Mr. von Baranoff, and then asked for items they needed equal in value for their gift. If they were not satisfied or asked for too much, then they took back the pelts they had presented as a gift" (cited in Dauenhauer, Dauenhauer, and Black 2008: 306). The Tlingits preferred the Americans and the British as trading partners, since those Europeans exchanged furs for alcohol, guns, and cannons. For more than five decades, the Tlingits were the only trading intermediaries between the European fur traders and the other Native groups.

Due to a high demand for fox and sable furs in the 1820s and 1830s, the Athapaskan tribes had to increase fur hunting, and that led to a considerable expansion of the Tlingit trading routes and trading contacts with them. Their trade system extended in several directions. The Tlingits of the Sitka ḵwáan bought furs from other ḵwáan(s) and sold them to Europeans. The Chilkat, Stikine, and Yakutat ḵwáan Tlingits traded with interior Alaska Natives and exercised control over trading paths into these regions (Tikhmenev 1863:349). Some groups of the coastal Tlingits visited Lituya and Yakutat Bays to hunt sea otter, and this afforded them additional opportunities for trade. The Yakutat Tlingits made their return visits to relatives in Hoonah, Sitka, and other southern areas, where they could also dispose of their furs and other goods. In addition, the Yakutat Tlingits made occasional trips to Nuchek in Prince William Sound and even to Kodiak Island (de Laguna 1972: 348). During trading operations, parties from different ethnic groups used the Chinook jargon. Initially it combined words from the languages of different Alaskan and Northwest Coast tribes, but later it included French, English, Hawaiian, and Russian words.

In the nineteenth century, the Haidas began acting as trade intermediaries as well. From the Russians they learned to grow potatoes, and very soon they were producing so many potatoes that it became possible to trade them with the British, the Russians, and the Tsimshians.

The Kaigani Haidas were the most active trading group who interacted with Russians in New Archangel during the special fairs arranged by the RAC for the Tlingit people. From the Tlingits, the Haida bought Chilkat blankets, moose skins, and copper plates. From the Tsimshians, they bought fish grease, and from the Kwakwaka'wakw, slaves.

An intensification of trade in Alaska during the Russian era resulted in an increased cultural exchange between Native groups. Because large hunting parties of Aleut and Kodiak Alutiiqs organized by the RAC visited Tlingit hunting areas, the Tlingits learned to use harpoons and other sea otter hunting tools. Thanks to the Tlingits, the Athapaskan groups became familiar with guns, fabric, and beads. In order to collect more furs, some Tlingits spent longer periods among the Athapaskans, staying in their settlements for two or three years. As a result, some Southern Tutchones, Tagish, and Tahltans even started to build Tlingit-style wooden log houses (Grinev 1986: 121).

Generally speaking, by the time the Russians sold Alaska, its aboriginal material culture represented a unique combination of traditional aboriginal elements that had remained more or less intact despite an intensive European influence, manufactured European goods, and traditional items that had been changed and modernized under the European influence. The introduction of new commodities and a strong demand for manufactured European goods prompted the establishment of long-distance trade and economic ties, which enhanced the cultural exchange.

Unfortunately, space limitations allow us only to outline the directions in which the topic of the cultural interaction between the Native peoples of Alaska and the Northwest Coast could be developed. In fact, it should be a subject for a separate in-depth research that is possible today thanks to the new data being discovered in archives and in newly published oral records. Thus it would be interesting to analyze the cultural interaction from the point of view of not only the Tlingit people, though they were certainly the core of this interaction, but also from the perspective of the other participating indigenous peoples of the region.

NOTES

1. This essay was translated from Russian and edited by Sergei Kan.
2. The Tlingits were not the only ones who traveled along the Northwest Coast. Records indicate that the Tsimshians also visited the Skeena and

the Stikine Rivers and the present-day Ketchikan and New Metlakatla areas to trade (Bradley 1992:7).
3. The Tlingit also acquired songs from their Alutiiq, Aleut, and Athapaskan neighbors to the north and the west—sometimes as gifts and sometimes as compensation for injuries and deaths [SK].

REFERENCES

Averkieva, Iuliia P. 1941. *Rabstvo u indeitsev Severnoy Ameriki* [Slavery among the Indians of North America]. Moscow: Izdatel'stvo Akademii Nauk SSSR.

———. 1960. K istorii obshestvennogo stroia u indeitsev severo-zapadnogo poberezh'ia Severnoi Ameriki (rod i potlatch u Tlingitov, Haida i Tsimshian) [On the history of the social organization of the Indians of Northwest Coast of North America (the clan and the potlatch among Tlingits, the Haidas, and the Tsimshians)]. Amerikanskii Ethnograficheskii Sbornik. *Trudy Instituta Etnografii* 58: 5–126.

Bradley, Joseph. 1992. *When the Aleuts Were on Tsimshian Territory: Tsimshian Oral Narratives.* Fairbanks: Tsimshian Chiefs.

Dauenhauer, Nora M., Richard Dauenhauer, and Lydia Black, eds. 2008. *Anóoshi Lingít Aaní Ka / Russians in Tlingit America: The Battles of Sitka, 1802 and 1804.* Seattle: University of Washington Press.

Davidov, Gavriil I. 1810. *Dvukratnoe puteshestvie v Ameriku morskih ofitserov Khvostova i Davidova, pisannoe sim poslednim* [Two voyages to America by the navy officers Kvostov and Davydov written by the latter]. Parts 1–2. St. Petersburg.

de Laguna, Frederica. 1972. *Under Mount Saint Elias: The History and Culture of the Yakutat Tlingit.* Washington: Smithsonian Institution Press.

Dzeniskevich, Galina I. 1987. *Atapaski Aliaski: Ocherki materialnoy i duhovnoy kulturi, konets XVIII–nachalo XIX v.* [Alaska Athapaskans: Material and spiritual culture of the late 18th–early 19th centuries]. Leningrad: Izdatelstvo Nauka.

Emmons, George. 1991. *The Tlingit Indians.* Seattle: University of Washington Press.

Gibson, James R. 1992. *Otter Skins, Boston Ships, and China Goods: The Maritime Fur Trade of the Northwest Coast, 1785–1841.* Seattle: University of Washington Press.

Golovnin, Vasilii M. 1861. "Zamechaniya V. M. Golovnina o Kamchatke i Russkoi Amerike v 1809, 1810 i 1811 godah" [V. M. Golovin's observations on Kamchatka and Russian America made in 1809, 1810, and 1811]. In *Materiali dlya istorii russkih zalesselniy po beregam Vostochnago okeana.* Prilozhenie k Morskomu sborniku, no. 2. St. Petersburg.

Grinev, Andrei V. 1986. "Tovaroobmen mezhdu indeitsami tlinkitami i atapaskami Skalistih gor v XIX veke" [Trade between the Tlingis and the

Mountain Athapaskans in the nineteenth century]. *Sovietskaya etnografiya* 5: 113-22.

———. 1991. *Indeitsi tlinkiti v period Russkoi Ameriki (1741-1867)* [Tlingit Indians during the period of Russian America (1741-1867)]. Novosibirsk: Izdatelstvo Nauka.

———. 1993. "Indeitsi eyaki v period Russkoy Ameriki" [Eyak Indians during the period of Russian America]. *Etnograficheskoe obozrenie* 5: 73-83.

———. 2005. *The Tlingit Indians in the Period of Russian America, 1741-1867.* Lincoln: University of Nebraska Press.

Hirschman, Erik T. 1999. "Empires in the Land of the Trikster: Russians, Tlingit, Pomo, and Americans on the Pacific Rim, 18th Century to 1910s." PhD diss., University of New Mexico.

Hope, Herbert. 2000. Kiksádi Survival March. In *Will the Time Ever Come? A Tlingit Source Book*, ed. Andy Hope III and Thomas Thornton, 48-79. Fairbanks: University of Alaska Press.

Gedeon, Ieromonakh. 1994. "Zapiski Ieromonaha Gedeona o pervom russkom krugosvetnom puteshestvii i Russkoi Amerike, 1803-1808" [Hieromonk Gedeon's notes on the first Russian round-the-world voyage and Russian America]. In *Russkaia Amerika po lichnym vpechatleniiam missionerov, zempleprokhodtsev, moriakov, issledovatelei i drugikh ochevidtsev.* Moscow: Mysl'.

Istomin, Aleksei A. 1985. "Russko-tlinkitskie kontakti (18-19 vv.)" [Russian-Tlingit contacts (18th-19th centuries)]. In *Istoricheskie sud'bi amerikanskih indeitsev*, 146-54. Moscow: Izdatel'stvo Nuka.

Kan, Sergei. 1999. *Memory Eternal: Tlingit Culture and Russian Orthodox Christianity through Two Centuries.* Seattle: University of Washington Press.

Khlebnikov, Kiril T. 1985. *Russkaya Amerika v «Zapiskah» Kirilla Khlebnikova* [Russian America in Kiril T. Khlebnikov's "Notes"]. Novo-Arkhangelsk [1832]. Vol. 1. Ed. V. A. Aleksandrov. Moscow: Izdatel'stro Nauka.

Korsun, Sergei A. 2002. "Sobranie I. G. Voznesenskogo po indeitsam Severo-Zapadnogo poberezhiya" [I. G. Voznesenskii's collection of Northwest Coast Indian artifacts]. In *Radlovskie chteniya. Materiali nauchnoy sessii*, 46-53. St. Petersburg: MAE RAN.

Liapunova, Roza G. 1975. *Ocherki po etnografii aleutov (konets 18 — pervaia polovina 19 v.)* [Essays on Aleut ethnography (end of the 18th-first of the 19th century]. Leningrad: Izdatelstvo Nauka.

———. 1987. *Aleuty: Ocherki etnicheskoy istorii* [Essays on the ethnic history of the Aleuts]. Leningrad: Izdatelstvo Nauka.

Lisianskii, Iurii F. 1977. *Puteshestvie vokrug sveta v 1803, 1804, 1805 i 1806 godah na korable "Neva"* [The voyage around the world in 1803, 1804, 1805, and 1806 on board the *Neva*]. Ed. A. I. Alekseev. Vladivostok.

Marsden, Susan, comp. 1992. *The Tsimshian, Trade, and North West Coast Economy: Tsimshian Oral Narratives.* Prince Rupert BC: School District 52.

Mishler, Craig, and William E. Simeone. 2004. *Han, People of the River: An Ethnography and Ethnohistory.* Fairbanks: University of Alaska Press.

Mobley, Charles. M. 1999. *The Ship Island Site: Tree-Ring Dating the Last Battle between the Stikine Tlingit and the Tsimshian.* Anchorage: Alaska Humanities Forum.

Nikolai, Igumen. 1994. "Iz zhurnala kenaiskogo missionera igumena Nikolaia" [From the journal of Igumen Nikolai, a Kenai missionary]. In *Russkaia Amerika po lichnym vpechatleniiam missionerov, zempleprokhodtsev, moriakov, issledovatelei i drugikh ochevidtsev,* 229–245.Moscow: Mysl'.

Okun, Semen B. 1939. *Rossiisko-Amerikanskaia Kompaniia* [The Russian-American Company]. Moscow and Leningrad: Nauka.

Olson, Ronald L. 1967. *Social Structure and Social Life of the Tlingit in Alaska.* University of California Anthropological Records 26.

Tikhmenev, Petr A. 1863. *Istoricheskoe obozrenie obrazovaniya Rossijsko-Amerikanskoy Kompanii i deistvii eiia do nastoyashego vremeni* [A historical overview of the establishment of the Russian-American Company and its operation until the present time]. Parts 1–2. St. Petersburg.

Vanderhoop, Evelyn. 2007. "Haida Traditional Woven Arts." Presentation at the Sharing Our Knowledge Conference of Tsimshian, Haida, and Tlingit Tribes and Clans. Sitka, March, 21–25, 2007.

Veniaminov, Ivan. 1840. *Zapiski ob ostrovah Unalashkinskogo otdela* [Notes on the islands of the Unalashka district]. Part 3. *Zapiski ob Atкinskikh aleutakh i koloshakh* [Notes of the Atka Aleuts and Kolosh]. St. Petersburg.

Wrangel (Vrangel), Ferdinand M. 1839. "Obitateli severo-zapadnih beregov Ameriki" [The inhabitants of the Northwest Coast of America]. *Syn Otechestva,* no. 7.

Zorin, A. V. 1994. "Rossisko-Amerikanskaia Kompaniya i tlingity v nachale XIX veka" [The Russian-American Company and the Tlingits in the beginning of the 19th century]. *Voprosi Istorii* 6: 170–73.

———. 2002. *Indeiskaya voina v Russkoy Amerike* [The Indian war in Russian America]. Kursk.

12

Relating Deep Genealogies, Traditional History, and Early Documentary Records in Southeast Alaska

Questions, Problems, and Progress

JUDITH BERMAN

As Galois and others have remarked, ethnography of the indigenous Northwest Coast did not begin until contact with Europeans and their descendants had been under way for a full century (Galois ed. 2004, 30; see also Quimby 1948, 247; Wike 1958, 1087). While the early European voyages of exploration to southeast Alaska resulted in only scattered encounters, after 1780, news of the fortunes to be made selling sea otter pelts in China brought an increasing number of visitors. By the 1790s, over a dozen English, Russian, American, and French merchant vessels were "coasting" in any given year, stopping at favored trading rendezvous for weeks and even months at a time. The seemingly early date of 1801, only two years after the establishment of the Russian colony at Redoubt Saint Michael (Old Sitka), in fact represents the peak of the maritime fur trade (Howay 1973; Gibson 1992, 299–310; Sturgis 1998, 18). In that year, over two dozen vessels competed to buy the otter skins offered by indigenous Alaskans. In one three-week period in 1801, nine ships arrived to trade in Tattiskey, a popular rendezvous in South Kaigani Harbor (AUP: 5/26/1801–6/17/1801).[1]

While southeast Alaskan Native life in the early contact era is still poorly known, there are at least two important sources of information that ethnohistorians have yet to exploit fully. The first of these is the body of manuscript records generated by fur traders and other early mercantile visitors. The surviving English-language logs and journals from the maritime trade number several dozen and are scattered in archives across the United States, Canada, and Great Britain. The records of the mostly land-based Hudson's Bay Company, which reached the vicinity of the Tlingit by the 1830s, include a series of journals from Fort Simpson, where many Tlingit went to trade, as well as the journals kept on company steamships that regularly traveled as far north as Klukwan. The contents vary widely from simple daily notations of weather and position to discursive entries replete with anecdotes of ship or post life and encounters with Native men and women. There are also French- and Russian-language sources from the period.

Many of these materials are familiar to historians of the fur trade who, however, have interested themselves primarily in its white rather than the indigenous participants (Gibson 1992; Howay 1973, 1940, 1941; Ogden 1932, 1941; Malloy 1998b, 2000). Of studies that have considered the interaction between Natives and visitors, most have focused on broad trends rather than the history of Native clans or communities (Fisher 1992; Gibson 1992; Howay 1925, 1942; Kan 1999; Malloy 1998a, 2000; Marsden and Galois 1995; Quimby 1948; Vaughan and Holm 1990; Wike 1958). At the same time, scholarly histories of individual Tlingit communities, still few in number, have tended to rely largely on published works (de Laguna 1960, 1972; Monteith 1998; though see Dauenhauer, Dauenhauer, and Black 2008; Langdon 1997; cf. Kan 1999). Manuscript sources have figured more prominently in ethnohistorical research outside of southeast Alaska (Acheson 1985, 1995; Grumet 1975).

The neglect of early documentary sources is doubtless due partly to the nature of the material. Basic information needed to translate the ship journals into accessible ethnohistorical data—for example, the locations of the trading sites mentioned in ship logs, or the clan and community affiliations of the Native people encountered there—can be difficult to extract. Moreover, the traders keeping the journals were often so culturally uninformed that they overlooked fundamental aspects of Native life—for example, clan organization—while devoting many pages of detail to such relatively peripheral cultural elements as the labret.

A second body of historical information offers promise in making the early manuscript materials more useful. This is indigenous historical tradition, a rich and elaborated domain in most Northwest Coast cultures (Berman 2004). Here the focus is precisely "that which is most important" to Native people (LSC: Shotridge to Gordon 1/7/1924). For the Tlingit, history provides the title to *at.óow* (tangible and intangible clan property), which occupies center stage in traditional culture;

at.óow in turn memorialize the lives and deeds of the deceased ancestors (Dauenhauer and Dauenhauer 1987, 25–28; Kan 1999, 6–7). To judge by the larger body of Tlingit historical tradition, however, cultural interest extends beyond the events explicitly connected with the origins of *at.óow*, and beyond the moral lessons dramatized in origin narratives, to the fine details of the past. A partial list of Tlingit cultural forms that express historical notions and transmit historical information would include genealogy, crest art, songs, names, and the genre that in Tlingit is traditionally called *sh kalneek*, narrative about the experiences of clan ancestors (de Laguna 1972, 210; R. Dauenhauer p.c. 4/17/2007). Performed "so that all people will know who they are," historical genres, taken as a whole, express a fundamental sense of rootedness in the past that anchors life and identity in the present day and provides a guide for the future yet to come (N. Dauenhauer 1995, 23).

Scholars have shown increasing interest in Northwest Coast historical traditions, primarily archaeologists exploring the precontact period (Acheson 1985, 1995; MacDonald 1984, 1989; Macdonald and Inglis 1981; MacDonald, Coupland, and Archer 1987; Wooley and Haggerty 1989), but also ethnohistorians using photography or material culture as primary data (Blackman 1981; MacDonald 1983; Weber 1985). A few writers have argued that the traditions are sufficient in themselves as a guide to the indigenous past (e.g., Marsden 2001; cf. Miller 1998). On the coast as a whole, there are as yet only a few extended attempts to combine oral traditions with primary textual sources (Acheson 1995; Dauenhauer et al. 2008; Marsden and Galois 1995). As Galois has written,

> [S]uch [traditional] narratives are important historical documents, [although] they call for careful analysis because they operate differently than do standard European accounts. . . . [W]hen viewed together, the narratives and journals inform each other and offer the possibility of a fuller and richer account of early encounters on the Northwest Coast. (Galois ed. 2004, 30)

The present essay is a progress report on research that attempts to combine traditional Tlingit forms of history with primary documentary sources in order to develop "a fuller and richer account" than we yet have of the early contact period. The goal is not simply to explore single encounters, or broader processes in the contact experience, but to enrich our understanding of the history of particular Tlingit *kwáans* (geographical divisions), communities, clans, and even individuals. The main focus of the project is the Taant'a Ḵwáan or Tongass division of the Tlingit, which has been one of the most poorly represented in ethnographic and historical literature (Monteith 1998, 34–36).

This essay deals primarily with the characterization of source materials, the methods of analysis, and some preliminary results, rather than with the underlying historiographic and epistemological questions. At the same time, the larger theoretical issues should be acknowledged. There is an ongoing, sometimes heated discussion in North American anthropology about the use of Native oral tradition as historical evidence (Echo-Hawk 2000; Whitely 2002). At one extreme in this argument, it has been asserted that indigenous forms of history should be taken as literal truth, in factual weight equal to or greater than the history of the dominant society (Deloria 1995). At the other extreme, it has been claimed that a nearly insurmountable incompatibility exists between the aims of oral historical traditions and "scientific historiography." This latter position considers oral tradition to be incapable of transmitting, except by pure chance, accurate records of historical fact (Mason 2006).

The present research adopts neither position. It assumes that there is an empirical substrate to human history—the devastating 1836 smallpox epidemic on the Northwest Coast being one such raw irreducible—and that through careful evaluation and interpretation of evidence this substrate may be partly discoverable. But it also assumes that the relationship between "what really happened" and the human perception and interpretation of it is always complex and always beset with epistemological uncertainties.

The overall perspective adopted here is that of the ethnography of communication (Hymes 1964). This viewpoint does not, at least in principle, privilege written over oral speech as far as the capacity to retain accurate historical information is concerned. In this view, all verbal representations of past events, whether indigenous oral traditions or the visitors' written records, whether eyewitness accounts or secondary interpretations made centuries later by academics, are equally examples of culturally constituted genres of speech. Trading journals, clan histories, and scholarly articles alike are communications addressed by a speaker to an audience, are equally contingent on the social situation in which they emerge, and are equally shaped by cultural proprieties regarding form, content, and use. Such communications, as

Boas said about lexicon and myth, embody the "chief interests" of the speakers (1911, 22; 1909, 309). Whether oral or written, all genres of expressive behavior whose main content is past events have embedded in them cultural notions about history, which is to say notions about the group's origins, purpose, and destiny. Historical speech, as Cruikshank has argued, always invokes a social order (1998, 92–94; cf. de Laguna 1972, 211).

Nor is written speech necessarily less susceptible than oral to memory lapses, unintended factual and verbal errors, purposeful omissions, or the record-maker's idiosyncrasies. The last-mentioned point is exemplified, where written documents are concerned, by two very different eyewitness accounts of the 1799 execution of the Haida war leader Scotsi (Jackman ed. 1978, 95–101; Sturgis 1998, 46–49; see also Malloy 1998b, 119–22, 149n29). Still, the differences should not be discounted. The journal keepers' observations were impeded by their ignorance of, and often lack of interest in, local culture and history. At the same time, their writings were largely records of personal experience and most often generated within days of the events they describe. Traditional historical narratives about this period, on the other hand, were recorded after an interval of a hundred or more years. During that time they were shaped in additional—and perhaps unknowable—ways by communal and individual processes of performance and transmission.

A further assumption adopted here is that the relationship of either indigenous or visitors' accounts to "what really happened" should not be assumed in advance, but should be investigated. The present research is such an examination. The following section will first discuss traditional historical materials, as they are less well known than the documentary sources, and then outline methods of evaluation. The third and final section will draw on both traditional and early documentary sources to sketch what can so far be said about the Tant'a K̲wáan during the early decades of contact.

Deep Genealogies, Succession Lists, and Narrative History

Of all the evidence of traditional Tlingit interest in historical detail, perhaps none is more telling than two bodies of extensive genealogical data recorded in the 1910s, 1920s, and 1930s. Both originate with Tlingit who were born in the nineteenth century, and both reach ten or more generations above them into the past. These are, first, a set of hand-drawn charts and accompanying notes in the papers of Ron-

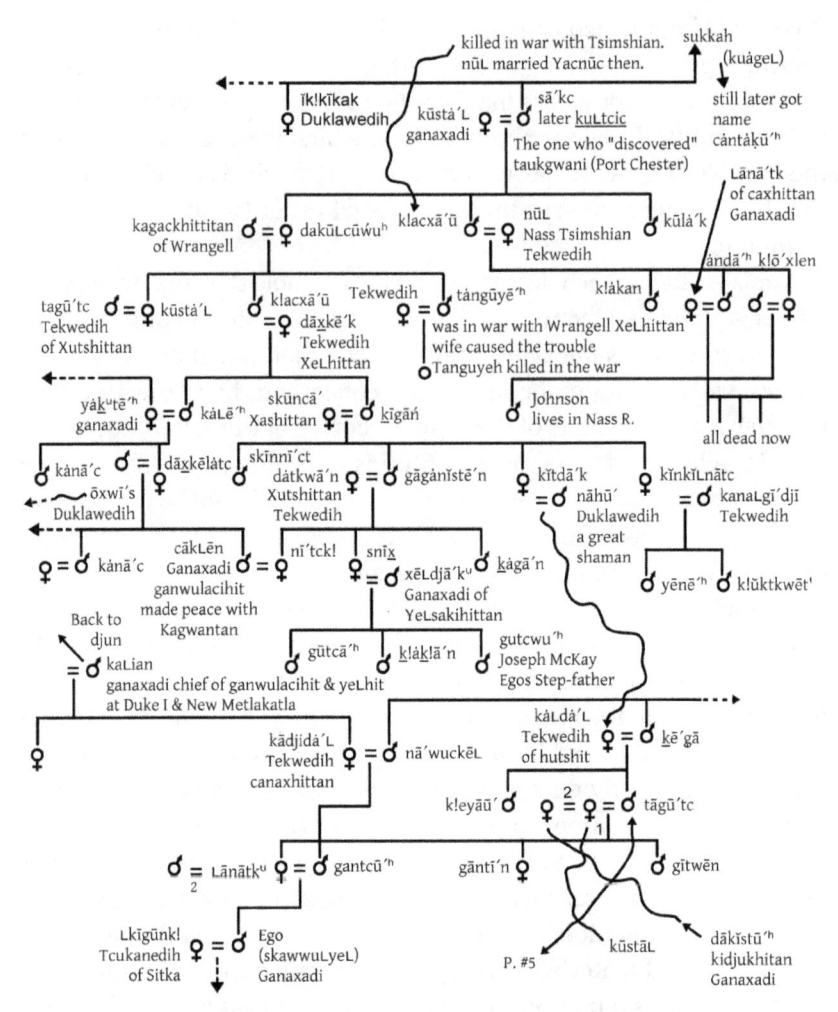

Fig. 12.1 Transcribed from a page of the George McKay genealogy (ROP). Dotted lines indicate continuation of the original chart. Olson made one or more major errors on this page; for example, his mother's parents "kūtsāL" and "tāgū'tc" are shown twice, near the bottom right and on the left toward the top.

ald Olson (ROP), and second, the genealogical files of Louis Shotridge (UEN, SMR, AHL).

Olson, a university-based anthropologist, conducted his primary fieldwork in southeast Alaska in 1933 and 1934, during which time he was adopted by, and received a name from, Cora or Clara Benson (Deinḵul.át) of the Klukwan G̱aanax̱teidí. He obtained substantial genealogical information from her as well as from Mrs. Don Cameron (Yandoosgéit),

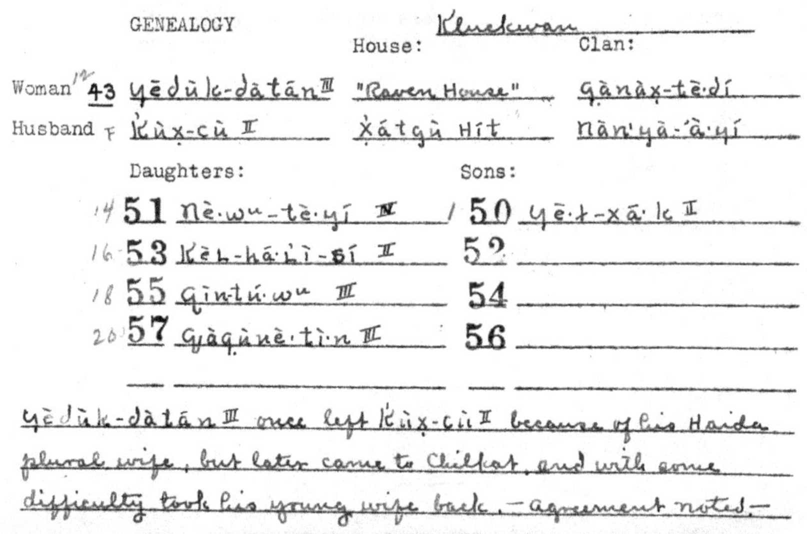

```
          GENEALOGY                     Klukwan
                      House:  _____  Clan: _____
Woman 12 43  yēdŭk-dàtàn Ⅲ   "Raven House"    gànàx-tēdí
Husband ғ    k̂ŭx-cù Ⅰ       x̂átgù Hit       nàn·yà-'à·yí
          Daughters:                    Sons:
       14 51 nè·wᵘ-tè·yí Ⅳ       / 50  yē·t-xā·k Ⅰ
       16 53 k̂èʟ-hà·ʟ̇ì-sí Ⅰ       52
       18 55 g̊inlŭ·wᵘ Ⅲ            54
       20 57 g̊àg̊ùnè·tì·n Ⅲ         56
```

yēdŭk-dàtàn Ⅲ once left k̂ŭx-cù Ⅰ because of his Haida plural wife, but later came to Chilkat, and with some difficulty took his young wife back. — agreement noted —

Fig. 12.2 Louis Shotridge genealogy card (UEN). Courtesy of the Penn Museum.

a Sitka Kiks.ádi; Charley Jones of Wrangell, who became Shéiksh VII of the Stikine Naanyaa.aayí; and George McKay (Skawoolyeil), a Taant'a Ḵwáan Gaanax̱.ádi.

The four genealogies recorded by Olson vary considerably in time depth and collateral spread. Those from Benson and McKay exhibit the greatest generational depth and are the ones that will be discussed here. McKay's Taant'a Ḵwáan genealogy reaches eleven generations above him to the Gaanax̱.ádi ancestress Joon, while the charts produced in sessions with Benson ascend an extraordinary nineteen generations before her own. Benson, as Olson wrote, "was able to give me accurate information on many hundreds of persons, not only from her own clan and tribe but also from tribes as distant as the Stikine" (1967, vi).

Figure 12.1 reproduces a page from the original McKay genealogy, showing in rather tangled form the four or five generations that preceded his own. As can be seen, Olson recorded it onto pages torn out of his field notebooks. Some of the genealogies, Benson's among them, have notations and other evidence that Olson discussed them afterward with his sources; McKay's does not. It appears to contain at least one major error, as generational disparities suggest that a large section is linked incorrectly to the rest.

The second body of deep genealogical information is that collected by Louis Shotridge (Stuwooḵáa), a Kaagwaantaan from Klukwan (Chilkat)

GENEALOGY OF THE KLUCKWAN RAVEN HOUSE FAMILY

Woman   Husband

Nùw^u-tè·yí (1)   A Djlnáx Tè·q^uè·dí man

   Daughters: Sons:

   Yè·dùk-dàtán (3)

Yè·dùk-dàtán (3)   Qùdè-wòàà·t (2)

   Nùw^u-tè·yí (5)

Nùw^u-tè·yí (5)   Tùx-sà·yí (4)

   Ctùyì·s-dù'ù (7)

Nùw^u-tè·yí (5)   x̣àyàx-qù·stí (6)

   Yé·t-kàtì·s (9)
          -No. 5 s second marriage.-

Yè·t-kàtì·s (9)   Dà·q^u-tánk (8)

   Yè·dùk-dàtán (11)

Yè·dùk-dàtán (11)   Kùx-où (10)

   Nùw^u-tè·yí (13   Yè·ì-xá·k (12)
   Kèʟ-há·ʟì-sí (15)
   Qìn-tú·w^u (17)
   Qàxùnè·tì·n (19)

Nùw^u-tè·yí (13)   Yì·s-yát (14)

   Yè·t-kàtì·s (21)   Yè·t-sú·w^u (16)
   À·n-qìngé (23)   À·n-àhá·o (18)

Upon the death of her husband Nùw^u-tè·yí (13) married
again to a man whos name is not obtained, this man
died also, and finally Nùw^u-tè·yí (13) was married to
Qàn-kìdá (20)

Fig. 12.3 First page of Shotridge chart of Raven House matriline, to Nuwuteiyí and Yisyát, the latter deceased by 1799 (SMR). Courtesy of the Penn Museum.

employed for many years by the University of Pennsylvania Museum. From 1915 to at least 1926 and likely later, Shotridge recorded genealogical data from a number of individuals, also, it seems, primarily in informal interviews (Shotridge 1917). This information he arranged on file cards, each of which listed a married couple, their respective clans, house groups, communities of origin, and their children.

Most of Shotridge's papers were destroyed after his death, so the original extent of his genealogical files cannot be gauged. The surviving cards refer to lineages from Klukwan, Klawock, and to some extent Sitka (UEN, AHL). Shotridge also supplied information about his own family tree, perhaps out of these files, to another anthropologist, Theresa Durlach, who published it in her monograph on Tlingit, Tsimshian, and Haida kinship (Durlach 1928). And he made some attempt to systematize his data into formal lineages. Figure 12.3 shows seven generations of the ranking line of descent within the Raven and Whale Houses of the Klukwan Gaanaxteidí (SMR). It is organized around the matriline of women who form its genealogical core.

In contrast, Olson's more spontaneous, ad hoc trees may provide a better picture of how his sources recalled genealogical data. Olson's charts depict networks of people connected by blood and marriage rather than organized by clan membership. That is, clan and house group affiliations are noted on the charts, but kin connections with even one's fellow house group members are as likely to be shown according to links through fathers—across clan boundaries—as through the maternal line.

The way in which the descendants of S'eiltín, the so-called Bride of Tongass, appear on Olson's charts exemplifies this cognatic aspect. S'eiltín was, according to McKay, the mother of two Taant'a Kwáan Gaanax.ádi clan leaders of the early nineteenth century, Kalian and Santagáw. She moreover figures in the histories of clans other than her own and is mentioned as far north as Yakutat (Olson 1967, 84-85; Shotridge 1929; Swanton 1909, 401; de Laguna 1972, 1226). McKay, from the same clan and lineage, did not detail his connection to her through the line of matrilineal descent within Drifted Ashore House, but rather via the children first of S'eiltín's eldest son, Kalian, through the Teikweidí Valley House, and second, of her youngest son, Santagaw, through the Dakl'aweidí Killer Whale House. McKay certainly possessed genealogical knowledge that is not represented in Olson's chart, but which does appear in other information he supplied to Olson. He may well have known how his matrilineal forebears connected him to S'eiltín. One

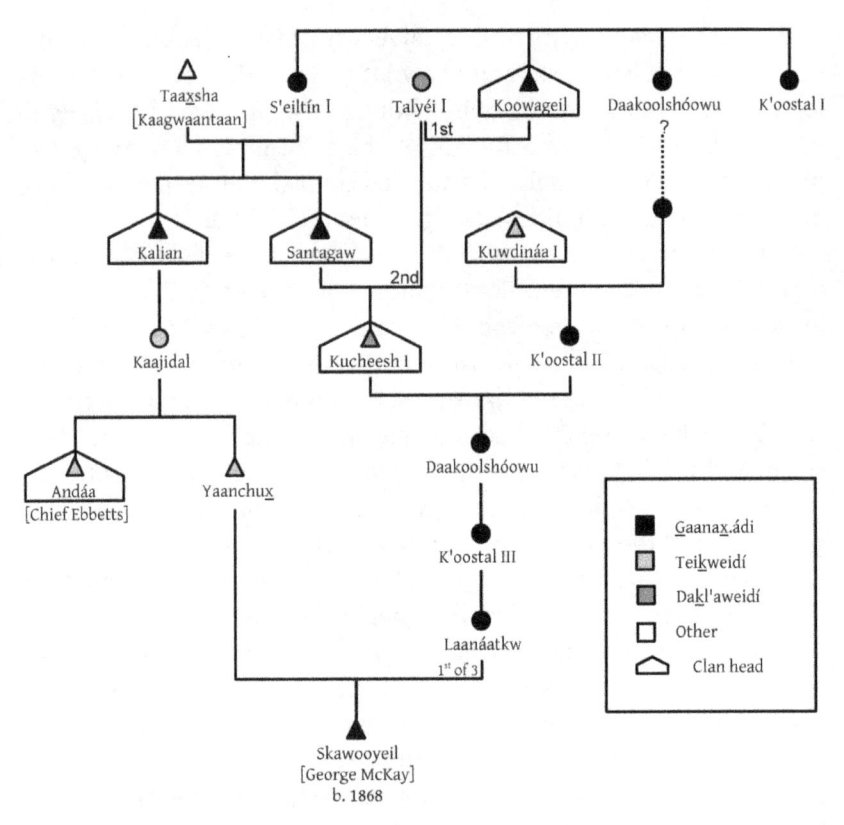

Fig. 12.4 McKay's descent from S'eiltín I and Taaxsha.

can speculate that the links in Olson's chart were those uppermost in his mind, and he or Olson never got around to adding information that lay deeper in his memory.

McKay's multiple connections to S'eiltín illustrate another characteristic of Olson's charts: the way important ancestors serve as reference points. A second example, from Cora Benson, is Nuwuteiyí. Though not figuring prominently in narrative history,[2] she was a pivotal figure in genealogy: the daughter of K'uxshóo II, head of the Stikine Naanyaa.aayí; the wife of Yisyát (or Yeesyát) I, leader of the Klukwan Kaagwaantaan; and in turn the sister and mother of two successive Gaanaxteidí clan heads, Yeilxáak and X'eitsóowu. All these men do figure in narrative tradition. On Olson's charts, Nuwuteiyí appears four times, and he and Benson followed three different lines of descent to the present.

Two other forms of traditional history in which genealogical information is embedded are the succession list of house masters or clan leaders and narrative history. Again, a fair number of examples have been recorded for both types whose subjects—as genealogy and other evidence suggest—reach back to the fur trade era and earlier.

There are quite a few more succession lists than genealogies available for the period before 1880. These lists provide little if any information about how the men in them were related to each other, outside of common membership in their house group; here, continuity of the position is the focus rather than the exact genealogical connection. Such lists are nevertheless valuable for working with fur trade documents, because clan leaders are the individuals whom early visitors mention most frequently in the records they left behind.

One such list, from Cora Benson, gives the succession of Gaanaxteidí leaders who, from the time of its founding, rebuilt the Klukwan Raven House: Kakáayi, Goos', Gunaneistí, Goonaxát,[3] Yeilgooxú, Kindaxgóosh, and Yeilxáak (Olson 1967, 8). This particular Yeilxáak, as will be discussed below, appears to be the Klukwan notable of the name who overlaps with the first decades of the fur trade.

A third traditional source of genealogical information is the narrative genre called in Tlingit *sh kalneek*, mentioned above. These narratives tell of the experiences of clan ancestors during the era that followed the end of the myth times and continue to the present day (de Laguna 1972, 210; R. Dauenhauer p.c. 4/17/2007; see also Olson 1967, vi). Available sources of Tlingit historical narrative include hundreds of pages recorded by Olson (1967, ROP), Shotridge (1919a, 1920, 1928, 1929, UEN), John R. Swanton (1909), Frederica de Laguna (1972), Edward Keithahn (1940), William Paul (1971), Dauenhauer and Dauenhauer (1987), and Dauenhauer et al. (2008) among others.

Some historical narratives contain an embedded succession list. While these often provide more genealogical information than unadorned lists, the information is rarely complete there, either. One example is the Naanyaa.aayí Dogfish House succession found in "The Authentic History of Shakes Island and Clan," which Charley Jones related to Keithahn (1940). Succession lists can similarly be assembled out of narrative and other materials for the ranking lineages of the Klukwan Gaanaxteidí and Kaagwaantaan—respectively, the lineages to which Benson and Shotridge belonged (see figures 12.5 and 12.6). On the Gaanaxteidí side, to the Raven House masters given above can be added those of Raven's daughter house, Whale: Xeits'óowu (its founder), Shkidlakáa, and Yeilgooxú (George Shotridge, father of Louis; UEN). The

Relating Deep Genealogies 197

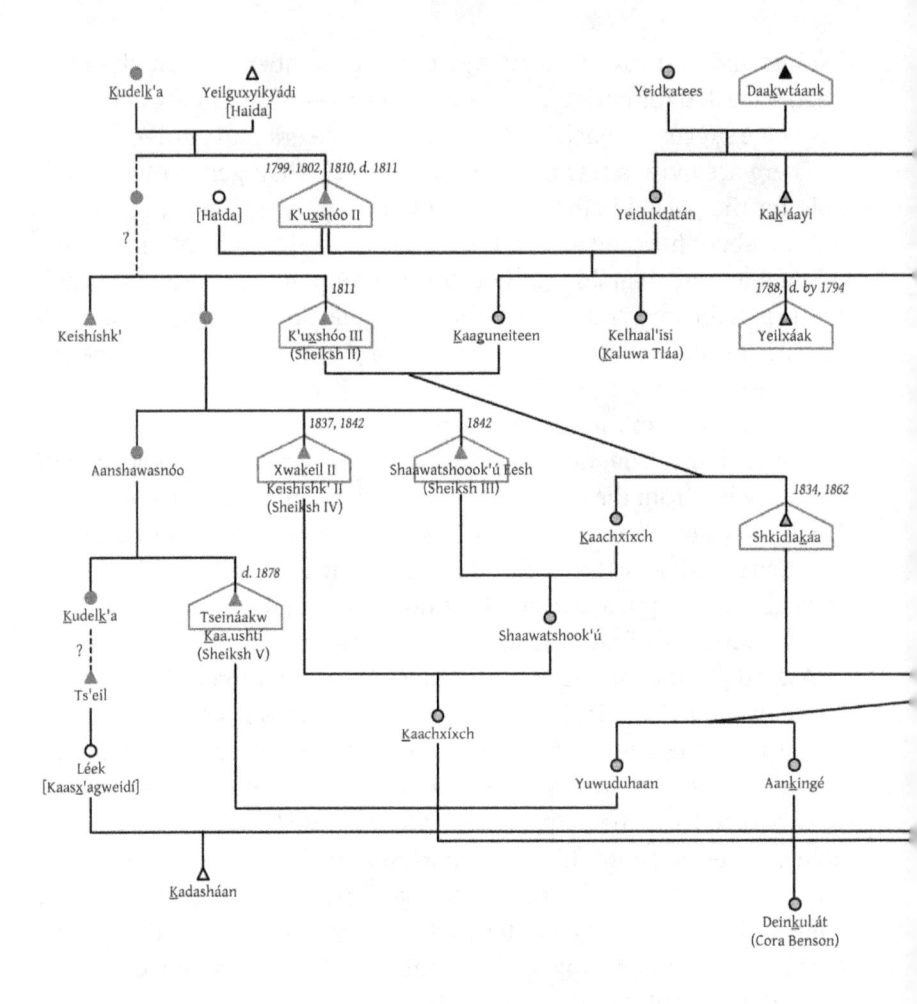

Fig. 12.5 Intermarried lineages of the Klukwan Kaagwaantaan and G̲aanax̲teidí, and the Stikine Naanyaa.aayi, ca. 1700–1870, with some dates of mentions in historical documents. Genealogical information is from ROP, UEN, AHL, Olson 1967, Emmons 1991, and Keithahn 1949. Not all known siblings or marriages are shown and birth order is not indicated.

known leaders of the Klukwan Kaagwaantaan begin with Daak̲wtáank, the founder of Bear House. Daak̲wtáank was followed by Yisyát I, K̲aa.ushtí, Laatx̲íchx̲ (Shartridge), and Yisyát II (Shotridge 1919a, 43–45; UEN, "History"; AHL). The larger body of genealogical and narrative materials indicates that other men filled the role of clan leader in both clans; these names seem to represent only those who rebuilt the lineage house or dedicated a new one.

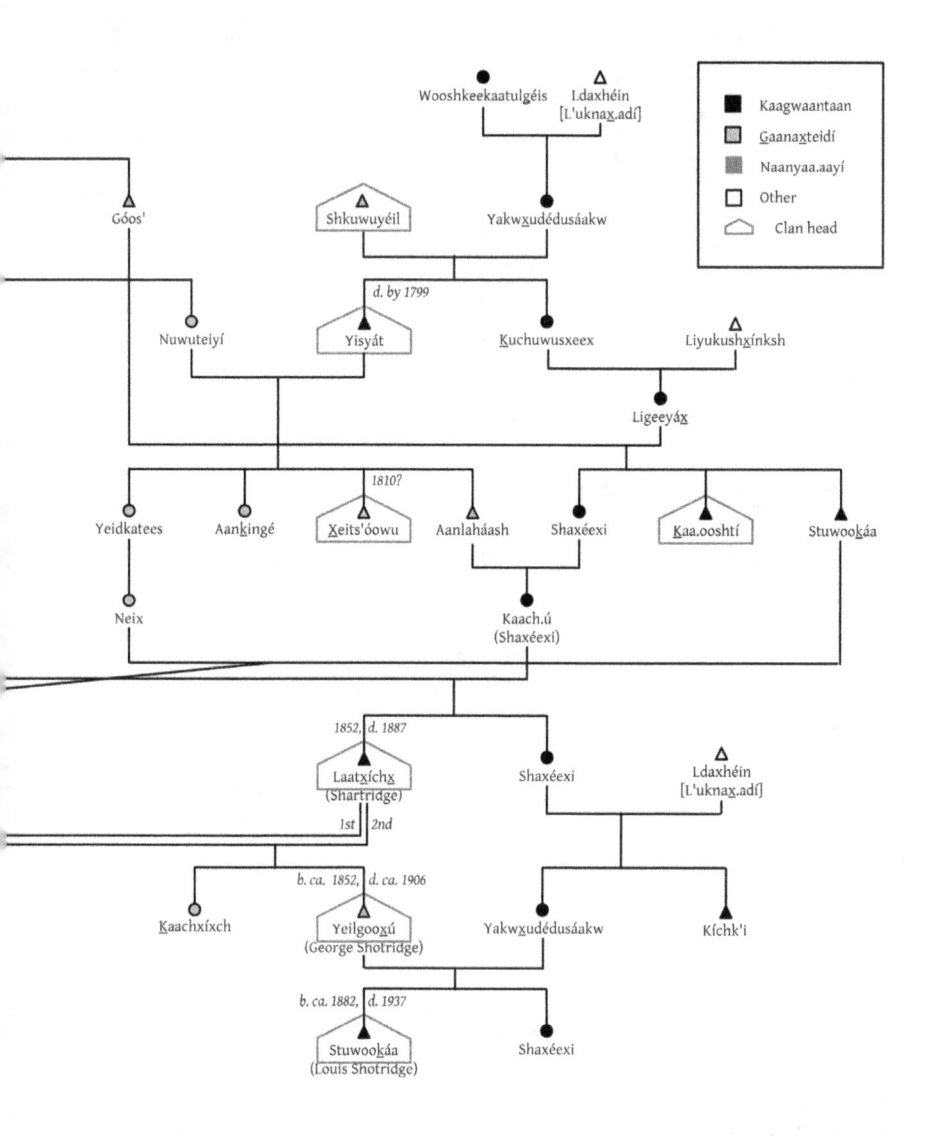

Traditional narrative history might seem to be the logical place to begin a comparison of indigenous and visitors' sources, but there are several reasons for starting with genealogy and succession lists. First, in Tlingit culture, genealogical knowledge forms the social, moral, and temporal armature for the other historical genres. As Nora Dauenhauer has said, genealogy "holds the system together" (1995, 23). Among other functions, genealogy binds what might otherwise be isolated episodes of narrative into a larger framework of history and time that connects ancestors to each other and provides continuity with the present.

Relating Deep Genealogies 199

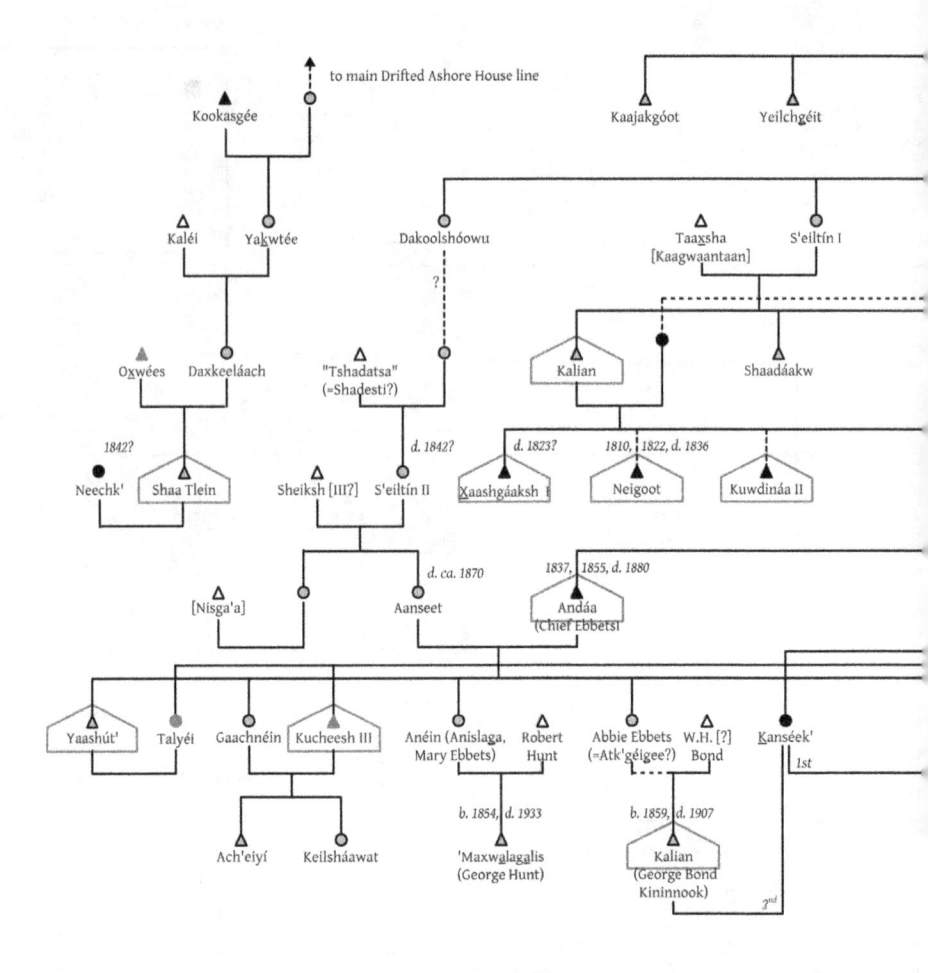

Fig. 12.6 Intermarried lineages of the Taant'a Ḵwáan Gaanax̱.ádi, Teiḵweidí, and Daḵl'aweidí, ca. 1730–1870, with some dates of mentions in historical documents. Genealogical information is from ROP, Olson 1967, Emma Williams, Esther Shea, Mary Jones, and Ken Lea's "Tlingit, Haida, and Tsimshian Genealogy of Alaska" at wc.rootsweb.ancestry.com. Not all known siblings or marriages are shown, and birth order is not indicated.

Second, genealogy and succession lists are one area where indigenous and outsider sources can directly supplement each other. The depth of available genealogical materials suggests they reach back to the fur trade era, and names occurring at this depth do, in fact, appear in traders' logs and journals. There is often evidence—if sometimes only circumstantial—that allows us to conclude that the two sets of sources refer to the same individual. With documentary sources as with traditional narratives, genealogy can provide a broader context—in this case of kinship and clan and community affiliation—for isolated references to Tlingit individuals. At the same time, log and journal entries are almost always linked to calendar dates, allowing the calibration of important events in Native biography and history—marriages, deaths, successions, conflicts, peacemaking, and the establishment of new communities—to the European calendar.

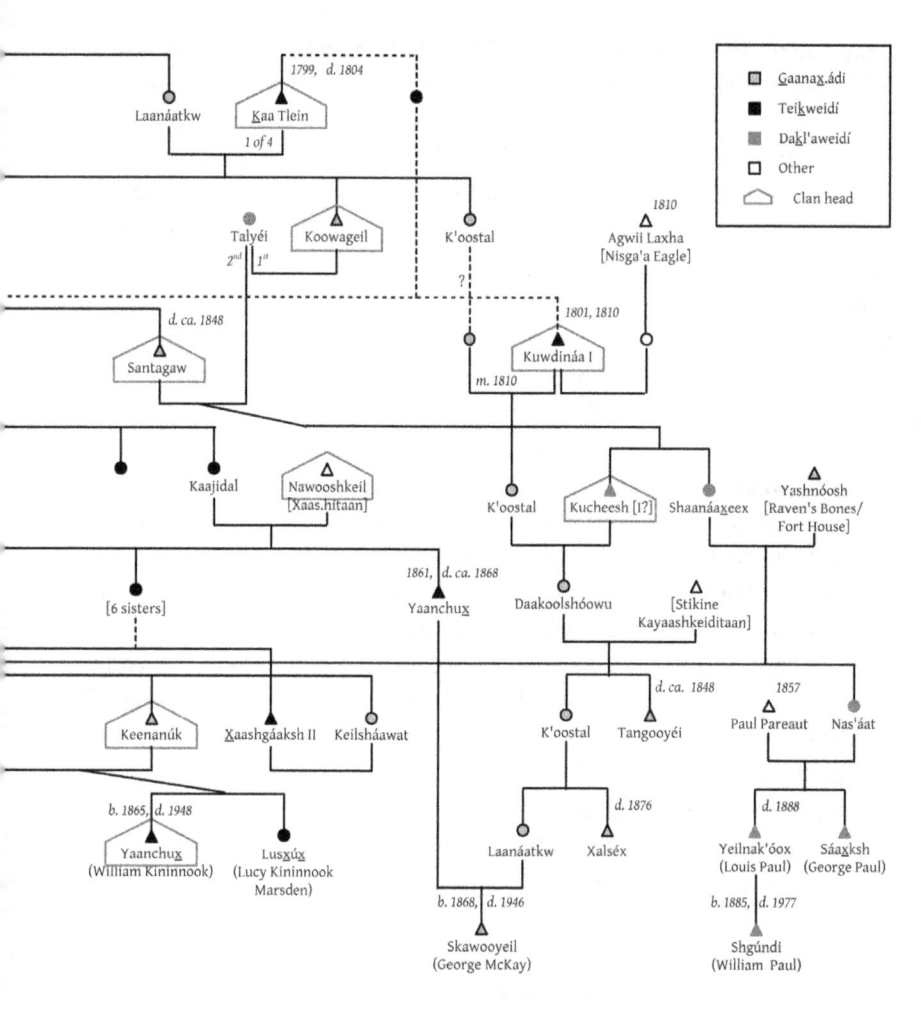

Third, genealogy seems to be the more stable form. When we compare narrative versus genealogical information originating from individuals of different clans, the genealogical place of a given ancestor changes little, while the events in which the ancestor is said to be involved can differ considerably. The variability of narrative history stems partly

Relating Deep Genealogies 201

from the nature of oral narrative. As with other narrative genres elsewhere in Native North America, a Tlingit history can carry a range of meanings, and individual narrators can shape performance according to the audience, situation, and the point they wish to make—in the process omitting some elements and emphasizing others (Cruikshank 1998, 25–44; Garfield and Forrest 1961, 12). Beyond this, however, Tlingit narrative history is influenced by the segmentary nature of traditional Tlingit social organization. Each clan possesses its own body of narrative (de Laguna 1972, 211). As a consequence, the larger body of Tlingit history is multivocal and, where conflict between clans is concerned, even *Rashomon*-like.[4]

Tlingit genealogy, on the other hand, deals with relationships *between* matrilineal clans: links between husbands and wives, fathers and children, grandparents and grandchildren. Part of the cultural importance of Tlingit genealogy may be the unifying function of cognatic networks, and descendants in a range of clans may therefore have an equal stake in maintaining the genealogical position of common ancestors. This may lie behind the traditional wide distribution of at least basic genealogical information. High-ranking individuals, meanwhile, "would know all about" the ancestry of those from other towns (Olson 1967, 12; de Laguna 1972, 465–66).

To evaluate the reliability of the Olson and Shotridge genealogical data, we will look first at the question of internal consistency and then at the question of how well these data correlate with documentary sources.

Olson's various charts in and of themselves exhibit a high degree of internal consistency. As he commented with regard to Cora Benson, "The genealogical charts I constructed [in our sessions] . . . meshed perfectly with data I obtained from other informants" (1967, vi). There is also substantial agreement between the Olson and Shotridge materials, and not just those dealing with Klukwan. The already mentioned Gaanax̱.ádi ancestress S'eiltín serves as an example here as well. Both Shotridge and McKay note her marriage to Taax̱sha (or Taax̱shaa), a Kaagwaantaan from Icy Strait in the north, and both sources also supply narrative history about the wedding. Shotridge first heard a story about it in Sitka, but went on to obtain versions from several "geographic divisions" (Shotridge 1929, 142), while McKay, it seems, heard the story from his Tongass Gaanax̱.ádi elders (Olson 1967, 84; see also Swanton 1909, 401, de Laguna 1972, 1226).[5]

Conflicts and ambiguities are not absent from the material. A major transcriptional error in McKay's chart has been mentioned. More often, inconsistencies point to the presence of error without it always being possible to locate where the error lies. For example, Shotridge and Benson differ as to the identity of their ancestor Shkuwuyeil's L'uknax̲.ádi father-in-law. Shotridge gives Yeil Tlein; Benson, Ldaxhéin; both men figure in histories from their era (Durlach 1928, 173, Shotridge 1919, 53, ROP; see figure 12.5). In this instance, an independent third source agrees with Benson's version (Swanton 1909, 161–65). The source was K̲adasháan (1909, 3), a Stikine Kaasx̲'agweidí but descended, like Shotridge and Benson, from the individuals in question.

In other instances, it is difficult to ascertain whether an apparent inconsistency actually *is* an error—whether by transcriber or source—or the result of an ambiguous reference. The tendency of names to repeat within a lineage, and of high-ranking individuals to bear multiple names, perhaps causes the most frequent interpretive difficulties. The Dogfish House of the Stikine Naanyaa.aayí presents perhaps the most extreme example, where something like six successive house masters, depending on the source, used the name Shéiksh over the course of the nineteenth century. Each of these men moreover bore at least one other name prior to acceding to the position (AHL). Another cause of ambiguity is the appearance of English kin terms like "nephew" and "brother" without additional details. Both can be used by Tlingit to refer to parallel (clan) cousins.

A second measure of reliability is the degree of correspondence between the genealogical materials and documentary sources. The succession lists given above for the Klukwan G̲aanax̲teidí Raven/Whale and Kaagwaantaan Killer Whale/Fin Houses supply an illustration.

The correlations that can be made with the greatest certainty are the most recent names on the lists. Louis Shotridge's father, George (Yeilgoox̲ú), who died ca. 1907 before completing his rebuilding of Whale House, was a good friend of Emmons and is also mentioned by missionaries and scientists visiting Klukwan as early as 1881. Yeilgoox̲ú at that time was about twenty-five years old (Willard 1995, 196, Krause 1956, 93, 99; Krause and Krause 1993, 133–42, 145, 153–54, 156; LSC: LS/GBG 8/28/1906).

The same observers also knew Yeilgoox̲ú's father of the opposite moiety, Laatx̲íchx̲, head of the Kaagwaantaan Fin House, whom they called Shartridge and variants.[6] In the 1880s, Laatx̲íchx̲ was the most

Relating Deep Genealogies 203

powerful clan leader in Klukwan (Willard 1995, 28, 41; Krause 1967. 93; Krause and Krause 1993, 140–41, UEN, "Organization"). Laatxíchx's death date was recorded on his tombstone as 1887, when he was said to have been seventy (Emmons 1991, 39, 263, 278).[7]

In her memory census of Klukwan, Cora Benson enumerated Laatxíchx first in the Kaagwaantaan Fin House and his father, Shkidlakáa, first in the Gaanaxteidí Whale House (Olson 1967, 8). Remembered by Native sources as a noted artist, Shkidlakáa's death date is at present unknown, but he is almost certainly the "Skitlakah" who figures as the most prominent man at Klukwan in the 1859–1860 trade journal of the *Labouchere* (LTJ 9/18/1859 et seq.; Shotridge and Shotridge 1913, 84; Emmons 1916, 23–24; 1991, 62). Emmons also cites an 1834 expedition in which Shkidlakáa guided Russian visitors up the Chilkat River (1991, 62).

Still moving backwards in time, Robert Kemp of the *Otter* named "Ziahduce & Kataneker" as "the 2 principle Chiefs" of the Chilkat in 1810 (RKO 10/10/1810). Interpretation of these names is less certain, but "Ziahduce" makes the most sense as an attempt to render the sounds, difficult for the English speaker's ear, of X'etidus'óowu (the long form of the name X'eits'óowu). He was a parallel cousin of Shidlakáa's and head of the Gaanaxteidí before him. Emmons, like Shotridge and Olson, names X'eits'óowu as the founder of Whale House and commissioner of its famous posts (Emmons 1916, 18; 1991, 62; UEN, "History"; Olson 1967, 8, 38; AHL). One narrative features both X'eitsóowu and his father, Yisyát, as leaders of their respective clans, suggesting, via sources given below, that X'eitsóowu became clan leader between 1794 and 1799 (UEN, "Warfare"). "Kataneker" resembles Kudenaháa, a high-ranking Kaagwaantaan name occurring elsewhere in the Killer Whale–Fin House lineage (ROP; UEN; Emmons 1907b, 7). He may be the unknown Killer Whale House man who immediately succeeded Yisyát I as head of the Kaagwaantaan, and who may also have been the second husband of Yisyát's widow, Nuwuteiyí.[8]

Eleven years earlier, in 1799, Samuel Curson recorded the death of "Eastgut . . . who resided at Chilcart" and who until that event had been "the oldest chief on the coast" (Jackman ed. 1978, 60). Via the y/gamma alternation found in older varieties of Tlingit, "Eastgut" is likely a rendering of Yisyát (or Yeesyát), the Kaagwaantaan clan leader whom genealogy gives as X'eits'óowu's father.[9]

Finally, in 1788, Russian explorers encountered the powerful "toion [chief] Il'khak" of Chilkat. This man was deceased by 1794 (Shelikov

1991, 94–98; Grinev 1995, 104–5).[10] "Il'khak" would be Yeilxáak, Yisyát's brother-in-law and the G̲aana̲xteidí leader before X̲'eitsóowu. Both Yisyát and Yeilxáak are important figures in narrative history (UEN, "Textile"; Olson 1967, 43, 19; de Laguna 1972, 134–35; Swanton 1909, 163–64; Dauenhauer and Dauenhauer 1987, 436–39).

Figures 12.5 and 12.6 represent two compilations of genealogical information, both still works in progress. Figure 12.5 shows a part of the two Klukwan lineages referred to above, together with the Stikine Naanyaa.aayí Dogfish House (X̲'átgu Hít) masters, with whom they were closely intermarried. Figure 12.6 lays out parts of two Taant'a K̲wáan lineages, the Teik̲weidí Valley House and G̲aana̲x.ádi Drifted Ashore House. Both figures include only people born between approximately 1700 and 1870—with the exception of Louis Shotridge himself, who was born ca. 1882 (TWC). The information comes primarily from Shotridge and Olson, with supplemental data from Keithahn (1940) and archival sources; with the exception of Shotridge's material, the spelling of names is often approximated from less than optimal transcriptions. The dates refer to mentions of the individual in historical documents. Substantial additional genealogical information, especially regarding Taant'a K̲wáan names, was also generously provided to me by the late Taant'a K̲wáan Teik̲weidí elders Emma Williams (Kalnaakw) and Esther Shea (Talyéi), as well as Mary Jones (Jeidgei), Saanya Neix̲.ádi, and a grandchild of Teik̲weidí.

Ambiguities or inconsistencies have been treated as follows. First, all other things being equal, the source nearer in social space is weighted as more reliable, on the assumption that the names and clan and house affiliations of one's immediate relatives would be remembered with greater accuracy than those of a family in a distant community to which one has fewer ties. A second principle is that, all other things being equal, a source closer in time to the genealogical datum is more likely to be accurate than one more removed in time. Vansina has discussed the way that, in oral tradition, the quantity of traditional history tapers off the further back in time the narrative is set. Eventually, for every oral-historical tradition, the "stream of tradition becomes a trickle," with time depth more or less determined by social structure (1985, 167–69, 197). While Shotridge, Olson, Keithahn, and others recorded historical information that extends deeper into the past—in Benson's case *much* deeper—all the Tlingit genealogical data are more detailed within a range of about two hundred years prior to collection.

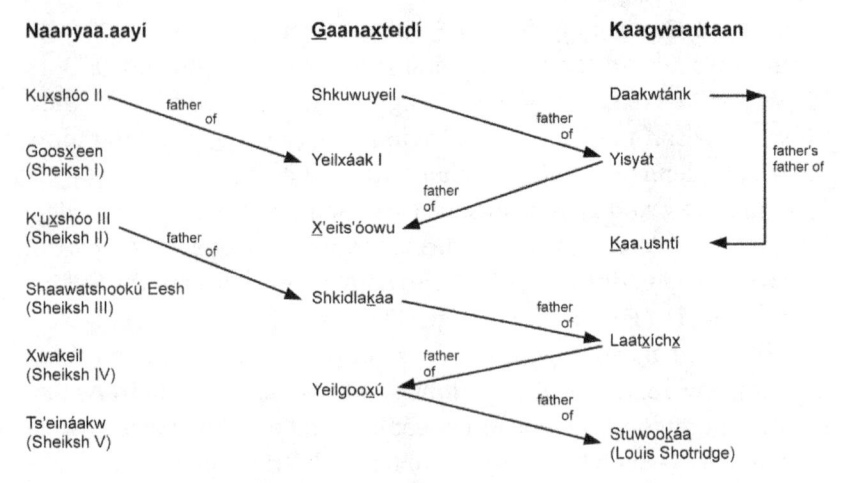

Naanyaa.aayí	Gaanaxteidí	Kaagwaantaan
Kuxshóo II —father of→	Shkuwuyeil —father of→	Daakwtánk →father's father of
Goosx'een (Sheiksh I)	Yeilxáak I ←—	Yisyát
K'uxshóo III (Sheiksh II) —father of→	X'eits'óowu —father of↗	Kaa.ushtí ←
Shaawatshookú Eesh (Sheiksh III)	Shkidlakáa —father of→	
Xwakeil (Sheiksh IV)	Yeilgooxú —father of↗	Laatxíchx
Ts'eináakw (Sheiksh V)		Stuwookáa (Louis Shotridge)

Fig. 12.7 Father-son relationships of the leading lineages of the Stikine Naanyaa. aayí and the Klukwan Gaanaxteidí and Kaagwaantaan clans, ca. 1750–1900.

A third method of resolving questions has been to examine siblings, spouses, and other biographical details more closely. Several placements within the Stikine Dogfish House lineage, for example, are clarified via the marriages with the Klukwan Raven House, for which more systematic information is available.

The Olson and Shotridge genealogical materials are of considerable interest in and of themselves, with the potential to provide insight into a number of social processes in the precontact and early contact periods. There is no space here to do more than mention one or two points. First, the remarkable consistency in lineage alliances between the Gaanaxteidí and their Eagle-moiety opposites, the Naanyaa.aayí and Kaagwaantaan, is echoed but not completely matched in the Taant'a Kwáan chart, which shows a greater variety of affinal choices. The Gaanax.ádi Drifted Ashore House married into the Teikweidí Valley House, as well as the Icy Strait Kaagwaantaan, the Stikine Naanyaa.aayí, and Nisga'a and evidently also Haida chiefly lineages.[11] The Teikweidí Valley House married Gaanax.ádi and Xaas.hitaan but also Coast Tsimshian, Nisga'a, and probably other groups including (hypothesized below) Stikine Raven clans.

Figures 12.5 and 12.6 also demonstrate that although genealogical position within the lineage is generally omitted from succession lists, it was not irrelevant in determining who came to fill the role of clan leader (cf. de Laguna 1960, 192). Figure 12.7 shows father-son relation-

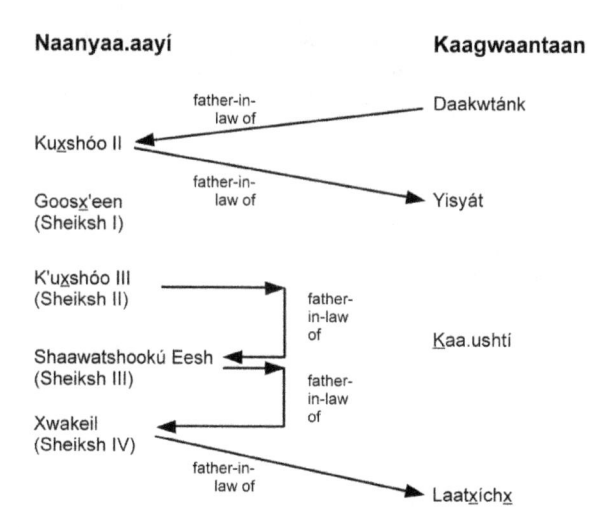

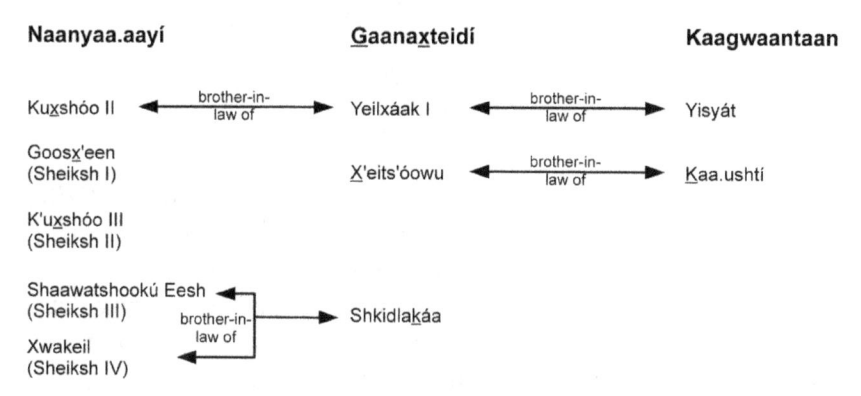

```
Naanyaa.aayí                    Kaagwaantaan

                father-in-
                law of          Daakwtánk
Kuxshóo II
                father-in-
Goosx'een       law of          Yisyát
(Sheiksh I)

K'uxshóo III
(Sheiksh II)
                        father-
                        in-law
                        of      Kaa.ushtí
Shaawatshookú Eesh
(Sheiksh III)
                        father-
                        in-law
Xwakeil                 of
(Sheiksh IV)
                father-in-
                law of          Laatxichx


Naanyaa.aayí            Gaanaxteidí             Kaagwaantaan

                brother-in-                brother-in-
Kuxshóo II      law of      Yeilxáak I      law of       Yisyát

Goosx'een                                   brother-in-
(Sheiksh I)                 X'eits'óowu     law of       Kaa.ushtí

K'uxshóo III
(Sheiksh II)

Shaawatshookú Eesh
(Sheiksh III)   brother-in-  Shkidlakáa
Xwakeil         law of
(Sheiksh IV)
```

Fig. 12.8 Affinal relationships of leaders of the Naanyaa.aayí and Kaagwaantaan (*top*) and of the Naanyaa.aayí, Gaanaxteidí, and Kaagwaantaanca (*bottom*), ca. 1770–1850.

ships among the clan leaders of figure 12.5. The fathers of Daakwtáank and Shkuwuyéil are unknown; of the remaining eight Gaanaxteidí and Kaagwaantaan clan heads, Kaa.ushtí is the only one whose father was not also a clan leader, and in his case both parents were the children of clan leaders. Figure 12.8 shows the degree to which clan leaders married the daughters of clan leaders. Again, these tendencies are manifest in the Taant'a Kwáan material, but with less consistency, in part perhaps because the information there is less complete (figure 12.9).

Relating Deep Genealogies   207

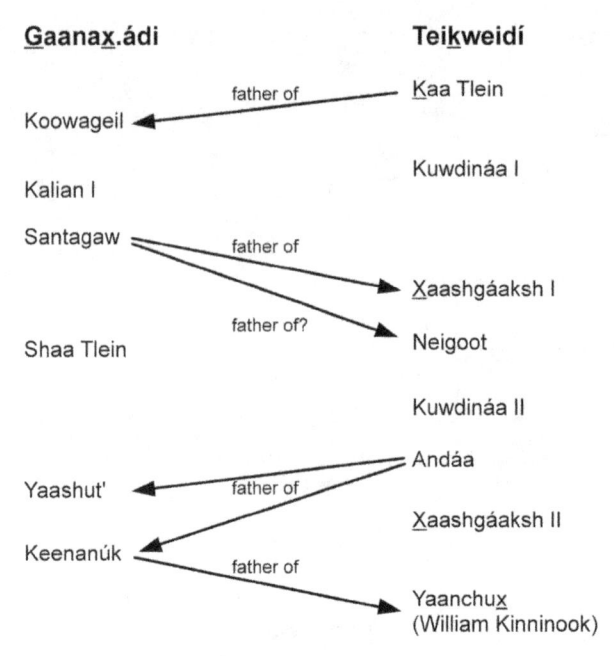

```
Gaanax.ádi                                Teikweidí
                        father of          Kaa Tlein
        Koowageil ◄─────────────────────

                                           Kuwdináa I
        Kalian I

        Santagaw ─────                
                        father of
                              ─────────► Xaashgáaksh I
                        father of?
        Shaa Tlein                    ──► Neigoot

                                           Kuwdináa II
                                        ─► Andáa
        Yaashut' ◄──────  father of
                                           Xaashgáaksh II
        Keenanúk ◄────
                        father of
                                        ─► Yaanchux
                                           (William Kinninook)
```

Fig. 12.9 Father-son relationships in the leading lineages of the Taant'a Kwáan Gaanax.ádi and Fig. Teikweidí clans, ca. 1770–1900.

Another point that may reflect differences in Klukwan, Stikine, and Taant'a Kwáan social processes is who gets mentioned by outsiders. According to Olson, each community historically possessed an *aankáawu*, or town chief, who was the master of the ranking house group of the highest-ranking clan (1967, 49; cf. GFN 7, 11:63).[12] His claim is supported by some evidence from the early fur traders suggesting that, like analogous "town chiefs" among the Haida and Tsimshian, the Tlingit *aankáawu* owned the privilege of initiating trade and setting its terms.

In Klukwan, the ranking clan leader came from the Gaanaxteidí Raven/Whale House lineage; for the Stikine, the Naanyaa.aayí Dogfish House lineage, and among the Taant'a Kwáan, as Olson mentions, the Teikweidí Valley House. In the Stikine and Taant'a Kwáan cases, the series of Dogfish and Valley House masters, respectively, are in fact the names most frequently mentioned by visitors in the eighteenth and nineteenth centuries. At Klukwan, on the other hand, at certain periods a Kaagwaantaan leader seems to be exercising the privilege of initiating or mediating trade. The more consistent pattern of alternation between fathers and sons in the Kaagwaantaan and Gaanaxteidí lead-

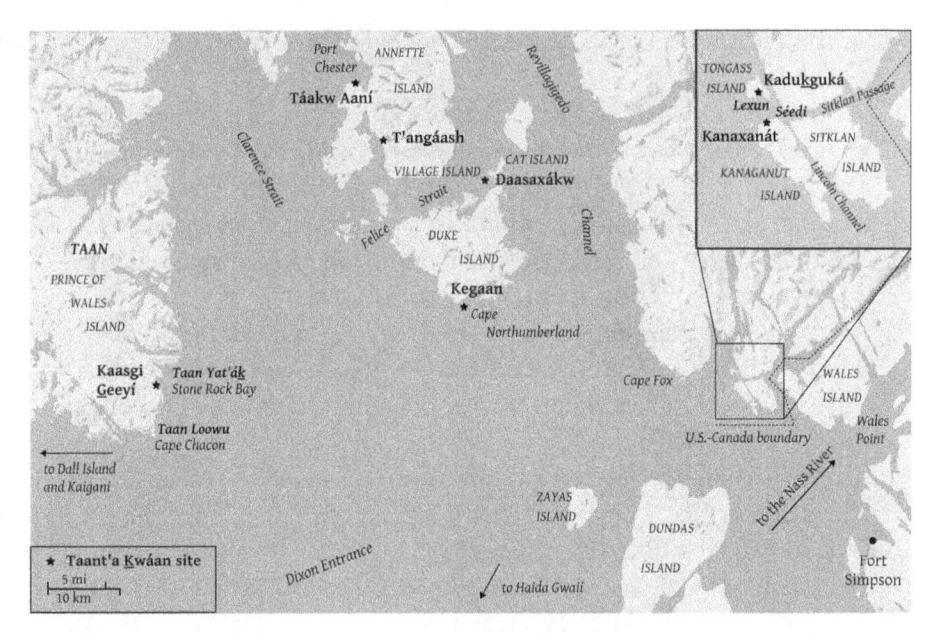

Map 12.1 Taant'a Ḵwáan town sites, ca. 1700–1900, from traditional history and documentary records. The precise locations of Kasgi G̱eeyí and Kegaan are unknown.

ership might be a factor here; at any given time, perhaps, the leader who was the father and senior might be the more influential (cf. Oberg 1972, 42–43). Shotridge may be referring to such a process in his assessment of his paternal grandfather, Laatx̱íchx̱ (Shartridge), as "the last leader who, to the last, maintained controll both [of] his side and the opposite of the leading families of Chilkat" (UEN, "History"; cf. Krause and Krause 1993, 141).[13]

Sketch of Taant'a Ḵwáan history to ca. 1880

As mentioned above, the McKay materials are less complete, the successions and genealogical relationships in them are more uncertain, and the documentary record is therefore more difficult to interpret. Another challenge is that place-names, both those appearing in traditional Taant'a Ḵwáan history and those used by visiting mariners, can be trickier to attach to physical sites. Further, unlike the Chilkat materials where the information comes from members of more than one clan, the history George McKay narrated to Olson focused on his own clan, the G̱aanax̱.ádi, while the Teiḵweidí are more prominent in the

Relating Deep Genealogies 209

fur traders' accounts. Despite these challenges, it is possible to sketch some initial findings.

The first named ancestor in McKay's genealogy is the female *ixt'* (shaman) Joon. She belonged to the southern branch of the Gaanax̱.ádi that settled at various sites on Prince of Wales Island—called in Tlingit Taan, or Sea Lion—and, according to traditional history, began to intermarry with Teiḵweidí already living there (Paul 1971, 10; Olson 1967, 82–84, 115; cf. 103–5; Swanton 1908b, 408f.).[14]

Some generations later, a group of Joon's Gaanax̱.ádi descendants, children of the Teiḵweidí, founded a new village with a part of their fathers' clan. Most sources place this community near Cape Chacon, in Tlingit called Taan Loowu "the nose of Taan," at the southern tip of Prince of Wales Island. The new town was built at Taan yat'áḵ, meaning "at the side of Taan's face," a location identified as Stone Rock Bay.[15] The residents named their town Kasgi Geeyí, "Shining Place," and became known as the Taan yat'aḵ Ḵwáan, or Taant'a Ḵwáan for short (Olson 1967, 3, 10, 57, 84; Paul 1971, 10; Goldschmidt and Haas 1998, 163, 171; GFN 7, 11:59).

McKay apparently supplied no clan history for the period in which the Taant'a Ḵwáan lived at Kasgi Geeyí, although there are indications that it was a turbulent time. Coast Tsimshian traditions referring to the Taant'a Ḵwáan community of "Skaigeh" (Kasgi Geeyí) at the tip of Prince of Wales Island tell of a Taant'a Ḵwáan push southward and the establishment of a new town on Dundas Island. According to Tsimshian clan histories, warfare with the Gitxaahla and other Tsimshian groups eventually forced the Taant'a Ḵwáan from the site (Marsden 2001, 72–73, 82; Cove and MacDonald eds. 1987, 36–37; 135–38, 147–49, 187–90). Another indication of former Taant'a Ḵwáan occupation of Dundas is the name given to the Raven's Bones and Fort House groups of the Gaanax̱.ádi: Waktléidi, "People of Dundas Island." Moreover, the Taant'a Ḵwáan claimed rights into the twentieth century at Dundas and neighboring Zayas Island, despite Tsimshian use (Olson 1967, 10, 56; Goldschmidt and Haas 1998, 169; see also Wooley and Haggerty 1989). Other traditions refer to the Haida displacing the Taant'a Ḵwáan from southern Prince of Wales Island shortly before contact. "The Haida people took it" (Goldschmidt and Haas 1998, 171, see also 79, 85; de Laguna 1960, 143–44; Emmons 1991, 15–16; Garfield 1947, 443–45; Olson 1967, 56; Swanton 1908b, 408–9, 1909, 88–89; cf. Vancouver 1984, 1040).

McKay's sketch of Gaanax̱.ádi history becomes more detailed with the story of L'eixi, a Gaanax̱.ádi Sea Lion House hunter said to have discovered the bounty of the reefs around Yei̱x (Duke Island).[16] According to McKay, it was L'eixi's hunting success at Yei̱x, rather than conflict with neighboring groups, that prompted the Taant'a Ḵwáan move from Kasgi G̱eeyí (Olson 1967, 84; cf. Swanton 1909, 233–36; Garfield and Forrest 1961, 65). Four clans raised houses near L'eixi's dwelling at the southern tip of Yei̱x: the G̱aana̱x.ádi, Teiḵweidí, Daḵ'laweidí, and Xaas.hitaan, descendants of the old G̱aana̱x.adi Xaas Hit (Skin House) at Kasgi G̱eeyí (Olson 1967, 10, 84–85; see also Marsden 2001, 72–73). They called the new town Kegaan and, like L'eixi, became rich from the bounty of Yei̱x (Olson 1967, 10, 11, 49, 56).

According to McKay, the first European and American sailing vessels reached Taant'a Ḵwáan territory after the resettlement at Kegaan (Olson 1967, 87). There are several recorded narratives of early G̱aana̱x.ádi sightings or contacts with sailing vessels, including one involving the then-elderly L'eixi and his wife (Olson 1967, 87–88; Paul 1971, 6, 10; UEN, "History"). These mostly describe chance meetings at sea rather than contacts at fixed sites, and mariners' accounts, which report any number of encounters with single canoes, cannot be definitely linked to any of them. European and American vessels became increasingly common in Dixon Entrance throughout the 1780s, so the earliest sightings probably took place before 1790.

Although George Vancouver's mapping expedition spent several weeks in Taant'a Ḵwáan territory in August 1793 (Vancouver 1984, 999–1023), and at least some of the Tlingit they encountered must have belonged to that division, the Taant'a Ḵwáan were not identified as a group in the first years of contact. Coasting vessels generally headed for known anchorages where trade had already proved profitable, and Haida Gwaii (the Queen Charlotte Islands), the Tsimshian coast, southeastern Dall Island, and Norfolk Sound (Sitka) were among the most popular destinations (e.g., Galois ed. 2004; BMJ; Ingraham 1971; Munro 1917, 112; Roe ed. 1967). By the end of the 1790s, sea otter populations were declining in many locations while the "mania" for northwest commercial voyages had only increased competition for pelts (RHA1 4/26/1802; Acheson 1995, 290, 294n14; Gibson 1992, 299–310; Howay 1973). In March 1799, Samuel Curson described the attempt of the officers of the *Eliza* to locate a new source of furs:

> It being known that not the fiftieth part of the Sea Otters' Skins got at Caiganee . . . were taken by the tribe themselves, and that the mass

of them were brought from other tribes caused us to make every inquiry to find where they generally went to trade.... Altatsee ... told us that he went sometimes up a vast distance to a place inland [the mouth of the Nass River].... [H]is brother [Cotseye also told us of a place] ... called Cockathanes and that the Caiganee tribe got the greatest part of their Skins [there].... He afterwards chalked out a sketch of the place on the cabin table. (Jackman ed. 1978, 66–67)[17]

En route to the Nass River a few months later, Curson

saw a large canoe following us up the Sound; they soon overtook us, and ... pressed us much to return to their village and buy their skins.... This canoe belonged to Cockathanes tribe and contained twenty four stout men ... plentifully furnished with muskets. (1978, 84–86)

While the *Eliza* did not venture to the village of the "Cockathanes tribe," preferring instead to look for the group at the Gitxaahla trading camp at the mouth of the Nass, Curson recommended to future traders that they seek out the Cockathanes and buy "the best part of their skins." These, he said, were available at a substantially lower cost than skins offered at Sitka and Kaigani (1978, 193).

By 1801, the "Cockathanes"—more often called Cocklanes, Cochlens, and similar variants—had become one of the traders' regular sources of furs.[18] The linguistic, genealogical, and geographic evidence they recorded indicate that the "Cockathanes" are the Taant'a Kwáan, making the *Eliza*'s 1799 encounter the earliest confirmed written account of contact with the visitors.

That the Cocklanes spoke Tlingit is indicated, among other evidence, by a vocabulary recorded by William Bryant ca. 1822, which includes, for example, "Coust er [kóoshda] Ld otter," "Clinket [lingit] Man," "Sharwott [shaawát] Woman," and "Hean [heen] Water" (WBR; see also RHA1 3/14/1802, 5/13/1802, Jackman ed. 1978, 86–87).[19]

Regarding genealogy, the "Cockathanes" individuals mentioned by traders bear Taant'a Kwáan names that appear in McKay's genealogy and narratives and are still recognized by Taant'a Kwáan today. The men who served as what the traders called "the head Cheif [sic] of Cocklanes" (SFO 2/29/1810) correspond with the series of names in the Teikweidí Valley House succession. The first of these is "Cockathane" himself, after whom, as the Kaigani told Curson, they had named the "Cockathanes tribe" (Jackman ed. 1978, 66). According to McKay, the Valley House master at first contact was, in Olson's transcription, "Kaklen," a name that today would be written Ḵaa Tlein (George Samuels p.c., 8/4/08). In McKay's genealogy, Ḵaa Tlein appears six generations below Joon.

Although there are ambiguities and puzzles in McKay's narrative, it is clear that after "Kaklen" came "Kudena," "Negut," and "Andah." In the traders' accounts, Ḵaa Tlein's successors include, in chronological order, "Coatenah," "Neacoot," and "Under." As understood by contemporary Teiḵweidí and written in the current orthography, these names would be Kuwdináa, Neigoot, and Andáa.

Geography is a more complicated matter, but in the end navigational and other details referring to "Cocklanes" point convincingly to well-documented Taant'a Ḵwáan sites. In the first years of direct trade, the mariners used "Cocklanes" and its variants for at least two and perhaps more locations. Curson's Kaigani sources located "Cockathanes" near "Intankoon," that is, "The mainland to the Eastward of Cape Murray [i.e., Cape Chacon] which makes the East point of this bay." Intankoon, then, might refer to Cape Fox or Wales Point near the mouth of Portland Inlet (Jackman ed. 1978, 66).[20] The harbor that Ralph Haskins of the *Atahualpa* called "Cocklanes" in 1802 lay among the small islands a few miles northwest of Wales Point (RHA1 3/14/1802).

By 1805, mariners were referring to the trading rendezvous near Wales Point as Clemelcitty, Clemming Ceede, and other variants that include the Russians' Tlekhonsiti (e.g., WWL 6/18/1805; TWL 5/9/1806; RKO 5/18-24/1810; CGT; MKV). Clemelcitty is a place-name recorded in the 1869 *Alaska Coast Pilot*, which described it as the "harbor . . . in the narrow straits forming a group of islands, about five or six miles northwest from Point Wales," the straits in question being Lincoln Channel and Sitklan Passage (Davidson 1869, 73). The site was evidently named after the "clemels" or "clamons," Chinook jargon for the elk hide armor much prized in the early days of the fur trade (e.g., BMJ 7/26/1793, 3/22/1794; RHA1 3/13/1802; TWL 6/22/1805; Roe, ed. 1967, 128). The variant Tlekhonsiti corresponds to a Tlingit toponym recorded by Shotridge, Lexun Séedi, which he glossed as "Lincoln Channel" (AHL). This derives from Tlingit *séet* "passage" and *lexun*, likely a Tlingit pronunciation of "clemon."[21] It does not seem improbable that the name "Lincoln" for the channel began as an anglicization of *lexun*.

Paul identifies "Clemelcitty" with the Taant'a Ḵwáan site of Kaduḵguká or Cottonwood Island, later the location of Tongass Village (Paul 1971, 10, 13). "Clemelcitty" for the mariners, however, referred to the harbor, and in the first half of the nineteenth century, the Taant'a Ḵwáan used both Kaduḵguká and a site on the opposite shore, on Kanaganut Island. Haskins's two ca. 1802 sketches of "Cocklanes Harbour" (RHA2) mark a "village" on either side, while an 1836 Russian map of the "harbor of Taiakhonsiti" shows a "Tangaz" settlement on Kanaganut but none on Tongass Island (CGT). The Kanaganut site is likely the "Kanaxanát" mentioned in McKay's histories, located on "a beach at the north end of Kanaganut Island" (Olson 1967, 93, 94, fig. 10).[22] As late as 1867–1869, when the earliest photographs show houses at Kaduḵguká, Davidson reported a "village on the south shore" opposite (Davidson 1869, 74).

A second geographical referent for "Cocklanes" is Tamgas Harbor on Annette Island, another site whose ownership and use by Taant'a Ḵwáan is well documented (Olson 1967, 56, 91; Goldschmidt and Haas 1998, 168). William Bryant, whose brig *Rob Roy* wintered at Tamgas Harbor in both 1822–1823 and 1823–1824, designated its lower portion as "Cocklanes" and the inner and more secure anchorage as "Tumgarse," though he also used the latter term for the trading locale as a whole (WBR 5/9/1822; 8/10/1822, 12/5/1922 et al.).[23] According to Shotridge, the Tlingit name for the Taant'a Ḵwáan site in the harbor was T'angaash (AHL; see also Olson 1967, 56).[24]

Samuel Furgerson referred both to a "Cocklanes Har." and "Cocklanes Sound"—the former being present-day Tamgas Harbor and latter Felice Strait and Revillagigedo Channel (SFO 9/17/1810, 11/12/1810). The traders may have applied the term "Cocklanes" to at least one other anchorage—the location Robert Kemp called "tessequah" and variants (RKO 8/8/1810 et seq.). Like Lexun Séedi and Tamgas Harbor, Tessequah was visited repeatedly by coasting vessels, but whether anyone besides Kemp distinguished it terminologically from other "Cocklanes" sites has not yet been determined (see RKO 8/8/1910, 9/23/1810, 10/28/1810, 12/11/1810). The similarity of names suggests that Tessequah is the traditional Taant'a Ḵwáan site of Daasaxákw on Village Island, off the northeast point of Duke Island (Olson 1967, 10, 41; Paul 1971, 12–13; Goldschmidt and Haas 1998, 79, 83, 167–69). This is supported both by Furgerson, Kemp's shipmate, who described their anchorage as on "the South side" of "Cocklanes Sound" (SFO 9/17/1810; RKO 8/26/1810, 12/1/1810).

No early nineteenth-century physical description for Daasaxákw has been located yet. Regarding Lexun Séedi, Haskins's ca. 1802 sketches identify a "village" on both the northern and southern shores, while the aforementioned 1836 map of "Taiakhonsiti" shows a line of sixteen structures on the Kanaganut side (RHA2; CGT). For the buildings at T'anga̲ash, Bryant, who distinguished between Native "fish huts" and "houses," used the latter term (WBR 9/30/1822, 10/13/1822; see also AUP 5/2/1801, 5/4/1801).[25] The houses were located on the lower harbor, "Cocklanes" proper (WBR 12/5/1822). Shotridge and McKay placed T'anga̲ash specifically at the outlet of Tamgas Lake; according to Nichols, it lay "just above" the stream (AHL, UEN; Olson 1967, 82, 56; see also Goldschmidt and Haas 1998, 79, 169; Nichols ed. 1891, 91).[26]

The mariners noted that the Taant'a Ḵwáan occupied these three sites on a yearly cycle, along with a fourth, their winter town. Bryant reported that Taant'a Ḵwáan moved from Tamgas Harbor to their "winter village" in December and from their winter quarters to "Clemel Ceede" at the beginning of March (WBR n.d. [3/1822], 12/6/1822, 2/23/1823; FSJ4 2/24/1858). The Russian map similarly notes "Taiakhonsiti" as the place where "the Tangaz Kolosh [Tlingit] live in spring" (*vesnoyu zhivut Tangazskiya Koloshi*) (CGT). Tamgas Harbor may be the "Cocklens Summer Village" mentioned by one journal-keeper (WWL 6/17/1805, 6/18/1805),[27] or this reference may have been to Daasaxákw. The *Otter* encountered Taant'a Ḵwáan at Tessequah in both August and December (RKO 8/8/1810, 11/29/1810, 12/11/1810; SFO 12/13/1810).[28]

One question raised by the fur traders' accounts is why—given they were seeking out the Taant'a Ḵwáan with such regularity—they were almost completely silent on the subject of the Taant'a Ḵwáan winter town of "Kegan" (Olson 1967, 84) or "xekan" (Waterman 1922, 13 in Monteith 1998). Bryant complained about the disappearance of trade when the Taant'a Ḵwáan departed Tamgas Harbor in winter, but his brig did not leave its anchorage to follow them, nor did he note where the town lay (WBR 12/6/1822). Kemp's journal contains a possible reference to Kegaan, made when the *Otter*, en route from Cape Chacon to the Stikine, stopped to repair a damaged hull "halfway between Cargann & Catsacklann" (RKO 1/21/1811). "Catsacklann" is surely the Stikine town of Ḵals'el Aan, and since Kemp transcribed Tlingit in his native Cape Cod accent, "Cargann" could be Kegaan.[29] But Kemp did not leave a record of its location, either.

Relating Deep Genealogies

While alternate locations have been given (Olson 1967, 84; Goldschmidt and Hass 1998, 79; Paul 1971, 9,10,12), both McKay and Waterman's source, Pete Williams, placed Kegaan near Cape Northumberland on Duke Island.[30] In August 1793, Vancouver saw an uninhabited "large village" near Cape Northumberland, situated "on a high detached rock . . . much more exposed to the inclemency of the weather than any residence of the natives I had before seen" (Vancouver 1984, 1021).[31] This may be the "appearance of a village" that the *Iphegenia* spotted in 1789 at the foot of "Mount Saint Lazaro," apparently present-day Mt. Lazaro at Cape Northumberland (1790, 362; Dall 1880, 174). However, archaeological surveys have so far failed to turn up evidence of a village in this vicinity (Martin Stanford p.c., 2/14/2008; Priscilla Schulte p.c., 3/24/2007).[32]

In 1810 Furgerson remarked that most coasting crews did not know "where these Indians live in the winter" (SFO 12/25/1810). Kegaan's location seems unlikely to have been a mystery to Bryant, who in 1822–1824 spent months at a time with the Taant'a Ḵwáan and commented upon the existence of such a village as well as three other sites occupied during their seasonal round (WBR). Another community not visited by the early traders, despite frequent commerce with its residents at other rendezvous, was Ḵals'el Aan, sited on the difficult channel of Zimovia Strait. The mariners' movements were restricted to "where it is practicable for [sailing] vessels to go" (RHA1 5/17/1801). Kegaan would have been situated, in Kemp's words, among "the Rocks and Shoales of Cape Northumberland" (RKO 8/26/1810). The 1891 *Coast Pilot* warned that "navigation of that vicinity [is] dangerous in the extreme . . . many sunken and dangerous reefs" (Nichols ed. 1891, 90).

While the *Coast Pilot* did not rate either Lexun Séedi or the vicinity of Daasaxákw as good anchorages, both were only a few miles from more adequate harbors (Pond Bay and Wales Harbor; 1891, 80–81, 97). Tamgas Harbor, on the other hand, offered "complete shelter in all weathers" (1891, 90), and in severe storms the fur traders did often seek refuge there. Bryant recommended Tamgas as "one of the finest harbours," despite being, as he wrote, "the most stormy Harbour on the Coast." Its bottom was "excelent holding ground" where anchors rarely pulled loose (WBR 7/11/1822).

Other writers of the era noted Tamgas Harbor's reputation as "the best in this part of the coast whence to obtain spars, and other wood" for ship repair (Dunn 1846, 286; TWL 4/11/1806).[33] A further attraction was that the Taant'a Ḵwáan, unlike most other Native groups, did not charge a fee for water and wood (Green 1915, 76–77; Gibson 1992, 126), nor had disputes with visitors ever escalated into violence (Malloy 1998a, 200–201). Taant'a Ḵwáan sites continued to be the destination of trading ships even after sea otters became scarce (e.g., FSC: J. Work to R. Finlayson 2/20/1844; FSJ4: 12/6/1860, 4/4/1862). At Tamgas Harbor, the Taant'a Ḵwáan were able to specialize as provisioners, serving Russian ships, visiting whalers, and fur traders alike who stopped there to buy the "Deer, Ducks, Geese & Swans" offered for sale along with furs (WBR 3/11/1822). With the establishment in 1831 of the Hudson's Bay Company at Fort Simpson, the Taant'a Ḵwáan became, as its officers wrote, the provisioners "on whom we principally depend" (FSJ3 3/3/1843). This role was so important that Tamgas Harbor was included in the formal agreement between the HBC and the Russian American Company, negotiated in 1839, as neutral ground "where either [side] may touch and trade provisions" (JDD 5/20-28/1840). When the U.S. Army arrived at Lexun Séedi, the Taant'a Ḵwáan began supplying Fort Tongass, too (Teichman 1963, 124).

Outside of their home territory, the place mariners most often encountered Taant'a Ḵwáan was on the Nass River, a day's canoe trip from Lexun Séedi (RHA1 3/14/1802, 3/28/1802; Paul 1971, 10). Participation in the oolichan fishery accounts for their presence on only some of these occasions; the indigenous trade through which the Taant'a Ḵwáan first attracted the attention of the visitors seems more frequently to have motivated the trip. The mouth of the Nass River was the site of busy trading camps owned by Coast Tsimshian groups, the most prominent in the early years of the trade being the "Shebassers" (Gitxaahla), renowned as sea hunters. At those camps, in addition to other Tsimshian groups, the early mariners found Taant'a Ḵwáan Tlingit, Nisga'a, and Haida from Kasaan, Kaigani, Masset, Skidegate, and Cumshewa (RHA1 3/24/1802, 4/12/1802, 6/27/1810; SFO 3/19/1810, 3/28/1810; RKO 6/27/1810; Sturgis 1998, 40; Olson 1967, 88; Marsden and Galois 1995, 171–72, 180–81n15).[34]

Most sources refer to a Nass River trading fair held once a year, in the spring, for oolichan oil (Marsden and Galois 1995, 172; Jackman ed. 1978, 66–67; Olson 1967, 88), while others note a separate fair in autumn for other commodities that, postcontact, included the Haida potato harvest (Sturgis 1998, 40; Scouler 1841, 219; Acheson 1995, 294n11). The mariners, however, report Taant'a Ḵwáan trade expeditions to the Nass in

March, April, May, June, September, and perhaps other months as well (Jackman ed. 1978, 66-67, 84-87; RKO 6/27/1810; RHA1 3/26/1802, 4/12/1802, 4/14/1802; WBR 9/28/1822).[35] The trade in oil, and the oolichan fishing privileges maintained by Taant'a Kwáan on the Nass, probably lay behind their reputation among other Tlingit for wealth (Shotridge 1929, 146; cf. Olson 1967, 94,100; Paul 1971, 10).

Bryant, in his one-line description of the Taant'a Kwáan, stated that "they are not numerous but are connected with other scattered tribes" (WBR n.d.), while Sturgis mentioned their "numerous friends" among other groups (1998, 40). The statements may refer to the higher rate of outmarriage that the Taant'a Kwáan chart shows relative to figure 12.5. This rate may have been the deliberate policy of a relatively small group in order to maximize trading and fishing privileges and security. It is probably not irrelevant that other Tlingit, traveling to trade with Tsimshian, employed Taant'a Kwáan as interpreters (Shotridge 1928, 357).

The Taant'a Kwáan mentioned most often in connection with trade, whether with visitors or other Native groups, are the Teikweidí clan leaders. The head of the Teikweidí, like other ranking "town chiefs" on the north Pacific coast, seems to have possessed the privilege of initiating trade and setting its terms. Others "would not commence a brisk trade until" this personage had completed negotiations (RHA1 5/10/1802, 3/17-26/1802; RKO 12/21-25/1809, 2/8/1810; Beresford 1789, 227; Acheson 1995, 279).

In March 1802, anchored at Lexun Séedi, Haskins encountered "Cocklane the Chief" (Kaa Tlein) returning from the mouth of the Nass where he had just purchased oil and furs from the Gitxaahla Tsimshian. Kaa Tlein had traded "two fathoms of cloth or one blanket" per skin, and he had also bought commodities with pieces of a whale washed ashore, "an article of no trifling demand" (RHA1 3/14/1802, 3/18/1802). The furs he immediately sold to Haskins's *Atahualpa*. For what price is not stated, but around that time, at the peak of the fur trade, other traders were paying as much as five fathoms of cloth per skin (Gibson 1992, 127).

Eight days after this transaction, Kaigani traders arrived at Lexun Séedi (RHA1 3/26/1802). Sometimes traveling as far as the Nass camps, they more often relied upon Taant'a Kwáan to bring them the furs harvested by Nisga'a and Tsimshian hunters. In this instance the Kaigani expressed disappointment and anger when they learned Kaa Tlein had sold his stock of otter pelts to the *Atahualpa* (Jackman ed. 1978, 66-67; RHA1 3/26/1802, 4/12/1802, 4/14/1802).

Haskins met "Old Cocklane," whom he judged to be "a clever old fellow" (RHA1 3/19/1802). Haskins described Ḵaa Tlein's elderly father, "born at Stikin," in some detail, and noted that Ḵaa Tlein had "*four* wives" and "grand children quite grown up" (3/22/1802). He did not, however, mention Ḵaa Tlein's children who, according to McKay, included Koowageil, the G̱aanax̱.ádi clan leader at the time, and Koowageil's sister S'eiltín, both of Drifted Ashore House.³⁶ S'eiltín is the so-called Bride of Tongass who had married Taax̱sha of the Kaagwaantaan and entered historical tradition in the north as an exemplar of virtue and beauty (Olson 1967, 84–85; Shotridge 1929; GFN 7,XI, 63). The sons of Taax̱sha and S'eiltín, Kalian and Santagaw—G̱aanax̱.ádi clan leaders following Koowageil—may have been among the grandchildren of Ḵaa Tlein who, in 1802, were "quite grown up."

A week after this meeting, Haskins encountered another of Ḵaa Tlein's relations, "Cotenett," "possessed of a great many skins" (RHA1 3/24/1802, 4/12/1802). This man, who appears variously in the journals as Coatenath, Coatenah, and Koodenah, had by 1810 become "the head Cheif [sic] of Cocklanes" (SFO 2/29/1810)—which agrees with McKay's designation of "Kudena" as Ḵaa Tlein's successor. While Haskins designated Kuwdináa as Ḵaa Tlein's brother, McKay called him a nephew. Kuwdináa may have been a parallel cousin in Ḵaa Tlein's Valley House lineage, whom Tlingit might have described either way.

We have three narratives of the events leading to Ḵaa Tlein's death and Kuwdináa's accession; Haskins's, obtained from eyewitness reports a few days after the events it describes; Sturgis's, written in 1848, over forty years later, although it may have been based on journals now lost; and McKay's, written down in the 1930s. The three accounts cannot be reconciled in every detail, but they do cover some common ground.

All three refer to trouble breaking out during one of Ḵaa Tlein's expeditions to the Nass. McKay identifies the opposite party in the conflict as the Gitxaahla; according to Sturgis, they came from Skidegate, while Haskins names the Gitxaalha ("Chebasser") as the opposites, with peripheral Skidegate and Cumshewa involvement (Olson 1967, 88; Sturgis 1998, 40; RHA1 3/24/1802, 4/12/1802). "The war commenced," Haskins wrote, while Ḵaa Tlein was at Nass buying oolichan oil at the beginning of April 1802.

[I]n one battle . . . he lost a slave, but killed six of the enemy. Nekeisks brother [a Kaigani Haida?] was killed, Nekeisk joined Cocklanes

Relating Deep Genealogies 219

party. The Skittagates and Cummeshewass people who were there sided with the Chebasser tribe. (RHA1 4/12/1802)³⁷

The subsequent "affray" in which "Cockalane... was killed" occurred, according to Sturgis, in the autumn of 1804, "at a sort of fair, which was annually held at Nass for the exchange of Indian commodities, and which was attended by a number of tribes" (Sturgis 1998, 40). McKay provides a more detailed account of what is presumably the same fatal Nass expedition. In his version the trouble began with a conflict between the Gitxaalha and another Tsimshian group. The Taant'a Ḵwáan were bystanders until Ḵaa Tlein's ten-year-old son, Skawoolyeil, was shot.³⁸ In Olson's words, "[T]he Tantakwan seized their guns and killed two Tsimshian, thinking the boy was dead. The Tsimshian returned the fire and killed Chief Kakklen." An ensuing feud was eventually followed by peace (1967, 89).

No physical description of Ḵaa Tlein's heir survives beyond McKay's statement that Kuwdináa was lame (Olson 1967, 88).³⁹ The traders mention his "very large and fine Canoe" (SFO 2/28/1810), which may have been the same "very large canoe" used by Ḵaa Tlein (RHA1 3/18/1802). In 1810 the *Otter* witnessed the passage of an expedition to the Nass led by Kuwdináa, accompanied by the Kaigani chief Khou (SFO 5/18/1810):

> there came along Side of us a great Number of the Cocklane Indians 4 of the Largest Canoes had 25 men in Each and 3 others with 10 So the whole Number was 130 men with arms & Equipments accordingly Besides one Large Canoe from Clarganee.... [It was] Caatanath and pretty much all the Rest of the tribe [going up] to Nauss to Settle Some old quarrel. (RKO 5/18/1810, 5/22/1810)

As the Gitxaalha historically possessed territory at or near the mouth of the Nass, this "old quarrel" could have been Kuwdináa's feud with the Gitxaalha over Ḵaa Tlein's death.

Two months later, Kemp's brig *Otter* assisted with the transport from Lexun Séedi in the same direction of "Coatanath the Chief of Cocklanes his wife and 20 Indians more.... Bound over to Kyoon to Recieve a wife of Aquilliker the Chief of one [of] the Nauss tribes" (RKO 7/10/1810). "Aquilliker" is probably the Nisga'a Eagle name Agwii Laxha, and "Kyoon" is a so far unidentified but perhaps Gits'iis site that lay somewhere to the north of Laxk'u (Tugwell Island) and near the mouth of the Nass (C. Roth p.c. 10/22/2007; RKO 8/1/1810; Marsden and Galois 1995, 171, 181n22).[40] Kuwdinaa's marriage to a Nisga'a chief's daughter may have been in the service of renewing the affinal ties through which the Teiḵweidí maintained their right to participate in the oolichan fishery (Goldschmidt and Haas 1998, 83; cf. Paul 1971, 10, 12–13; Olson 1967, 94, 100; Sturgis 1998, 40).

The date and circumstances of Kuwdináa's death are at present unknown. Apparently the first heir to follow him was X̱aashgáaksh, a great-grandson of Ḵaa Tlein and a son of Kalian, the G̱aanax̱.ádi leader after Koowageil (Olson 1967, 81). Little information has been located about X̱aashgáaksh, however, and the far more visible Valley House leader after Kuwdináa was Neigoot. "Nacoot" was "a young Chief" in 1810, when he visited the *Otter* at "tessequah" to sell beaver skins (SFO 8/21/1810, RKO 8/8/1810). By 1822–1824 Neigoot had become "head Chief" of the Cocklanes (Malloy 1998a, 201, 2000, 15; WBR 3/11/1822).[41] He may in fact have been X̱aashgáaksh's brother (Olson 1967, 43).[42] Traditional history tells how X̱aashgáaksh was shot in the stomach, and later died, in a dispute with another Taant'a Ḵwáan clan (1967, 87), and Bryant, while wintering at Tamgas Harbor in December 1923, wrote of a similar event: "during this time the Indians have been fighting on account of Nacoots brothers [*sic*] being shot by one of them[.] 4 killed" (WBR 11/23 to 12/21/1823).

Neigoot was well known to Bryant, who initially judged him "a pretty troublesome fellow," but later called him "a grate drunkard but the cleverest indian on the coast" (WBR 3/11/1822, 8/25–26/1822). Neigoot's quirks of personality emerge in the trade journals and in traditional history. McKay and Shotridge both recount the story of a pig, purchased from fur traders, which Neigoot eccentrically adopted as a family member. When it died, he required his opposite clan, the G̱aanax̱.ádi, to undertake the full mourning ceremonies and even raised a pole to commemorate the animal (Olson 1967, 38, 88). "No one ever knew whether or not the chief did this thing as a source of amusement, but everyone ... had to go through with ... the solemnity of the occasion" (UEN, "History"). At another time, Bryant watched as Neigoot precipitated a quarrel between three Kaigani chiefs' wives, then stood by "enjoying the frollick" (WBR 9/1/1822). A traditional story describes how Neigoot's fiercest warrior, encountering a mirror for the first time, attempted to fight his own image. Neigoot, looking on, "only smiled" (UEN, "History"; cf. Olson 1967, 88).

A number of sources tell the story of a Teikweidí leader named Neigoot who received the name Ebbets and a letter from an early ship captain (Olson 1967, 42, 87–89; UEN, "History"; Garfield and Forrest 1961, 50; Scidmore 1893, 52). Both were passed down in the Valley House lineage for many years, with the daughters of Andáa, a later Teikwedí clan leader, using the title as their English surname. This story has been said to refer to Captain John Ebbets, whose known voyages to the Northwest Coast took place between 1801 and 1810 (Bancroft 1884, 1:311, 318–20, 2:139–40). A Richard Ebbets also journeyed to Tlingit country in 1814–1815, first as clerk then captain of the *Forester*, and John Ebbets apparently made a voyage as late as 1825, though not as a ship's master (Ogden 1941, 165–66, 172).

From the pig story we can infer that Neigoot had married a Gaanax.ádi woman, like his predecessors Kaa Tlein and Kuwdináa. Also like these men he may have had more than one wife. If so, a second may have belonged to a Stikine Raven clan, as there is some evidence of an ongoing relationship between Valley House and one or more Stikine lineages. For example, Kaa Tlein's father, who was apparently Taant'a Kwáan and therefore likely Gaanax.ádi, was according to Haskins born at Stikine, suggesting an opposite-moiety Stikine (Naanyaa.aayí?) father. When Neigoot held a "housewarming" in the winter of 1822–1823, presumably for the rebuilt Teikweidí Valley House at Kegaan, he invited Stikine and Kasaan guests (WBR 1/30–2/7/1823).[43] And the mariners found Neigoot a number of times in company with Stikine visitors, including, in 1822, one of the Shéikshes (WBR 3/10/1822, 3/12/1822, 5/9/1822, see also 12/10–21/1822, 1/4/1824; SFO 8/22/1810; RHA1 3/22/1802). This Shéiksh or his successor was later instrumental in arranging peace between the Taant'a Kwáan and Xeil Kwáan (Olson 1967, 96; Paul 1971, 11).

A Gaanax.ádi woman named S'eiltín (II) provides a more definite link between the Taant'a Kwáan and the Stikine during this period. She came from the same Drifted Ashore House lineage to which Kaa Tlein's daughter belonged, although the precise connection between the two S'eiltíns is unknown. Based on dates associated with her grandchildren (see below), S'eiltín II could not have been born much later than 1790. She is said to have become the eldest wife of one of the Stikine Shéikshes, and her father was "Tshadatsta," which may be the Naanyaa.aayí name Shadesti (Barbeau 1950, 651; Llwyd 1909, 7).[44] The husband was perhaps Shéiksh III (Shaawatshook'u Éesh), or, if she married young,

Shéiksh II (K'uxshóo III), while the father could have been Haskins's "Chidestee." This man and "Cockshoo" (K'uxshóo II or III) were, in 1801, "two of the first chiefs of the Great Stikin" (RHA1 5/4/1801; Jackman 1978, 89).[45] S'eiltín II may be the "Shelteen a Tongass woman of consequence" who "died suddenly" in June 1842 (FSJ:6/12/1842).[46]

Another Taant'a Ḵwáan woman who served as an exemplar in traditional history is Kaajidal, the sister of X̱aashgáaksh and possibly also of Neigoot. The mother of eight Valley House children, she twice ended conflict between the Teiḵweidí and her husband's clan, the Xaas.hitaan. The first time was at Kegaan as a young bride, after X̱aashgáaksh's shooting, and the second, after the Taant'a Ḵwáan left Kegaan, by which time her son Andáa was grown (1967, 87, 92–93). In 1822 Bryant met Neigoot's "Chesi" (sister)[47]—who may have been Kaajidal, although McKay's chart gives X̱aashgáaksh a second, unnamed female sibling as well (WBR 9/24/1822, 9/30/1822; ROP).

In the G̱aanax̱.ádi succession at Kegaan during this time, S'eiltín I's brother Koowageil was followed by, first, her oldest son, Kalian, and then her youngest son, Santagaw. When still boys, Kalian and Santagaw were sent down from the north, where their parents lived, to be raised by Koowageil in Kegaan (Olson 1967, 85). As a young man, Santagaw was said to have been a heavy gambler who reformed upon learning of his uncle's wife's bad opinion of the habit. After Koowageil died, Kalian became the clan leader of the G̱aanax̱.ádi at Kegaan, while Santagaw married the widow, Talyéi (Olson 1967, 85). Kalian became "a famed chief" and led the G̱aanax̱.ádi during a war with the Saanya Ḵwáan (1967, 85–87). No definite reference to these two men in visitors' records has been identified, and when Kalian came into his position is unknown, but according to McKay, Santagaw was clan leader by the time the Taant'a Ḵwáan moved from Kegaan (Olson 1967, 91).

They built a new town at the entrance to the Annette Island anchorage of Port Chester, site of present-day Metlakatla. McKay's account gives no reason for relocating, but the difficulties of commerce at Kegaan may have prompted the move; certainly many Taant'a Ḵwáan had been living much of the time at Tamgas Harbor where they could do business with visiting merchant vessels. The move probably postdated 1823; Bryant, wintering at Tamgas Harbor, seems likely to have mentioned a winter village only a few miles away at Port Chester. The first clan leader to break ground for a new lineage house was said to be Kucheesh, head of the Taant'a Ḵwáan Daḵl'aweidí and son of Talyéi and

Relating Deep Genealogies

Santagaw. Santagaw and the Gaanax̱.ádi followed Kucheesh to Annette Island and so, too, did the Teiḵweidí (Olson 1967, 91).

The new settlement was called, simply, Táakw Aaní "winter town," but whites quickly attached the name "Tungass" to it. According to information from Ivan Petroff, the Taant'a Ḵwáan numbered around 900 at this time, before the devastating 1836 smallpox epidemic. On reaching southeast Alaska, the epidemic struck the "settlement of Tongass" first and "most severely," reducing its population by nearly a third, to around 650 (Bancroft 1886, 560). Neigoot was one of the victims (Dunn 1836, 284, 1991, 346, Monteith 1998, 127).

Population figures from the era are unreliable; estimates of Taant'a Ḵwáan numbers during the eighteenth and nineteenth centuries vary wildly. This in part is doubtless because outsiders rarely, if ever, encountered the whole *kwáan* at any one location. Tsimshian traditions describe the division (which they called Gitaganits) as "many in number," apparently living in at least three winter villages on Prince of Wales, Dundas, and Duke Islands at the beginning of the eighteenth century (Marsden 2001, 72–74, 79–84; Wooley and Haggerty 1989). Captain Sturgis, whose voyages to the northwest coast began in the 1790s, called the Taant'a Kwáan "a powerful tribe" (1998, 40), and in 1810 Kemp counted 130 Taant'a Kwáan men in Kuwdináa's Nass expedition who could have been primarily Teiḵweidí (RKO 5/18/1810). Scott heard in the 1860s that "not many years ago this was a warlike and numerous tribe" (1904, 352) and in the twentieth century, other Tlingits also remarked upon its reputation of having been "once large and aggressive" (Goldschmidt and Haas 1998, 79), even "one of the largest [*kwáans*] . . . in old times" (GFN 7, 11:30; Monteith 1998, 80–81).

Bryant in 1822–1824, however, labeled them "not numerous" (WBR n.d.), and Tolmie, an HBC officer whose observations may have postdated the 1836 smallpox epidemic, described the "Tun Ghaase" as "a small tribe" (Scouler 1841, 218). Scott, calling them "much reduced" from earlier times, estimated a population of only 250 in 1867 (Scott 1904, 352). In 1879, Morris guessed at a figure of 700, and for the 1880 census, Petroff counted 315 Taant'a Ḵwáan individuals (Morris 1879, 145, 148; Petroff 1884, 36–37; see also Boyd 1996; Paul 1971, 8–9, 15; Scidmore 1891, 52; Olson 1967, 3; Emmons 1992, 431–32, 434).

Petroff's two counts, in 1836 and 1880, would indicate a reduction of two-thirds over forty-five years. The latter figure in fact follows another major smallpox epidemic in 1862 and several serious conflicts, including a war involving the Haida adventurer Sgaagia, remembered in both Taant'a Ḵwáan and Haida eyewitness accounts, that led to heavy loss of life on both sides (Swanton 1905, 64–70; Shotridge UEN, "Warfare"; Olson 1967, 73–75, 94–95).[48]

At any rate, Táakw Aaní stood for only a short time. Another conflict erupted, this initially between the Xeil Ḵwáan and Gaanaxh.ádi. In a night raid on Tamgas Harbor, the Xeil Ḵwáan shot and killed Santagaw, the then-elderly head of the Gaanaxh.ádi.[49] Years later, Shaa Tlein told McKay the story of the fierce gun battle, in which he had been one of the leaders, when they killed or drove off all of the raiders (Olson 1967, 93). But they nevertheless abandoned the fort the same day and "arrived off Point Davidson in the evening. They slept in their canoes that night. The northern lights seemed to flicker among the canoes and to make a soft sound of wuh wuh. It was the spirits of the dead doing this. . . . The people slept badly and dreamed of the fighting" (Olson 1967, 93).

With the death of Santagaw, Shaa Tlein led the Gaanaxh.ádi to Moira Sound, where they built a second and temporary fort. Several months later, during salmon season when the other Taant'a Ḵwáan clans were also absent from Táakw Aaní, a few Xeil Ḵwáan returned to Annette Island and set fire to the whole town (Paul 1971, 11; Olson 1967, 94). When enough food had been obtained for the winter, the Gaanaxh.ádi moved to the old campsite of Daasaxákw on Village Island, where they built a third and more secure fort. Apparently no more serious confrontations occurred, and a peace settlement was negotiated by the Teiḵweidí and the Shéiksh of the time (Olson 1967, 95–96; Paul 1971, 12).

Meanwhile, however, the other three Taant'a Ḵwáan clans had been left homeless as well. They chose not to rebuild Táakw Aaní, and at the entrance to Port Chester in 1883, Nichols saw "the ruins of an old Indian village, entirely overgrown with trees."[50] Over time the Taant'a Ḵwáan began to erect lineage houses at Daasaxákw. Village Island became "nearly covered" with fifteen houses, along with outbuildings and "numerous" poles; another seven houses were raised on neighboring Cat Island (Nichols ed. 1891, 97; Paul 1974, 12; Olson 1967, 94). The name Tongass once again followed the Taant'a Ḵwáan, with Daasaxákw becoming the third site after T'angaash (Tamgas Harbor) and Táakw Aaní (Port Chester) to receive the name.

Shaa Tlein, the Gaanaxh.ádi leader at Daasaxákw, belonged to Drifted Ashore House and was a nephew—apparently a classificatory one—of his predecessor, Santagaw. His connection to other branches of the

Drifted Ashore lineage is one of its unknowns. McKay called him his mother's mother's brother, but according to McKay's chart, this cannot be literally correct. He was, however, likely a parallel cousin of McKay's actual mother's mother's brother, Tanguyéi, a casualty of the battle at Tamgas Harbor (Olson 1967, 82, 93). Shaa Tlein and his wife may have been the pair that traveled to Fort Simpson and the Gitxaahla village in 1842 to pay the debts of the deceased "Shelteen" (who was perhaps S'eiltín II). The journal identifies them as "Natch a Tongass woman with her husband"; Shaa Tlein's wife was Néechk' of the Teikweidí Bear House (FSJ3: 6/19/1842). Both McKay and George Hunt knew Shaa Tlein in childhood, and McKay spent considerable time in his company. Both men told how Shaa Tlein had worked as a pilot for trading vessels and that (in the 1830s, Hunt said) he and his companions signed on to hunt sea otters for a visiting merchant vessel (BPC: Hunt/ Boas 8/2/1920). It was likely one of the traders illegally operating in California. The *Griffon* (in 1828) and *Bolivar Liberator* (in 1834) are known to have brought "Tongass hunters" to Spanish waters, though others may have done so as well (Ogden 1941, 125, 174, 178). Shaa Tlein subsequently traveled as far as Oahu and (McKay said) the Philippines (Curtis 1915, 6; Olson 1967, 41; BPC: Hunt to Boas 1/6/1919).[51]

The succession in the Teikweidí Valley House after Neigoot's 1836 death is murky. In 1842 the Fort Simpson journal reported that "Abits [Ebbets] the chief of that place ["Tongass"] is at the point of death" (Grinev 2005, 172; FSJ3 6/12/1842). This man may have been Kuwdináa II. An "heir of Negut" of this name is mentioned who was both a grandson of the Sitka Kaagwaantaan—perhaps meaning a grandchild of S'eiltín and Taaxsha—and apparently also a son of Kalian. As such, he would have been a younger brother of Xaashgáaksh and possibly also of Bryant's Neigoot (Olson 1967, 41, 43, 46, 89, 91 92, 94).[52]

The Teikweidí line becomes clearer with the rise of two Valley House brothers, Yaanchux and Andáa, both sons of Xaashgáaksh's sister Kaaajidal. Russian sources mention Andáa as early as 1837 (Grinev 2005, 172), but it is not clear when the two brothers assumed leadership of the Teikweidí (Olson 1967, 88–89). Yaanchux, the younger, was McKay's birth father. According to McKay, it was Yaanchux who raised the Valley House at Daasaxákw. He was said to be so wealthy that he stayed in the village while slaves did his work (Olson 1967, 41, 94, 100). If the last is true, it may explain why Fort Simpson trading journals rarely mention Yaanchux (FSJ5 6/20/1860, 6/26/1860). They do, on the other hand, note "'Under' or 'Ebbetts'" arriving frequently to trade and attend feasts, as often as every three months during the years 1855–1860 (FSJ4 10/19/1855 et seq.).

In McKay's narrative, the brothers fell out over the unruly behavior of Andáa's sons, and one day an enraged Yaanchux̱ seriously wounded his older brother (Olson 1967, 41). The Fort Simpson journal reported "the attempted murder of Ibbets by his relation Yancha" in June 1861, presumably the same event (FSJ5 6/21/1861). Andáa recovered but with a part of the Teik̠weidí moved from Daasaxákw to Lexun Séedi (Olson 1967, 41). A few years later a Stikine man of an unspecified clan, angry over an accidental death, shot and killed Yaanchux̱. Reuniting, the Teik̠weidí factions launched a successful raid northward against Yaanchux̱'s killers (Olson 1967, 41–42). In the spring of 1868, when Emil Teichman visited newly established Fort Tongass on Tongass Island, he was met by "a canoe manned by ten armed Indians [who] suddenly blocked our entrance to the bay . . . holding their muskets between their knees." They allowed Teichman's party to pass and visit the island, where Teichman was told of an ongoing feud with Stikine people. In this, "the Tongass had recently inflicted a defeat on their enemies and were now expecting an attack on their own territory. The . . . canoe which we had seen guarding the harbour . . . kept watch day and night" (Teichman 1963, 125; cf. Paul 1971, 13). Teichman had evidently arrived just after the raid McKay describes.

Although McKay gives the falling out between Yaanchux̱ and Andáa as the reason for Andáa's removal from Daasaxákw (Olson 1967, 41), the site had major disadvantages, including exposure to storms and a shortage of drinking water and firewood (Paul 1971, 12; AHL; Field 1888, 684; cf. Nichols ed. 1891, 92, 97–98). "Slaves carried water from other islands" (GFN 7, 11:61). At the same time, Lexun Séedi had been used extensively throughout this period as both a trading rendezvous and a camp and resource site, sufficiently important to the British that they claimed it in their 1840 division of trading rights with the Russians (JDD 5/20–28/1840; FSJ4, FSJ5; cf. Simpson 1847, 206).[53] It would have been a logical destination for Andáa, an active trader at nearby Fort Simpson. The site chosen for new lineage houses, however, was Kaduk̠guká rather than the Kanaganut shore (Olson 1967, 10–12, 42, ROP).

When Major Scott of the U.S. Army visited Tongass Island in 1867, he found "Ebbitt, chief of the Tongas . . . very anxious to have an American trading post established on the island," hoping it would "concentrate . . . the scattered members of his own tribes [sic]" (Scott 1868,

308–9). With Yaanchux̱'s death, the rest of the Teik̲weidí did indeed join their fellows at the new town. The G̲aanax̱.ádi appear to have waited a little longer to build winter houses at Kaduk̲guká. George Hunt mentions visiting relatives at both Daasaxákw and Kaduk̲guká in the 1860s and perhaps early 1870s (BPC: Hunt to Boas 9/28/1918, 8/2/1920; KM IV:4882–907, V: 5420, 5552). Hunt's mother's brothers, Yaashút' and Keenanúk, were Andáa's sons and Shaa Tlein's heirs. They raised a new Raven House first at Daasaxákw to honor Shaa Tlein while he was still living, and later, another at Kaduk̲guká, where it replaced the old Drifted Ashore house (Olson 1967, 96).

Yaashút', the older brother, was a practicing shaman. McKay provided an account of his initiation and training, and another describing his services for the Teik̲weidí on the raid to revenge Yaanchux̱'s death (Olson 1967, 42, 96, 112–13).[54] Keenanúk, the younger brother, worked, like Shaa Tlein before him, as a pilot for visiting vessels (Curtis 1915, 6, Teichman 1963, 127–28). Both brothers were familiar faces to the HBC traders at Fort Simpson (FSJ4: 2/4/1856; 9/1/1857, 9/15/1857, 9/16/1857, 3/9/1858). Like too many during these years, however, Yaashút' was shot and killed, this time in an intra-clan clash at Kaduk̲guká in 1876 in which his brother was also wounded (AMH; Olson 1967, 96–98).

Eventually, a total of seventeen houses were raised at Kaduk̲guká (Olson 1967, 41, 10, 96). Once again the designation of Tongass followed the Taant'ak̲wáan, so that Kaduk̲guká, Cottonwood Island, became present-day Tongass Island. Photographer Eadweard Muybridge visited Kaduk̲guká shortly after the U.S. military arrived in May 1868, as part of a U.S. Coast and Geodetic Survey expedition. His images show several camp or smoke houses as well as structures of milled wood (figure 12.10; Paul 1971, 4–5). The dwellings' sleeping rooms, wrote another visitor of the time, were "as neatly furnished as most whaling ships' cabins" and built with joinery of comparable skill (Colyer 1869, 535).

In figure 12.10, men in Bear tunics stand with an older man wearing a frontlet and chilkat robe, in front of the recently erected Sea Bear pole that was a Valley House crest (*kuwi* [?] *xóozi*; Olson 1967, 11, 46; KM V:5536–5552). These are surely Teik̲weidí men, and one of them, most likely the man in the frontlet, is Andáa. Muybridge, under his studio name Helios, sent a carte de visite of this image back to Kaduk̲guká with a handwritten message, "to the brave and noble Chief of the Tongas with Helios' respect." This picture was passed down in the Hunt family and survives today (Andy Everson p.c. April 10, 2012).[55]

Fig. 12.10 Andáa with other Teikweidí men at Kadukguká on Tongass Island, 1868. Photo by Eadweard Muybridge. Presbyterian Historical Society, Philadelphia.

Andáa remained at Kadukguká until his death in 1880 (Scidmore 1891, 52). Colyer, who met "Mr. Ebbitts, chief of the Tongass" in 1869, described him as "an intelligent and kind-hearted old man" (1869, 537).[56] He had at least two wives (FSJ4 3/9/1858; ROP). One, about whom little is known, belonged to the Gaanax.ádi Sea Lion House; a daughter of this union was still living in 1938 (GFN 7, 11:61). The other wife belonged to the Drifted Ashore House lineage. She was Aanseet, daughter of Shéiksh and S'eiltín II, and she may be the woman wearing the robe and painted hat in Muybridge's photos. Aanseet drowned on a visit to the Nass River, where a daughter had married a Nisga'a chief (Collison ed. 1981, 111–12; GFN 7, 11:65).[57] She was later memorialized by a crest pole that was removed to Seattle's Pioneer Square, where a copy still stands.

Given a long-standing practice of outmarriage among the Taant'a Kwáan, it is not surprising that they would have sought to bring whites into their affinal network. The coasting ships did not remain long enough, but a number of marriages took place between HBC employees and Taant'a Kwáan women, a few of which can be mentioned here.

A young G̲aanax̲.ádi woman known in English as Kate married Captain Swanson of the HBC steamship *Labouchere*. Olson records her Tlingit name as "Xich," and though she cannot be precisely linked to McKay's genealogy, he mentions her as a cousin (ROP; FSJ5 6/12/1860; LTJ 9/29/1860). The pole at Kaduk̲guká featuring a carving of a ship, a copy of which was later installed at Ketchikan City Park, is said by one source to have been raised in Kate's honor, though other interpretations have been offered (Garfield and Forrest 1961, 66; Barbeau 1950, 407–8; cf. Olson 1967, 38).

A second marriage took place between Paul Pareaut and Nas'áat, the Dak̲'laweidí granddaughter of Santagaw and Talyéi. Pareaut was one of the HBC men visiting Tongass, "the land of their wives," in the summer of 1857 (FSJ4 8/1/1857; also 7/14/1858).[58] The children of this union included the missionary and teacher Louis Paul, in turn the father of civil rights lawyer William Paul (Paul 1971, 4-5).

Finally, one of Andáa's daughters, Mary Ebbetts (Anein), wed Robert Hunt, an HBC employee at Fort Rupert on Vancouver Island, whom she first met during an 1850 trading voyage to Victoria (BPC: Hunt/Boas 11/12/1921, 12/24/1921). Their second child and eldest son, George, was born in Fort Rupert in February 1854 (BPC: Hunt/Boas 4/7/1916, 1/6/1919; Barbeau 1950, 651). In his early adulthood George Hunt was employed by the HBC as well, but after making his first object collection in 1879, he went on to work for over fifty years as a museum collector and ethnographic fieldworker, most notably with pioneering anthropologist Franz Boas (Berman n.d.).

That Northwest Coast ethnography begins with Hunt, eighty years after the *Eliza* first encountered the "Cockathanes," says a good deal about the historical lacuna in the discipline. Of other early indigenous figures in ethnography, K̲adasháan of the Stikine Kaasx̲'agweidí, one of Swanton's sources, was the eldest son of Laatx̲íchx̲, himself the great-grandson of Yisyát, Curson's "Eastgut"; in other words, K̲adasháan was in the fifth generation from the beginning of the fur trade era. Louis Shotridge, the son of K̲adasháan's half-brother, Yeilgoox̲ú, came from the sixth generation; and George Hunt belonged to the seventh generation of the Taant'a K̲wáan, beginning with his ancestor K̲aa Tlein, to engage with the global economy.

Conclusion

Although still incomplete, the interim results of this project argue for the validity of the approach. Using genealogy and succession lists to link indigenous and documentary sources has shown several things. First, traditional succession lists show a convincing degree of overlap with the sequence of clan leaders mentioned by fur traders and others. Second, through such lists and related genealogical information, it is possible to correlate the two sources temporally. Third, once this is done, it is possible, with varying degrees of certainty and levels of detail, to identify subjects treated in both sets of source materials. These include unique historical episodes like Ḵaa Tlein's death; larger-scale events such as Taant'a Ḵwáan relocations through a series of winter town sites over the nineteenth century; and ongoing social or economic processes that include marriage patterns, seasonal movement between resource sites, and exchange with other indigenous groups as well as with visiting mariners.

The study shows the degree to which the two sets of materials can be complementary. Indigenous sources tend to provide individual motivation and the cultural and social background of events; documentary sources provide calendar dates, eyewitness descriptions, and sometimes geographical or other kinds of specificity.

It is hoped that further research will help to confirm or disprove the correlations made here and fill the gaps in the expanding picture of Taant'a Ḵwáan history. Unknowns that at present beg for answers include the location of Kegaan; more specific dates for founding and abandonment of Taant'a Ḵwáan winter towns; and the degree to which the striking number of Taant'a Ḵwáan clan leaders who died in violent conflicts during this period is a consequence of the fur trade due to, for example, competition for furs, increased contact between clans with a history of unfriendly relations, and the introduction of alcohol.

Whether the methodology or results of this study are applicable elsewhere in North America is an open question. While there is evidence of similar types of deep historical memory elsewhere on the Northwest Coast, the cultural meanings of history and time, and the genres in which such concepts are expressed, differ in other North American cultural provinces (cf. Vansina 1985, 24,117–18).

ACKNOWLEDGMENTS

More people have helped in the course of this study than it is possible to mention here. I owe a particular debt to the late Emma Williams and Esther Shea, who helped decipher Olson's transcriptions of Taant'a

Ḵwáan names; Esther provided most of the spellings used here. My Ketchikan visits were enriched by the hospitality of Mary Jones and her late husband, Willard, much missed, and over the years Mary has also generously shared her family history files as well as other genealogical tidbits culled from her wide correspondence. I am grateful as well to George Samuels for further details of Teiḵweidí names and history and for encouraging me to believe that this would be a project with value for contemporary Taant'a Ḵwáan. I would also like to thank the Tongass tribe and Dan Monteith for, years ago, making available their collection of publications on Tongass history; Priscilla Schulte and Martin Stanford for information regarding archaeological surveys in Duke Island and vicinity; Chris Roth for patiently answering my many questions about Nisga'a and Tsimshian locales and names; Nora and Dick Dauenhauer and James Crippen for aid in spelling Tlingit; Steve Langdon for pointing me to further archival resources; and last but not least, Sergei Kan and the late Andrew Hope III, another who will be greatly missed, for their valuable comments on the drafts of this paper. None of these people should be held responsible for the mistakes I inevitably will have made.

The helpful staff of the numerous archives visited are also too numerous to list in this space, but I especially would like to acknowledge the staff of the Nantucket Historical Association; Katherine Griffin of the Massachusetts Historical Society for information regarding authorship of the *Eliza* and *Pearl* logs; and Alex Pezzati of the University of Pennsylvania Museum Archives for his help with the Shotridge papers over the course of many years. Funding for fieldwork and archival research was provided by the Jacobs Research Fund of the Whatcom Museum of History and Art, the Philips Fund for Native American Studies of the American Philosophical Society, a National Endowment for the Humanities Travel to Collections grant, and a travel grant from the Center for Native American Studies at the University of Pennsylvania.

ARCHIVAL WORKS CITED

AHL   Louis Shotridge papers, Alaska Historical Library. Juneau AK.
AMH   Letter of Abbits to Mary [Ebbets] Hunt, 1876. In the possession of Sally Lyon McMahon.
AUP   Logbook of the *Polly* 1800–1802. Author unknown. Massachusetts Historical Society, Boston.

BMJ   Remarks & Observations in a Voyage Made on Board Ship Jefferson Josiah Roberts Commander from Boston North America to the NW Coast the Same & Round the Globe, 1791–1793. Kept by Bernard Magee [first officer]. Massachusetts Historical Society, Boston.

BPC   Franz Boas Professional Correspondence. American Philosophical Society, Philadelphia.

CGT   Plan Gavani Taiakhonsiti: Sniat s Briga Chichiagova 1836 Goda. Rare Maps Collection (CG3512 T381 [verso]), Alaska and Polar Regions Collections, Elmer E. Rasmuson Library. University of Alaska, Fairbanks.

ECV   Remarks on Board the Ship *Vancouver:* from Boston to the N. West Coast of America and China, 1804–1806. Kept by Ebenezer Clinton. Beinecke Library, Yale University, New Haven (WA MSS 92).

FSC   Fort Simpson Correspondence, Provincial Archives of British Columbia, Victoria.

FSJ1   Journal of the Hudson's Bay Company at Fort Simpson 1834–1838. Bancroft Library, University of California, Berkeley.

FSJ2   Fort Simpson Journal 1838–1840, Hudson's Bay Company Archives, Provincial Archives of Manitoba, Winnipeg.

FSJ3   Fort Simpson Journal 1842–1843, Provincial Archives of British Columbia, Victoria.

FSJ4   Fort Simpson Journal 1855–1859, Hudson's Bay Company Archives, Provincial Archives of Manitoba, Winnipeg.

FSJ5   Fort Simpson Journal 1859–1862, Provincial Archives of British Columbia, Victoria.

FSJ6   Fort Simpson Journal 1863–1866, Hudson's Bay Company Archives, Provincial Archives of Manitoba, Winnipeg.

GFN   Garfield Field Notebooks, Viola Garfield Papers. Manuscripts and University Archives Division, University of Washington Libraries, Seattle.

JDD   Sir James Douglas, Diary of a Trip to the Northwest Coast [1840]. British Columbia Provincial Archives, Victoria.

JSP   Logbook of the Ship *Pearl* 1804–1808. Kept by John Suter. Massachusetts Historical Society, Boston.

KM   Kwakiutl Materials by Franz Boas and George Hunt [Freeman #1941]. Franz Boas Collection of American Indian Linguistics. American Philosophical Society, Philadelphia.

LTJ   Fur Trade Journal of the Steamer *Labouchere* 1859–1860. Author unknown, British Columbia Provincial Archives, Victoria.
LSC   Louis Shotridge Correspondence, University of Pennsylvania Museum Archives, Philadelphia.
MKV   Merkatorskaia Karta Vostochnago Okeana S Sieverozapadnya Beregom Ameriki i Prelagaiushchim K Nemu Koloshenskim Arkipelagom, Alaska and Polar Regions Collections, Elmer E. Rasmuson Library, University of Alaska, Fairbanks.
RKO   Shipping Logbook of Brig *Otter* 1809–1811 (Log 1809 O). Kept by Robert Kemp. Phillips Library, Peabody Essex Museum, Salem.
RHA1 Voyage from Boston to the North-West Coast of America, 1800–1803, vols. 1–2 [Ship *Atahualpa*, Capt Wildes master] (WA MSS S-126). Kept by Ralph Haskins. Beinecke Library, Yale University, New Haven.
RHA   23rd Vol of a Journal Kept by R. Haskins on the Ship *Atahualpa* Bound on a Voyage from Boston 'Round the World, 1800 to 1803 [Capt Wildes master]. Columbia River Maritime Museum, Astoria OR.
ROP   Ronald Olson Papers, Bancroft Library, University of California, Berkeley.
SFO   Journal of a Voyage from Boston to the North-West Coast of America, 1809–1911, on the Brig *Otter* (WA MSS 207). Kept by Samuel Furgerson. Beinecke Library, Yale University, New Haven.
SMR   Louis Shotridge Miscellaneous Records, University of Pennsylvania Museum Archives, Philadelphia.
TWC   Twelfth Census of the United States (1900). National Archives.
TWL   Supercargo's Log for the Brig *Lydia*, 1805–1807 [Samuel Hill, master] (WA MSS S-214). Kept by Thomas Walker, Beinecke Library, Yale University, New Haven.
UEN   Louis Shotridge Unpublished Ethnographic Notes, University of Pennsylvania Museum Archives, Philadelphia.
WWL   Supercargo's Log of the Brig *Lydia*, 1805–1807 (WA MSS S-214). Kept by William Walker Jr. Beinecke Library, Yale University, New Haven.
WBR   Journal of a voyage Round the World on the Brig *Rob Roy* in the years 1821, 1822, 1823, 1824, and 1825. Kept by William Bryant. Nantucket Historical Association.
WTG   Thomas T. Waterman, Tlingit Geographical Names for Extreme Southeast Alaska with Historical and Other Notes, 1922 (NAA MS 2938). National Anthropological Archives, Smithsonian Institution, Washington DC.

NOTES

1. Tattiskey lay between several Kaigani villages on Dall and Long Islands. The appearance in early sources of both Tattiskey and Tattis Cove (and variants of both names) lends confusion to the issue of its exact location. According to two ca. 1802 maps sketched by Ralph Haskins, "Tatterskee" proper, the preferred anchorage, lay in South Kaigani Harbor, while "Tattersco" or the "Cove" refers to Datzkoo Harbor (RHA2; see also MKV; Sturgis 1998, 46; Davidson 1969, 91; Dall 1880, 55–56; Gibson 1992, 206).
2. An exception is Olson 1967a, 19; another possible reference to her is Emmons 1907a, 342–43.
3. The spelling of this name is particularly uncertain.
4. The respective versions of the nineteenth-century war between the Kaagwaantaan and Naanyaa.aayí provide one example, where each side ascribes its origin to different causes (Olson 1967, 77–79). Modifications might also be made to *forestall* conflict, especially after peace had been made. For example, Mrs. Cameron's mother, who told her the history of a war between the Kaagwaantaan and Teiḵweidí, withheld the name of the man who caused the death that ignited it (Olson 1967, 50; cf. UEN: "Emblems").
5. Swanton gives the groom's name as G̱unahéen. This is a Kaagwaantaan Wolf House name and may also have been used by Taax̱sha.
6. This name has been given incorrectly as Shaadaxícht (Milburn 1994, 551, 1997, 44, 76n41, 42). According to Shotridge, the full version is L-shaaduxích-x̱, "Not clubbed," and refers to the Dogfish crest of Laatx̱íchx̱'s Naanyaa.aayí paternal grandfather, K'ux̱shóo III (Shéiksh II), from whom the name originated (Emmons 1991, 262; UEN, "History"; Durlach 1928, 174)
7. Laatx̱íchx̱ is mentioned as the leader of an 1852 overland raiding party that destroyed the Hudson's Bay Company post of Fort Selkirk, and restored the Tlingit fur trading monopoly in that region (Emmons 1916, 10, 1991, 15).
8. Shotridge says that this man's "name is not obtained" (SMR; UEN, "History").
9. Similarly, Olson recorded the Teiḵweidí name Yaanchux̱ as Gantcúh (ROP).
10. The published English translation of Shelikov's account (1991) spells it "Ilchak." For the original Russian transcription of the name—given here in Library of Congress transliteration with /kh/ for the Russian /x/—I am indebted to Sergei Kan (p.c. 3/15/2011).
11. According to George Hunt, the Taant'a Ḵwáan G̱aanax̱.ádi acquired the names Keenanook and Neshot (=Nishoot?) via the marriage of Raven

Relating Deep Genealogies 235

to the daughter of "Edensu" of "YäkwEn" (KM VI, "Raven or Yáł story of the łenget").

12. Oberg states that each moiety had an *aankáawu*, the highest-ranking house master of its ranking clan (1972, 142–43).
13. The Krause brothers reported that the G̲aanax̲teidí Raven House posts were in 1881–1882 stored in "one of Tschartritsch's warehouses."
14. Differences in McKay's various statements about the origins of the Taant'a K̲wáan G̲aanax̲.ádi (Olson 1967, 83, 84, 115) are perhaps explained by the fact that only some houses claimed descent from Joon's daughters (see also Monteith 1998, 80–81, 105–7).
15. Waterman's account from Pete Williams (1922, 13 in Monteith 1998, 115) agrees in placing Kasgi G̲eeyí at Stone Rock Bay, while Olson gives Moira Sound as an alternate location (1967, 3). Moira Sound is not near the "head" of Taan and seems a less likely source for the name Taan yat'ak̲. According to Paul, Cape Chacon was the site of the winter town while Moira Sound, Annette Island, Cape Northumberland, and Tongass Island, each one day's paddling from the next, were traditional camp- sites used, among other things, for trips to the annual Nass oolichan run (1971, 10).
16. L'eixi does not appear in the original McKay genealogy; for another account see Waterman 1922, 13 in Monteith 1998, 115.
17. That the Haida at Kaigani did not hunt most of the furs they offered for sale was observed by other traders (e.g., WBR n.d.)
18. E.g., AUP 5/2/1801, 5/4/1801; RHA1 6/25/1802; JSP flyleaf list (5/22–28/1805); WWL 6/18/1805; TWL 3/13–15/1806, 4/8–16/1806, 6/18–19/1806; ECV 6/6/1806.
19. Under the heading "Tumgarse"; Bryant's use of the terms "Tumgarse" and "Cocklanes" is discussed below. The identification of the *Rob Roy* journal's author as William Bryant was made by Malloy (2006). For another early word list, see Scouler (1841, 231–35).
20. "Entancoon" also occurs on a ca. 1801 or 1802 sketch by Haskins (with RHA2).
21. Since Tlingit has no /m/, the form of the word "clemel"—doubtless related to Heiltsuk *tl'u'ls* "elk"—suggests that traders acquired the term via the Haida or Tsimshian, and Haida use of the jargon word is attested (e.g., WBR 1822). Monolingual Tlingit speakers of earlier generations converted foreign bilabials to /w/ or a velar like /x/, and for /n/ alter- nated between [l] and [n] (Dauenhauer and Dauenhauer 2001, 72; J. Crippen p.c. 7/20/2009).
22. For Kanaxanat, Shotridge gives Kax̲ana.aat, for which he proposed the derivation a-káx̲-ana.aat, "a journey-way or 'passage'" (AHL).
23. That American mariners initially wrote the name as Tumgarse—with an /m/ rather than an /n/—suggests they did not first hear it from Tlingit speakers. Russian use of /m/ and /n/ in the name varies (CGT; MKV).

24. Olson provides a similar name (Tangáash) for Zayas Island (1967, 57; Goldschmidt and Hass 1998, 183). It seems possible that, as Zayas and Dundas Islands were at one time Taant'a Ḵwáan territory, the name T'angaash originated there.
25. The harbor the *Polly*'s journalist called Cocklains may have been Lexun Séedi (AUP).
26. Olson's text in this particular passage has the Taant'a Ḵwáan "winter village" at first contact on Tamgas Creek, which may be evidence of the permanence of the structures there but contradicts McKay's narratives about Kegaan (see also Paul 1971, 10, 11).
27. Walker described the "Summer Village"—which he distinguished from "Clemencette" near Point Wales—only as somewhere north of Dundas Island.
28. In light of the statements by other observers, it is difficult to interpret Haskins's notation of the two sites on Lincoln Channel, Kaduḵguká and Kanaxanát, as "winter village" and "summer village," respectively (RHA2).
29. It is not Kaigani, as this Kemp consistently writes "Clarganee" (RKO 4/15/1810 et seq.).
30. Olson's text reads, "on the south shore [of Duke Island] near Cape Cumberland," presumably meaning "Cape Northumberland" (1967, 84).
31. Vancouver's vantage has been taken as present-day Vancouver Island off Cape Northumberland, but Davidson judged it to be only "a small island of a large number lying south of the cape" (1869, 76).
32. A Teiḵweidí fort said to have been occupied for a short time on Kelp Island southeast of Duke Island may be Vancouver's "village," as well as the fort mentioned both by Waterman and in Coast Tsimshian tradition (Olson 1967, 89; Marsden 2001, 73). Kuwdináa was said to be the Teiḵweidí leader when it was built, however, which would date it after Vancouver's expedition.
33. Kemp mentions both his brig and the *Derby* engaging in ship repair at nearby Tessequah as well (RKO 8/6/1810–9/23/1810).
34. Marsden and Galois state, "In 1787, the Gispaxlo'ots . . . had . . . preferred access to trade at the mouth of the Nass" (1995, 170, see also 181n19)." However, neither that name nor that of the Gispaxlo'ots leading chief, Ligeex, appear in documents from the first decades of the fur trade. Initially Seeks (either the Gitxaahla or Ginaxangiik Killerwhale chief of the name), and then Ts'ibasaa ("Shebasser" and variants, the leading chief of the Gitxaahla Killerwhales), are the Coast Tsimshian men appearing most often in association with these camps (see also Jackman ed. 1978, 66–67, 87–89; RHA1 3/14/1802, RHA2; Roe ed. 1967, 67–72, 89–94).
35. Trade between the Taant'a Ḵwáan and the Nass River was not initiated solely by the Taant'a Ḵwáan. In June 1806, the crew of the *Lydia* witnessed the departure of a Nass River (Nisga'a or Coast Tsimshian?) trad-

ing expedition bound for Clemelcitty, "about twenty large canoes loaded with fish and oil" (TWL 6/9/1806).
36. Four other children appear on McKay's chart (Olson 1967, 84–85, 88; ROP). The Tongass "Cowgelth" or "Cogwealth," a "half-Nass man" who appears in the Fort Simpson journals, is clearly a Koowageil from a later generation (FSJ5 9/1/1859, 11/11/1859).
37. The affiliation of Nekeisk, a "chief of considerable consequence . . . rich in furs" (RHA1 4/12/1802), is at present unknown. A Kaigani-Gitxaalha conflict occurred in the same month, and Edensaw's brother and another relative were killed (RHA1 4/24/1802). It seems possible that Nekeisk's brother could be one of these Kaigani men.
38. As the clan that sought immediate retaliation against the Gitxaalha was the Xaas.hitaan, it can be inferred that Skawoolyeil belonged to that clan (Olson 1967, 88).
39. That statement may apply to a second, later Kuwdináa (see below).
40. That it may have been Gits'iis is suggested by Kemp's reference to the "Nestorkoonots tribe Liveing up at Kyoon." "Nestorkoonots" is perhaps Niisyaganaat, paramount chief of the Gits'iis Tsimshian. If "Kyoon" is in fact in Gits'iis territory, it may have been located on Work Channel or the adjacent mainland on the southern side of the Nass estuary (RKO 11/2/1810; C. Roth p.c., 10/31/2007).
41. The name Neigoot appears in contexts in which the identity of the bearer is murky. This could be because more than one Teikweidí man used it (Shotridge 1929, 148). A Kuwdináa II who may have been the successor of Bryant's Neigoot might have used the name (Olson 1967, 89, 91), and the next Valley House master, Andáa, is known to have used it (Scidmore 1891, 52–53; Scott 1904, 349; Paul 1971, 9; see FSJ4 10/19/1855, 10/9/1857, 6/7/1862).
42. Bryant's Neigoot has incorrectly been identified as Nisga'a (Gibson 1992, 167). Some historians may have confused the name with Nishoot or "Neachoot," which, according to George Hunt, is a Taant'a Kwáan Gaanax.ádi name originally acquired from the Haida (KM VI "Raven or Yáł story of the łenget") and shared with the Gitzaxhlaahl Ravens (WBR 7/28/1822; Marsden and Galois 1995, 174, 176).
43. According to moiety exogamy rules, Kaa Tlein's father would have belonged to a Raven-moiety clan and, similarly, Neigoot's Tlingit guests would have been Raven-side opposites of his Wolf-moiety Teikweidí clan.
44. Llwyd gives the meaning of "Tshadatsta" as "Everybody looks up to him," information supposedly from George Hunt.
45. He is also perhaps the 1799 Stikine "Hatestey" whose name was mentioned to Curson (Jackman ed. 1978, 89).

46. The name S'eiltín is connected with two headdresses purchased by Shotridge in the 1920s, one from the Sitka Wolf House (University of Pennsylvania Museum number NA8474) and the other from Wrangell (NA11755). Shotridge called both the hair of the Bride of Tongass, and a photograph in his article confusingly depicts both laid side by side, with the Wrangell headdress on the left (1929, 154). It seems possible that one comes from the S'eiltín who married into the Kaagwaantaan Wolf House, and the other from S'eiltín II, who married into the Naanyaa.aayí Dogfish House. The two clans were rivals during much of the nineteenth century.
47. Spelled and glossed as such in Bryant's Kaigani word list (WBR n.d.).
48. Swanton's narrator was Sgaagia himself. The conflict may be that referred to in Fort Simpson correspondence from 1844 (FSC: J Work/C Dood 8/2/1844, J Work/McLaughlin 11/17/1844).
49. At a fort called Ch'eex̲'aani "Thimbleberry Town" (Olson 1967, 93; Emmons 1916, 16; de Laguna 1972, 446).
50. "Some Indian houses," however—almost certainly Taant'a Ḵwáan—were then still extant at "the bight near Copper Point [where] a fine salmon stream empties from Trout Lake" (Nichols ed. 1891, 93).
51. According to Hunt, Shaa Tlein returned with a box of abalone shells, perhaps the highly desirable California abalone, that brought him considerable wealth back home (Curtis 1915, 6; Olson 1967, 41; BPC: Hunt to Boas 1/6/1919, 8/2/1920; see also Boas 1966, 190–91). In Sturgis's day, a single California shell of the right color and luster could buy a prime sea otter pelt (Sturgis 1998, 30; see RHA1 4/20/1802; Ogden 1941, 28–30).
52. Niblack's image of the "feast house of Chief Kootenah at Tongass Village," taken perhaps in 1885–1887 (1890, pl. LV, fig. 294), may refer to Andáa's successor, as Andáa died in 1880. Lucy Kininnook Marsden's reference to a "Kodinat," who was an "Indian Doctor," is even more ambiguous (GFN 7, 11:71).
53. Simpson speaks of the inhabitants of both "Tomgass, and the Isles des Clamelsettes."
54. He is perhaps the shaman Yaashút' mentioned by Emmons, whose helper spirit was called *hintak xóozi* (undersea bear), a "slave" of G̲unaakadeit (1991, 365).
55. From Maggie Frank (daughter of Emily Hunt Wilson and granddaughter of George Hunt) to her grandson, artist Andy Everson, who has it today.
56. The name Colyer supplies for Chief Ebbets, "Quack-ham," cannot be identified, unless it is a corruption of Ḵaa Tlein (1869, 537).
57. Barbeau says "sister" (1950, 651, 654).
58. The "Louis Pareut," a "retiring servant" who departed Fort Simpson in 1860, may be the same man (FSC: H Moffatt/AG Dallas 2/4/1860).

WORKS CITED

Acheson, Steven R. 1995. "In the Wake of the Iron People: A Case for Changing Settlement Strategies among the Kunghit Haida." *Journal of the Royal Anthropological Institute* 1 (2): 273–99.

———. 1985. "Ninstin Village: A Case of Mistaken Identity." *BC Studies* 67: 47–56.

Bancroft, Hubert Howe. 1884. *History of the Northwest Coast.* Pt. 1, 1543–1800; pt. 2, 1800–1846. Vol. 27 of the *Works of Hubert Howe Bancroft.* San Francisco: A. L. Bancroft.

———. 1886. *History of Alaska, 1730–1885.* Vol. 33 of the *Works of Hubert Howe Bancroft.* San Francisco: A. L. Bancroft.

Barbeau, Marius. 1950. *Totem Poles.* 2 vols. Bulletin 119, Anthropological Series no. 30. Ottawa: National Museum of Canada.

Beresford, William. 1789. *Voyage Round the World, but Particularly to the North-West Coast of America; Performed in 1785, 1786, 1787, and 1788, in the* King George *and* Queen Charlotte, *Captains Portlock and Dixon.* London: Goulding.

Berman, Judith. 2004. "'Some Mysterious Means of Fortune': A Look at Northwest Coast Oral History." In *Coming to Shore: Northwest Coast Ethnology, Traditions, and Visions,* ed. Marie Mauzé, Michael Harkin, and Sergei Kan, 129–62. Lincoln: University of Nebraska Press.

———. 2007. "Relating Deep Genealogy, Oral History, and Early European Accounts: Questions, Problems, Progress." Paper presented at Sharing Our Knowledge: A Conference of Tsimshian, Haida, and Tlingit Tribes and Clans, March 22–25, 2007, Sitka AK.

———. n.d. "Raven and Sunbeam, Pencil and Paper: George Hunt of Fort Rupert BC." Manuscript in author's possession.

Blackman, Margaret. 1981. *Window on the Past: The Photographic Ethnohistory of the Northern and Kaigani Haida.* National Museum of Man Mercury Series, Canadian Ethnology Service Paper 74. Ottawa: National Museums of Canada.

Boas, Franz. 1966. *Kwakiutl Ethnography.* Ed. Helen Codere. Chicago: University of Chicago Press.

———. 1911. Introduction to Boas, ed., *Handbook of American Indian Languages,* 5–83. Bureau of American Ethnology Bulletin 40. Washington: Government Printing Office.

———. 1909. *The Kwakiutl of Vancouver Island.* The Jesup North Pacific Expedition, Memoirs of the American Museum of Natural History V. New York: American Museum of Natural History.

Boyd, Robert. 1996. "Commentary on Early Contact Era Smallpox in the Pacific Northwest." *Ethnohistory* 43 (2): 307–28.

Collison, William Henry. 1981. *In the Wake of the War Canoe.* Ed. Charles Lillard. Victoria BC: Sono Nis.

Colyer, Vincent. 1869. *Alaska: Report of the Hon. Vincent Colyer*. Annual Report of the Commissioner of Indian Affairs, 533–616. Washington DC: Government Printing Office.

Cove, John J., and George F. MacDonald, eds. 1987. *Tsimshian Narratives, Collected by Marius Barbeau and William Beynon*. 2 vols. Mercury Series Directorate Paper no. 3. Ottawa: Canadian Museum of Civilization.

Cruikshank Julie. 1998. *The Social Life of Stories: Narrative and Knowledge in the Yukon Territory*. Lincoln: University of Nebraska Press.

Curtis, Edward S. 1915. *The Kwakiutl*. The North American Indian 10. Norwood CN.

Dall, William Healey. 1880. *Pacific Coast Pilot: Coasts and Islands of Alaska, Dixon Entrance to Cape Spencer with the Inland Passage*. United States Coast and Geodetic Survey. Washington DC: Government Printing Office.

Dauenhauer, Nora Marks. 1995. "Tlingit *at.óow*: Traditions and Concepts." In *The Spirit Within: Northwest Coast Art from the John H. Hauberg Collection*, ed. Helen Abbott, Steven Brown, Lorna Price, and Paula Thurman, 20–29. Seattle: Seattle Art Museum.

Dauenhauer, Nora Marks, and Richard Dauenhauer. 2001. "Tracking 'Yuwaan Gageets': A Russian Fairy Tale in Tlingit Oral Tradition." In *Native American Oral Traditions: Collaboration and Interpretation*, ed. Larry Evers and Barre Toelken, 58–91. Logan: Utah State University Press.

Dauenhauer, Nora Marks, and Richard Dauenhauer, eds. 1987. *Haa Shuka, Our Ancestors: Tlingit Oral Narratives*. Seattle: University of Washington Press.

Dauenhauer, Nora Marks, Richard Dauenhauer, and Lydia T. Black, eds. 2008. *Anóoshi Lingít Aaní Ká, Russians in Tlingit America: The Battles of Sitka, 1802 and 1804*. Seattle: University of Washington Press.

Davidson, George. 1869. *Coast Pilot of Alaska (First Part): From Southern Boundary to Cook's Inlet*. United States Coast Survey, Pacific Coast. Washington DC: Government Printing Office.

de Laguna, Frederica. 1960. *The Story of a Tlingit Community: A Problem in the Relationship between Archeological, Ethnological, and Historical Methods*. Washington DC: Government Printing Office.

———. 1972. *Under Mount Saint Elias: The History and Culture of the Yakutat Tlingit*. 3 vols. Smithsonian Contributions to Anthropology 7. Washington DC: Smithsonian Institution Press.

Deloria, Vine, Jr. 1995. *Red Earth, White Lies: Native Americans and the Myth of Scientific Fact*. New York: Scribner.

Dunn, John. 1844. *History of the Oregon Territory and British North-American Fur Trade: With an Account of the Habits and Customs of the Principal Native Tribes on the Northern Continent*. London: Edwards and Hughes.

Durlach, Theresa Mayer. 1928. *The Relationship Systems of the Tlingit, Haida, and Tsimshian*. Publications of the American Ethnological Society 11. New York: Stechert.

Echo-Hawk, R. 2000. "Ancient History in the New World: Integrating Oral Traditions and the Archaeological Record in Deep Time." *American Antiquity* 65:267–90.

Emmons, George T. 1907a. "The Chilkat Blanket." *Memoirs of the American Museum of Natural History* 3 (4): 329–50.

———. 1907b. "The Use of the Chilkat Blanket." *American Museum Journal* 8 (5): 65–72.

———. 1916. "Whale House of the Chilkat." *American Museum of Natural History Anthropological Papers* 19 (1): 1–33.

———. 1991. *The Tlingit Indians*. Ed. Frederica de Laguna. Vancouver BC: Douglas and McIntyre.

Field, Kate. 1888. "A Trip to Southeastern Alaska." *Harper's Weekly Supplement*, September 8, 1888.

Fisher, Robin. 1992. *Contact and Conflict: Indian-European Relations in British Columbia, 1774-1890*. 2nd ed. Vancouver: UBC Press.

Galois, Robert, ed. 2004. *A Voyage to the North West Side of America: The Journals of James Colnett, 1786-89*. Vancouver: University of British Columbia Press.

Garfield, Viola. 1947. "Historical Aspects of Tlingit Clans in Angoon, Alaska." *American Anthropologist* 49 (2): 438–52.

Garfield, Viola, and Linn A. Forrest. 1961. *The Wolf and the Raven: Totem Poles of Southeastern Alaska*. Seattle: University of Washington Press.

Gibson, James. 1992. *Otter Skins, Boston Ships, and China Goods: The Maritime Fur Trade of the Northwest Coast, 1785–1841*. Montreal: McGill-Queens University Press.

Goldschmidt, Walter R., and Theodore H. Haas. 1998. *Haa Aaní, Our Land: Tlingit and Haida Land Rights and Use. (Possessory Rights of the Natives of Southeastern Alaska.)* Ed. Thomas F. Thornton. Seattle: University of Washington Press.

Green, Jonathan. 1915. *Journal of a Tour on the North West Coast of America in the Year 1829*. New York: Hartman.

Grinev, A. V. 2005. *The Tlingit Indians in Russian America, 1741–1867*. Trans. Richard L. Bland and Katerina G. Solovjova. Lincoln: University of Nebraska Press.

Grumet, Robert Steven. 1975. "Changes in Coast Tsimshian Redistributive Activities in the Fort Simpson Region of British Columbia, 1788–1862." *Ethnohistory* 22 (4): 295–318.

Howay, F. W. 1925. "Indian Attacks upon Maritime Fur Traders of the Northwest Coast, 1785–1805." *Canadian Historical Review* 6: 287–309.

———. 1940. *The Journal of Captain James Colnett Aboard "The Argonaut" from April 26, 1789, to November 3, 1791*. Edited with introduction and notes. Toronto: Champlain Society.

———. 1941. *Voyages of the "Columbia" to the Northwest Coast, 1787–1790 and 1790–1793*. Edited with introduction and notes. Boston: Massachusetts Historical Society.

———. 1942. "Anglo-American Competition in the Fur Trade." In *British Columbia and the United States*, ed. H. F. Angus. Toronto: Ryerson.

———. 1973 [1930]. *A List of Trading Vessels in the Maritime Fur Trade, 1785–1825*. Kingston ON: Limestone Press.

Hymes, Dell. 1964. "Introduction: Toward Ethnographies of Communication." *American Anthropologist*, n.s., 66 (6) pt. 2: 1–34.

Ingraham, Joseph. 1971. *Journal of the Brigantine Hope on a Voyage to the Northwest Coast of America, 1790–2*. Ed. Mark D. Kaplanoff. Barre MA: Imprint Society.

Jackman, S. W., ed. 1978. *The Journal of William Sturgis* [journal kept by Samuel Curson]. Victoria: Sono Nis Press.

Kan, Sergei. 1999. *Memory Eternal: Tlingit Culture and Russian Orthodox Christianity through Two Centuries*. Seattle: University of Washington Press.

Keithahn, Edward. 1940. *The Authentic History of Shakes Island and Clan*. Wrangell AK: Wrangell Historical Society.

Krause, Aurel. 1956. *The Tlingit Indians: Results of a Trip to the Northwest Coast of America and the Bering Straits*. Translated by Erna Gunther. Published for the American Ethnological Society. Seattle: University of Washington Press.

Krause, Aurel, and Arthur Krause. 1993. *To the Chukchi Peninsula and to the Tlingit Indians, 1881/1882: Journals and Letters by Aurel and Arthur Krause*. Fairbanks: University of Alaska Press.

Langdon, Stephen J. 1997. "Efforts at Humane Engagement: Indian-Spanish Encounters in Bucareli Bay, 1779." In *Enlightenment and Exploration in the North Pacific, 1741–1805*, ed. Stephen Haycox, James K. Barrett, and Caedmon A. Liburd. Seattle: University of Washington Press.

Llwyd, J. P. D. 1909. *The Message of an Indian Relic*. Seattle: Lowman and Hanford.

MacDonald, George F. 1983. *Haida Monumental Art: Villages of the Queen Charlotte Islands*. Vancouver: University of British Columbia Press.

———. 1984. "The Epic of Nek̲t: The Archaeology of Metaphor." In Margaret Seguin, ed., *The Tsimshian: Images of the Past, Views for the Present*, 65–82. Vancouver: University of British Columbia Press.

———. 1989. *Kitwanga Fort Report*. Mercury Series Directorate Paper no. 4. Hull QC: Canadian Museum of Civilization.

MacDonald, George F., G. Coupland, and D. Archer. 1987. "The Coast Tsimshian ca. 1750." In *Historical Atlas of Canada*, vol. 1, ed. R. Cole Harris and Geoffrey J. Matthews. Toronto: University of Toronto Press.

MacDonald, George F., and Richard I. Inglis. 1981. "An Overview of the North Coast Prehistory Project." *BC Studies* 48: 27–63.

Malloy, Mary. 1998a. *"Boston Men" on the Northwest Coast: The American Maritime Fur Trade, 1788–1844.* Kingston: Limestone Press.

———. 1998b. Introduction and annotations to *"A Most Remarkable Enterprise": Lectures on the Northwest Coast Trade and Northwest Coast Indian Life*, by Captain William Sturgis. Marstons Mills MA: Parnassus.

———. 2000. *Souvenirs of the Fur Trade: Northwest Coast Indian Art and Artifacts Collected by American Mariners, 1788–1844.* Cambridge MA: Peabody Museum.

———. 2006. "Author Exposed! Young Sailor Is Revealed as 'Anonymous' Keeper of Excellent Voyage Narrative." *Historic Nantucket* 55 (1): 4–9.

Marsden, Susan. 2001. "Defending the Mouth of the Skeena: Perspectives on Tsimshian-Tlingit Relations." In *Perspectives on Northern Northwest Coast Prehistory*, ed. Jerome S. Cybulski. Archaeology Survey of Canada Paper 60. Hall QC: Canadian Museum of Civilization.

Marsden, Susan, and Robert Galois. 1995. "The Tsimshian, the Hudson's Bay Company, and the Geopolitics of the Northwest Coast Fur Trade, 1787–1840." *Canadian Geographer* 39: 169–83.

Mason, Ronald J. 2006. *Inconstant Companions: Archaeology and North American Indian Oral Traditions.* Tuscaloosa: University of Alabama Press.

Meares, John. 1790. *Voyages Made in the Years 1788 and 1789, from China to the North West Coast of America.* London: Logographic Press.

Milburn, Maureen. 1994. "Louis Shotridge and Florence Shotridge." In *Haa Kusteeyí, Our Culture: Tlingit Life Stories*, ed. Nora Marks Dauenhauer and Richard Dauenhauer, 548–61. Seattle: University of Washington Press.

———. 1997. "The Politics of Possession: Louis Shotridge and the Tlingit Collections of the University of Pennsylvania Museum." PhD diss., Fine Arts, University of British Columbia.

Miller, Jay. 1998. "Tsimshian Ethno-Ethnohistory: A 'Real' Indigenous Chronology." *Ethnohistory* 45 (4): 657–74.

Monteith, Dan. 1998. "Tongass, the Prolific Name, the Forgotten People: An Ethnohistory of the Tongass Tantakwaan People." PhD diss., Anthropology, Michigan State University, East Lansing.

Morris, William Governeur. 1879. *Report upon the Customs District, Public Service, and Resources of Alaska Territory.* Washington DC: Government Printing Office.

Munro, Wilfred Harold. 1917. *Tales of an Old Sea Port.* Princeton: Princeton University Press.

Niblack, Albert. 1890. *The Coast Indians of Southern Alaska and Northern British Columbia.* Report of the United States National Museum, 1888. Washington DC: Smithsonian Institution.

Nichols, Henry E., ed. 1891. *Pacific Coast Pilot, Alaska, Part I: Dixon Entrance to Yakutat Bay, with Inland Passage from Strait of Fuca to Dixon Entrance.* 3rd ed. United States Coast and Geodetic Survey. Washington DC: Government Printing Office.

Oberg, Kalervo. 1973. *The Social Economy of the Tlingit Indians.* Foreword by Wilson Duff. Seattle: University of Washington Press.

Ogden, Adele. 1932. "The Californias in Spain's Pacific Otter Trade, 1775–1795." *Pacific Historical Review* 1 (4): 444–69.

———. 1941. *The California Sea Otter Trade, 1784–1848.* Berkeley: University of California Press.

Olson, Ronald L. 1967. *Social Structure and Social Life of the Tlingit in Alaska.* Anthropological Records 26. Berkeley: University of California Press.

Paul, William. 1971. "The Real Story of the Lincoln Pole." *Alaska Journal* 1(3):2–16.

Petroff, Ivan. 1884. *Report on the Population, Industries, and Resources of Alaska, 10th Census: 1880,* vol. 8. Washington DC: U.S. Department of the Interior.

Quimby, George I. 1948. "Culture Contact on the Northwest Coast, 1785–1795." *American Anthropologist* 50 (2): 247–55.

Roe, Michael, ed. 1967. *The Journal and Letters of Captain Charles Bishop on the North-West Coast of America, in the Pacific and in New South Wales, 1794–1799.* Hakluyt Society, 2nd ser., no. 131. Cambridge: Cambridge University Press.

Scidmore, Eliza Ruhamah. 1893. *Appleton's Guide-book to Alaska and the Northwest Coast: Including the Shores of Washington, British Columbia, Southeastern Alaska, the Aleutian and the Seal Islands, the Bering and the Arctic Coasts.* New York: D. Appleton.

Scott, Robert N. 1904. "Colonel Scott's Report on the Indians, 1867." *Proceedings of the Alaska Boundary Tribunal,* 347–57. Washington DC: Government Printing Office.

Scouler, John. 1841. "Observations on the Indigenous Tribes of the N.W. Coast of America." *Journal of the Royal Geographical Society of London* 2: 215–51.

Shotridge, Louis. 1917. "My Northland Revisited." *Museum Journal* 8 (2): 105–15.

———. 1919. "War Helmets and Clan Hats of the Tlingit Indians." *Museum Journal* 10 (1-2): 43–48.

———. 1928. "The Emblems of the Tlingit Culture." *Museum Journal* 19 (4): 350–77.

———. 1929. "The Bride of Tongass: A Study of the Tlingit Marriage Ceremony." *Museum Journal* 20 (2): 131–56.

Shotridge, Louis, and Florence Shotridge. 1913. "Chilkat Houses." *Museum Journal* 4 (3): 81–99.

Simpson, Sir George. 1847. *Narrative of a Journey Round the World, during the Years 1841 and 1842.* London: Colburn.

Sturgis, Captain William. 1998. *"A Most Remarkable Enterprise": Lectures on the Northwest Coast Trade and Northwest Coast Indian Life.* Ed. Mary Malloy. Marstons Mills MA: Parnassus.

Swanton, John R. 1905. *Haida Texts and Myths, Skidegate Dialect.* Smithsonian Institution. Bureau of American Ethnology Bulletin 29. Washington DC: Government Printing Office.

———. 1908. "Social Condition, Beliefs, and Linguistic Relationship of the Tlingit Indians." *Bureau of American Ethnology 26th Annual Report,* 391–485. Washington DC: Government Printing Office.

———. 1909. *Tlingit Myths and Texts.* Bureau of American Ethnology Bulletin 39. Washington DC: Government Printing Office.

Toelken, Barre. 2003. *The Anguish of Snails.* Logan: Utah State University Press.

Vancouver, George. 1984. *A Voyage of Discovery to the North Pacific Ocean and Round the World, 1791–1795.* Ed. W. Kaye Lamb. London: Hakluyt Society.

Vansina, Thomas, Jr. 1985. *Oral Tradition as History.* Madison: University of Wisconsin Press.

Vaughan, Thomas, and Bill Holm. 1990. *Soft Gold: The Fur Trade and Cultural Exchange on the Northwest Coast of America.* Portland: Oregon Historical Society Press.

Weber, Ronald L. 1985. "Photographs as Ethnographic Documents," *Arctic Anthropology* 22 (1): 67–78.

Whiteley, Peter M. 2002. "The Scientific Importance of Dialogue." *American Antiquity* 67(3): 405–15.

Wike, Joyce. 1958. "Problems in Fur Trade Analysis: The Northwest Coast." *American Anthropologist,* n.s., 60(6):1086–1101.

Willard, Carrie M. 1995. *Carrie M. Willard among the Tlingits: The Letters of 1881–1883.* Sitka: Mountain Meadows Press.

Wooley, Chris B., and James C. Haggerty. 1989. "Tlingit-Tsimshian interaction in the Southern Alexander Archipelago." Paper presented to the 16th Alaskan Anthropological Association, Anchorage, March 3–4, 1989.

13

Whose Justice?

Traditional Tlingit Law and the Deady Code

DIANE PURVIS

Back in the 1870s and 1880s, southeast Alaska was a region with a frontier atmosphere. General stores, stables, and saloons dotted the landscape. Troubles and disputes occurred, but unlike other Old West towns, there were no sheriffs to keep order. Sitka and Wrangell were the only locations that could be called towns. Adjacent to these towns were Tlingit settlements, operating under their traditional law system. In 1799, when the Russians set up their post in Sitka, Russian laws or regulations did not concern the Tlingit; they simply did not apply. There was no formal non-Tlingit law until the Organic Act was passed in 1884. After 1867, the only basis for law came from the Treaty of Cession, a document signed when Alaska was sold to the United States. In this document, the citizenship was confirmed for the Americans and the remaining Russians. There was a clause that referred to the "civilized and uncivilized" tribes of Alaska. These tribes were subject to the laws that the federal government may make from time to time. This loose structure caused several problems as time went on.

This paper examines the differences in legal interpretations between the Tlingit, the various branches of the military, and the Oregon court that had jurisdiction over Alaska until the passage of the Organic Act. To accomplish this comparison, it is necessary to examine Tlingit law, military statutes, and the interpretations of Judge Matthew P. Deady of Portland. The 1834 Trade and Intercourse Act was at the heart of the controversy. This act regulated commerce and trade relationships in Indian country, and Indian country was defined as all lands west of the Mississippi. Further, if a region was Indian country, the Native inhabitants were in control of their land and self-governing. A certain set of laws applied to the Native tribes which held that offenses between

Natives and committed in Indian country were subject to the Native judicial system, not civil courts. It was difficult to fit Alaska into the definition of Indian country, since the territory had a much different set of circumstances than the Natives of the lower United States, most notably the lack of treaties or reservations. That fact made it necessary to look at other aspects to determine aboriginal land title and what code of law should be followed.

The Tlingits of Alaska had occupied southeast Alaska for at least nine thousand years (Ackerman 1979, 195). Their social structure was based on matrilineal clans. At the head of each clan house was a *hít s'aatí*, who was responsible for keeping the spiritual goods of the clan house safe. As spiritual head, he also occupied a position of influence within the greater social system, although the *hít s'aatí* of one clan usually did not have jurisdiction or influence over another clan. This clan nobleman was not a true chief in that his administrative influence was restricted to his own segment of his clan, but when the military came to Alaska after 1867, they assumed these men were chiefs and acted accordingly. The Tlingit social system was based on clan prestige and a strict code of law designed to keep the balance between clans so that the values of harmony and reciprocity could be maintained.

Before the arrival of the Europeans and the Americans, the Tlingit law system included a strict code of ethics and a structured indemnity system. Acts determined to be an offense were punished by exact compensation, including that the punishment be carried out on an individual of the offending clan whose rank was equal to the victim. In reality this meant that a murder was punished by a member of the offending clan giving up his life (Oberg 1934). In the 1880s the rules were modified so that often an exchange of goods could settle a murder charge, but equity and restitution were maintained. With the assimilative measures of the Americans, the Tlingit law system underwent several adjustments. When the Russians sold Alaska to the United States in 1867, Tlingit territory came under the authority of the Army, the first American oversight agency in Alaska. The Army left in 1877, and for two years southeast Alaska was ruled by custom collectors. In 1879, the Navy was called in to investigate a report of an Indian uprising in Sitka. This brought Capt. Lester Beardslee and the USS *Jamestown* to southeast Alaska. Faced with the fact that there was no established law code in Alaska, he became the de facto governor, and the *Jamestown* became the courthouse. Beardslee was aware of the history of Oregon court decisions and the question of previous inequities. As far as the law, Captain Beardslee brought with him the orders of the secretary of the Navy and the revised statutes of the naval code. His orders were to keep the peace.

Beardslee was charged with administering law and order in Sitka and the outlying areas of the Alexander Archipelago. He quickly realized that without an understanding of the Tlingit law code, his task would be made more difficult. He looked at the role of the *hít s'aatí* and other leaders in Tlingit society and decided that if he deputized these men, he could create a conduit for peace between the Tlingit village and the Sitka town. In 1879, the first man he deputized was a Kaagwaantaan who had demonstrated leadership in the face of adversity. His name was Annahootz, and he would come to play a decisive role in Tlingit and southeast Alaska history.

The prominent Oregon judge was Matthew P. Deady, who had studied law under an Ohio attorney and was admitted to the Ohio bar in 1847. In 1849 he decided to strike out west and settle in Portland. He quickly rose to a position of acclaim in legal circles. The "Salem Clique," an influential political group, considered him an important member and promoted his short-lived dabbling with political office, but it was soon apparent that the law was Deady's calling. He served as associate justice of the Supreme Court of Oregon until Oregon became a state on February 14, 1859. He then accepted the appointment as the U.S. district judge for Oregon. In this position he now had jurisdiction over the Washington and Alaskan Territories. Deady made legal decisions between 1868 and 1886 that would greatly affect the Tlingit and set precedents that would be influential factors for indigenous self-determination, the implementation of Alaska Native sovereignty, and general criminal law in Alaska. During this critical period, it was his interpretation of "Indian country" that set the stage for dramatic conflicts.

In Deady's position, he was able to define and redefine laws that applied to various ethnic groups in Alaska and Oregon. Some of his viewpoints and legal decisions went against the tide of conventional thinking. When the rights of Chinese immigrants in Oregon were in question, he sided with the immigrants because they were industrious and performed their jobs with diligence (Mooney 1984, 1988). Deady even crusaded for the protective rights of the Chinese immigrants based on federal and constitutional laws, even though they could not qualify as American citizens. His justification for this crusade was the Treaty of

Burlingham, which guaranteed the protection of Asian immigrants in America. This treaty was close in language to a "most favored nation" agreement. In terms of the American Native tribes, his viewpoint was characteristically paternal. Although Native Americans could not be considered citizens of Oregon, he believed that their culture should be protected. An example of this belief was that he never pronounced the major river in Oregon as Willamette, but rather Wall-a-met, which was derived from the local Indian language. His reason for keeping the traditional name was because it held "strength, dignity, and euphony."[1] He even gave credence to the fact that the Indian wars were created by the non-Native population. In further evidence of his defense of Native cultures, which may have bordered on the Noble Savage philosophy, he kept a picture of Chief Joseph on the wall of his chambers. He admired Chief Joseph because he sought freedom against U.S. domination even though his actions led to his arrest by the federal government. To Deady, that made Chief Joseph a martyr for a just cause (Deady 1975, 1:618).

The slavery issue was active in the 1860s, and Deady, a pro-slavery Democrat, supported the continuation of slavery because it was the present law and had not been overturned. This issue alone demonstrates that Deady's interpretation of the law was restrictive rather than broad, and though he tried to combine law and equity under common law, his bent was toward the strict adherence to the letter of the law. He did not always allow a critical analysis of the circumstances in each case, and this factor weighed on his decisions concerning Indian country. In the strictest sense of the word, Judge Deady was a legalist (Mooney 1984).

Should the law be followed to the letter in every case, or should each case be reviewed individually to find what the most equitable outcome might be? In Oregon, Deady had several cases where he was called upon to review landownership issues. In settling these cases, he went beyond the written law and settled cases based on the fairness principle (Mooney 1993). The fairness principle was contrasted with formalism, which looked at the broad implications of the law instead of being guided by unique situations (Mooney 1988, 21). In honoring the fairness and equality of law, he set civil procedures so that all persons were competent witnesses, regardless of race or religion. Since this was not in keeping with the political views of the time, this action drew censure in political circles, including the 1864 Oregon legislature. His decision was overturned to exclude "Negroes, mulattoes and Indians . . . in an action or proceeding to which a white person is a party" (Peters

1981, 399). Although his thinking could be defined as politically progressive at times, he also voiced the same racist ideas that were prevalent during this era, including classifying a person as Indian if there was the least bit of Indian heritage, even measuring this blood quantum to the sixteenths. In that way, the individual would not be allowed to vote.[2] A review of Deady's decisions indicates many dichotomies. At one turn, he seemed to be upholding the rights of minorities, and then at other times his judgments showed blatant ethnic discrimination (Niedermeyer 1988).

The Oregon code of law, which Deady was credited with creating, applied to Alaska until the Organic Act of 1884. Deady's code, however, continued in Alaska with the passage of the Organic Act because the Oregon laws and statues were the basis for the Alaskan Organic Act. This act provided for the appointment of a governor, judges, and attorneys, plus the creation of a court system. Finally Alaska had its own law, its own trial system, and a better chance for due process. No longer would prisoners and witnesses need to be sent down to Oregon for trial. Deady continued to serve as an appellate judge, and in an 1886 case that he heard on appeal he changed the judgment of the original Alaskan case involving a Tlingit man named Kie that turned into the ultimate test for Indian country in the Alaska territory. This outcome pointed to Deady's residual influence in Alaska and Tlingit matters. An important clause in the Organic Act guaranteed that the indigenous inhabitants of Alaska would not be disturbed on their traditional lands. If this law had been enforced, it would have turned the tide on Tlingit land entitlement, their political base, and self-determination, including legal matters.

Historically, Deady's court had a large impact on the definition of Indian country in Alaska, and this was a factor in Tlingit criminal cases that were sent to Portland. There were times where Deady claimed jurisdiction in Alaska based on his definition of Alaska as Indian country, and then, in a reversal in some cases, he would claim that he did not have jurisdiction in Alaska and send the freed suspect on a ship headed back to Alaska. These jurisdictional issues revolved around his definition of the 1834 Trade and Intercourse Act and what portion of the act applied to Alaska in his opinion. In this determination, his legalism was evident. This issue is portrayed and analyzed using specific cases below.

Russia sold Alaska to the United States in 1867, and the Army took over the command of the territory. In 1868 the Alaska Act was passed extending limited trade and intercourse laws.[3] The Alaska Act stated that the already established local laws were still in effect. For southeast Alaska, that was problematic. The Russians did not have a code of laws, and the military laws did not apply to the indigenous people. Tlingit law was the only codified system at the time, and it had a historical background that dated back thousands of years.

Capt. Jeff C. Davis was in charge of the troops in Alaska from 1867 to 1877. During this time, he believed the only way he could control the Tlingit population was to declare southeast Alaska "Indian country." This declaration provided that no alcohol would be transported for the purposes of sale to the indigenous people and essentially extended the twentieth and twenty-first provisions of the 1834 Intercourse Act across Alaska. Secretary of State William Seward cited an earlier decision of the famous Chief Justice John Marshall in the *Worcester v. Georgia* case, which stated among other things that the current Trade and Intercourse Act extended to any new territories, and their inhabitants would abide by the existing laws. Seward reasoned that this applied to Alaska and gave this as a directive to the Army. Another precedent was the *Mackey et al. v. Cox* decision, which concluded that the Nonintercourse Act laws were not limited by specific boundaries occupied by Indians, who had not extinguished their titles (Harring 1994, 213). This 1855 decision would be important on at least two levels. There was no treaty which stated that the Tlingit extinguished their rights to their customary lands. Further, while interpreting the Trade and Intercourse Act, Deady held that the law did not apply to Alaska because the law could not be extended west of the Rocky Mountains, completely ignoring the 1855 precedent. His rigid interpretation of the Trade and Intercourse Act stated that if Congress had intended that the law should be extended to Alaska, then Congress would have explicitly made this statement. Again this was a decision that did not analyze the special conditions of Alaska in terms of customary aboriginal rights and land use.

Whether Deady's interpretation was valid or not did not matter because the Army had the order to act as though the region were Indian country. The first case that tested this classification was *United States v. Seveloff*, heard by Judge Deady. In this case, Ferueta Seveloff was charged with selling liquor to an "Indian." Seveloff was part Alaskan Native himself. The Indian Intercourse Act of 1834 was evoked to prove that a violation had taken place in Indian country with the importation of alcoholic substances into Indian country. In the final decision, Judge

Deady ruled that Alaska was not Indian country, and so Seveloff had not committed a crime. As precedent for the decision, Deady used the *United States v. Tom* case, where Charles H. Williams had previously found that Oregon was not covered by the Trade and Intercourse Act. Deady claimed that decision also covered Alaska territory. In *U.S. v. Tom*, the final opinion was that Indian country did not apply to territories unless Congress expressly wrote this determination. The demurrer in *Seveloff* was approved on the basis that the 1834 Indian Trade and Intercourse Act did not specifically include Alaska, and therefore Seveloff could not be prosecuted under that law.

From *U.S. v. Tom*, a new language was set where decisions of this kind were based on what was in the best interests of the non-Natives who were coming to settle the wild areas of Oregon and Alaska. In doing so, Deady completely ignored the meaning of the federal interpretation of the nonintercourse acts. Hamar Foster, an expert on indigenous legal cases in the Pacific Northwest, had the following to say about Deady's interpretation: "So when the Treaty of Washington confirmed in 1846 that Oregon was part of the United States, the new territory was 'Indian country' as defined by the 1834 act and subject to federal Indian law (Foster 2003). Once again Deady had his own interpretation that negated the stipulations set by federal law, which superseded state or territorial law. When the federal government tried to right the balance through the Alaska Act, Deady ignored this, too.

Apparently the Alaska Act of 1868, which explicitly forbade the importation of spirituous liquors, was not strong enough for Judge Deady. The Alaska Act created custom districts with certain powers and fortified the Army in its duty to ban alcohol. Still there were no district courts, and so prisoners faced Judge Deady's court. The Alaska Act did not make a direct statement concerning Indian country, although its language was close to the Trade and Intercourse Act, which did establish Indian country in the contiguous United States.

Deady's interpretation of Indian country in the *Seveloff* case left the wild frontier of Alaska without a criminal law code. Apparently the federal government did not agree with Deady's decision, because directly after the *Seveloff* decision in 1873, certain sections of the Trade and Intercourse Act were added to the 1868 Alaska Act to bolster the law. The changes extended commerce and navigation laws to Alaska that were closely aligned with the 1834 Trade and Intercourse Act and treated Alaska as Indian country. The military was charged with keeping the law and order, which left them caught in the middle. Faced with the realities of Alaska, the Army and later the Navy either broke the tenets of Deady's decision or left the outcome for the Tlingit to resolve in cases that did not involve non-Natives. This latter occurrence could be interpreted as a precedent in itself.

Within the Treaty of Cession, the "uncivilized tribes" did not receive the same privileges as non-Natives. Even the foreign-born Russians were afforded more legal protection and equality. The Alaska Native, according to the treaty, was instead held open to the laws and regulations that the federal government might decide upon. There was not even a clarification concerning the difference between "civilized" and "uncivilized" tribes. While the foreign-born Russians were U.S. citizens, the Tlingit, born on American soil, were not and would not be until 1924. The Fourteenth Amendment (1886), which guaranteed the right to citizenship if born in American territory, did not apply to the Tlingit until after they had fought for the right of suffrage.

Deady had previously made his decision about American Natives and their American citizenship. In *McKay v. Campbell*, he ruled that an Indian who was part Oregon Chinook was not automatically a citizen by birth. The decision stated that being born in America did not guarantee citizenship without the support of the government. Further, in a statement that sounds contradictory, Deady claimed the Indian tribes had always been seen as distinct, and because of this they retained the right to self-government. Without citizenship these people were without the basic American rights guaranteed by the Constitution. This had further ramifications for Natives in Oregon or Alaska, because lack of citizenship ostensibly implied that there was no protection from the whims of court case interpretation. Being the case, the Fourteenth and Fifteenth Amendments could not be used to strengthen the arguments or the foundation of Native legal action. If they were not U.S. citizens, then they must be citizens of their own indigenous Nations and subject to those laws. In Alaska, Native laws and rights had not been extinguished by treaty or lands ceded by reservations. The Tlingit were still the owners of their land, but their rights were not protected like those of other tribes in the contiguous United States. In fact, without special guards, Native rights were equal to the non-Native population in statement if not by action. Much of this stemmed from the fact that there were no treaties or reservations, and this fact played a large role in the Tlingits' future.

To contrast the Deady code with Tlingit law, it is important to clearly understand that the Tlingit legal system was aligned with the ideal of an eye for an eye. If an infraction occurred, a person of the offending clan who was of equal rank to the victim had to suffer a punishment equal to the original offense. This was not an act of revenge as some historians and ethnologists have stated, but it was a necessary imperative to maintain the balance and reciprocity between clans in Tlingit society. With the *Seveloff* case in mind, if Seveloff's sale of liquor had caused a person or persons to become sick or injure themselves, then under Tlingit law Seveloff would be held responsible and would have to suffer an equal punishment. In this case, Seveloff was not part of a clan, so he would be solely responsible for the incident.

Deady's narrow interpretation of the law, based on strict adherence to federal statutes, created a situation where deadly force was not convictable in Alaska. There were cases that Deady dismissed because he could not find any law against attempted murder in Alaska. The letter of the law was used instead of common law and common sense, both of which Deady claimed to champion. A case that illustrates this point was *United States v. Williams*. The defendant had pleaded guilty to attempted murder, but Judge Deady could not find a specific law for Alaska that covered this case, so the man was released. Judge Deady, however, had no problem with finding murder laws when it involved the Tlingit.

United States v. Kot ko wot and Okh kho not was such a case. These two Tlingit men were accused of killing Tom Brown and sent to Oregon for trial. After a speedy appearance in Judge Deady's court, Kot ko wot was convicted and sentenced to hang, while Okh kho not, who had pleaded not guilty, was released. In terms of Tlingit law this was justice: a life for a life. What was unbearable to Kot ko wot's clan was that Deady further ordered that his body be dissected. This horrified his clan because now he was prevented from going to the next life, and this final punishment was not equal to the man's crime. An injustice had occurred according to the Tlingit law code. With a closer examination, the motivation for the crime was later revealed. The victim, Tom Brown, was the manager of the hot springs near Sitka. Previously, five Kiks.ádi clansmen had been killed in an accident aboard the *San Diego*, and no restitution was forthcoming. An apparently frustrated Kot ko wot wanted to settle the case and decided that indemnity could be satisfied by the death of Tom Brown, whose only crime was being in the wrong place at the wrong time. This action was consistent with the Tlingit belief that any "white" man was equal to another, and so justice was done.[4]

In Deady's diary he gave this case a passing mention: "[Sidney] Dell defended them by my appointment and made an excellent speech to the jury" (Deady 1975, 1:278). Equity appears to be missing in this case. The judge appointed the defense and applauded a speech made in the prisoner's defense, but Kot ko wot was executed and further humiliated by a dissection. Perhaps this could even be considered extralegal. If English law was followed, which was often the case in the American legal system, then the 1752 Murder Act must be reviewed. This English act allowed dissection after murder cases to advance medical science. There is evidence that this law applied to those poor souls of lower rank and quickly fell into disuse.[5] A further inspection of the Oregon statues revealed an 1878 statute titled "An Act to Promote Medical Science," which stipulated that any person executed for a crime could be taken to a medical facility and dissected for the good of science.[6] The language of the act not only approves this action but seems to encourage it. There was one stipulation in the law that directly applied in this case: the remains could not leave Oregon. That meant that the Kiks.ádi clan was unable to have proper funerary rites—another strike against justice.

Kot ko wot's trial was in early 1879, and within months Commander Lester Beardslee arrived in Sitka. He quickly learned about Kot ko wot's case and Deady's court. He gave the following report: The two suspects were first taken into custody by Annahootz, a leading *hít s'aatí* of the Kaagwaantaan clan.[7] When the suspects were taken to Portland, they were accompanied by Kaagwaantaan witnesses. Here was the first problem. Kot ko wot was a Kiks.ádi, and the two clans were historic rivals. In effect, these would have been the prisoner's enemies and would conceivably testify against him, a fact that was later confirmed by the Kiks.ádi clan. This series of events put Commander Beardslee in a difficult position. Beardslee entered the following citation in his report from one of Kot ko wot's clansmen: "The man was hung upon the testimony of two of his enemies; he was in a strange country where he had no friends, and had he not been guilty it would have been the same, he could not have proved it. He was guilty, and it is right he was killed, but he should have had a fair trial" (Deady 1975, 1: 278).

U.S. v. Kot ko wot and Okh kho not was not reported in the federal records. Judgments were not reported when the judge believed the case was unimportant. It is strange that the execution of a man would seem unimportant. The witnesses at the trial were Armie, Ata-chin, Hack-satan, A. W. Waters, E. G. Hughes, and George Kostrometinoff. The first three men were the Kaagwaataan witnesses. Kostrometinoff was an interpreter in Sitka and later became a marshal. Of interest when reading the judgment was the following phrase: "in the territory of Alaska, said territory being Indian Country." This must have slipped past Judge Deady, because he had ruled in the 1872 *Seveloff* case that Alaska was not Indian country.

In 1882, the Tlingit man Kitatah found himself in front of Deady's court accused of the robbery and the murder of two non-Natives. He was sentenced to be executed. Again that would be just according to Tlingit law, but the dissection of the man was against the Tlingit law, and it again created a situation that far outweighed the offense. In his diary Judge Deady wrote about moving Kitatah's execution date so "that the Indian witnesses could see him swing." He further mentioned that the accused wanted to talk to Katlian and Kostrometinoff. Katlian was a leading *hít s'aatí* among the Kiks.ádi and a clan brother of Kitatah. Katlian's passage to Oregon and his appearance as a witness were significant. Later Judge Deady went to the medical building to give a lecture, and he wrote in his diary that he happened to observe the "mangled remains" of the prisoner Deady 1975, 2:393–94). These were the only two executions that Deady ordered after thirty years on the federal bench. Deady remained on the bench for four more years, and there were no further murder trials. If these murders had involved only Tlingits, then the decisions would have been left to the Tlingit law system, as consistent with the precepts of Indian country. With these apparent questions of law, equity, and humanity in Deady's system, perhaps it was a good thing that there was rarely money to send offenders all the way down to Oregon. Beardslee and later Cdr. Henry Glass wrote in their reports that they wished to settle matters in Alaska, as there were considerable problems with the Oregon court and Judge Matthew Deady.

The Native police system, set up by Commander Beardslee in 1879, worked better in Tlingit cases, and Beardslee worked hard to keep the system strong and equitable. For example, there was the Big Charley case to consider. The Big Charley verdict was the first punishment administered under the auspices of the Tlingit police and the de facto governor, Beardslee. Big Charley was accused of assaulting a Tlingit woman; he had a history of violence. The Sitka Ranche held a council made up of leading Tlingit men, the *aanyatx'i*. This was the first tribal court recognized by the naval authority, and they found Big Charley guilty. Justice was upheld based on the Tlingit law of paying for an injury. A "severe punishment" was placed on Big Charley, and after his incarceration he became an upstanding member of the community and in the employ of the Navy (Beardslee 1882, 48).

Beardslee was required to follow the Revised Statutes of the naval code, which were specific about the territories under naval jurisdiction. He referred to section 2145, which gave him oversight authority in Alaska and the responsibility for punishment of crimes in Indian country. Section 2146 allowed the indigenous people control over Indian-related matters in their own territory. Beardslee was well aware of the controversy concerning Indian country, but he "deduced" from these statutes that the United States had jurisdiction over Alaska, and he was put in place to maintain the jurisdiction. The United States recognized Indian rights in local criminal cases. For a time it would seem that Beardslee believed the power that the U.S. Navy gave him superseded Judge Deady's court, and with this reasoning the Tlingit should be afforded some degree of sovereignty to settle their own matters, as was the case for other tribes who had not extinguished their rights or their land.[8]

If the Tlingit could prove they were sovereign, they could enforce their own law code in their territory and avoid Judge Deady's court. The matter of Tlingit sovereignty was problematic. The question, however, would be addressed in *United States v. Kie*. Kie, a Tlingit man, was accused of murdering his wife, who was also Tlingit. Under Tlingit law, this action was justified in that the wife had committed adultery. Kie was Stikine, and his wife was a Chilkat, two historically rival clans, so her clan may have raised an objection if they did not believe the charges. Apparently there were no protests, and the matter was settled for the Tlingit community.[9]

The non-Native population was incensed by the apparent injustice and called for Kie to be tried in a court of law. By this time the Organic Act was in effect, and there was a court in Sitka. Kie was convicted and sentenced to ten years in jail plus a fine. This conviction was disputed because Tlingit territory was considered Indian country and American laws could not be applied. Judge Deady heard this case on appeal and once again reiterated his view of Alaska in terms of Indian country. He reasoned that the conditions in Alaska did not have any direct parallel to the laws or court decisions in the lower United States that had already set a precedent, including the expanded definition of Indian country set forth by the *Ex parte Crow Dog* case (*United States v. Kie.* 7 West Coast Rep. 6. Case No. 15,528a. May Term 1885, District Court, D. Alaska. Cited in *YesWeScan! The Federal Cases*; Harring 1994, 219–20).[10] Part of his decision was based on the fact that there were no treaties or reservations in Alaska, and he continued to stick to the fact that the federal government had never stipulated that Alaska was Indian country. At this point there was no treaty to protect indigenous rights, and there was no land purposely set aside for the Tlingit by way of a reservation. The Tlingit were actually hindered by the lack of federal involvement in their territory. On the other hand, there was no document that extinguished aboriginal land claims. The clans owned the lands by right of occupation as they had from time immemorial.

Once again the only treaty in effect was the hastily written Treaty of Cession, which was acquired when United States bought the Alaska territory from Russia. In an illogical argument, Deady considered this treaty extinguished aboriginal ownership. Following his reasoning, Russia owned Alaska, and when the foreign territory was sold, it implied that Indian title was extinguished. The new American ownership did not change these terms. There was nothing in the language of the treaty that even vaguely conveyed this idea.

Judge Deady ruled against Kie because the Tlingit system did not have jurisdiction over Indian cases. Kie's case then went back to Alaska, where he was sentenced to seven years in prison. There was no record whether he actually served this time or not. It was known that he was suffering from untreated venereal disease, and he may have died.

During the trial, Kie's attorney cited the *Crow Dog* decision in South Dakota as defense that the United States did not have jurisdiction in Indian cases. The case *Ex parte Crow Dog* case set an important precedent for the definition of Indian country across the nation. In this 1882 case, it was found that Crow Dog was accused of killing a Brule Sioux man. The offender's and victim's families met in a tribal council and settled on a just compensation with an exchange of goods, which was much like the Tlingit's customary indemnity system. The Sioux legal structure, similar to the Tlingit, was in place to restore the harmony of the community. This was not a fair settlement according to the non-Native authorities, and Crow Dog was taken into custody. He went to trial, and after one year he was sentenced to hang. In a review of the case, it was found that the non-Native courts did not have jurisdiction in Indian country, and Crow Dog had a case for false imprisonment. It should be noted that the South Dakota Sioux did have several reservations and treaties. This continued be an important factor in decisions.

In a turn-around, Deady used the principles of *Crow Dog* to further restrict Alaska's definition of sovereignty and prove it was not Indian country. In his analysis he used the South Dakota conditions to illustrate that those same conditions did not pertain to Alaska, and therefore Alaska could not be considered Indian country, especially in light of the lack of reservations and treaties. Of interest to the case at hand was the opinion of Justice Stanley Matthews from the *Crow Dog* case, where he stated that the Native Americans should not be subject to laws they do not understand and that do not conform to their culture. They are in effect being judged by the values of a foreign government and are not tried by their peers. Matthews was upholding traditional tribal councils and their decisions. To some evaluators of Deady's law, *Crow Dog* did prove that Alaska was Indian country (Harring 1989, 289). If this legal logic is substantial, then Deady's former rulings were wrong, as several Western legal historians have attested.

The *Crow Dog* case left the Indian country question murky and in abeyance for Alaska. There was the question of sovereignty, landownership, and the guarantees in the Organic Act that recognized that the Alaska Natives would not be disturbed in their homelands. It was clear that the Tlingit did not extinguish their land rights, they were occupying their homelands, and they were following their own law code. These were the tenets for establishing Indian country. Judge Deady's inclination to change definitions in cases appeared to be based on what would favor the settlers over the original inhabitants. If this was true, his decisions were specious and jingoistic.

Traditionally the Tlingit had a clearly defined landownership system. Each clan held ownership of certain houses, creeks, rivers, beachfronts, berry picking patches, and other resources. If another clan violated this strict ownership pattern, they would be expected to pay damages. This was a major element of the Tlingit legal system. Following this analysis, the Russians and later the Americans were foreigners, and when they took these resources without proper payment, they were in violation. In Tlingit eyes, the changing of the flags in 1867 did not extinguish landownership, and with landownership came the right to their legal system and their sovereignty. This pattern then had parallels to the dictums of Indian country, which guarantees that those living in Indian country have the right to make and follow their own laws. The decisions of Judge Deady directly attacked landownership, sovereignty, and the Tlingit code of law.

The court in Oregon was far from Alaska and the realities of Alaskan living. The question arises: What did Judge Deady know about Alaska? He did take a cruise to Alaska in August 1880. This would have been between the 1879 trial of Koh ko wot and the 1882 trial of Kitatah. In his diary, Deady expresses disdain for Sitka and Klawock, calling them, respectively gaudy (Russian Orthodox icons) and dirty. In Sitka, he had the opportunity to meet Commander Beardslee and his wife as well as other officials. He noted the large number of Natives aboard the *Jamestown*, but he carefully kept his distance from any of the Tlingit in both Sitka and Klawock (Deady 1975, 1:311).

There is no question that Deady's decisions had an effect on later legal arrangements in Alaska. Deady had his own view of the law, which did not agree with federal Indian policy or the important precedents that had already been set. Following the history, it would appear that he had his own agenda, which did not include Native rights in that far-off land of Alaska. Although the Tlingit continued to retain their traditional legal system, which was based on balance and equity, they did not have the resources to defend themselves from any of Deady's decisions. The more distant villages in the panhandle remained untouched, but not so for the Tlingit residents of Sitka and Wrangell, who experienced the forces of rapid American acculturation. At least two indigenous rights experts have reviewed the decisions of Deady, and both claim that his cases set a precedent to eliminate sovereignty among Alaska Natives today.[11]

Historically the Tlingit have been highly politicized. Their traditional legal system was set up on the premise of equity, balance, and the maintenance of harmony in a volatile world. They would not stand by and see their lands taken or rights trampled on. Their ancient law system had always incorporated the principles of law and equity. The Tlingit obviously did not call their lands and waterways Indian country, but merely Tlingit territory, *Lingit aani,* and they fiercely protected it from all trespassers. The movement to reclaim their rights escalated in the late 1800s and early 1900s. Leaders stood up to defend Native rights and their position in the greater American society. In 1912 the Natives of southeast Alaska formed the first Native American organization to fight against discrimination legally, economically, and socially. This organization was called the Alaska Native Brotherhood (ANB). In 1915 it was followed by the ANB's partner, the Alaska Native Sisterhood (ANS). Faced with a shrinking land base and questionable property rights, the Tlingit and Haida banded together to fight for their jurisdictional rights in southeast Alaska. After a long battle, the Tlingit-Haida Jurisdictional Act was won in 1959, the same year as statehood. The ANB, ANS, and the Tlingit and Haida Central Council remain strong political forces in Alaska today.

NOTES

1. *Oregonian*, October 15, 1874, at 1, col. 2
2. *McKay v. Campbell*, 2 Sawy. 118; 5 Am. Law T. Rep. U.S. District Court D. Oregon, November 7, 1871. In this case, James Campbell was denied the right to vote in a local election based on his Chinook ancestry. Judge Deady used his own formula to establish that the plaintiff was 9/16ths Chinook.
3. "An Act to Extend the Laws of the United States Relating to Customs, Commerce, and Navigation over the Territory Ceded to the United States by Russia to establish a Collection District therein, and for other purposes," 40th Cong., 2nd sess., chapters 272, 273 (1868). Referred to in the text as the Alaska Act.
4. There are historical cases where a Tlingit was injured and to satisfy the indemnity a non-Ntive was made to pay for the crime. According to the Tlingit, all non-Natives were of equal status.
5. Laws of Oregon, chapter 57, "Of the Promotion of Medical Science" Statutes 3730, 3731, 3732, October 15, 1878.
6. Oregon Laws of 1878, p. 6, section 1, "An Act to Promote Medical Science."
7. The *hít s'aatí* was the spiritual head of an individual clan or clan house. When the Russians and Americans arrived, they assumed these men were chiefs. Since in some sense this was true, the name stayed. Commander Beardslee deputized these chiefs, placed them under the Navy muster roles, and assigned them as Native police to keep order in the Tlingit area and often to act as liaison.
8. Capt. L. A. Beardslee, USN, Reports of . . . Relative to Affairs in Alaska and the Operations of the USS *Jamestown* under His Command, While in the Waters of That Territory, S. Exec Doc 71, 47th Cong., 1st sess., 1879, vol. 4, 14–15.
9. In the Tlingit social system, clans were divided between the Eagle and Raven moieties. A man from an Eagle moiety must marry a woman from

a Raven moiety. Historically, there was often rivalry or feuding between the clans of opposite moieties. See Oberg 1934.

10. In her analysis of Deady's decisions, Deborah Niedermeyer claims that the *Crow Dog* decision proved that Alaska was Indian country and weakened Deady's jurisdiction. She refers to a phrase in *U.S. v. Tom* which states that any decision about Indian country must entertain the best interests of the "white" population tantamount to the idea of manifest destiny. In this way, Deady was influenced by the need to populate Oregon and Alaska with non-Native pioneers.

11. Personal communication with Sidney Harring and Hamar Foster, October 16, 2006.

REFERENCES CITED

Published Works

Ackerman, Robert. 1979. "Early Cultural Complexes in the Northwest Coast." *Canadian Journal of Archaeology* 3: 195.

Deady, Matthew P. 1975. *Pharisee among Philistines: The Diary of Judge Matthew P. Deady, 1871–1892*. 2 vols. Ed. Malcolm Clark Jr. Portland: Oregon Historical Society.

Foster, Hamar. 2003. "Trespassers on the Soil: *United States v. Tom* and a New Perspective on the Short History of Treaty Making in Nineteenth-Century British Columbia." *BC Studies* 138: 51–84.

Harring, Sidney L. 1989. "The Incorporation of Alaskan Natives under American Law: United States and Tlingit Sovereignty, 1867–1900." *Arizona Law Review* 31 (2): 279–327.

———. 1994. *Crow Dog's Case: American Indian Sovereignty, Tribal Law, and United States Law in the Nineteenth Century*. New York: Cambridge University Press.

Mooney, Ralph James. 1984. "Matthew Deady and the Federal Judicial Response to Racism in the Early West." *Oregon Law Review* 63: 561–637.

———. 1988. "Formalism and Fairness: Matthew Deady and Federal Public Land Law in the Early West." *Washington Law Review* 63 (April): 317–70.

———. 1993. "The Deady Years." In *The First Duty: A History of the U.S. District*, ed. Carolyn M. Buan. Portland: U.S. District Court of Oregon Historical Society.

Niedermeyer, Deborah. 1988. "The True Interests of a White Population: The Alaska Indian Country Decisions of Judge Matthew P. Deady." *New York University Journal of International Law and Politics* 21: 195–257.

Oberg, Kalvero. 1934. "Crime and Punishment in Tlingit Society." *American Anthropologist*, n.s., 36 (April–June): 145–56.

Peters, Robert N. 1981. "The 'First' Oregon Code: Another Look at Deady's Role." *Oregon Historical Quarterly* 82 (383): 394–401.

Legislation and Legal Cases

An Act to Extend the Laws of the United States Relating to Customs, Commerce, and Navigation over the Territory Ceded to the United States by Russia to Establish a Collection District Therein, and for Other Purposes." 40th Cong., 2d sess., ch. 272, 273 (1868). Referred to in the text as the Treaty of Cession.

Ex parte Crow Dog, 109 U.S. 556, 3 S.Ct. 396, 27 L.Ed. 1030 (1883).

Trade and Intercourse Act, ch. 161, 4 Stat. 729 (1834).

Johnson v. McIntosh 21 U.S. Wheat 543, 1823.

Laws of Oregon, ch. 57, "Of the Promotion of Medical Science," Stats 3730, 3731, 3732. October 15, 1878. Oregon Laws of 1878, pg. 6, sec. 1, "An Act to Promote Medical Science.

McKay v. Campbell, 2 Sawy. 118, 5 Am. Law T. Rep. U.S. District Court D. Oregon, November 7, 1871.

United States ex rel Mackey v. Cox, 59 U.S. 100, 18 How. 100, 15 L.Ed. 299 (1855).

United States v. Kot ko wot and Okh kho not, U.S. Circuit Court Oregon, Judgment 487, roll 21 (1879).

United States v. Kie, 26 F. Cas. 776 original. Appeal: *United States v. Kie* 27 F. 351 (1886).

United States v. Kitatah in the District Court of United States for the District of Oregon. March 1882. Pacific Alaska Region (Seattle), Judgment 487, roll 21.

United States v. Seveloff, 27 F. Case 1021, CCD Or 1872 (No. 16, 252).

United States v. Tom, 109 U.S. 556 (1883).

United States v. Williams, 2f. 61 (D. Or. 1880).

Worcester v. Georgia, 31 US (6 Pet) 515 8l.Ed. 483 (1832).

14

Bringing to Light a Counternarrative of Our History

B. A. Haldane, Nineteenth-Century Tsimshian Photographer

MIQUE'L ICESIS DANGELI

Shu'goot Laxsgyiik ada Táakw Shaawát di waayu.
Rachael Askren ada Mootgm'goot waas di nooyu.
Corrine Reeve waa na ndi nits'iit'dszu.
Cora Booth na waa agwi nits'iit'dszu.
Laxsgyiik di pteegu. Gispaxlo'ots di wil 'nat'ału.
Wil Uks T'aa Mediik di wil 'waatgu.

As is protocol among my people, I have introduced myself by honoring the matrilineal line that defines my identity. In Sm'algyax[1] I shared with you both my Tsimshian and Tlingit names, the names of my mother and grandmother, and that we are of the Gispaxlo'ots Eagle Clan of Metlakatla, Alaska.[2]

Metlakatla was founded in 1887 by 823 Tsimshian people who, under the guidance of lay Anglican missionary William Duncan, migrated from Metlakatla, British Columbia, in quest of government-sanctioned land rights and the liberty to follow nondenominational Christianity.[3] In the wider missionary project that followed European colonization in many parts of the world, our community was considered a Christian utopia. Photographs and stories of Metlakatla were strategically circulated by Duncan and his supporters, such as Henry Wellcome, in books and newspapers throughout Canada, the United States, and Britain as evidence of its "success," the formation of an economically self-sufficient Christian Native community. The international dissemination of these materials and later anthropological publications widely promoted Metlakatla as typifying the colonial agenda of missionization and assimilation of indigenous peoples.[4] Today this depiction continues to dominate our community's representation in written histories of the Northwest Coast.[5]

I am a direct descendant of the Tsimshians who moved to Metlakatla with Duncan in 1887. My great-great-grandparents, Charles and Sara Milton Brendible and Harry and Sarah Usher Lang, were married by him. My great-grandmother, Cora Brendible Lang-Booth, who passed away when I was fourteen years old, attended his school. This history is recent to us. Based on my experiences in Metlakatla and our *adaawx* (oral history), it is my assertion that this colonial narrative, which depicts our conversion to Christianity as a complete rejection of our Tsimshian traditions and so-called assimilation into Euro-American culture, has overshadowed the stories of resistance and cultural continuity that persist in our community. The primary objective of this essay and my ongoing research is to challenge this colonial narrative by bringing to light a counternarrative of Metlakatla's history that was captured through the photographic lens of one of our own people, Benjamin Alfred Haldane (1874–1941).

Throughout my life I have heard aunts, uncles, grandparents, and elders talk about his musical abilities, photography, and the general store that he owned. They did not refer to him as Benjamin but as B. A. Although he is considered one of the first professional Native photographers on the Northwest Coast, few publications before my research discussed his work, and none explore his life and career extensively (Sexton 1979; Parham 1996; Savard 1996).[6] Adhering to the ethics and protocols of researching in indigenous communities, I received permission from B. A.'s family and our Metlakatla Indian Community Council to do this research for my master's thesis and subsequent publications.[7] As it is also the responsibility of researchers to give back to the communities in which they work, I have held several public presentations in Metlakatla to share my research as it progresses, distribute my written work, and receive feedback from our community.[8] I am grateful for their support and would like to say Ap' luk'wil T'oyaxsut nüüsm to the elders of the Haldane family for their participation in these forums and their support throughout my research: B. A.'s granddaughter, Loretta Baines (daughter of Wilfred and Fannie Haldane), and B. A.'s great-grandchildren, who are the grandchildren of Wilfred and Fannie Haldane: Fran Majors (daughter of Clara Haldane Chalmers-Dundas), Alice

Ann Nelson (daughter of Pauline Haldane Dundas) and Wayne Hewson (son of Mary Haldane Hewson).[9] I would also like to thank B. A.'s granddaughter, Lindarae Shearer (daughter of Raymond Haldane), for inviting me into her home to discuss my research, and B. A.'s grandson, Francis Haldane (son of Boyd Anthony Haldane) for his beautiful words of encouragement in Sm'algyax during our meeting in Anchorage.

The images that are the focus of this essay frame B. A.'s imagery and practice as performing strategic acts of what Hulleah Tsinhnahjinnie defines as "photographic sovereignty." Descending from Diné, Seminole, and Muskcogee peoples, Tsinhnahjinnie is an internationally renowned photographer and the director of the C. N. Gorman Museum. In her 2003 essay "When Is a Photograph Worth a Thousand Words?" Tsinhnahjinnie uses the concept of photographic sovereignty to articulate the agency of indigenous people in ethnographic images taken by nonindigenous photographers. Empowering the vantage point of the subject, she challenges the so-called expert narrative of the image by contextualizing indigenous people in the various epistemologies, ceremonies, spiritualities, oral histories, and biographies within which they functioned at that time and to which they continue to be connected today. Viewing images through this lens, Tsinhnahjinnie insists on returning power to the indigenous people in these photographs by telling their stories of resistance, resilience, and survival (2003, 41). Although her use of this concept is primarily confined to images taken by nonindigenous photographers, Tsinhnahjinnie makes space for further examination of photographic sovereignty as it applies to the interpretation of images taken by early Native photographers and particularly B. A. Building on Tsinhnahjinnie's position, I empower the vantage points of both B. A. and the Native people in his images. From this location, I will contextualize his photography within its sociopolitical circumstances so as to illuminate the ways in which both his practice and imagery assert a particular type of photographic sovereignty.[10]

Of the Laxgyibuu (Wolf Clan) from the Ginadoiks tribe[11] of the Tsimshian, Haldane was born to Matthew and Ada Haldane on June 15, 1874, in Metlakatla, British Columbia.[12] He was thirteen years old when he participated in the mass migration to Alaska, which established our community in 1887. Two years later, his formal schooling was cut short when after completing the third grade reading material he was expelled by Duncan, who stated, "There was nothing more for him to learn."[13] Like other missionaries at this time, Duncan tried to keep his Native converts at a level of education that he presumed would not threaten his authority. However, B. A. did not allow this experience to discourage him from continuing his education on his own. Working in the salmon cannery from sixteen until nineteen, he purchased a variety of books and "studied every day of the year."[14] An avid reader with a remarkable aptitude for learning, B. A. taught himself both music and photography from books.[15] He played the piano, pipe organ, cornet, trombone, and violin. He also composed orchestral music and translated ancient Tsimshian songs to sheet music (Davis 1904, 123; Arctander 1909, 338–39; Murray 1985, 264). From the time he was a young adult until late in his life, B. A. directed many bands and choirs in addition to teaching music and organizing brass bands in Native communities throughout southeast Alaska and British Columbia.[16]

Around 1890, when B. A. was sixteen, he began his career as a photographer by taking individual and family portraits in Metlakatla using homes in our community as backdrops. Nine years later, he established a business as a "scenic and portrait photo-grapher" and opened a portrait studio in Metlakatla with the standard props, backdrops, and floor décor of the period.[17] In his research on nineteenth-century Native photographers on the Northwest Coast, Dan Savard has shown that B. A. was "the lone professional" among photographers such as George Hunt (Kwakwaka'wakw) and Louis Shotridge (Tlingit) because he was the only one who owned a studio (2005, 84). By the 1890s, Native people and families on the Northwest Coast were commissioning studio portraits in unprecedented numbers, which may have caused B. A. to develop his business to meet this demand. Carol Williams argues that this substantial rise in Native commissioning of portraits during the late nineteenth century indicates an increasing desire for control over their representations, which made them purposeful and strategic consumers (2003, 138, 141). Those who traveled from various communities throughout the Alaska and British Columbia to have their portrait taken in B. A.'s studio may have found additional prestige and meaning in having their images made by another Native. His portraiture style also adhered to Victorian conventions emphasizing wealth and respectability, which were commonly reserved for images of Euro-American settlers (figure 14.1).

In the late 1890s, B. A. started to teach music and take photographs in Native communities along the Northwest Coast in southeast Alaska, Washington state, Vancouver Island, and villages along the Nass and

Fig. 14.1 David Kininnook of Saxman, Alaska, taken by B. A. Haldane, 1907. ARC 297521, Wellcome Collection, National Archives–Pacific Alaska Region.

Skeena Rivers in northern British Columbia (figure 14.2). As a teacher of music, B. A. was often called Professor Haldane (Parham 1996, 37). By 1905, he had organized Native brass bands in Ketchikan, Saxman, and Howkan, Alaska (Roppel 1983, 70). In 1899, B. A. spent the winter in the Nass River taking photographs and teaching music to the local bands.[18] In 1903 and 1914, B. A. returned to the Nass River area where

Fig. 14.2 George Hamilton, Haidah (Haida) from Howkan, Alaska, taken by B. A. Haldane, 1906. ARC 297515, Wellcome Collection, National Archives–Pacific Alaska Region.

he took photographs of potlatches and ceremonies that Duncan referred to as "heathen festivities." As an early resident of Metlakatla, B. A. lived under the "Declaration of Residents" eight rules constructed by Duncan that outlawed the practice of ancient ceremonies and beliefs and made it mandatory to observe the Sabbath, attend school, and to be clean,

Fig. 14.3 Nisga'a family, Laxgalt'sap (Greenville BC), 1903. Image PN 16970, courtesy of Royal BC Museum, BC Archives.

industrious, and honest, with additional rules regarding landownership and loyalty to the U.S. government. Rule 5 stated that residences of Metlakatla were "to never attend heathen festivities or to countenance heathen customs in other villages" (Kohlstedt 1957, 47). In light of this rule and the 1884 Canadian legislation outlawing potlatching, the sociopolitical circumstances in which B. A.'s practice and imagery exercised a particular type of photographic sovereignty is apparent.[19]

Strikingly different from most of B. A.'s images, the Nisga'a people in these photographs are wearing and displaying their traditional forms of wealth. The 1903 image is of a high-ranking Nisga'a family of the village Laxgalt'sap, now know as Greenville (figure 14.3).[20] In his study of Raven's Tail weaving on the Northwest Coast, Steve Henrickson has found that "this is the only the known photograph of a raven's tail robe in ceremonial use" (1992, 65). The 1914 photographs were taken in Gitlaxt'aamiks, now known as Aiyansh, of Sm'oogyit Ksdiyaawk, with Chief James Skean and his family (figure 14.4) (Francis 1996, 53).[21] At the time that these images were taken, the Canadian law against potlatching had been in place for over twenty years. However, the large amount of eagle down that is noticeably dispersed on the floor, people, and ceremonial objects in both photographs strongly indicates that these images were taken directly after a potlatch. By 1905, colonial authorities regarded photographs taken at potlatches as concrete evidence of illegal activities (Williams 2003, 149). In a 1907 court case, Kwakwaka'wakw people were prosecuted as violators of the potlatch law on the "evidence" of photographs taken years earlier (Savard 2005, 72). Thus the Nisga'a people in these images and

Fig. 14.4 Chief James Skean and his family, Gitlaxt'aamiks (Aiyansh BC),1914. Image PN 4330, Courtesy of Royal BC Museum, BC Archives.

B. A. were putting themselves at considerable risk of prosecution. In the sociopolitical conditions of both Canada and Alaska, the commissioning and creation of these images asserted their sovereignty by continuing to hold and witness potlatches in the face of the potlatch law and Duncan's governance.

Living under Duncan's Declaration of Residents, B. A. could have also put in jeopardy his home and business in Metlakatla by witnessing these potlatches and taking images. However, his well-established position as a leader in our community allowed his work not only to flourish against Duncan's "authority" but also to strengthen Metlakatla's long-standing resistance. This is particularly evident in his photograph of Edward Marsden (Tsimshian) and Lucy Kinninook's (Tlingit) wedding reception in 1901 (figure 14.5). The son of Samuel and Catherine Marsden, Edward Marsden was born on May 19, 1869, in Metlakatla BC. Upon the death of his father in 1878, Catherine asked Duncan to help raise their children as the couple had grown close to him over the many years they took turns preparing his meals while she was his housekeeper (Murray 1985, 222). Duncan trained Edward in many aspect of the church, including how to play the organ for services. He was eighteen years old when he participated in the mass migration that established our

Fig. 14.5 Group in native dress taken on occasion of Edward Marsden's wedding day at Metlakahtla. ACR# 297646, Wellcome Collection, National Archives–Pacific Alaska Region. *Left to right:* Solomon Burton, Henrietta Dundas, Alice Mather, Mrs. Adam Gordon Sr., and Mrs. Edward Chalmers.

community in 1887. After years of opposition from Duncan, who was admittedly against Edward furthering his education, he left Metlakatla to attend Sheldon Jackson's Industrial School in Sitka. Edward went on to graduate from Marietta College in Ohio in 1895 and was later ordained at Lane Theological Seminary. Against Duncan's orders, he began a movement to build a Presbyterian church in Metlakatla, which was fully established by 1922.

B. A.'s photograph of Edward and Lucy's wedding reception was taken in the area of Metlakatla commonly called "the ballpark," where celebrations continue to be held today. This image shows five people from our community, identified as Solomon Burton, Henrietta Dundas, Alice Mather, Mrs. Adam Gordon Sr., and Mrs. Edward Chalmers, openly wearing ceremonial regalia, which was prohibited by Duncan. Since both their fathers were chiefs, Edward and Lucy's invitation to wear regalia to their wedding may have been an assertion of their family's high rank (Beattie 1955, 119).[22] Taking into consideration Edward's history of resisting Duncan's authority, the public nature can be seen as protest against Duncan forcing people to relinquish ownership of their ceremonial possessions both upon being baptized and upon moving to Alaska. Despite his demand, the fact that people continued to own and use their regalia is made clear by their actions. It is evident in this image and in B. A.'s photographs of potlatches in villages along the Nass River that his imagery and practice functioned as a dual means of photographic sovereignty from both his perspective as a photographer and the perspectives of those he photographed. This duality is also apparent in other photographs that he took in Metlakatla.

In 1930, anthropologist Viola E. Garfield was in Metlakatla for six weeks to conduct her fieldwork for her master's thesis, "Change in the Marriage Customs of the Tsimshian." Garfield was intimately familiar with people in our community after her yearlong position as a schoolteacher in 1922. In her observations of Metlakatla, Garfield noted,

> Many teachers and village heads leave the village without realizing any of the current aboriginal belief, thought, and practices possessed by the people. They do not know of the night ceremonies with weeping and feasting for the dead, nor of the clan affiliations, which color many village activities, especially those of the church. (1931, 10)

Garfield is the only anthropologist who took an active interest in the continuation of Tsimshian traditions in our community. In her 1930 survey, she recorded the clan and tribal genealogy, Tsimshian name and rank, and their role in the pre-marriage, marriage, and post-marriage arrangements of nearly every Tsimshian family in Metlakatla. In her thesis, Garfield stated that all Tsimshian people in Metlakatla "preserve their tribal affiliations so that any individual can give both the name of his clan and tribe." (1931, 8). B. A.'s photographic practice supports Garfield's findings, since his images were used by people in our community, as well as B. A. himself, to assert their clan identity. In a self-portrait made around 1900, B. A. represents his career, both as a photographer and musician, and declares his Tsimshian identity (figure 14.6). Placing himself at the center of the composition, B. A. is flanked by his photographic equipment on his left, including a large camera, a lantern, and a Kodak Brownie camera on the floor. On his right are objects relating to his teaching of and love for music including a megaphone, a gramophone with five sets of earphones, and an open case of cylindrical records. Although B. A. had a variety of props

Fig. 14.6 B. A.'s self-portrait in his Metlakatla studio. THS 89.2.14.21, Tongass Historical Society, Ketchikan Alaska.

that he could use to hold himself up, he chose to visually connect to his body a model totem pole with his Laxgyibuu (Wolf Clan) crest represented by the bottom figure. In this image, B. A. confidently positions himself as physically and metaphorically supported by our cultural values and beliefs.

Two of B. A.'s images of children in Metlakatla are visual testaments to the fact that adherence to clan protocols and participation in our cultural traditions continued to be transgenerational. In his portrait of two little girls, a model totem pole has been placed in the center to make an explicit visual reference to their clan lineage (figure 14.7). The placement of the crocheted garment over the chair in front of the model totem pole conceals the other figures and emphasizes the children's' connection to the crest represented at the top. In another of B. A.'s images, also taken outside a home in Metlakatla, a boy is shown dressed in a button robe and holding a paddle (figure 14.8). The strings of beads hanging off each side of his paddle indicate its use in dancing. Its large size along with the adult-sized button robe suggests that these are being handed down to him, probably by a matrilineal uncle, which is an inheritance protocol for Tsimshian men. Unlike the recurring props seen in B. A.'s studio, it is clear that the families who commissioned these images brought with them carvings and regalia deliberately to

Bringing to Light a Counternarrative of Our History 275

Fig. 14.7 Young girls with model totem pole. ARC#297489, Wellcome Collection, National Archives–Pacific Alaska Region.

use this new form of visual record for documentation purposes. Considering the activities surrounding clan inheritance and protocols in Metlakatla as recorded by Garfield and in our *adaawx*, the composition of these two images suggests that they were commissioned for internal purposes: to be circulated throughout our community to serve the same function as bringing out crest objects at a potlatch in order to publicly validate ancestry.

Fig. 14.8 Boy wearing button robe and holding a paddle. ARC#297489, Wellcome Collection, National Archives–Pacific Alaska Region.

B. A.'s photography was also used by members of our community to assert ceremonial and hereditary privileges. Sidney Campbell (ca. 1849–1934) was a child when Duncan arrived on the coast of British Columbia in 1857. Sidney also participated in the migration to Alaska in 1887. Of the Gisbutwada (Killer Whale Clan) of the Ginadoiks tribe of the Tsimshian, his Sm'algyax name was Neeshlut.[23] It was given to Sidney during his initiation into the society and activities as a Gitsontk at Fort Simpson, British

Bringing to Light a Counternarrative of Our History 277

Fig. 14.9 Sidney Campbell with his totem pole in Metlakatla, Alaska, ca. 1905. Image from glass plate negative, William Duncan Memorial Church Archives, Metlakatla, Alaska.

Columbia (Shane 1984, 163). As an exclusive society of powerful carvers among the Tsimshian, Nisga'a, and Gitxsan people, the Gitsontk made objects that were used in the dancing and initiation ceremonies of secret societies. These activities were formed around the concept of Halaayt, a complex set of beliefs and practices concerning the supernatural and its powers. Sidney is one of the few documented members of the Gitsontk (160). Sometimes referred as "Chief Neesh-loot" in recognition of his rank, he was also known for his vast knowledge of Tsimshian songs and *adaawx*. B. A. photographed Sidney as he continued to carve ceremonial objects in Metlakatla including full-size totem poles (figure 14.9). There is no evidence that this totem pole was raised in Metlakatla. However, Sidney raised two fully carved and painted totem poles in Ketchikan, Alaska, a city fifteen miles south of Metlakatla (figure 14.10). The creation and raising of these totem poles occurred at least seventy years before this practice was thought to have been "revived" in our community.

Garfield utilized Sidney's knowledge in her 1930 fieldwork. As the majority of our community were fluent Sm'algyax speakers, Josephine

Fig. 14.10 The sign between the totem poles reads, "These Totems were carved by Chief Neesh-Loot and his Native Tribesmen." Alaska State Library, Mary Nan Gamble Collection (1935-1945), Image 9270-39.

Fig. 14.11 Sidney Campbell and Josephine Hewson Hayward, ca. 1930, University of Washington Libraries, Special Collections, NA3546.

Hayward, shown here with Sidney, also worked for Garfield as a translator (figure 14.11). In this image and another taken with Viola, Sidney is holding model totem poles, both of which resemble the full-sized poles he carved in Ketchikan and the three models that are held in the collection of his family members in Metlakatla today.

Around 1910, B. A. photographed Sidney and a group of men with whom he shared his Gitsontk teachings in an area on the outskirts of

Fig. 14.12 Sidney Campbell is identified as the fourth man from the left in a note signed "M. W. Minthorn, 1926," on the back of a badly damaged print in the archives of the Duncan Cottage Museum. On a photocopy of this image found in his records, Metlakatla Historian Ira Booth (1912–1996) confirmed Minthorn's identification. Booth also identified the rest of the men: (*left to right*) Paul Mather, Joel Baines, Bob Nelson, Sidney Campbell, Henry Booth, and Walter Calvert. Image from glass plate negative, William Duncan Memorial Church Archives, Metlakatla, Alaska.

our community (figure 14.12). In this image Sidney is wearing an *amhalaayt* (chief's headdress), a painted hide or canvas apron and leggings, and *gwisnap'a'la* (button robe), which he also brought over with him from British Columbia despite Duncan's demands.[24] The remote location in which B. A. took this photograph compared with his images of people in regalia at Edward Marsden's wedding alludes to the effort of Sidney and these other men to remove themselves from public, which is the protocol of the Gitsontk during their ceremonies.

While these ceremonial activities were purposefully kept secret, others made it their objective to publicly reinstate their hereditary positions as chiefs. In 1924 and 1925, Matilda Minthorn, a missionary and teacher who had worked closely with Duncan, corresponded with Henry Wellcome, one of Duncan's most influential supporters, concerning the movement in our community to reestablish our hereditary chiefs:

> Mrs. Hudson told me that Moses [Hewson] had spoken to them of the fact that his tribe had offered to choose him for the chief in the place of Alfred Atkinson. That tribe almost in a body went to the Presbyterian Church. This looks like a scheme of Marsden's to cripple Mr. Duncan's church or to combine the two. They tell me that when Mr. Duncan was leaving Fort Simpson to begin the new colony of Old Metlakahtla, that this tribe was not intending to go, but an epidemic of small pox broke out and they fled to Mr. Duncan for refuge. They came without convictions, and never were willing even under his teaching to drop the office of chief. Of course it affects others, and Joseph Hayward, whose father gave it up under Mr. Duncan, is now desiring to claim his station in that line.[25]

Joseph Hayward was fourteen years old when he came to Metlakatla with his mother, whom he identified to Garfield as "sister of Saoks, Kitkatla Chief" of the Gisbutwada (Killer Whale Clan).[26] In 1919, Joseph went to his mother's village of Kitkatla in order to receive his uncle's name and chiefly position. Years later, Joseph passed the name "Saoks" and hereditary privilege to his brother John Hayward (Roth 2008). In the mid-1930s, B. A. photographed John Hayward in Metlakatla wearing his chief's regalia, *amhalaayt* (chief's headdress), *gwishalaayt* (also known as a Chilkat blanket), and holding two raven rattles (figure 14.13).[27] John's commissioning of this image further substantiates the argument that B. A.'s photography was used by community members to validate their clan lineage as well as also their hereditary positions, such as chief, and other ceremonial rights and privileges such as those owned by Sidney Campbell. Thus, B. A. engaged his practice and imagery as a mutual means of photographic sovereignty, which he and the people incorporated into their cultural practices as complex and subversive means of resisting colonial authority.

When I began my research in the summer of 2005, only a few of B. A.'s photographs remained in our community. Most of the memories shared with me by elders and his family members involved grief over the loss of his photographs in house fires and by people who unknowingly discarded them. We also have a tradition of burning the important personal belongings of loved ones who have passed away. Many of B. A.'s photographs have made this journey. In 2003, 163 glass plate negatives were salvaged from the waste facility in Metlakatla by Dennis Dunne, one of our community members.[28] These negatives are of

Fig. 14.13 John Hayward, Metlakatla, Alaska, ca. 1920. University of Washington Libraries, Special Collections, #NA3456.

Fig. 14.14 A mother and child photographed in B. A.'s studio, ca. 1910. This is one example from the 163 of B. A.'s glass plate negative salvaged from our local waste facility by Dennis Dunne in 2003.

portraits taken in B. A.'s studio around 1910 of men, women, and children. Their edges have been scarred by the heat and flames from which they were rescued, the traces of which act as permanent reminders of our near loss of this rich source of our history (figure 14.14). Until recently, there were ten crates of glass plate negatives that survived in two makeshift archives in Metlakatla. Neither facility was equipped

Fig. 14.15 A detail of "Looking to Our Past to Inspire Our Future: A Photographic Exhibit of Metlakatla's History." Visitors are holding their canvas bags, and one is shown using the note pad and pen inside to fill out her request for prints, August 4, 2007. Photo by author.

with the type of climate control and conservation methods needed for their preservation. In 2005, I sought and received permission from our council to relocate the negatives to Ketchikan to be placed on loan in the archive of the Tongass Historical Society until we are able to secure our own museum and archive.[29]

As a part of my effort to give back to our community for their support of my research and to increase their access to B. A.'s images and other historical photographs of Metlakatla, I curated "Looking to Our Past to Inspire Our Future: A Photographic Exhibit of Metlakatla's History" from the corpus B. A.'s photographs that I located in institutions and museums across North America. Over three hundred people attended the opening on August 4, 2007, which was the first exhibit opening in our community's history (figures 14.15 and 14.16). To honor our ceremonial protocols at the exhibition opening, as we would do at our potlatches, each visitor was gifted with a canvas bag and coffee mug with the exhibition logo and a bound copy of my M.A. thesis in acknowledgment of their role as witnesses to the history that was shared through the images and the words spoken by our people. Some of the most prestigious items to be distributed during the mass give-

Fig. 14.16 B. A.'s granddaughter and great-granddaughters posing with his self-portrait in Looking to Our Past to Inspire Our Future. *Left to right*: great-granddaughter Alice Ann Nelson, granddaughter Loretta Baines, and great-granddaughter Fran Majors, August 4, 2007. Photo by author.

away at the end of our potlatches are silkscreen prints embellished with Tsimshian designs memorializing the event. Following this tradition, all visitors to the exhibition also received a note pad and pen in their canvas bags so that they could request prints of any of the images in the exhibit free of charge. Over five hundred photograph requests were place by community members, elders, and children as young as nine.

Within the last thirty years, there has been a great resurgence of potlatching, totem pole raising, dancing, and other Tsimshian traditions in Metlakatla. This shifting ground has brought up many unresolved issues concerning the effects of colonialism on our community. For the generations who have internalized the colonial narrative of our history, insecurity has developed that our cultural knowledge and connections to our traditions are not as strong as those of our Nation who remained in British Columbia. From the very first time that I brought the images that I have discussed in this essay home to Metlakatla to be presented to our community, these feelings about ourselves have dramatically shifted and caused our people to see their lived experience and the Tsimshian teachings that they were raised with in a different light. Among the more than fifty men, women, and children who were in attendance that day on February 28, 2006, there was a strong response of pride in the visual affirmation of the ways in which our ancestors strengthened and maintained Tsimshian cultural traditions, values, and belief in the early years of our community. In response to my presentation, B. A.'s great-grandson, artist and carver Wayne Hewson, stated:

> It made me proud of the fact that my grandfather helped record history, not just ours but all the people he traveled to, and that he continued to attend potlatches. In our family, the descendants of Haldane women, we were always told by our mothers that we are from the Killer Whale Clan of the Gitlaan and to be proud of who we are. These photographs show that our people were proud and that we didn't give up our culture.

Wayne has eloquently summarized the overall objective of my research on B. A.'s photography. After viewing B. A.'s images and learning of the findings of this research, he has reflected back on the clan and tribal identity that his mother, grandmother, and aunts made integral to the identity of their children. I hope that this will encourage others in our community to do the same. By acknowledging these cultural teachings and knowing Metlakatla's history from our ancestors' perspectives, and being aware of the inherent biases of its dominant colonial narrative, we can strengthen our cultural traditions by recognizing its persistence. This does not discredit the dedication of those who are leaders in what is considered the revival of our culture but shows the potency of their efforts as a part of a continuum. This is a part of the overall objective to my research to repatriate B. A.'s photography back to our community, restore the names of these beautiful people, families, and children in his images, and empower our voices by placing them at the forefront of our history and culture.[30]

NOTES

1. Sm'algyax is the name of our language. Dialects of Sm'algyax are spoken by the Tsimshian, Nisga'a, and Gitxsan peoples of Northern British Columbia and the Tsimshians of Metlakatla, Alaska.
2. My great-great-grandfather, Charles (Brensen) Brendible, was the first Tlingit to live in what was formerly the Tlingit village of Taakw K̲wáan after it was settled as the Christian community of Metlakatla in 1887.

Metlakatla is located on Annette Island in southeast Alaska. The core of our social organization is based on the inheritance of one of four matrilineal clans: Laxsgyiik (Eagle Clan), Laxgyibuu (Wolf Clan), Gisbutwada (Killer Whale Clan), and Ganhada (Raven Clan).
3. William Duncan (1835–1918) was sent by the Church Missionary Society (CMS) of England to work among the Tsimshian at Fort Simpson, British Columbia, in 1857. In 1862 Duncan moved with a small group of converts to Metlakatla with the intention of isolating them from the influences of their unconverted relatives and the vices introduced by the traders. The population of Metlakatla quickly increased to three times its original size with people who were seeking refuge from the smallpox epidemic. Duncan governed this community with "the Rules of Metlakahtla," fifteen rules that outlawed potlatching, face painting, and belief in supernatural powers and medicine men and made it mandatory to attend religious instruction, send children to school, be industrious, build nice houses, and pay the village tax. These rules were not entirely effective as at least some people continued Tsimshian traditions and beliefs in secrecy or under the guise of Christian practices. Until the 1880s, Metlakatla was sustained by revenue from its stores, local industries such as the salmon cannery and sawmill, and donations from all over the world, as well as the financial support of the CMS. Duncan was opposed to Tsimshian converts participating in high church Anglican rituals, such as drinking wine at communion, because he thought the symbolism of the blood and body of Christ would be misunderstood. This belief, which Duncan later argued was an assertion of his religious freedom, was one of the many disputes between Duncan and his superiors at the CMS, which led to his dismissal in 1882. Duncan began to lobby for Tsimshian land rights in order to regain control over Metlakatla from the CMS. In August 1886 Duncan received a verdict from Chief Justice Matthew Begbie that supported the CMS's takeover of the Metlakatla mission and denied the Tsimshian people their aboriginal claim to the land. These conflicts led to the decision to move to Alaska and lobby the U.S. government for land rights, which resulted in the Annette Island Indian Reserve being established by an 1891 congressional act.
4. See Davis 1904; Drucker 1965, 199–204; Barnett 1941; Beynon 1941.
5. See Kohlstedt 1957; Bowman 1983; Murray 1985; Dunn and Booth 1990, 294–97; Reader's Digest 1995, 254–55; Time-Life Books 1993, 160–67.
6. I am indebted to Dan Savard, senior collections manager at the Royal British Columbia Museum (RBCM), for bringing my attention to the interest in B. A.'s photography outside of our community in a paper that he presented at the Borders in the Art of the Northwest Coast" Conference at the British Museum in London in 2000. He then sent me copies of the photographs that are housed at the RBCM that are attributed to B. A.

7. Please note that the following publications and my thesis are under my maiden name, Mique'l Askren: "From Negative to Positive: B. A. Haldane, Nineteenth-Century Tsimshian Photographer" (master's thesis, University of British Columbia, 2006); "Bringing Our History into Focus: Redeveloping the Work of B. A. Haldane, 19th-Century Tsimshian Photographer," *BlackFlash: Lens, Site, Scene* 24, no. 3 (2007): 41–47; "Benjamin A. Haldane (Tsimshian, 1874-1941)," in *Our People, Our Land, Our Images: International Indigenous Photographers*, ed. Hulleah J. Tsinhnahjinnie and Veronica Passalacqua, 2 (Davis: C. N. Gorman Museum, University of California and Heyday Books, 2006).
8. My methodological approach to community-based photograph research is the focus of my essay "Looking to Our Past to Inspire Our Future: Strengthening Native Communities through Historical Photograph Research," in *Visual Sovereignty: Indigenous Photography*, currently being edited by Hulleah J. Tsinhnahjinnie and Veronica Passalacqua. This book is due to be released by the University of Washington Press in Seattle in 2014. Please note that this publication is under my married name, Dangeli.
9. *Ap' luk'wil T'oyaxsut nüüsm* in Sm'algyax is translated as expressing thank you very much; however, *T'oyaxsut nüün* has a much deeper meaning when conveyed in English. It literally means "I am bound to you," referring to the eternal connection between the people that results from the context of this exchange.
10. I have argued this point less extensively in my essay "Memories of Fire and Glass: B. A. Haldane, 19th-Century Tsimshian Photographer," in *Visual Currencies: The Native American Photograph in Museum and Galleries*, ed. Henrietta Lidchi and Hulleah J. Tsinhnahjinnie, 90–107 (Edinburgh: National Museums of Scotland, 2010). Please note that this work is under my maiden name, Askren.
11. Ginadoiks means "people of the rapids." They are one of the nine tribes of Tsimshian people on the lower Skeena River who moved to Lax Kw'alaams (also known as Port Simpson) in order to protect and control their trade routes as they were encroached upon by the Hudson Bay Company establishment of the Fort Simpson trading post in 1834.
12. Registrar of Infant Baptisms 1875, Metlakatla Christian Church, Metlakatla, BC.
13. B. A. Haldane to Elmer E. Brown, U.S. Commissioner of Education, May 22, 1909, A–L file, folder 329, document 1, box 112, Sir Henry S. Wellcome Collection, 1856–1936, Record Group 200, National Archives–Pacific Alaska Region, Anchorage (hereafter Wellcome Collection).
14. Benjamin Haldane, Native Statement, January 17, 1917, A–L file, folder 279, box 108, p. 10, Wellcome Collection.
15. Viola Garfield, "1930 Survey of Benjamin Haldane: Notes—Tsimshian Marriage—Clan and Tribal Affiliation," Viola Garfield Papers, box 4,

folder 3, accession number 2027-72-25, University of Washington Libraries, 1 (hereafter Garfield Papers).
16. B. A. married Martha Calvert, daughter of Aldolphus and Matilda Calvert of Metlakatla, Alaska, in 1896. In chronological order their children are Wilfred Walter (January 30, 1897), Anna Laura (June 24, 1899), Egbert Oscar (a.k.a. Oscar Egbert) (December 30, 1901), Boyd Anthony (a.k.a. Tony Boyd) (September 28, 1903), a girl who died in infancy (May 1905), Raymond Victor (February 13, 1907), Francis Floyd (September 22, 1908), Alexander Frederick (April 22, 1910), Sandy (died in infancy) (November 1911), Emma Louise (July 14, 1913), and Dennis Everett (September 11, 1915). I am grateful to genealogist Chris Roth along with B. A.'s grandchildren Loretta Baines and Francis Haldane and his wife, Kathy, for providing me with the names and birthdates of B. A.'s children.
17. The earliest dated portrait taken in his studio is an 1899 image of George McKay, a Tlingit from Saxman, Alaska. ARC# 29751, Wellcome Collection.
18. Haldane, Native Statement, 9.
19. Missionaries and the Department of Indian Affairs saw potlatching as a hindrance to the assimilation of First Nations people into Euro-Canadian society. In 1884, the Canadian government revised the Indian Act in order to criminalize the potlatch and other First Nations ceremonies. First Nations people continued the practice in secret throughout the nineteenth and early twentieth centuries. Few cases were prosecuted in court, the best known being Dan Cranmer's 1922 potlatch where Kwakwaka'wakw people were forced to relinquish ownership of their ceremonial possessions or go to jail. Several people chose to go to jail. Finally, in 1951 the law was dropped.
20. This photograph was identified as taken in Gitlakdamiks (Aiyansh). However, in 2001, Chief Morris Haldane (not related to B. A.) of Gingolx (Kincolith) BC wrote in the notes that accompany this image at the RBCM that his grandfather Peter Calder, who is the third person from the left in this image, told him that it was taken in Laxgalt'sap (Greenville).
21. These photographs became a part of Canadian anthropologist Marius Barbeau's collection and have become well-known images because of their misattribution to him. However, the original of the 1903 image (PN 16970, Royal British Columbia Museum) was embossed using the seal from B. A.'s studio and "Haldane" was noted as the photographer of the 1914 photographs (PN 4330 and PN 4329, Royal British Columbia Museum) by Dr. Charles F. Newcombe. These dates also correspond with the documentation confirming that B. A. was teaching music in villages in the Nass River area.
22. I have yet to be able to locate which tribe of the Tsimshian Samuel Marsden's chief name comes from. Beattie notes that his name was Shooquanaht (1955, 15).

23. Viola Garfield, "1930 Survey of Sidney Campbell: Notes—Tsimshian Marriage–Clan and Tribal Affiliation," Garfield Papers. Sidney's Tsimshian name was spelled by Garfield as "Ni'asluits." I have seen his name spelled "Ni.sluut" and "Neesh-loot" in other sources. I prefer the spelling "Neeshlut" because it reflects how his name is remembered by his family in our community. Myranell Bergtold, interview, Metlakatla, May 26, 2006.
24. On the illustration page adjacent to p. 67 of John W. Arctander's *The Apostle of Alaska*, a portrait of Sidney Campbell taken around 1880 in British Columbia shows him wearing the same apron, leggings, and *amhalaayt* (chief's headdress), but with a painted robe instead of the *gwishnapala* (button robe). It was included in Arctander's book without Sidney's name, however, and instead the caption of this image is "regalia of a Tsimshian Chief."
25. Matilda Minthorn to Henry Wellcome, January 31, 1925, A–L file, folder 265, document 15, box 107, Wellcome Collection.
26. Viola Garfield, "1930 Survey of Joseph Hayward: Notes—Tsimshian Marriage–Clan and Tribal Affiliation," Garfield Papers.
27. I am thankful to my Auntie Bernita Brendible for bringing to my attention that the man in B. A.'s photograph is her grandfather, John Hayward. The note Viola Garfield made in the album where this photograph originally resides states "Joseph Hayward" underneath the image. However, after following up on Auntie Bernita's observation by cross-referencing this image with other known images of John and Joseph Hayward, it is evident that this is John Hayward. In my correspondence with tribal genealogist Christopher F. Roth, author of *Becoming Tsimshian: The Social Life of Names,* he asserted that the Hayward brothers held the name in succession.
28. Our community is grateful to Dennis not only for saving the negatives but also for ensuring their preservation by placing them in the archives of the Tongass Historical Museum in Ketchikan, Alaska. We are also thankful to Richard Van Cleave, senior curator of collections for Ketchikan museums, for inventorying and scanning the negatives, and to the Tongass Historical Museum for housing.
29. I would like to thank Pastor Byron Parker of the William Duncan Memorial Church, Roy Williams, Tom Brendible, Stan Patterson, and Butch Hayward for loading these heavy crates into their trucks and traveling to Ketchikan on the ferry with the negatives to help unload them at the THS archives. I am working to establish a museum and cultural center in our community after I complete my doctoral program so that we can manage the care of these and other historical material ourselves.
30. When I presented this paper at the clan conference, I was surprised and honored by the story that Haida elder and renowned language teacher

Erma Lawrence shared with us about being one of B. A. Haldane's music students when she was a child in Howkan, Alaska. It was my first time presenting my research at a conference held in Alaska, and I thank her along with all those who attended, including the representatives sent by Metlakatla Indian Community, Mayor Victor Wellington and Councilwoman Rachael Askren (my mother), for making it such a wonderful experience.

REFERENCES

Arctander, John W. 1909. *The Apostle of Alaska: The Story of William Duncan of Metlakahtla.* New York: Fleming H. Revel.

Barnett, Homer G. "Personal Conflicts and Cultural Change." *Social Forces* 20, no. 2 (1941): 160–71.

Beattie, William Gilbert. 1955. *Marsden of Alaska: A Modern Indian.* New York: Vintage Press.

Beynon, William. "Tsimshian of Metlakatla, Alaska." *American Anthropologist* 43, no. 1 (1941): 83–88.

Bowman, Phylis. *Metlakatla — The Holy City!* Port Edward: privately published, 1983.

Dangeli, Mique'l Icesis. 2006. *From Negative to Positive: B. A. Haldane, Nineteenth-Century Tsimshian Photographer.* MA thesis, University of British Columbia.

Davis, George. 1904. *Metlakahtla: A True Narrative of the Red Man.* Chicago: Ram's Horn.

Drucker, Philip. *Cultures of the North Pacific Coast.* San Francisco: Chandler, 1965.

Dunn, John A., and Arnold Booth. "Tsimshians of Metlakatla." In *Handbook of North American Indians,* vol. 7: *Northwest Coast,* ed. Wayne Suttles. Washington: Smithsonian, 1990.

Francis, Daniel. 1996. *Copying People, 1860–1940: Photographing British Columbia First Nations.* Sakatoon: Fifth House.

Garfield, Viola. 1930a. "Survey of Benjamin Haldane: Notes — Tsimshian Marriage — Clan and Tribal Affiliation," Viola Garfield Papers, box 4, folder 3, accession number 2027-72-25, University of Washington Libraries.

———. 1930b. "Survey of Sidney Campbell: Notes — Tsimshian Marriage — Clan and Tribal Affiliation." Garfield Papers.

———. 1930c. "Survey of Joseph Hayward: Notes — Tsimshian Marriage — Clan and Tribal Affiliation." Garfield Papers.

———. 1931. "Change in the Marriage Customs of the Tsimshian." MA thesis, University of Washington.

Henrickson, Steve. 1992. "Yeilkoowu: The Reemergence of Ravens Tail Weaving on the Northwest Coast." *American Indian Art* 18 (1): 58–67.

Hewson, Wayne. February 28, 2006. Personal interview, Metlakatla AK.
Kohlstedt, Edward Delor. 1957. *William Duncan, Founder and Developer of Alaska's Metlakatla Christian Mission.* Palo Alto: National Press.
Minthorn, Matilda. January 31, 1925. Correspondence to Henry Wellcome. A–L file, folder 265, document 15, box 107, Wellcome Collection.
Murray, Peter. 1985. *The Devil and Mr. Duncan: A History of the Two Metlakatlas.* Victoria BC: Sono Nis Press.
Parham, R. Bruce. 1996. "Benjamin Haldane and the Portraits of a People." *Alaska History* 11 (1): 37–45.
Reader's Digest. *Through Indian Eyes: The Untold Story of Native American Peoples.* Pleasantville: Reader's Digest, 1995.
Roppel, Patricia. 1983. *Southeast Alaska: A Pictorial History.* Norfolk: Donning.
Roth, Christopher F. *Becoming Tsimshian: The Social Life of Names.* Seattle: University of Washington Press, 2008.
Savard, Dan. 2005. "Changing Images: Photographic Collections of First People of the Pacific Northwest Held in the Royal British Columbia Museum, 1860–1920." *BC Studies* 145: 54–91.
Sexton, Tom. 1979. "A Sampling of 19th-Century Alaskan Images: A Photographic Reading." *Alaska Journal* 9(3): 60–71.
Shane, Audrey P. M. 1984. "Power in Their Hands: The Gitsontk." In *The Tsimshian: Images of the Past, Views for the Present,* ed. Margaret Seguin, 160–73. Vancouver: University of British Columbia Press.
Time-Life Books. *Keepers of the Totem.* Alexandria: Time-Life Books, 1993.
Tsinhnahjinnie, Hulleah. 2003. "When Is a Photograph Worth a Thousand Words?" In *Photography's Other Histories,* ed. Christopher Phinney and Nicolas Peterson, 40–52. Durham: Duke University Press.
Williams, Carol. 2003. *Framing the West: Race, Gender, and the Photographic Frontier in the Pacific Northwest.* New York: Oxford University Press.

Part 3 | *Subsistence, Natural Resources, and Ethnogeography*

15

Haida and Tlingit Use of Seabirds from the Forrester Islands, Southeast Alaska

MADONNA L. MOSS

Puffin, puffin, flew in from the sea
Puffin, puffin, flew in from the sea
Make yourself meaty, puffin!

FORRESTER ISLAND BIRD SONG BY JESSIE NATKONG.
RECORDED IN 1985 IN HYDABURG, ALASKA, BY JOHN ENRICO

Hunn et al. (2003) recently demonstrated the cultural importance of gull egg collecting by the Huna Tlingit in Glacier Bay National Park, located near Juneau, Alaska. Their compelling study showed the efficacy of Tlingit traditional environmental knowledge in promoting long-term sustainable use of gull eggs. Other than this single study, however, little is known about Tlingit or Haida use of seabirds in southeast Alaska. In other sources, the importance of birds has been minimized based on the dietary contribution of birds over the course of the year relative to that of other foods (e.g., Fladmark 1975, 51; Jacobs and Jacobs 1982, 123; de Laguna 1972, 395). Yet seabirds are important, not just as food sources but because their skins can be made into clothing and bags, beaks and feathers are used to ornament regalia, and bones can be fashioned into needles, tubes, whistles, and other objects. Beyond such uses, Hunn et al. reveal the cultural significance of gull egg collecting as both a celebration of seasonal change and a time for families to enjoy an excursion to offshore islands. The Marble Islands studied by Hunn et al. are one of the few known locations of Tlingit seabird use; St. Lazaria Island near Sitka is another. Although biologists have identified at least ninety-one seabird colonies in southeast Alaska (Nelson and Lehnhausen 1983), Native use of most of these has not been documented.

The Forrester Islands lie beyond the Prince of Wales Archipelago in the eastern Gulf of Alaska (map 15.1). These islands are part of the Alaska Maritime National Wildlife Refuge managed by the U.S. Fish and Wildlife Service, headquartered in Anchorage. The Forrester Islands' importance as wildlife habitat was officially recognized in 1912, when President William Howard Taft signed Executive Order 1458, making it illegal to hunt, capture, or disturb any bird or their eggs on the islands. This action set aside the Forrester Islands as a bird sanctuary (reservation). Not only do the Forrester Islands provide steep cliffs for bird colonies but three of these islands support spruce forests that have loose soils that burrowing seabirds require for nest-building. The islands are positioned close to the continental shelf where upwelling provides birds with abundant food relatively close to shore. The absence of terrestrial mammalian predators is an additional reason that the Forrester Islands are the largest seabird colony in the eastern Gulf of Alaska, providing nesting grounds for over one million birds.

The results of archaeological investigations in 2004 and 2005 demonstrate that sites on the Forrester Islands have significant potential to yield important new information on the Native use of seabirds. Five sites, four located on Forrester Island itself and one site on nearby Lowrie Island, contain abundant faunal remains of seabirds, demonstrating Native use of seabirds during the precontact period, as many as 1,600 years ago. Zooarchaeological data are reported here along with ethnographic information that indicate the range of important species and suggest various ways the birds were obtained. The reports of early field naturalists, particularly those of Harold Heath and George Willett, provide key biological information in addition to previously unknown ethnographic details. This archaeological and historical information provides crucial documentation of Alaska Native use of seabirds from the Forrester Islands. I suspect that some of the oral history of seabird hunting and egging has been repressed over the years, since seabird use was controlled by federal law and international treaties in the early twentieth century. Archaeological data show that Native use of seabirds has a long history on the Forrester Islands, despite the relative inaccessibility of the islands.

The Forrester Islands

The Forrester Islands are situated in a remote part of southeast Alaska, approximately 35 km offshore Dall Island in the Prince of Wales Archi-

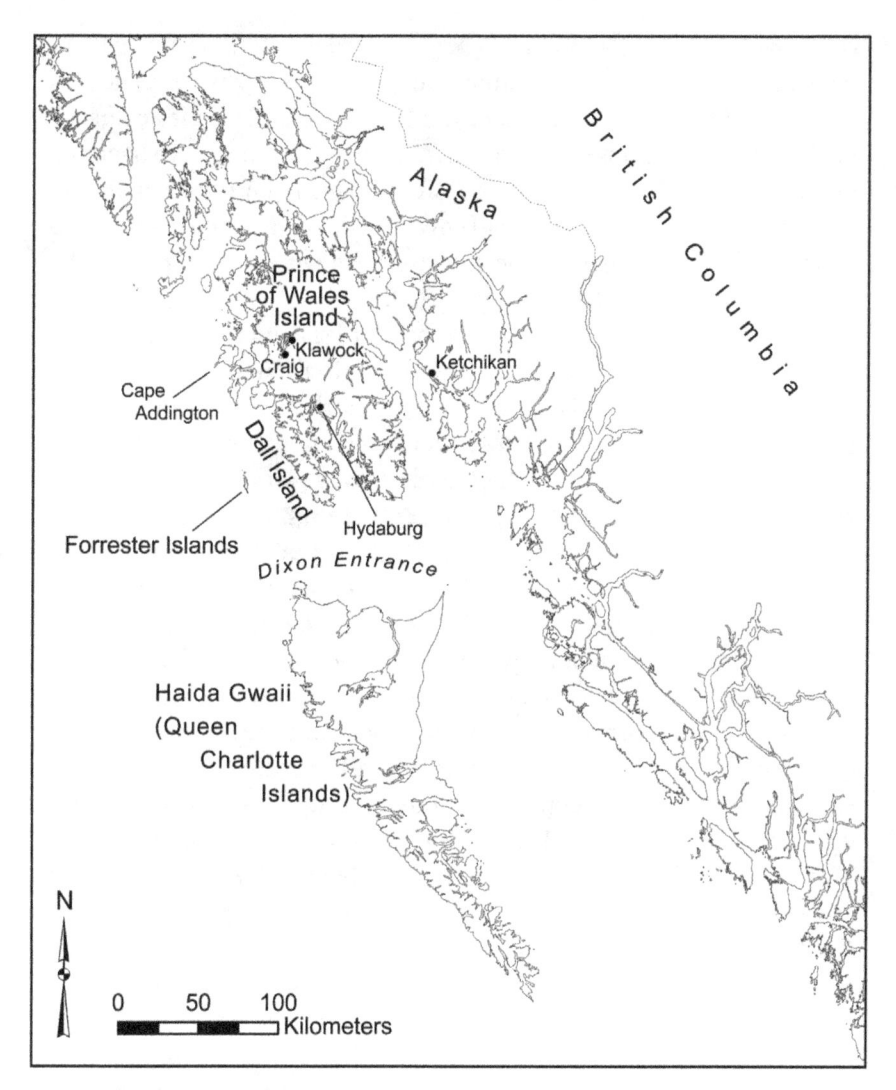

Map 15.1 Location of the Forrester Islands. Map prepared by Jacob Bartruff, Department of Geography, University of Oregon.

pelago and 135 km west-southwest of Ketchikan. What was once known as the Forrester Island National Wildlife Refuge is now part of the Alaska Maritime National Wildlife Refuge. From north to south, the Forresters include North Rocks, Lowrie Island, Cape Horn Rocks, Sea Lion Rock, Forrester Island, Petrel Island, and South Rock.

Forrester Island was named by Captain George Dixon in 1787 for his steward, George Forrester (Orth 1971 [1967], 346). It was called Santa

Christina Island in 1774 by Juan Perez, San Carlos Island in 1775 by Maurelle, and Douglas Island by William Douglas in 1788. Lowrie Island was named in 1879 by William Dall of the U.S. Coast and Geodetic Survey for Captain Lowrie, one of Cook's men, who in 1786 may have been the first English-speaking navigator to visit the Queen Charlotte Islands and "possibly the first who saw this [Lowrie] island" (602). Petrel Island presumably was named for the storm-petrels who nest there, but the name was not published until 1917 (752).

The Forrester Islands were set aside as a bird sanctuary in 1912. Harold Heath of Stanford University conducted an initial study of birds on Forrester, Lowrie, and Petrel Islands in 1913 (Heath 1915), sponsored by the U.S. Fish Commission and the National Association of Audubon Societies. George Willett of the U.S. Biological Survey worked on the Forresters in 1914, 1915, 1916, 1917, and 1919 (Willett 1915, 1917, 1920). In 1927, Willett became affiliated with the Los Angeles County Museum. These early efforts highlight the national significance of the Forrester Islands as bird habitat. Although many seabirds require steep, rocky cliffs for nesting, other species require heavy, protective vegetation that supports loose soils in which they can burrow. The Forrester Islands provide both types of seabird nesting sites (U.S. Fish and Wildlife Service 1966).

At least two of the islands (Lowrie and Forrester) are substantial enough in size to have supported human occupation during the precontact period, and Petrel Island may also have been occupied. Ethnographic use of the islands is indicated by Niblack (1890, 278), Swanton (1905, 235), Heath (1915), Garfield and Forrest (1948, 122–24), Langdon (1977, 94), Emmons (1991, 6), and Thornton (1995, 303). Part of the reason the Forresters have not been surveyed for archaeological sites before is because they are administered by the U.S. Fish and Wildlife Service to protect marine mammals and migratory seabirds; the wildlife refuge has been spared the commercial and industrial land use that often threatens archaeological sites in Alaska. The Alaska Department of Fish and Game (ADF&G) established a research camp on Lowrie Island in 1992, and every year since, biologists have lived on the island seasonally.

Both Forrester and Lowrie Islands are densely vegetated, but on Lowrie, the ADF&G biologists' trail system facilitates overland foot travel. Lowrie Island is composed of a series of rocky sea stacks that have been uplifted over several millennia. No foot trails cut across the thick vegetation of Forrester Island. The sheer cliffs along much of the shoreline of both islands preclude easy access to the beach. Between the sheer cliffs are short segments of boulder beaches, often with large piles of drift logs.

Archaeological Investigation of the Forrester Islands

The 2004 Lowrie Island project and the 2005 Forrester Island survey represent the only archaeological work conducted on the islands. Lowrie and Forrester Islands provide an interesting set of contrasts. Forrester Island may be twenty times larger than Lowrie, and while the highest peak on Forrester reaches 1,340 ft. (408 m), the high point of Lowrie Island is less than 200 ft. (61 m). Lowrie Island is the haulout locale for approximately 7,000 Steller sea lions today. Although numerous sea lions are found in the waters between the two islands, Forrester Island itself is not a major haulout. On Lowrie Island, the ADF&G biologists' trail system allows one to walk through the interior, while Forrester Island has no extant trails. In 2004, I surveyed Lowrie Island on foot from the ADF&G base camp on a project sponsored by ADF&G and the University of Oregon. I also conducted a test excavation of Elderberry Cave, collecting samples from seven arbitrary levels, each 10 cm thick. The 2005 project began with interviews of Haida elders in Hydaburg, led by University of Alaska Anchorage anthropologist Stephen Langdon and Hydaburg Cooperative Association environmental planner Anthony Christianson. Then U.S. Fish and Wildlife Service archaeologist Debra Corbett and I conducted an archaeological survey from a boat. From Forrester Island, samples for radiocarbon dating and faunal analysis were recovered from surface or shallow contexts.

Of eight archaeological sites identified during these two projects, five sites have yielded good samples of seabird remains. These include four sites on Forrester Island: Waterfall Cave (49-DIX-54), Red Lichen Cave (49-DIX-62), Soft Shell Cave (49-DIX-63), and the Saddle Site (49-DIX-55) and one site on Lowrie Island, Elderberry Cave (49-DIX-53). The radiocarbon dates from these five sites are presented in table 15.1. All seven dates were run by Beta-Analytic (Coral Gables, Florida) on *Mytilus californianus* shells. As shown, $^{13}C/^{12}C$ ratios were measured on all samples to correct for isotopic fractionation, and this has been incorporated into the adjusted ages. These adjustments average 402 years, with a standard deviation of 10.9 years. The calendar ages are derived from the CALIB Radiocarbon Calibration Program Revision 5.0.1 (© 1986–2005, M. Stuiver and P. J. Reimer; Hughen et al. 2004;

Table 15.1 Radiocarbon ages from five sites having seabird remains, Forrester Islands, Alaska

SITE 49-DIX-		LAB #, BETA-	UNCORRECTED ^{14}C AGE
53	Elderberry Cave	194561	520 ± 70
53	Elderberry Cave	194562	1810 ± 60
54	Waterfall Cave	208745	550 ± 70
54	Waterfall Cave	208746	660 ± 50
55	Saddle Site	208747	450 ± 50
62	Red Lichen Cave	208749	1810 ± 70
63	Soft Shell Cave	208750	1800 ± 60

Stuiver and Reimer 1993; Stuiver et al. 1998a, 1998b), with dates presented as a range at one sigma. The calendar age range incorporates the estimated correction for the local oceanic reservoir effect of -280 ± 50 years (Moss et al. 1989). The end points of the age ranges have been rounded to the nearest 10 years. Along with the historic occupation at another Forrester Island site, Eagle Harbor (49-DIX-061), these sites represent occupation between AD 360 and the World War II era.

The time depth of human occupation on both Lowrie and Forrester Islands is comparable to that of Cape Addington, 49-CRG-188 (Moss 2004). The 2004 test excavation at Elderberry Cave (49-DIX-53) revealed that the lowest level of the deposit represents occupation dated to AD 390–570, and the uppermost level is dated to AD 1590–1810. No break in occupational debris was identified during the excavation of Elderberry Cave, indicating long-term use of that cave. The oldest date from Forrester Island itself is from Red Lichen Cave, but use of nearby Soft Shell Cave is nearly as old, and both overlap with the earliest occupation of Elderberry Cave. People used these three caves on the west coast of the Forrester Islands ca. 1,600 years ago.

Although the sequence of dates from the Forrester Islands is not continuous, the gaps between AD 600 and 830 and between AD 1000 and 1450 are likely more apparent than real, probably resulting from limited radiocarbon sampling. These apparent gaps do not show up in the Cape Addington Rockshelter sequence (Moss 2004, 60), indicating

ADJUSTED $^{13}C/^{12}C$ AGE	ESTIMATED CALENDAR AGE RANGE (A.D.)	PROVENIENCE
900 ± 70	A.D. 1590-1810	Unit 1: 0-10 cm
2210 ± 60	A.D. 390-570	Unit 1: 70 cm
950 ± 70	A.D. 1520-1710	surface
1070 ± 50	A.D. 1460-1590	0-20 cm
860 ± 50	A.D. 1660-1830	probe: 0-20 cm
2220 ± 70	A.D. 360-570	surface
2190 ± 60	A.D. 410-590	surface

that people were using Noyes Island during these times. All of the dates from Forrester Island come from surface or shallow contexts, and I do not claim that they bracket the entire duration of human occupation. The oral historical information we gathered in Hydaburg testifies to use of the Forrester Islands into the nineteenth and twentieth centuries.

Sites with Seabird Remains

In the following abbreviated site descriptions, specific locational information has been omitted to protect the confidentiality of site locations. More detailed site descriptions are recorded on the Alaska Heritage Resource Survey filed with the Alaska State Office of History and Archaeology and with the U.S. Fish and Wildlife Service in Anchorage. I identified the vertebrate remains from the Forrester Island sites by direct comparison with specimens in the North Pacific comparative collection of reference faunal specimens at the Department of Anthropology, University of Oregon (see http://darkwing.uoregon.edu/~mmoss/Zooarchaeology-at-oregon/). In addition, specimens representing two storm-petrel species were loaned from the Burke Museum of Natural History and Culture, University of Washington. I identified the eggshells from one site using collections of the University of Oregon Museum of Natural and Cultural History.

Waterfall Cave. 49-DIX-54 is the only archaeological sea cave thus far identified on the east side of Forrester Island, where the island is more

TABLE 15.2 Bird remains from five archaeological sites, Forrester Islands, Alaska

TAXON	COMMON NAME	49-DIX-54 WATERFALL NISP	G	49-DIX-55 SADDLE NISP	G
Alcidae	alcid family	7	0.9	3	0.3
Brachyramphus marmoratus	Marbled Murrelet				
Cerorhinca monocerata	Rhinoceros Auklet	49	29.5	69	12.4
Haliaeetus leucocephalus	Bald Eagle				
Larus spp.	Gull			1	0.2
Lunda cirrhata	Tufted Puffin	2	2.2	5	1.1
Oceanodroma spp.	Storm-petrel	1	0.1	1	0.1
Phalacrocorax pelagicus	Pelagic Cormorant			3	1.8
Ptychoramphus aleuticus	Cassin's Auklet	8	1.6	70	7.6
Puffinus spp.	Shearwater				
Synthliboramphus antiquus	Ancient Murrelet				
Uria aalge	Common Murre			2	0.6
Aves unidentified		20	0.7	44	1.3
TOTAL AVES		87	35.0	198	25.4

Note: Weights have been rounded to the nearest 0.1 gram.

protected than the surf-beaten west side. Near the center of the 25 m x 15 m cave, we found a hearth containing charcoal, ash, unburned wood, mussel shells, and bones, and an associated cobble tool. The site was occupied between AD 1460 and 1710. The recovered faunal sample came from 0-15 cm below the surface, and contained mussel and barnacle shells, fish and bird bone. Of 93 bones, 73 were identified to at least the family level. Both halibut (*Hippoglossus stenolepis*) and lingcod (*Ophiodon elongatus*) are represented, but most were bird bones (table 15.2). Of those identified to family, 49 (73%) are rhinoceros auklet (*Cerorhinca monocerata*). Cassin's auklet (*Ptychoramphus aleuticus*), tufted puffin (*Lunda cirrhata*), and Leach's storm-petrel (*Oceanodroma leucorhoa*) were also identified. While the site occupants fished the nearby waters

49-DIX-62 RED LICHEN		49-DIX-63 SOFT SHELL		49-DIX-53 ELDERBERRY		TOTAL	
NISP	G	NISP	G	NISP	G	NISP	G
3	0.8	7	2.1	49	2.9	69	7.0
				1	0.1	1	0.1
1	1.9					119	43.8
				5	7.8	5	7.8
5	4.2	5	5.2			11	9.6
37	24.1	19	12.9	71	22.6	134	62.9
				3	0.2	5	0.4
4	3.8	4	5.8	13	17.8	24	29.2
1	0.2	6	0.9	34	5.5	119	15.8
6	8.8	1	0.9			7	9.7
		1	0.1	3	0.8	4	0.9
36	38.9	87	75.4			125	114.9
5	1.1	14	3.0	40	3.3	123	9.4
98	83.8	144	106.3	219	60.8	746	311.3

for halibut and lingcod, rhinoceros auklets and other alcids apparently were a primary target of their subsistence efforts, and the subsurface hearth indicates that people cooked and camped in the cave.

Saddle Site. 49-DIX-55 is also located on the east side of Forrester Island, where a low-lying saddle crosses the island from east to west. Shell midden was found in a 25 m x 5 m area vegetated with widely spaced spruce trees and a groundcover of thick grasses. Blackened soil, charcoal, fragmented mussel shell, and numerous bird bones were found to a depth of 20 cm and dated to AD 1660–1830. The shell midden was not particularly shell-rich, and the bones were more heavily fragmented than those recovered from the floors of the cave sites on Forrester Island. Of 198 bones, 154 were identified to at least the family level (table 15.2). Most common were Cassin's auklet (NISP=70, 45%) and rhinoceros auklet (NISP=69, 45%), and tufted puffin, pelagic cormorant (*Phalacrocorax pelagicus*), common murre (*Uria aalge*), gull (*Larus* spp.), and Leach's storm-petrel were also identified. The site lies within an area that Robert Sanderson of Hydaburg identified as a place the Kaigani Haida went to collect seabird eggs in the twentieth century. Clearly people were obtaining not just eggs but the birds themselves.

Red Lichen Cave. 49-DIX-62 is a sea cave located along the steep rocky shoreline of the west side of Forrester Island. The site was named for the pincushion orange lichen that grows on the rock surfaces surrounding the cave entrance. The 58 m x 10 m cave is 10.6 m above high tide. Two samples recovered from the cave floor were rich in bird bone, but also contained lingcod bones, mussel and limpet shells, and bird eggshells. Many of the bones are relatively large fragments, but show extensive surface weathering, including staining with organic growth, acid-etching, and exfoliation. All but 5 of the 105 bones were identified to at least the family level. The bones of a large lingcod were found (NISP=7), but all others are from birds (table 15.2). Most are tufted puffin (NISP=37, 40%) and common murres (NISP=36, 39%), but shearwater (*Puffinus* spp.), adult and juvenile gull, juvenile cormorant, rhinoceros auklet, and Cassin's auklet are also present. Eggshells from the site were identified as common murre. The site falls within the general area Sanderson identified as a place for gathering gull eggs.

Soft Shell Cave. 49-DIX-63 is another sea cave (52 m x 10 m), located close to Red Lichen Cave, and adjacent to a colony of glaucous-winged gulls on the west side of Forrester Island, about 9 m above high tide. In addition to bird bone, the faunal sample contained mussel shell, black katy chiton (*Katharina tunicata*) shell, and lingcod bone, and was dated to AD 410–590. Of 149 bones, 135 were identified to at least the family level. Most of the bones (NISP=87, 67%) are common murre, with tufted puffin (NISP=19, 15%), Cassin's auklet, gull, cormorant, shearwater, and ancient murrelet (*Synthliboramphus antiquus*) also present. Some of the gull and cormorant bones are from juvenile birds. The most striking aspect of these results is that the common murre is the most abundant species among the faunal remains, whereas the site is immediately adjacent to a glaucous-winged gull (*Larus glaucescens*) colony.

Elderberry Cave. 49-DIX-53 is a former sea cave (12 m x 5 m) occurring well within the forest fringe on the west side of Lowrie Island, 12–15 m above high tide. A single 0.5 m x 1.0 m test pit was excavated at the center of the cave entrance just inside the dripline to a depth of 70 cm. The lowest level of the deposit is dated to AD 390–570, and the uppermost level is dated to AD 1590–1810. All bone, whole shell valves, and artifacts retained in the ¼ inch mesh screen were recovered. A bone point and two pieces of worked bone were found. California mussel was the most common shellfish, but littorines (*Littorina sitkana*) and limpets (*Lottia digitalis, Tectura persona*) were also abundant. Fish and mammals included rockfish (*Sebastes* spp.), prickleback (stichaeid), lingcod, halibut, salmon (salmonid), harbor seal (*Phoca vitulina*), and Steller sea lion (*Eumetopias jubatus*). The bird remains from seven levels have been combined in table 15.2. Of those identified to family, tufted puffins are most abundant (NISP=71, 40%). All but one of the 49 specimens identified to the alcid category are ribs that may likely belong to these puffins, but ribs are elements that zooarchaeologists generally do not assign to bird species. Next in abundance are Cassin's auklet (NISP=34, 19%) and pelagic cormorant (NISP=13, 7%). Bald eagle (*Haliaeetus leucocephalus*), fork-tailed storm-petrel (*O. furcata*), ancient murrelet, and marbled murrelet (*Brachyramphus marmoratus*) were also identified.

Zooarchaeological Results in Ethnographic and Biological context

In this section, I aim to integrate the zooarchaeological data with ethnographic information, biological background, and field observations to better understand how Native people used the birds of the Forrester Islands. In a few instances, the archaeological data provide some indication of changes in seabird species availability or abundance that suggest habitat change over time. I start by addressing the apparent discrepancy between the archaeological findings at Soft Shell Cave with the contemporary abundance of gulls adjacent to that site, and then discuss key species at other sites.

Glaucous-winged gulls lay their eggs during the first week of June, and Hydaburg elders told us they aim for June 8 as the best date to collect gull eggs. Gulls are indeterminate layers; so if one or two eggs are removed from a nest, a gull will lay a few more to replace those lost (Ehrlich et al. 1988, 165). I observed a few gull nests just within the entrance to Soft Shell Cave, but they did not contain eggs. This could be because the eggs had hatched, and gulls are known to remove eggshells from their nests as a defense against predators (167). Eggs hatch by the first week in July, but the chicks require another month to eight weeks to fly. My visit to Soft Shell Cave occurred on August 10, when some but not all young were fledged. I was able to approach two gull chicks within a meter, showing how vulnerable the young birds are at this time of year. Birds such as these could be easily chased into the cave where they could be killed.

Despite the proximity of the gull colony, 67% of the bird bones from the Soft Shell Cave sample were common murres. Next in abundance were tufted puffins (15%), but only a few gulls were present, including one juvenile. Apparently gulls were not the main species targeted by the people who used Soft Shell Cave. Murres do not build nests; the female lays a single egg on bare rock. Some seacliff rookeries accommodate multiple seabird species, stratified by elevation and available habitat (Ehrlich et al. 1988, 197). Murres usually are positioned below gulls at such sites, although I did not see any murres. The gull nesting site adjacent to Soft Shell Cave has bare rock ledges where murres could lay their eggs, and Willett (1915, 299) stated that the principal murre rookeries were "on the west side of Forrester Island," Cape Horn Rocks, and on Petrel Island. Willett stated that murres begin laying eggs on July 20 and that the earliest young murre he saw was on August 13. Therefore, if murres were using the rookery, I should have seen murres tending their eggs on August 10.

One explanation for this discrepancy is that the rookery adjacent to Soft Shell Cave accommodated murre breeding in the past, but not now. As a sea cave, Soft Shell Cave has been formed by wave action. The drift logs found within the cave indicate this process, but now the cave entrance is just above the reach of the waves, as the land in this area is still undergoing isostatic rebound. The large boulders that litter the shoreline in front of the cave have broken off the cliff side, and the gull-nesting site is at the base of what appears to be a landslide track. One possibility is that at some point in the past, the cliffs dropped directly into the sea, before the fringe of fallen boulders developed at the base of the cliffs. When murres learn to fly, the parents stand between their chick and the cliff edge to prevent the chick from jumping off before it should (Bennett 2001; Lichen 2001, 38). The murre chick's first attempt at flight involves stepping off the cliff edge and fluttering 800 to 1500 ft. (244–457 m) down to the sea. Today, at the rookery adjacent to Soft Shell Cave, there is enough of a boulder perimeter in front of the cliffs that if a murre chick stepped off a ledge, it would tumble onto rock. The cliffs in this area may have been a murre rookery before the boulder fringe developed; the radiocarbon date suggests that murres were the focus of use at this site about 1,500 years ago. With the breakdown of cliffs and the emergence of a beach of massive boulders, today's cliffs no longer would seem to suit the needs of murres.

Red Lichen Cave is located only 40 m south of and at an elevation 1.6 m higher than Soft Shell Cave. Its entrance is heavily vegetated, demonstrating that it formed earlier than did Soft Shell Cave. Its dated occupation is just slightly older than that of Soft Shell Cave. At Red Lichen Cave, the percentages of murres and puffins are each about 40%. Clearly, Red Lichen Cave was also occupied during a time when murres were locally abundant, breeding in the site vicinity. Puffins are relatively abundant in the samples taken from both sites. In stratified seacliff colonies, puffins typically nest above both murres and gulls, using their claws to dig burrows into loose soil atop or alongside cliffs. I could not see puffin nest sites above Soft Shell Cave; one would need ropes to climb the cliffs in this area to observe suitable nesting habitat.

In both Soft Shell and Red Lichen samples, gulls and cormorants were represented by juveniles as well as adults, indicating midsummer use. Juveniles were apparently not the primary target of subsistence, however, since they make up small proportions of both assemblages. Although bird eggshells were present in both caves, the only eggshell samples are from Red Lichen Cave, and these have been identified as common murre. Hence the evidence indicates that murres and their eggs were targeted by the people using theses caves 1,600 to 1,400 years ago. The evidence may also suggest that a rookery that accommodated murres in the past shifted to one dominated by gulls in the last 1,000 years or so.

Although not numerous, smaller alcids and shearwaters were found at both west coast caves. This is the first case of the genus *Puffinus* to be identified in an archaeological site in southeast Alaska. Shearwaters were not represented among the 33 species inventoried by Heath (1915), although Willett (1915, 300) stated that the sooty shearwater was "seen occasionally throughout the summer, generally a half mile or more off shore, but on one occasion between Forrester and Lowrie islands." In 1917, Willett collected a "slender-billed" shearwater (now known as the short-tailed shearwater) floating dead a few hundred yards off the north end of Forrester Island (Willett 1920, 138). Pelagic shearwaters may have been deliberately hunted by Kaigani Haida or Tlingit, or stranded birds could have been collected.

On the east side of Forrester Island, the use of birds differed from that of the west side. At the Saddle Site, the most abundant species were Cassin's auklet and rhinoceros auklet, each at 45%. Tufted puffin, pelagic cormorant, common murre, gull, and Leach's storm-petrel were also identified. From Waterfall Cave, most of the remains were rhinoceros auklet (73%), and Cassin's auklet, tufted puffin, and Leach's storm-petrel were also identified.

Heath devoted considerable space to rhinoceros auklets and their extensive burrows, built in spruce forests "where the shadows are of such depth that ferns and underbrush find but scanty foothold. . . . In such localities over four hundred burrows have been counted in an area six hundred feet square" (1915, 31). Heath measured such burrows and found them to be at least 8 ft. long and some up to 20 ft. long. Both Cassin's auklets and ancient murrelets also occupy some of these burrows. Rhinoceros auklets lay their eggs during the first half of June, then incubate them for three weeks. Heath wrote that "the natives are unanimous in declaring that they now know of no other nesting site of the Rhinoceros Auklet in southeastern Alaska" (32). During his fieldwork, Heath was assisted by "Captain John," "an unusually keen and accurate naturalist of the Haidah tribe" (23), and I assume when Heath refers to "Natives," he means Haida. Heath reported that according to the Natives, rhinoceros auklets were far more numerous in the past than at the time of his 1913 visit:

> In those earlier times the sky was literally darkened as they [rhinoceros auklets] put out to sea, and the sound of their cries was a veritable babel. The diminution might naturally be ascribed to the activity of the natives, who relish this species above all others, but the natives themselves meet such a claim with the evidence of many scores of years when, with a much larger tribe than at present, they gathered eggs and birds in vastly greater numbers without any appreciable decline in the bird colony. Their explanation rests solely upon the belief that the decrease is due entirely to the rank growth of underbrush and ferns, which form a tangled mat too dense to permit of ready flight to and from the burrows. In former times, even within the memory of some of the older men of the tribe, the country was much more open; and it is certainly a readily observed fact that this species avoids the thickets and seeks out more open ground. Occasional nests are found in salmon berry patches, but well worn runways invariably lead into the open. (33)

Willett (1915, 297) explained that all rhinoceros auklet nesting colonies are located on the east side of Forrester Island and that burrows can occur just above the beach to 500 ft. up the hillsides. Auklets use their bills to break up the soil and their feet to move it out of the way. At the entrance to their burrows, they leave mounds of grass, moss, leaves, and earth from their digging. Willett reported that egg laying begins during the last week of May. Rhinoceros auklets are rarely seen during the day; they fly to the more protected waters around Dall, Prince of Wales, and Suemez Islands to feed. The mating pair take turns incubating the eggs; one mate sits on the eggs from 2:00 a.m. or so until 11:00 p.m., while the other takes the 11:00 p.m. to 2:00 a.m. shift. During the middle of the night, when the birds were changing positions, the Haida built bonfires amid their burrows to confuse the birds. Willett reported that auklets were then easily dispatched with spruce boughs.

In the Saddle Site environs, former sea stacks are now stranded in the forest, and the ground is pocketed with bird burrows, most likely those of rhinoceros auklets. Saddle Site residents were probably gathering both rhinoceros and Cassin's auklets from their burrows in the immediate vicinity of the site. I was unable to survey the cliffs around Waterfall Cave for comparison.

The tiny Cassin's auklet, 7½ in. long, compared with a rhinoceros auklet at 15 in. long (Armstrong 1995, 182, 185), was surprisingly abundant in the Saddle Site sample. Cassin's auklets build their burrows on Petrel and Forrester Islands. They, too, are attracted to firelight, and the Haida reportedly captured them much like they did rhinoceros auklets. Heath (1915, 34) wrote that Cassin's auklets "figure largely in the native's bill of fare, and large numbers were annually taken by means of snares or were attracted by bonfires and subsequently knocked down." On Lowrie Island, Cassin's auklet carcasses are frequently found on the trails. Most of these adult birds seemed to have died at night by colliding with trees. The birds arrive on the Forrester Islands at the beginning of March and reportedly spend two months digging their burrows (Ehrlich et al. 1988, 206). The females incubate the eggs and are fed at night when the males return from foraging. Heath wrote that fishermen reported to him that "in the early morning these birds had struck their tents, and in a stunned condition were readily taken" (34). Like rhinoceros auklets, Cassin's auklets would appear to need some clearings to make night flying less hazardous.

The question Heath raised with his Haida contacts about the reason for the decrease in the number of rhinoceros auklets by 1913 might be answered archaeologically. With large enough samples from enough well-dated assemblages, perhaps we could identify whether or not the abundance of rhinoceros auklets appeared stable or changed during precontact times. Provisionally, information from the Haida suggests another example of habitat change.

Tufted puffins are present in assemblages from both east and west sides of Forrester Island and are the most abundant bird recovered from Elderberry Cave on Lowrie Island. Both Heath (1915, 29) and Willett (1915, 296) considered tufted puffins to be the most abundant alcid on the Forrester Islands. They described puffins as skilled bait thieves, easily taken by hook and line or gaff hook. Willett wrote of the attitude of those commercial fishermen hand-trolling for salmon during the summer of 1914:

> The fishermen detest these birds because of their penchant for stealing the herring that is used as bait in trolling for salmon. After the fisherman has placed a fresh herring on the hook and lets the line out to trolling distance, the puffin will dive and neatly remove the bait from the hook. I have seen this done when the bird was forced to go down at least fifteen fathoms. Apparently a puffin will attach itself to a particular trolling boat and will follow it for hours. The fishermen attribute to the bird a surprising amount of cunning. One Norwegian assured me solemnly that the parrot would rise up on the crest of a wave and look into the boat in order to count the herring therein. . . . Frequently the puffins will get all the herring the fisherman has and he will be obliged to cease fishing. . . . This habit of stealing bait is confined to this species. (296)

It seems likely that precontact Native fishermen would have caught such a puffin long before the bird had stolen all their bait. Moreover, the Haida and Tlingit probably "fished" for puffins and other seabirds in the waters around the Forrester Islands prior to the birds' legal protection.

In discussions of the Forrester Islands, contemporary Haida elders emphasized egg collecting. Hunn et al. (2003) have shown that gull egg collecting by the Huna Tlingit in Glacier Bay is important, not only to provide a subsistence resource but to mark spring as a time of renewal when the Huna reassert their claim to a special place. Certainly the Forrester Islands were and are a special place to the Haida and Tlingit. Camped on Dall or other islands in late April, when they saw flocks of returning rhinoceros auklets, they knew that seabird nesting on the Forrester Islands was about to begin. These groups had to await good weather to canoe across to the Forresters. As Heath (1915, 30) wrote, "They repaired to this summer resort for their annual egg and bird collecting holiday." Fine weather signaled the richness of the food gathering season to come.

Ethnographically, the Tlingit shot birds with bows and arrows, snared them, and fished for gulls using baited double-pointed bone gorges (Emmons 1991, 138). Yet bird hunting (as opposed to egg collecting) was not described by the elders in Hydaburg. Since migratory birds on the Forresters have been protected by law for a century, perhaps this is not something that people discuss openly. Taft's Executive Order of 1912 made it illegal to hunt, capture, or disturb any bird or their eggs on the Forrester Islands (King 2005, 1–2). Heath (1915, 36) witnessed evidence of gull egg "poaching" in 1913, but the extent of aboriginal use of Forrester Islands seabirds after refuge designation is unknown. Nonetheless, the observations by early twentieth-century naturalists, along with the archaeological evidence, testify to significant Native use of seabirds, particularly tufted puffins, common murres, rhinoceros auklets, Cassin's auklets, cormorants, and gulls. Further study of the archaeological sites on the Forrester Islands can reveal more about the sustained Native use of these birds over the centuries.

The Illegality of Migratory Bird Hunting

When the Forrester Islands were designated a bird sanctuary in 1912, the taking of birds from the islands—during any season—was outlawed. More broadly, between 1916 and 2003, the hunting of migratory birds during the spring and summer by Alaska Natives was illegal, even though Tlingit and Haida bird hunting and egg collecting are traditional subsistence activities. The 1916 Migratory Bird Treaty with Canada was the first of several international treaties aimed at curbing the massive decline of bird populations due to commercial hunting in the late nineteenth and early twentieth centuries. The act did not prohibit bird hunting during autumn—primarily for ducks and geese—an activity in which both Native and non-Native hunters participated. While the intent was to protect migratory birds and allow for variable levels of fall sports hunting, the treaties ignored the customary use of birds by Alaska Natives and other indigenous northern peoples during spring and summer (Moss and Bowers 2007).

The 1956 Fish and Wildlife Act designated the Department of the Interior as the key agency for managing migratory birds in the United States. The Migratory Bird Treaty Act Protocol Amendment of 1995 aimed to redress long-term discrimination against Alaska Natives by providing for "customary and traditional use of migratory birds and their eggs for subsistence use by indigenous inhabitants of Alaska," but states that "it is not the intent of the Amendment to cause significant increases in the take of species of migratory birds relative to their continental population sizes" (U.S. Fish and Wildlife Service 2003, 1). This placed the management agencies involved, the U.S. Fish and Wildlife Service and the Alaska Department of Fish and Game, in the awkward position of having to document harvests that had been technically illegal.

Nevertheless, the U.S. Fish and Wildlife Service and the Alaska Department of Fish and Game surveyed subsistence harvest, and in 2000 the Alaska Migratory Bird Co-Management Council was established with representatives from both agencies in addition to Native organizations. The Council issued its first annual harvest regulations for the spring and summer of 2003. The 2004 harvest regulations identified Hoonah as the only southeast Alaskan community eligible for spring and summer migratory bird harvest. Huna people were permitted to collect glaucous-winged gull eggs on national forest lands along Icy Strait and Cross Sound, but not in their traditional territory in Glacier Bay National Park. Starting in 2005, harvest regulations have identified both Hydaburg and Craig, located in southeast Alaska, as eligible communities. They were permitted to collect gull eggs from "small islands and adjacent shoreline of western Prince of Wales Island from Point Baker to Cape Chacon, but also including Coronation and Warren islands" (Department of Interior 2005, 18250; 2006a, 10410). The Forrester Islands were excluded from the harvest area in 2005 and 2006 and were not mentioned in the proposed regulations for 2007 (Department of Interior 2006b).

Implications for the Future: Wildlife Use and Management

This study is not the first to identify evidence of seabird use in southeast Alaska. From Cape Addington Rockshelter (49-CRG-188) on Noyes Island in Tlingit territory, the bones of eleven seabird taxa were identified: short-tailed albatross (*Phoebastria albatrus*), northern fulmar (*Fulmaris glacialis*), storm-petrel (*O. furcata*), cormorant, gull, pigeon guillemot (*Cepphus columba*), rhinoceros auklet, tufted puffin, Cassin's auklet, marbled murrelet, and common murre (Moss 2004). The wide range of taxa represented at this site suggested offshore hunting of seabirds, although not all of these were taken at colonies (e.g., albatross). While working on that study, I wrote that the location, scale, and frequency of Tlingit seabird use across southeast Alaska were poorly known (Moss 2003, 97).

My purpose has been to document the long-term use of migratory birds on the Forrester Islands by the indigenous people of southeast Alaska. Investigations of five archaeological sites have yielded good samples of seabird remains. The presence of immature gulls and cormorants and murre eggshells at two of the sites clearly shows summer harvest of seabirds. The ethnographic and historical information discussed above in relation to the other three sites also indicates spring and summer use of seabirds. Taken together, the data from Cape Addington and the Forrester Islands sites have shown that the Kaigani Haida, the Tlingit, and their ancestors have been harvesting seabirds during the spring and summer over the past sixteen centuries. These results provide longitudinal support for the rights of southeast Alaska Natives to harvest seabirds. I hope that the data described herein will be useful to wildlife managers, particularly to the U.S. Fish and Wildlife Service and the Alaska Migratory Bird Co-Management Council.

Further study, including the identification of additional sites, systematic collection of larger samples, additional radiocarbon dating of samples, and more faunal analyses will be necessary to address some of the research questions that emerged in this study. For example, the study of the Soft Shell and Red Lichen Caves suggests that common murres were more numerous in the vicinity than they are today, and more research is necessary to confirm and explain this pattern. The suggestion by Heath (derived from his discussions with Haida men) that the population of rhinoceros auklets had decreased by the early twentieth century is another inference that may find support or refutation through more in-depth archaeological study. These are two of many examples where the study of the archaeological record can help us understand patterns of wildlife abundance that evolved with the history of Native use of the Forrester Islands.

The data presented here provide support for the rights of southeast Alaska Natives to harvest seabirds, particularly the communities on the west side of Prince of Wales Island, including Hydaburg, Craig, and Klawock. Zooarchaeological results from this study of five Forrester

Island sites indicate aboriginal use of eleven seabird taxa, including (in order of abundance): tufted puffin (*Lunda cirrhata*), common murre (*Uria aalge*), rhinoceros auklet (*Cerorhinca monocerata*), Cassin's auklet (*Ptychoramphus aleuticus*), pelagic cormorant (*Phalacrocorax pelagicus*), gull (*Larus* spp.), shearwater (*Puffinus* spp.), storm-petrel (*O. leucorhoa, O. furcata*), ancient murrelet (*Synthliboramphus antiquus*), and marble murrelet (*Brachyramphus marmoratus*). As indicated in the epigraph to this paper, the "meaty puffin" and other seabirds were highly valued as resources and messengers of the harvest season.

ACKNOWLEDGMENTS

I am grateful to Debra Corbett for her support of and enthusiasm for the work on the Forrester Islands. The 2004 Lowrie Island project was conducted under an Archaeological Resource Protection Act permit from the U.S. Fish and Wildlife Service, funded by the Alaska Department of Fish and Game and the University of Oregon. I am indebted to Ken Pitcher, Lauri Jemison, and Erik Schoen of ADF&G for their assistance on the 2004 project. Corbett and I worked together in the planning and execution of all stages of the 2005 fieldwork. Financial support from the U.S. Fish and Wildlife Service is gratefully acknowledged. I also thank Steve Langdon and Tony Christianson for their work with the people in Hydaburg, who provided crucial cultural context for this project. We gratefully appreciate the contributions of Haida experts: Bob Sanderson, Charles Natkong, Alma Cook, Claude Morrison, Woodrow Morrison, Anna Peele, and Bob Peele. Thanks are also due Mike McKimens and the crew of the *Na Pali*, Skeet Arasmith, Patty Lazzar, and Pete Smith for getting us on and around Forrester Island. Terry Fifield helped with logistics in Craig, and Ken Pitcher, Steve Lewis, and Jim Baichtal generously provided key information. Robert Faucett, Burke Museum, made possible the loan of storm-petrels as comparative specimens used in the faunal analysis. Pam Endzweig and Elizabeth Kallenbach facilitated access to the egg collection at the University of Oregon Museum of Natural and Cultural History. I also appreciate the efforts of the thoughtful anonymous reviewers and the work of Rick Stepp and Kari MacLauchlin.

This paper was reprinted from *Journal of Ethnobiology* 27, no. 1 (2007): 28–45.

REFERENCES CITED

Armstrong, Robert H. 1995. *Guide to the Birds of Alaska.* Anchorage: Alaska Northwest Books.

Bennett, Jody. 2001. "*Uria aalge*, Common Murre." University of Michigan Museum of Zoology Animal Diversity Web. Available at http://animaldiversity.ummz.umich.edu/ (verified July 5, 2001).

Department of Interior, Fish and Wildlife Service. 2005. "50 CFR 92 Migratory Bird Subsistence Harvest in Alaska: Harvest Regulations for Migratory Birds in Alaska during the 2005 Season; Final Rule." *Federal Register* 70 (67): 18244–250.

———. 2006a. "50 CFR 92 Migratory Bird Subsistence Harvest in Alaska: Harvest Regulations for Migratory Birds in Alaska during the 2006 Season; Final Rule." *Federal Register* 71 (39): 10404–410.

———. 2006b. "50 CFR 92 Migratory Bird Subsistence Harvest in Alaska: Harvest Regulations for Migratory Birds in Alaska during the 2007 Season; Proposed Rule." *Federal Register* 71 (239): 75059–75066.

Ehrlich, Paul R., David S. Dobkin, and Darryl Wheye. 1988. *The Birder's Handbook: A Field Guide to the Natural History of North American Birds.* New York: Simon & Schuster.

Emmons, George T. 1991. *The Tlingit Indians.* Ed. Frederica de Laguna. Seattle: University of Washington Press and Vancouver: Douglas and McIntyre, in association with the American Museum of Natural History, New York.

Enrico, John, and Wendy Bross Stuart. 1996. *Northern Haida Songs.* Lincoln: University of Nebraska Press.

Fladmark, Knut R. 1975. *A Paleoecological Model for Northwest Coast Prehistory.* Archaeological Survey of Canada Mercury Series 43. Ottawa.

Garfield, Viola E., and Linn A. Forrest. 1948. *The Wolf and the Raven.* Seattle: University of Washington Press.

Heath, Harold. 1915. "Birds Observed on Forrester Island, Alaska, during the Summer of 1913." *Condor* 17: 20–41.

Hughen, K. A., M. G. L. Baillie, E. Bard, A. Bayliss, J. W. Beck, C. Bertrand, P. G. Blackwell, C. E. Buck, G. Burr, K. B. Cutler, P. E. Damon, R. L. Edwards, R. G. Fairbanks, M. Friedrich, T. P. Guilderson, B. Kromer, F. G. McCormac, S. Manning, C. Bronk Ramsey, P. J. Reimer, R. W. Reimer, S. Remmele, J. R. Southon, M. Stuiver, S. Talamo, F. W. Taylor, J. van der Plicht, and C. E. Weyhenmeyer. 2004. "Marine04 Marine Radiocarbon Age Calibration 0–26 Cal Kyr BP." *Radiocarbon* 46: 1059–86.

Hunn, Eugene S., Darryll Johnson, Priscilla Russell, and Thomas F. Thornton. 2003. "Huna Tlingit Traditional Environmental Knowledge, Conservation, and the Management of a 'Wilderness' Park." *Current Anthropology* 44 (4): S79–S103.

Jacobs, Mark, Jr., and Mark Jacobs Sr. 1982. "Southeast Alaska Native Foods." In *Raven's Bones*, ed. Andrew Hope III, 112–30. Sitka: Sitka Community Association.

King, Robert W. 2005. "Rowboats and the Bird Sanctuary: The Salmon Troll Fishery at Forrester Island, 1912–1914." Paper presented to the Alaska Historical Society, Kodiak.

de Laguna, Frederica. 1972. *Under Mount Saint Elias: The History and Culture of the Yakutat Tlingit.* Smithsonian Contributions to Anthropology 7. Washington: Smithsonian Institution.

Langdon, Stephen J. 1977. "Technology, Ecology, and Economy: Fishing Systems in Southeast Alaska." PhD diss., Anthropology, Stanford University, Palo Alto. Ann Arbor: University Microfilms.

Lichen, Patricia K. 2001. *Brittle Stars and Mudbugs: An Uncommon Field Guide to Northwest Shorelines and Wetlands.* Seattle: Sasquatch Books.

Moss, Madonna L. 2003. "Comment on Huna Tlingit Traditional Environmental Knowledge, Conservation, and the Management of a 'Wilderness' Park." *Current Anthropology* 44 (4): S96–S97.

———. 2004. *Archaeological Investigation of Cape Addington Rockshelter: Human Occupation of the Rugged Seacoast on the Outer Prince of Wales Archipelago, Alaska.* University of Oregon Anthropological Paper No. 63. Eugene: University of Oregon.

Moss, Madonna L., and Peter M. Bowers. 2007. "Migratory Bird Harvest in Northwestern Alaska: A Zooarchaeological Analysis of Ipiutak and Thule Occupations from the Deering Archaeological District." *Arctic Anthropology* 44 (1): 37–50.

Moss, Madonna L., Jon M. Erlandson, and R. Stuckenrath. 1989. "The Antiquity of Tlingit Settlement on Admiralty Island, Southeast Alaska." *American Antiquity* 54 (3): 534–43.

Nelson, J. W., and W. A. Lehnhausen. 1983. *Marine Bird and Mammal Survey of the Outer Coast of Southeast Alaska, Summer 1982.* Anchorage: U.S. Fish and Wildlife Service.

Niblack, Albert P. 1890. "The Coast Indians of Southern Alaska and Northern British Columbia." In *Annual Report of the U.S. National Museum for 1888*, 225–386. Washington: Smithsonian Institution.

Orth, Donald J. 1971 [1967]. *Dictionary of Alaska Place Names.* Geological Survey Professional Paper 567. Washington: Government Printing Office.

Stuiver, M., and P. J. Reimer. 1993. "Extended ^{14}C Data Base and Revised CALIB 3.0 ^{14}C Age Calibration Program." *Radiocarbon* 35: 215–30.

Stuiver, M., P. J. Reimer, E. Bard, J. W. Beck, G. S. Burr, K. A. Hughen, B. Kromer, F. G. McCormac, J. Plicht, and M. Spurk. 1998a. "INTCAL98 Radiocarbon Age Calibration, 24,000–0 cal BP." *Radiocarbon* 40: 1041–83.

Stuiver, M., P. J. Reimer, and T. F. Braziunas. 1998b. "High-Precision Radiocarbon Age Calibration for Terrestrial and Marine Samples." *Radiocarbon* 40: 1127–151.

Swanton, John R. 1905. *Contributions to the Ethnology of the Haida.* New York: G. E. Stechert.

Thornton, Thomas F. 1995. "Place and Being among the Tlinit." PhD diss., Anthropology, University of Washington, Seattle. Ann Arbor: University Microfilms.

U.S. Fish and Wildlife Service. 1966. Wilderness study report. Forrester Island wilderness study area, Forrester Island National Wildlife Refuge, First Judicial Division, Alaska. U.S. Department of Interior, Fish and Wildlife Service, Bureau of Sport Fisheries and Wildlife.

———. 2003. Alaska Subsistence Migratory Bird Harvest Surveys. Available at http://alaska.fws.gov/ambcc/ambcc/Harvest/subharvweb.pdf (verified January 7, 2005).

Willett, George. 1915. "Summer Birds of Forrester Island, Alaska." *Auk* 32: 295–305.

———. 1917. "Further Notes on the Birds of Forrester Island, Alaska." *Condor* 19: 15–17.

———. 1920. "Additional Notes on the Avifauna of Forrester Island, Alaska." *Condor* 22: 138–39.

16

Deiki Noow

Tlingit Cultural Heritage in the Hazy Islands

STEVE J. LANGDON

Tlingit visions of existence stretch to the earliest moments of transformative creation when things as they are now experienced came to be. The activities of Yéil, the being known as Raven, are detailed in a mythic cycle of accounts in which manipulations, duplicity, farce, and unforeseen consequence unfold and produce the contexts of life today. The adventures and antics of Yéil in traditional accounts are invariably positioned in real space and known locations if not chronological time. Often the Tlingit oral tradition includes information about props or items involved in Yéil's antics that continue to be present and confirm the factuality of the account. For example, the Raven mythic account in which Yéil persuades little birds to assist him in tricking king salmon to jump on the beach was told to me by an elder of the T'akdeintaan clan, who added that Raven's footprints could still be seen on the beach north of Lituya Bay. But Raven mythic accounts are but one of many layers through which the Tlingits demonstrate ancestral linkages to places, thereby affirming for non-Tlingits and confirming to other Tlingits the basis for their distinctive relationships to these places, and those relationships establish certain rights recognized in Tlingit legal practice. The various layerings extend from time immemorial, as in the Raven myths, down to the experiences of people living today. While these manifestations of specific places might be seen as separate conceptual and temporal layerings, a more nuanced reading reveals how the layers interpenetrate, influencing and infusing meaning and purpose into experience on an ongoing basis (Thornton 2004, 2008).

The location known to southern Tlingit as Deiki Noow (Far Out Fort) is a site of enormous cultural heritage elaboration, providing opportunities to encounter the characteristics of the Tlingit construction of

Fig. 16.1 *Deiki Noow* from *Kuxk'*. Photograph by Steve J. Langdon.

place and the many meanings through which people and place are connected. In each generation, Tlingit youth (primarily males) raised by families with knowledge of Deiki Noow may encounter a wide range of accounts that will be available for interpretation and at some point may have personal experiences of encounter with Deiki Noow. The knowledge of previous generations as well as personal experiences will in turn be passed on to family members, community members, the larger Tlingit community, children, and grandchildren, sustaining the continuing process of creation so central to the Tlingit practice of *shuká*.

Understanding the significance of place in Tlingit existence has benefited greatly from research undertaken and published by Thomas Thornton. He outlines four "structures of emplacement" through which Tlingit construct relationships between "being and place": social organization, language and cognitive structure, material production, and ritual processes. These are certainly evident in the following discussion, which articulates two additional structures: the interpenetration of levels of meaning and forms of practice and the anatomy of encounter that explores the flow of engagement between persons, ideas, experi-

Fig. 16.2 *Deiki Noow* from the air. Photograph by Steve J. Langdon.

ences, and places as an ongoing constructivist enterprise where agency and interpretation matter.

This chapter explores the meaning layers and their interpenetrations that Tlingit associate with Deiki Noow ("Far Out Fort"), which has been called the Hazy Islands since first recorded by George Vancouver in 1794 (Orth 1971). In doing so, the account will stretch from the beginnings of existence-as-it-is-known, through clan traditions, historical documents, and oral traditions, to personal recollections and experiences. A portion of my information derives from the interviews I conducted in 2004 and 2005 with Kake and Klawock Tlingit elders about Deiki Noow. The chapter ends with a discussion of a visit to Deiki Noow by a group of Tlingit men from Kake whom I accompanied in June 2007 that demonstrates how that experience was informed by the past and looked to the future and links activities conducted at that time to the core components of Tlingit culture. It constitutes explication of an anatomy of encounter.

Context: Environment, Society, and Culture

Deiki Noow or Big Hazy is one of five small islands or islets. The Hazy Islands are eight miles west of Coronation Island, which in turn is the most westerly of the islands of the Prince of Wales Archipelago in south-

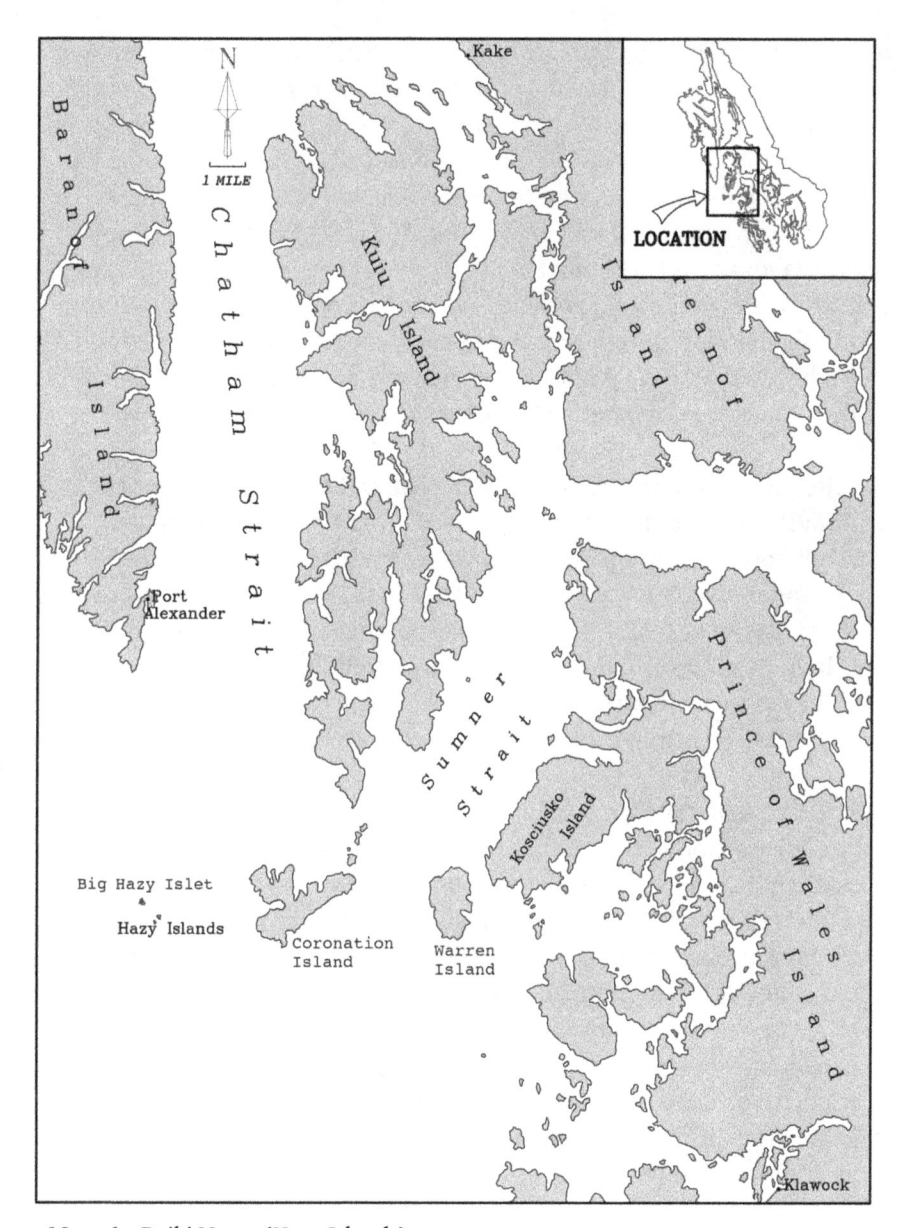

Map 16.1 Deiki Noow (Hazy Islands).

east Alaska. They are the last land in the north Pacific Ocean between southeast Alaska and Japan or Hawaii depending on the direction chosen. Big Hazy Island, as the largest of the group, rises abruptly and steeply from the surrounding waters and is geologically different from the four flatter islands. Big Hazy also has two sea caves, one facing east and the other south, that are tidally influenced. The U.S. government designated the islands as a refuge in 1912, and they were declared federal wilderness in 1970. The islands are presently administered by the U.S. Department of Fish and Wildlife as a refuge subunit of the Alaska Maritime National Wildlife Refuge, Gulf of Alaska Unit, into which they were placed in 1980. The islands are characterized in refuge online literature as follows:

> Remote, without anchorages or campsites, beaten by frequent storms under high winds, the rocks called Hazy Islands are seldom seen. Far offshore, beaten by wind and wave, Big Hazy Island and her four smaller sisters stick out of the frigid sea, providing predator-free nesting areas for large populations of common murres, pigeon guillemots, glaucous-winged gulls, horned puffins, and tufted puffins. Brandt's cormorants nest here, one of only two islands they inhabit in Alaska. (http://www.wilderness.net, accessed March 5, 2009)

Tlingit use of the islands in particular for the harvesting of seagull and murre eggs is not reflected in this characterization of the islands, a point that will be discussed at greater length below.

The ten species of birds that reside in the Hazy Islands are central to the administrative mission of the U.S. Fish and Wildlife Service to treat the islands as "refuge." Sea lion and harbor seals are also found here. The marine mammals were reported by interviewees to have been harvested occasionally on visits to the islands in the past. Killer whales were also sometimes seen. In the twentieth century, long-line fishing for halibut and salmon trolling periodically brought some Tlingit into the vicinity.

The islands are often covered by fog (hence their name), which makes them difficult to locate. Second, the tides and currents run powerfully around and between the islands due to their location at the crossroads of current movements in and out of Chatham Strait to the north and due to the relatively shallow bottom surrounding the islands. This affects a third observation of significance, namely, the rapidity and intensity of wave action resulting from the shallow waters generate choppy, short, high waves that must be monitored and carefully navigated. In conjunction with the lack of any protection from westerly and northwesterly winds and the steep rocky shores of Big Hazy Island, these wave patterns make for extremely dangerous landing conditions. The bottom area surrounding the Hazy Islands is poorly suited for anchoring a vessel. Finally, weather conditions change capriciously. Tlingit customarily travel to the Hazy Islands to collect eggs in June and July, which are generally the months with relatively mild weather. Often, however, weather conditions prevent immediate transit to the islands, and therefore Tlingit have been accustomed to waiting in more sheltered bays around Coronation Island for calmer waters.

Linguistically and culturally, a distinction is commonly made between Tlingit groups along geographic lines in which Frederick Sound is used as a dividing point (Emmons 1991; Kroeber 1939; Olson 1967). Above Frederick Sound, the ḵwaans are collectively known as the northern Tlingit, and those below are known as the southern Tlingit. It is evident that far more ethnographic attention has been devoted to the northern Tlingit groups than to the southern (de Laguna 1960, 1972; Kan 1989, 1999; Oberg 1973). However, in his extremely important but as yet unpublished manuscript, "History of Tlingit Tribes and Clans," George Emmons stated the following concerning the Klawock ḵwaan:

> This tribe has never been given its proper place among the Tlingit families, but has been included in the Henyeh kwan. It is a very old division, possibly older than the latter people, and included the inhabitants of Port Bucarelli who are described by Maurelle who accompanied the Spanish expedition under Bodega y Quadra in 1775. This region seems to have been a center of life in the early days, but . . . the population decreased until during our occupation this tribe has become almost extinct. Smallpox ravaged this locale several times during the last century and whole villages were practically wiped out and deserted, which may reasonably account for this condition.

This can be read to imply that certain foundational components of Tlingit cultural concepts and practices are likely to be found among the southern Tlingit and that careful attention to materials from these groups could yield new and significant insights. The southern Tlingit ḵwaan(s) of the western or ocean-fronting portion of the Alexander Archipelago will be at the center of this discussion due to the special knowledge of, experience at, and relationship with Deiki Noow held by their members. The relevant kwaans whose ancestors and present members are most connected to Deiki Noow include Keex̱', Klawak, Heinya, and Kuyu.[1] In the mid-nineteenth century, only the Kuyu and Heinya kwaan(s), due to their proximity to Deiki Noow, would have regularly encountered and traveled to the islands; however, the devastating impact of the 1862 smallpox epidemic on the Kuyu kwaan and the slightly later relocation of the Heinya kwaan clans from Tajik' aan to Klawock where they resided in association with the drastically diminished Klawock kwaan has resulted in those groups being now consolidated with the Keex̱' (Kake) and Klawak (Klawock) Tlingit. The discussion of the place of Deiki Noow in Tlingit cultural heritage is of great importance to the members of the Naastedí clan, who have a special relationship with the island as demonstrated by their *at.óow* and the L'eeneidí with whom they were closely aligned due to intermarriage and proximity of clan territories to Deiki Noow. Through marriage relations and kwaan amalgamation, members of other clans also participated in outings to Deiki Noow and absorbed mythic accounts, oral traditions, and stories of personal experience.

Tlingit social organization places a person of the Tlingit nation (speech and cultural community) within a set of relations based on personal name, ancestors who held the name, and the matrilineal institutions of house, clan, and moiety (Emmons 1991; Dauenhauer N 2000; de Laguna 1972; Olson 1967; Thornton 1997). The father and paternal grandfather are also significant in the social position of an individual. Clans, houses, and individuals in turn are linked to specific ancestral events and places, knowledge of which was carefully sustained in the oral traditions of the clans (Thornton 2004, 2008). A person also exists in a social matrix of status or rank positions based on name and genealogical relationship to others of higher or lower status or rank in the house and clan (de Laguna 1972; Emmons 1991; Olson 1967). This social location and position of a Tlingit person are central to the manner in which they are connected to others as well as to the manner in which they can and should behave (Thornton 1994).

Key Tlingit cultural concepts and practices inform the thinking and behavior of individuals past and present. Most important for consideration as they apply to the Deiki Noow exegesis are *at.óow*, *shagóon*, *shuká*, and *kusteeí*; each has an abstract/conceptual meaning and a specific experiential referent.

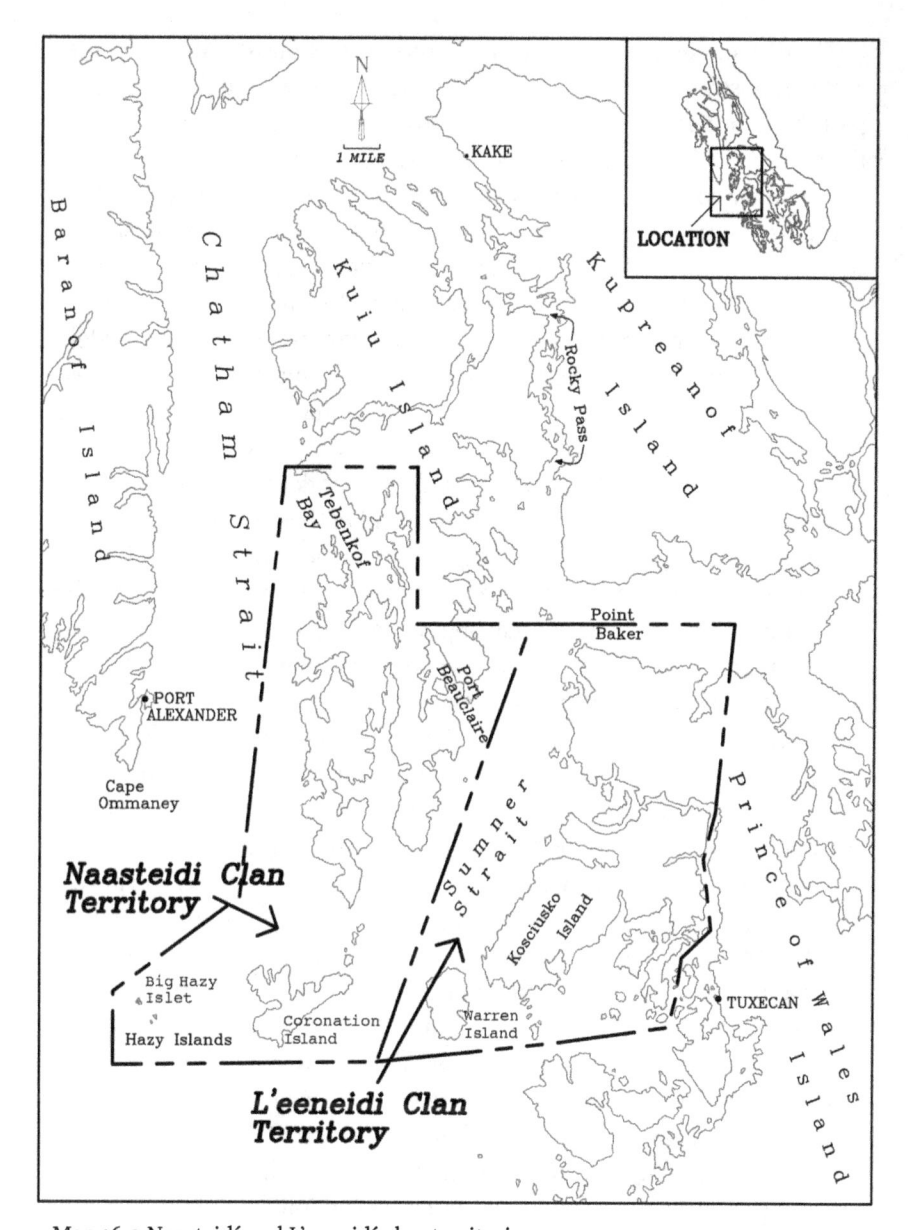

Map 16.2 Naasteidí and L'eeneidí clan territories.

The concept of *at.óow* is considered the cornerstone of Tlingit culture, as it demonstrates the linkage of living persons to events and places in the past. Nora and Richard Dauenhauer have provided a clear discussion of the nature and import of this concept in Tlingit life (1987, 24-29, 1990; N. Dauenhauer 2000). The essential qualities of this concept are that it constitutes ownership obtained by purchase that is typically demonstrated by a physical object. What is purchased can vary, but it can include locations, events, persons, and things; *at.óow* of the highest significance to a clan has been purchased by the loss of human life. Lily White, widely respected elder of the Chookaneidei clan of Huna Ḵwaan, described *at.óow* as an event that was experienced by a matrilineal ancestor that resulted in a great loss (often of human lives) from which a story, an object (hat, tunic, robe), a song, and a dance are derived (personal communication, 2003). In her view, only when all of these elements exist and are integrated can the characterization *at.óow* be applied. The physical objects are typically stored with a caretaker and brought out for public display only on occasions of great significance such as the *koo'éex'* (mortuary potlatch) when they may or may not be accompanied by a telling of the oral tradition and/or a performance of the song and dance associated with the object. A "thing" that is *at.óow* is available only to members of the clan for use—any other uses, without clan authorization, are a violation of Tlingit law, and the injured parties will seek indemnification for the material loss and shame that they have experienced.

Shagóon refers to past circumstances with special emphasis on ancestors through whose performance the cultural traditions of the clan were created or sustained. It also encompasses a sense of the general character and practices of the clan, which have been received from ancestors by the present generation. *Shuká* is defined more broadly, as it is "ambiguous faces two directions" referred to as "ahead and before." Further, it "references those born ahead of us who are now behind us, as well as the unborn who wait ahead of us" (N. and. R Dauenhauer 1993, 19). There is an implication of obligation when this term is invoked, the obligation to sustain cultural practice (*at.óow* and *shuká*) for the use and benefit of future generations.

The concept of *kusteeí* references the collective experiences, materials, practices, and "way of life" of Tlingit people and embeds the foremost value of respect for all and for the collective enterprise of which they are a part. Each of these concepts will be explored as they apply to Deiki Noow as concept and practice.

Raven Myths

There are two Raven myths that pertain to Deiki Noow, one of which was recalled from childhood by many of the elders I interviewed. It concerned Raven's acquisition of freshwater from a spring located on Deiki Noow. Clara Peratrovitch of Klawock, a Tlingit elder and widely respected culture bearer of the L'eeneidí (Raven dog salmon) clan, had the most detailed version of the story that I was given in Klawock.

I was raised in fishing camps and winter camps, away from the village. We only came by dugout canoe to get supplies probably once a week or once a month. So when the winter nights were long and days were short, a lot of the stories were told to me over and over. One of the stories was where the Raven wanted to bring water to the mainland and there was only one place designated for water and it was out at Hazy Island. They call it in Tlingit Deiki Noow. There was a little old lady that lived on that island that guarded the water. Nobody else was allowed to use it. She had a box and in that box was the water. The mainland people needed water to survive on and to continue life. So Raven volunteered to go out and get water from Deiki Noow for the people. When he told the people he was going out there he said, "I am going to Deiki Noow and bring water to you people." And the people responded, "You're never going to make it. She guards it with her life. She never goes to sleep. She guards it so that nobody can have that water but herself. She doesn't share it with anybody." Raven argued and said, "I am going to bring water." So Raven went on his journey to Deiki Noow. And sure enough, Ganuk was there. That was the little old lady's name. As he approached the island, Ganuk was ready where she sat by her water. Raven walked up to her residence where she was staying and he said, "I had a long flight. I flew from the mainland, and I'm very thirsty." He said, "I've been walking around looking for water, and I can't find it." And Ganuk said, "Come on in, sit down." She opened up her box and got a dipper and gave him a cup of water. And she closed the box again—she put her arm on it, leaned on it, and sat by it. As time went on, Raven said, "I want to tell you a story." He said, "I'll tell you a story, and I want you to listen very carefully." So Raven kept on telling her story after story after story. After three days and three nights, on the fourth day, she started showing signs that she was getting tired. So Raven went and told more stories; he went on and on and on and toward the morning, her eyes would close automatically. She'd shut her eyes and he'd nudge her. He said, "Hey, Ganuk, wake up. I'm telling you a story. I want you to listen to me." And so Ganuk would sit up; she took her arm off the box—now that was the first good sign or the second good sign. The first good sign was her closing her eyes; she couldn't keep her eyes open anymore. When she took her arm off the box and leaned back, Raven said, "Get comfortable so you can listen to me carefully." And so she did. And he went and told the story continuously. Pretty soon her eyes closed again. And he'd nudge her and say, "Wake up, listen to me. I'm telling you a story. It's not good if you fall asleep before I finish." She couldn't open her eyes. Her eyes were just shut; she couldn't move. She wouldn't move; he'd push her, but she wasn't moving. So after the fourth time, he went and slid the lid over sideways. So here's the box, and he slid the lid over just far enough so he can get his beak in there and siphon all the water he can hold. All of a sudden he was getting to the point where he couldn't hold any more and he was going to close the lid when Ganuk woke up. Raven flew to the smoke hole and almost got stuck because all the water he siphoned up had expanded his body. The smoke hole shrunk up on him, and he barely made it out of there. As he was flying, as soon as he made it out—Kaaw!—he made a sound. Then the box became a rock and the lid remained half over the box. He flew on, and as he was flying to the mainland, the drops that fell from his beak became rivers, creeks so that the people from the mainland were able to get all the water they could use. Lakes, rivers—and that's how Raven got the water for the mainland. To this day, when you go out there, where it is I have no idea, I have never been out there, but my dad said when they went out there, they went looking for that and in this one area, I guess in the middle of the island, is this boxlike well. It's half full and the lid, it's flat and looks like a lid, and the box it has water in there. When you take water out of there, it is pure water. It's not rainwater; it's continuous pure freshwater out there. It's like a box. The lid became a rock." (Peratrovitch 2003)

While there were many less elaborate versions of this myth given in the interviews, two are especially important for the details that they add. Franklin James of the Shangukeidí clan was raised in Kake and later Klawock. He traveled to Deiki Noow once as a child but did not go ashore. He was told the Raven story on many occasions by his grandparents who raised him. In his version, Raven heads offshore in search of the island, but it is hidden by the fog. Only by following the sound of the waves landing on the shores of Deiki Noow is Raven able to locate the island (James 2004). Charles "Topsy" Johnson, also a Shangukeidí clan member, provided additional elaboration on the myth as well as much additional information, a substantial amount of which was based on personal experiences. His father, who was of the Sukteeneidí clan, took him to the islands as a boy. Johnson states that the water dripping from Raven's beak as he departed Deiki Noow and headed east past Coronation Island was responsible for the ragged shoreline on the north shore of Sea Otter Sound, a body of water sitting between Prince of Wales, Kosciusko, and Heceta Islands and homeland to a portion of the L'eeneidí clan. This jagged coast, termed a "dancing shoreline," was the model for the bottom of the *naxein* (Chilkat robe) that is made by the multiple flowing strands of mountain goat string (Johnson 2004).

In *Tlingit Myths and Texts*, Swanton (1909, 83) provides a version of the myth of the Raven acquiring freshwater that refers to "De Ki-nu (Fort Far Out)" as the location of the story.

The other Raven myth in which Deiki Noow figures is less well known and was not reported by any elder during the interviews.[2] Louis Shotridge obtained an account which describes a remarkable encounter between Yéil and the other mythic figure, Ganuk. Shotridge's typescript, supplemented by bracketed handwritten inserts from William Paul, reads as follows:

> Amid ocean Ye.l and Ganu.k met. While one paddled in opposite direction of the other, . . . Ye.l accosted Ganu.k in a hilarious manner: "Ah, this be thine honorable presence my good brother-in-law." Not allowing the other to voice an opinion on his familiary, the Ye.l went on to relate many incidents which in turn had developed into events, exhibiting this and that from his own point of view. In this untimely hindrance Ganu.k was very much annoyed. To him it was obvious that this crafty being was in pursuit of something, but he was determined not to be persuaded to betray what was sacred. And Ye.l continued "My good friend, this incident then is proof that I am the most ancient in the world." The Ganu.k, who had maintained pride of knowing himself to be the most ancient of all beings, expressed his disapproval only by a grunt, and after a moment of

silence spoke for the first time: "What thou feignest out of thine own mind will provoke truth only out of fool tongue. I beseech my friend, proceed on thine journey." With this remark he pushed his own canoe clear of the other [and put on his "fog hat"]. With great disappointment the Ye.l afloated, looking after the Ganu.k, and only a few strokes thither the departing canoe began to disappear to the Ye.l [while Ganu.k said, "If you know so much you will know how to get to shore."] Ye.l knew what was happening, so quickly made a turn to catch up with his friend, but then the mysterious fog immediately shut off the course in all directions. At last the Ye.l realized that his fool tongue had placed him in danger and knew that unless he apologized and admitted his false pretense, that which annoyed him would go from bad to worse. Thus Ganu.k's power provoked his sense of weakness to entreat for mercy. At first Ye.l expressed his apology in a manly voice: "Sir, I shall have to admit that thou has at present proved by thine power, thine lengthy existence." But Ganu.k did not seem to have heard this and was silent. Again, but this time it was in a manner of beseech, and finally Ye.l had to implore the mercy of the ancient God of Rain: "My good brother-in-law, my brother-in-law, I implore thee, put thine ear to my words. In sooth, it has been told abroad that thou art the most ancient of all beings." Right close behind, the Ganu.k spoke in a very calm manner: "Ah, my good friend, thou still linger, me thinks ere thou has erred well upon thine timely journey." With these words, [Ganu.k took off his fog hat and immediately] there was no fog, and in the shadow of his thought the Ye.l paddled away on his journey.

A fascinating and crucial footnote for this discussion is that Shotridge's typed copy of the legend was at some point reviewed by William Paul, who added the following clarifying note: "Shotridge also omits the site via de-kin (Hazy Island) so of Coronation Id, so of Kuiu Id."[3] It can be inferred from this note that Paul had heard the myth, which included the actual geographic location of the event, and felt it to be of such importance that he added the locational information to Shotridge's account.

Swanton (1909, 10–11) provides the following version of the same myth, which he heard in Sitka:

One day Ganuk the Petrel was at sea in his boat when he met Raven. Raven began to question the Petrel, asking him where he came from and how long he had lived in the world. Ganuk told him he had been living since the world was made. Raven replied that this had been just a short while before and that he had been first in the world. They quarreled until Ganuk became angry and put on his hat. Immediately Raven's canoe was surrounded by a thick fog, and he could not see where he was. Worried at his predicament, Raven conceded to the Petrel shouting, "You are older than I." But Ganuk was not so easily placated and began to sprinkle Raven with rain. The Petrel teased Raven for some time before relenting and removing his fog hat. As the fog lifted, Petrel saw Raven nearby, paddling blindly about in all directions. Thus it is that Ganuk is considered to be the most ancient character in the Tlingit world.

There are several intriguing aspects embedded in this myth that deserve exegesis. One of the aspects is the exchange over who is the oldest being, in which Raven asserts that the beginning of time had only recently occurred. As we were informed in Shotridge's version, Deiki Noow is the site of the exchange, therefore indicating its presence near the beginning of time as well. The primeval quality of Deiki Noow, based on its geological, not mythic, qualities, was also commented upon by elder Leonard Kato of Klawock. He juxtaposed the slippery, shaley nature of the steep rocky formation of Deiki Noow with the hard, jagged quality of the other nearby low-lying islets. In fact, most of the interviewed elders who had climbed up Deiki Noow commented on the slippery, loose rocky surface of Deiki Noow and how it had required them to be extremely careful on their descent to avoid falling. Further, Topsy Johnson referred to it as the "old, old island." He recalls that they were instructed by their elders to take any loose rock they found and "shore it" in order to prevent a rockslide.

A second aspect of the account is that the Ganuk hat, as *at.óow*, is associated with the Kaagwaantaan, a leading Eagle/Wolf clan found primarily among the northern Tlingit ḵwaans. The "purchase" of this mythic account by the Kaagwaantaan and its conversion to their *at.óow* is discussed in the next section.

As arguably the most powerful northern Tlingit clan, it is interesting that the Kaagwaantaan chose to create *at.óow* out of what might be considered a myth of broad general applicability to all Eagle/Wolf clans or even all Tlingit. It is a myth shared widely and passed on in many Tlingit households to this day. The Kaagwaantaan initiative is in

Fig. 16.3 *At.óow*–Kagwaantaan Ganuk hat. Courtesy of the Penn Museum, image no. 150251.

keeping with the possibilities for *at.óow* noted by the Dauenhauers, who state, "It can be an image from the oral literature such as an episode from the raven cycle on a tunic, hat, robe, or blanket" (1987, 25). The representation of this legend, which positions Ganuk as more ancient and therefore, in some sense, "higher" than Raven, as clan *at.óow* by the Kaagwaantaan would appear to be an interesting and perhaps provocative jab at primacy among Tlingit operating at the level of moiety representation and clan position. Berman (2004, 131) points out that this hat is specifically referenced in Louis Shotridge's article "The Bride of Tongass," about the marriage of a Kaagwaantaan man from Icy Strait to a high status *Taant'akwaan Gaanax.adi* (Shotridge 1929). Taxsha wears the hat during his party's arrival at the wedding site. This formal presentation of the Ganuk *at.óow* is indicative of its cultural significance and perhaps presents implicitly the claim to the highest standing of Kaagwaantaan among the Eagle clans and to the existential precedence of Eagles over Ravens. Finally, the importance of the presentation of the Ganuk hat at the wedding must also be seen in light of the Tlingit principle of "balance" according to which the Kaagwaantaan were under considerable pressure to demonstrate their similar standing to the Gaanax.adi, the oldest of the Raven clans. Emmons signified his understanding of this clan's generally recognized status as the oldest Raven clan (Emmons 1991, 436).

The special *at.óow* relationship of the Naastedí clan to Deiki Noow is more directly experiential than the mythic connection asserted by the Kaagwaantaan. The Naastedí are an Eagle/Wolf clan whose name and oral traditions indicate that they lived on the Nass River in northern British Columbia prior to their migration to Alaska. After their departure from the Nass River, the clan moved to various locations in southeast Alaska before settling down on Kuiu Island (Emmons n.d.). Naastedí traditional clan territory extends from Tebenkoff Bay on the west side of Kuiu Island on down and takes in Coronation Island and the Hazy Islands. Deiki Noow was therefore available for viewing on a regular basis during the travels of Naastedí people throughout their territory. The most significant and sacred of clan *at.óow* are generally those that involve the sacrifice or loss of life of ancestral clan members in association with activities of importance to the clan. In this case, there is a key Naastedí oral tradition concerning a man who traveled to Deiki Noow to collect bird eggs, probably murre eggs, and died on the island when weather prevented him from returning home. In carrying out research on totem pole restoration projects conducted in various southeast Alaska communities in the late 1930s, Viola Garfield recorded the story from an unidentified Tlingit source in Klawock.[4] The following is a summary of the oral tradition that appears in *The Wolf and the Raven* (Garfield and Forrest 1951, 139):

> Long ago a man went to the island but was caught in a storm before he could land. His canoe was wrecked and the wind and the waves washed him right through an underwater hole in the rocks. His spirit still dwells there, where he may be heard during storms. People going to the island put a little food in the water and ask this spirit for good weather and a safe journey. The island spirit helps those who observe the rules of good conduct and respect for wild life. Misfortune is sure

to come to those who are frivolous or who disregard the strict laws of food conservation and proper use of resources. The spirit withdraws his protection from such people, and they are in danger of losing their canoes or their lives.

The Naastedí *at.óow* associated with this account is a totem pole that was erected in the village of Tajik' aan, which was the major settlement of the Heinya ḵwaan throughout the nineteenth century. The pole was restored by Tlingit carvers under the auspices of the federal Civilian Conservation Corps in Klawock and subsequently erected there in the late 1930s.

Pole in Klawock Totem Park

While it is the loss of life that provides the Naasteidí *at.óow* a basis for "purchase," what was purchased was "the exclusive right to gather murre eggs from the island" (Garfield and Forrest 1948, 139). The murre then became a crest that was used as a tattoo design and carved on wooden articles, serving to "publicize their ownership of the island as well as to identify members" (139). The most prominent expression of this aspect of the Naastedí relationship with Deiki Noow as *at.óow*, however, is in the carved images that appear on the totem pole. Garfield provides the following description of the replacement for the original pole that was located in Tajik' aan but only a portion of which was salvaged when it was moved to Klawock for recarving:

> Two murres were carved for the top of the copy. They were painted with black heads, brown backs, and white breasts. Carved models of their eggs were pegged to the front of the shaft. The eggs were painted grey with brown, blue, and green markings or green with brown, white, and blue markings, no two of the twenty-six alike. According to legend, the murres spend much of their nesting time painting their eggs so that each pair can recognize its own among the great number lying about on the bare rocks. (139)

The two murres sit side by side on an attached horizontal piece at the top of the pole, presumably representing a ledge of the island where they are nesting. On the bottom of the pole was carved a human image that represented the man who lost his life at Deiki Noow providing the basis for claiming the island as Naastedí *at.óow* (139).

Fig. 16.4 *At.óow*-Naasteidí pole originally located at Tajik'aan depicting murres on ledges at Deiki Noow with eggs. Each egg was painted with a different pattern, replicating the actual appearance of murre eggs on Deiki Noow. Photograph by Steve J. Langdon.

It is important to note that Naastedí *at.óow* refers to the right to collect murre eggs at Deiki Noow but not seagull eggs. Members of other clans as well as the Naastedí apparently traveled to Deiki Noow and the other islands to collect seagull eggs as part of a more general pattern of common use.

Additional Clan Materials

Beyond the pole images and crest images used as tattoos and carved on wooden objects, Naastedí property associated with Deiki Noow includes a set of personal names. Raymond Roberts, the caretaker of Naastedí *at.óow* and tradition, states that many Naastedí personal names are associated with activities at or characteristics of Deiki Noow. The following names along with their approximate translations are from members of his immediate family or other Naastedí, and they demonstrate Naastedí relations to Deiki Noow and conditions nearby:

Aanyaaélich: waiting for the right wave, waiting for the smallest of four waves
Daat Awu.aat: walking around the island while picking eggs
Kl'kushi: soil conditions leading to hard luck
Hahlahen: coloration of murre eggs (?)
Gus'han: murre birds sitting on top of the rocks near their nest
Daal ku woox': broad chest (white chests of murres lined up on ledges)
Nashageesh: foam or bubbles on the water
Eehus: fog bank or misty conditions
Najuk: murre birds flying and crying in anger

These names provide information about conditions around Deiki Noow, what to look for, what to be prepared for, and what activities will be undertaken. The first name provides critical information about the dangers associated with landing on Deiki Noow, as failure to attend to wave conditions could lead to people being dumped into the water or canoes crashing on the rocks. Thus knowing when to jump to shore or pull the canoe up was of enormous significance. This pattern of naming is in keeping with other Tlingit linkages between names and environmental characteristics that are elucidated by Thornton (2008) in his examination of Sitka Kaagwaantaan elder Herman Kitka's telling of the Aakwatatseen (Salmon Boy) myth. Among the Naastedí, personal names provide important instructions about behavior and critical information about environmental conditions that must be attended to. By embedding such critical information in personal names, the information would be a constant reminder that would become stored in the habitus of those most likely to need that information.

Roberts provided another oral tradition concerning Naastedí heritage at Deiki Noow associated with the smallpox epidemic in the mid-nineteenth century that killed many people and led the survivors to relocate to Klawock. The Naastedí matriarch who led the remnant band to Klawock to settle insisted on strongly conveying to her descendants the importance of their heritage at Deiki Noow. One of her sons, Robert Peratrovitch Jr., who became the mayor of Klawock and the founder of a salmon cannery that operated there from the mid-1920s to the 1940s, was a receptive vessel of this training. In support of his salmon canning operation, he had a large fish packing vessel built for moving salmon from the fishing grounds to the cannery which he named "Deikinoow." This is one of the very few vessels ever constructed or owned by Tlingit that was given a Tlingit name.

Place-Names

At the very center of Tlingit thought is the relationship between person and place because that nexus is the essence of being and the crucible of character (Thornton 2000, 2004). Given that linkage, Deiki Noow provides a particularly powerful crucible due to the danger and difficulties inherent in travel to and from the islands. To successfully accomplish a mission to Deiki Noow is an important demonstration of ability and will, qualities that are highly regarded in Tlingit culture such that individuals seek opportunities for their demonstration. There are seven Tlingit place-names associated with the Hazy Islands. All seven were provided by elders from Kake, while only Deiki Noow proper was offered by elders from Klawock.

The name Deiki Noow is typically translated at "Far Out Fort," composed of *"noow"* (sometimes *"nu"*), the standard Tlingit reference to a protected constructed locale, separate from a village or camp, that is located on a steep island or promontory and has various constructed facilities for protection and occupation associated with it. The other portion of the word, translated as "far out," refers to things offshore or on the outer coast. It can be seen in the Tlingit name for the Haida, Dekinaa, referring to their residence on lands out in the ocean: Haida

Deiki Noow

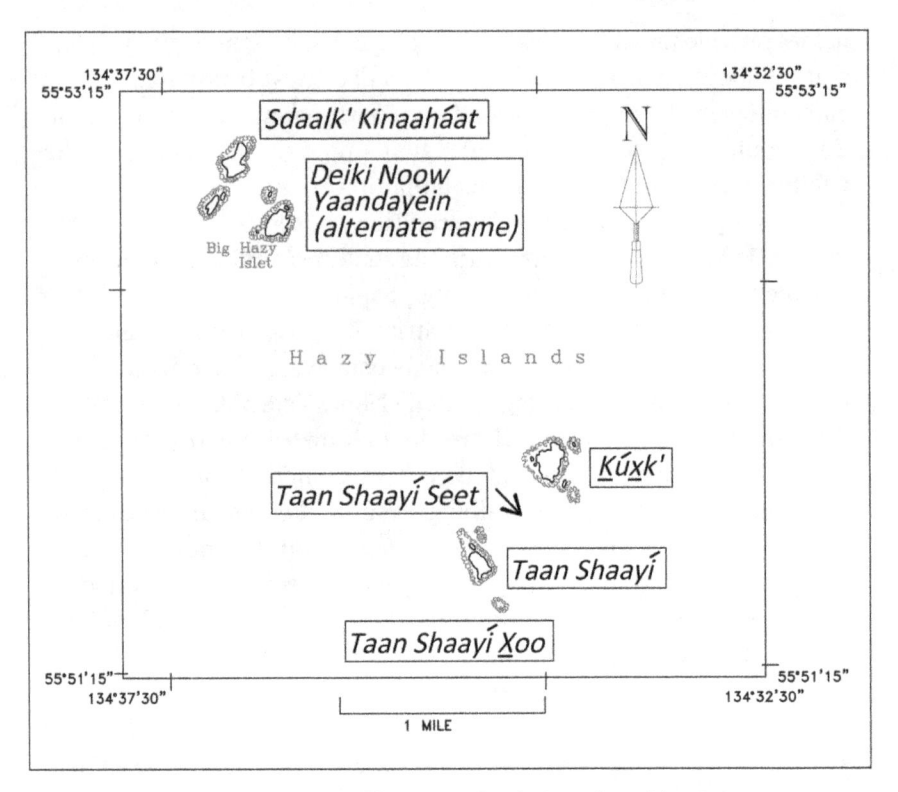

Map 16.3 Tlingit place-names in the Hazy Islands (see also table 16.1).

Gwaii (Queen Charlotte Islands). It can also be seen in the reference to the Dekigaanaxadi, a subgroup of the Klawak ḵwaan Ganaaxadi who lived on Baker Island, which is an outer coastal member of the Prince of Wales Archipelago (Olson 1967, 109).

On its surface, the name implies a fortified locale occupied at some point in the past by humans. Garfield's sources said that "a clan of the Wolf [moiety] . . . once had a fortified town on Hazy Island called Fort Far Out" (Garfield and Forrest 1948, 137). Several interviewees gave similar views, notably Clara Peratrovitch of Klawock and Topsy Johnson of Kake, who provided the most information on oral traditions concerning Deiki Noow from their respective communities.

In addition, Johnson (2004) stated that "the Naastedí there have that totem pole on Deikinoow itself, the old island, that totem pole. A totem pole with an eagle's nest on top. That's their Naastedí *at'óow*." This statement is intriguing in that it implies human occupation in association with the totem pole. It might also refer to the original design

TABLE 16.1 Tlingit place-names associated with the Hazy Islands

TLINGIT NAME	ENGLISH NAME	LOCATION	TRANSLATION
Deiki Noow	Big Hazy Island	Largest of Hazy Islands	Far Out Fort
Sdaalk' Kinaahaat (alternate name)	None	Largest of Hazy Islands	No place to anchor or No harbor
Yaandayein	None	Second largest of Hazy Islands	Moving Island
Taan Shaayí	None	Large southern island	Sea Lion Head
Taan Shaayí Xoo	None	Small southern most of the Hazy Islands	Among the Sea Lion Head
Taan Shaayí Séet	None	Channel between two southern islands	Sea Lion Head Passage
Kuxk'	None	Island immediately east of Big Hazy Island	Personal name of ancestor who always went to this island for seagull eggs

of the pole in Tajik' aan or another pole altogether. There is a parallel between the nest on the top of the pole at Deiki Noow and the murre "nest" on the top of the pole in Klawock. In addition, the eagle would also be Naastedí *at.óow*, but it would therefore be a separate pole. There are other possible meanings to Deiki Noow—given the distance to, danger in, and difficulty of traveling to the islands, structures that would be next to impossible to build onsite would not be necessary as the fort's "natural" characteristics—hidden, distant, dangerous—would protect the Naastedí from enemies when they were there. Also, it may have been regarded as a fort for the birds who went there for protection when they were raising their young. No archaeological research has been undertaken on the island to seek evidence of precontact human occupation. Such research might provide further light on the question.

There is a second or alternate meaning that was applied to Deiki Noow proper, or it might also be applied to the entire area of the islands. Sdaalk' Kinaaháat informs the speaker that this site has no anchorage, a reality that must be taken into consideration as an account provided by elder Clarence Jackson demonstrates. Several years ago he visited the Hazy Islands in a modern purse seine vessel equipped with a small skiff

Fig. 16.5 Deiki Noow and Yaandayein up close. Photograph by Steve J. Langdon.

with which to land his party on Ḵúx̱k'. He decided to anchor out and take the entire party ashore, as it was a calm day. After several hours of egg picking, in which no one was on board the purse seine vessel, Jackson happened to glance up to see if the boat was still anchored. His heart stopped when he did not see it floating where he expected to on the east side of the island. He climbed over to the west side of the island, where he saw the vessel drifting southwestward out into the Pacific Ocean. He quickly went down to the skiff and was able to start the motor, travel to the drifting vessel, and reboard it (Jackson 2005).

The name *Yaandayéin* is revealing in demonstrating what I term perceptual and "perspectival" information in Tlingit place-naming. The name refers to the perception that this island, once seen, does not appear to get larger as one approaches it. Our perceptual expectation is that as we travel toward an object, it will seem larger. The fact that this island does not correspond to expectations could lead the viewer to believe it is a mirage. This name, however, would alert the observer to pay attention and not jump to precipitous conclusions. Indeed, Tlingit ecological knowledge provides the further insight that while the island appears to be very distant and at the same distance for a long period of time, when you arrive, it is suddenly upon you.

The name Kúxk' is associated with a particular elder who regularly returned to this small island east of Deiki Noow to gather eggs. It was the only island that he visited. This practice appears to be in keeping with place-naming practices of southern Tlingit in assigning a personal name as a place-name more so than northern Tlingit. However, the name does not indicate a clan property or *at.óow* association with the island, according to interviewees.

The final name references the similarity of appearance of the larger of the two southernmost islands to a sea lion head. This is also a widespread pattern in Tlingit place-naming as well as that of many other human groups (Thornton 2008). It is also the location of a sea lion rookery.

Place-names associated with Deiki Noow provide important information for visiting the islands. The names also reference appearance, customary social uses, and rookery locations.

Other Traditional Accounts

Two more traditional accounts concerning events at Deiki Noow that were provided by interviewees cannot be classified as clan traditions or *at.óow* stories. Their placement in time is uncertain, as they may reference events prior to or after contact, but both are of substantial cultural significance because they mention events that implicate traditional Tlingit concepts of spirituality and relationship across time, space, and species.

Evans Kadake (2004) provided the following account:

A man went out to Hazy Island to harvest seagull eggs. The weather picked up, and the storm lasted for a long, long time. Weeks and months went by. His canoe got away, and he was stranded on that island for a long, long time. He was given up for dead, and everyone had lost hope. But his wife did not give up hope. Every time that mealtime would come along, she would take a big portion of food and put it in the fire. . . . And so in our language they would say, "*Gantu yéigi x'eidé*" (for the spirit of the fire), and they would put the food into the fire. And they would be feeding that person spiritually. I don't know how long this person stayed out on Hazy Island before he got rescued. By the time they got him, he had a really long beard, and they were surprised to see him alive. He came back to tell the story, and he said, "The strangest thing happened to me. While I was out on the island, every time it was time to eat I began to feel full. I never got hungry." This is a believe-it-or-not story. I can't prove it myself, but I believe what happened was true. There are a lot of things spiritually that man don't know yet.

In addition to its referencing traditional Tlingit spirituality and the conveyance of food across space, time, and existence through burning, Kadake's account speaks to the values of never giving up and continuing to believe in positive outcomes when evidence suggests otherwise.

Kake elder Clarence Jackson provided another oral tradition of a man being stranded at Deiki Noow who survived and eventually returned safely to Kake.

Once a man traveled to Deiki Noow to collect seagull eggs. While he was there the waves grew stronger and higher and smashed his canoe because he had not pulled it up high enough to protect it. Being stranded, the man thought long and hard about how he might get off the island and back to safety. Eventually, his thoughts were understood by a seagull who communicated with him that he should dive into the water and down under Deiki Noow where he would find an underwater cave where the sea lion chief lived. So having nothing better to do, the man dove into the water, found the underwater cave and climbed up inside it. Indeed he then found the sea lion chief who asked him why the man had come to see him. The man replied that the seagull had told him to come and see him. The sea lion chief then asked, "What is it you want from me?" The man asked if there was any way that the sea lion chief could assist him in returning to the islands where he lived. The sea lion chief thought for a while and then said, "See that old sea lion skin over there? Take it and make a big ball out of it and then blow air into it." So the man went and got the skin and did as he was told. He returned to the sea lion chief and asked, "Now what should I do?" The sea lion chief replied, "Get onto that ball and push yourself off into the ocean. Think only about where you want to be and absolutely do not think at all about where you have been, about Deiki Noow." With those instructions in mind, the man got his sea lion skin ball, jumped on it, and pushed off from shore, paddling toward the islands in the distance. But try as he might to think only of where he intended to go, his mind wandered back to where he had been, to Deiki Noow. And just as soon as it slipped into his thoughts, he was back on the island again. The sea lion chief, seeing him back at Deiki Noow, asked, "What are you doing back here?" And the man replied, "I tried to do as you told me, but I thought about where I had left from and just as quickly I was back here again." The sea lion chief then said, "You must follow my instructions, or you will never make it back to your home again." The man tried two more times, but each time he failed as he began to think about where he had been. Finally, on his fourth attempt, he thought only about where he wished to be, and when he awakened, he was back in Kake. (Jackson 2008)

In Jackson's account, two themes are present. The first theme is that of listening to and learning from other species—seagull and sea lion—because they have important lessons to teach. The second relates to the necessity and power of letting go and remaining positive in envisioning where you wish to go.

Historical Accounts: Documentary and Oral

A substantial body of archaeological research has been conducted in Tebenkoff Bay, the major site of Naastedí winter settlement (Maschner 1992). The excavation of several village sites, notably locations recognized by Raymond Roberts as ancestral Naastedí communities, is thought to demonstrate a substantial population (300–500) occupying the bay from the mid-1500s to the mid-1800s (Maschner 1992; Roberts 2004). The population of the Kuiu subdivision of the Tlingit was estimated by Veniaminov in 1834 to be 150 and by Verman in 1861 to be 262 (Emmons 1991, 431, 433). The Kuyu ḵwaan Tlingit possibly encountered early European explorers and certainly engaged in trading with later Euroamerican fur traders. Indeed Rowan Bay, located on the west side of Kuiu Island immediately north of Tebenkoff Bay, is named after an early Euroamerican trader from Boston who was on the coast in the late eighteenth century. Two waves of smallpox epidemic wreaked havoc on southern Tlingit villages in the nineteenth century—in the mid-1830s and again around 1862. There may have been an earlier episode of population decimation as well arising from Spanish exploration in the vicinity in 1779 (Boyd 1994; Langdon 1997). In fact, Mr. Roberts believes that the Naastedí oral tradition of the smallpox epidemic that precipitated the departure from Tebenkoff Bay was the result of an encounter at that time with traders in the vicinity of Deiki Noow. The Naastedí split and went in two directions at the time of their departure from Kuiu Island. One segment traveled north and settled among the Keex' ḵwaan, while, as discussed earlier, another segment traveled south to join the Klawak ḵwaan. In both Kake and Klawock, the heritage and practice of traveling to Deiki Noow has been sustained since the time of departure from Kuiu Island, nearly 150 years ago.

Following the purchase of the European rights to discovery in Alaska from the Russians in 1867, the U.S. government initiated institutional mechanisms to govern the new territory. A most significant activity was that of making the new lands and waters "legible" to the state and potentially to citizens who might be interested in making use of the resources in Alaska (Scott 1998). To that end, the activities of the Coastal Survey in making charts of Alaskan waters was a substantial undertaking that dates to the late 1870s. Gradually the shores and waters of southeast Alaska were made "legible" through these acts of governmentality. As yet not subjected to systematic scholarly scrutiny are the materials created by the crews of the Coast Survey vessels in undertaking this mission. However, by chance I happened to find an early reference to Tlingit use of Deiki Noow in a Coast Survey handwritten manuscript from 1887 housed in the National Archives. In that document, a narrative of navigational information for travel in the vicinity of Sumner Straits, Ensign Simon Cook who served aboard the USS *Patterson* on this mission, reported as follows:

> Egg Harbor, the western bight on the north side [of Coronation Island] lies at the foot of Pin Pk. . . . [It] is a good anchorage for small craft in 5 to 7 fthms of water. It is a rendezvous for the Indians who await favorable weather to go to the Hazy Ids for Gull and Murre [?] eggs. (Snow 1887)

This terse statement implicates several unarticulated processes, most significantly the source and manner in which Snow acquired this information. It certainly could not be obtained from mere observation of Tlingit in the vicinity and therefore must have been learned from someone. Further, Snow does not tell us why the small bight is named Egg Harbor. Was it also a site of egg collection, or was its status as jumpoff point for seabird egg collection the reason for its naming? Benjamin James, a L'eeneidí clan member raised along the shores and waters of Sumner Strait, reported that his grandfather took him on seagull collecting missions into a large sea cave at the southwestern end of Coronation Island as well as to Deiki Noow (Benjamin James 2004).

As part of the conservation movement, the Hazy Islands were declared part of the National Wildlife Refuge system in 1912. The harvesting of resources from the Hazy Islands was declared illegal through this designation, which must have been communicated to the local Tlingit at some point as Frank Johnson states that "before it was made a bird reservation by the United States, our people visited the island every summer to gather birds' eggs." Interviewees reported continuing use of the islands for seabird egg harvesting after its designation as a wildlife refuge.

Klawock and Kake accounts from the historical area range from approximately 1900 as a specified date to the initial years of the twenty-first century. The oldest recorded historical account of actual Kake Tlingit activity on Deiki Noow, told by Frank Johnson, a member of the Sukteeneidí clan, is entitled "Wrecked on Hazy Island":

> It must have been in July of 1900 (see seagull eggs are picked in June) when a large canoe load of Kake residents went there. Usually only men go out after birds' eggs, but it was so fair and calm that instead of leaving the women on the safe, sandy beaches of Coronation Island they were allowed to go.
>
> The landing was easy and uneventful. Everyone had an exciting time picking eggs and just walking about on the barren rocks. The great ground swells began slowly to increase in volume and ferocity. Hardly anyone paid much attention, as it was normal for that when the tides change or as the winds come up.
>
> Suddenly it was noticed that the waves were about too high and a sudden southwest wind came up. The wind and the waves were so violent they could no longer launch the boat safely. They were stuck on a barren island. Instead of abating, the waves were now so huge only the men made it to the great canoe at personal peril to themselves. The men pulled the canoe up as high as they could above the giant waves and into the shelter of a large projection of rock. Bedding, food, and all heavy and moveable goods had to be unloaded in a hurry. The women helped.
>
> The storm greatly and rapidly increased. This was no ordinary storm. Though the bedrock here was solid and the height of the island seemed safe during most days, the waves kept increasing so much that spray came over the highest point and came down to soak everyone. The canoe had to be bailed out after each extra-large wave. Finally an extra-large one came crashing down and split the canoe in about

half and smashed one end into small pieces and swept much of the precious camp equipment and food overboard. They rushed down to recover whatever they could.

My father got a hold of the mast and noticed a cavity in the rock shaped like a dishpan upside down. The women screamed. A huge wave was coming. He ran towards the cavity and braced himself with the mast. The wave completely covered him but he found that some air was trapped in the reverse cavity.

The wave went down and he came out just in time to see two men about to be carried over a precipice by the waves. Father was strong and fast on his feet. He ran and waited in the shallow lip where they were about to go over. One of the men yelled, "Take this one. I can make it up." The women screamed again, and another great wave was coming. He thought he let the man go. He was caught away from the comparative safety of the hollow place. In the excitement he dragged the man by his long hair. The rock was largely limestone and hence jagged, but he got him to a place where others got a hold of him. His hands were terribly cut and bleeding profusely.

Only a few essential things were saved. The eggs were gone, and all of the food except a very small amount was gone. The oars and paddles were saved as were the wet blankets and a few clothes.

The storm gradually abated and the waves lessened in force. Altogether it lasted several days and the people were exhausted. The sun came out. The women made a fire using broken pieces of the canoe. There was no other wood then immediately available. My father was in a rage when he saw the canoe pieces starting to burn. His younger sister had made the fire. "Why did you do such a thing?" he screamed at her. "Do you not realize that we must somehow get ashore by ourselves even if some other party comes for us? Do you not realize some strange people may rescue us and then claim us all as slaves?" It was the Indian law at that time to take rescued people as your slaves. No one spoke, for what he voiced was true.

Miraculously a few simple tools (awls, knives, hatchets, and adz) had been carried [up] and were saved. They always carried fresh twigs, stripped off bark, called "zoo" for mending cracks in red cedar canoes. The men went to work. They carefully pieced together remnants. Only short pieces from both bow and stern were missing and pieces of the toolbox were used. The women used parts of their dresses to caulk the canoe. They killed seals and put them down on the bottom of the canoe, which helped, to stop leaks. The waves slowly went down, then they made it to Coronation Island's sheltered bays and eventually back to Kake."

This harrowing account is once again a testament to the ferocity of the ocean and the danger of not attending to weather conditions at Deiki Noow. At the same time, it provides a wealth of pertinent ethnographic data and geological information. Most important to the Tlingit valuation of character, it is a story of tenacity, courage, preparation, and how the knowledge and application of traditional techniques of survival made it possible for those threatened to survive.

The accounts provided by Klawock and Kake elder interviewees primarily referenced a new technological era in which the primary means of transportation was no longer by canoes, great or otherwise. By the early 1920s, many Tlingit families had acquired small, combustion-engine powered plank boats, many built by the men with their well-developed woodworking skills in boat houses located on the shores of their communities. These vessels then became the primary vessels for travel from place to place, for fishing and for heading out to Deiki Noow. These vessels were invariably named by interviewees and were a central dimension in the recollection of experiences at Deiki Noow.

During the first half of the twentieth century, the level of community affiliation to an extent superseded that of clan among southern Tlingit. As village consolidation enlarged villages and brought members of new clans into them, a sense of community identity began to emerge. For older generations, clan traditions and *at.óow* were still central, but younger generations raised in schools with age mates tended to develop new associations. In discussing who went on the vessels that traveled to Deiki Noow from Kake and Klawock, it is clear that kinship networks, both of descent and marriage, were the foundations for selecting persons. Invitations were never open-ended to anyone in the village to join a planned trip to the islands, but a broad range of close and mostly distant kin were involved in these activities through much of the twentieth century.

A central topic put to the interviewees was the men's actual experiences in traveling to Deiki Noow and collecting seagull or murre eggs. It is important to note that this collection would occur at two separate times. Seagull eggs were reported as being harvested from June 5 to 12 with the target dates for being in the Hazy Islands differently reported from one person to the next. Seagull eggs can be obtained on all of the islands, so it is not necessary to go to Deiki Noow, despite the fact that they are most abundant there. The collection of murre eggs, however, occurs around July 4, some three weeks after the seagull egg collection and therefore involves a second trip to the Hazy Islands if both species are to be harvested by a family group in the same year. In addition, murre eggs can only be obtained from the higher ledges on Deiki Noow (Peratrovitch 2004; Roberts 2004). Murre eggs are reported to be blue with the intensity of the coloration varying (George 2009). Only two men, Theodore Roberts and Robert George of Klawock, reported visiting Deiki Noow to collect murre eggs. Roberts did this around 1930 when he was eight years old, and George went in the mid-1970s after returning from military service in Vietnam.

The men traveled to Deiki Noow as boys when they were between eight and fourteen in the 1930s and early 1940s. In preparing for their first trip to Deiki Noow, they reported hearing many stories from their elders about the steep slopes and slippery rocks and were excited to visit and collect eggs. All had heard the story of Raven acquiring freshwater from Deiki Noow, and many stated that they had made efforts to find the freshwater source. Clarence Jackson and Charles Johnson reported that they had found the spring on the small island Ḵúxk'. Mr. Johnson stated:

> The one nearest shore of course is the one with the fresh water, Ḵúxk'. That's where Ganuk had the fresh water well. That was part of our deal. My dad took me around. All that I remember is we're up on top there and down there's freshwater. We went down there and there is quite a lot of rock and looks like part of the thing is to the side, like this thing is off to the side like that [uses hand to demonstrate]. And my dad reached in there and started scooping out the water. There was all kinds of moss and stuff in there and grass was growing around there and moss and stuff. Pretty soon he was reaching down as far as he could and he reached, he used his hat, I don't know why but he used his hat as a scoop and he said it would take a while to fill and he showed me around. We walked around looking at different plants and then he said my grandfather got wrecked there in the canoe. They got careless there and they got caught there and the canoe got wrecked but he managed to toss it up again and then he went back to shore. But after some time, I guess an hour—it

might have been longer or might have been less time—but we went back there and I said the water should be back up so we went back there and we could see the water level back up. It didn't overflow. I think it might have overflowed a little because it was wet and my dad got some, what you call wild rhubarb, looked like wild celery, but they're grown on the mainland and some of the islands and stuff and maybe used for cooking, and they are a form of rhubarb. But he made cups out of the leaves of it. The big leaves he made cups out of it and the water was cold and really, really quite a treat. That was our introduction to that one. Two times I got to go to that one, but I don't remember where exactly. All I know is you had to go down into a kind of depression there between the island, kind of a cone like or something. (Johnson 2004)

Another topic that was addressed in the interviews was actual experiences on Deiki Noow. These experiences were well remembered by most of the men. Clarence Jackson recalled that he was trained not to speak when he landed on the islands. If he encountered sea lions or seals, he was not to make eye contact but to move quickly past them, demonstrating that he had no interest in them. Interviewees from both villages reported instructions to not look down on their way up or down or when they reached the top of Deiki Noow. They were specifically told not to look down into the water when they were on the top of Deiki Noow. Leonard Kato (personal communication, 2005) reported that on his way up, he did look out into the water and saw a seal diving down and going under the island. He interpreted this as an indication that there was an underwater cave to which the seal was going.

One fascinating account of preparation for ascending Deiki Noow was provided by James Martinez (2005) of Klawock.

When I got ashore on Deiki Noow, my dad called me over and told me to go find one of those little crabs. So I did and brought it back to him. Then he said to put the little crab up under my shirt and scratch my chest a little bit with the claws until some blood come out. This way he said it would be easier for me to get up to the top.

The men recalled that they wore special oversized sweatshirts with ropes tied around their waists when they climbed up the steep slopes of Deiki Noow. Eggs were placed inside the sweatshirts so that both hands could be free to pick eggs and to assist in maintaining balance. When they came down from the top, it was often quite slippery, and they would slip and slide. With a full load of eggs, it was a major accomplishment to reach the bottom without breaking any. Several men remembered that they had fallen either coming down or jumping into the waiting skiffs and a number of eggs had broken all over them. This was always a highlight of the recollection and shared with peals of laughter.

An important topic of the interviews was the rules of harvest of the eggs. Young harvesters were informed that seagulls would dive at them but would generally not strike them, so they were to keep their heads down at all times. This would allow them to focus on the circumstances they found in the nests. The essential rule of harvest conveyed by individuals from both Klawock and Kake were as follows:

1. Never take all of the eggs from a nest. Always leave at least one egg.
2. Get a general sense of how many nests there are and how many have eggs.
3. If there are lots of nests with multiple eggs, then take all but one from a nest.
4. If there are fewer nests with eggs, use your judgment—for example, if there are four you may take one, two, or three depending on general abundance.
5. Do not touch eggs unless you are going to take them.

Research conducted on seagull egg collecting by Tlingit of Huna kaawu in their traditional territory indicates that there are a various rules, but the core principle, as among the Klawock and Kake Tlingit, was never take a single egg and always leave at least one egg in the nest (Hunn et al. 2003).

Once the eggs were harvested, they were brought to the skiffs for transport back to the primary vessel. Here they were carefully stored in boxes in the hatch so that they would stay cool. The next step was to check the eggs for their stage of maturation. Each egg was placed in a bucket of seawater. If the egg sank or stayed at the bottom, then it was in an early stage of development and would be in a liquid state with a yellow center. If it floated, however, a chick had begun to develop in the egg. The eggs were then sorted as they would be differently distributed and utilized. On the way back from Deiki Noow, interviewees reported

Fig. 16.6 Seagull egg in grass nest on Kuxk'. Photograph by Steve J. Langdon.

that typically some of the eggs would be consumed. Usually they would be hardboiled, but occasionally they were fried or scrambled.

Distributional practices for the eggs reported by interviewees differed between Kake and Klawock. In Kake, especially up until the 1960s, vessels returned to the city dock where everyone in the community was invited to come down. Eggs were then distributed to all, with elders receiving the eggs that had been identified as having chicks inside of them. In Klawock, the eggs were distributed to the families of those who participated in the trip. However, village elders in general were provided with the eggs with chicks. They were regarded as a special delicacy, and one man recalled that his mother loved the juicy crunchiness of the chicks.

In both communities, eggs were joyfully received and generally put to immediate use. It was reported in both communities that seagull eggs had a richer flavor than chicken eggs. They were especially valued for use in cakes where they produced very fluffy delicacies. They were also used in pancakes. Eggs were reported to be stored by some in seal oil in cool locations such as cellars where they might be preserved for a limited time.

Wesley Brown reported that as a boy he brought back an egg and decided he wanted to hatch it and have a baby seagull. So the egg was placed under the stove in the house and eventually it hatched. The bird imprinted on Wesley, who was caring for it and constantly around it, and he now had a pet. He laughingly reported how the bird followed him around the village for several years thereafter. Brown's seagull was a topic of humorous remembrance by other elder interviewees in Kake as well. A related story was told by Gordon James, who was raised in Kake. He recounted that once his party had brought back an infant seal from Deiki Noow as it appeared to have been abandoned or been left without a mother. Back in Kake, it was kept in their home for a few months and fed out of a bottle. Subsequently, they put the seal back into the ocean. It stayed around the docks for a few weeks, but it eventually disappeared, presumably leaving to go on its own travels.

Encounter

In June 2007, five Kake men, my research assistant, Kelly Gwynn, and I traveled to the Hazy Islands to collect seagull eggs. The trip was the outgrowth of the research and interview process that started in 2004 in Klawock and had been extended to Kake in 2005. Mike Jackson, a political and cultural leader who had agreed to the project and with whom the research was conducted, decided that it was important to make a trip to the islands under the auspices of the Organized Village of Kake (OVK) as part of the documentation process associated with the traditional cultural property nomination. We decided to make videos of the activities as part of the documentation of the visit and the cultural heritage of Deiki Noow as well.[5] In addition, he had a strong personal interest in traveling to the islands as he had never visited them. Perhaps most significantly, the recent death of the beloved Charles Johnson, who had so enjoyed traveling to Deiki Noow and who, as a cultural historian, was the repository and source of so much of the cultural knowledge about Deiki Noow, was an important consideration as well. One of the tribal council members, Nick Davis, an experienced commercial fisherman who knew the waters around Hazy Islands and who like all other Kake Tlingit had grown up listening to stories of Deiki Noow adventures, was also eager to go. He offered to take a party to the islands in his Nordic Tug. With the commitment of a vessel large enough to transport a group of people to the islands, Jackson contacted me, and I was able to obtain funding to travel to Kake with my assistant to join the party and record the trip to Hazy Islands.

Preparation. Jackson recruited three young men as well as two elders in addition to himself and Davis, the vessel owner. The young men, as in previous generations, were excited to visit the islands, collect seagull eggs, and perhaps find the spring. Jackson visited key elders to obtain information about timing and landing in the Hazy Islands, learning that it was best to arrive and begin activities right at daybreak if possible, as ocean conditions were likely to be calmest at this time. Wesley Brown again reminded Jackson to watch the horizon for the first appearance of Deiki Noow, which he simulated by holding a fist with his thumb sticking up. Buckets, boxes, coolers, food, fuel (for the skiff that would be used to land the party on the island), and life vessels were collected and transferred. We hoped to depart around 10:00 p.m. in order to arrive at the Hazy Islands by 7:00 a.m.

Departure. The crew was finally all aboard at about 11:45 p.m. Mike sat everyone down in the cabin and began a discussion about where we were going, what we were doing, and the significance of the trip. He introduced himself in customary Tlingit fashion (personal name, clan, father's clan, and grandfather's clan) and then mentioned the elders from whom he had obtained his knowledge. Then he pointedly stated that on the trip "Topsy will be with us," and he held up a sheathed knife that was owned by Charles Johnson. Each man in turn then introduced himself in the Tlingit fashion, noted from whom he had learned about Deiki Noow, and stated why it was important to him to be going there. At the end of the session, Mike said that we needed to all watch carefully to see the islands and held his fist in front of him with the thumb sticking up.

Travel and arrival. Our trip proceeded smoothly down Chatham Strait in clear weather for the first six hours. Just north of Cape Ommaney we entered a thick fog bank. We were completely engulfed by the mist, and so our movement and location were tracked by the vessel's radar. When we passed Cape Ommaney and headed out into the unprotected waters of the north Pacific Ocean, a small but noticeable westerly swell began to be felt on the starboard side. Tension and expectation began to rise as we moved closer to the islands.

Everyone was at high attention looking for the first glimpse of Deiki Noow. All of a sudden, we broke out of the fog bank and two islands loomed on the horizon. The island on the left corresponded to the manner in which the thumb held up sign shown to Mike Jackson by elders as an indicator of how the island would first show itself. The smaller island farther offshore to the west that appeared was unexpected. However, since we had traveled closer to the island in the fog bank, at its first appearance it was already of good size, too. The excitement at seeing the islands was palpable.

Almost immediately, Jackson sat down on the bow of the vessel and began singing loudly and with great energy. With his right arm outstretched and forearm bent upward at a ninety-degree angle, he joyfully announced our arrival with a Killer Whale song of introduction to inform the islands and the spirits that resided there that we were coming. After several minutes of singing, he stopped and told me that once the song had been sung at Kake and that more than forty killer whales had passed by while it was being sung.

Landing and egg collection. After looking at the steep slopes of Deiki Noow and knowing that we had a relatively limited time to harvest eggs due to our midmorning arrival, Mike decided that we would go ashore on Ḵúxk'. As the skiff approached the island, a landing spot was located in a small bight where a large number of sea lions were swimming and basking. On the way in, a single large male posed imperiously and alone on a rock at the entrance. We landed safely and offloaded the necessary equipment in two trips. The three young men were equipped with backpacks, the contemporary substitute for oversized sweatshirts, and boxes. Tyrone immediately headed out in search of eggs. When he returned, he showed how he had used the grass from the rocks to create neo-nests in the box in which each egg was placed. This effectively prevented the eggs from rolling around and accidentally breaking as he transported them across the rough, rocky, but not particularly steep terrain of Ḵúxk'.

The three men scattered across the island. Later they reported that many of the nests were already empty, but there had been a number of nests with multiple eggs. One gave an interesting report of how at one nest he observed a seagull mother pecking at a dozing sea lion that was about to roll over in its sleep onto the nest, threatening to crush the egg. He was impressed by the seagull mother's diligence in protecting the egg.

Departure from the island and travel back to Kake. After about two hours of egg collection, Mike announced that it was time to go. He had received a citizen band message from Captain Davis that the westerly wind was picking up and choppy swells were building. As safety was paramount, he wanted everyone back aboard immediately so that we could get under way. Davis wanted to be able to travel directly north to Cape Ommaney and up Chatham Strait rather than having to first go east to Coronation Island and then north, which was the traditional route. Large white-capped waves driven by the westerlies would make it an uncomfortable if not dangerous passage directly north if we delayed any longer. So everyone quickly got down to the landing and boarded all the eggs and equipment for transport back to the Nordic Tug.

Travel across the open north Pacific Ocean waters back to the protected waters of Chatham Strait was rough but uneventful. As we neared Kake, Davis radioed in our expected time of arrival. Mike told him to announce that the next morning the eggs would be distributed at the city dock.

Arrival at city dock and egg distribution ceremony. The next morning, Mike came down to the boat and subjected each egg to the float test. It turned out that none floated, so we would not be able to give an egg with a chick to an elder as a special treat.

The vessel was moved from the harbor to the dock where a crowd of thirty Kake residents, Native and non-Native, had congregated. Mike came ashore and welcomed them to the distribution. He introduced each member of the party and thanked them for their contribution. He gave an account of the experience, noting the rules of harvest, the difference between egg maturation stages, and why the documentation of their use by film was necessary. He then asked the elders to come forward, and the young men distributed the eggs to them. Mrs. Ruth Demmert, the Tlingit culture bearer and linguist, was first to receive her eggs. She asked the young man who gave them to her to count in Tlingit the number of eggs in the bag she was given. Distribution of the eggs to others continued.

About halfway through the distribution, Mike Jackson's wife, Edna, arrived on the dock with their granddaughter. The child was immediately brought over to the coolers where the eggs were stored and shown one. Then she was walked over to the bucket of water being used to test the eggs. She put her hand in and pulled one out to look at it. All of her behavior was joyfully received by her family and the other residents in attendance.

Several elders who received eggs gave thanks to Mike and the party, stating that it brought back fond memories of earlier days when this was a regular experience. One of them told a story about sea lion behavior in the islands.

After the egg distribution had been completed, the crew was given the opportunity to speak about and share their experiences. Each of the men expressed strong positive emotions, indicating that it was something that they would always remember and would surely pass on to their children.

News of the 2007 Deiki Noow journey, including the collection of seagull eggs, passed by word of mouth to other members of the Kake community living in other places. I was later informed by Mike Jackson that elder George Davis, who resides in Juneau but was interviewed for the research, was delighted to learn of the trip, the return of the seagull eggs to the community, and the participation of young Kake Tlingit in the activity.

Discussion

The trip to Deiki Noow was a powerful episode of Tlingit cultural heritage expression through action. It was built upon the *at.óow* understandings of the clan traditions and the oral traditions handed down through the generations. The spirits present in the islands were acknowledged and remembered through the arrival song. The most recent ancestor with a strong tie to the islands was brought to the islands, and his spirit was envisioned as present when we were in the islands—*shuká* was invoked. Practices in the islands were directly linked to those with experiences who provided the knowledge and direction on how to be safe, how to collect the eggs, and how to determine the life stage of the eggs. The young people were told about the experience, and the little girl was brought directly into contact with eggs—*shagoon* was enabled. The experience was shared broadly among those who came to receive eggs and learn about Deiki Noow—*kusteeyí* was sustained.

Conclusion

Deiki Noow is a place of enormous cultural significance to the southern Tlingit, particularly those associated in recent generations with the communities of Kake and Klawock. It was present at the time of creation and may be in Tlingit thought to be the oldest land in the world. It is the ancestral source of the world's freshwater and the location of a critical cosmological encounter between Yéil and Ganuk. It is the foundation of *at.óow* based on clan tradition of loss by the Naastedí and of mythic significance by the Kaagwaantaan. It is a site of pilgrimage where young men test and prove themselves, linkages are made with ancestors and heritage, and memorable adventures occur. It is a location where wonderfully tasty seagull and murre eggs can be acquired. But, as the accounts of great danger and many losses depict, it is also a place

TABLE 16.2 Tlingit Cultural Heritage in Practice: *Deiki Noow* 2007.

CONCEPT	TLINGIT CULTURAL DEFINITION	PRACTICE/APPLICATION
AT.ÓOW	Symbolic property "purchased by an ancestor" that is "consecrated" through ceremonial use and formal dedication within the context of . . . potlatch or party." Mostly objects	*Nasteedi* poles – first at *Tajikaan* and now in Klawock memorializing ancestor who lost life and special relationship with murre eggs; *Kagwaantaan* hat that memorializes Raven-GanUk legend
SHAGÓON	Remembering and honoring persons that have gone before who have special meaningful experiences for clan members in regard to the specific event or place—both immediate parent and ancestor Mostly visual images or designs	Direct mention of Charles Johnson, revered ancestor who carried and transmitted knowledge of *Deiki Noow*, at the outset of the tip; Carrying and display of Johnson's pocket knife at the outset of the trip
SHUKÁ	Connecting past, present and future generations with specific ties to persons and events of clan significance—faces past and future; includes both at.oow and shagoon	Respectful sharing of seagull eggs from *Deiki Noow* with elders; infants present at ceremonial distribution and introduction to seagull eggs
KUSTEEYI	Encompassing "life", "way of life" or "culture"	Raven myth of freshwater acquisition; Inviting all members of the Kake community to come and hear about the trip to *Deiki Noow* and participate in the distribution of seagull eggs; this event replicated past occasions which were publicly remembered on the occasion of the sharing of the seagull eggs from *Deiki Noow*

where character has been built and the lessons from those tragedies can continue to educate new generations. While abstractions from the stories of Deiki Noow can be used in a variety of contexts and place can become a mental metaphor as well as a physical location, the foundations of heritage going forward lie in the continuing reconstruction and regeneration of cultural heritage through direct experiences of ancestral places. These dimensions of Deiki Noow's multiple appearances in Tlingit lives make it an exemplar of Thornton's (2004, 365) contention that knowledge of places is foundational to the installation and development of individual and social character among Tlingit. As Tyrone Davis said upon his return from the Hazy Islands in June 2007: "Any chance you get to go to Deiki Noow, you better take it. There is nothing like it."

ACKNOWLEDGMENTS

This paper is dedicated with affection, appreciation, and deep respect to the memory of Andrew Hope III. I knew Andy for over forty years, first meeting him as a high school student when I was a counselor in an Upward Bound program. Our shared interests were many through the years and merged powerfully when he undertook a "Place-Based Educational Curriculum" initiative in the early 2000s. He was extremely interested in my work and provided a number of opportunities for me to develop and present my ideas. I hope this paper contributes to understanding and strengthening *shuká*, continuing the relationship of Tlingit people with their heritage in the places they have occupied for thousands of years. Andy cared deeply about this outcome and hoped future generations of Tlingit, as well as others, would encounter the joy and wonder of the Tlingit meaning of places.

The tribal governments of Klawock and Kake gave permission for and supported the research that is the basis for this essay. Their commitment to the research and to seeking traditional cultural property status for Deiki Noow is appreciated. Sincere and deep gratitude is expressed to all the elders from Kake and Klawock who gave so generously of their time, knowledge, and experience with Deiki Noow. They include Kake: Ronald Bean, Wesley Brown, Archie Cavanaugh, George Davis, Clarence Jackson, Mike Jackson, Rocky Jackson, Raymond Jackson, Dale Jackson, Franklin James, Charles Johnson, Evans Kadake, Marvin Kadake, Harold Martin, Ray Nielson, and Calvin Wilson; and Klawock: Robert Armour, Robert George, Leonard Kato, James Martinez, Alva Peratrovitch, Clara Peratrovitch, Theodore Roberts, Byron Skinna, Vaughn Skinna, Jim Williams, and Ronald Williams.

Special thanks are also extended to Mike Jackson, who coordinated the research and trip in Kake, to Nick Davis, who provided the vessel and the safe transport to and from the Hazy Islands, and to Kelly

Gwynn, who provided excellent camera work and post-production work. Greatly appreciated are the Tlingit language translations provided by Ruth Demmert. Heartfelt thanks are also extended to Dr. Deborah Corbett of the Fish and Wildlife Service for her commitment to seeing the cultural heritage of Alaska Native people in the islands of the Alaska Maritime Wildlife Refuge documented and celebrated. Funding for this research was provided by the U.S. Fish and Wildlife Service, the Sealaska Heritage Institute, and the University of Alaska Anchorage, all of whom are thanked for their generosity. Any errors or misinterpretations presented in the essay are the sole responsibility of the author.

NOTES

1. Another southern Tlingit ḵwaan, ironically appearing on the map of Tlingit ḵwaan(s), clans, and houses prepared by Andrew Hope III (2003), the *Tajik ḵwaan* are here treated as a part of the *Heinya ḵwaan*.
2. I am indebted to Judith Berman, who acquainted me with this myth involving *Deiki Noow* and provided me with the oral tradition that Louis Shotridge collected in association with the Kaagwantaan hat he collected in 1917 (Kaplan and Barsness 1994). Neither Swanton's nor Shotridge's version places the protagonists in a specific location.
3. Judith Berman identified the handwritten notes inserted on Shotridge's typescript of the Raven and Ganuk at Deiki Noow myth as having been written by William Paul.
4. Garfield erroneously attributed the oral tradition to the "Winter People," which would be the Takuaneidí clan, one of the neighboring Raven clans with whom the Naasteidí married extensively.
5. *Deiki Noow 2007: Kake Tlingit Seagull Egg Collection in the Hazy Islands*, a video documentary of the trip sponsored by the Organized Village of Kake to the Hazy Islands, is available from the Department of Anthropology at the University of Alaska Anchorage.

REFERENCES

Berman, Judith. 2004. "Some Mysterious Means of Fortune": A Look at North Pacific Oral History. In *Coming to Shore: Northwest Coast Ethnology, Traditions, and Visions*, ed. Marie Mauze, Michael Harkin, and Sergei Kan, 129–62. Lincoln: University of Nebraska Press.

Boyd, Richard. 1999. *The Coming of the Spirit of Pestilence: Introduced Infectious Diseases and Population Decline among Northwest Coast Indians, 1774–1874*. Vancouver and Seattle: University of British Columbia Press and University of Washington Press.

Dauenhauer, Nora Marks, and Richard Dauenhauer. 1987. *Haa Shuka, Our Ancestors*. Seattle: University of Washington Press.
———. 1990. *Haa Tuwunaagu Yis, For Healing Our Spirit: Tlingit Oratory*. Seattle: University of Washington Press.
Dauenhauer, Nora. 2000. "Tlingit At.óow." In *Celebration 2000: Restoring Balance through Culture*, ed. S. Fair and R. Worl, 101–6. Juneau: Sealaska Heritage Foundation.
De Laguna, Frederica. 1960. *The Story of a Tlingit Community [Angoon]*. Bureau of American Ethnology Bulletin 172. Washington DC.
———. 1972. *Under Mount Saint Elias: The History and Culture of the Yakutat Tlingit*. 3 vols. Washington DC: Smithsonian Institution Press.
Emmons, George. 1991. *The Tlingit Indians*. Ed. F. de Laguna. Washington DC: Smithsonian Institution Press.
———. n.d. "History of Tlingit Tribes and Clans." Manuscript.
Garfield, Viola, and Lynn Forrest. 1948. *The Wolf and the Raven: Totem Poles of Southeastern Alaska*. Seattle: University of Washington Press.
Hunn, E., D. Johnson, P. Russell, and T. Thornton. 2003. "Huna Tlingit Environmental Knowledge, Conservation, and the Management of a 'Wilderness' Park." *Current Anthropology* 44 (December): S79–103.
Jackson, Clarence. 2004. *Deiki Noow*. Interview transcript. Manuscript in author's possession.
James, B. 2004. *Deiki Noow*. Interview transcript. Manuscript in author's possession.
James, F. 2004. *Deiki Noow*. Interview transcript. Manuscript in author's possession.
James, G. 2003. *Deiki Noow*. Interview transcript. Manuscript in author's possession.
Johnson, C. 2004. *Deiki Noow*. Interview transcript. Manuscript in author's possession.
Johnson, F. n.d. "Wreck on Hazy Islands." Manuscript in possession of Organized Village of Kake, Alaska.
Kadake, E. 2004. *Deiki Noow*. Interview transcript. Manuscript in author's possession.
Kan, Sergei. 1989. *Symbolic Immortality: The Tlingit Potlatch of the Nineteenth Century*. Washington DC: Smithsonian Institution Press.
———. 1999. *Memory Eternal: Tlingit Culture and Russian Orthodox Christianity through Two Centuries*. Seattle: University of Washington Press.
Kaplan, Susan, and Kristin J. Barsness, eds. 1986. *Raven's Journey: The World of Alaska's Native People*. Philadelphia: University Museum, University of Pennsylvania.
Kroeber, A. L. 1939. *Cultural and Natural Areas of Native North America*. Berkeley: University of California Press.

Langdon, Steven J. 1997. "Efforts at Humane Engagement: Indian-Spanish Interaction in Bucareli Bay, 1779." In *Enlightenment and Exploration in the North Pacific, 1741–1805*, ed. Steven Haycox, Caedmon Liburd, and James Barnett, 162–81. Seattle: University of Washington Press.

Martinez, J. 2003. *Deiki Noow*. Interview transcript. Manuscript in author's possession.

Maschner, Herbert D. G. 1992. "The Origins of Hunter and Gatherer Sedentism and Complexity: A Case Study from the Northwest Coast." PhD diss., University of California, Santa Barbara.

Oberg, Kalervo. 1973. *The Social Economy of the Tlingit Indians*. Seattle: University of Washington Press.

Olson, Roland. 1967. *The Social Structure and Social Life of the Tlingit in Alaska*. University of California Anthropological Records 26. Berkeley: University of California Press.

Orth, Donald J. 1971. *Dictionary of Alaska Place Names*. Geological Survey Professional Paper 567. Washington DC: Government Printing Office.

Peratrovitch, Clara. 2003. *Deiki Noow*. Interview transcript. Manuscript in author's possession.

Scott, James. 1998. *Seeing Like a State: How Certain Schemes to Improve the Human Condition Have Failed*. New Haven: Yale University Press.

Shotridge, Louis. 1929. "The Bride of Tongass: A Study of the Tlingit Marriage Ceremony." *Museum Journal* 20 (2): 131–56.

Snow, S. 1887. "Descriptions and Sailing Directions Obtained on the Coast of Alaska in 1886." U.S. Coast Survey manuscript. National Archives, Washington DC.

Swanton, J. 1909. *Tlingit Myths and Legends*. Bureau of American Ethnology Bulletin 39. Washington DC: Government Printing Office.

Thornton, Thomas F. 1997. "Know Your Place: The Organization of Tlingit Geographic Knowledge." *Ethnology* 36 (4): 295–307.

———. 2000. "Person and Place: Lessons from Tlingit Teachers." In *Celebration 2000: Restoring Balance through Culture*, ed. Susan Fair and Rosita Worl, 79–86. Juneau: Sealaska Heritage Foundation.

———. 2004. "The Geography of Tlingit Character." In *Coming to Shore: Northwest Coast Ethnology, Traditions, and Visions*, ed. Marie Mauze, Michael Harkin, and Sergei Kan, 363–84. Lincoln: University of Nebraska Press.

———. 2008. *Being and Place among the Tlingit*. Seattle and Juneau: University of Washington Press and Sealaska Heritage Institute.

———, ed. 2012. *Haa Léelk'w Hás Aaní Saax'ú- Our Grandparents' Names on the Land*. Juneau: Sealaska Heritage Institute; Seattle: University of Washington Press. http://www.wilderness.net/index.cfm?fuse=NWPS&sec=wildView&WID=235. Accessed March 5, 2009.

17

Place as Education's Source

THOMAS F. THORNTON

Lately, a good deal of effort has been put into making schooling more relevant and responsive to Alaska Natives through a broadening of cultural standards, an emphasis on Native ways of knowing, and investments in place-based education (see Barnhardt and Kawagley 2011a, 2011b). Two hundred years ago, this was not necessary because Alaska Natives had *full control* over their educational destinies, and the curriculum was carried out *in situ* (i.e., in place) and *in vivo* within a wholly indigenous cultural framework. One hundred years ago, this was not necessary because Alaska Natives had virtually *no control* over their educational destinies due to state and missionary imperatives to "civilize" and assimilate them into white society, which had no place for their so-called "primitive" ways. This meant not only ignoring Native ways of knowing (what philosophers call epistemologies) but actively undermining them so they did not threaten socialization into the dominant values systems. Thus Alaska Natives were forbidden to speak their own language—the lifeline of cultural reproduction—and even were taken from their home communities—the nexus of place-based education—in the service of assimilation goals.

Now, in the post ANCSA (Alaska Native Claims Settlement Act of 1971) era of self-determination, cultural reawakening, and revitalization, the situation is different. The dominant educational institutions, schools, are ideologically sympathetic toward inclusion of non-Western civilizations and cultural diversity, at least, but they remain structurally rather hostile to it. The critical problem, then, is this: How do you take a state-sponsored educational system initially designed to destroy Native cultures and make it not only tolerant but inclusive of diverse Native ways of knowing? It requires not only infrastructural change, such as building schools in existing rural communities, as the 1976 Molly Hootch court decision enabled (*Tobeluk v. Lind*, Alaska Superior Court

No. 72-2450), but also a new set of systemic commitments to place as the foundation of Native education in Alaska.

Infrastructural change definitely has not been enough, as a recent editorial by Father Michael Oleksa attests:

> Ask any rural teacher when they consider their program a success and they will say when their graduates leave the village. Ask then how many actually do leave for further training at AVTEC UA, or Job Corps, and the percentage is usually fairly low. Ask then what in their curriculum is relevant to the 80 to 90 percent of their students who have no intention or wish to leave, and they'll admit that there is nothing in the existing curriculum that would excite or interest that group. Ask then why this does not explain the high truancy and dropout rates.
>
> The problem with Molly Hootch isn't that we built too many schools. The problem is that the reform only built schools, without reforming the way we educate or orient educators whom we import mostly from Outside. We have never seriously reconsidered the substance of the curriculum. The village school remains an alien institution whose aim is the destruction of the community in which it operates. We systematically take bright, beautiful 5-year-olds and in 10 years transform them into angry, alienated, suicidal 15-year-olds. For every successful graduate we have five catastrophes. The whole structure needs radical reform. (*Anchorage Daily News*, December 7, 2008)

Following the footsteps of others, I wish to argue that place-based education should be the foundation of any systemic reform.

Education in Resonant Places

In southeast Alaska, part of the effort toward incorporating place-based Alaska Native epistemologies into the curriculum was led by the late Andrew Hope III, through a major National Science Foundation funded project known as the Alaska Rural Systemic Initiative. Among other things, this project funded a cultural atlas prototype based on Tlingit-named places in the vicinity of Angoon. Our endeavor was to build a place-based education curriculum module. Andy Hope saw it as a realization of something I promoted in an essay for the first clan conference in 1993, entitled "Building a Tlingit Resource Atlas" (Thornton

2000a). Working with the late Lydia George, Jimmy George Jr., and Michael Travis, I helped put together a web-based cultural atlas, now stored on the Alaska Native Knowledge Network (Angoon Cultural Atlas 1998) in which a person could start within a Tlingit cultural geography, either a named place, a named house, or even a cultural emblem or crest, and move to the corresponding cultural property associated with that entity. There was logic to it in that clans and houses were often named for geographic places they belonged to (e.g., Deisheetaan, from Deishu Hít Taan, "End of the Trail House People"), and their cultural property represented places which defined their history and identity and to which they laid claim. Tlingit cultural geography has integrity that way: claims to property are supported through a multimediacy of identity, language, art, and dwelling.

Seeing the beauty and integrity of these connections inspired me to write a book, *Being and Place among the Tlingit*, in which I explored them in some detail, emphasizing the particular roles of social structure, language, livelihood, and ritual in developing and maintaining Tlingit senses of place as a foundation for culture and well-being (Thornton 2008). In the conclusion to that book I argued that the health of these vital cultural structures was inextricably linked to the places from which they evolved.

> The key to future success lies in cross-cultural recognition of biological and cultural health as two sides of the same entity: place. Environmental health and communal health were never separate in Tlingit place consciousness. "Taking care" of places and communities meant never going "against nature" (*ligaas'*, the Tlingit word for "taboo") and cultivating places through respectful engagement with their constituent beings as a means of promoting *biocultural health*. (196)

The same goes for educational health in rural southeast Alaska. It is unlikely to be successful unless it attends to place and the land and sea-based knowledge, skills, and institutions that have proven adaptive in enabling Alaska Natives to dwell sustainably over millennia, rather than those that have supported the rapacious colonization and exploitation of the "Last Frontier" in little more than a century.

In introducing *Haa Léelk'w Hás Aaní Saax'ú, Our Grandparents' Names on the Land* (Thornton 2012), a guide to southeast Alaska Native place-names, I emphasized the potential of using indigenous geographic nomenclature as an educational foundation for understanding places, citing what I called the "3 Rs." First is resilience; as linguistic artifacts, place-names are remarkably resilient: we hold them in our minds and they help us remember critical contexts of physical geography, events, and experience, from historical episodes to the location of critical fish, wildlife, and plant resources. Second is the remarkable resonance that Native place-names exhibit as potent signifiers of identity, relationships, and belonging. This in turn engenders the third "R," respect, for if you feel a social, economic, political, spiritual, and emotional sense of belonging to a landscape, you tend to respect it, you tend to take care of it (Thornton and Kitka 2010). The land is not just your commodity or a stock of resources; you are intimately related to its places, and they to you.

The corollary to this is also critically important. That is, if you don't have respect for places, if they do not resonate with your being in some fundamental and resilient way, then you are less likely to take care of them over time. This is why the growing global economy is so hard on places: its principles of economic integration are too often championed at the expense of environmental and place integrity. The people consuming the constituent elements of places are ever farther removed from them, except perhaps when they stampede toward certain "must-be-experienced" places as tourists. But tourism is consumption, not dwelling, and most consumers never develop the intimate dwelling relations necessary to care for places in a sustainable way. For this reason, conservation, especially conservation of sustainable livelihoods that develop from a placed-based education, remains a critical cultural problem.

So what is to be done?

The Three "L's": Language, Livelihood, and Land-Sea Stewardship

The answer to the problem of place in the modern world is to restore places to their foundational role as our individual and communal ground of being (Casey 1997). This is not to say that we must all become slavish creatures to the places we are born into or currently inhabit, but rather that we become more cognizant and intentional about the process of, as Wes Jackson (1994) puts it, "becoming native to this place." This means, in part, reorienting ourselves and our basic institutions to places from a native perspective. It also means conserving and bolstering Native institutions that have been the wellsprings of a resilient, resonant, and respectful orientation to the land over time. These institutions, what we might call the three "L's"—language, livelihood (or subsistence), and land-sea stewardship—are fundamentally educational institutions, from which evolves a sense of "becoming native to this land" in places like *Lingít Aaní*.

The first step in the process is learning something of the language of the existing landscape. Mastering a new language is hard, especially one like Tlingit or Haida, which is fundamentally different from English in its phonology and grammar and has a limited body of speakers and texts. Yet learning even a few intricacies of Tlingit as it applies to places can be truly educational. Did you know, for example, that Tlingit uses metaphors of the body and of kinship to relate places to one another? Thus a cliff may have a "face," a bay a "mouth" (not unlike English), while a large mountain may have a "wife" or smaller "child" mountain next to it. Similarly, Tlingit is remarkably descriptive in characterizing the elements of place. Consider Angoon: in Tlingit, *Aangóon* means "Isthmus Town," a very neat characterization of the town's peninsular position. But Tlingit is also descriptive of natural and cultural processes over time. Another example from the Angoon Cultural Atlas (1998) illustrates this point: Sitkoh Bay (*Sít'kú*, Glacier Area) describes a bay shaped by glaciers that long ago melted. As we recorded in the atlas:

> Tlingit traditional knowledge and Western science each provide important details about Sitkoh Bay. Deisheetaan clan history tells how the name *Sit'kú* was derived from the presence of glacial ice in Sitkoh Bay and Chatham Strait many years ago. Although we don't find glaciers there today, geomorphology studies suggest that a large valley glacier carved out Sitkoh Bay during the Wisconsin Ice Age (18,000 to 12,000 years ago). Glacial ice probably also clogged the waters of Chatham Strait during the so-called Little Ice Age (700 to 225 years ago). The oldest Deisheetaan stories about Sitkoh Bay begin with the phrase *Aangalaku*, meaning "Before the Flood," perhaps corresponding to the warming of the glaciers and consequent rise in water levels (and flooding) that occurred at the end of the Wisconsin Ice Age. Thus Sit'ḵú is both a very old name and a very descriptive one.

Sitkoh Bay also played host to a village, *L.awdagaan*, "No Sunshine," so named for the settlement's north-facing aspect, a noteworthy exception to the general rule of locating Tlingit villages with a southern exposure. In other respects, however, the Sitkoh Bay village is paradigmatic in its siting: defensible several fort sites are identified in the place-names, such as *Chaatlk'aanoow* (Fort on Top of the Halibut) yet accessible (a good beach for landing canoes, *Xakwgeeyí*, Sandbar Bay), with good sources of freshwater (e.g., *Tinaa Gooní*, Copper Shield Spring Water), and, most importantly, a good multi-species salmon stream, so named for its prized sockeye (*Gathéeni*, Sockeye Salmon Stream). How and why was this village established? By whom? Why was it necessary to defend it? Why was sockeye so important within Tlingit ecology? Why did they pack cohos from the lake down to Peril Strait (*Anax L'ukduyaa Yé*, Where They Pack Cohos)? What is the significance of the Raven's Cave (*Yéil Katóogu*) that is depicted on Deisheetaan regalia? And what happened to the sea otters at *Yáxwch'i Áak'u* (Sea Otter Lagoon)? The answers are in the stories behind the names, and they are central to understanding the natural and cultural landscape of central southeast Alaska. A teacher within any curriculum—science, humanities, social studies, even mathematics—in either primary or secondary school could build lessons or modules around these questions and the social-ecological relationships they evoke. In such a curriculum, students would learn that these places are alive, and the places, in turn, would enliven student connections to curricular topics in the most meaningful and memorable ways.

The southeast Native language of place, from the content of place-names to the conceptualization of a world in which animals, plants, even glaciers contain animate spirits which humans must respect, reflect the importance of maintaining a balance in one's interactions with nature (Swanton 1908, de Laguna 1972, Cruikshank 2005). As the language of place also reveals, the main mode of interaction with places has been livelihood, making a living on the land. "Subsistence," in this context is not simply an allocation scheme or a set of "use" rights for natural resources, but rather a fundamental way of sensing and caring for places. Livelihood explains why sockeye streams are highly prized. Livelihood explains why people traveled from place to place during different stages of the seasonal round and avoided certain places during other times. Today livelihoods have changed or become hybridized. No Alaska Native community lives completely off the land, but in rural areas households typically draw their livelihood from the land—on average a pound or more of wild foods per day per person (Alaska Department of Fish and

Game, CPDB 2008)—as well as the cash economy. This keeps people on the land in vital, productive, biocultural diversity-enhancing ways.

In cases where traditional hunting, fishing, and gathering livelihoods have been severely attenuated, there is evidence of deleterious effects on physical, social, and cultural health. As one recent study of an aboriginal Canadian community that has suffered such effects as a result of assimilation and settlement policies argues: "This disconnection from the country has a profound effect on the Innu's identity and their sense of connection to places and to each other" (Samson and Pretty 2006, 543). Arguably, in all northern hunting cultures the land, "the country," is synonymous with health, and thus "country-based activities [are] vital for both economic and cultural survival" (544). This is true even in areas where there is sufficient commercial development to support wage jobs. But it is especially true where the commercial economy is limited or unstable. As Peter Naoroz (see Federal Subsistence Board 2008) of Angoon's Kootznoohoo Corporation put it:

> Subsistence is our highest priority in the community. It is the most important thing that goes on in Angoon right now. It is our economy.... [W]e have a small charter fleet, [but] we've lost our last commercial boat out of the area. There is other commercial activity around there, but [for] Angoon, almost 90 percent of the economy is subsistence. So for all intents and purposes it's our most important economic driver.

The high priority of subsistence suggests that place-based livelihoods should be an integral component in any northern rural educational system. But, of course, they are not. School buildings and school calendars militate against following the seasonal round of hunting and gathering activities. Only in a few cases, such as Barrow, are school days suspended or rearranged to give priority to major subsistence activities like bowhead whaling.

A number of authors have argued for systemic changes to promote a more responsive school curriculum, calendar, food policy, and economic development strategies that will encourage livelihoods in which people continue to make their living on the land (whether in the cash or subsistence economy, or a mixture of the two) and gain vital nutrition, skills, and values from the land (cf. Samson and Pretty 2006; Thornton 2001, 2008). To date, however, the benefits of place-based livelihoods have hardly been recognized by state departments of education and health. Educational and health policies continue to be put into place that increase dependence on outside resources rather than local ones. In books like *Last Child in the Woods: Saving Our Children from Nature-Deficit Disorder* (Louv 2005) one senses the potential crisis that looms as a result of this alienation. The evidence is overwhelming that direct exposure to natural places is essential for healthy childhood development and human physical and emotional health. Country foods and subsistence livelihoods provide this exposure in a uniquely integrative way.

Sustainable livelihoods require the third "L," sustainable and adaptive *land-sea stewardship* systems. The dominant tenure system today is that of the state management. In scale and conceptualization, states are poorly matched to manage most ecosystems. State borders are often arbitrary latitude or longitudinal lines rather than meaningful ecosystem boundaries. And within states the patchwork of land and resource management systems that develop may be more an artifact of property rights or jurisdictional boundaries rather than true ecological units. Only recently have states begun to realign their management systems with natural ecological zones. An example of this is the U.S. Environmental Protection Agency's move to a "watershed approach" to environmental management as "the most effective framework to address today's water resource challenges." This makes not only ecological sense but also economic sense in the long run: "Watersheds supply drinking water, provide recreation and respite, and sustain life. More than $450 billion in food and fiber, manufactured goods, and tourism depends on clean water and healthy watersheds" (EPA 2008). In Europe the watershed management approach has led to the landmark European Water Framework Directive to manage large watersheds like the Rhine River, the catchment area of which encompasses nine countries.

Place-based education should be in the business of realigning resource management units with meaningful ecological systems and the communities that depend on them. This point was made in a recent Federal Subsistence Advisory Council meeting by Peter Naoroz, representing the village corporation of Angoon, who objected to an important local sockeye stream (Kanalku Creek) being managed as a "puddle" by the state simply because it was not a big commercial producer of salmon.

And it really goes back to looking locally. We're talking about Kanalku sockeye, a very small stream in Angoon but an important stream

> because it's the closest stream to the town and it's some of the best sockeye in the area. Well, our Board of—the State looks at . . . Snettisham [outside of Angoon's traditional area] as part of Kanalku. They got a million sockeye returning to Snettisham, and so we don't have a problem. They look at the whole region and they don't look at some of the smaller streams. And I actually was in a meeting where Kanalku was described as a puddle; not only did I take great offense to that on behalf of my people, but because it's just bad management. If you can't describe your smallest and health[iest] streams in terms of what their health level is, then you have no business managing a larger region. (Federal Subsistence Board 2008, 74)

As this example shows, when nature is controlled by outside interests, be they private property owners, commercial interests, or even government protected areas, indigenous livelihood and land stewardship systems may be compromised. At best they may operate in a circumscribed manner. At worst they may be totally undermined.

When we consider the fate of stream tenure and stewardship systems like the ones that operated at Kanalku, where the sockeye were so distinctive in their long, slender proportions that they had a separate name, *s'axa xáat* (slender sockeye), it is obvious that something valuable has been lost. The people charged with caring for the health of these streams have been put out of a job, and the land and sea are not being managed with place-based well-being in mind.

How would it look if they were managed with such well-being in mind? To begin with, the management scale would be at the local social-ecological level. Indeed, in raising their concerns about the Kanalku fishery, Angoon submitted a proposal requesting precisely this, that the state "manage for the amounts necessary for subsistence by location," meaning the community and watershed level, "rather than by management area." An even more radical proposal would be to empower Angoon to manage the fishery according to their traditional stewardship system. This included a *héen s'aatí* (stream master), typically the head of clan house (*hít s'aatí*) who studied the conditions of a watershed, including its fish stocks, and regulated interactions accordingly. This system thrived under Tlingit social structure because it was typically the house group that held contingent proprietorship over small streams like Kanalku and the house leader who organized the timing, means, and quantity of fish harvests. If fish returns were poor, the *héen s'aatí* might call for limits or even a moratorium on fishing. This stewardship system was based on a combination of intimate local knowledge of the stream, active monitoring of watershed conditions, and effective tenure over the resource base.

This system was actively challenged by the state, most aggressively at Sitkoh Bay in the late nineteenth century, where Deisheetaan leaders tried to prevent commercial cannery fishers from taking too many sockeye at Sitkoh Creek and were threatened with military force (Thornton 2000b; Thornton et al. 1990). Though the Tlingit stewardship system is no longer formally recognized, its logic still persists in some areas, where stream masters are recognized and consulted on how to fish particular streams (Thornton 2008). In Angoon, a kind of communal management prevails over streams like Kanalku, which are proximal to the community and can be monitored closely. At Kanalku, this has included "a voluntary closure for years" when fish returns were poor due to stream conditions (Federal Subsistence Board 2008). There also have been community-based efforts to improve the productivity of the stream, some originating from descendants of its original Tlingit stewards. Still the Tlingit land-sea stewardship system remains invisible, even antithetical, to the state, which to date has rarely supported local initiatives to improve stream management.

The Angoon Cultural Atlas outlines the biocultural logic behind the Tlingit stewardship systems over natural and cultural property. Recognition and reinvigoration of the indigenous stewardship systems of Southeast Alaska could improve management of resources critical to livelihoods. States would gain better information and monitoring of community streams, which ultimately would lead to better governance of bioculturally diverse marine social-ecological systems. New stream masters could tend to critical watersheds and educate people about how they sustain communities and how communities must sustain them. This, in turn, could serve to build a new kind of co-management and collaborative reciprocity between states and local communities, including tribes and clans.

Toward a New Paradigm

Like education itself, language, livelihood, and land-sea stewardship are human processes, not merely institutions or curricula. They involve sensing, interpreting, and acting on the world at a human scale. They are ways of building and sustaining community and identity. They are

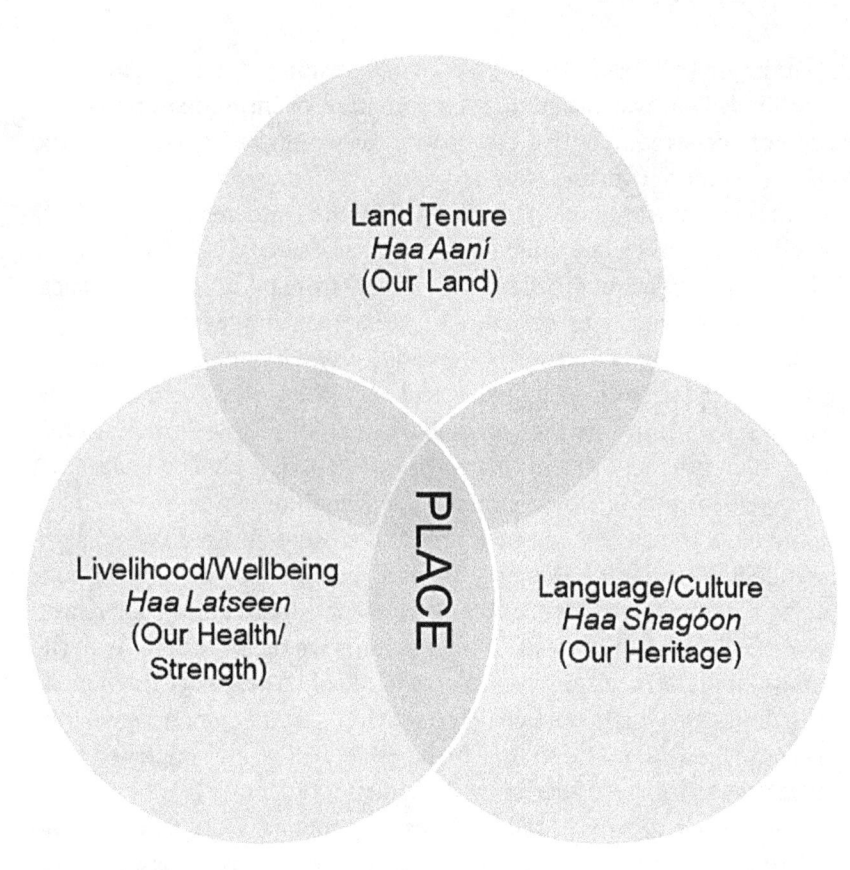

```
                    Land Tenure
                    Haa Aaní
                    (Our Land)



                         ┌─┐
                         │P│
  Livelihood/Wellbeing   │L│   Language/Culture
     Haa Latseen         │A│      Haa Shagóon
     (Our Health/        │C│     (Our Heritage)
      Strength)          │E│
                         └─┘
```

Fig. 17.1 Place-based model of education and health.

sources of healthy, integrated biological and cultural diversities that have enabled humans to adapt to life on earth for millennia (Pretty et al. 2009). In the contemporary renaissance of Alaska Native culture, an emerging consensus toward revitalization of indigenous place-based education and identity is emerging. One feels it in places like "Celebration," Tlingit Immersion Programs, Dog Point Fish Camp, and increasingly in state-sponsored schools themselves, where a new generation of Tlingit teachers is reorienting the curriculum to center on the process of "becoming native to this place" in ways that meet the challenges of the future without sacrificing the wisdom of the past.

This emerging model of place-based education may also be linked to well-being, as illustrated in figure 17.1.

Place stands at the center within the three "L's" that support it. Each circle has a corresponding set of processes that underpin it. For example, subsistence can be seen as a critical aspect of livelihood, though it is also an important process in the maintenance of land-sea stewardship, as well as language and culture. Ritual, especially the memorial potlatch or *koo.éex'*, a kind of "total emplacement phenomenon" (Thornton 2008), could be added as an additional dimension which supports *Haa Kusteeyí* (Our Culture). Together these pillars support the histories and identities of Tlingit communities like Angoon (cf. de Laguna 1960), their atlases of space, time, and destiny (Thornton 2010). But they are not exclusive to Tlingit people; non-Tlingits have been incorporated and adopted into this system of education and living for as long as it has been in existence. Indeed the incorporation of new elements, be they new livelihoods or languages, is one of the strengths of the Tlingit model of education and well-being, contributing to its resilience and adaptive capacity. The dominant non-Native model of education generally has lacked this same adaptive capacity largely because of its failure to attend to place and the critical processes of dwelling that sustain places, so that they, in turn, may sustain us as infinite and resonant repositories of resources and learning.

The great Lakota leader Sitting Bull (Tatanka Iyotaka) famously said, "We belong to the Earth; Earth does not belong to us," an insight born of a place-based education and intelligence too often lacking in the modern world. Fortunately, in Tlingit country, the cultural and natural resources are available to undertake the task of re-emplacing education for those who are committed to learning how we belong to the Earth and the best ways to inhabit it. Ultimately, this is a project of re-sourcing and repatriating education into places.

REFERENCES CITED

Alaska Department of Fish and Game, Community Profile Database. Alaska Department of Fish and Game, Division of Subsistence, Anchorage. Accessed December 2008, http://www.subsistence.adfg.state.ak.us/geninfo/publctns/cpdb.cfm

Angoon Cultural Atlas. 1998. Prepared by Jimmy George Jr., Thomas F. Thornton, and Michael Travis. Prototype version archived on the Alaska Native Knowledge Network, accessed December 2008. http://ankn.uaf.edu/Cultural Atlases/course/view.php?id=3.

Barnhardt, Ray, and Angayuqaq Oscar Kawagley. 2011a. *Alaska Native Education: Views from Within*. Fairbanks: Alaska Native Knowledge Network, University of Alaska.

——. 2011b. *Sharing Our Pathways: Native Perspectives on Education in Alaska*. Fairbanks: University of Alaska Press.

Casey, Edward. 1997. *The Fate of Place: A Philosophical History.* Berkeley: University of California Press.

Cruikshank, Julie. 2005. *Do Glaciers Listen? Local Knowledge, Colonial Encounters, and Social Imagination*. Vancouver: University of British Columbia Press.

de Laguna, Frederica. 1960. *The Story of a Tlingit Community: A Problem in the Relationship between Archaeological, Ethnological, and Historical Methods*. Bureau of American Ethnology, Bulletin 172. Washington DC: Government Printing Office.

——. 1972. *Under Mount Saint Elias: The History and Culture of the Yakutat Tlingit*. 3 vols. Washington DC: Smithsonian Institution Press.

EPA (Environmental Protection Agency). 2008. Retrieved December 15, 2008: http://www.epa.gov/owow/watershed/approach.html.

Federal Subsistence Board. 2008. Southeast Alaska Federal Subsistence Regional Advisory Council meeting, public meeting, vol. 2. Juneau, September 23. Transcript retrieved December 15, 2008: http://alaska.fws.gov/asm/pdf/ractrans/Region%201%20transcripts%2023%20sep%2008.pdf.

Jackson, Wes. 1994. *Becoming Native to This Place*. Lexington: University Press of Kentucky.

Louv, Richard. 2005. *Last Child in the Woods: Saving Our Children from Nature-Deficit Disorder.* Chapel Hill NC: Algonquin Books.

Pretty, Jules, Bill Adams, Fikret Berkes, Simone Ferreira de Athayde, Nigel Dudley, Eugene Hunn, Luisa Maffi, Kay Milton, David Rapport, Paul Robbins, Eleanor Sterling, Sue Stolton, Anna Tsing, Erin Vintinnerk, and Sarah Pilgrim. 2009. "The Intersections of Biological Diversity and Cultural Diversity: Towards Integration." *Conservation and Society* 7 (2): 100–112.

Samson, Colin, and Jules Pretty. 2006. "Environmental and Health Benefits of Hunting Lifestyles and Diets for the Innu of Labrador." *Food Policy* 31 (6): 528–53.

Swanton, John R. 1908. *Social Condition, Beliefs, and Linguistic Relationships of Tlingit Indians*. Twenty-Sixth Annual Report, Bureau of American Ethnology, 391–485. Washington DC: Government Printing Office.

Thornton, Thomas F. 2000a. "Building Tlingit Resource Atlases." In *Will the Time Ever Come? A Tlingit Sourcebook*, ed. Andy Hope and Thomas Thornton, 98–116. Fairbanks: Alaska Native Indigenous Knowledge Network, University of Alaska.

2000b. "Person and Place: Lessons from Tlingit Teachers." In *Celebration 2000*, ed. Fair and Worl, 79–86. Juneau: Sealaska Heritage Foundation.

2001. "Subsistence in Northern Communities: Lessons from Alaska." *Northern Review* 23 (Summer): 82–102.

———. 2008. *Being and Place among the Tlingit*. Seattle: University of Washington Press.

———. 2010. "A Tale of Three Parks: Tlingit Conservation, Representation, and Repatriation in Southeast Alaska's National Parks." *Human Organization* 69 (2): 107–18.

———. 2012. *Haa Léelk'w Hás Aaní Saax'ú, Our Grandparents' Names on the Land*. Seattle and Juneau: University of Washington Press and Sealaska Heritage Institute.

Thornton, Thomas F., and Herman Kitka Sr. 2010. "The Tlingit Way of Conservation: A Matter of Respect." In *Indigenous Peoples and Conservation: From Rights to Resource Management*, ed. Painemilla, Rylands, Woofter, and Hughes, 211–18. Washington DC: Conservation International.

Thornton, Thomas F., Robert F. Schroeder, and Robert G. Bosworth. 1990. *Use of Sockeye Salmon at Sitkoh Bay, Alaska*. Technical Report 174. Juneau: Alaska Department of Fish and Game, Division of Subsistence.

Part 4 | *Material Culture, Art, and Tourism*

Fig. 18.1 Haida canoe pulled up on the beach at South Pond in front of Haida and Kwagulth houses, World's Columbian Exposition, 1893, from *The Glories of the World's Fair, Chicago: The Fair* (1894).

18

Skidegate Haida House Models

ROBIN K. WRIGHT

Early in 1892, a group of at least seventeen Haida carvers were commissioned to carve a model of their village of Skidegate on Haida Gwaii (formerly known as the Queen Charlotte Islands, British Columbia) for the World's Columbian Exposition in Chicago, Illinois. This model of Skidegate village (*Hlgagilda 'Llnagaay*) is unique, in that no other aboriginal village in Canada or the United States was systematically documented in this way by its own nineteenth-century residents. James Deans, who commissioned the models, created a written record of the stories he acquired from the Skidegate residents telling the history of each house and model pole, and he recorded the names of seventeen of the Haida artists whom he commissioned (Deans 1893). Their names are Adam Brown, Peter Brown, John Cross, George Dickson, William Dickson, Daniel Ellguwuus ('Iljuwaas), Phillip Jackson, Joshua (Kinnajesser), Moses McKay, Phillip Pearson, John Robson (Gyaawhllns), Amos Russ, David Shakespeare (Skilduunaas), Peter Smith, Tom Stevens (Tl'aajaang quuna), George L. Young, and Zacherias.

Fredrick Ward Putnam was in charge of the Anthropology Building at the fair. He hired Franz Boas to oversee much of this installation, and Boas in turn hired James Deans, a Victoria amateur archaeologist and former employee of the Hudson's Bay Company, to go to Haida Gwaii and collect this set of Haida houses. In addition to the model village, Deans collected three boxcar loads of Haida material, including a full-sized house and frontal pole and a forty-two-foot canoe (figure 18.1). Next to the Anthropology Building was South Pond. This pond is still there today and has a marina that opens onto Lake Michigan. This is where the big Haida canoe was pulled up on the beach next to two full-sized houses.

This full-sized house on the left, Great Splashing of Waves House, belonged to Tom Stevens in Skidegate. The frontal pole from this house

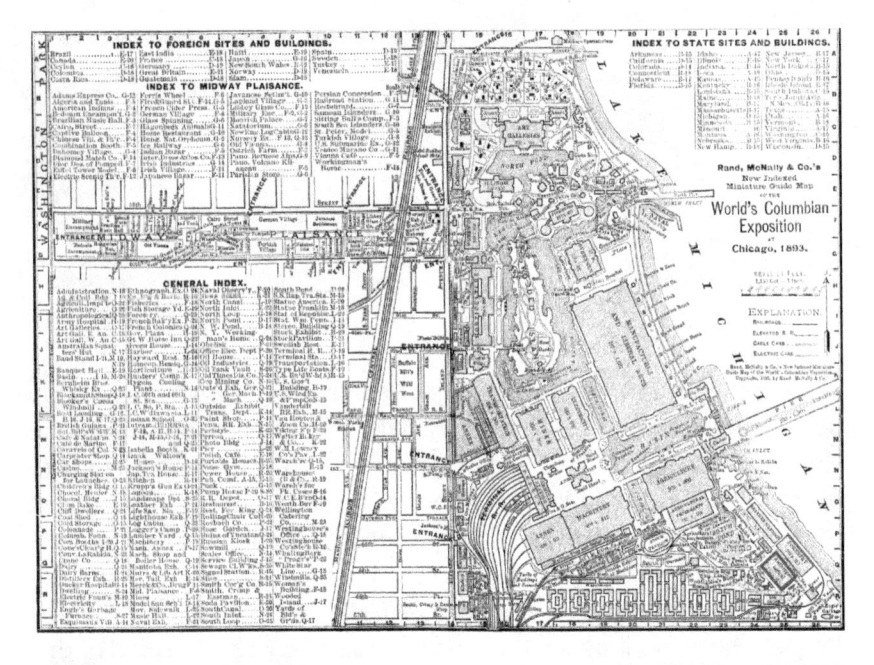

Fig. 18.2 (*top*) Map sketch of World's Columbian Exposition grounds, Chicago, 1893. Chicago Historical Society, ICHI-30461.

Fig. 18.3 (*bottom*) Skidegate Haida model houses installed in the Anthropology Building at the World's Columbian Exposition, 1893. Peabody Museum, Harvard University, negative no. N28375A. Photograph by Charles Dudley Arnold.

Fig. 18.4 Skidegate Haida model houses installed in the Anthropology Building at the World's Columbian Exposition, Chicago Public Library catalog no. CDA108. Photograph by Charles Dudley Arnold.

now stands in the foyer of the Field Museum, along with a pole from X̱áayna, seen to the right. Next to it is a house that belonged to Nakumgilisala of Nuwitti (Tlatlasikwala First Nation, now in Port Hardy, BC).

The World's Columbian Exposition was a grand place with huge neoclassical buildings, but the Anthropology Building opened late and was stuck way down at the south end of the fairgrounds next to the stockyards. It did not look very spectacular at all, but with the help of Google Earth it is possible to compare the map of Chicago then and the world's fairgrounds and find the exact spot where the Anthropology Building was, and it's now a golf course. The map of the world's fairgrounds shows a black block in the lower right where the Anthropology Building was (figure 18.2).

One photograph of these house models has been published in a number of sources (Cole 1985, 124; Jacknis 1991, 96). Figure 18.3 shows eighteen of the twenty-nine model houses that were in the exhibit. Those at the right are obscured due to the raking angle of the photograph. These large models measure about three feet by three feet square, with four to five foot tall model poles in front. I was able to locate another photo at the Chicago Public Library that had never been published (figure 18.4).

This shows eleven model houses from the center section of the village. This view overlaps with figure 18.1, showing seven of the houses that are obscured at the right of that photo plus four more. This center photo confirms that the model mortuary pole (third pole from the left), now

Skidegate Haida House Models 383

Fig. 18.5 Extreme right end of Skidegate Haida model house. Image #337267s, American Museum of Natural History Library.

in the Museum fur Völkerkunde in Vienna (cat. no. 1762), was actually part of this installation. Grizzly Bear's Mouth House, carved by John Robson and David Skilduunaas, appears partially at the far right (Field Museum cat. no. 17990). The tall striped model memorial pole at the center of figure 18.3 (Field Museum cat. no. 17842) appears at the far right in figure 18.2. This memorial pole is said by Deans to have been raised by Tom Stevens in honor of Hungo Dass. Stevens likely carved this model pole. We also found a photo of the extreme right end of the village installation that shows the last two houses, Copper House and Cah Guintt House (Figure 18.5).

We know from Deans's list that has Charles Newcombe's handwritten margin notes that there were two other houses installed to the left of Copper House, Food House and Eagle House, which don't appear

Fig. 18.6 View from the back of model Haida, Tsimshian, and Nuxalk houses installed in separate display behind the Skidegate village installation in the Anthropology Building at the World's Columbian Exposition, 1893, image no. 337268s, American Museum of Natural History Library.

in these photos. Hopefully a photo of that section of the installation may still be found.

In addition to the houses in the Skidegate village installation, there were three more model Haida houses that were displayed in a different area in the Anthropology Building: Earthquake House (Field Museum cat. no. 17825), Raven House from Sgaang Gwaii (Vienna cat. no. 51775), and a shed roof grave house (Field Museum cat. no. 17824). A fourth photograph shows this display from the back (figure 18.6).

You can see one tall frontal pole to the left that may be Earthquake House. No other photograph of this missing model exists. The other models in figure 18.6 include Tsimshian model houses, collected by Mrs. Morrison, a Tsimshian woman from Port Simpson, and Nuxalk model houses (shown to the right).

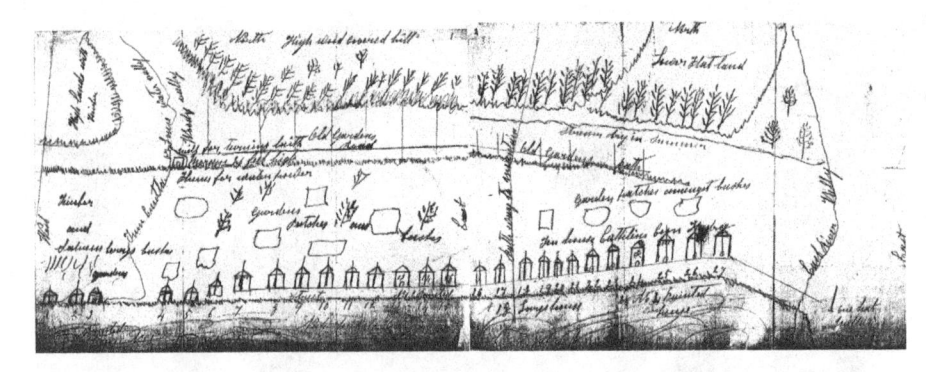

Fig. 18.7 Deans's sketch. Field Museum of Natural History, Anthropology Archives, acc. 21.

James Deans drew a sketch of the village (figure 18.7) and numbered all of the twenty-nine houses as an aid for Boas to install the houses.

Deans also went to Chicago to assist with the installation.[1] This sketch, compared with the photographs, shows that Boas did not follow Deans's instructions fully, moving some of the houses to a separate display. The Deans sketch shows three houses that were not in the village of Skidegate set slightly apart to the left: one from the village of X̱áayna (Field Museum cat. no. 17823), the Sgaang Gwaii model house (Vienna cat. no. 51775), and Captain Gold's House (figure 12, Field Museum cat. no. 17819) from First Beach. Only two of these models (17823 and 17819) were actually installed in this position at the fair. The Sgaang Gwaii House was apparently placed with the Tsimshian and Nuxalk models.

The installation of the Skidegate model houses at the fair did not represent the exact locations of the original old houses in the village, though this model was intended to represent the village of Skidegate in 1864. The first photographs of Skidegate were not taken until George Dawson, of the Canadian Geological Survey, arrived there in 1878 (figure 18.8).

We've attempted to locate the exact spot on the beach where some of these old photographs were taken of Skidegate (figure 18.9). The village today has some changes to the shoreline, with big breakwater rocks that have been put on both ends of the beach, but you can see the curve of the beach and the skyline that is the same as it was in 1878.

In our attempt to connect the model poles with the original old houses that they were intended to represent, we are looking at Charles Newcombe's lists of Skidegate houses and his 1901 notes and sketches,

Fig. 18.8 (*top*) Hlgagilda 'Llnagaay (Skidegate village), Haida Gwaii BC. Photograph by George M. Dawson, 1878, negative no. 253.

Fig. 18.9 (*bottom*) Hlgagilda 'Llnagaay (Skidegate village), Haida Gwaii. Photograph by Robin K. Wright 2006.

where he matched the houses he numbered in his notes with information recorded from village residents to photos of the village (Newcombe 1901). Newcombe helped to catalogue the model houses after the fair at the Field Museum, and his margin notes on Deans's list are also helpful (Deans 1893c). We are looking at John Swanton's lists as well (Swanton 1905, 286–87). Of course, these lists are numbered differently, named differently, and it's complicated to figure out for sure which houses some of the models represent. We have compared George MacDonald's map of Skidegate and his house names, which are drawn

Skidegate Haida House Models 387

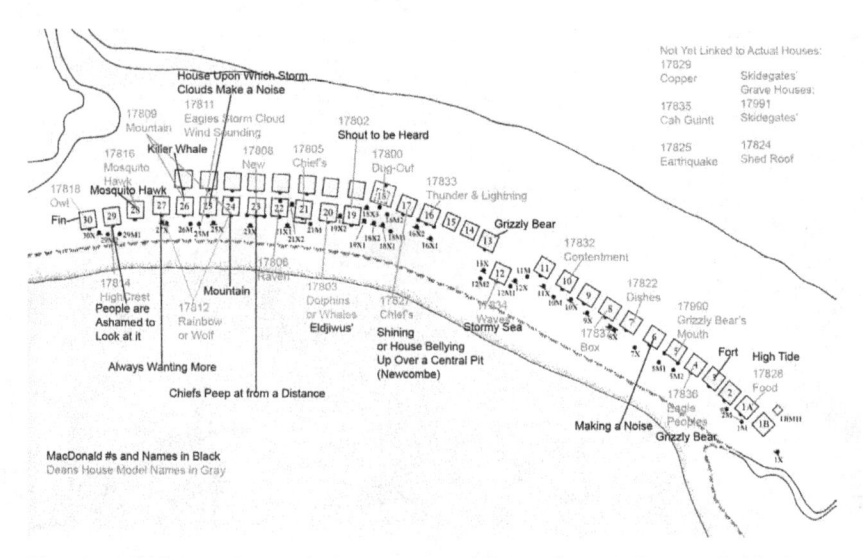

Fig. 18.10 Skidegate site rendering. MacDonald's numbers and names in black, with Deans's house model correlations in light gray. Reprinted with the permission of the publisher from *Haida Monumental Art* by George MacDonald © University of British Columbia Press 1983: 38. All rights reserved.

largely from Swanton's, Newcombe's, and Deans's lists, with the house model names (in light gray) matching those that we can (figure 18.10). You can see that we haven't figured this out completely. Mountain House could be one of two houses, as could Rainbow or Wolf House. There are several houses listed in the corner of this diagram that we can't link with known houses, so it's an ongoing process.

One of the model houses that we know the most about is the model of Captain Gold's House. The original house had a fully painted house front and moon mortuary panel placed at the peak of the gable. It stood at *Hlgaaxid 'Ilnagaay* (known as First Beach) to the west of Skidegate (figures 18.11 and 18.12). The knowledge shared by Richard Wilson, the current Captain Gold, has been very important to this project. I first met Captain Gold, who was then called Wanagan, when he was the caretaker at the village of Sgaang Gwaii in the 1980s, and he has generously shared his great knowledge of genealogy with me over the years. I interviewed a number of elders during this project, and an excerpt of our interview with Captain Gold follows:

> My name is Captain Gold of the NaiKun Kigawaay clan from Rose Spit area. I have the English name Richard Wilson, and over the

Fig. 18.11 Captain Gold's House, First Beach, Haida Gwaii, courtesy of Royal British Columbia Museum BC Archives, negative no. PN9059. Photographed in 1884 by Richard Maynard.

years I received the name Wanagan from my father's mother in the past, and that was my name until my mother's brother passed away, and then I got Captain Gold from him, plus two other names, Sgana Yuwans and Nangkilslas. Nangkilslas is the name of Raven during the time of creation. Sgana Yuwans is like great supernatural being or something like that. The first Captain Gold has a recorded name that appears in *Haida Monumental Art*, dealing with Kaysun or dealing with Chaatl at the time. So he'd be the first Captain Gold. The name came about in the 1851 time period, and then the second Captain Gold was the nephew of that first one. He came from the area of First Beach where Pearl Pearson's house is right now. He moved out to join the first Captain Gold out at Kaysun, and then he passed on shortly after that. And when he passed on, the nephew was very young. But my family was living with the group out near that Kaysun area and joined them on the final moves after smallpox into Chaatl and then into Skidegate.

One of the intriguing things about the model of Captain Gold's House is that it was made by a man named Zacherias, according to James Deans's notes. Thanks to the work of Bill Holm, we think that the old original painting on the house of Captain Gold was made by a man he dubbed

Fig. 18.12 Model of Captain Gold's House, First Beach, Haida Gwaii, attributed to Zacherias Nicholas. Photograph by Bill Holm, Field Museum catalog no. 17819.

"The Master of the Chicago Settee." Those of you who know about the attribution of Haida artists' work will have read Holm's 1981 article "Will the Real Charles Edenshaw Please Stand Up?" Holm differentiates the work of six or seven artists, one of whom is the Master of the Chicago Settee. It has been one of my lifetime goals to figure out what his Haida name reallywas. We are getting closer to that goal. We now believe that the same person who painted the large house also painted the model house, and that man is Zacherias. But who was Zacherias? In the baptismal and census records of Skidegate, there is a Zacherias Nicholas. Captain Gold believes this man was a Raven from Sgaang Gwaii. We were thrilled to find that Percy Williams remembered the man:

> Zacherias Nicholas is a name I used to hear all the time. I'm surprised there was nobody named after him. It's a beautiful name . . . important name. Even not meeting him or hearing about him, I feel he was a very important man. Zacherias, I like that name.

For those of us who have done work on attribution, this is really exciting. Having only had descriptive names, it's wonderful to suddenly be able to put real names and real people together with the works of art and have the memory of those people. Percy Williams goes on in the interview to say he remembered that Zacherias lived to be an old man and that he liked to go out and hunt and fish. We have now found the official marriage and death records for Zacherias Nicholas. He was born around 1861, baptized in 1888, and married to Isabella (the widow of Tom Stevens) in 1906. He died exactly as Williams remembered. His body was found in a cabin at Slatechuck Creek in March 1927. The model mortuary pole, which stood next to the model of Captain Gold's House (figure 18.3), has also been attributed to the Master of the Chicago Settee, now Zacherias Nicholas (see Wright 2009).

Barbara Wilson is someone who has helped us with the research on Cumshewa houses. A number of Cumshewa families lived in Skidegate. Owl House at the west end of Skidegate belonged to a Cumshewa woman. Only one small owl from the corner post of the model of this house remains in the Brooklyn Museum. The house itself and the frontal pole are missing, as are twelve others from the original twenty-nine models.

> My Haida name is Kii'iljuwus, and my English name is Barbara Wilson. I'm the eldest sister of the next in line to be Chief Cumshewa. And as the eldest sister, I'm actually his only sister. I only have a cousin; she's my second cousin. We are the last females of our age; we're the matriarchs of our clan. . . . And so this education we talk about extends to people my own age, because we grew up in a time when our parents told us to leave the old ways behind, to move on because we had to survive in a white man's world. And so, as I learn stuff, you know, I pass it on to my cousin, and she hopefully passes it on to her children, and I pass it on to mine and my brothers, and we spend a lot of time self-educating ourselves. And now here we are, you know, it's what twenty to thirty years later, and our kids dance, our women weave and make clothing, and our men carve and tell stories, and it's just like, it's like one of those . . . you know how they talk about Snow White. Somebody kissed her. Somebody kissed the Haida nation, and we woke up. That's what it's like, you know. I'm overwhelmed when I think of how grateful I am to those people who hung on to bits and pieces, so that we could start putting the puzzle back together again.

Skidegate Haida House Models

I feel more and more the urgency of the work that we're doing. Since we started interviewing the Skidegate elders in 2006, several have passed away, some before we had a chance to record their memories on tape.

ACKNOWLEDGMENTS

Haaw.wa (thank you) to Captain Gold (Richard Wilson), Irene Mills, Nika Collison, Kwiaahwah Jones, and Nathalie Macfarlane, director of the Haida Gwaii Museum, for sharing their genealogy research with me. Thanks as well to Percy Williams and the late Niis Wes, Ernie Wilson (Chief Skedans), his daughter Barbara Wilson, the late Johnny Williams (Chief Kitkun), the late Billy Stevens, and the late James Young for their help with the house model research. Interviews with some of them are on the Bill Holm Center web site at http://www.washington.edu/burkemuseum/bhc/haida_models/skidegate/. Thank you as well to Bill Holm, my teacher, from whom I continue to learn. There are still thirteen of the model houses with their frontal poles that have gone missing. The photos of them are on our web site: http://www.washington.edu/burkemuseum/bhc/haida_models/model_houses/missing.php. Please help us find them! We hope to bring them back together for a traveling exhibit and commission new models for those that we don't find.

The Skidegate Haida House Model Project has been supported by the Bill Holm Center for the Study of Northwest Coast Art, Burke Museum; Canadian Embassy Senior Fellowship; Haida Gwaii Museum at K̲aay Llnagaay; National Endowment for the Humanities; University of Washington Royalty Research Fund; and the University of Washington College of Arts and Sciences.

NOTE

1. No Haida people were invited to go to Chicago with Deans, but Boas had arranged for George Hunt, Boas's collector/collaborator from Fort Rupert, to bring a group of Kwakwaka'wakw people, fifteen adults and two children, to the fair to be the living components of his anthropology exhibit. In April 1983, they set out for Chicago, escorted by James Deans, who stayed with them until the fair closed in October. The group was housed temporarily in three small rooms in the stock pavilion until they could move into the two traditional cedar plank houses (*tl'aajang'kuna's*

Skidegate House, and a Nuwitti house belonging to Nakumgilisala) that were erected on the fairgrounds (see figure 18.2).

BIBLIOGRAPHY

Cole, Douglas. 1985. *Captured Heritage: The Scramble for Northwest Coast Artifacts.* Seattle: University of Washington Press.

Deans, James. 1893a. "Order of Haidah Houses as They Used to Stand in Skidegats Town, Q.C. Islands, BC." Field Museum of Natural History Archives, acc. 21.

———. 1893b. "Collections from North Pacific Coast, Department of Ethnology, World's Columbia Exposition, Haida Indians, Collection of James Deans." Field Museum of Natural History Archives, acc. 21.

———. 1893c. "Model No. 1 of Haidah Houses in Skidegate (James Deans ms. with notes by C.F.N.)." In BC Provincial Archives, Add. MSS. 1077 Newcombe Family. vol. 38, folder 4, Haida Industry Notes: section III, pp. 15–95. Victoria BC.

Holm, Bill. 1981. "Will the Real Charles Edenshaw Please Stand Up?" In *The World Is as Sharp as a Knife: An Anthology in Honour of Wilson Duff*, ed. D. Abbott, 175–200. Victoria: British Columbia Provincial Museum.

Jacknis, Ira. 1991. "Northwest Coast Indian Culture and the World's Columbian Exposition." In *Columbian Consequences*, vol. 3: *The Spanish Borderlands in Pan-American Perspective*, ed. D. H. Thomas, 91–118. Washington: Smithsonian Institution Press.

MacDonald, George F. 1983. *Haida Monumental Art, Villages of the Queen Charlotte Islands.* Vancouver: University of British Columbia Press.

Newcombe, Charles F. 1900–1911. Add. Mss. 1077: Newcombe Family Papers, unpublished notes, British Columbia Provincial Archives, Victoria.

Swanton, John Reed. 1905. *Contributions to the Ethnology of the Haida.* Leiden and New York: E. J. Brill and G. E. Stechert.

Wright, Robin K. 2001. *Northern Haida Master Carvers.* Seattle: University of Washington Press.

———. 2009. "Zacherias and the Chicago Settee: Connecting the Master to the Masterpiece." *American Indian Art Magazine* 1 (Winter): 68–75.

19

The Evolution of Tlingit Daggers

ASHLEY VERPLANK MCCLELLAND

The Tlingit tribe inhabits the coastal region of southeast Alaska and is known for its finely crafted daggers, which date from precontact times to the early twentieth century. The use and meaning of Tlingit daggers may have changed over time, but they remain an important symbol of pride and honor to the Tlingit people. Within the Tlingit community, daggers have functioned as implements of warfare, ceremonial status symbols, declarations of family heritage, and moneymakers for the tourist trade. A survey of these objects and their history makes it possible to chart the effects of contact and trade on the construction of daggers and to assign a relative date. The styles and materials utilized by Tlingit dagger makers over a long period have been catalogued using formal analysis and provide a more complete understanding of their evolution. Combining this stylistic evidence with published historical records and Tlingit oral histories allows the documentation of cultural and temporal reasons for changes in both form and function. This paper examines daggers from both a chronological and contextual framework to clearly define their physical and functional evolution.

The majority of daggers can be placed within three progressive categories: double-bladed, hafted-pommel, and made-for-sale.[1] Through a stylistic analysis of blades, guards, hilts, and pommels, these daggers have been categorized and a tentative timeline for their development has been created. Aspects of the dagger that are fundamental to any analysis are the blade, guard, hilt, and pommel (see figure 19.1). The blade can come in a variety of shapes and materials, but this paper will only focus on copper, iron, and steel. Guards may be made of copper, leather, horn, ivory, baleen, wood or iron. Their main function is to provide a protective barrier for the hand between the top of the blade and the bottom of the hilt. Double-bladed examples feature an upper and lower guard. The hilt is the area where the user places his hand,

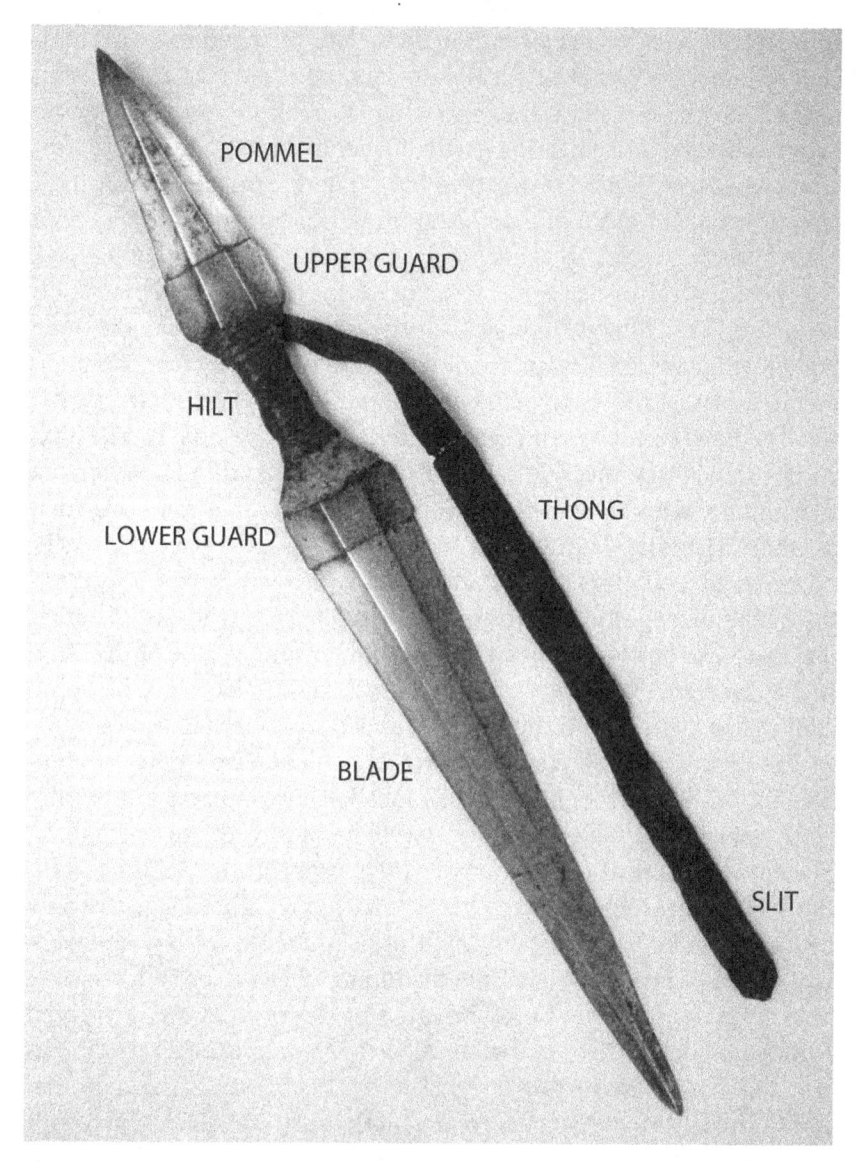

Fig. 19.1 Dagger vocabulary. Courtesy of the National Museum of Natural History, catalog no. E9288.

just above the blade. The pommel is the extension above the hilt and may be wood, horn, ivory, bone, baleen, copper, iron, or brass.

An important element of daggers used for warfare is the thong, a long piece of leather or hide that extends from the upper back of the hilt. Many daggers have not retained their original hilt wrapping, yet

The Evolution of Tlingit Daggers   395

those that are intact show that the thong was attached in a standardized method. Thongs are typically present only on daggers utilized in battle. They have a slit at the end for the warrior to insert his middle finger and wrap the remaining length of leather around his wrist (Beresford 1789, 188). Some daggers also have a hand strap, a wide strip of leather attached at the top and bottom of the hilt providing an area under which the user slips his hand.

When prefabricated blades were used, more effort was placed on designing the non-metal pommel, which would be hafted onto the trade blade. "Hafting" is the term used to describe the attachment of a pommel to a blade. This change in construction allowed artists to expand their pommel creativity and carve materials such as wood, bone, ivory, and horn. Hafting involves the tang of the blade, a thin metal tongue that extends from the top of the blade, and the pommel material, such as wood. The hilt material is often an extension of the pommel, reaching down to create the guards. A hafted pommel will have a bifurcated leg, with the tang slipped between and wrapped with hide, or the pommel can have one leg that extends down to cover one side of the tang. In this case, a separate slat of pommel material is placed on the opposite side of the tang and the hilt is wrapped with cloth or hide.

One of the oldest styles of Tlingit daggers assessed here, double-bladed, is the most technically advanced. These daggers are usually composed of one piece of metal and were hand-forged (see figure 19.2). The dates of fabrication for this style range from precontact times until the mid-nineteenth century. Next came hafted-pommel daggers, which became popular after contact in the late-eighteenth century and were continuously produced until the beginning of the twentieth century. This style typically used prefabricated blades or blades hand-forged from commercial files. These blades were then connected to Tlingit-made pommels (see figure 19.3). The final category is the nonfunctional, made-for-sale daggers created at the very end of the nineteenth century and the early twentieth century. The majority of these third phase daggers were created as objects for sale during Alaska's booming tourist industry. They were typically constructed from sheet copper and embellished with traditional Tlingit decorative materials such as abalone, hair, and fur (see figure 19.4).

Tlingit oral histories verify the ancient discovery of copper and iron and the function of these materials within the Tlingit community. Archaeological data allows scholars to assign possible dates for

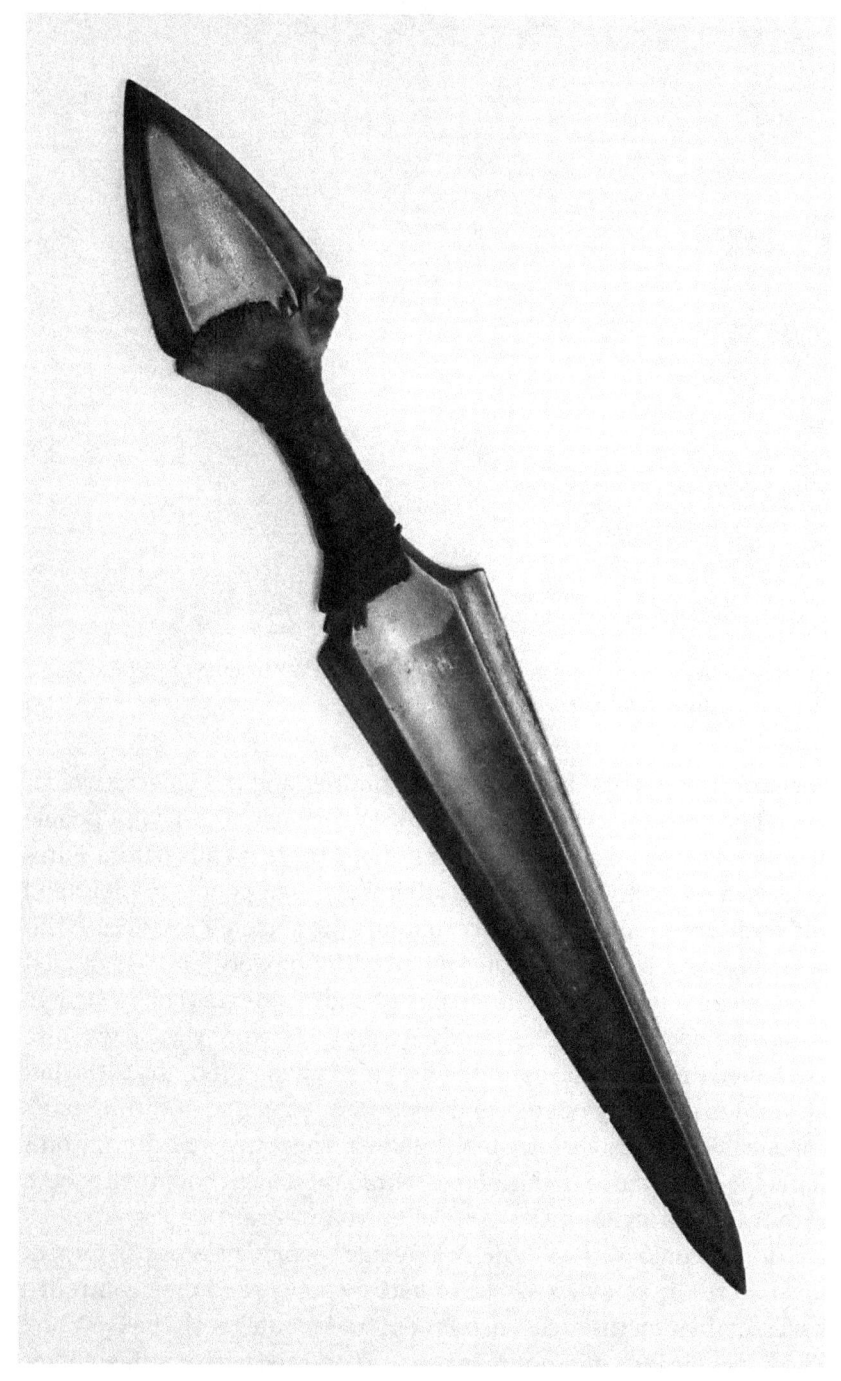

Fig. 19.2 Double-bladed dagger. Courtesy of the author.

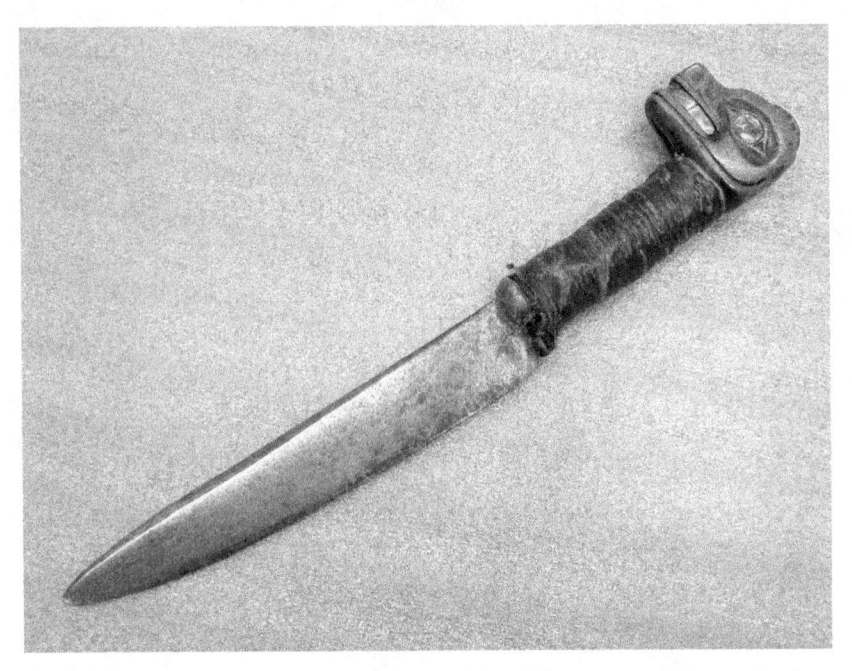

Fig. 19.3 Hafted-pommel dagger. Courtesy of the Burke Museum of Natural History and Culture, catalog no. 1209.

the entrance of metal into these communities and the longevity of its use. This data supports the oral histories that state the Tlingit people had the skill and knowledge to work both these metals before Euro-American contact. Oral traditions link the Tlingit people to their land and their ancestors, and they corroborate the ancient presence of daggers in Alaska. De Laguna notes that the Tlingit word for dagger, *djixanat'*, meant "something close to one's hand" (1964, 124) or, as George Ramos stated it, "something handy" (2007). The word *gwalaa* was also used, meaning "to strike with the fist" (de Laguna 1960, 109). The latter term is probably related to the warfare technique of hitting one's opponent in the head before stabbing them. These two traditional words show the importance of this object within the Tlingit community both before and during the early years of Euro-American contact.

Prior to contact, the Ahtna Athabascan people of Alaska's Copper River were the primary source of native copper, and they controlled its dissemination through a network of trade routes with the Eyak and Tlingit people (Swanton 1909, 154–65). The Ahtna tribe dominated this trade for hundreds of years, but the copper economy began to change

Fig. 19.4 Made-for-sale dagger. Courtesy of the National Museum of the American Indian, catalog no. 4630.

in the late eighteenth century. Ships began to trade commercial sheet copper on the coast, thus increasing its supply and lowering its value.

Many Tlingit oral narratives state that iron was first discovered on the shore, salvaged from a shipwreck. Another possibility is that iron was acquired by trade with other aboriginal populations. Drift iron, however, was described by Native Americans all along the Pacific coast, from California to the Aleutian Islands. The similarities of these stories lend authenticity to the shipwreck salvage claim, and the black stream current, Kuro Shiwo, from Japan frequently washed disabled Japanese vessels, known as junks, onto North America's coast (Brooks 1964, 7).

English explorer Captain Cook ventured into Alaskan waters in 1778, but the best description of Tlingit daggers comes from Jean-François de Galoup, comte de La Perouse. Sailing under the French flag, La Perouse arrived in Lituya Bay, Alaska, in 1786. In his journal he records his interactions with Northwest Coast tribes and clearly outlines their use of iron. "Of all our articles of trade, they appeared to have no great desire for any thing but iron. . . . They were not unacquainted with this metal. Every one had a dagger of it suspended from the neck, not unlike the criss of the Malays, except that the handle was different, being nothing more than an elongation of the blade, rounded, and without any edge" (La Perouse 1798, 340). This account confirms a long tradition of metal working knowledge among the Tlingit before this date, yet the daggers La Perouse described were clearly not the double-bladed type.

An English captain participating in the Pacific fur trade, George Dixon, reached Tlingit territory in 1787. At this time, iron was still the most desirable barter good. "[Iron] toes are the article of traffic held in the first estimation at this place; but they always refuse small ones, wanting them in general from eight to fourteen inches long" (Beresford 1789, 182). While in Port Mulgrave, Alaska, the Dixon expedition recorded the appearance of two copper daggers, one with a flattened bifurcated pommel, the other with a small pommel blade (Beresford 1968, 188). This drawing provides the first image of a double-bladed dagger and depicts the early presence of a single-raised median. These two daggers were collected by Dixon, but only this drawing remains.

An artist by the name of Suria visited Yakutat, Alaska, in 1791 with Malaspina's Spanish expedition and recorded images of the Tlingit people and their possessions. In one drawing, he portrays a well-built Tlingit man who appears to be wearing nothing more than a bearskin robe and a spruce root hat. In his hand, he grasps a dagger with a rounded

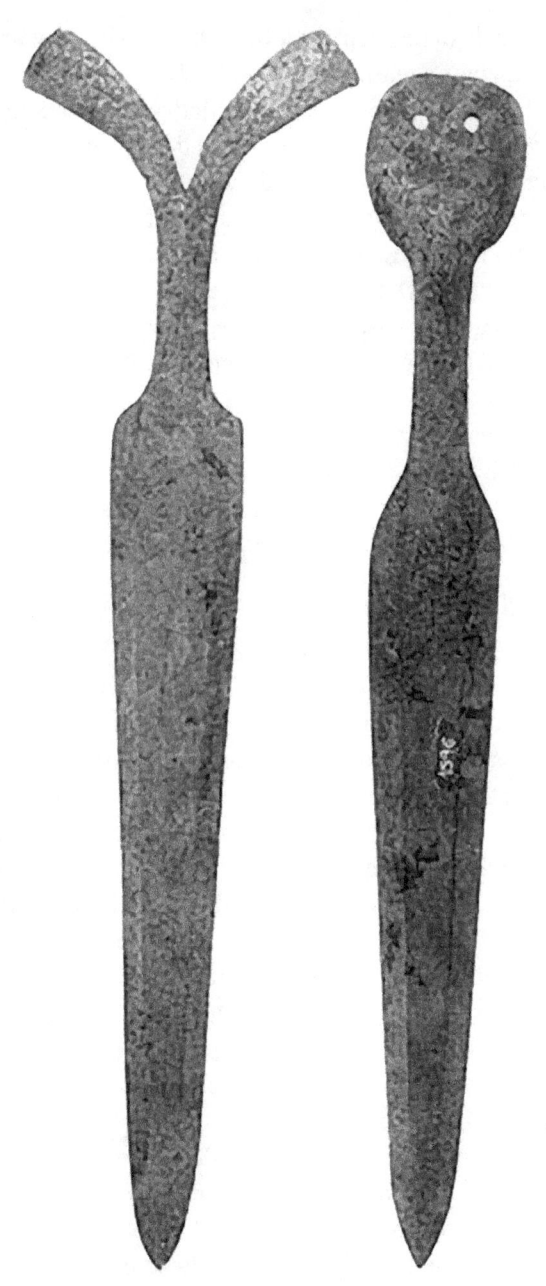

Fig. 19.5 Malaspina daggers, collected in 1791. Courtesy Museo de Americas.

pommel. Another drawing depicts a fully suited Tlingit warrior with a split pommel dagger sheathed at his side. Two daggers collected by Malaspina on this voyage, now housed in Madrid's Museo de America, are similar to this description (Emmons and de Laguna 1991, 326) (see figure 19.5). One pommel is round and depicts the face of a being, the eyes pierced through, while the other has a flattened bifurcated pommel. Both daggers have single-raised medians.

The physical form of the Tlingit dagger has changed many times during its existence, and there is a distinct progression of styles that can be documented before and after contact. The Dixon and Malaspina examples appear to be all one piece and have simple pommel designs. Despite this simplicity, the metal work is still advanced. The two iron daggers collected by Malaspina during his 1791 expedition provide further evidence that there were already multiple styles of Tlingit daggers in existence in the late eighteenth century (Niblack 1888, 283).

Double-bladed Daggers

The term "double-bladed" refers to the pommel of a dagger, which forms a smaller blade above the hilt to complement the longer blade below. Numerous examples of double-bladed daggers exist, which allows a thorough survey of forms and construction techniques. These daggers were seldom constructed using prefabricated blades, which are a common feature on the hafted-pommel style. Instead, they were hand-forged by masterful Tlingit metalsmiths. Encountering a double-bladed dagger that is not hand-forged should immediately raise questions about its authenticity.

The following information concerning the form of double-bladed daggers is based on a group of eighty-eight that were personally inspected by the author. Despite the variety of pommel imagery on double-bladed daggers, the forms of hand-forged blades fall into three stylistic categories. The first and most popular blade style has a wide, raised-line down the central median (see figure 19.6). These blades are usually well crafted, and the median line carries on from tip to tip, tapering at either end. The second major blade style has two slender raised ribs running down the blade (see figure 19.7). These lines flank a concave channel that moves down the center of the blade and tapers at the tip. These lines create three wide concave areas and are technically difficult to fabricate. On some examples, these lines appear on both faces of the blade and attest to the skill of these early metal workers. The third and

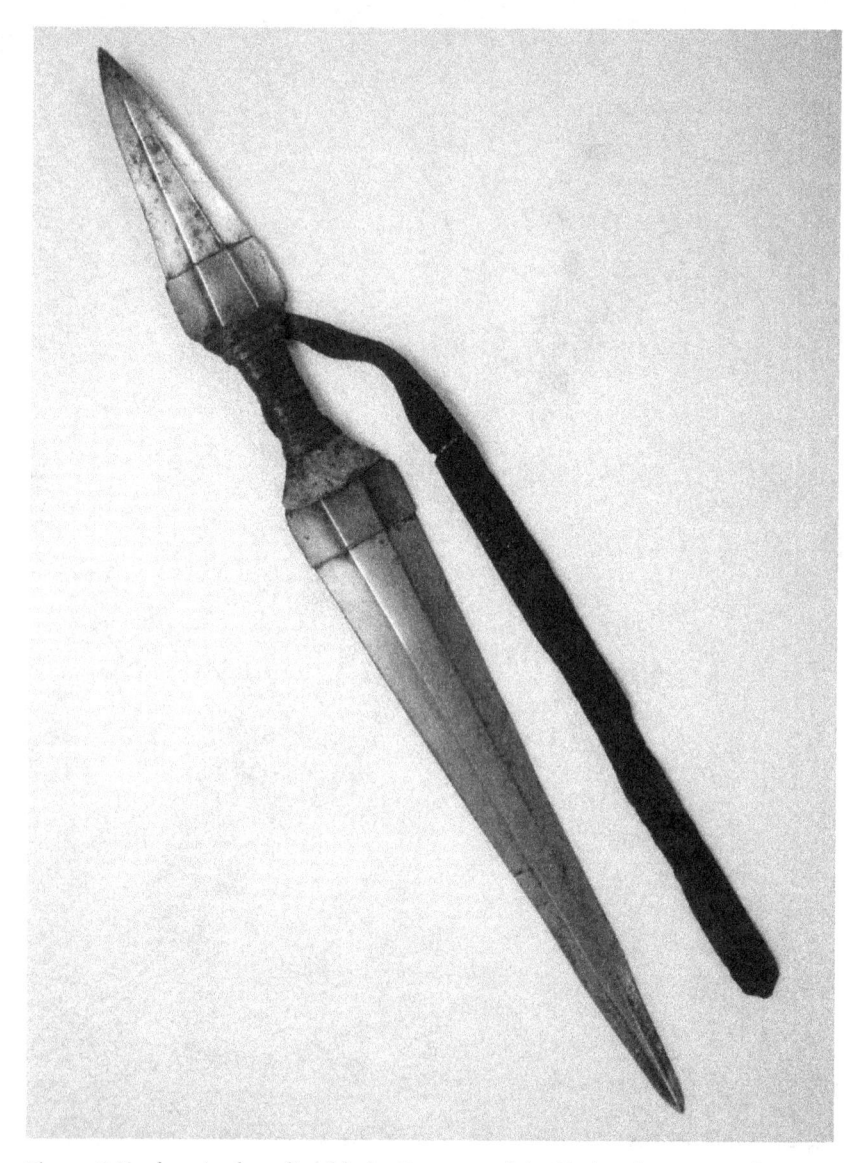

Fig. 19.6 Single-raised-median blade. Courtesy of the National Museum of Natural History, catalog no. E9288.

most sophisticated style contains up to six raised lines that run down the blade, parallel to each other at the top and converging to form one raised median line toward the tip (see figure 19.8). Between these thin lines are deep, narrow concave areas commonly referred to as flutes or fullers. These channels run the length of the blade, narrowing as they go.

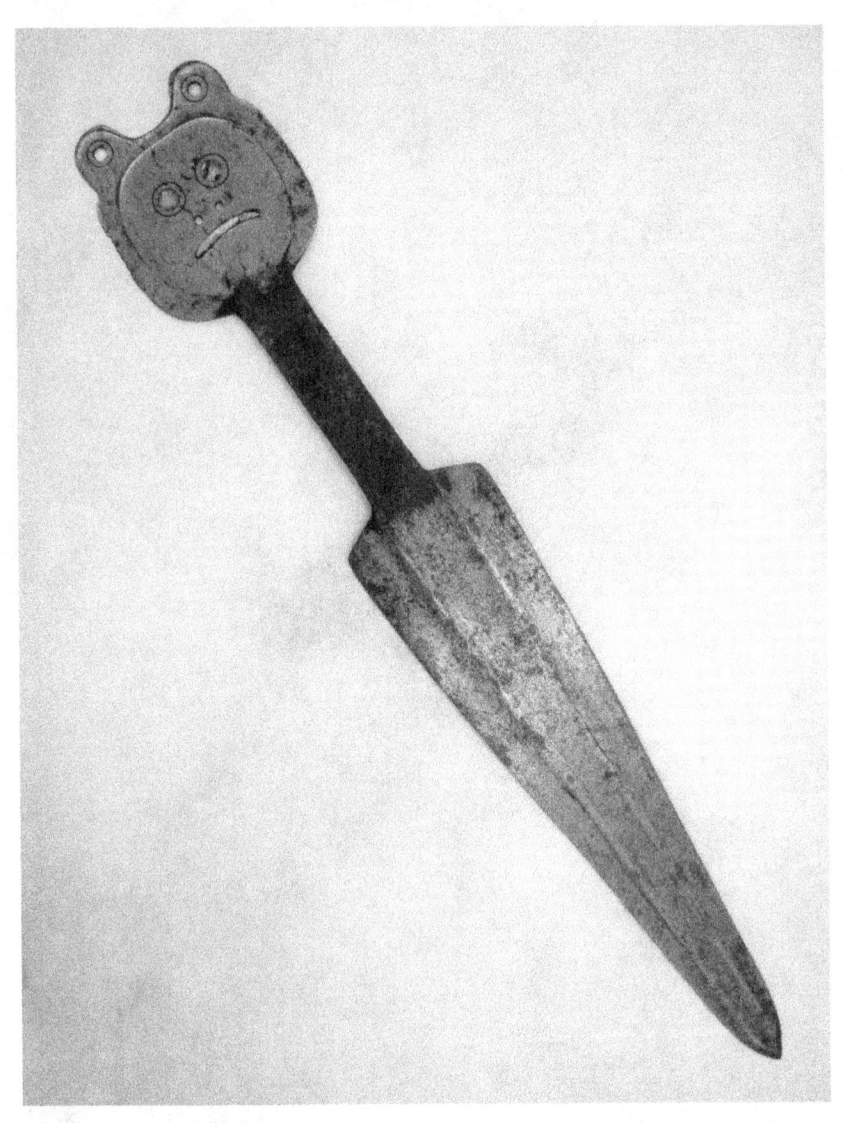

Fig. 19.7 Double-raised-line blade. Courtesy of the National Museum of the American Indian, catalog no. 14260.

Practically every double-bladed dagger had some type of median shift on the front, and this medial portion is an essential piece in identifying an authentic Tlingit double-bladed dagger. Another important signifier can be found on the reverse side of the blade. If a blade is not worked on both sides, then its back is gracefully concave, sloping to the sharpened edges.

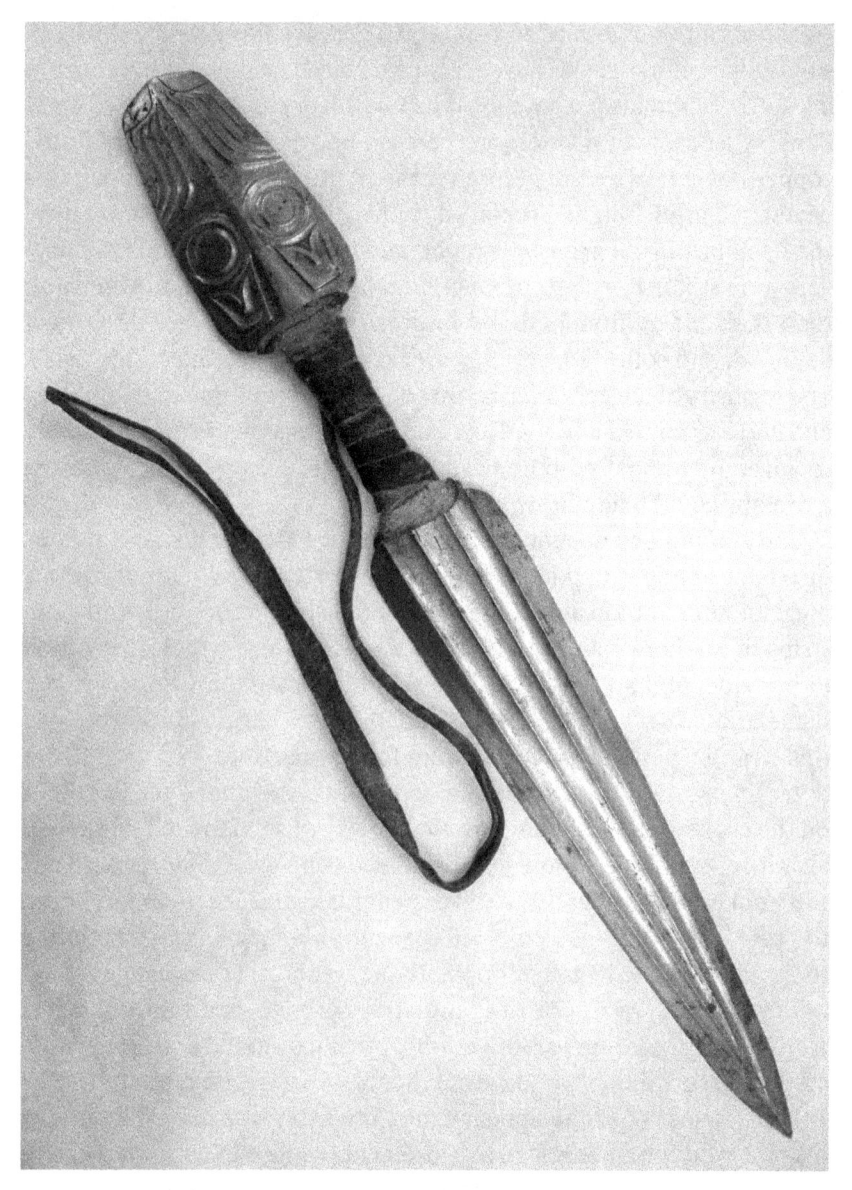

Fig. 19.8 Fluted blade. Courtesy of the National Museum of the American Indian, catalog no. 12596.

Almost all double-bladed copper daggers were constructed from a single piece of metal and have the single-raised median with a concave back. There are also examples of copper blades with two raised lines flanking a concave channel, yet there are no known examples of fluted copper daggers. This suggests that the multiple-flute blade style was developed after iron had replaced copper. The Tlingit people realized the benefits of iron prior to contact, and although copper bladed daggers were still in use, their production ceased and stronger iron versions took their place. Rounded and bifurcated pommels were described, depicted, and collected, yet they are not common in collections today. The majority of daggers in museum collections are of the double-bladed and hafted-pommel variety. The double-bladed style was probably only replaced by the hafted-pommel style due to the convenience of using a prefabricated blade for the latter.

Early one-piece dagger examples do not have permanent guards; instead, the upper and lower guards are created by wrapping a thick piece of animal hide around the hilt and lashing it in place with thin strips of leather or sinew. The hide used was longer than the hilt on either side, and so it covered the shoulders of the lower and upper blade and protected the warrior's hand. Many daggers have retained this wrapping and provide examples for comparison.

As time passed, both iron and copper became abundant materials on the coast. Due to this and the availability of steel tools, Tlingit metalsmiths began to get more creative and daring with their forms. They were not only piercing the metal but engraving it. The pommels began to grow larger and take on more recognizable forms. Images relating to the owner's life began to populate the weapon. These images could relate to crests, oral histories, ancestral heritage, and more. Daggers were given great names, inlaid with precious shells, and some were stored in special bentwood cases when they were not in use.

Soon copper began to appear again, not as a blade material but as a decorative flourish. Metal artists used copper and brass as decorative highlights and began to apply copper over the hilt, creating permanent guards. At times these guards were sculptural, engraved, and inlaid. Some were fluted to match the dagger blade, and others were simple and plain, merely following the single-raised median of the blade. Despite the visual representations, the overall effect of placing shiny copper flat against steel creates a striking appearance.

To achieve this, most Tlingit metalsmiths had a standard copper guard application process. It involved two pieces of appropriately shaped copper, usually sheet copper acquired through trade, that were placed over the hilt and shoulders of the blades. The copper was first placed on the back of the dagger, then the front. The edges of the front piece were then folded over the back and hammered flat. In rare cases, the copper guards were constructed from one sheet of copper that was wrapped around the hilt and shoulders. This single edge was then folded over one side on the back and finished in the same manner as above.

The technical pinnacle of Tlingit metalsmithing appears to have occurred in the early nineteenth century. This is most likely the period when Tlingit metalsmiths began to forge highly sophisticated one-piece steel daggers. The blades of these daggers were elegantly fluted, so as to create a jagged and deadly wound. The pommel displayed wealth materials and clan crests. Status was an integral part of Northwest Coast society, so one can infer that the more elaborate and sophisticated the dagger, the higher the status of its owner. The symmetry and sleekness of these flutes testify to the patience and skill of the creator. The pommel blades of these daggers vary in their detail and workmanship. Some are merely fluted with copper guards, while others show the elaborate and sculptural formline crest art tradition (see figure 19.9). In the late eighteenth century, fur traders also brought large amounts of firearms and ammunition to the coast. The introduction of the musket was the beginning of the end for warfare daggers. They were no longer considered the most valuable asset to warriors during battle, and the number of hand-forged double-bladed iron daggers began to decrease.

Hafted-pommel Daggers

The daggers discussed in this section are not made of one piece of metal or one type of material. Instead, they are two parts hafted together to make a whole. Typically it is a Tlingit carved pommel married to a prefabricated trade-blade or a Native-forged blade from a file (see figure 19.10). These daggers visually declared a man's clan affiliation or alluded to his elevated status. The use and creation of hafted-pommel daggers overlaps with that of the double-bladed style, and so they also served as warfare daggers. These two types were being used for battle simultaneously after trade commenced, but eventually the hafted-pommel style became more popular and numerous among Tlingit men.

The large number of hafted-pommel daggers in museum collections reflects the quickness of their construction. This survey involved an

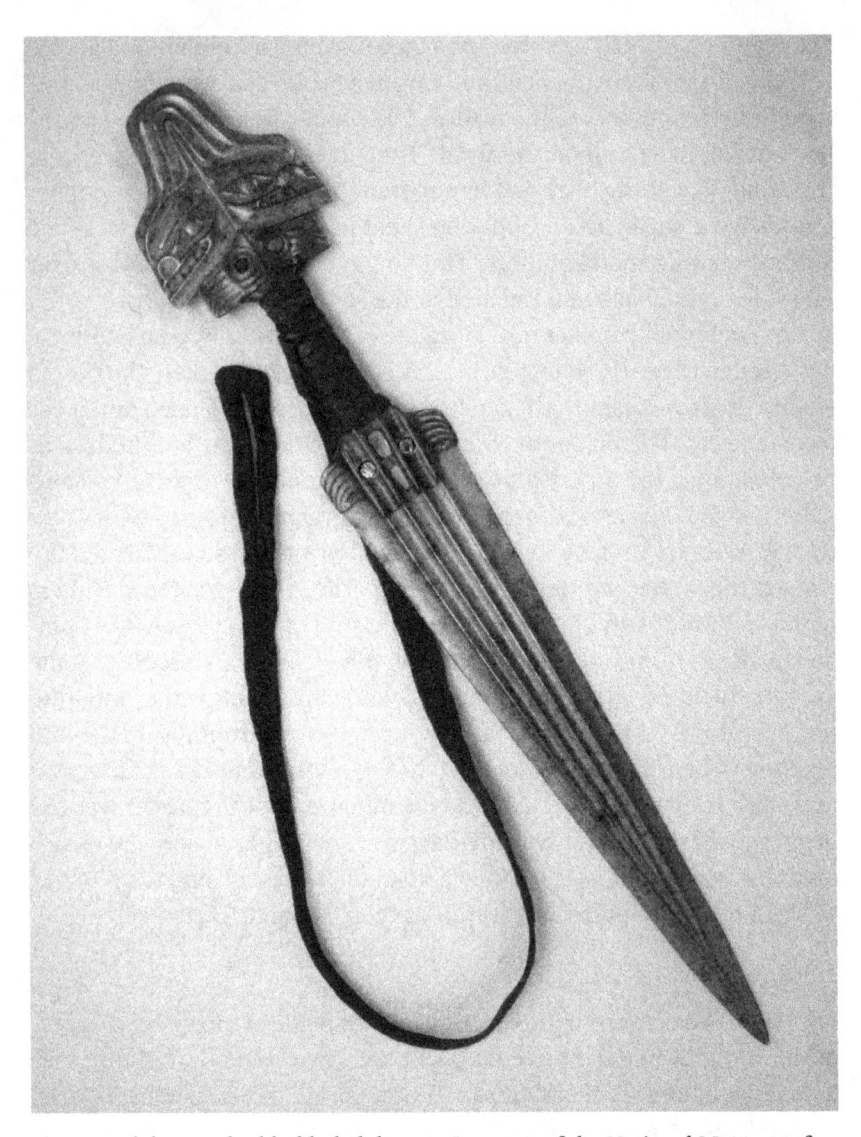

Fig. 19.9 Elaborate double-bladed dagger. Courtesy of the National Museum of Natural History, catalog no. E221184.

inspection of 117 hafted-pommel daggers. Many of the blades were Native-forged from steel files, which still required metalworking skill and knowledge, but some utilized Western-forged blades that simply required hafting. The range of quality and design on this style varies widely, and it is known that some hafted-pommel daggers were far more valuable than others.

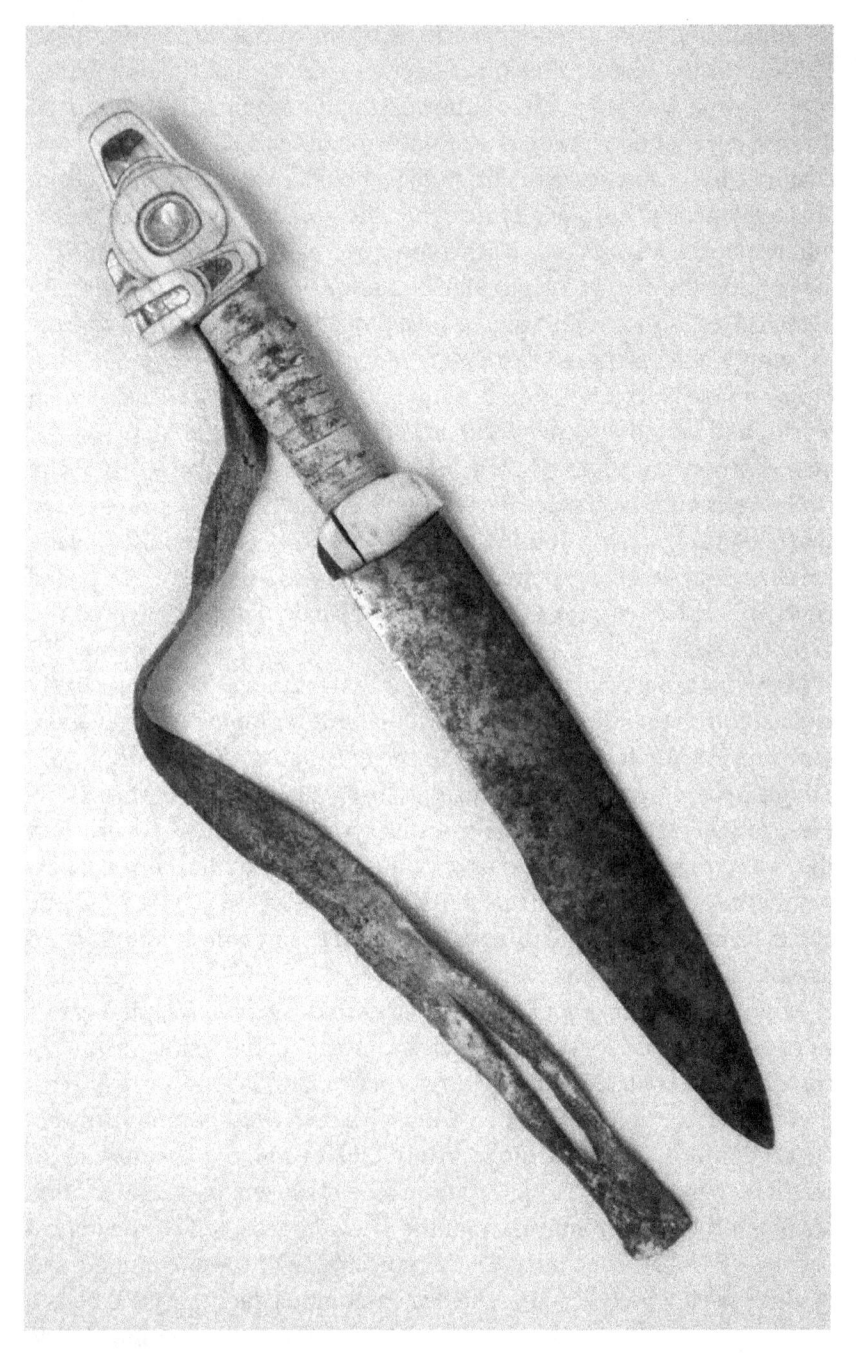

Fig. 19.10 Hafted-pommel dagger. Courtesy of the National Museum of Natural History, catalog no. E20643.

Contact and trade created an artistic boom on the Northwest Coast. This was also a pivotal time for daggers. By the turn of the nineteenth century, iron was abundant on the coast and less valuable. This made it more accessible to those not of noble birth, and daggers were now available to the masses. Numerous dagger blades were hammered from old steel files and are visually recognizable because of the hatch marks that remain. Many of these Native-modified blades were made of steel and mimic the two most popular blade forms found on the double-bladed style, either with a single-raised median or two-raised-lines.

Many blades acquired through contact can be differentiated from Tlingit-made blades. They are usually flat on both sides, with no hatch marks, and are not completely sharpened on both edges. Many Tlingit men sharpen the edges of their bartered knives into daggers and the evidence is clearly visible. Early double-bladed examples reveal two sharpened edges that continue up to the guard, while a modified blade will have one fully sharpened edge and a second partially sharpened edge. It is extremely rare to see a Tlingit-made blade hammered flat on both sides.

Many hafted-pommel daggers do not have thongs. This most likely means that they either lost their original hilt wrappings or they were never meant for the battlefield. By the early nineteenth century, the Tlingit people had long recognized the superiority of firearms. However, the dagger's function as a status symbol remained strong, and they were proudly displayed as *at.oow* at potlatches and other prestigious events. This function allowed daggers to take on a more symbolic and ceremonial role, one that strengthened their owner's identity and prestige (see figure 19.11).

At the turn of the twentieth century, hafted-pommel Tlingit daggers were being created for sale. Often these latter versions feature a quickly carved wooden pommel hafted onto a nonfunctional copper blade or a prefabricated iron trade-blade. Many of these hafted-pommel daggers do not conform to the old standards of fabrication, but their structure is still recognizable as Tlingit. At times the blade will feature Victorian scroll motifs or other imagery that the Tlingit creator felt would appeal to the non-Native consumer. The sophistication of these pommels and blades varied widely, making the hafted-pommel dagger style the easiest to replicate, fake, or misattribute. Although the hafted-pommel style is less standardized, there are still a number of construction techniques and design elements that can aid in discerning the origin of a specific

Fig. 19.11 Gusht'eiheen and Keet Gwalaa. This double-headed Killer Whale dagger was used in ceremonies by Gusht'eiheen in the late nineteenth century. Courtesy of Alaska State Library, ASL-P1-022.

dagger. Dagger makers who are not intimately acquainted with the northern Northwest Coast style of carving will usually make numerous mistakes in their attempt to replicate it.

Hafted-pommel daggers allowed carvers the freedom to express themselves and possibly make some money. Many hafted-pommel daggers were crafted for use and for sale in the late nineteenth century, but their

The Evolution of Tlingit Daggers 411

function within Tlingit society had changed. Potlatches were being suppressed, and many traditional Tlingit objects began to disappear from everyday life. By the turn of the twentieth century, both colonists and tourists populated the northern Northwest Coast, expanding the market for "Indian curios." Regular steamship cruises through Alaska's Inside Passage created a completely new market for daggers, and Tlingit artisans took the initiative.

Made-for-sale Daggers

Made-for-sale daggers were created between the late nineteenth and early twentieth centuries. At this time, daggers were no longer used as weapons, and large iron daggers were no longer being hand-forged. The production of daggers spiked again, only now the majority of blades were copper, not iron (see figure 19.12). This cyclical use of copper confirms that these later daggers were not meant for battle. The design and construction of some daggers were more elegant than others, yet Tlingit copper work executed at this time has recognizable features. Many of these copper daggers share a similarity with their false patinas, large wooden guards and two-piece blades. Other types of daggers produced for sale at this time also display extravagant details that distinguish them as nonfunctional, and their collection dates link them to this made-for-sale period.

With this copper-bladed dagger style, aesthetics trumped strength, and these daggers were objects for display, not use. This survey inspected twenty-eight historic made-for-sale daggers. The majority of these daggers feature a copper blade with a single-raised median. Unlike eighteenth-century single-raised blades, these blades are not one piece. The slender ribs were created separately and riveted onto the blade. The dagger maker worked hard to conceal the copper rivets, and typically the area around them shows signs of this. Other examples replicate the look of the traditional two-raised-line style, while others attempt to capture the sophistication of the fluted style. Despite the medial reference to historic blades, the artists were not actually creating the raised lines, just simulating the look.

Many of these copper blades have a flat back, while others overly accentuate the concave shape. Regardless, the blade maintains the same thickness from side to side as if it were cut from a sheet of copper, and the edges are rarely sharpened. These smiths were obviously aware of the standard Tlingit dagger styles and used shortcuts to copy

Fig. 19.12 Made-for-sale dagger. Courtesy of the National Museum of the American Indian, catalog no. 2872.

them. Also, the majority of made-for-sale daggers do not have thongs attached, which is another sign that they were not created as weapons.

These made-for-sale daggers were Native-made, but not all of the dealers who sold to collectors acknowledged that they were contemporary versions, and most displayed an artificially aged patina. Because they were created by Native American metalsmiths, they were and are authentic, yet some collectors thought they were buying a historic object. Dedicated collectors of Native American objects, such as George Gustav Heye, gave explicit directions to his agents to only collect old objects and avoid anything that was contemporary. "No Tourist Material" was Heye's mantra, yet he purchased some of these made-for-sale daggers (Lenz 2004, 86–105). There are variations within this made-for-sale style, but the majority use copper for the blade.

A large number of these daggers in museum collections were purchased from the dealer Bernard A. Whalen. Whalen split his time between Skagway and Los Angeles, but his store, Alaska Indian Curios, was based in California. This is where Heye purchased six of these copper daggers in 1904 (Lenz 2004, 91). Other known dealers at the time were P. E. Kern of Skagway, Alaska, Dr. Robert and Belle Simpson of Juneau, and Grace Nicholson of Pasadena, California. The specifics of each dealer's involvement are not fully known, but it is probable that they were aware of the deceit taking place.

These daggers were meant to look old. It is not known if their aged patinas were intended to deceive or to just make them more appealing to tourists. The investigative work that Emmons conducted in the late nineteenth century links these objects to a specific Californian curio dealer with ties to Alaska. Unfortunately, he does not list the dealer by name, but this dealer may be B. A. Whalen. He was the one dealer with consistent ties to Alaska and California and had sold at least five of these daggers. Emmons also verifies that the California dealer supplied the materials for the objects, making it unlikely that these pieces were made from native copper.

Most tourists, on the other hand, knew that they were buying a contemporary work and appreciated it for what it was: a souvenir of their tour through Alaska's rugged and wild Inside Passage. The Tlingit people were well known for their fierce warfare tactics and their well-crafted daggers. The large, bold pommels of the made-for-sale copper daggers appear to exaggerate the otherness of the Tlingit people, which by Victorian standards made the curios more appealing.

The majority of pommels created during this time represent a grizzly bear.[2] What other animal is more closely associated with the last frontier than this fierce creature? This visual association with the untamed wilderness of Alaska most likely contributed to the success of this imagery. Numerous bear pommel daggers were carved from sheep horn and covered with real fur. Their features were given an extra dazzle with abalone inlay and riveted copper highlights. Some examples have formline elements carved in the ears. Other pommels were crafted from two pieces of sheet copper riveted together, giving them a bulbous appearance. These forms were then engraved with formline design and inlaid with abalone. The "primitive-looking" pommels were then attached to large copper blades. Tourists were not looking for an ancient ethnographic specimen; they were looking for something to remind them of their adventure in an exotic locale.

There were, however, multiple styles of copper Tlingit daggers being sold along the Inside Passage. It is likely that some of these daggers are old copper double-bladed daggers that have been engraved or embellished to make them more attractive to Western buyers. The quality and design of these engraved daggers are not uniform, and there does not seem to be a specific dealer who sold them in large quantities. Some have wonderful formline designs on them and others have designs with no hint of traditional formline. They are crafted in the classic manner, with the typical median shift and the concave back, which suggests these daggers were forged much earlier and embellished later.

Many daggers have been separated from their communities and historical context. A large number have lost their given names and powerful oral histories, yet they still have valuable information to share. When Tlingit daggers are viewed together with their contextual history, the complexity of their role within Tlingit society is revealed. They are not merely weapons; they are emblems of strong and proud Tlingit warriors. Each dagger was capable of visually distinguishing its owner and his rank, representing status in a culture whose identity was enmeshed with hierarchical social levels and constant warfare. These daggers convey evidence of a sophisticated metal working tradition that allowed room for innovation and change in response to Tlingit sociocultural changes during the eighteenth and nineteenth centuries. Without understanding the traditional role of daggers within Tlingit society, one cannot truly understand their significance today.

NOTES

1. The main difference between daggers and knives is that daggers have two sharpened edges, while a knife generally has only one. Daggers are for stabbing or thrusting, and knives are for cutting. Of course, daggers were used to cut, but their most effective function in warfare was to create a stab wound that would not easily heal. After contact, Tlingit metalsmiths often modified prefabricated knife blades to give them the customary two edges instead of one, or they would take a file and hand-forge it to their own standards.
2. For more detailed information on this subject, see Verplank (2008).

REFERENCES

Beresford, William. 1789. *Voyage Round the World; but more particularly to the North-West of America: Performed in 1785, 1786, 1787, and 1788, in the King George and Queen Charlotte, Captains Portlock and Dixon.* London: George Goulding.

Brooks, Charles Wolcott. 1964. *Japanese Wrecks Stranded and Picked Up Adrift in the North Pacific Ocean.* Fairfield: Ye Galleon Press.

de Laguna, Frederica. 1960. *The Story of a Tlingit Community.* Washington DC: Smithsonian Institution Press.

———. 1964. *Archeology of the Yakutat Bay Area, Alaska.* Washington DC: Smithsonian Institution Press.

Emmons, George T. 1896. AMNH accession record for 1896-24.

———. 1991. *The Tlingit Indians.* Ed. Frederica de Laguna. Seattle: University of Washington.

La Perouse, Jean F. G. 1798. *A Voyage Round the World Performed in the Years 1785, 1786, 1878 and 1788.* London: J. Johnson.

Lenz, Mary Jane. 2004. "No Tourist Material: George Heye & His Golden Rule." *American Indian Art Magazine*, Autumn, 86–105.

Niblack, Albert P. 1888. *The Coast Indians of Southern Alaska and Northern British Columbia.* Washington DC: Smithsonian Institution Press.

Ramos, George. 2007. "Tlingit Warfare." Presentation at Sharing Our Knowledge: Tlingit, Haida and Tsimshian Clan Conference, Sitka, Alaska, March.

Shotridge, Louis. 1920. *The Ghost of Courageous Adventurer.* Shotridge Manuscripts, container 1. University Museum Archives, University of Pennsylvania, Philadelphia.

Swanton, John R. 1909. *Tlingit Myths and Texts.* Washington DC: Government Printing Office.

Verplank, Ashley. 2008. "The Evolution of Tlingit Daggers: Form Follows Function." Master's thesis, Art History, University of Washington.

20

Tourists and Collectors

The New Market for Tlingit and Haida Jewelry at the Turn of the Century

KATHRYN BUNN-MARCUSE

Like other emblematic Northwest Coast artworks (totem poles, crest art), the history of Northwest Coast jewelry has been described in terms of a nineteenth-century "golden age," followed by an early twentieth-century "decline" and a subsequent renaissance by a few key artists. By emphasizing examples of cultural deterioration, this simplistic narrative profoundly undermines the tangible legacy of cultural endurance. The early twentieth century, often characterized as "the dark years" in Northwest Coast history, was ignored for many years in Northwest Coast art historical accounts, which leaped from the late nineteenth century to the late twentieth century—from Charles Edenshaw directly to Bill Reid. This lacuna created a "signification gap" that "came to be seen as a period of 'decline and loss'—the premise for the recovery of earlier, more 'authentic' art forms" as part of the Northwest Coast renaissance led by Reid and others in the 1960s (Crosby 2004, 119).

This chapter focuses on the jewelry-making practices of many Tlingit and Haida artists in Alaska and northern British Columbia from the 1880s to the 1940s. I posit that northern Northwest Coast art production was *not* in substantial decline at the beginning of the twentieth century and that it was instead turning to new markets for patronage. While a change in aesthetics and techniques did occur, the production of artworks was still a critical artistic pursuit. Evidence from the tourist economy in Alaska and northern British Columbia, specifically Haida and Tlingit jewelry production, provides one example of continued artistic production. Discrepancies between anthropological reports and those of tourists, travelers, and Indian agents serve to illustrate the biases of contemporary anthropologists who—consciously or otherwise—discounted jewelry production for at least two reasons: (1) they viewed jewelry's status as an "acculturated," rather than "traditional," art form, and (2) they saw it as a manufactured tourist commodity—each of which made it seem "inauthentic." The beliefs and biases of the anthropologists and professional collectors contrast sharply with the reality of the market economy during the first decades of Alaskan tourist travel. Artists of the time were capitalizing on their indigenous identity as a key marketing technique in a field beginning to be pressured by mass-made (but indigenously inspired) souvenirs. Their techniques for producing and marketing indigenous work also serve to underscore the lively trade in Native-made jewelry, in contrast to apparently false anthropological reports on the dearth of artistic production.

Jewelry—specifically silver and gold bracelets—has been a symbol of clan and personal identity on the Northwest Coast for generations even though it has rarely been the subject of anthropological inquiry. Jewelry has been a key component in public displays of identity and in personal constructions of identity and social relations. Bracelets can signify gender, rank, and status in ceremonial and other contexts. Used as personal adornment and potlatch payment, jewelry enhances the status of its owner and expresses both individual and clan identity (Bunn-Marcuse 2007). Like basketry, jewelry was a thriving art form at the turn of the century, bringing greatly needed income to artists and their families as well as serving ongoing cultural functions and values. The importance of these forms to artistic and cultural endurance during difficult decades of colonial rule and economic disenfranchisement has been overlooked.

The Myth of a "Golden Age" in Decline

From the 1880s clear through to the 1980s, anthropologists and art historians frequently wrote that Northwest Coast art lost its way at the end of the nineteenth century. In 1957, ethnologist and folklorist Marius Barbeau wrote that the "inventiveness and progress [of Haida artists] developed from 1820 onwards reached a peak only during the last four decades of that century," implying an inevitable decline (Barbeau 1957, 1).

It has been said that there were only a handful of artists who carried on the knowledge of earlier generations. Bill Reid called the nineteenth century "the time of the greatest flowering of the art" (Duff et al. 1967). Consistent with this story of a "golden age," it is also regularly assumed that the number of artists dwindled, leaving only Edenshaw to pass the art tradition to Charlie Gladstone and then to Bill Reid. Doris Shadbolt bemoaned that even Charles Edenshaw—heralded as the great nineteenth-century Haida master—went "from creating great ceremonial art to works for curio trade" (Shadbolt 2004, 31).

The impression that art-making in general and jewelry production in particular declined after the nineteenth century is widely held and long-standing. Even turn-of-the-century sources underestimated the numbers of working silversmiths. As early as 1882, U.S. Navy lieutenant George T. Emmons reported there were only four silversmiths in Alaska (Emmons 1991, 189). However, contemporary evidence shows that Emmons misjudged the number of silversmiths in Alaska. (Emmons, while not an academically trained anthropologist, worked for a number of East Coast museums, collecting both objects and ethnographies and ultimately publishing a number of reports on the Tlingit. His work was directed by Franz Boas, F. W. Putnam, Frederick Douglas, and other museum anthropologists.) Emmons's misunderstanding demonstrates typical anthropological assumptions of the time, which were biased against art made for the tourist trade.

Indeed, anthropologists and collectors have always complained of the limited availability of "good" (i.e., old) material; the late nineteenth and early twentieth century on the Northwest Coast was no exception. Contemporary writings described a proliferation of jewelry and other arts on the Northwest Coast, but anthropologists and collectors continually deprecated then-current works. In 1899 Boas declared that "it is rather difficult nowadays to obtain good works of art of these Indians [Kwakiutl]. During my last few trips I have hardly seen any thing that can compare with the good old carvings" (Jacknis 2002, 379). Fifteen years later, Thomas Deasy, Indian agent on the Queen Charlotte Islands, wrote that it was "very difficult" to obtain the bracelets he was seeking and that "few Indians are doing that kind of work, now" (Deasy 1914, October 19).

He later wrote that

> the Indians are giving up this kind of work, and it was difficult to have one of them make [a pair]. They are each made from one dollar piece, of American money, and I had the Indian make them with the distinct Haida characters of years ago. (Deasy 1914, November 15)

Deasy's second letter highlights the common perception that the art of the moment is never as qualitatively pleasing as older art. His request for bracelets made "with the distinct Haida characters of years ago" suggests that this was an older form, no longer in practice, but ironically he overlooked the fact that the contemporary artist he commissioned was fully able to produce the supposedly classical aesthetic forms.

Well into the twentieth century, museum collectors continued to desire older material and to discount current productions. By the 1930s, there may well have been fewer silversmiths at work—and even fewer who could practice the art full-time. Nonetheless it was still possible to buy newly made bracelets, yet collectors snubbed them.

A series of letters to and from Emmons clearly demonstrate this bias in favor of older works. In 1937 Edward A. Hill-Trout wrote to Emmons, "About the pipes and bracelets I could have them made, but you wouldn't want that. However, I'll look around for old ones." The following month his list of available items included "modern silver bracelets and rings" (Newcombe 1890s–1930s, A-01769, vol. 60, folder 1). In 1941 Emmons wrote to Douglas at the Denver Art Museum, "You asked me about old bracelets, I have not been able to get but two from natives through fifteen or more years." A further note from Emmons suggests that he is looking for older bracelets and avoiding new ones that could be had: "The . . . bracelets are native made and have come from old families of the past or older generations and have been put away for years. I have but one from an Indian. They have none except new ones" (Emmons 1932–1944, November 3, 1941).

These letters from collectors in the field reflect the biases of museum professionals who held the purse strings and set the standards for what would be purchased. Biases against the abilities of contemporary artists can be seen throughout these correspondences. Emmons's letters suggest that while he was aware that new bracelets were still being made in the 1940s, he deemed them to be unworthy of collecting. "Now the old bracelets have gone I have only gotten one from a native for ten or more years. Those made by them today are newer often in scroll work" (Emmons 1932–1944, May 11, 1941). Barbeau concurred, averring that new bracelets available for purchase were inferior. "In any case, hardly any pieces are left for purchase now. *Those made nowadays are not worth a collector's attention.* There are plenty of them for sale in Prince Rupert" (Barbeau 1916–1954, 252.1). Yet Barbeau's assessment contrasts sharply with evidence that quality artworks were readily available for sale. The fact is that museum collectors were biased against market-bound pieces that eluded their preconceived standards of "authenticity."

Tourists saw that which anthropologists did not. Numerous contemporary tourist accounts document art-making in both Alaska and Haida Gwaii (Anonymous 1885; Duncan 1889; Emmons 1991, 190–91; Schwatka 1900; Scidmore 1885, 129, 179–80). Raibmon notes,

> High-minded disparagement of tourist arts reflected very little Aboriginal perspective. For Tlingit vendors and artists, tourists were a less discerning and far larger market than professional collectors, who preferred old pieces manufactured for Aboriginal use than for sale to Whites. (2005, 151)

The Flourishing Jewelry Trade

Up and down the Northwest Coast, all cultural groups were well versed in trade from time immemorial. In Alaska and British Columbia, indigenous artists recognized that the new tourist market offered a great trade opportunity, with many tourists arriving at designated ports at scheduled times. There was a thriving art industry in the Queen Charlottes in 1882, where indigenous artists were "noted for their carvings both in slate and wood, and for the manufacture of silver ornaments, bracelets and ear rings" and may have realized as much as $600 to $700 per year from art sales (O'Reilly 1882, 108–9). Travelers to the coast recorded that every village had its own silversmith, and bracelets and rings were to be had at almost every port-of-call. At least one traveler found a silversmith everywhere she stopped, including Tongass, Wrangell, Howkan, Kasaan, Hoonah, Metlakatla, and Sitka (Scidmore 1885). Indeed the Sitka newspaper, the *Alaskan*, reported: "Every village can boast of several carvers who make their living chiefly by making silver jewelry" (Anonymous 1885).

In fact, the Alaskan economy depended heavily on tourism and especially on the production of Alaska Native curios. The 1890 census report estimated that the town of Sitka was supported by the trade of Sitka and Yakutat natives. "The native 'curios' are sold to the many tourists who visit southeast Alaska during the summer" (Boursin 1893). In southeast Alaska tourism grew dramatically throughout the late 1880s. Between 1885 and 1890, the Pacific Coast Steamship Company sold 25,048 tickets for their Alaskan tours, increasing from 1,600 the first season to over 5,000 in later years. The federal government estimated that each tourist spent between $50 and $100 on curios, adding up to between $1.25 and $2.5 million over those six years (United States 1893, 250–51).[1]

The curio trade was so vast that the Portland newspaper, the *Oregonian*, insisted that the enormous quantities of jewelry for sale by local Indians were in fact manufactured in San Francisco, implying that the artists who sold dozens of bracelets to each steamer could never have made all their own wares. The *Oregonian* claimed: "Visitors to Alaska often invest in silver jewelry supposed to be the manufacture of the Indians. It is in fact made in San Francisco and shipped to Alaska to be peddled out by the Indians to curio-hunters" (reprinted in the *Alaskan*: Anonymous 1885).

This type of slander must have been alarming to those dependent not just on Native artwork but also on the continuing perception that those works were *authentic* Native productions.[2] Not surprisingly, the *Alaskan* followed up its reprint of the *Oregonian*'s accusations with a vehement response, defending the local manufacture of Native curios:

> The *Oregonian* is either very ignorant of the abilities of the Alaska Indians or else is willfully trying to injure what has become an industry of many Indians of the archipelago. A person has only to make a trip among these islands and visit the villages of the natives to see all kinds of carving, from the tall totems . . . down to the finer workmanship in silver and gold displayed on ear-rings, finger-rings, bracelets, blanket pins, etc. Scarcely an article in use by them but what has some meaning design worked upon it. Their carvings are done on wood, stone, copper, silver and gold, and some of their finest work would be a credit to any skilled workman. . . . The Indian women are just as fond of displaying jewelry as their more enlightened sisters, and if they lack in quality they make up in quantity, as I have seen a dozen bracelets and sixteen finger-rings displayed on one pair of arms. . . . Every village can boast of several carvers who make their living chiefly by making silver jewelry.
>
> A few months ago a trader had a few articles made in San Francisco and brought to Alaska to sell, but it was found out on the way here, and such was the indignation of the resident whites, as well as the Indians, that I do not think he sold a pair, and it will probably be his last attempt. Persons purchasing jewelry from the Indians may rest assured that they are getting Indian manufacture. (Anonymous 1885)

The *Alaskan*'s discussion of the (supposedly unsuccessful) California-made knock-offs may have been a damage-control effort to quell rumors

Fig. 20.1 Silver bracelet by Rudolph Walton. Sheldon Jackson Museum, Sitka, 1A-550. Photograph by the author.

that could have seriously damaged the local economy. The *Alaskan* flatly denied that fakes were a part of the tourist market (although, as I will show, there were indeed imported, manufactured bracelets for sale on the Northwest Coast).

Some artists used the fear of fakery to their advantage. The Tlingit artist Rudolph Walton focused on providing not only Native-made goods but a personal interaction with the artist (Raibmon 2005, 150).

A newspaper article encouraged consumers to patronize Walton directly:

> We call attention to the advertisement of Rudolph Walton, a former mission boy. We can state that he is thoroughly reliable and deserves patronage. Gold and silver rings and bracelets are on hand and made to order. . . . All of the engraving is done by himself and the engraving is in the curious designs common to the Alaskan Indian. . . . We can assure you will get a courteous reception as Rudolph speaks English well. (Hall 2004, 41)

Many tourist publications urged visitors to buy curios directly from the artists or their families:

> You can buy Indian baskets in Seattle, and nearly any Eastern city, but baskets thus obtained lack the value of those bought from the

Fig. 20.2 Tlingit woman selling baskets and bracelets, Sitka, 1886–1890. University of Washington, Special Collections, detail NA2258.

old Indian woman, in the far-off wilds of Alaska. You will prize such acquisitions. Never will you forget that Indian village, with its totem poles and dried fish; its smoky huts and dirty children; its stolid "citizens" and numerous dogs; and the terrible time you had reaching an understanding with the Indian sales lady, and your unsuccessful effort to get a basket or mat at less than the marked price. The basket you bought in Alaska, perhaps at an Indian village . . . outvalues a dozen store baskets. (MacDowell 1905)[3]

Still, the reality of the situation in Alaska was not as simple as "authentic" vs. "fake"; the buying experience was a key part of the tourist adventure. There were many levels of authenticity to choose from, whether the buyer knew it or not.

One avenue to authenticity was achieved by buying directly from the person using the desired object.[4] Tourists, like anthropologists and professional collectors, bought jewelry directly from the person wearing it. It was well known then, as now, that an object that had seen indigenous use would carry more value than one on display in the tourist stores (Raibmon 2005, 155). Lukens and Scidmore both mention buying a bracelet directly off the silver-decked arm of Princess Thom, the famed Tlingit saleswoman of Sitka (Scidmore 1885, 176). Schwatka reported:

> Some of their women wear a dozen or more bracelets on each arm, covering them up to the elbows and beyond, but this seems to be only a means of preserving them until the arrival of white customers, when they are sold at from one to five or six dollars a pair according to their width. (1900, 42)

When Scidmore visited with the silversmith at Hoonah, he brought out all his wares, as well as three women in his family who each displayed "her wrists covered with rows of closely fitting bracelets" (1885, 129). Wearing bracelets intended for sale was an effective marketing tactic on the part of women traders as described by Scidmore:

> Indian women crouched on the wharf with their wares spread before them . . . extending arms covered with silver bracelets to the envious gaze of their white sisters. . . . They are keen traders and sharp at bargaining, and no white man outwits these natives. (90–91)

At another level, tourists could watch a silversmith make a bracelet starting with a silver or gold coin, or silverwork could be bought directly from an artist who had prepared a number of pieces for sale on steamer days. Stores owned by Native artists competed directly with white-owned stores and had an edge over them by having the artist at hand. The Tlingit silversmith Jim Williams and his wife owned their own store in Skagway whose name—the Native Curio Shop—emphasized the indigenous nature of their products (Hall 2004, 43).

Fig. 20.3 Tlingit silversmith Johnny Kasank. Image RBCM PN 9220 courtesy of Royal British Columbia Museum.

A third level of authenticity was to buy from white-owned stores who employed Native artists to carve on order. Native participation was strategically marketed to promote the stores. The Bethelsen and Pruell store in Ketchikan advertised "genuine Indian Silver Bracelets and spoons made by Mr. Mather, a Metlakatla Indian who was with Father Duncan when he first brought his Indians to Alaska" (Hall 2004, 44). Another store in Skagway hired Native artists to make souvenirs, including gold, copper, and silver jewelry for the gold miners and the tourists who followed in their wake. "[Peter Kern's] Indian Curio Workshop turned out almost anything that could accommodate a Native motif. He trained them to produce gold, copper, and silver jewelry and make souvenir spoons by the hundreds" (Hall 2004, 42). A curio store in Kasaan hired Chief Sonihat to produce silver rings and "kept him so busy filling their orders he never had much left over to sell to the tourists when they come in on the boat" (McKeown 1951, 225).

At another level, many stores offered a combination of Native-made

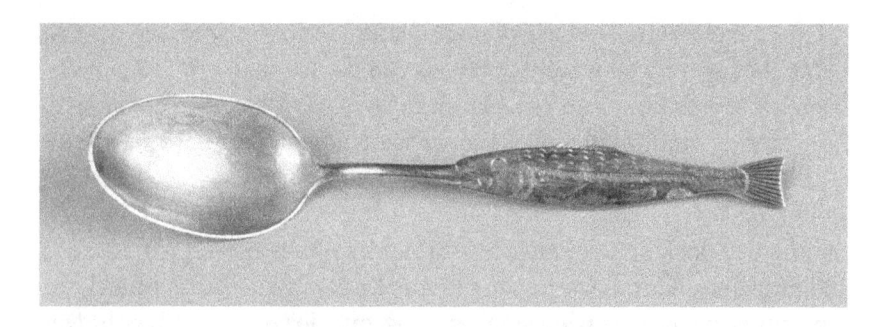

Fig. 20.4 (*top*) Silver spoon with fish handle by Jim Williams. Courtesy of the Burke Museum of Natural History and Culture, catalog no. 1-1867.

Fig. 20.5 (*bottom*) Commercially produced fiddle-back spoon with engraved handle attributed by the author to Tom Price. Image RBCM 7925 courtesy of Royal British Columbia Museum. Photograph by Nancy Harris.

and manufactured objects. In the 1920s, the Tlingit artist Jim Williams was hired to engrave the handles of manufactured spoons and bracelet blanks (Hall 2004, 43). Hall writes:

> When Jim lived at Auke Bay near Juneau, he was sent assorted tea and coffee spoons, 52 bracelet heads, 40 straight bracelets of varying widths, 18 child's bracelets and 4 wiggly tail bracelets, all to be engraved. These spoons and bracelets were pre-made blanks readied for engraving by hand that had become standard in the curio industry. (60)

A few hand-engraved bracelets from the turn-of-the-century are marked "sterling" inside, revealing the use of sheet silver marked by the manufacturer or perhaps the store owner.

Tourists and Collectors   427

One traveler noted the use of manufactured spoons by native smiths, "As the fever for souvenir spoons spread the Alaskan was led to hammer silver dollars into clumsy imitations of fiddle pattern spoons, or merely etch totemic designs on the traders' plated ware." (Scidmore 1893, 43)[5]

Charlie Gunnock of Kake supplied Kirmse's store in Juneau with spoons and bracelets. A letter from 1916 records Kirmse's order to Gunnock for the engraving of two dozen stock spoons, one dozen sheet silver bracelets, and one paper cutter, for which he was paid $18.75 (Hall 2004, 45).

Evidence from almost every village shows that contemporary scholars like Emmons and Barbeau greatly underestimated the number of silversmiths in Alaska. Indeed, Haida teacher G̲waganad (Diane Brown) lists many artists who were practicing in Haida Gwaii when she was young: Tim Pearson, John Cross, Tom Moody, Arthur Moody, Charlie Gladstone, Luke Watson, Lewis Collison, Isaac Hans, Rufus Moody, and Henry Young Sr.[6] She writes that Rufus Moody taught art to youngsters, many of whom are still carving. She refutes the notion that Bill Reid brought Haida art out of a veritable dark age. "It's always been said that Bill brought back Haida art. The Haida art didn't go anywhere. It was always there" (G̲waganad 2004, 66).

By my own calculations, there were at least thirty-four Tlingit silversmiths and five Kaigani Haida smiths working in southeast Alaska in the 1880s.[7] Through archival and published research I have determined that there were over one hundred silversmiths on the Northwest Coast in the late nineteenth and early twentieth century. While the cataclysmic effects of disease on indigenous peoples are undeniable—decimated by up to 90 percent in some areas—the robust number of artists in the communities is a testament to both the importance of art to the culture and the economic opportunities afforded by the tourist trade.

As I will show, the errors of prior scholarship are typical of anthropological assumptions of the time and reveal both a scholarly bias and a field collectors' prejudice against art made for the tourist trade.

"Why Not Tourist Art?"

The writings of Emmons and Barbeau indicate a collectors' bias against artworks that did not meet certain preconceived standards of authenticity.[8] Their standards were primarily grounded in late nineteenth-century anthropological value judgments. Anthropologists sorted artists and their productions hierarchically, seeking out artwork that fit Western conceptualizations of authenticity and tradition. These judgments led collectors to exclude artwork influenced by European materials and practices, such as silver and gold jewelry and spoons, button blankets, and beaded items. While the "arts of acculturation" did enter into museum collections, they were often portrayed as such in museum exhibits and scholarly writings, isolating them from more "traditional" pieces and thus calling their authenticity into question for viewers and readers.[9]

These attitudes were compounded by contemporary gender discrimination. Scholarly attitudes toward the use of trade cloth parallel anthropologists' attitudes toward jewelry. The handling of cloth

> was considered feminine, which also rendered it less valuable. This Victorian mindset kept most settlers and tourists from understanding the subtle nuances of Tlingit cloth use, and instead enabled them to make generalizations about aesthetics and fashion in ways that reinforced perceived cultural differences. (Smetzer 2005, 7)

In the Victorian world, jewelry—like cloth—was part of the feminine realm and relegated to the category of "adornment" rather than "art."

> Nowadays, in most villages, a native silversmith will be found who makes bracelets, rings and other ornaments from silver dollars, and *these fulfil the feminine craving for adornment, but are poor substitutes for the interesting native art* which has now vanished. (Harrison 1925, 86)

Because of its associations with the feminine, professional male anthropologists generally ignored jewelry to focus instead on artwork that fit within Western categories of the "great arts"—painting and sculpture. The bracelet, as feminine accessory, was acknowledged, if at all, only in passing as an aside in anthropological investigations into more "worthy" topics such as ceremonialism, kinship identification, or technology.

This gender bias also influenced anthropologists' self-characterization as professional collectors, not casual touristic consumers:

The distinction between dilettante tourists and professional collectors was often aligned with the binary characterization of emotional women and rational men. Women were cast as tasteless hobbyists, indiscriminate consumers of mass culture's curios who drove up prices for more serious, professional male collectors of authentic high art and artifacts. Marketing techniques reinforced this assumption; newspaper articles about popular Indian arts invariably appeared on the daily women's pages. (Raibmon 2005, 151)

Tourists' demands ran contrary to collectors'. Vendors understood that "a plentiful stock is an indispensable prerequisite for attracting buyers" and that multiples, while key for tourist sales, could "empt[y] the object of value for the rare art collector" (Phillips 1995, 111).

As alluded to earlier, there is yet another reason anthropologists and those who collected for them may have discounted contemporary artwork: manufactured jewelry was, in fact, widely available. By way of example, a 1910 invoice from the Seattle production company of Joseph Mayer & Bros. records an order by Kirmse's store for eleven lots of Indian spoons and eleven lots of Indian bracelets (Emmons 1894–1915; Emmons 1942; Emmons 1991, 189–90, 248–49). The invoice also records an order for fourteen handle carving sets, implying that Kirmse was not only selling commercially stamped jewelry but also providing tools and blanks to hand-engrave pieces for the store. The practice of hand-engraving stock pieces increased artist efficiency while still allowing the artworks to be marketed as original indigenous productions.

In practice, it can be difficult to differentiate some of the stamped bracelets from handmade ones; particularly vexing are stamped bracelets to which hand-engraving was added (as may be implied by the Kirmse order) and stamped bracelets that reproduced small imperfections on the original engraving from which the cast was made.

Silver bracelets for sale through the Olde Curiosity Shop catalogs were implied to be of Haida manufacture, but were commercially made. Catalog pages from the 1910s show bracelets of the type manufactured by Mayer & Company (Duncan 2000, 184, 238n33). Many of the Tlingit designs cast by Mayer & Company (and now by Metal Arts) were designed by Tlingit artist Bill Wilson.

A stamped floral bracelet, which has been attributed to Joseph Mayer himself (rather than having the design for the stamping die commis-

Fig. 20.6 (*top*) Tlingit silver bracelets, n.d. The bracelet on the left has a convexly curved (or coved) band while the bracelet on the right has a flat band, which may imply that it is a stamped production piece. Denver Art Museum Collection: Museum Purchase, 1942.168a& b. Photograph by Nancy Harris.

Fig. 20.7 (*bottom*) Silver bracelet designed by Bill Wilson and produced by Mayer & Bros. Courtesy of Metal Arts Group. Photograph by Chalmers-McDonald.

sioned from a Native artist) is most likely the composition of Tlingit artist Jim Jacobs (Metal Arts 2006a).[10]

Comparisons to hand-carved bracelets by Jim Jacobs suggest that perhaps he was the original creator of this design.

Finally, correspondence between the jewelry company, Harry Birks and Sons, and Barbeau suggests that the company was trying to secure a collection of Native-made silver bracelets, possibly as prototypes for a manufactured line of Northwest Coast–style bracelets (Barbeau 1916–1954, 251.1).

Toward a Nuanced Understanding of Collecting Practices

To a certain degree, I have overstated the gender and professional biases shown toward contemporary jewelry by anthropologists and collectors in general and Emmons in particular. What is clear is that anthropological interests in silverwork focused on the tools and techniques for manufacture over any social meaning or ceremonial use. Although he

Fig. 20.8 (*top*) Floral bracelet designed by Jim Jacobs and produced by Metal Arts Group. Courtesy of Metal Arts Group. Photograph by Chalmers-McDonald.

Fig. 20.9 (*bottom*) Silver bracelet by Jim Jacobs. Sheldon Jackson Museum, Sitka SJ I.A.611. Photograph by the author.

made at least three complete descriptions of the silver jewelry-making process, and he collected a set of silversmith's tools for the American Museum of Natural History, Emmons recorded only *one* silversmith's name, Jim (Jim Jacobs, a.k.a Silversmith Jim) in all his time on the Northwest Coast.

But even Emmons's biases did not leave him completely blind to the realities of the situation. Despite his assertions that few artists had knowledge of jewelry-making, he noted an overwhelming market for their products. As the tourist trade grew, he recorded that silversmiths could not keep up with demand; bracelets "simply were exhausted except in outlaying villages between 88 & 98 when white tourists came." While Emmons despaired of jewelry quality and its associations with the tourist trade, he did collect nearly eighty silver, gold, and copper bracelets as well as spoons for Canadian and American museums (Emmons 1932–1944, May 11, 1941). He identified several bracelets as being specifically "of the very narrow type made first about 1880 for the newly developing tourist trade" (see figures 20.6 and 20.7) (Emmons 1932–1944, March 28, 1942).

His collection notes read:

> These very narrow bangle type bracelets were made by Tlingit smiths at Wrangel and Sitka in 1880 for the tourist trade then just beginning. The wider native type bracelets took too long to make to keep the trade supplied. A raven is represented here with the head at one end and the tail at the other. (Emmons 1932–1944, May 11, 1941)

And while he decried the influences of Euro-American design motifs, he also acknowledged that the floral designs were worn by Tlingit women themselves (Duncan 2000, 213). My research shows that such designs were very much in demand by Native customers, not just white tourists. Floral and scrollwork designs, adapted from European sources such as woodworking, fabrics, and printed materials, were popular with Native and non-Native customers alike (Bunn-Marcuse 2000). Florence Davidson remarked that flowers and leaves were extremely popular motifs at the turn of the century when she was young. She remembered her father, Charles Edenshaw, commenting that everyone ordered "flowers and leaves" to the extent that he became bored with executing floral motifs (Blackman personal correspondence to Nancy Harris, August 8, 1981).

Theorizing a Unitary Market

The question, then, is whether there is really any distinction between the categories of "authentic" and "tourist" jewelry as posited by Emmons. The terms "made for sale" and "made for use" suggest fixed, distinct categories, whereas in all probability any such categories were extremely fluid, existing (if at all) only at the moment of transfer from artist to new owner. As such, I believe that at the turn of the century there was actually a single unitary art market with as much artistic variability in quality and technical skill as there is today.

Emmons's collections illustrate that anthropological writings which asserted different categories for artworks produced for consumers do not reflect the realities of the market. Having already established Emmons's bias against tourist art, one can surmise that while he sought "authentic" jewelry made for Native community members, there was actually a great overlap in style and motifs among the bracelets that Emmons collected and descriptions of bracelets purchased by tourists, like Eliza Scidmore. A comparison of bracelets illustrated by Scidmore as being

Fig. 20.10 Silver bracelets illustrated in Scidmore (1885:61).

available for purchase by tourists with those collected within a few years of Scidmore's trip shows the similarities.

Many bracelets for sale were indistinguishable in type and style from those made for use within the community. Both types were popular with Native customers of the time. While artworks produced after 1910 may have a different aesthetic from earlier works, the broader point is that there was a flourishing market for jewelry—among Natives and non-Natives—which included those displaying nineteenth-century form line design systems *and also* pieces that no longer followed all of those formal tendencies.

"Tourist Art" Endures

Stamped jewelry is still popular today and widely available along the Northwest Coast and on the web. The same pieces available in the ca. 1920 Curiosity Shop catalog are still for sale. Among these are pieces produced by Metal Arts Group. The dies used by this company were originally commissioned by Mayer Brothers of Seattle (Metal Arts 2006a).

Interestingly, these Mayer Brothers/Metal Arts pieces are marketed on the basis that stamped bracelets were as popular with Native consumers as non-Native:

> In the early 1900s Mayer Brothers, a jewelry manufacturer in Seattle, set up to produce silver bracelets to sell to the Indians up the

Fig. 20.11 (*top*) Tlingit silver bracelets collected at Fort Wrangell in 1879. Denver Art Museum Collection: Museum Purchase, 1938.189. Photograph by Nancy Harris.

Fig. 20.12 (*bottom*) Tlingit silver bracelet collected by Emmons in 1942 but dated by him to 1885–86. Denver Art Museum Collection: Museum Purchase, 1942.167. Photograph by Nancy Harris.

> coast, using designs from Tlingit carvers. *These trade bracelets became favored items to be given away at potlatches.* Production has continued to this day. . . . The primary market continues to be in Alaska, and the jewelry is sold to both Indians and tourists. The Indians buy mainly the traditional designs, with the most popular bracelet still being the Lovebirds. (David Morgan Store 2006a, emphasis added)

That Tlingit women owned both stamped and hand-engraved designs is evidenced by Emmons's collection of the two floral bracelets (see figure 20.6) discussed above: one stamped, the other hand-engraved but bearing remarkably similar designs. The virtual replication of this same design on numerous hand-engraved bracelets suggests the use of

Tourists and Collectors   435

a pattern book; perhaps the makers of engraved bracelets were replicating the stamped design.

The marketing material quoted above reworks the concept of authenticity by emphasizing the purchase and use of stamped jewelry by Native people, and subtly invites the contemporary customer to participate in the same process, clearly inverting white consumers' earlier preference for indigenously made pieces in favor of commercially produced but indigenously used ones. The historical depth of the stamped bracelet designs adds to the sheen of "authenticity." A stamped "lovebirds" head and tail bracelet for sale online is a century-old Tlingit design:

> We are pleased to offer a range of trade bracelets and matching rings designed by Bill Wilson, a Tlingit raised in Hoonah, Alaska. The bracelets are struck from the original dies made in the early 1900s for trade with the Indians of the Pacific Northwest. Typical of the early patterns, the bracelets are relatively narrow, with the design on the terminals. The bracelets and rings are available in sterling silver. The rings are also available in 14 kt. gold. (David Morgan Store 2006b)

Though often associated with the tourist trade, these designs were actually made for both the Native and non-Native market, starting in the late nineteenth century and continuing through the present day.

Conclusion

This chapter examined turn-of-the-century anthropological biases against the arts of acculturation and tourist art in generaland the indifference to jewelry outside of its role in established avenues of anthropological inquiry, ignoring community needs and interests. These biases affected the development of the scholarly canon, laid down at a time when Northwest Coast indigenous people experienced great cultural upheaval resulting from population loss, missionization, acculturation, and potlatch criminalization. Depopulation and forced assimilation led to the seeming disappearance of public indigenous practices, such as the potlatch and the raising of new totem poles and big houses; anthropologists lamented the passing of "authentic" indigenous cultures and assumed that current artistic practices were too acculturated to reflect a "genuine" expression of culture. Bias against artworks made with European materials or techniques and those made for sale to non-Natives

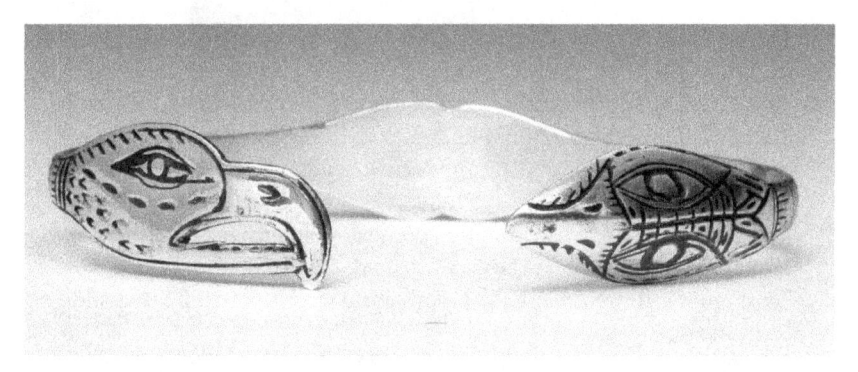

Fig. 20.13 "Love Birds" bracelet designed by Bill Wilson and produced by Metal Arts Group. Courtesy of Metal Arts Group. Photograph by Chalmers-McDonald.

appears to have kept scholars from recognizing that these items provided a channel for creative cultural endurance.

Anthropologists' claims that no "good, old" work was being made, or that the Native artists were giving up precious metal jewelry-making, were wrong and are disproved by the objective facts of the tourist market at that time. The reality is that Native artists and their products were critically important to the Alaska economy, attracting tourists and their dollars to the new American territory. Scholars of the period had cultural biases that influenced their subjective perception of authenticity and caused them to overlook contemporary artworks as well as the functions and values of those works. Questions of authenticity that may have appeared stark to scholars of the period were in fact quite nuanced. A range of products—all indigenously inspired, if not actually Native-made—existed for purchase, from the handmade to the mass production piece. Works of all types—regardless of method of manufacture—have been worn and treasured by their owners, whether as a travel souvenir or as a precious symbol of cultural and clan affiliation.

NOTES

1. These numbers are impressive, totaling between 17 and 34 percent of the $7.2 million that the United States paid for all of Alaska in 1867, only twenty years earlier.
2. Paige Raibmon has noted, "Maintaining the authentic cachet of one's work became more important, as charges of degraded authenticity increased in conjunction with the growing popularity of tourists arts" (2005, 150).

3. This could have been written about any number of curio items, including bracelets.
4. I use the term "authenticity" here in the full understanding of its problematic and relativist history. Rather than put it in quotations referencing current discussions of the nineteenth-century biases that attend it, I let it stand as a term that was fully in use in the period and trust that the reader will place it within that context. For further discussions of the term, see Raibmon 2005, 3206.
5. For an in-depth treatment of Alaska's curio stores, see Hall 2004 and Duncan 2000.
6. In 1939 Arthur Moody told Barbeau that his father, Tom Moody, was the only one working in silver at Skidegate at the time. Moody noted, "There used to be lots of good silver carvers before small pox in Vancouver at that time most of them passed away and now it is nearly all gone" (Barbeau 1916–1954, 247.10). While interviewing Mrs. Walter Stevens, Barbeau learned that no one in the village was working in silver except for Charlie Gladstone (240.46). This claim was repeated in a 1945 article in the *Vancouver Sun* reporting that Gladstone was the only artist carving silver in Skidegate at the time (Thornton 1948). If Moody and Gladstone were working contemporaneously, one wonders who else might have been producing jewelry during those same years, yet were ignored by anthropologists?
7. The research on Tlingit smiths in Alaska had been a long-term project of Peter Corey and Irene Schuler working with the Sheldon Jackson Museum in Sitka. They have been very generous in sharing that research.
8. Ruth Phillips examined the biases against tourist art of northeastern North America in her article of the same name (Phillips 1995).
9. For example, Erna Gunther's exhibit and catalog, *Indians of the Northwest Coast*, for the Taylor Museum in Colorado and the Seattle Art Museum lists button blankets and items made of silver and gold or sheet copper under "new materials" (Gunther 1951).
10. In 2006, this floral bracelet was attributed to Joseph Meyer by the Metal Arts website; in 2011, they changed their attribution to Tlingit artist Bill Wilson, who designed a number of the bracelets that they still produce. My research suggests this floral design originated with Tlingit artist Jim Jacobs.

WORKS CITED

Anonymous. 1885. "The Indian Carvers." *Alaskan*, December 26.
Barbeau, Marius. 1916–1954. Notebooks, notes, and correspondence. Ottawa: Canadian Centre for Folk Culture Studies, Canadian Museum of Civilization.
———. 1957. *Haida Carvers in Argillite*. Ottawa: Department of Northern Affairs and Natural Resources National Museum of Canada.

Boursin, Henry. 1893. "The Mines of Alaska." In *Report on Population and Resources of Alaska at the Eleventh Census: 1890.* Washington: Government Printing Office.

Bunn-Marcuse, Kathryn. 2000. "Northwest Coast Silver Bracelets and the Use of Euro-American Designs." *American Indian Art Magazine* 25 (4): 66–73, 84.

———. 2007. "Precious Metals: Silver and Gold Bracelets from the Northwest Coast." PhD diss., University of Washington.

———. Forthcoming. "Streams of Tourists: Navigating the Tourist Tides in Late Nineteenth-Century SE Alaska." In *Cultural Tourism Movements: New Articulations of Indigenous Identity*, ed. Alexis Bunten, Nelson Graburn, and Jenny Chio. Chicago: University of Chicago Press.

Crosby, Marcia. 2004. "Haidas, Human Beings, and Other Myths." In *Bill Reid and Beyond: Expanding on Modern Native Art*, ed. K. Duffek and C. Townsend-Gault, 108–30. Vancouver: Douglas and McIntyre.

David Morgan Store. 2006a. Indian Jewelry of the Pacific NW. http://www.davidmorgan.com/nwindianjewelry.html?cPath=5&. 8/9/2006.

———. 2006b. Trade Bracelets & Rings. http://www.davidmorgan.com/tradebracelets.html. 8/9/2006.

Deasy, Thomas. 1914. Correspondence to Edward Sapir. Canadian Museum of Civilization.

Duff, Wilson, Bill Holm, and Bill Reid. 1967. *Arts of the Raven: Masterworks by the Northwest Coast Indian.* Vancouver: Vancouver Art Gallery.

Duncan, Kate. 2000. *1001 Curious Things: Ye Olde Curiosity Shop and Native American Art.* Seattle: University of Washington Press.

Duncan, William. 1889. In *The Metlakahtlan*, vol. 1. Metlakatla.

Emmons, George. 1894–1915. Collection Notes. Anthropology Department Archives, American Museum of Natural History.

———. 1932–1944. Correspondence with Frederic Douglas. Denver Art Museum.

———. 1942. Collection Notes. Denver Art Museum.

———. 1991. *The Tlingit Indians.* Seattle: University of Washington Press.

Gunther, Erna. 1951. *Indians of the Northwest Coast.* Colorado Springs and Seattle: Taylor Museum of the Colorado Springs Fine Arts Center and the Seattle Art Museum.

Gwaganad (Diane Brown). 2004. A Non-Haida Upbringing: Conflicts and Resolutions. In *Bill Reid and Beyond: Expanding on Modern Native Art*, ed. K. Duffek and C. Townsend-Gault, 56–63. Vancouver: Douglas and McIntyre.

Hall, June. 2004. *Alaska Souvenir Spoons and the Early Curio Trade.* Juneau: Gastineau Channel Historical Society.

Harrison, Charles. 1925. *Ancient Warriors of the North Pacific: The Haidas, Their Laws, Customs, and Legends, with Some Historical Account of the Queen Charlotte Islands.* London: H. F. and G. Witherby.

Jacknis, Ira. 2002. *The Storage Box of Tradition: Kwakiutl Art, Anthropologists, and Museums, 1881–1981*. Washington DC: Smithsonian Institution Press.

MacDowell, Lloyd. 1905. *Alaska Indian Basketry*. Tourist flyer.

McKeown, Martha Ferguson. 1951. *Alaska Silver*. New York: Macmillan.

Metal Arts. 2006a. http://www.metalartsgroup.com/artists.php?aid=24. 9/22/2006.

———. 2006b. Bracelets by Bill Wilson. http://www.metalartsgroup.com/products.php. 5/1/2007.

Newcombe, Charles. 1890s–1930s. Newcombe Family Correspondence. British Columbia Archives.

O'Reilly, P. 1882. *Report of the Deputy Superintendent—General of Indian Affairs*. DOI Affairs, ed. Dominion of Canada.

Phillips, Ruth. 1995. Why Not Tourist Art? Significant Silences in Native American Museum Representations. In *After Colonialism: Imperial Histoires and Postcolonial Displacements*, ed. G. Prakash, 98–128. Princeton: Princeton University Press.

Raibmon, Paige. 2005. *Authentic Indians: Episodes of Encounter from the Late Nineteenth-Century Northwest Coast*. Durham: Duke University Press.

Schwatka, Frederick. 1900. *Along Alaska's Great River: A Popular Account of the Travels of Alaska Exploring Expedition along the Great Yukon River, from Its Source to Its Mouth, in the British North-West Territory, and in the Territory of Alaska. Together with the Latest Information on the Klondike Country*. Chicago: G. M. Hill.

Scidmore, Eliza Ruhamah. 1885. *Alaska: Its Southern Coast and the Sitkan Archipelago*. Boston: D. Lothrop.

———. 1893. "Some American Spoons." *Jeweler's Circular and Horological Review*, September 27, 42–43.

Shadbolt, Doris. 2004. "The Will to Be Haida." In *Bill Reid and Beyond: Expanding on Modern Native Art*, ed. K. Duffek and C. Townsend-Gault, 26–37. Vancouver: Douglas and McIntyre.

Smetzer, Megan. 2005. "From Bolts to Bags: The Transformation of Cloth in Nineteenth-Century Southeast Alaska." Paper presented at the Native American Art Studies Association Conference, Arizona.

Thornton, Mildred Vally. 1948. "Totems Fall, but Haidas Thrive." *Vancouver Sun*, January 31.

United States Department of the Interior. 1893. *Report on Population and Resources of Alaska at the Eleventh Census: 1890*. Washington: Government Printing Office.

21

Opening the Drawer

Unpacking Tlingit Beadwork in
Museum Collections and Beyond

MEGAN A. SMETZER

Several years ago, as a homesick Alaskan in an art history master's program on the East Coast, I decided to do an independent study project that would reconnect me with home. Since I had grown up in Fairbanks, I intended to research Athapaskan beadwork, as I knew many beaders and was familiar with that artistic production. In order to begin this process, Aldona Jonaitis invited me to explore the beadwork collections at the University of Alaska Museum of the North. After opening drawer upon drawer of Athapaskan beadwork, I opened one that held beaded objects whose shapes and patterns were unfamiliar to me. I was informed that these were octopus bags made by Tlingit women. As a lifelong Alaskan, I was taken aback because I had been unaware of the rich history of beading in southeast Alaska. In order to learn more about these beautiful objects and the women who made them, I decided to focus instead on Tlingit beadwork. My initial research on octopus bags grew into my PhD thesis, which examines the wide range of beaded regalia, souvenirs, and other objects that have circulated and gained meaning within southeast Alaska and beyond since the nineteenth century.

Background

As I began my research, it quickly became apparent that despite the extensive academic scholarship on Northwest Coast art, very little has been written about Tlingit beadwork. This omission is notable given the ubiquity of beadwork in historic photographs, particularly those from the 1904 Sitka potlatch and images from the late Victorian era tourist trade, in addition to the beadwork worn, sold, and displayed at

Celebration. As my research progressed and I learned that beadwork has had significance in southeast Alaska for over one hundred years, I determined that this oversight in the literature has a great deal to do with the construction of the "canon" of Northwest Coast art. This seemingly comprehensive scholarly literature has focused almost exclusively on carved and painted objects, such as totem poles and masks, as well as on weaving, including spruce root baskets and Chilkat robes. Interlocking Euro-American discourses that developed in the late nineteenth century regarding authenticity, tradition, the hierarchy between fine and applied arts, and issues of commodification have contributed to the scholarly oversight of beaded regalia and souvenirs. Because beadwork is almost entirely composed of materials acquired through trade such as glass seed beads and cloth, it has been largely ignored or dismissed as a sign of assimilation and cultural degeneration.

Methodology

My approach to Tlingit beadwork has been to leave aside these imposed Euro-American categorizations and look carefully at the ways in which beadwork has circulated and gained meaning from the late nineteenth century to the present. Because of its ubiquity and the lack of academic analysis, beadwork occupies a unique position within Tlingit visual and material culture. The study of its roles within Tlingit society past and present and its discursive positioning by outsiders reveals the complex interactions among the indigenous peoples of the region, both interior and coastal, and those who arrived later, including fur traders, colonists, missionaries, tourists, and settlers.

To fully illustrate the complex histories that inform the production and circulation of beadwork, I utilized four interrelated research strategies. First, I developed an approach to beadwork that draws on important theoretical work emerging in relation to the material and cultural production of indigenous peoples, particularly in the South Pacific, that positions academically marginalized artistic production in a way that foregrounds indigenous values and counters Euro-American categorizations. Second, I read the ethnographic and photographic records of southeast Alaska "against the grain" to identify Tlingit voices embedded within them as a way of accessing the perspectives of late nineteenth- and early twentieth-century Tlingit on beadwork that were not written down. Third, and most significantly, I attended to this gap in the literature through conversations with beaders and elders, whose knowledge is unparalleled and has rarely been recorded. Finally, I drew on the classic art historical techniques of stylistic and iconographic analysis to assemble and analyze, for the first time, a visual compendium of over 1,100 pieces of Tlingit, Inland Tlingit, and Tahltan beadwork that are currently located in museum collections across North America.

Beadwork in Museums

As the compilation of this database was the precondition for all the other analyses, it was crucial to identify those museums with noteworthy collections of beadwork and examine, document, and analyze the contents. Because this database underlies the entire thesis and is also the most potentially useful aspect of this research in southeast Alaska, I will introduce the process I undertook to develop it and share some of the findings.

For several reasons, I chose to focus on beadwork in museums, as opposed to that currently being used in Tlingit communities. First, prior to my thesis, a comprehensive survey of beadwork in museum collections had not yet been undertaken. In order to do so, I sent eight hundred letters to museums across North America to determine their holdings of Tlingit, Inland Tlingit, and Tahltan beadwork. Of those that responded, museums with only one or two pieces sent photographs and related provenance materials for inclusion. I traveled to those museums with larger collections to photograph the pieces and research-related archival information. This process has resulted in an extensive catalogue that makes up the second half of my thesis. While still a work in progress, the 1,100 objects in its current incarnation are organized alphabetically by object type. Each piece is illustrated with a thumbnail image and includes provenance information, materials and dimensions, museum location and accession number, approximate date of construction, place of origin and maker, if known, collector, if known, and other relevant information. A second reason for focusing on beadwork in museum collections is that the important work of recording regalia currently being worn and used in southeast Alaska, beaded and otherwise, is being carried out by Chilkat weaver Clarissa Rizal and artist/videographer Donna Foulke as part of the "Regalia Documentation Project," which they have implemented in conjunction with Celebration since 2004. Finally, as an Alaskan, but a non-Native one, I see this project as an act of reciprocation, a way of giving back to the place and people who have contributed to the shaping of who I am.

I would like my thesis to be the initial step in this process. As I talk to more people and get feedback on the thesis and catalogue, I hope that this will lead to collaborative projects that will be useful to community members and future researchers in southeast Alaska and beyond.

The institutional repositories of beadwork reveal a great deal about how it has been valued. Beginning in the late nineteenth century, objects produced by indigenous peoples throughout the world were systematically collected by anthropologists and others working for newly developed museums that attempted to classify and quantify humans and their material production. On the Northwest Coast, the era of greatest museum collecting took place between 1875 and the 1920s.[1]

The mandate of these museums, as part of a larger colonial endeavor, was to collect a wide range of items from Native North American groups in order to preserve what they felt was a precontact way of life that was rapidly disappearing and to trace processes of cultural evolutionism through the material record. For this reason, collectors focused on objects that did not obviously show a history of contact. Anthropologist Franz Boas made this bias explicit by referring to the "contamination by European wares" as a significant stylistic problem.[2] Beadwork, made from commercial cloth and imported glass beads, did not conform to anthropological ideals regarding purity and was rarely purchased by the major anthropological museums. Beadwork slowly began to enter museum collections, primarily smaller university museums, during the second half of the era. Not surprisingly, with the exception of the National Museum of the American Indian (NMAI), the majority of Tlingit beadwork in museum collections is located in Alaska. The Alaska State Museum, the Sheldon Jackson Museum, and the University of Alaska Museum of the North have the largest collections of regalia and souvenirs in the state.

Ethnographic Collectors

The few ethnographic collectors from this era who acquired beadwork usually had long-standing relationships with individuals and communities in southeast Alaska. These men primarily collected regalia, a preference that stemmed from the ethnographic weight given to objects that had been used in important ceremonial events within Tlingit communities over those made for sale or everyday use. George Thornton Emmons (1852–1945) was the first to collect multiple examples of regalia, beginning around 1905. Most of these pieces are at the NMAI, although the Burke Museum at the University of Washington has several octopus bags that Emmons collected for the Yukon-Pacific Exposition in 1909. Another significant collection resides at the University of Pennsylvania Museum (UPM), acquired in the 1910s and 1920s by Louis Shotridge (c1882–1937). Many pieces of beaded regalia worn at the 1904 potlatch are found here. Though not technically an ethnographic collector, Axel Rasmussen (1886–1945) shared a similar ethnographic perspective with Emmons and Shotridge and collected many objects used in ceremonial practices, including beaded regalia, during his tenure as superintendent of schools in Wrangell and Skagway during the mid-twentieth century. The bulk of his collection is housed at the Portland Art Museum in Oregon.

Settler Collectors

A second group of beadwork collectors consists of individuals who came to Alaska as missionaries, primarily male, and schoolteachers, primarily female from the late nineteenth century to the middle of the twentieth. Though many of these settlers left Alaska after several years, they developed relationships with communities and collected or were gifted objects that were sold in slightly different form to tourists. These "special access collectors" brought home wall pockets, dolls, moccasins, bead-covered bottles, and so forth. What differentiated these items from souvenirs made for sale was their almost exclusive cloth construction and the occasional use of beaded crests, a practice that increased during the first half of the twentieth century. These nonceremonial beaded objects, which were often used in Tlingit homes, indicate the significance of cloth within Tlingit social practices. The collection of Presbyterian missionary A. R. Mackintosh, who was stationed at Haines circa 1890-1910, is now at the University of Alaska Museum of the North. The Yale Peabody museum acquired the dolls, moccasins, and purses collected by Ethel Klemm during her years as a schoolteacher in Ketchikan and Haines in the 1930s. A third collection at the Sheldon Museum and Cultural Center in Haines, put together by Steve and Elizabeth Sheldon, includes many pairs of moccasins from the 1920s to the 1940s, which were obtained in trade for groceries and other necessities.

Tourist Collectors

Although there are no large groups of beaded souvenirs gathered by an individual tourist in a single museum collection, many museums have

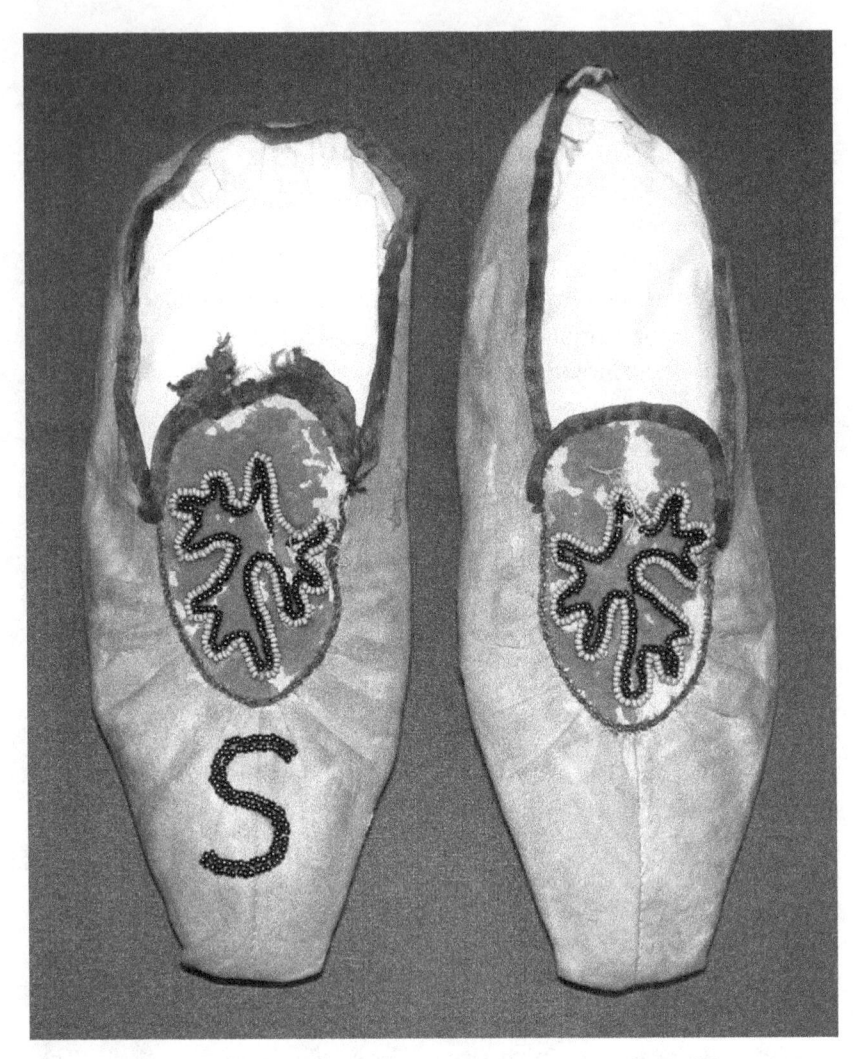

Fig. 21.1 Moccasins purchased at Sitka, Alaska, in 1888. Courtesy of the Penn Museum, object nos. 97-84-386a and 97-84-386b. Photograph: Megan A. Smetzer.

examples of souvenirs acquired from the nineteenth century onward. These pieces tend to be moccasins and wall-pockets made primarily from hide and fur but embellished with small pieces of woolen cloth and beaded floral or seaweed motifs. Souvenirs, particularly from the late Victorian era (1880–1920), were usually purchased by women and have little to no accompanying documentation. One significant exception provides a tantalizing glimpse of the interaction that took place between a Tlingit beader and a Euro-American tourist. The moccasins (L84-386 a, b), housed in the University of Pennsylvania Museum, are made of Native tanned hide and are ornamented with red cloth aprons and blue silk trim (figure 21.1).

On each apron, a foliate or seaweed motif is outlined in a double row of turquoise and black beads. One moccasin displays a double row of black beads in the shape of the letter "S" applied directly to the tanned hide below the apron. The museum catalog indicates that the moccasins were collected in 1888 by Mary Schaeffer, donated to the Academy of Natural Sciences in 1904, and transferred to the University of Pennsylvania Museum in 1944. Cramped handwriting in the Academy's accession book states: "The sailing of the vessel prevented the maker & donor from completing the second S." A note accompanying the moccasins states, "Moccasins made by Sitka Indian Woman." These pieces of information are significant because they disclose the name of the collector, the year in which she collected the moccasins, and the location from which she collected them. Moreover, they indicate the time constraints of a typical tourist who was dependent on tides and the steamer's schedule. These few details open a window to the past in a way that is rarely recorded. Though the name of the Tlingit woman who made the moccasins remains unknown, her skills as a sewer and beader are apparent in the object itself.

Analysis of Database

As the history of the moccasins attest, during the height of museum collecting at the turn of the nineteenth century, ethnographers and other collectors rarely recorded the names of makers. One result of the compilation of this database is the ability to bring to the forefront those few women, primarily from the twentieth century, whose names have been recorded. Up to this point, I have identified forty-four beaders who have pieces in museum collections.[3] And, as this research disseminates throughout southeast Alaska, I anticipate that the beadwork of more artists will be recognized and their names can be associated with the pieces. This is a significant process as a series of conversations I held with Pamlea Bogda indicate.[4] While leafing through a binder of beadwork photographs, Pamlea noticed that a pair of sealskin moccasins trimmed with rabbit fur and embellished with an eagle beaded onto a background of red wool looked just like the ones her grandmother, Annie White of Hoonah, used to make (figure 21.2).

Fig. 21.2 Sealskin moccasins made by Annie White from Hoonah, Alaska, ca. 1960s. Identified by Pamela Bogda. All rights reserved, Image Archives, Denver Museum of Nature & Science, a1074a, b. Photograph by Megan A. Smetzer.

When we examined the museum provenance, we found that the moccasins had been made in the 1960s and given to a man who had been a schoolteacher in Hoonah. Further research in the Ethel M. (Clayton) Montgomery Papers (MS 136), housed at the Alaska Historical Library indicated that Annie White had been beading moccasins and selling them through the Alaska Native Arts and Crafts Cooperative at that time.

A second example of the kind of knowledge only available through community consultation derives from conversations I held with Johnnie Marks and Florence Marks Sheakley.[5] Both Johnnie and Florence suggested a use for dance collars with three beaded pouches suspended from a beaded neckpiece (figure 21.3, 21.4). They believe these dance collars, worn during the late nineteenth century, were probably used to hold money. The reconnection of community-based knowledge with museum and archival holdings is one of the ongoing aspects of this research and is a valuable resource for all parties concerned.

Fig. 21.3 (*top*) Late nineteenth- or early twentieth-century dance collar with pouches. University of Alaska Museum of the North, 771-8. Photograph by Megan A. Smetzer.

Fig. 21.4 (*bottom*) Angoon dancers from the Teikweidí clan. The man standing directly below the dragonfly at the center of the photograph has been identified as Yeilnaawú (Dick Yetlna). He appears to be wearing the dance collar (UAMN 771-8) illustrated in fig. 22.3. Elbridge W. Merrill Collection, Alaska State Library, P57-28.

Fig. 21.5 Sam Davis seated with octopus bags and other regalia. Octopus bag to Davis's right is similar to bags in the University of Alaska's Museum of the North Collection (720-7 and 724-17). Octopus bag to his left (fig. 22.6) is now in the Portland Art Museum Collection (48.3.817). This photograph was taken in Vincent Soboleff's store, ca. 1910. Vincent Soboleff Collection, Alaska State Library, P1-50.

A third result of this project has been to identify the museum location of some of the beaded pieces that are depicted in photographs from the late nineteenth and early twentieth centuries. For example, in a photograph of Sam Davis in the Kootznahoo store in Angoon, taken by Vincent Soboleff at the turn of the nineteenth century, an octopus bag depicted on Davis's left is now in the collection of the Portland Art Museum (figure 21.5, 21.6). According to Axel Rasmussen's records, he purchased this bag from the photographers Lloyd Winter and Percy Pond in the 1930s. The bag to Davis's right is quite similar to two bags located at the University of Alaska Museum of the North (720-7 and 724-17). This similarity, particularly in terms of the central motif, provides previously unrecorded information regarding a possible community of origin for these two bags.

Fig. 21.6 Octopus bag, early twentieth century, Angoon. Appears in PCA 1-50. PAM 48.3.817. Collected by Axel Rasmussen from photographers Winter and Pond, 1934. 52.7 x 27.3 cm.

Case Studies

Before outlining the four case studies within which I focus on the specific social, cultural, and political contexts and discourses relevant to the understanding of the production and consumption of beadwork, I would like to briefly define my terminology. On a general level, I utilize the term *beadwork* to include a wide range of objects constructed from hide, fur, and/or commercially made wool and cotton cloth embellished with beads in identifiable patterns.[6] Although beads made from natural materials have been used to adorn Tlingit clothing and other goods since before contact with Euro-Americans, I focus primarily on the use of glass seed beads, which in the nineteenth century were imported primarily from Venice for trade with indigenous peoples in North America. These small, uniformly sized beads continue to be sewn in great quantities to cloth or tanned hide in characteristic patterns. Though I cannot go into great detail here, I identify three major types of beaded motifs, which are floral/foliate/seaweed, crest, and geometric, and three major types of objects, which include regalia made for ceremonial occasions, objects made for use within Tlingit homes and/or gifts, and souvenirs made for sale.

Each of the case studies draws on three theoretical formulations that have proved helpful in explaining these historical and contemporary phenomena. Ruth Phillips's work on souvenirs and material culture, Nicholas Thomas's notion that objects and contexts disrupt one another, and James Clifford's articulation theory counter the interlocking Euro-American discourses regarding authenticity, tradition, the gendered hierarchy between fine and applied arts, and the issues of commodification that have led to the marginalization of many objects made by indigenous women. Instead, I consider these kinds of objects as the material embodiment of the complex and uneven relationships between indigenous women and others and also as a means for disrupting and altering the contexts within which they circulated and gained meaning.

I utilize the term *embodiment* in two ways. First, I consider material objects as physical representations of historical processes. Following Phillips's argument in regard to indigenous clothing, objects developed in contact situations must be considered both as an example of "self-imaging" in relation to the Euro-American/Canadian gaze and also as the "materialization of negotiation and inventions that occurred in the process of its fabrication."[7] Because many of these objects often combine aspects of long-standing cultural practices with newer ideas and materials, they manifest shifting interactions at specific moments. In this sense, beaded objects can be considered sites of historical negotiations that carry information into the present regarding their producers and consumers as they are situated within specific cultural practices and in terms of contemporaneous art historical and anthropological discourses.

Second, I build upon this idea of indigenous objects as embodiment through Thomas's concept that objects and contexts disrupt one another. He argues against art being understood as a mere illustration of cultural symbols and relations. Rather, he has "presumed that art is effective in defining those social relations and meanings, and may radically redefine them."[8] Though I am not necessarily arguing that indigenous objects have agency in Alfred Gell's sense, I maintain that their physical existence enabled indigenous people to resist, and even shift, imposed notions about disappearing cultural practices and reinforce significant issues surrounding identity.[9]

My definitions of embodiment are further framed by Clifford's articulation theory, which contends that attention should be paid to the ways in which indigenous communities selectively draw on aspects of the past and combine them with present realities in order to address contemporary issues. A key concept introduced by Clifford, critical to the repositioning of these objects, is that "authenticity is secondary."[10] Articulation theory provides a means for moving beyond the entrenched academic paradigms informed by assertions of inauthenticity and the loss of tradition, because it recognizes that inventiveness is a normal process of cultural continuity. And it is this sense of inventiveness that assists in the reconsideration of beadwork.

The late Victorian era encompasses the first two case studies. In the first, I analyze the ubiquity of beadwork in the 1904 potlatch photographs (figures 21.4, 21.7). I argue that contemporaneous Euro-American settlers may have understood beadwork's prominence in these images as a clear signal of the degeneration and disappearance of Tlingit people and their cultural practices through assimilation. Colonial officials, ethnographers, and others may have understood beadwork as a weak substitute for "pure" cultural expression, a perspective reinforced by the rhetoric that this was to be the "last potlatch." Viewed from another point of view, however, beaded dance collars, tunics, cartridge belts, and octopus bags make strong statements about continuity and resis-

Fig. 21.7 Sitka hosts and Yakutat guests at the 1904 Sitka potlatch. Individuals identified in *Under Mount Saint Elias* (p. 1139). E. W. Merrill Collection, Alaska State Library, PC57-21.

tance. The beaded bib-shaped dance collar, for example, parallels, in both shape and crest embellishment, eighteenth-century wood and hide armor (figure 21.8). I believe that the turn-of-the-century makers and wearers of this evocative collar style would have understood it as a reference to the strength of Tlingit warriors and an assertion of Tlingit identity in the face of increasing colonial pressures.[11]

In the second case study, I situate beadwork as a significant strategy by which Tlingit women exploited the developing tourist market in order

Fig. 21.8 Dance collar, late nineteenth or early twentieth century. Reverend Andrew P. Kashevaroff Collection, Alaska State Museum, Juneau, 2001.10.11.

to survive economically and culturally. I argue that because of their qualities, beaded souvenirs such as moccasins and wall pockets, fulfilled missionary and tourist ideals regarding assimilation through the use of introduced materials and the engagement with the cash economy. At the same time, because it was considered inauthentic and nontraditional, particularly by ethnographers, beadwork produced for sale provided a smokescreen for beaded regalia being made within communities for ceremonial purposes. In order to bring the complexities of this situation to light, I trace the career of Gadji'nt, known popularly to tourists as Mrs. Tom or Princess Thom, who successfully marketed herself and her souvenirs, converted to Presbyterianism, and also participated in significant Tlingit cultural practices (figure 21.9).

In the mid-twentieth century, which scholars have often categorized as a time of little or no art making, beadwork was both an economic outlet and a way to maintain and continue cultural practices. I draw this conclusion from my conversations with beaders and from the records of the Alaska Native Arts and Crafts Cooperative. These documents indicate that more than five hundred women of all generations produced beadwork for sale through ANAC from the late 1930s through the 1970s. Moccasins were the most popular item made for sale, outsold only by Inupiat and Yup'ik ivory carvings. Dolls were also

Fig. 21.9 Two native Sitka women. Alaska Historical Library, William R. Norton collection, P226-813. Identified as Princess Thom and Mrs. Mausbauer in Frances Knapp and Rheta Louise Childe's 1896 book, *The Tlinget Indians* (p. 106).

produced, and they illustrate a significant shift that represents, in part, the increasing political autonomy of Alaska Native people throughout the twentieth century. Beginning in the 1930s, Tlingit-made dolls were of a generic "Alaska" type, exhibiting both fur ruffs and beaded dance collars. By the 1950s, a shift was occurring, and dolls wearing regalia were being increasingly produced (figure 21.10).

ANAC records indicate that mid-century doll makers did not like making the generic "dolls that tourists want."[12] Rather they began asserting specific Tlingit identities through the regalia clad dolls.[13]

My final case study examines the multiple roles played by beadwork at Celebration. I have been attending Celebration since 2000 and have witnessed the ways in which beadwork is worn and used in a variety of settings. The Mount Saint Elias Dancers, for example, differentiate themselves from the other dance groups by pointing out the significance of their beaded regalia and how it visually illustrates long-standing relationships with interior peoples. Beadwork is often sold at the Native Artist Market and has been included in the juried art shows.

Fig. 21.10 Mid-twentieth-century dolls, probably made by Mary Baker of Juneau. Sheldon Jackson Museum, Sitka, 1.A.307a, b. Photograph by Megan A. Smetzer.

Finally, beadwork has also been used to indicate important political relationships. During a fund-raiser for her gubernatorial campaign in 2002, Agnes Bellinger presented Fran Ulmer with a beaded headband and pendant depicting eagles and spoke of her family's support for Ulmer's ultimately unsuccessful gubernatorial run.

Each one of these case studies, in conjunction with the catalogue, is intended to illustrate that beadwork has been thoroughly entwined with Tlingit social, economic, and cultural practices over the past century and a half. Though made from introduced materials, beadwork has drawn meaning from long-standing Tlingit traditions and concepts that have enabled it to serve a wide range of functions and to act as a way of perpetuating significant cultural practices into the future. The dynamic roles played by Tlingit beadwork, whether regalia, souvenirs, or nonceremonial pieces made for internal use, underline the innovation and creativity of the women who have made and used it. Regalia have been implicated in issues of identity, becoming a metaphor for strength and resilience in the face of colonial pressures. Among Tlingit communities and by Tlingit individuals, beadwork has served as a marker of difference and an expression of long-standing relationships with other indigenous groups. Beaded souvenirs have helped to fulfill tourists' expectations of indigenous peoples through materials and embellishment. At the same time, these expectations contributed to what I term *colonial blindness*, which allowed for the continuation of some cultural practices during eras when those practices were considered degenerating, dying, or disconnected from tradition. The acceptance and transformation of new materials such as beads and cloth indicate the flexibility with which Tlingit people have accommodated colonial impositions, at the same time that they have furthered significant and long-standing cultural practices.

As this essay indicates, attention must be paid to those concepts and objects that have continued to accrue meaning or play roles through the significant cultural disruptions caused by colonialism. Rather than focusing on imposed categorizations of authenticity and tradition, it is more useful to examine accommodation, resilience, and inventiveness. It is my hope that this approach to these beautiful objects, in combination with the catalogue of beadwork in museum collections, will have value and use in southeast Alaska, and lay the groundwork for future explorations of the practices and histories of Tlingit beadwork.

ACKNOWLEDGMENTS

I would like to thank the many beaders and elders who have taken the time to share their experiences of beading and knowledge of beadwork. My thesis has been greatly enriched through these conversations. I would also like to acknowledge the Sealaska Heritage Institute for inviting me to be a visiting scholar in 2006, which enabled me to pursue additional lines of inquiry raised through the writing process.

NOTES

1. Cole, *Captured Heritage*.
2. Boas, *Primitive Art*, 144.
3. Maria Ackerman, Mary Baker, Big Emma (Tahltan), Esther Billman, Lillian Demmert, Vesta Dominicks, Lillian Hammond, Annie Hotch, Margaret Howard, Flora Huntington, Mrs. B. A. Jack, Nancy Jackson, Mary James, Annie James, Johnnie Joe's Aunt (Tagish), Minnie Johnson, Mrs. Johnson, Ida Kadashan, Annie Kinnauiaq Kadvulik, Joyce Katzeek, Anna

Katzeek, Mary King, Esther Littlefield, Emma Marks, Anny Marks, Mary Martin, Alvina Martinez, Stella Martins, Elsie Mellott, Maria Miller, Tillie Paul, Annie Fulton Ross, Florence Marks Sheakley, Mrs. Moses Smith, Mildred Sparks, Mrs. St. Clair, Jennie Thlunaut, Fannie Ukase, Bessie Visaya, Emma Weaver, Annie White, Sara Williams, Lily Yaquan.
4. Pamlea Bogda, personal communication, March 2006.
5. Johnnie Marks and Florence Marks Sheakley, personal communications, March 2006.
6. For further information on the history of glass beads in North America and elsewhere, see, for example, Dubin, *North American Indian Jewelry and Adornment*; Dubin, *The History of Beads*; Frances, "Beads and Bead Trade in the North Pacific Region," 341; Orchard, *Native American Beadwork*.
7. Phillips, "Making Sense out/of the Visual," 606.
8. Thomas, "Technologies of Conversion."
9. On agency, see Gell, *Art and Agency: An Anthropological Theory*; and Pinney and Thomas, eds., *Beyond Aesthetics: Art and the Technologies of Enchantment*.
10. Clifford, "Indigenous Articulations," 479.
11. Smetzer, "Tlingit Dance Collars and Octopus Bags."
12. Ethel M. (Clayton) Montgomery Papers, 1934–1989, Alaska State Library, MS 136, box 3, folder 9.
13. Smetzer, "From Ruffs to Regalia."

REFERENCES

Boas, Franz. 1928, 1955. *Primitive Art*. New York: Dover.
Clifford, James. 2001. "Indigenous Articulations." *Contemporary Pacific* 1 (2): 468–90.
Cole, Douglas.1985. *Captured Heritage: The Scramble for Northwest Coast Artifacts*. Norman: University of Oklahoma Press.
Dubin, Lois Sherr. 1995. *The History of Beads: From 30,000 BC to the Present*. New York: Harry N. Abrams.
———. 1999. *North American Indian Jewelry and Adornment: From Prehistory to the Present*. New York: Harry N. Abrams.
Frances, Peter, Jr. 1988. "Beads and Bead Trade in the North Pacific Region." In *Crossroads of Continents: Cultures of Siberia and Alaska*, ed. William W. Fitzhugh and Aron Crowell, 341. Washington DC: Smithsonian Institution Press.
Gell, Alfred. 1998. *Art and Agency: An Anthropological Theory*. Oxford: Oxford University Press.
Orchard, William. 1929, 1975, 2002 *Native American Beadwork*. Mineola NY: Dover.

Phillips, Ruth B. 2004. "Making Sense out/of the Visual: Aboriginal Presentations and Representations in Nineteenth-Century Canada." *Art History* 27 (4): 593–615.

Pinney, Christopher, and Nicholas Thomas, eds. 2001. *Beyond Aesthetics: Art and the Technologies of Enchantment.* New York: Berg.

Smetzer, Megan A. 2009. "From Ruffs to Regalia: Tlingit Dolls and the Embodiment of Identity." In *Women and Things, 1750–1950: Gendered Material Culture*, ed. Mary Daly Goggin and Beth Fowkes Tobin, 75–90. Hampshire, England: Ashgate, 2009.

———. 2008. "Tlingit Dance Collars and Octopus Bags: Embodying Power and Resistance." *American Indian Art Magazine* 34 (1): 64–73.

Thomas, Nicholas. 2000. "Technologies of Conversion: Cloth and Christianity in Polynesia." *Hybridity and Its Discontents: Politics, Science, Culture*, ed. Avtar Brah and Annie E. Coombes, 198–215. New York: Routledge.

22

Balancing Protocol and Law for Intellectual Property

Examples and Ethical Dilemmas from the Northwest Coast Art Market

ALEXIS C. BUNTEN

"If I make it, it's original!"
—NORTHWEST COAST ARTIST, SITKA, 1998

Just over 1.5 million people visited Alaska in 2011, outnumbering state citizens by a two to one ratio and spending an average of $941 per trip. The basic economic principle of supply and demand suggests that Alaska Native art should be rare, given that only .04 percent of the United States population is Alaska Native.[1] To the contrary, the market for Alaska Native commercial arts is flooded with inventory, ranging from cheap, mass-produced souvenirs to original commissions to antique objects auctioned at hundreds of thousands of dollars. Estimates report that most of what is offered for sale is not made by Alaska Natives at all, making it difficult for Alaska Natives to take part in the cash economy.

The Alaska Department of Commerce and Economic Development stated that about half of the $80 million in retail purchases made by tourists in Alaska each year are presented as Native arts and crafts, but 75–80 percent of what is displayed as Native work is counterfeit (Hollowell 2000).[2] Another report released by the U.S. Interior's Office of Inspector General concludes that the extent of the problem is "difficult to quantify" due to inadequate information about the size of the market, poor statistics, public misconception, and conflicting perceptions of the criteria to identify an object as fake Alaska Native art (U.S. Government Accountability Office 2011, 9–10). Imitation Alaska Native products vary from high-end original artworks to mass-produced pieces from Asia. Most galleries and souvenir shops have no problem displaying Native-made art next to non-Native work adorned with misleading labels, such as "authentic" and "Alaska made." Some non-Native artists market their pieces with indigenized names, such as the Cambodian-born "Chupak," whose agent marketed his work as "made in a Native Alaskan village" (Hollowell 2004, 59). Other tricks used to confuse visitors wanting to purchase Alaska Native art include adding certifications of authenticity to reproductions of original Native-made pieces whose copyright has been purchased (Hollowell 2000). In line with the logic of classical economic theory, the marketplace is clearly more interested in maximizing profit than in putting money into the hands of the actual Alaska Native artists.

While the Western notion of original art is that it is available to anyone who wants to make it, most of the iconography seen in Northwest Coast art forms is governed by cultural protocol that places strict rules on who has the right to produce new artworks. When individuals produce Northwest Coast style art without possessing some kind of "birthright" or permission to use these forms, they compete with those who do. I interviewed Northwest Coast artists throughout southeast Alaska, the traditional homeland of the Tlingit people, to gain an understanding of how they experience the commercial market for Alaska Native arts.[3] Here's a sample of what they had to say about the market.

> It's nice to know that things will be off this continent and people will be showing it saying, "Hey, I got this. This was made by a real Alaska Native!" It feels good.

> The shops around here, and especially some of these old time shops, have taken advantage of artists for years and years, and it still goes on to this day. It's a shame. And the way the shop owners look at it, they are doing the artists a favor, you know?

> I'm learning to make a living from my art. That's the thing that's taking me the longest to learn is how to deal with the gallery. But it takes time to work your way up.

> A lot of [Native artists] have no background in the business actually. They have no idea how it operates. If anything, they can work on the business as well as have the love, the passion, and the skills

because it's so much of a balancing act between the two to be successful. A lot of them have been burned so much by the gift shops and stores to where they don't trust anyone from outside the region to deal with. There's really no one here that promotes except basically Natives that promote Natives.

There are a lot of non-Natives that do it, and they are rich. They are making all the money, and the artists aren't.

I don't think there's going to be much of a future if there's other people doing it. If there's other people trying to take it over. There's a lot of ivory carvings that weren't even done by Natives. They were done in Bali or something. And I go to a lot of other places and see all these plastic totem poles, plastic whatever poles. They're not trying to do nothing for us.

In addition to having to compete in a marketplace saturated with pieces made by non-Natives, Alaska Native artists must navigate complex legal, cultural, and ethical issues in order to successfully take part in the commercial art world. These considerations are especially complex for Northwest Coast artists, who need to make decisions about the ownership of certain images and art forms and in which cross-cultural contexts they can be used. While the market pushes Alaska Native artists to produce a wider variety of objects to compete with a growing array of imposter goods, cultural protocol can serve to restrict the imagery, designs, and materials used in contemporary art production.

Legal protections under the category of intellectual property (IP) law safeguard Alaska Native artists from unfair competition and misrepresentation. This chapter introduces the basic tenets of IP law, comparing it with Tlingit protocol for *at.óow*, or customary law. Through a series of real-life cross-cultural "dilemmas" that Northwest Coast artists routinely negotiate as they make and share their work across cultural divides, this chapter outlines the vast cultural differences between U.S. IP law and traditional Tlingit protocol.

Intellectual Property Law and At.óow

"Intellectual property" is a catchall term that refers collectively to trademarks, copyrights, rights to designs, patents, and trade secrets. Arts and crafts as tangible objects fall under the protection against unauthorized reproduction, misrepresentation, and unfair competition covered by IP law. From a business perspective, intellectual property is considered a valuable asset because it can provide market exclusivity, build brand reputation, and generate income.[4] However, United States IP law has several limitations for Native Alaskans: it only applies to commercial contexts, and it does not protect against international theft.

While IP law offers protection for individual artists and Native business entities that own the rights to a particular art piece, trademark, or design, it does not recognize the traditional Tlingit sociopolitical units that govern ownership and rights to most of the concepts, stories, and imagery associated with Northwest Coast art forms. IP law is fundamentally British in origin and therefore supports a Western notion of individual ownership as opposed to a more indigenous notion of collective ownership, whereas Tlingit protocol for intellectual property fits under the concept of *at.óow* (owned thing), a concept central to a Tlingit worldview linking the social, spiritual, and material aspects of the universe.

For the Tlingits who follow traditional protocol, collective ownership and political power are structured by the kinship-based clan system.[5] Tlingit elder Paul Jackson described the concept to me:

> *At.óow* is something that the clan has. Something in their history has happened so they would put it on something—a totem pole, a carving, or a robe, a Chilkat robe—and this becomes part of the history of the people, and they would take care of it from generation to generation, and it becomes *at.óow*. And there are many things that we call *at.óow*. And *shuká* is our ancestors where we come from, and this is where we learn to do the many things that we do.

According to Dauenhauer and Dauenhauer (2000, 104), *at.óow* may include the "land (mountain, a historical site, a place), a heavenly body (the sun, a constellation), a spirit, a personal name, an artistic design, or an object. It can be an image from oral literature, like an episode from the Raven cycle executed on a tunic or hat; it can be a story or song about an event in the life of an ancestor, and even ancestors themselves. *At.óow* can also be spirits of various kinds: shaman spirits and spirits of animals." Tlingit silver carver Louis Minard defined traditional Northwest Coast artistic style in terms of *at.óow*: "The way it was developed in the past. The traditional formlines. The way our ancestors developed it. So that is traditional but only for them. When we carve and we think it's done exactly as it was done in the past, and today a lot of them are doing the contemporary which they sell to the public, but for our people, its always the traditional formlines with the traditional detail because it's their property and their crests, and they are the owners of it." For Louis, the crest designs depicted within the formline design belong exclusively to clans. The most important aspect of *at.óow* is that it is *clan-owned*, defined by the clan through usage, and in turn, it defines clan-based identity. As such, *at.óow* is a powerful political tool used to assert identity-based rights to oral history and land claims in additional to images and other kinds of intellectual property that fit within the concept of traditional knowledge. If *anybody* can appropriate the formline design or representations that fall under *at.óow*, then it follows that Tlingit identity itself is subject to theft.

Issue 1: Who Has the Right to Make Northwest Coast Art?

The concept of *at.óow* is more complicated than these descriptions suggest. There are protocols for obtaining *at.óow*, inheriting it, displaying it, and using it in ceremonies. Only certain people authorized by the clan have the authority to approve the reproduction or fabrication of clan-owned objects or the use of certain imagery within various contexts. I asked the artists how these rules translate to the commercial art market. Their responses indicated a controversy over *who* may make Northwest Coast art. Some felt that an artist's ethno-racial background is irrelevant, so long as they understand the culture behind the art form, whereas others felt strongly that only Alaska Native artists should be allowed to make it. Comments against non-Natives making the art altogether revealed some artists' frustrations with economic insecurity caused by the glut of non-Native pieces in the marketplace.

> It helps to be born and raised in the culture. Some non-Natives can adopt in the culture or are born into it. But to do the art, you have to look into its background and respect the culture.

> The main thing is knowing the stories, knowing your cultural background. Knowing who your family is, knowing the stories that came to your family.

Any Native art is how the people are doing it, Native and non-Native. For me, I think it's pretty much people doing their own traditional styles, but there are lots that copy styles and mix them up.

Louis Minard: We try to keep this within our own people because the art form belonged to our people, the Tlingit. Also the Haida, Tlingit, and the Tsimshian formlines are the same with a little detail that would be changed, which the Haidas use and the Tsimshians use. But the formlines are the same, which is the property of our people. The three tribes are the same, and it is their traditional property, so we try to keep it within our people. I don't like to pass it on to white people, because they have money to live on. Why should they live on this art? My feeling is this: If they get into here, we let one in, the door will open for all the rest of them. So I want it to stay. I have refused a lot of people from the white community who want to come in and become a silver carver or a silver engraver in NWC Indian art. I feel it belongs to our people. It's their property.

Jimmy Marks: Right now we have a lot of Caucasian artists entering the competition, and I don't think they really have a knowledge of what it's supposed to mean. They just carve, and they put us out of business. Also, those plastic totem pole makers. They are going to put us out of business. They put them up in Alaska shops, and you look in the back and it says they are made in Taiwan, and that really works on our traditional way of life, you know?

Issue 2: Should Artists Ask Permission to Use *At.óow* in Making Commercial Work?

At.óow includes images and stories that have been acquired by a clan and passed down from generation to generation. All Tlingit clans possess a symbol or crest. For example, the Dakl'aweidí clan owns the symbol of the killer whale, and can therefore be referred to as the killer whale clan. Regardless of whether a clan crest is depicted on an old piece that is used in ceremonies or a brand-new artwork, it is still considered *at.óow*. Northwest Coast artists must decide what kinds of stories and images they will and won't include in their commercial work. If they are very strict about following protocol, they will use very little traditional symbolic imagery. Artists who try to respect traditional protocol get around this issue by using "generic" crests and other imagery, not specific to one clan or lineage. Continuing the example, there are multiple killer whale designs owned by different killer whale "sub-clans" or "houses." Therefore, it could be argued that a killer whale design that is not directly copied from a living object of *at.óow* does not breech traditional law. Some artists ask permission from clan leaders to depict particular designs, and others do not bother. Here's what they had to say about this issue.

There should be no traditional designs or sub crests on anything you make to sell. Baskets should have no traditional designs, and other objects should only be decorated with eagle or raven crest symbols.

We will modify the formlines and also rearrange the details so it does not look like the traditional emblem of our peoples. So if we make a difference, then our people don't fuss at us for selling their property.

I feel free to carve any of the crests that are of my clan.

Ester Shea: You have to ask permission even before you use your own design.

If I have permission to use a crest design from one person in a clan, it could be honoring the clan. It's hard to ask permission for crest designs.

I try not to depict a story without permission. It's really complicated because as far as ownership goes, *at.óow*. Ownership was something that was already created, not something potentially created, so traditional leaders don't have the authority to demand ownership of what I'm about to create. But some people in this area want to assert power they don't have. Maybe they feel they have been disrespected in the past, so they feel resentful toward those who disrespected them.

There's certain things that a person should not do, and if you want to do it, make sure you have permission before you do.

If I had complaints from a clan member because I was carving their crest, first of all, I would investigate if they actually did own the crest, and if that was the case, I would make amends or payment. Compensate for use of that crest, but it just doesn't happen that often. Today, everybody just carves whatever they want to carve, and today that tradition of respecting whose crests you are carving is gone.

Today everyone just carves what they want to carve, and that tradition of respecting whose crests you are carving is gone. There are certain stories that clans own that you may really want to get permission when carving a totem or something like that.

Northwest Coast artists' opinions about whether and how to address permissions to reproduce *at.óow* are varied. While they may risk social censure for "stealing" clan designs without permission, artists (of any ethno-racial background) are not legally required to obtain the rights to them from authorized clan representatives. U.S. intellectual property law can only protect the kind of traditional knowledge, designs and objects encapsulated within the concept of *at.óow* if it is commoditized for commercial sale. *At.óow* outside of the commercial realm is therefore beyond the protection of this body of law and, as such, can be copied or used by anybody for any reason without legal repercussion. According to IP law, anybody has a legal right to make any kind of art they want to, as long as they remain within the boundaries of the law as protects the owners of intellectual property against misrepresentation and unfair competition.

Issue 3: Can Artists Replicate Objects in the Public Domain?

One example that illustrates the stark difference between *at.óow* and Western law is the question of public domain. Public domain refers to works that are not eligible for copyright protection or that have expired copyrights. Most nineteenth-century and earlier Tlingit art held by museums is probably *at.óow* for two reasons. First, any objects made before 1923 are not protected under copyright. Second, most of the great masterworks of Northwest Coast art that remain in public or private hands today were not signed following a Western script system. Without a signature to verify the original artist, the object becomes part of the public domain, known in legal terminology as an "orphan work."

According to traditional Tlingit protocol, any *at.óow*, regardless of location (inside or outside clan hands) or authorship, is considered clan-owned in perpetuity. Therefore, clan consent is still required to replicate parts or all of the objects themselves, including the ideas behind the symbolism depicted. According to IP law, permission is not needed to copy works in the public domain. Moreover, objects in the public domain can be replicated, mass-produced, and distributed in any number of forms, media, and ways including digitally. The clan that customarily "owns" an object of *at.óow* held in the public domain does not have the legal right to stop somebody from replicating it.

While it does not legally safeguard *at.óow* from commercial reproduction, the public domain helps artists to hone their craft precisely because it allows rare pieces to be reproduced in any number of forms. Often the only access that artists have to older, traditional Northwest Coast art is through books that depict images of works that have been preserved in museums. Most of the artists I spoke with told me that they study objects that are in the public domain for inspiration.

Q: What do you look for in objects that are in the public domain?
A: Traditional style. Old style is what I call it. I look at the old stuff and try to get that look and feel.
Q: Where do you draw references for your art?
A: Books. Mental library of stories.
Q: Do you ever reference books or museum pieces?
A: I do. I look at a lot of books.
Q: Do you ever reference anything to do your work?
A: I've got a good collection of books. I like the books that have all the old artwork in it.
   I used to look at books and get ideas from the books. I'd also get ideas from my uncles.
Q: How did you start learning how to do the art?
A: Just looking at my books. Just always studying stuff and trying to practice doing what I was looking at.

If an artist makes a replica of an object in the public domain, he or she acquires the copyright over any new or added features and over the specific form of the replica. This legal nuance means that indigenous artists can "take back" copyright by remaking older designs in new forms (Hollowell 2000). There are some limitations to this strategy, however. The new piece, called a "derivative work" in legal terminology, must differ somehow from the preexisting piece. A well-executed photograph of a two-dimensional painting or an exact replica of a clan hat using 3D scan and print technology, for example, would likely not be considered "derivative" in the legal sense.[6] Moreover, the copyright only belongs to the producer of the derived work; legal ownership of the original piece of *at.óow* does not automatically revert back to the clan.

Issue 4: How Can an Artist Retain the Copyright to Original Designs?

Copyright is the right of an author to control the use of his or her literary and artistic creations. These may include:

1. literary works
2. musical works, including any accompanying words
3. dramatic works, including any accompanying music
4. pantomimes and choreographic works
5. pictorial, graphic, and sculptural works
6. motion pictures and other audiovisual works
7. sound recordings
8. architectural works

As soon as any of the things listed are created, the creator "owns" the copyright to his or her own work. Copyrights give the owner the exclusive legal right to reproduce, publish, sell, or distribute the works created. It also allows the owner to control how his or her creations are used by others, granting the owner the right to stop others from copying, adapting, displaying, distributing, or selling copyrighted work without permission. Copyright is important to establish and maintain because once a creation is given or sold to others, it becomes possible for others to make uses of it.

Artists can forfeit or sell the copyright to their original works. Many Northwest Coast artists are unaware that they do not retain the copyright over objects they make as employees of an art or cultural center. If an artist is hired explicitly to make art objects, the copyright to everything he or she makes belongs to the employer.

In general, the artists I talked to said they avoided selling the copyright to their original designs. Most understand that selling copyright is a single transaction in which they earn money only once, whereas the buyer can make money for any number and means of reproduction without paying the original artist royalties.

Artists also know that when they are being asked to sell the copyright to their designs, the buyer may intend to mass reproduce it in various forms. Selling copyright is a tricky issue, because artists need to make a living, and most of them don't have the access to the capital, means, and know-how to reproduce their own artwork. They are aware that cheaper, mass-produced pieces advertised as "authentic" Native designs often outcompete more expensive hand-crafted objects, and many don't like the idea of non-Natives profiting off of what was originally Native-owned intellectual property. Artists concerned about being exploited, or exploiting themselves, are justified by the off-season timing of wholesalers looking to purchase designs. As one artist put it, selling copyrights kills the market.

> I had this friend, and you know how they put these designs on jackets and all that stuff? A friend of mine came up to me and said, "Oh yeah, they are doing that stuff, and they're selling it for too much, and I am going to do it better and sell it for cheaper." I looked at him and said, "Right on, man. The next person is gonna come right behind you and do the exact same thing and so forth and so forth, and pretty soon none of you guys are going to make money. That's the way to go." He looks at me and said, "I never even thought of it that way." I said, "Yeah, none of you guys ever do. You come and kill your own market. You guys think you are all being better than them, and all you are doing is just killing us all."

Here's what others had to say about selling the copyright to their designs.

> This guy wanted me to do a bunch of castings of my work. And I was ready to go do it. And I took off and I thought about it and thought about it, and I was like, no, I can't do that. If I go and do it, it's like stabbing myself in the back.
>
> There was one guy that's a wholesaler and he travels around, and most of the things were kind of like originals to casts. I have some cast pieces out there, and I sold the rights for them right off. And he travels all around. Like the pins and totem poles. Those are all his, so I don't get any royalties back. He usually catches me in the winter when things are getting tight.

Q: Does it cheapen the art?
A: Oh yeah, people don't want to buy what we are putting out because they see that the plastic is cheaper. There are a lot of people that just do it to make money off it.

Balancing Protocol and Law for Intellectual Property 471

Artists are more ambivalent about doing commissions than selling copyright outright. Commissions can provide good opportunities for Northwest Coast artists. They supply steady work during the slow months outside the tourist season. While many commissions are private, federal and state agencies regularly commission public art. By making art more accessible to more people, public arts bring outside attention to Northwest Coast artists, increasing cross-cultural understanding and raising their profiles. Doing a commission leads to a domino effect for many artists. Once they have one, they are more likely to be sought after for more. However, artists who sign on to commissions need to understand that the commissioning agent owns the intellectual property associated with the commissioned piece. As the copyright owner, the commissioning agent can reproduce the design in any amount or medium, and the original artist would then need permission to reproduce his or her own piece.

One artist told me that he will not copy designs that someone else has made. If he is asked to do a special design, he won't do it. "I am protecting myself and my copyright."

Another artist explained why he enjoys commissions, but neither he nor his clients seemed to understand that the copyright for his original work belongs to the client.

> I like the challenge. Keeps it fresh. Like it would be something different. It would be mine and it wouldn't be duplicated. Some people request that they don't be duplicated. So they want to tell people they have the original.

After years of being in the business, Jimmy Marks (1941–2009) explained that he charged more for commissions than for pieces he produced for the tourist market. "I get more money, also. Another old Indian trick!"

Jimmy had the right idea. Artists who agree to do commissions should charge more because in addition to making a custom piece for a client, they are also selling the copyright to it. If the client wishes, he or she can reproduce the artwork in the same or another medium for future sales, making the commissioned piece more valuable than one purchased in a store or gallery. To clarify, if an artist makes a piece and sells it to a shop, gallery, or even directly to a tourist or a collector, the artist retains the copyright to his or her design even after it is sold. Finally, unlike *at.óow*, copyrights do not belong to the owner in perpetuity. They only last seventy years after the creator's death.

Issue 5: Should Alaska Native Art Be Trademarked?

Unlike copyright, trademarks don't protect designs from misuse, and unauthorized reproduction. The U.S. patent and trademark office describes a trademark as a branding device that includes any word, name, symbol, device, or any combination of these used to identify and distinguish the goods and services of one seller or provider from others, or to indicate the source of the good and services.[7] The legal purpose of a trademark is to protect corporations from having their products imitated or wrongfully appropriated by others. Unlike copyrights, which expire, but similar to *at.óow*, trademarks remain valid as long as they are in use. However, trademarks only cover material used in commercial trade and have no ability to protect noncommercial forms of cultural or intellectual property included in *at.óow*.

The state of Alaska manages the Silver Hand program to promote Alaska Native arts and enable consumers to identify and purchase Alaska Native art.[8] The Silver Hand label program is a kind of trademark that enables Alaska Native art to be more easily identified and differentiated from non-Native works or copies that may be available. Any Alaska Native artist who is a full-time state resident and can verify tribal enrollment can apply for a permit that allows them to label their art with the Silver Hand logo. This logo can only be applied to original art, not reproductions and manufactured work, and can only be used by individuals or organizations granted written permission by the Alaska State Council on the Arts.

Northwest Coast artists I spoke with have a good understanding of how the program works as well as its limitations.

> I think it's good, but I think the state needs to invest more time and effort into promoting it. It's great that we can use that. If all Natives used it, it would put everybody else out of business who is making replicas.
>
> But I think about that program of the Native arts with the Silver Hand on it. That's a good problem there to help someone that doesn't know how to tell that it is Native made and getting revived because it was a big issue about things getting made in Bali. That's where guys would even change their names to Eskimo-sounding names, and they got tags that said Alaska made, and it wasn't.

While the Silver Hand program distinguishes Alaska Native art from those that are made by non-Natives, the use of this kind of trademark only works when consumers are educated about specific labels and how labels function as an indication of the originality and/or authenticity of the products. When consumers are misled, it does not work.

> To see somebody like Jack Tripp get the Silver Hands representative, knowing full well he is selling Anglo art right next to the Silver Hand products, so that everybody is misled into thinking that everything along the wall is Silver Hand. That makes me sick to see that they wouldn't even investigate who they were giving this to.

While trademarking programs like the Silver Hand cannot stop non-Natives from appropriating or mass-producing Northwest Coast style art for the market, it does give discerning consumers the ability to differentiate the fakes from genuine Native-made art.

The Indian Arts and Crafts Act of 1990 provides an additional layer of protection for Alaska Native artists. This is a truth-in-advertising law designed to prevent the sale of art falsely advertised as Native-made. This law makes it illegal to directly or indirectly offer or display for sale any art or craft product in a manner that falsely suggests it is made by a Native American or the product of a particular tribe or Native arts organization. If found guilty in court for a violation of the Indian Arts and Crafts Act, the offending party would be responsible for any statutory damages, including payment. A first-time violator faces civil or criminal penalties up to a $250,000 fine or a five-year prison term, or both.[9] If a business violates the act, it can face civil penalties or can be prosecuted and fined up to $1,000,000. A 2009 amendment to the act allows all federal law enforcement officers including officers working for the Bureau of Indian Affairs, the National Parks Service, and the U.S. Customs and Border Protection, in addition to the FBI, to investigate a suspected violation.

As frightening as the penalties seem for breaching the Indian Arts and Crafts Act, it has not prevented the continued wholesale appropriation of Native American art. Between 2006 and 2010, the Indian Arts and Crafts Board received 649 complaints of alleged infringements (U.S. GAO 2011, 14). The Board determined that 148 of these claims were violations of the law, with 49 percent involving retail stores, 33 percent internet sales, and the remaining 18 percent involving various venues including powwows, arts markets, and individual sellers. Upon further investigation, no cases were filed in federal court. Due to "higher law enforcement priorities," the board has dealt with these violations by sending warning letters and educational brochures to the offending parties. Because the Indian Arts and Crafts Act is relatively untested in court, its effectiveness as a deterrent against unlawful representation of "Indian" arts and crafts is negligible. As long as non-Native labels made to look like Native designs can compete with Native-made art, trademarks will have to be accompanied by consumer education to tell the authentic pieces from the fakes.

Issue 6: What Can You Do If Someone Steals Your Design?

The law makes it very difficult for Northwest Coast Native artists and communities to make a legal case against non-Natives who appropriate the art form for commercial gain. If an artist's original design is stolen, the artist can file a lawsuit for violation of copyright or obtain a court order to stop the sale of the infringing goods and seek monetary damages. But legal action can be too confusing, time-consuming and expensive for most artists to pursue. At the very least, the artist would need to consult and mostly likely hire an IP attorney.

Although existing U.S. law offers Northwest Coast artists some recourse if their IP is violated or stolen, it has limitations that do not consider traditional protocol governing the works. First, IP law only protects Native artists who are engaging within the Western marketplace, such as those who create art for sale or apply for a patent. Second, copyright protections are automatic, but trademarks must be registered in order to protect artists' IP. Third, if the theft is international in nature, artists have no recourse because U.S. IP law can only be upheld within the United States.

Much of what falls under the Tlingit definition of *at.óow* is outside the context of U.S. IP law. For example, many clan crests were designed long ago and fall under the category of public domain. However, an artist's specific rendition of a crest may be copyrighted to that artist, whether or not the artist has permission from the clan to use it. Another problem with U.S. IP law is that it does not protect group-owned intellectual property unless the group is represented by a corporation or other legally recognized sovereign unit. Individual Tlingit clans who want to file a lawsuit must be represented by an Alaska Native corporate or tribal entity; they cannot file a suit as a clan per se.

Outside the reach of U.S. law, clans may exert pressure on individual Northwest Coast artists thought to use clan imagery or designs without permission. Several artists told me that if the clan members feel that their *at.óow* has been misappropriated, social pressure is applied to the offending party.

> I do see elders, mostly old women, who say, "You can't carve that. That's my crest. Who gave you permission?" And that happened to me once when I carved a little crest design. So finally I just gave the necklace to the lady. And after that I just asked her if I could carve that particular crest design and she said, "Go ahead." [laughter] And she was happy. She was a Tlingit elder woman. It made me feel good in a way to settle that. If I had complaints from a clan member because I was carving their crest, first of all I would investigate if they actually did own the crest, and if that was the case, I would do the same thing I did with this woman. I would make amends or payment.

If an artist is not a part of the Tlingit social structure and is therefore unmoved by social pressure, traditional means of regulating the use of *at.óow* won't work. This does not apply to all non-Native artists. Often non-Natives are drawn to the art and the culture in respectful ways; many of them are adopted into clans and follow traditional Tlingit protocol. They understand what one Native artist explained: "Respect means knowing that you shouldn't be giving it away or just giving the forms to anybody. You got to have respect for where it came from, who is doing it, for other people that are involved."

Unlike those who approach the art form with respect, outsiders looking to commercialize Northwest Coast art for the sole purpose of making money are not moved by traditional protocol if it doesn't affect their bottom line. IP law helps to regulate unlawful appropriation of Native intellectual property by those whose motivations are solely monetary in nature. However, U.S. IP law is limited in scope and does not protect most of what falls under the traditional definition of *at.óow*.

Conclusion

The capitalist underpinnings of contemporary U.S. IP law seemingly conflict with *at.óow* in ways that render the law impossible to protect intellectual property held by Tlingit clans in perpetuity. With the development of the commercial market for Northwest Coast arts, what once fell under the exclusive domain of *at.óow* has become commoditized. Some of these forms of intellectual property easily fall under the protection of U.S. IP law, whereas other aspects of it do not. Issues of ownership, public domain, and commercial usage blur the lines between traditional protocol and open public access to many Northwest Coast art forms and designs. Finally, not all artists or Tlingit people follow traditional clan-based protocols, but everyone in America must obey the law.

A hypothetical comparison of U.S. IP law and *at.óow* sheds light on the shortcomings of the law for indigenous peoples in general. As currently conceived, written, and interpreted, U.S. IP law does not shelter *at.óow* from unauthorized appropriation. Because they are neither individuals nor business entities, Tlingit clans cannot make a legal claim against infringements of their *at.óow*. Copyrights and patents are finite, whereas *at.óow* is considered clan-owned in perpetuity. Finally, any violations of *at.óow* that are not commercial in nature are ineligible for legal protection.

In some ways *at.óow* almost matches legal concepts central to U.S. IP law, but it always falls short. In different contexts, *at.óow* can act like a copyright, a trademark, and a license. Similar to the way that commissions today render copyright to whoever commissions an artwork, clans traditionally owned the rights to control any *at.óow* that they commissioned. Like a trademark, *at.óow* "brands" a particular clan. And like a license, the clan must give permission for *at.óow* to be used once or multiple times for personal, ceremonial, or commercial reasons. Despite these promising overlaps in rights over usage and reproduction of intellectual property, as a nonbusiness entity a clan has no ability to copyright, license, or trademark the designs it owns.

This set of dilemmas that Northwest Coast Native communities and artists face underscores an overall tension between indigenous needs and Western IP law in general. IP laws do not consider the values of indigenous communities, whose societies are often organized along principles of collective ownership and decision making processes that consider the past ancestors as well as future generations. In a paper on the topic of indigenous knowledge and intellectual property, Dr. Jane Anderson explains:

> Indigenous peoples' interests in intellectual property law raise issues that involve both legal and non-legal components. Problems are not always commercial in nature and can involve ethical, cultural, historical, religious/spiritual, and moral dimensions. For example, inap-

propriate use of sacred cultural artifacts, symbols, or designs may not cause financial loss but can cause considerable offense to the relevant community responsible for the use and circulation of that artifact, symbol, or design (2010, 2).

Although current IP law does not accommodate indigenous peoples well, a team of experts involving Dr. Anderson and many others (including IP lawyers who are members of indigenous communities themselves) are working together to find ways to stretch the boundaries of existing national and international IP laws to meet the needs and objectives of indigenous communities. They have built international networks through the Intellectual Property and Cultural Heritage Project and the World Intellectual Property Organization, and they have developed print (some are listed in Dr. Anderson's issues paper) and Internet resources such as mukurtu.org, an open source platform for managing digital heritage built for indigenous community usage.

As it currently stands, U.S. IP law is in direct conflict with the United Nations Declaration on the Rights of Indigenous Peoples, Article 31, 2007, which states:

> Indigenous peoples have the right to maintain, control, protect, and develop their cultural heritage, traditional knowledge, and traditional cultural expressions, as well as the manifestations of their sciences, technologies, and cultures, including human and genetic resources, seeds, medicines, knowledge of the properties of fauna and flora, oral traditions, literatures, designs, sports and traditional games, and visual and performing arts. They also have the right to maintain, control, protect, and develop their intellectual property over such cultural heritage, traditional knowledge, and traditional cultural expressions.

Instead of standing by while Northwest Coast Native intellectual property is appropriated for sale or any other unauthorized usage, I urge Native leaders and artists to take a proactive stance by learning the perimeters of the law. While this chapter raises issues that have continued to plague Northwest Coast artists for at least the past fifteen years (since I conducted the artist interviews shared in this chapter), new kinds of IP problems have surfaced, such as the management of digital knowledge. Since the colonization of Alaska, Tlingit people have paved the way for the most important Alaska Native causes from civil rights to land claims. The challenges presented in this chapter call for Tlingit leaders to promote the reformation of Western-based legal frameworks to include indigenous knowledge systems and ways of being.

NOTES

1. I came up with this statistic by dividing the total number of American Indians/Alaska Natives alone or in combination with other races as self-reported in the 2010 U.S. Census (138,312) by the entire U.S. population (308, 745, 538).
2. A 2002 McDowell report suggested that Alaska Native artists' income totaled about $20 million that year; however, no specific data were collected from the Alaska Native arts market (U.S. Government Accountability Office 2011, 10).
3. The interviews took place in 1998 as part of my senior honors thesis research at Dartmouth College. I spoke with more than thirty predominantly Tlingit artists in or from Klukwan, Haines, Juneau, Hoonah, Kake, Sitka, Ketchikan, Metlakatla, and Haidaburg. All artists interviewed signed a release that granted me permission to share their ideas in subsequent publications.
4. See the answer to the question "Can IP generate income?" in the brochure *Introduction to Intellectual Property (Trademarks, Copyrights, Patents and Trade Secrets) for American Indian and Alaska Native Artists*, distributed by the Indian Arts and Crafts Board, U.S. Department of the Interior.
5. See the appendix to this volume where the traditional Tlingit social structure is outlined.
6. From the U.S. book of copyright law: "A 'derivative work' is a work based upon one or more preexisting works, such as a translation, musical arrangement, dramatization, fictionalization, motion picture version, sound recording, art reproduction, abridgment, condensation, or any other form in which a work may be recast, transformed, or adapted. A work consisting of editorial revisions, annotations, elaborations, or other modifications, which, as a whole, represent an original work of authorship, is a 'derivative work'" (104).
7. From http://www.uspto.gov/trademarks/index.jsp.
8. From http://www.eed.state.ak.us/aksca/native.htm.
9. If the misrepresented goods are valued at less than $1,000, the maximum punishment for a first-time offender is a year in prison and a $25,000 fine.

REFERENCES

Anderson, Jane. 2010. "Indigenous Traditional Knowledge and Intellectual Property." Issues paper. Durham NC: Duke University School of Law, Center for the Study of the Public Domain.

Dauenhauer, Nora. 2000. "Tlingit At.óow." In *Celebration 2000: Restoring Balance through Culture*, ed. Susan Fair and Rosita Worl, 101–6. Juneau: Sealaska Heritage Foundation.

Dauenhauer, Nora Marks, and Richard Dauenhauer. 1990. *Haa Tuwunáagu Yís, for Healing Our Spirit: Tlingit Oratory*. Seattle: University of Washington Press.

Hollowell, Julie. 2000. "Intellectual Property Protection for Alaska Native Arts." *Cultural Survival* 24, no. 4. http://www.culturalsurvival.org/publications/cultural-survival-quarterly/united-states/intellectual-property-protection-alaska-nativ.

Huntington, Howard. 2010. "Dangerous Territory: How the Indian Arts and Crafts Act Can Ruin Your Business." *In-House Defense Quarterly*, Winter.

McDowell Group. 2002. *Economics of Alaska's Arts Industry*. Report prepared for the Alaska State Council on the Arts. Juneau.

———. 2012. *Alaska Visitor Statistics Program*. Alaska Visitor Statistics Program VI. Prepared for the Alaska Department of Commerce, Community, and Economic Development.

Torsen, Molly, and Jane Anderson. 2010. "Intellectual Property and the Safeguarding of Traditional Cultures: Legal Issues and Practical Options for Museums, Libraries, and Archives." Written for the World Intellectual Property Organization (WIPO)

U.S. Census Bureau. 2010. "The American Indian and Alaska Native Population." In *2010 Census Briefs*, January.

U.S. Government. 2011. Copyright Law of the United States. Title 17: United States Code. Chapter 1: Subject Matter and Scope of Copyright. December.

U.S. Government Accountability Office. 2011. *Size of Market and Extent of Misrepresentation Are Unknown*. Brochure. Indian Arts and Crafts Board, Department of the Interior, April.

U.S. Patent and Trademark Office. 2010. *Introduction to Intellectual Property (Trademarks, Copyrights, Patents, and Trade Secrets) for American Indian and Alaska Native Artists*. Brochure. Indian Arts and Crafts Board, Department of the Interior, July.

Wachowiak, Melvin J., and Vicky Karas Basiliki. 2009. 3D Scanning and Replication for Museum and Cultural Heritage Applications. *Journal of the American Institute for Conservation* 48: 141–58.

Part 5 | *Repatriation*

23

A Killer Whale Comes Home

Neil Kúxdei woogoot, Kéet S'aaxw, Mark Jacobs Jr., and the Repatriation of a Clan Crest Hat from the Smithsonian Institution

R. ERIC HOLLINGER AND HAROLD JACOBS

The Angoon Dakl'aweidí clan leader Mark Jacobs Jr., although confined to a wheelchair and in great pain from his illness, was filled with renewed strength as Herman Davis Sr. and David Davis Jr., Coho clan leaders from the opposite side,[1] placed the Killer Whale hat (Kéet S'aaxw) on Mark's head. This act completed the return of the hat to the Dakl'aweidí clan under Tlingit law, and it was the first time in more than one hundred years that the hat had been worn in a Tlingit ceremony.

Just eleven days later Mark Jacobs began his "walk in the forest" with the Kéet S'aaxw and the other *at.óow* of his clan by his side.[2] The repatriation of the Kéet S'aaxw by the Smithsonian's National Museum of Natural History on January 2, 2005, marked the climax of Jacob's lifetime of efforts to preserve and protect the traditions and cultural heritage of the Tlingit people.[3]

In February 1942 Mark went to see Archie Bell (Daanaawú), his mother's maternal uncle who was dying. Losing his eyesight, Archie Bell had told his niece, Annie Jacobs, that she conducted herself like a man and that she was to take care of the house and its artifacts for her children, naming her sons, Harvey and Mark, specifically. His niece told him that Harvey was already on active duty and Mark was soon to leave. In 1983, Annie turned the Killer Whale House over to Mark, and at that time he was given the traditional housemaster's name of Gusht'eihéen (Spray behind the Dorsal Fin), a name Archie Bell had himself inherited from his great-uncle.

Mark knew that clan-owned objects had been illegally leaving Tlingit possession for generations, sold to collectors by the Tlingit who had

483

Fig. 23.1 Mark Jacobs Jr. wearing the Killer Whale hat after the repatriation. Photo by David Dapcevich.

no rights to the objects, and ending up in museums or private collections. When a national movement began for the repatriation of human remains and funerary objects from museums, Mark advocated that the new repatriation law also address objects of cultural patrimony, which would include Tlingit clan objects. The Native American Graves Protection and Repatriation Act (NAGPRA) was passed in 1990 and created a process by which Native Americans, Alaskan Natives, and Hawaiians could seek repatriation of human remains and certain categories of objects of their ancestors. Mark used NAGPRA to request the return of many of his own clan's objects held in museums around the country. The repatriation of the Killer Whale hat from the Smithsonian is the story of one of those returns.

The Smithsonian Institution is not subject to NAGPRA. Instead, it is subject to the repatriation mandates in the National Museum of the

Fig. 23.2 The Killer Whale hat as illustrated in Swanton (1908: plate 58).

American Indian (NMAI) Act, which was passed in 1989 and served as the model on which the NAGPRA was founded. The NMAI Act required all the Smithsonian museums to inventory their collections and provide those inventories to tribes, which could then request repatriation of human remains and funerary objects to which they were culturally affiliated. The NAGPRA included expanded categories of objects that could be claimed by adding sacred objects and objects of cultural patrimony, and the Smithsonian adopted a policy to return such items when requested. This policy later became law with an amendment to the NMAI Act. In 1996, inventories of Tlingit objects in the collections of the National Museum of Natural History were mailed to the Central Council of Tlingit and Haida Tribes of Alaska as well as all Native villages in southeast Alaska.

In January 1997 Mark Jacobs and his son, Harold, traveled to Washington DC to attend the annual meeting of the National Congress of the American Indians. Harold had seen a picture of the Killer Whale hat in Swanton's 1908 book and, knowing it was at the Smithsonian, he arranged for Mark to visit that museum to view the hat and consult with the museum's Repatriation Office. When the two of them saw the hat, Harold told his father in Tlingit that it was probably the first time

Figs. 23.3a and 25.3b Mark Jacobs Jr. with the Killer Whale hat at the Smithsonian Institution. Photographs courtesy of Eric Hollinger.

the hat had heard the Tlingit language spoken in a very long time. Mark tried on the hat and posed for a photograph, and the museum provided copies of the accession records associated with the collection of the hat. When they returned to Alaska, Mark authorized the Kootznoowoo Cultural and Educational Foundation of the Village of Angoon to submit a request for repatriation on behalf of the Dakl'aweidí clan.

The museum received the claim as well as many others from tribes and clans across Alaska and across the country and began researching these various cases in order to prepare a report with recommendations to the secretary of the Smithsonian. A long backlog of repatriation requests and a series of staff changes prevented the Repatriation Office from beginning work to address the case until 2003, when repatriation case officer Eric Hollinger was assigned the responsibility. The late Richard Dalton, T'aḵdeintaan clan leader from Hoonah, was on the Smithsonian's Native American Repatriation Review Committee at the time, and he advised the museum staff to visit the Tlingit communities to consult with the clan leaders making requests and to learn as much as possible about the Tlingit culture. The museum hired ethnologist Anne-Marie Victor-Howe, a researcher at Harvard University's Peabody Museum with considerable experience of working with the Tlingit community, to assist with consultations and research. Hollinger, Victor-Howe, and Repatriation Office program manager William Billeck traveled to Juneau to consult with Mark Jacobs Jr., Harold Jacobs, and other Dakl'aweidí clan house leaders including Edwell John of the "Killer Whale Chasing the Seal House".

Mark shared with the museum staff the origins and history of the Dakl'aweidí clan and talked about the importance of clan crest objects and the deeper meanings of *at.óow*. Mark explained their belief that the hat at the Smithsonian had been made by Yéilnaawú. Yéilnaawú was the brother-in-law of Gusht'eihéen and a well-known Deisheetaan artist who had painted the killer whales on the front of the Killer Whale House in Angoon and made a number of clan crest hats. Mark brought out his main Killer Whale hat, which had been made by Yéilnaawú and had been originally owned by the Gusht'eihéen who, more than one hundred years earlier, had also owned the hat in the Smithsonian. Mark pointed out the clear similarities in the design and painting of both hats suggesting that they had been created by the same artist. The museum staff heard from the Dakl'aweidí clan leaders how clan crest hats were needed by clan leaders today for use in their most important ceremonies.

The museum's assessment of the repatriation request was compiled in a report along with assessments of other claimed Tlingit objects (Hollinger et al. 2005). In addition to the consultation information provided by Mark and the other Dakl'aweidí house leaders, the museum considered a wide range of historical records and anthropological literature. The repatriation legislation requires the claimants to show that they are culturally affiliated to the object, that the object is a sacred object and/or an object of cultural patrimony, and that the museum lacks the right of possession to the object because it has been illegally alienated from the tribe or clan.

According to the museum's records, John R. Swanton, an ethnologist for the Smithsonian's Bureau of American Ethnology, collected the Killer Whale hat in Sitka in 1904 while conducting field research on Tlingit myths and customs in southeast Alaska. Swanton kept detailed field notes, which showed that he had purchased the hat from the son of Gusht'eihéen for twenty dollars. He wrote in his notebook that it was "worn as a true emblem by Gushteheen—a Killisnoo man of the

Dakl'aweidí (Daxtawedi) family" (Swanton 1904b). Gusht'eihéen was the hereditary name and title held by the leader or caretaker of the Angoon Killer Whale House (Kéet Hít) of the Dakl'aweidí clan (de Laguna 1960, 189). Swanton also described this hat in a March 15, 1904, letter sent from Sitka to William H. Holmes, head of the Bureau of American Ethnology. In that letter Swanton wrote:

> Besides these I have obtained a fine killer-whale hat inlaid with abelone [sic] shell. It was made as a real emblem although it has only been worn four years. These emblem hats are much more interesting and involve much finer work than the masks. The father of this man, who is living at Killisnoo, has two more of them for which he wants forty dollars a piece. Very likely, if one were on the spot, he could get them for thirty a piece. These seem to be the most treasured Tlingit possessions. (Swanton 1904a)

These collectors' records corroborate Mark Jacobs's opinion that the hat was culturally affiliated to the Dakl'aweidí clan and had been owned by the Killer Whale House leader named Gusht'eihéen. Mark presented evidence that he was a descendant of the original Gusht'eihéen. Gusht'eihéen's title and his role as the Killer Whale House caretaker transferred to his matrilineal nephew Daanaawú (Archie Bell). After his death they were transferred to Daanaawú's maternal niece, Sxaalgen (Annie Paul Jacobs), and upon her death the role and title transferred to Mark. This established that Mark was a lineal descendant of the Gusht'eihéen under the Tlingit matrilineal kinship system.

The evidence also supported the claim that the Killer Whale Hat was a sacred object and an object of cultural patrimony as defined by the repatriation legislation. Historical and anthropological literature corroborated the consultation information that clan hats display the crest of the clan and were and are used in ceremonial contexts. Ethnographer George Thornton Emmons, who worked among the Tlingit during the 1880s and 1890s, wrote:

> The most valuable and significant crest objects, however, were the carved wooden hat or the highly ornamented hat of finely woven spruce root. Such hats, *sach* [*sáaxw*], were shown only upon occasions of the greatest importance, when the clan was represented as a whole and large amounts of property were distributed. Or, the hat

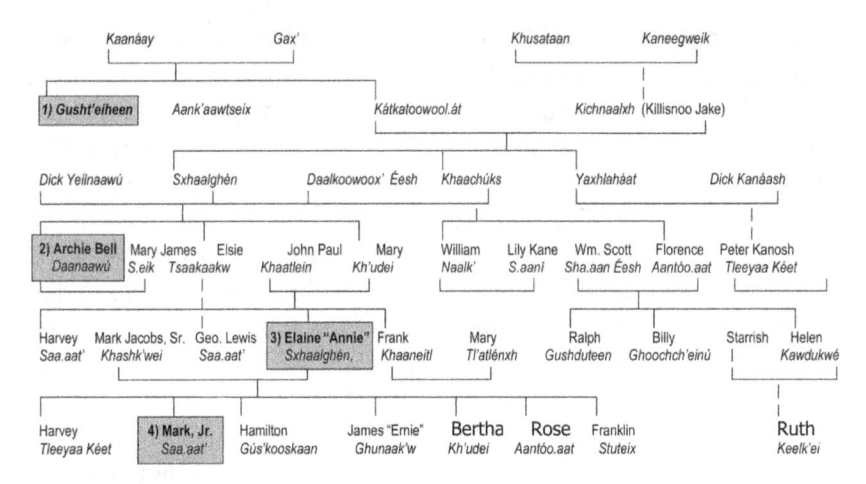

Fig. 23.4 Kéet Hít (Killer Whale House) lineage.

was placed beside the dead chief as he lay in state. A clan might own one or several such hats, representing only the principal crests, and each time they were exhibited their value would be increased by the amount of property given away. [A distribution of property to invited "opposites" is necessary to validate the owners' claims to the crests displayed.] The wealth was contributed by the whole clan, so, although the hats themselves descended from the clan chief to his successor, the chief was only the custodian, and the hats were actually the property of all the clan. Similar hats were possessed by the heads of households [lineages], and were used upon like occasions to represent these lesser bodies, but they did not have the same significance [importance] as the clan hats. (Emmons 1991, 34–35; bracketed comments were by the editor, Frederica de Laguna)

Clan and house crest objects or *at.óow* such as clan hats were owned communally. True crest objects were commissioned by clan or house leaders, were made by a craftsman of the opposite moiety, and were dedicated and validated or "brought out" at a ceremonial potlatch. According to de Laguna (in Emmons 1991, 33), "such physical representations of the crest must be made by the 'opposites' and have no value unless the latter are compensated as makers and witnesses at the potlatches in which these objects are displayed." It is these validated objects that become known as *at.óow*, which means "an owned or purchased thing" (Dauenhauer and Dauenhauer 1987, 25). Swanton's asser-

A Killer Whale Comes Home 489

tion that the Killer Whale hat was made as, and was, a "true emblem" suggests that compensation of the maker and validation in the context of a potlatch had been completed. Kan (1989, 202) provided an excellent summary of this use in memorial potlatches when he wrote, "By using the objects once owned by their ancestors, the speakers placed the dead in the ritual domain, thus dramatizing the solemnity of the occasion and reiterating the historical depth of the ties between the two opposite matrilineal groups." Thus the Smithsonian recognized that *at.óow*, such as the Killer Whale hat, have a significant ceremonial and spiritual or sacred role in Tlingit society and were both sacred objects and objects of cultural patrimony to the clan as a whole.

The repatriation request pointed out that the museum lacked the right of possession because the son of the Gusht'eihéen would not have had the right to sell the hat under Tlingit law. The Gusht'eihéen is known to have had four sons, and although it is not known which of the sons was responsible for selling the hat, it is clear that they were all members of their mother's clan rather than their father's. The Killer Whale hat, along with the other *at.óow* in their father's care, would have been the property of the Dakl'aweidí clan, and Gusht'eihéen's sons, as members of an opposite clan, would not have had the authority to sell or otherwise alienate it. The Smithsonian recognized that the evidence showed that the museum lacked the right of possession, and the hat belonged to the Dakl'aweidí clan.

While the Repatriation Office's report recommending that the museum return the Killer Whale hat was working its way through the administrative approval process of the Smithsonian, Hollinger learned that Mark Jacobs had fallen gravely ill and was in the hospital in Sitka. The Dakl'aweidí clan's *at.óow* had all been moved into his hospital room to be with Mark because he was not expected to survive. Traditionally the *at.óow* are brought to a clan leader when he is near death. Photographs from the late 1800s show *at.óow* assembled around dying clan leaders and clan leaders lying in state.

George Thornton Emmons described this ancient practice:

Upon the approach of death to a man, when all hope had been abandoned, his family assembled and chanted their clan war songs. The dying man was placed behind the fire, facing the door, and was dressed in clean clothes and surrounded by the family's ceremonial paraphernalia. It was a fixed belief of the Tlingit that at this time

Fig. 23.5 Tlingit clan leader lying in state with Killer Whale clan property. Alaska State Museum, ASL-P91-24. Photograph by Edward DeGroff.

the dying person was in direct communication with the spirits of the departed, and that they talked to him, telling him to have no fear, that they would guide and protect him on his journey to the future life where all his ancestors awaited him. And thus death was made easy and there was no struggle. The Tlingit had no fear of death. (Emmons 1991, 270)

Hollinger recognized the serious condition that Mark was in and the significance of the clan's act of bringing the Dakl'aweidí *at.óow* and placing them around him. Knowing that the Killer Whale hat was also an *at.óow* of the Dakl'aweidí clan, the Repatriation Office, Ethnology Division curators, and Department of Anthropology all agreed to ask the museum administration to expedite the review process and approve the recommendation for repatriation of the Killer Whale hat in an effort to return this *at.óow* as rapidly as possible. The director of the National Museum of Natural History, Cristian Samper, concurred with the recommendation and instructed the Repatriation Office to arrange for the return of the Killer Whale hat to Mark Jacobs Jr. and the Dakl'aweidí clan as quickly as possible.

The Jacobs family was contacted at the Southeast Alaska Regional Health Consortium (SEARHC) to begin coordinating efforts to effect the repatriation, and the Kootznoowoo Cultural and Education Foundation and the Central Council Tlingit and Haida Indian Tribes of Alaska were notified. Museum staff moved rapidly, and head conservator Greta Hansen constructed a special box designed to hold the hat safely during transport and protect it from rapid changes in temperature and humidity that might cause the wood to split. On New Year's Eve 2004, Director Samper personally attended the final packing of the hat for the return, and on New Year's Day 2005 Hollinger flew with the hat to Sitka. On January 2, the hat was officially repatriated to Mark and the Dakl'aweidí clan in Mark's hospital room.

Although signing of papers was enough for Western law, the repatriation still needed to be formally recognized under Tlingit law, so several hours later, clan leaders gathered in the hospital's cafeteria for a Tlingit ceremony to complete the process. The Dakl'aweidí clan *at.óow* were assembled there along with approximately thirty Tlingit representing clans from both the Raven and Eagle moieties. Mark Jacobs Jr. publicly acknowledged that he was dying, and clan leaders from the Raven's side opened the box and revealed the Killer Whale hat, placing it beside the Coho hat of the L'ooknax.ádi clan.

The Raven leaders, Herman and David Davis, then carried the hat over to Mark and placed it upon his head. Everyone sang a special Killer Whale clan song, *Eeshan di Kéet*. Speaking in Tlingit through his pain, Mark gave a moving speech thanking the Raven's side for witnessing the transfer of the hat, and clan leaders of both the Eagle's side and the Raven's side gave speeches thanking the opposite side for showing support for Mark and for witnessing the return of the Killer Whale hat. Mark was unable to endure the entire ceremony, and he asked for a prayer before being returned to his room while the speeches and acknowledgments continued.

The Killer Whale hat was placed with the Dakl'aweidí clan *at.óow*. After everyone had been given an opportunity to speak, the Killer Whale hat was placed on the head of Mark Jacobs's maternal nephew, Pete Karras Jr., who danced with the other Killer Whale clan members. For the first time in more than one hundred years, the Killer Whale hat was brought out and danced in a traditional Tlingit ceremony. A Killer Whale had finally come home.

Sadly, Mark passed away just eleven days later. Fortunately, the Killer Whale hat was at his side along with the other *at.óow* of the clan helping Mark to communicate with his ancestors. Like his predecessors, Mark was comforted through the hat by his ancestors as they made him know that they would guide and protect him on his journey

Fig. 23.6 Clan leaders from the Raven side placing the Killer Whale hat on Mark Jacobs Jr. Photograph courtesy of Eric Hollinger.

to join them. The hat was also present at the funeral ceremony held a few days later in the Sitka tribe's community house; an astounding thirty-one crest hats were present for this service. including the repatriated Killer Whale hat.

With Mark's passing, the Dakl'aweidí clan *at.óow* became "masterless objects" because they have no recognized caretaker until the new clan leader is chosen. While in that limbo, the *at.óow* are at risk of being sold by the family of the clan leader against Tlingit law. That may have been the way many clan crest objects were alienated from the community and ended up in museums or private collections. At the "Sharing Our Knowledge" clan conference held in Sitka, March 22–25, 2007, at an impromptu and emotional ceremony carried out during the conference banquet, Harold Jacobs transferred all of his father's *at.óow* back to the Dakl'aweidí clan and to the new clan leader, Edwell John Jr. This act, witnessed by clan leaders of the Eagle and Raven sides as well as hundreds of conference attendees, helped to ensure that the clan's crest objects remain safely in the possession of his father's clan.

New clan leaders are usually formally installed at a memorial for the deceased clan leader that is usually held one year after their passing. However, for very important clan leaders, such as Mark Jacobs Jr., more time is necessary to raise adequate funds and prepare a memorial appropriate for their status. In Mark's case, it took two and a half years before the clan was prepared for the ceremony, known as a *koo.éex'*. Mark's memorial was held September 1–2, 2007, at Sheldon Jackson College in Sitka. Witnessed by Eagle side and Raven side clan leaders, Edwell John Jr. was installed as the clan leader (*naasháadei háni*) and given the name Woochxh kádúhaa, while all of the Dakl'aweidí clan *at.óow*, including the Killer Whale hat from the Smithsonian, were formally transferred to his care. The hat was placed on Ben Didrickson, a spokesman from the Klukwan branch of the Dakl'aweidí from the Dorsal Fin House, who was also named as co-caretaker of the *at.óow* along with Edwell John Jr. During the ceremony the hat was held upside down to hold the money in the "killing of the money" for the ceremony. The hat was then danced in by Armando DeAsis (Naalk), who is also a direct descendant of the Gusht'eihéen who originally owned the hat.

The hat is now back in use in the ceremonial context it was meant for, as it is regularly brought out for Tlingit ceremonies. One of Mark Jacobs's last acts as leader of the Dakl'aweidí clan was to accept the return of the Killer Whale hat on behalf of his people. The story of Mark Jacobs and this hat continues to help educate people in both the Tlingit and non-Tlingit communities about why repatriation is important. For the museum community, it reminds us that we are the caretakers of important cultural property and the heritage of many cultures. For the Tlingit, in many ways, it is the story of a Killer Whale finally coming home.

NOTES

1. "Side" is the English term used in the Tlingit community instead of the anthropological term "moiety."
2. "To walk in[to] the forest" is a common Tlingit expression signifying a person's transition from the world of the living to that of the dead.
3. For details on Mark Jacobs Jr.'s life, see the chapters by Harold Jacobs and Sergei Kan (this volume).

REFERENCES CITED

Dauenhauer, Nora Marks, and Richard Dauenhauer. 1987. *Ha Shuka, Our Ancestors: Tlingit Oral Narratives.* Seattle: University of Washington Press.

de Laguna, Frederica. 1960. *The Story of a Tlingit Community: A Problem in the Relationship between Archeological, Ethnological, and Historical Methods.* Bureau of American Ethnology, Bulletin 172, Smithsonian Institution. Washington DC: Government Printing Office.

Emmons, George Thornton. 1991. *The Tlingit Indians.* Ed. Frederica de Laguna. Seattle: University of Washington Press and New York: American Museum of Natural History.

Hollinger, R. Eric, Betsy Bruemmer, and Anne-Marie Victor-Howe. 2005. Assessment of Tlingit Objects Requested for Repatriation as Objects of Cultural Patrimony and Sacred Objects in the National Museum of Natural History, Smithsonian Institution. Repatriation Office, National Museum of Natural History, Smithsonian Institution, Washington DC.

Kan, Sergei. 1989. *Symbolic Immortality: The Tlingit Potlatch of the Nineteenth Century.* Washington DC: Smithsonian Institution Press.

Swanton, John R. 1904a. Swanton to Holmes, March 16, 1904, Swanton John R. 1900–1903, box 21, Swanton-Tweedale Correspondence, Letters Received, 1888–1906, Papers of the Bureau of American Ethnology, National Anthropological Archives, National Museum of Natural History, Smithsonian Institution, Washington DC.

———. 1904b. Swanton to Holmes, March 15, 1904; Swanton John R. 1900–1903, box 21, Swanton-Tweedale Correspondence, Letters Received, 1888–1906, Papers of the Bureau of American Ethnology, National Anthropological Archives, National Museum of Natural History, Smithsonian Institution, Washington DC.

———. 1908. "Social Conditions, Beliefs, and Linguistic Relationship of the Tlingit Indians." In *Twenty-Sixth Annual Report of the Bureau of American Ethnology for the Years 1904–1905,* 391–512. Washington DC: Government Printing Office.

24

Building New Relationships with Tlingit Clans
Potlatch Loans, NAGPRA, and the Penn Museum

STACEY O. ESPENLAUB

In the United States, the Native American Graves Protection and Repatriation Act (NAGPRA) was signed into law in 1990. The law provides a legal mechanism for federally recognized Indian tribes, Native Alaskan corporations, and Native Hawaiian organizations to make claims for certain categories of objects held by museums and other institutions that receive federal funding. Among the categories of objects identified by NAGPRA are "objects of cultural patrimony" and "sacred objects." The Penn Museum is proud of its achievements in addressing NAGPRA because it has approached this law not simply as a legal responsibility but as an opportunity to develop new and substantive relationships with Native groups. While the museum is working assiduously to implement NAGPRA, it is also committed to making its collections accessible to Native American communities.

One example of this is the "potlatch loans" the museum has undertaken since 2003. In that year, the Central Council of Tlingit and Haida Indian Tribes of Alaska (CCTHITA) invited the museum to loan clan hats for use in a memorial potlatch. And when this incredible request presented itself, the museum enthusiastically pursued the opportunity to make the objects available for loan. The museum agreed to this unusual request because it offered an opportunity to learn about contemporary Tlingit memorial potlatches and to appreciate the ongoing significance of clan objects in the celebration of Tlingit culture. Through these activities, the museum has reestablished its historically close connection to the Tlingit people beginning with Tlingit associate curator Louis Shotridge, and this goodwill has led to new acquisitions and collaborations. And for the first time in nearly ninety years, Tlingit objects held in the collections of the Penn Museum are being used in contemporary memorial potlatches.

Loan Requests

Potlatches are a distinctive cultural expression of the Tlingit and other indigenous peoples of the Northwest Pacific Coast of the United States and western Canada. Potlatches are familiar to many as political feasts where goods are given away or sometimes destroyed to enhance social prestige. But they are also social and religious contexts for healing, dispute resolution, and communion with ancestors. Traditionally potlatches take place under very specific contexts such as a memorial for a deceased relative, the rebuilding of a clan house, or the dedication of a totem pole. Today they are also held to mark important anniversaries and personal accomplishments. As Preucel and Williams explain, "The potlatch is thus a complex and multi-layered communication system where participants express their relationships among themselves, with their ancestors, and with their future generations" (2005, 11). Sergei Kan as well as Nora Marks Dauenhauer and Richard Dauenhauer provide an in-depth look at the complex nature and importance of the potlatch to the Tlingit (Kan 1989; Dauenhauer and Dauenhauer 1990).

Prior to the 2007 clan conference, four separate loan requests were made by the CCTHITA. These were made on behalf of two Tlingit clan leaders, Herman Davis, Sitka L'uknax̱.ádi [Coho Salmon] clan, and Andrew Gamble, Sitka Kaagwaantaan [Wolf] clan, for use of clan objects during memorial potlatches to honor Tlingit individuals who had died. The first potlatch the museum attended was held on November 15, 2003, in honor of Sarah Davis, the sister of the L'uknax̱.ádi clan leader Herman Davis. The most dramatic potlatch the museum attended was the Centennial Potlatch in 2004. This event was to commemorate the so-called Last Potlatch held in Sitka, Alaska, in 1904. In 2005, the museum attended a potlatch in honor of Cecilia Kunz, an important and beloved member of the Juneau community, and her daughters, Lorraine and Martha Kunz. The fourth loan request was for the L'uknax̱.ádi /T'akdeintaan memorial party held in the fall of 2006 in honor of Katherine Mayberry, Betty Garrity, Alice Williams, and Eli Biggs, the brother of clan member Chuck Miller, with whom the museum had worked.

Loan Considerations and Preparations

The Penn Museum carefully considered each loan request, and several departments were involved in facilitating the loans, including the American section, the registrar's office, the conservation department,

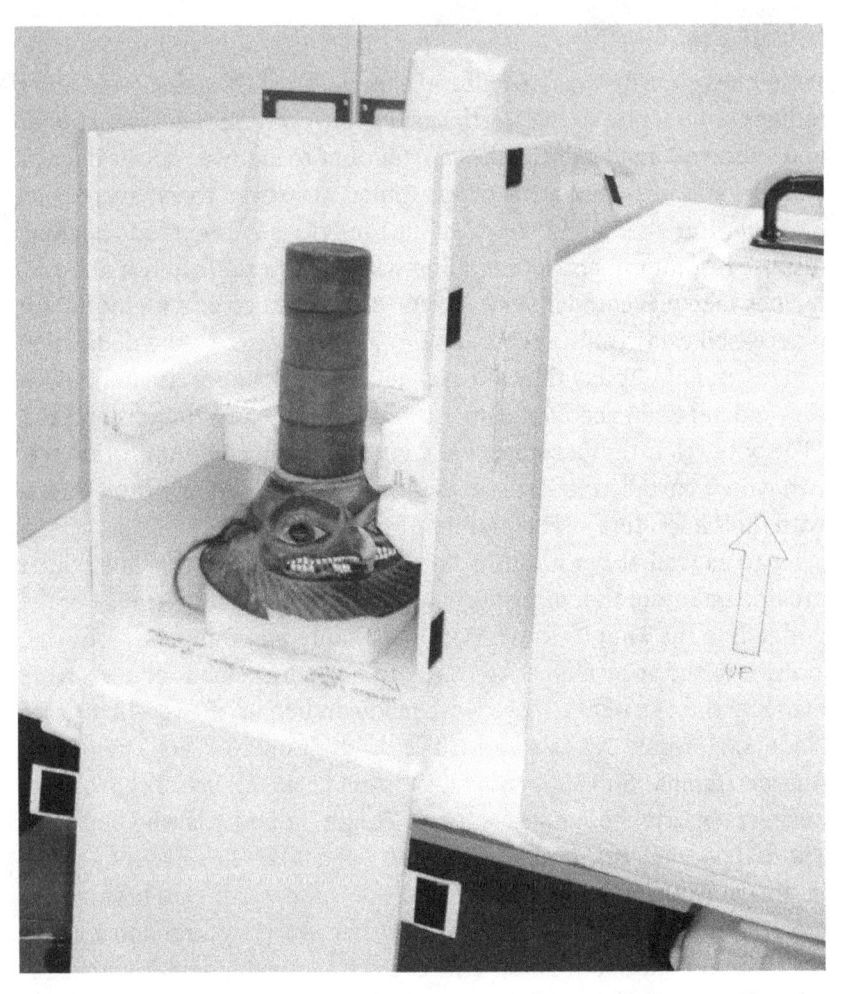

Fig. 24.1 Interior view of foam-core box containing the Petrel hat, 2004. Photo by Stacey O. Espenlaub.

the director's office, and the university's office of general counsel. A number of factors were considered in preparation for each of the loans: (1) object condition,(2) funding, (3) packing, (4) method of travel, and (5) security. The museum's director, who provided the necessary funds, nearly $10,000 for each loan request, generously supported each trip.

Lynn Grant from the Penn Museum's Conservation Department evaluated each object's condition and made recommendations regarding stabilization for use and travel. Unfortunately, there were a few objects that were originally requested for loan that were either too fragile (the

Fig. 24.2 Foam-core boxes containing the Tlingit clan hats en route to Sitka, Alaska, 2004. Photo by Stacey O. Espenlaub.

Noble Killerwhale hat) or too large (the Wolf baton and the Barbequing Raven hat) to travel. Certain objects needed to be stabilized for travel and use, and colleagues at the Alaska State Museum were consulted. They generously provided advice and diagrams for object stabilization. The hats are intrinsically delicate. The conservators decided that boxes, which are precisely tailored to the object and rely on internal protection, external cushioning, and extremely careful control of transit conditions to prevent damage, were needed. Atalier, a professional art shipping service, provided containers for each of the objects.

In order to mitigate any potential damage during transportation, the museum decided that a staff member would hand-carry each of the hats to its destination.

Tickets were purchased for the museum staff members and for each of the hats themselves. A security guard escorted the museum staff and the hats from the time they left the museum in Philadelphia, through each airport until they arrived in Alaska. Upon arriving in Alaska for each of the trips, the objects were greeted at the airport by a delegation of clan members. For example, in 2003, forty people including

Fig. 24.3 The Wolf hat on display for the public at the Sitka National Historic Park prior to the centennial potlatch at the Sitka National Historic Park, 2004. Photo by Stacey O. Espenlaub.

Mark Jacobs Jr. with the Killer Whale dagger greeted the Raven-of-the-Roof hat. The Eagle moiety dagger was present in order to balance the arrival of the Raven moiety hat. The museum also needed to consider storage for the objects during our stay in Alaska when they were not in attendance at the potlatches. For the three loan trips to Sitka, curator Sue Thorsen generously provided storage and exhibit space for the hats at the Sitka National Historic Park. And for our trip to Juneau, Steve Henrikson, curator of Collections, facilitated storage for two hats at the Alaska State Museum.

Prior to each event, a number of preparations were made. A special loan and use agreement, created just for the potlatch trips, was signed. The hats were fitted with material in order to be worn for dancing during the potlatches. The conservationist made recommendations about whether or not the hats could be worn during the potlatches. In one instance, after meeting and talking with the clan leader, a curatorial decision was made to allow the Wolf hat to be worn and to strengthen the chin strap accordingly. The conservationists had recommended that this hat not be worn.

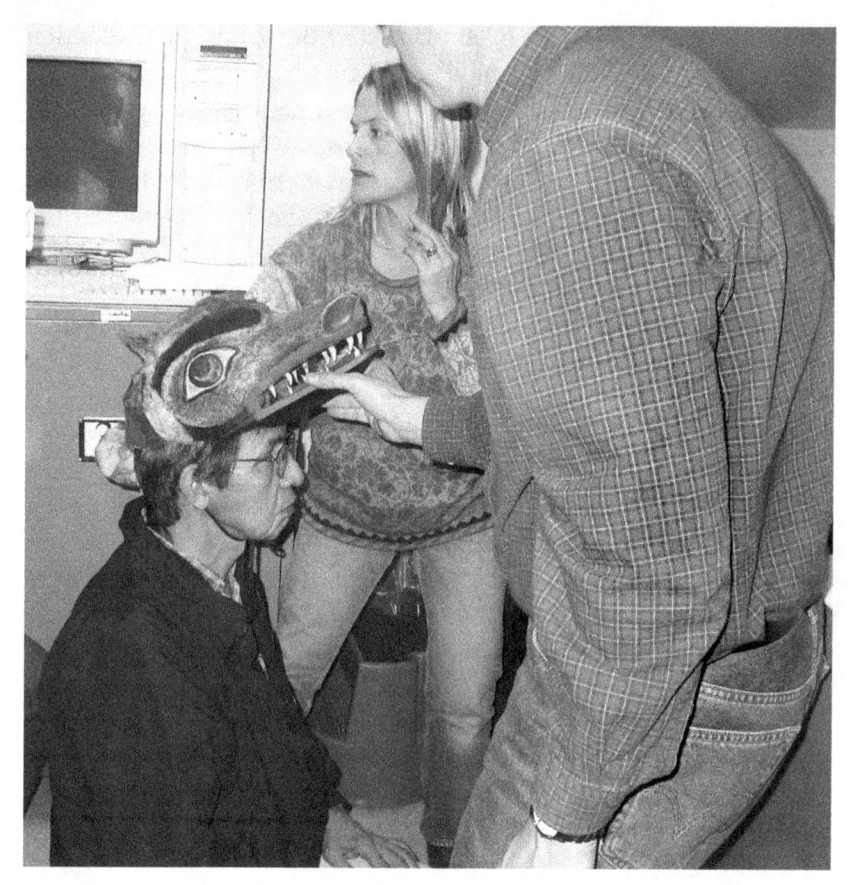

Fig. 24.4 Andrew Gamble, Lucy F. Williams, and Robert W. Preucel trying on the Wolf hat prior to the centennial potlatch, 2004. Photo by Stacey O. Espenlaub.

Use during the Potlatches

Potlatches are structured according to a standard protocol; however, there is variation across communities (Preucel and Williams 2005, 12). A memorial potlatch begins with the hosts welcoming the guests; it quickly turns to the mourning period when the hosts sing their clan mourning songs. Immediately the guests respond by singing their clan songs, holding up their clan regalia, and making consolation speeches. Once the mourning period is over, the potlatch turns more celebratory with the singing of clan love songs and dancing. Next the fire dishes, meals, gifts, goods, and fruit bowls are distributed. All the while, clan guests are donating money to members of the host clan, which is redistributed later when those who supported and helped the host clan are publically recognized. This takes place after the naming and adoption ceremonies. Lastly, after the money and gifts have been given and all speeches and dances are performed, the guests perform their own dance called the "return dance" to thank their hosts.

Tlingit objects from the Penn Museum were collected by Louis Shotridge, a Tlingit curator who assisted in the development of the Northwest Coast collection (see papers by Preucel and Williams, this volume). Shotridge was a curator at the Penn Museum from 1912 to 1932. He kept detailed documentation for the objects he collected, and each of the hats that were loaned has its own distinctive history relating to the clan's origins, histories, and myths. Objects are used throughout the memorial party, and the Penn Museum objects were featured prominently during each of the potlatches. Five objects from the Shotridge collection have been loaned for potlatches: the Eagle Hat (UPM# NA11742), the Raven-of-the-Roof Hat (UPM# NA10511), the Wolf Hat (UPM# NA8507), the Shark Helmet (UPM# 29-1-1), and the Petrel Hat (UPM# NA6864).The Raven-of-the-Roof and the Eagle hats were each requested for use three times. The eagle is the moiety crest of the Kaagwaantaan and an emblem of strength and vision. The right to use the eagle as a crest was granted to them by their Tsimshian neighbors. During the Centennial Potlatch (2004), according to protocol, the Eagle hat (*Ch'aak S'aaxw*) is placed on the head of the Kaagwaantaan clan leader by two clan members of the opposite Raven moiety during the mourning portion of the ceremony.

Later the Eagle hat was danced alongside a copy made by Augustus Bean for the Alaska State Museum at the Centennial Potlatch. The Eagle hat song, which was rediscovered in the archives of the Library of Congress, was also sung. At the end of the Raven moiety memorial party in 2005, the Kaagwaantaan clan leader wore the Eagle hat, and along with the other guests he took part in the Return dance, thanking the L'uknax̱.ádi hosts for their hospitality.

The Raven-of-the-Roof hat, the first object loaned, tells the story of a dispute between the Chilkat G̱aanax̱teidí clan and the Sitka L'uknax̱.ádi clan regarding use of the Raven emblem. The dispute ended when a man and a woman from the two different clans fell in love and married. During the 2005 potlatch for Cecila Kunz, the Raven-of-the-Roof and the Eagle hats were both present. An inspiring moment came when a member of the Eagle moiety, Joe Howard Sr., wearing the Eagle hat, and Edward Kunz, the son of Cecilia Kunz, wearing the Raven-of-the-

Fig. 24.5 (*top*) Ray Wilson and Herman Davis placing the museum's Eagle hat on Andrew Gamble, head of the Sitka Kaagwaantaan clan, 2004. Photo by Lucy F. Williams.

Fig. 24.6 (*bottom*) Joe Bennett Jr. holding the Shark helmet. Photo by Lucy F. Williams.

Fig. 24.7 Joe Howard Sr. dancing the Petrel hat at the centennial potlatch, 2004. Photo by Lucy F. Williams.

Roof hat, danced the hats together. Harold Jacobs indicated that this was one of the few times that these two hats could be danced together. This is related to the complex rules for use of objects during a memorial party (Dauenhauer and Dauenhauer 1990, 20).

The Wolf hat, Shark helmet, and Petrel hat were loaned to the *Kaagwaantaan* clan for the Centennial Potlatch in 2004. The wolf is the main crest of the *Kaagwaantaan* clan. According to Swanton, the clan received the right to use the crest after a hunter removed a bone from the teeth of a wolf. The wolf then appeared to him in a dream and made him lucky. Jerry Gamble,

Fig. 24.8 Andrew Gamble Jr., Kaagwaantaan clan leader, Herman Davis, L'ooknax.ádi clan leader, and Tom Young Jr., Kaagwaantaan Box House leader, all wearing ceremonial regalia including three clan hats from the UPM Collections, NAGPRA consultation visit, January 2008. Photo by Robert W. Preucel.

the brother of the Kaagwaantaan clan leader, Andrew Gamble, wore the Wolf hat (*Gooch S'aaxw*) during the mourning period. On the second day, the hat was danced alongside three other wolf hats as part of the blanket dances (*Yeikutee*) performed to entertain the Raven guests.

The Shark helmet was made to represent a shark, one of the first emblems associated with the Kaagwaantaan clan. Because the Shark helmet (*Toos' Shadaa k'wat S'aaxw*) had once been associated with warfare and bloodshed, the clan leaders decided that it should not be worn. Instead, a clan member carried the helmet during the mourning period of the potlatch, and another used it during the United States veterans' appreciation ceremony.

The Petrel hat (*Ganook S'aaxw*) commemorates the story of Petrel and his rivalry with Raven and refers to his ability to control the weather, wind, fog, and rain. According to Harold Jacobs, it is one of the oldest clan hats in existence. At one point, an elder of the Chookaneidí clan danced the Petrel hat while someone sang the song to accompany the dance. His dance steps imitated the Petrel and wove in and around four stacks of blankets positioned between the Raven guests and Eagle hosts. During each of the potlatches the Museum was publicly acknowledged and thanked for making the hats available.

NAGPRA and the Penn Museum

The Potlatch loans took place within the larger political context of the Native American Graves Protection and Repatriation Act. Many tribes, including the Tlingit, have been using NAGPRA as a means of restoring and revitalizing their culture. In fact, at the 2004 Centennial Potlatch, the museum staff witnessed the repatriation and subsequent use of the Sea Monster hat from the Field Museum of Natural History in Chicago (Preucel and Williams 2005, 16).

Prior to our first loan in 2003, the museum had received four claims from different Tlingit communities for a number of objects collected by Louis Shotridge. Since 2003, the museum has hosted six consultation visits from Tlingit communities.

One of the goals of the Central Council in making these loans is to have the museum understand the context in which these object were intended to be used and to see clan objects in motion. The Central Council has now submitted two NAGPRA claims to the museum for the repatriation of the five hats and other clan objects.

It is impossible to say at this time how many of the Tlingit objects in the Penn Museum's Shotridge collection may be repatriated, since this is a decision yet to be made by the trustees of the University of Pennsylvania. However, the repatriation of a portion of the collection is likely, given that similar artifacts have already been repatriated by major museums.

Conclusion

For the Penn Museum, NAGPRA is not just about compliance but about building new relationships and developing new projects with Tlingit people that strengthen our historical relationship and reflect what is relevant in today's Northwest Coast Tlingit communities. For example, we recently purchased two new objects for our Tlingit collection, a dagger and a woven dance apron. The dagger made by Harold Jacobs is a copy of the famous Killer Whale dagger. The original Killer Whale dagger, made from a meteorite, was repatriated by the Seattle Art Museum to the Dakl'aweidí of Angoon. The apron, made by Teri Rofkar of the T'akdeintaan clan of Hoonah, combines design elements from both

Tlingit and Maori weaving traditions. Teri made the apron in honor of her mentor, the late Emily Schuster, a Maori weaver from New Zealand. The museum has recently received two grants to strengthen its relationship with Tlingit communities and artists. The museum received a National Endowment for the Arts grant project to support Teri Rofkar to analyze and prepare a catalogue of the museum's four hundred Tlingit baskets. Additionally, the museum received a grant from the Institute of Museum and Library Services to digitize the Louis Shotridge collection in order to make it accessible to students, scholars, the Tlingit Indian community, and the general public (see Williams, this volume).

To date, we have made five separate potlatch trips, and each has been a remarkable experience for members of the museum to see these objects in use and to hear the eloquence of the Tlingit language. Pursuing these loan requests has afforded the museum the opportunity to see the objects come alive and to understand how they are used during contemporary potlatches to support the clan hosts. These objects make tangible clan crests, histories, ancestors, and spirits.

ACKNOWLEDGMENTS

I acknowledge my travel companions, Lucy F. Williams, Robert W. Preucel, and William Wierzbowski, and thank our many colleagues at the Penn Museum who supported the loan trips, including Jeremy A. Sabloff, Richard M. Leventhal, Margaret Spencer, Xiuqin Zhou, Jack Murray, Juana Dahlan, Julia Lawson, Lynn Grant, Jamie Gorman, Monica Means and Brenda Fraser. I am grateful to have been able to share these experiences with Sue Thorsen, Steve Henrikson, Sergei Kan, and Helen Robbins. My final thanks go to our Tlingit colleagues who have supported and graciously hosted us in Alaska, especially Harold Jacobs, Herman Davis, and Andrew Gamble. *Gunalchéesch*

REFERENCES

Dauenhauer, Richard, and Nora Marks Dauenhauer. 1990. *Haa Tuwunaagu Yis, for Healing Our Spirit: Tlingit Oratory*. Seattle: University of Washington Press.

Kan, Sergei. 1989. *Symbolic Immortality: Tlingit Potlatch of the Nineteenth Century*. Washington DC: Smithsonian Institution Press.

Preucel, Robert W., and Lucy F. Williams. 2005. The Centennial Potlatch. *Expedition* 47 (2): 9–19.

APPENDIX

An Outline of the Traditional Tlingit Social and Ceremonial System

SERGEI KAN

As a people, the Tlingit traditionally shared a common language and cultural heritage. By "traditional" I mean a social and ceremonial system that had not yet been significantly affected by direct and indirect influences of Western colonization, including Christian missionization, the rise of the nuclear family at the expense of the matrilineal system, migration to urban centers, and modern education.

The eighteen or so local groups constituting the Tlingit nation were not political units but have often been called "tribes" for convenience. The Tlingit refer to them as *kwáan* (sing.), "inhabitants of such-and-such a place," for example, Sheet'ká *kwáan*, "the inhabitants of Sitka" or "the people of Sitka." They were distinguished from each other by subdialectical and minor cultural differences; in other words, they were "local communities, made up of representatives of several clans, united by propinquity, intermarriage, and love for their common homeland" (de Laguna 1990, 203).

In each *kwáan* there was at least one main village, occupied in the winter but usually deserted in the summer, when they departed for their fishing and hunting camps. New settlements might be established within the *kwáan*'s territory if an immigrant group was allowed to settle there or if an old village was being abandoned as a result of warfare, disputes, or disease.

The basic unit of Tlingit society was the clan (*naa*), whose members traced their descent through a line of common matrilineal relatives. It claimed territory, which included rights to various natural resources, ownership of which meant that clan members were the first ones to enjoy the first products of the season, frequently shared at a feast. Many clans were restricted to a single *kwáan* or village. However, some of the largest and most important clans were represented in several *kwáans*. Despite strong clan solidarity, such subclans were rather independent and were the de facto property-holding and political units. Most clans or subclans (their localized subdivisions, e.g., the Sitka area branch of the Kaagwaantaan clan) were divided into several matrilineages identified with a house group and hence called "houses" (sing. *hít*) by the Tlingit. The house was the smallest unit of society, possessing its own head (*hít s'aatí*, master of the house), territory within or subordinate to the larger plots owned by the clan as a whole, heraldic crests in addition to or as variants of the crest of its clan, personal names and ceremonial prerogatives (sing. *at.óow*), and history. Some lineages were probably remnants of the once important clans that had joined stronger clan groups for protection or had been incorporated into them. Others must have been formed by subdivisions of a clan, just as a house might grow and develop offshoots, referred to as "daughter houses."

The entire Tlingit nation was also divided into two matrilineal halves (moieties), known as Ravens and Eagles (or Wolves); a Raven could only marry an Eagle and vice versa. The Tlingits of one moiety have often referred to those of the other as "the opposite side." Moieties had no leaders and owned no property but were central to the Tlingit worldview and social life, because they regulated marriage and exchange of ritual services at life crises, death being the most important one. Taken as a whole, the main material and immaterial attributes of the individual's social persona were believed to be derived from and shared with his or her matrilineal kin and constituted his or her clan's *shagóon* or *shuká*, best translated as "origin/destiny," established in the past by its matrilineal ancestors and continuing to order its members' lives, generation after generation. The clan's totemic animal(s), the crest(s) representing them, and all of the other representations and manifestations of these crests (e.g., dances, songs, ceremonial clothing, lands owned by the clan) collectively constituted its *shagóon* or *shuká*. Because of the constant recycling of the names and spirits (via reincarnation) as well as material and other possessions (*at.óow*) of the clan's deceased members by their descendants, the living and the dead matrilineal kin were intimately linked to each other; in theory, clans were immortal, their membership consisting of their deceased as well as the living (and the yet unborn) members. The sacredness of the crest was illustrated by its extremely reverential treatment by its owners. When a crest-bearing object deteriorated beyond repair, its name was usually transferred to a new object depicting the same crest. Thus the crest, like the clan, remained immortal, surviving its temporary representations, just as a human being's essential spiritual attributes survived the body after death.

Similarly, an individual's birth name (which sometimes implied an ancestor's reincarnation) and especially the "heavy" ceremonial names or titles were derived from a stock owned by the matrilineal group. Although new birth and ceremonial names were periodically coined, the most valuable ones were those inherited from the ancestors. Since each matrilineal group owned a limited stock of such names and recycled them every few generations, one could say that the names themselves (especially the ceremonial/potlatch titles) were its true members. As long as there were appropriate individuals to inherit these names, the matrilineal group remained alive, and if there were not enough people to carry them, members of related houses and clans were adopted and given the names. Each "big" or "heavy" name had its own value, based on the previous owner's prestige and status and especially on the number and scale of potlatches he or she had been actively engaged in (see below). The new owner inherited the name's value but could raise or lower it, depending on his or her conduct.

Marriage was one of the central institutions of the Tlingit social order and a powerful mechanism for establishing and perpetuating cooperation and reciprocity between matrilineal groups belonging to the opposite moieties. The preferred (but not the only) form of marriage was with the members of one's father's clan or house. Members of the elite occasionally married aristocrats from neighboring non-Tlingit nations, if such a marriage could bring significant political, economic, or social gains.

The father-child link and the link through marriage were considered symbolically equivalent, even when in reality they were not; they furnished the basic pattern upon which all inter-moiety relationships were built. Thus, while membership in a moiety, clan, and house were central to the person's identity, he or she was also proud of being referred to, informally and especially on ceremonial occasions, as the "child of such-and-such a clan."

Tlingit society was ranked, but there were no formal grades--ranking was inexact and subject to dispute and reevaluation. The heads of houses and other high-ranking members of these matrilineal groups as well as their immediate matrilineal relatives constituted the aristocracy or nobility (sing. *aankáawu* or *aanyádi*; pl. *aanyátx'i*). Its members' status was defined by aristocratic birth, inherited and acquired wealth, personal accomplishments, ritual knowledge, and character, with age and accumulated wisdom adding to their prestige. The "commoners" were simply the aristocrats' junior kin (or at least they viewed themselves as such). House groups within the clan and clans within the moiety and the *kwáan*, as well as between moieties, were also ranked, but on no exact scale. High-ranking clans had large membership, owned more crests and wealth, and were aggressive and successful in war, trade, and ceremonial activities.

Access to and knowledge of the matrilineal group's *shagóon* was unequally distributed among its members. Older persons had more knowledge of and were more closely identified with it. The heads of the matrilineal groups made few important decisions unilaterally; instead, they consulted the council of mostly older aristocrats, which existed at the house as well as the clan level. All of the main activities supervised by the heads of matrilineal groups resulted in the accumulation of surplus food, furs, and exotic trade items in the hands of the aristocracy, whose duty it was to use most of that wealth to sponsor smaller feasts for their own matrilineal kin and larger ones (like the potlatch) involving the opposite moiety.

While much of Tlingit religious life was individual-oriented, and there was apparently no collective worship of powerful spirits or deities, death-related ritual activities were extremely elaborate and formed the core of the entire sociocultural order. It was in the funeral and especially the elaborate memorial ritual, come to be known in the post-contact times as the potlatch, but which the Tlingits referred to as the *koo.éex'* (literally "invitation"), that the above-mentioned oppositions, conflicts, and contradictions of this order were played out as well as manipulated, so as to overcome (or at least mask) them. These rituals provided a rather sharp contrast with daily life, allowing for the largest concentration of people, dispersed during the spring and the summer or living in other communities, providing an arena for a stronger (though still heavily ritualized) expression of some powerful emotions, and giving the participants an opportunity to subtly air their disagreements and eventually achieve (some) consensus on the distribution of power and prestige in their social universe by using oratorical metaphors, gift-giving, and other forms of symbolic action.

Most potlatches were the last major stage in a cycle of rites aimed at disposing of the remains of the deceased (especially a high-ranking one) and mourning and memorializing him or her. The house or even the entire localized clan of the deceased acted as the mourners and were assisted and comforted by one or several matrilineal groups linked to them through marital and ritual ties. Since the matrilineal kin of the departed were prohibited from touching the remains, they had to rely on their "opposites" who cremated them and performed all of the other appropriate ritual tasks, for which they were publicly thanked and generously remunerated in a future potlatch hosted by the mourners.

A *koo.éex'* given in honor of a high-ranking person, and especially a house head or a clan head, memorialized several recently deceased members of his group and involved the official installation of his heir, who assumed the deceased man's ceremonial title and regalia. A big *koo.éex'* was an elaborate affair with a large number of guests. Huge amounts of food and material goods had to be accumulated for such a ceremony in which the guests had to be lavished with delicacies and gifts. The *koo.éex'* began with the hosts expressing their grief for the last time and then ritually expelling it from their bodies. The guests offered them speeches of condolence, seen as another manifestation of their "love" for their in-laws and paternal relatives. The hosts expressed their own gratitude and love to them through feasting, gifts, oratory, songs, and dances. The latter were also an opportunity for the hosts to demonstrate in a proper ritual setting the various expressions and symbols of their ancestral heritage (*shuká*) and thus affirm their claims to them in the presence of the "opposites" acting as witnesses. The dead were believed to be present in the *koo.éex'* alongside the living, since only in this setting, when their names were invoked, could they receive generous portions of food and gifts.

Eventually the mood of the ceremony turned from sadness to joy, with the hosts proudly demonstrating their wealth and parading their *at.óow*. The distribution of gifts was the climax of the entire affair, with the amount given to each guest serving as a statement of the hosts' view of his or her specific rank. In the course of the memorial *koo.éex'* the mourners ritually ended their grief and restored the order in their ranks by passing the ceremonial titles and the regalia of their recently deceased matrilineal kin to their descendants.

Thus the memorial potlatch had several major economic, social, religious, and psychological functions. Because of the need to distribute large amounts of food to the guests, it stimulated production and accumulation of resources. The imbalance in their mourners' relationship with their opposites, caused by a symbolic debt the former had accumulated prior to the potlatch, was restored. The ritual also helped smooth over many intra- and intergroup tensions and conflicts, since cooperation and solidarity of matrilineal kin and of opposites were supposed to outweigh competition. One could say that it temporarily froze the social hierarchy, since the amount of food and gifts contributed by each host and given to each guest represented their current standing in it. By honoring the dead, the *koo.éex'* participants restored order in the entire social universe and were believed to protect the hosting group from additional deaths. Finally, it helped the mourners cope with their grief by utilizing such powerful emotions as love toward one's maternal kin and "opposites" as well as pride in one's public performance.

Despite the major changes that the Tlingit culture had undergone in the 1870s and 1880s, when the Western colonization of their country began in earnest, and in the late 1970s and early 1980s, when I began my ethnographic research in several Tlingit communities, I was fortunate to be able to work closely with a number of the more conservative individuals and families who continued to subscribe to many of the rules and principles outlined here.

Nonetheless, for all intents and purposes, clans and lineages no longer operated as unified sociopolitical groups led by the aristocracy, Ravens were no longer obligated to marry Eagles, and sponsoring a memorial potlatch for one's departed mother or sibling was no longer obligatory. At the same time many of the families have continued to perform the *koo.éex*, and it is in the context of this ritual that the Tlingit people still interact as members of matrilineal moieties, clans, and houses, display their ceremonial *at.óow*, and invoke, invigorate, and learn about the key traditional cultural values.[1]

SOME OF THE TLINGIT CLANS MENTIONED IN THE BOOK

Eagle (Wolf) Moiety	Raven Moiety
Kaagwaantaan	Lukaax.ádi
Dakl'aweidí	T'akdeintaan
Wooshkeetaan	Deisheetaan
Chookaneidí	L'uknax.ádi
Shangukeidí	Kiks.ádi
Sik'nax.ádi	Gaanaxteidí
Teikweidí	L'eineidí
Yanyeidi	Ganaxádi

NOTE

1. This overview is based on my own earlier summaries of Tlingit culture (see Kan 1999, 3-24).

REFERENCES

De Laguna, Frederica. 1990. "The Tlingit." In *Handbook of North American Indians,* vol. 7: *Northwest Coast.* Ed. Wayne Suttles, 203-28. Washington DC: Smithsonian Institution.

Kan, Sergei. 1999. *Memory Eternal: Tlingit Culture and Russian Orthodox Christianity through Two Centuries.* Seattle: University of Washington Press.

CONTRIBUTORS

JUDITH BERMAN is a research associate in the School of Environmental Studies and adjunct assistant professor at the Anthropology Department at the University of Victoria. Her Northwest Coast research includes many years' exploration of the work of indigenous ethnographers George Hunt and Louis Shotridge and of the ethnohistory of the early contact period.

KATHRYN BUNN-MARCUSE, PhD, is the assistant director of the Bill Holm Center for the Study of Northwest Coast Art at the Burke Museum and a visiting lecturer in art history at the University of Washington. Her publications on Northwest Coast art and culture have focused on jewelry and body adornment, cultural tourism, and the filmic history of the Kwakwaka'wakw.

ALEXIS C. BUNTEN is the project ethnographer for Intellectual Property in Cultural Heritage (IPinCH) at Simon Fraser University and a senior researcher for the FrameWorks Institute. Dr. Bunten's areas of expertise include the heritage industry, cultural production and consumption, interpretation, cross-cultural communication, community development, tourism, and the anthropology of work.

MIQUE'L ICESIS DANGELI is a Tsimshian from Metlakatla, Alaska. She served her community for eight years as the director of the Duncan Cottage Museum and curator of the Annette Island Service Unit's Healing Art Collection. Mique'l is now a PhD candidate in Northwest Coast Native art history at the University of British Columbia.

NORA MARKS DAUENHAUER was born in Juneau, Alaska. Her first language is Tlingit. She has worked extensively with Tlingit oral literature, doing fieldwork, transcription, translation, and explication. Her own poetry, prose, and drama have been widely published and anthologized. She is a freelance writer and independent scholar and in 2012 was named Alaska state writer laureate.

RICHARD DAUENHAUER lived in Alaska since 1969. He was a former poet laureate of Alaska, and his poetry, translations, and essays have been widely published. With Nora Dauenhauer he wrote and edited Tlingit grammars and bilingual editions of Tlingit oral literature. He was a freelance writer and independent scholar. Richard died on August 19, 2014.

STACEY O. ESPENLAUB is the Euseba and Warren Kamensky NAGPRA coordinator at the University of Pennsylvania Museum of Archaeology and Anthropology. She is pursuing a PhD in anthropology at the University of Pennsylvania.

R. ERIC HOLLINGER is the case officer for the Midwest, Northeast, Great Basin, and California Repatriation Program, Department of Anthropology, Smithsonian Institution.

ANDREW HOPE III (1949–2008) was a Tlingit educator, poet, and political and cultural activist. He edited two important collections of essays: *Raven's Bones* (1982) and *Will the Time Ever Come? A Tlingit Source Book* (edited with Thomas F. Thornton) (2000). He developed the idea of the Tlingit clan conference and organized several of them in the 1990s as well as the 2007 one.

ISHMAEL HOPE, born in Sitka and living in Juneau, is a storyteller who shares stories from his Iñupiaq and Tlingit heritages. He also is a writer, poet, actor, and an enthusiastic learner and educator of Alaska Native art and culture.

HAROLD JACOBS is the cultural resource specialist of the Central Council of the Tlingit and Haida Tribes of Alaska. He is a major expert on repatriation issues involving Tlingit house and clan-owned sacred objects (*at.óow*).

MARK JACOBS JR. (1923–2005) was a well-known Tlingit elder, the leader of the Dakl'aweidí (Killer Whale) clan of Angoon, and the housemaster of Killer Whale House. He was a highly knowledgeable tribal historian, a World War II veteran, and a prominent Alaska Native politician.

SERGEI KAN is professor of anthropology and Native American studies at Dartmouth College. He has conducted ethnographic and archival research in southeastern Alaska since 1979 and is the author of numerous publications on the history and culture of the Tlingit. His latest book is *Russian American Photographer in Tlingit Country: Vincent Soboleff in Alaska* (2013).

STEVE J. LANGDON is professor emeritus of anthropology at the University of Alaska, Anchorage. His research has focused on precontact, historic, and contemporary fisheries, cultures of place, and ethnohistory of the Tlingit and Haida people of southeast Alaska, especially of groups occupying the Prince of Wales Archipelago.

ASHLEY VERPLANK MCCLELLAND is a University of Washington PhD candidate studying Native American art history. She is the rights and reproductions manager for ethnology at the Burke Museum in Seattle, a curator for the Shaw Island Historical Museum in the San Juan Islands, and manager of a private art collection in Medina.

PETER METCALFE is a writer-publisher and communications specialist. Born and raised in Juneau, he has worked for every major Native organization in southeast Alaska, including most of the Alaska Native Claims Settlement Act corporations, producing books on southeast Alaska Native history, newsletters, annual reports, and television documentaries. He also produced the video documentation of the 1993, 2007, and 2009 clan conferences.

MADONNA L. MOSS is a professor of anthropology at the University of Oregon. As an archaeologist, she studies the long-term history of the Tlingit and Haida. She is the author of *Northwest Coast: Archaeology as Deep History* and co-editor with Aubrey Cannon of *The Archaeology of North Pacific Fisheries*. She is currently working on "The Archaeology of Herring" using ancient DNA to understand contemporary fisheries.

ELENA PITERSKAYA is a Russian anthropologist who received her PhD in 2007. She is the author of several articles on Native Alaskans during precolonial and colonial periods as well as the Creoles. Currently she is the assistant editor of the new Russian journal *Medical Anthropology and Bioethics*.

ROBERT W. PREUCEL is director of the Haffenreffer Museum of Anthropology and professor of anthropology at Brown University. Trained as an anthropological archaeologist, he is particularly interested in the relationships of archaeology and society. His fieldwork projects include the archaeology of a post Pueblo Revolt community in New Mexico (the Kotyiti Research Project). He is the author of numerous articles and several books including *Archaeological Semiotics* (2006).

DIANE PURVIS has written about Alaska Native constitutional law coupled with environmental law. Currently she is working with the Sealaska Heritage Institute on a manuscript concerning the 1955 Supreme Court *Tee-Hit-Ton* case. In addition, she is completing a group of essays on Alaska Native historic legal issues. She has also been a cultural studies instructor in Alaska for over twenty years.

JUDITH RAMOS is a Tlingit from Yakutat, Alaska. She is an assistant professor in the Department of Alaska Native Studies and Rural Development Program at the University of Alaska Fairbanks. She is a graduate student in the indigenous studies PhD program and Resilience and Adaptations Program fellow at the same university.

MEGAN A. SMETZER is an art historian based in Vancouver, British Columbia. She teaches, publishes, and lectures on historic and contemporary Northwest Coast indigenous art, focusing on women's work and the production of transcultural art. She is currently working on her book *Painful Beauty: A History of Tlingit Beadwork*.

THOMAS F. THORNTON is senior research fellow at Oxford University's Environmental Change Institute, where he directs the graduate program. His books include *Being and Place among the Tlingit* (2008) and *Haa Léelk'w Has Aaní Saax'ú: Our Grandparents' Names on the Land* (2012).

LUCY FOWLER WILLIAMS is associate curator and Jeremy A. Sabloff Senior Keeper of American Collections at the University of Pennsylvania Museum of Archaeology and Anthropology. Her publications include *Native American Voices on Identity, Art, and Culture: Objects of Everlasting Esteem* (edited with William S. Wierzbowski and Robert W. Preucel) (2005).

ROBIN K. WRIGHT is the Bill Holm Center Endowed Professor of Art History, director of the Bill Holm Center for the Study of Northwest Coast Art, and curator of Native American art, Burke Museum, University of Washington. She received the Lifetime Achievement Award from the Native American Art Studies Association in 2011.

INDEX

Page numbers in italic indicate illustrations

Abraham, Susie, 79, *83*
Alaska Native Brotherhood (ANB), 67, 91–92, 102, 149
Alaska State Museum, 499–500
American Museum of Natural History, 485–92
ANB. *See* Alaska Native Brotherhood (ANB)
Angoon AK, 8, 20, 25, 483, 487

Boas, Franz, 29n3, 44–45, 419

clan conference. *See* Conferences of Tlingit Tribes and Clans (clan conference)
collaborative research, 7, 99–115, 265–87
Conferences of Tlingit Tribes and Clans (Clan Conference): of 1993, 1–2, 151; of 1995, 1; of 1997, 1; of 2007, 1, 19, 31n16, 151–52, 493; of 2009, 19

Dakl'aweidí clan, 88, 98, 483–94, 506
Dangeli, Mique'l Icesis, 19–20, 265–67, 285–87
Dauenhauer, Nora Marks, 14–16, 21–22, *30*, 30n9, 31n12, 153–56
Dauenhauer, Richard, 14–16, 21–22, 30n6, 31n12, 157–67
Davis, Herman, *3*, 492–93, 497, *503, 505*
Deady, Matthew P., 247–62
Deiki Noow (Hazy Islands), 320–61

de Laguna, Frederica, *8*, 9, 20, 29n2, 30n5, 31n6, 79–86

Emmons, George T., 42, 45, 57, 99, 419

Gaanax.ádi clan, 193
Gaanax.tedí clan, 45, 53, 69, 192–93, 502
Gamble, Andrew (Andy), 112, 115n6, 497, *501, 503, 505*
Gordon, George Byron, 44–54
Grinev, Andrei V., 21

Haidas, 51, 297–316; house models of, *51*, 381–92
Haldane, Benjamin Alfred, 19–20, 265–87
Henrikson, Steve, 3, 500
Hinckley, Ted, 20
Hope, Andrew (Andy) III, *xviii*, 1, 2, 6, 16–19, 31n14, 116n9, 360, 365; poetry of, 137–52

Jacobs, Adelaide Bartness, *29*, 91
Jacobs, Harold, 11–12, 28–29, 95–96, 113, 493, 506
Jacobs, Mark, Jr., *3*, 11–12, *14*, 28, 93–94, 95–96, *104*, 110–11, *111*, 483–94; biography of, 88–94, 100–103, *112*, 115n1; death of, 492–94; as ethnographic consultant and scholar, 97–115; and Killer Whale headdress repatriation, 483–94;

521

Jacobs, Mark, Jr. (*continued*)
and Sergei Kan, *14*, 109–10, *115*;
navy service of, 90–91, 118–36
Jacobs, Mark, Sr., 101–2
John, Edwell, 5, *111*, 487, 493–94

Kaagwaantaan clan, 41, 49, 53, *72–73*, 74, 103, 111–12, 115n6, 235n4, 333–35, 497; Petrel (Ganuk) headdress of, *72*, *498*, *504*, 505; Shark headdress of, *73*, 503, *505*; Wolf headdress of, 501, 504–5; Wolf House potlatch of (2004), 497–506
Kake (Keex') AK, 326
Kan, Sergei, 11–13, *14* , 20–21, 30n8, 97–115
Kéet Hít (Killer Whale House of the Dakl'aweidí clan of Angoon), 100–101, 489
K'ineix Kwáan clan (Kwáashk'i Kwáan clan), 79
Klawock (Klawak) AK, 326, 339
Kunz, Cecilia, 497

Langdon, Steve, 23–24
Luknax.ádi clan, 52, 74, 79, 114, 497, 502; Raven of the Roof headdress of, *9*, 502

Metlakatla AK, 19–20, 265–87
Moss, Madonna, 25, 31–32n20
museums, 41–78, and potlatch loans, 496–507; and repatriation, 483–507

Naastedí clan, 327, 336–37
National Museum of Natural History, 28
National Museum of the American Indian, 484–85

photography, 27–29, 265–87

repatriation of Tlingit *at.óow* (sacred collectively owned possessions), 483–507

Russians in Alaska, 21–22, 172–74

Shotridge, Florence, 42, 45, 54–55
Shotridge, Louis, 10, 22, 41–78; biography of, 42–46, 64–65; as collector, 66–73, 502, 506–7; as ethnographer, 60–78, 193–95; as exhibitor, 46–54; as photographer, 70; as teacher, 54–57
Sitka AK, 481–506
Swanton, John R., 99, 487–88

Taant'a Kwáan (Tongass), 22, 31n17, 209–30
Teikweidí clan, 53, 226, *229*, *449*
Thornton, Thomas F., 23–25, 338–39, 364–75
Tlingits: art and intellectual property of, 461–80; *at.óow* (sacred collectively owned possessions) of, 27–28, 113, 510–11; and Christianity, 97–98; genealogies of, 191–209; house models of, *48*; laws of (vs. American law), 247–62; oral literature and narrative history of, 14–17, 153–67, 191–209, 329–36; place names of, 339–43, 364–75; potlatch of (*koo.éex'*), 15, 79, 103, 105–7, 109–12, 138–39, *454*, *456*, 496–506, 512–14; Raven myths of, 329–33; and relations with other Alaska Native peoples, 175–80; and seagull eggs harvesting, 343–45, 351–58; social structure, 509–12; songs of, 79–87, 95–96; and use of seabirds by, 297–316; warfare of, 95–96; weapons of, 394–416
Tsimshians, 45, 183n2, 265–87
"tourist" arts and crafts, 27, 417–58; beadwork, 441–58; silversmithing, 417–37

University of Pennsylvania Museum
of Archaeology and Anthropology,
9–10, 41–78, 496–507

Whale House (Gaanax.tedí clan,
Klukwan AK), 45, 53, 69

World Columbian Exposition, 27,
382–88

World War II in Alaska, *12*, 118–36

Yakutat AK, 8, 79–86, *454*,

zooarchaeology, 297–316